GERMAN-ENGLISH
ENGLISH-GERMAN
DICTIONARY

GERMAN-ENGLISH
ENGLISH-GERMAN
DICTIONARY

GEDDES&
GROSSET

This edition published 2000 by Geddes & Grosset, an imprint of
Children's Leisure Products Limited

© 2000 Children's Leisure Products Limited,
David Dale House, New Lanark ML11 9DJ, Scotland

ISBN 1 85534 967 1

Printed and bound in Indonesia

Contents

Abbreviations / Abkürzungeu

acc	accusative	Akkusativ
adj	adjective	Adjektiv
adv	adverb	Adverb
art	article	Artikel
auto	automobile	Automobil
aux	auxiliary	Hilfs-
bot	botany	Botanik
chem	chemistry	Chemie
col	colloquial term	umgangssprachlich
com	commerce	Handel
compd	in compounds	Kompositum
comput	computers	Informatik
conj	conjunction	Konjunktion
dat	dative	Dativ
etw	something	etwas
excl	exclamation	Ausruf
f	feminine noun	Femininum
fam	colloquial term	umgangssprachlich
fig	figurative use	Übertragen
gr	grammar	Grammatik
jdm	somebody (dat)	jemandem
jdn	somebody	jemanden
imp	impersonal	unpersönlich
inform	computers	Informatik
interj	interjection	Ausruf
invar	invariable	unveränderlich
irr	irregular	unregelmäßig
jur	law term	Rechtswesen
law	law term	Rechtswesen
ling	linguistics	Sprachwissenschaft
m	masculine noun	Maskulinum
mar	marine term	Marine
mat, math	mathematics	Mathematik
med	medicine	Medizin
mil	military term	militärisch
mus	music	Musik
n	noun	Substantiv
n	neuter	Neutrum
nom	nominative	Nominativ
pej	pejorative	abschätzig
pl	plural	Plural
pn	pronoun	Pronomen
prep	preposition	Präposition
rad	radio	radio
rail	railway	Eisenbahn
rel	relative	Relativ-
relig	religion	Religion
sl	slang	Slang
teat	theatre	Theater
tec	technology	Technik
TV	television	Fernsehen
vb	verb	Verb
vi	intransitive verb	intransitives Verb
vr	reflexive verb	reflexives Verb
vt	transitive verb	transitives Verb
zo, zool	zoology	Zoologie

German–English Dictionary

A

ab *prep* from:—*adv* away; down; off.

abändern *vt* to alter.

Abänderung *f* alteration.

abbrechen *vt vi* to break off; to stop.

abbringen *vt* to divert; to dissuade.

Abbruch *m* breaking off; demolition.

abdanken *vi* to resign.

Abdankung *f* resignation.

abdecken *vt* to uncover; to clear (table).

abdrehen *vt vi* to turn off.

Abdrift *f* drift.

Abend *m* evening:—**guten ~** good evening.

Abendblatt *n* evening paper.

Abendessen *n* dinner.

Abendmahl *n* Holy Communion.

abends *adv* in the evening(s).

Abenteuer *n* adventure.

abenteuerlich *adj* adventurous.

aber *conj* but, however.

Aberglaube *m* superstition.

abergläubisch *adj* superstitious.

abermals *adv* again.

abfahren *vi* to leave; to cover (distance):—*vt* to remove.

Abfahrt *f* departure; descent.

Abfall *m* waste; slope; decline.

Abfalleimer *m* rubbish bin.

Abfalleisen *n* scrap iron.

abfallend *adj* sloping.

abfertigen *vt* to dispatch; to clear (customs); to serve (customer).

Abfertigung *f* dispatch, clearance.

abfliegen *vi* to take off, fly off.

abfließen *vi* to flow away.

Abflug *m* departure, take-off.

Abfluß *m* outflow.

Abfuhr *m* removal; defeat.

abfüllen *vt* to fill.

Abgabe *f* delivery; pass (ball); tax.

abgabenfrei *adj* duty-free.

Abgang *m* departure.

Abgas *n* exhaust (gas).

abgeben *vt* to hand over; to pass (ball).

abgehen *vi* to leave.

abgelegen *adj* isolated.

Abgelegenheit *f* remoteness.

Abgeordnete(r) *f(m)* deputy, member of parliament.

abgesehen von apart from.

abgesondert *adj* separate.

Abgott *m* idol.

Abgötterei *f* idolatry.

abgöttisch *adj* idolatrous.

abgrenzen *vt* to demarcate.

Abgrund *m* abyss.

abgründig *adj* abysmal.

Abhang *m* slope.

abhängen *vt* to take down; to detach:—*vi* to hang up (telephone):—**~ von** depend on.

abhängig *adj* dependent; sloping.

Abhängigkeit *f* dependence.

abholen *vt* to collect; to meet.

Abitur *n* German school-leaving examination.

Abkehr *f* turning away; departure.

abkehren *vt vr* turn away.

Abkommen *n* agreement.

Abkommling *m* descendant.

abkürzen *vt* to abbreviate.

Abkürzung *f* abbreviation.

abladen *vt* to unload.

Ablage *f* storeroom.

ablagern *vt* to store.

Ablauf *m* drain; course; expiry.

ablaufen *vi* to drain away; to happen; to expire.

ablehnen *vt vi* to refuse.

ablehnend *adj* critical.

Ablehnung *f* refusal.

Abnahme *f* removal; purchase; decrease.

abnehmbar *adj* removable.

abnehmen *vt* to remove; to purchase: —*vi* to decrease.

Abnehmer *m* purchaser, customer.

Abneigung *f* reluctance, dislike.

abnutzen *vt* to wear out.

Abnutzung *f* wear.

Abonnement *n* subscription.

Abonnent(in) *m(f)* subscriber.

abonnieren *vt* to subscribe.

Abordnung *f* delegation.

Abort *m* lavatory.

abräumen *vt* to clear up.

abrechnen *vt* to deduct:—*vi* to settle.

Abrechnung *f* settlement; account.

Abreise *f* departure.

abreisen *vi* to leave.

abrüsten *vi* to disarm.

Abrüstung *f* disarmament.

Absage *f* refusal; cancellation.

absagen *vt vi* to call off.

Absatz *m* sales; paragraph; ledge, landing; heel.

abschaffen *vt* to abolish.

Abschaffung *f* abolition.

abschalten *vt vi* to switch off.

Abscheu *m* loathing.

abscheulich *adj* horrible.

Abschied *m* departure:—~ nehmen take one's leave.

Abschlag *m* reduction.

abschlagen *vt* to knock off; to take down; to refuse.

abschlägig *adj* negative.

abschließen *vt* to lock; to conclude.

abschließend *adj adv* final(ly).

Abschluß *m* conclusion.

Abschnitt *m* section.

abschreiben *vt* to copy; to write off; to write down, deduct.

Abschreibung *f* depreciation, write-off.

Abschrift *f* copy.

abseits *adv* aside, apart, offside.

Absicht *f* intention.

absichtlich *adj adv* deliberate(ly), intentional(ly).

absolut *adj* absolute.

Abstand *m* distance.

Abstinenz *f* abstinence.

Abstinenzler(in) *m(f)* teetotaller.

abstoßend *adj* repellent.

abstrakt *adj adv* abstract(ly).

Abstrich *m* cut, deduction; (*med*) smear.

abstufen *vt* to grade.

absurd *adj* absurd.

Abszeß *m* abscess.

Abt *m* abbot.

Abtei *f* abbey.

Abteil *n* compartment.

abteilen *vt* to divide.

Abteilung *f* department, section.

Abtreibung *f* abortion.

abtreten *vt* to wear out; to hand over:—*vi* to resign.

Abtritt *m* resignation.

abwandeln *vt* to adapt.

abwandern *vi* to migrate.

Abwanderung *f* migration.

abwärts *adv* down(wards).

Abwasch *m* washing-up.

abwaschen *vt* to wash off, wash up.

Abwasser *n* sewage.

Abweg *m* detour, wrong way.

Abwehr *f* defence.

abwehren *vt* to fend off.

abweichen *vi* to deviate; to differ.

abwesend *adj* absent.

Abwesenheit *f* absence.

abwischen *vt* to wipe (off).

abzahlen *vt* to pay off.

Abzahlung *f* repayment, hire purchase.

ach *excl* oh:—~ **ja!** oh, yes!:—~ **nein?** you don't say?:—~ **so!** I see.

Achse *f* axis, axle.

Achsel *f* shoulder.

Achselhöhle *f* armpit.

acht *num* eight.

Acht *f* ban; attention.

achtbar *adj* respectable.

achte(r, s) *adj* eighth.

achten *vt* to respect:—*vi* to pay attention.

achtlos *adj* careless.

achtsam *adj* careful.

Achtung *f* attention, respect.

achtzehn *num* eighteen.

achtzig *num* eighty.

ächzen *vi* to groan.

Acker *m* field.

Ackerbohne *f* broad bean.

Adel *m* aristocracy.

ad(e)lig *adj* noble.

Ader *f* vein.

Adler *m* eagle.

Admiral *m* admiral.

adoptieren *vt* to adopt.

Adoption *f* adoption.

Adrenalin *n* adrenaline.

Adresse *f* address.

adressieren *vt* to address.

Affäre *f* affair.

Affe *m* monkey.

affektiert *adj* affected.

Afrika *n* Africa.

Afrikaner(in) *m(f)* African.

afrikanisch *adj* African.

Agent *m* agent.

Aggression *f* aggression.

aggressiv *adj* aggressive.

Ägypten *n* Egypt.

Ägypter(in) *m(f)* Egyptian.

ägyptisch *adj* Egyptian.

ahnen *vt* to suspect.

ähnlich *adj* similar.

Ähnlichkeit *f* similarity.
Ahnung *f* suspicion.
Ahorn *m* maple.
Ähre *f* ear (corn, etc).
Aids *n* Aids.
Akademie *f* academy.
Akademiker(in) *m(f)* graduate.
akademisch *adj* academic.
Akkord *m* chord.
Akrobat(in) *m(f)* acrobat.
Akt *m* act.
Akte *f* document, file.
Aktenschrank *m* filing cabinet.
Aktentasche *f* briefcase.
Aktie *f* share.
Aktiengesellschaft *f* joint-stock company.
Aktion *f* campaign, action.
Aktionär(in) *m(f)* shareholder.
aktiv *adj* active.
Aktiva *pl* assets.
aktivieren *vt* to activate.
Aktivität *f* activity.
aktuell *adj* topical, up-to-date.
Akustik *f* acoustics.
akut *adj* acute.
Akzent *m* accent, stress.
akzeptieren *vt* to accept.
Alarm *m* alarm.
Albanien *n* Albania.
albern *adj* absurd.
Album *n* album.
Algebra *f* algebra.
Alibi *n* alibi.
Alimente *pl* alimony.
Alkohol *m* alcohol.
Alkoholiker(in) *m(f)* alcoholic.
alkoholisch *adj* alcoholic.
All *n* universe.
all (aller, alles) *pn* all:—*adj* all, every, any.

Allee *f* avenue.
allein *adj* alone:—*conj* only.
allerdings *adv* certainly.
Allergie *f* allergy.
allergisch *adj* allergic.
alles *pn* everything.
allgemein *adj* general.
Allianz *f* alliance.
allmählich *adj* gradual.
Alltag *m* everyday life.
alltäglich *adj adv* everyday.
Alpen *pl* (the) Alps.
Alphabet *n* alphabet.
alphabetisch *adj* alphabetical.
Alptraum *m* nightmare.
als *conj* when; as; than:—~ **ob** as if.
also *conj* therefore.
alt *adj* old.
Alt *m* alto.
Alter *n* age.
altern *vi* to age.
Alternative *f* alternative.
altmodisch *adj* old-fashioned.
Aluminium *n* aluminium.
am = **an dem**.
Ameise *f* ant.
Amerika *n* America.
Amerikaner(in) *m(f)* American.
amerikanisch *adj* American.
Ampel *f* traffic light.
Amsel *f* blackbird.
Amt *n* office; post.
amtlich *adj* official.
amüsant *adj* amusing.
amüsieren *vt* to amuse:—*vi* to enjoy oneself.
an *prep* at, on, near, to.
Analyse *f* analysis.
analysieren *vt* to analyse.
Ananas *f* pineapple.
Anarchie *f* anarchy.
Anatomie *f* anatomy.

Anbetracht *m:*—**in** ~ (+*gen*) in view of.
anbieten *vt* to offer.
Anblick *m* sight.
anblicken *vt* to look at.
anbrechen *vt* to break into:—*vi* to begin (night, day).
Anbruch *m* beginning.
Andacht *f* attention.
andächtig *adj* devout.
andauern *vi* to continue.
andauernd *adj* continual.
Anden *pl* (the) Andes.
andere(r, s) *adj* other; different.
ändern *vt vr* to change.
andernfalls *adv* otherwise.
anders *adv* differently; else.
anderswo *adv* somewhere else.
anderthalb *adj* one and a half.
Änderung *f* change.
andeuten *vt* to indicate.
Andeutung *f* indication.
andrehen *vt* to turn on.
androhen *vt* to threaten.
aneignen *vt* sich (*dat*) **etwas** ~ to acquire.
Anemone *f* anemone.
anerkannt *adj* recognized.
anerkennen *vt* to recognize.
Anerkennung *f* recognition.
Anfall *m* attack, fit.
anfallen *vt* to attack:—*vi* to occur; to accrue.
Anfang *m* beginning.
anfangen *vt* to begin.
Anfänger(in) *m(f)* beginner.
anfänglich *adj* initial.
anfangs *adv* at first.
anfassen *vt* to touch; *vr* to help.
anfechten *vt* to dispute; to trouble.

anfordern *vt* to demand, call on; to requisition.

Anfrage *f* inquiry.

anfragen *vi* to inquire.

anfügen *vt* to attach; to add.

Anführungszeichen *pl* quotation marks *pl*.

Angabe *f* statement; specification.

angeben *vt* to give; to specify.

angeblich *adj* alleged.

Angebot *n* offer, tender; supply:—~ **und Nachfrage** supply and demand.

angebracht *adj* appropriate.

angehören *vi* to belong.

Angelegenheit *f* matter, issue.

angeln *vi* to fish.

Angeln *n* fishing.

angemessen *adj* appropriate.

angenehm *adj* pleasant.

angenommen *adj* assumed, assuming.

angesichts *prep* in view of.

angespannt *adj* tense.

Angestellte(r) *f(m)* employee.

Angewohnheit *f* habit.

angreifen *vt* to attack; to touch.

Angriff *m* attack.

Angst *f* fear, anxiety.

ängstigen *vt* to frighten:— *vr* to worry.

ängstlich *adj* nervous.

Anhalt *m* support.

anhalten *vt vi* to stop.

Anhaltspunkt *m* clue, criterion.

anhand *prep* with.

Anhang *m* appendix.

anhangen *vt* to hang up,

add on.

Anker *m* anchor.

Anklage *f* accusation.

anklagen *vt* to accuse.

Ankläger *m* plaintiff.

ankommen *vi* to arrive.

ankündigen *vt* to announce.

Ankündigung *f* announcement.

Ankunft *f* arrival.

Anlage *f* layout, structure; installation.

Anlaß *m* occasion; reason.

anläßlich *prep* on the occasion of.

anlegen *vt* to lay, design; to invest; to aim.

Anleihe *f* loan.

anmaßend *adj* arrogant.

Anmaßung *f* arrogance.

anmelden *vt* to announce.

Anmeldung *f* announcement.

anmerken *vt* to note (down).

Anmerkung *f* comment.

annähern *f* to approach.

annähernd *adj adv* approximate(ly).

Annäherung *f* approach.

Annahme *f* acceptance.

annehmbar *adj* acceptable.

annehmen *vt* to accept, assume.

anonym *adj* anonymous.

Anonymität *f* anonymity.

anordnen *vt* to arrange; to order.

Anordnung *f* arrangement, order.

anpassen *vt vr* to adapt.

Anpassung *f* adaptation, adjustment.

anreden *vt* to speak to.

anregen *vt* to touch; to stimulate.

Anregung *f* suggestion; stimulus.

Anruf *m* call.

anrufen *vt* to call; to invoke.

ans = **an das.**

ansässig *adj* resident, located.

Ansatz *m* beginning; extension.

Ansatzpunkt *m* starting point.

anschaffen *vt* to buy, acquire.

Anschaffung *f* purchase, acquisition.

anschalten *vt* to switch on.

anschauen *vt* to look at.

Anschauung *f* opinion, view.

Anschein *m* appearance.

anscheinend *adj adv* apparent(ly).

Anschlag *m* impact; advertisement.

anschließend *adj* adjacent; subsequent:—*adv* then.

Anschluß *m* connection; supply; annexation:—**im ~ an** further to.

Anschrift *f* address.

Anschuldigung *f* accusation.

ansehen *vt* to look at.

Ansehen *n* respect; reputation.

ansetzen *vt* to affix; to develop:—*vi* to try; to begin.

Ansicht *f* view:—**zur ~** on approval: —**meiner ~ nach** in my opinion.

Anspruch *m* claim.

anspruchslos *adj* undemanding.

anspruchsvoll *adj* demanding.

Anstalt *f* institution.
Anstand *m* decency.
anständig *adj* decent.
anstatt *prep conj* instead of.
anstecken *vt* to stick on; to infect:—*vi* to be infectious.
ansteckend *adj* infectious.
Ansteckung *f* infection.
anstellen *vt* to turn on; to recruit, employ.
Anstellung *f* employment, position.
Anstieg *m* climb, rise.
Anstrengung *f* effort.
Antarktis *f* the Antarctic.
antarktisch *adj* antarctic.
Anteil *m* share.
Antenne *f* antenna.
Antibiotikum *n* antibiotic.
antik *adj* antique.
Antike *f* antique; antiquity.
Antilope *f* antelope.
Antrag *m* application; proposal.
antreiben *vt* to propel.
Antrieb *m* drive.
Antwerpen *n* Antwerp.
Antwort *f* answer.
antworten *vi* to answer.
Anwalt *m* **Anwältin** *f* lawyer, solicitor.
anweisen *vt* to instruct.
Anweisung *f* instruction; remittance.
anwendbar *adj* applicable.
anwenden *vt* to use.
Anwendung *f* use.
anwesend *adj* present.
Anwesenheit *f* presence.
Anzahl *f* number.
Anzeige *f* advertisement.
anzeigen *vt* to advertise, announce.
anziehen *vt* to put on; to dress; to attract:—*vr* to get dressed.
Anziehung *f* attraction.

Anziehungskraft *f* attraction; magnetism; gravitation.
Anzug *m* suit.
anzünden *vt* to light, ignite.
Anzünder *m* lighter.
Apathie *f* apathy.
apathisch *adj* apathetic.
Apfel *m* apple.
Apfelsine *f* orange.
Apfelwein *m* cider.
Apostel *m* apostle.
Apostroph *m* apostrophe.
Apotheke *f* chemist's, pharmacy.
Apotheker(in) *m(f)* pharmacist.
Apparat *m* item of equipment; telephone; camera:—**am ~!** speaking!: —**am ~ bleiben** hold the line.
Appell *m* appeal.
Appetit *m* appetite:—**guten ~** enjoy your meal.
appetitlich *adj* appetising.
Applaus *m* applause.
Aprikose *f* apricot.
April *m* April.
Aquarell *n* watercolour.
Aquarium *n* aquarium.
Äquator *m* equator.
äquatorial *adj* equatorial.
Araber *m* **Arabin** *f* Arab.
Arabien *n* Arabia.
arabisch *adj* Arabian.
Arbeit *f* work.
Arbeiter(in) *m(f)* worker.
arbeiten *vt vi* to work.
arbeitslos *adj* unemployed.
Arbeitslosigkeit *f* unemployment.
Arbeitsplatz *m* job; place of work, workstation.
Arbeitszeit *f* working hours.

Archäologe *m* archaeologist.
Archäologie *f* archaeology.
Architekt(in) *m(f)* architect.
Architektur *f* architecture.
Archiv *n* archive.
arg *adj* bad, evil:—*adv* badly.
Arg *n* malice, harm.
Argentinien *n* Argentina.
Ärger *m* anger; trouble.
ärgerlich *adj* angry; annoying.
ärgern *vt* to annoy:—*vr* to get annoyed.
Ärgernis *n* annoyance.
Arglist *f* cunning, deceit.
arglistig *adj* malicious.
arglos *adj* guileless.
Arglosigkeit *f* innocence.
Argument *n* argument.
Argwohn *m* suspicion, distrust.
Arie *f* aria.
Aristokrat *m* aristocrat.
Aristokratie *f* aristocracy.
Arithmetik *f* arithmetic.
arithmetisch *adj* arithmetic(al).
Arktis *f* Arctic.
arktisch *adj* arctic.
arm *adj* poor.
Arm *m* arm.
Armband *n* bracelet.
Armbanduhr *f* wristwatch.
Armee *f* army.
Ärmel *m* sleeve.
Ärmelkanal *m* (the) English Channel.
ärmlich *adj* poor, shabby.
Ärmlichkeit *f* poverty, shabbiness.
armselig *adj* poverty-stricken.
Armut *f* poverty.
Aroma *n* aroma.
aromatisch *adj* aromatic.

Arrest *m* arrest, detention.
arrogant *adj* arrogant.
Arroganz *f* arrogance.
Arsch *m* arse, bum.
Art *f* way; sort; species.
Arterie *f* artery.
artig *adj* well-behaved.
Artikel *m* article.
Artillerie *f* artillery.
Arznei *f* medicine.
Arzt *m* **Ärztin** *f* doctor.
ärztlich *adj* medical.
As *n* ace; A flat.
Asbest *m* asbestos.
Asche *f* ash(es).
Aschenbecher *m* ashtray.
Aschermittwoch *m* Ash
   Wednesday.
Asien *n* Asia.
Asiat(in) *m(f)* Asian.
asiatisch *adj* Asian.
Aspekt *m* aspect.
Assistent(in) *m(f)* assistant.
Assoziation *f* association.
Ast *m* branch.
ästhetisch *adj* aesthetic.
Asthma *n* asthma.
Astrologe *m* astrologer.
Astrologie *f* astrology.
astrologisch *adj* astrological.
Astronaut *m* astronaut.
Astronom *m* astronomer.
Astronomie *f* astronomy.
Asyl *n* asylum.
Asylbewerber *m* asylum-
   seeker.
Atem *m* breath.
atemlos *adj* breathless.
Atheismus *m* atheism.
Atheist *m* atheist.
Athen *n* Athens.
Äther *m* ether.
Äthiopien *n* Ethiopia.
Athlet *m* athlete.
Atlantik *m* Atlantic
   (Ocean).
Atlas *m* atlas.

atmen *vt vi* to breathe.
Atmosphäre *f* atmosphere.
atmosphärisch *adj* atmospheric.
Atmung *f* breathing.
Atom *n* atom.
Atomkraftwerk *n* nuclear
   power station.
Atomkrieg *m* nuclear war.
ätzen *vt* to corrode.
Ätzdruck *m* etching.
ätzend *adj* corrosive, caustic.
auch *adv* also.
auf *prep + dat* on, in, at; +
   acc on, in, at, to; up:—~
   und ab up and down.
Aufbau *m* building, structure.
aufbauen *vt* to build.
aufbewahren *vt* to keep.
Aufbewahrung *f* storage.
aufbleiben *vi* to stay open,
   stay up.
Aufbruch *m* departure;
   uprising.
aufdecken *vt* to uncover:—
   vi to lay the table.
Aufenthalt *m* stay; stop;
   delay.
Auferstehung *f* resurrection.
Auffahrt *f* approach; entry;
   driveway.
auffallen *vi* to fall, hit; to
   be conspicuous.
auffallend, auffällig *adj*
   conspicuous.
Aufgabe *f* job; homework;
   giving up.
Aufgang *m* ascent; stair-
   way; germination.
aufgeben *vt* to give up; to
   send; to hand in.
aufgeregt *adj* excited.
aufgeweckt *adj* intelligent,
   alert.
aufgrund *prep* on the basis

of, because of.
aufhalten *vt vr* to stay.
aufheben *vt* to lift; to
   cancel:—*vr* to offset,
   cancel out.
Aufheben(s) *n* fuss.
aufhorchen *vi* to listen
   closely.
aufhören *vi* to stop.
aufklären *vt* to clarify; to
   enlighten.
Aufklärung *f* enlighten-
   ment.
Auflage *f* edition; circulation; imposition; tax.
auflesen *vt* to pick up,
   gather.
auflösen *vt* to dissolve,
   disintegrate; to solve.
Auflösung *f* solution;
   break-up; termination.
aufmachen *vt* to open:—*vr*
   to set off for.
Aufmachung *f* format; layout; outfit.
aufmerksam *adj* alert:—**auf
   etw ~ machen** to point out.
Aufmerksamkeit *f* alert-
   ness.
Aufnahme *f* absorption;
   beginning; inclusion;
   photograph; recording.
aufnehmen *vt* to lift; to
   absorb; to begin; to photograph; to record.
aufpassen *vi* to listen,
   watch, pay attention.
Aufprall *m* impact.
aufräumen *vt vi* to clear
   away.
aufrechnen *vt* to calculate;
   to charge; to settle.
aufrecht *adj adv* upright.
aufregen *vt* to excite:—*vr*
   to get excited.
aufregend *adj* exciting.
Aufregung *f* excitement.

Aufruf *m* call, summons.
aufrufen *vt* to call up;
to call out.
Aufruhr *m* uproar; revolt.
aufrühren *vt* to stir up.
aufs = **auf das.**
aufschließen *vt* to open,
unlock:—*vr* to close ranks.
Aufschluß *m* information.
Aufschrei *m* cry.
aufschreien *vi* to cry out.
Aufschrift *f* inscription;
label.
Aufschwung *n* upturn.
Aufsicht *f* supervision.
Aufstand *m* rebellion.
aufständisch *adj* rebellious.
aufstehen *vi* to be open; to
stand up; to rebel.
aufstellen *vt* to put up; to
display; to prepare; to set
up.
Aufstellung *f* arrangement;
preparation; list.
Aufstieg *m* ascent.
Auftrag *m* job; order:—**im**
~ **von** on behalf of.
auftreten *vi* to step; to
appear; to enter; to occur.
Auftreten *n* appearance,
occurrence.
Auftritt *m* entrance;
appearance; scene.
auftun *vt vr* to open.
aufwachen *vi* to wake up.
Aufwand *m* expenditure;
extravagance.
aufwärts *adv* upwards.
aufwecken *vt* to wake up.
aufweisen *vt* to display.
aufwenden *vt* to spend; to
devote.
aufwendig *adj* expensive.
Aufzug *m* lift, elevator;
procession.
Augapfel *m* eyeball; apple
of one's eye.

Auge *n* eye; bud.
Augenblick *m* moment.
augenblicklich *adj* momen-
tary; present.
Augenbraue *f* eyebrow.
Augenheilkunde *f* ophthal-
mology.
Augenmerk *n* attention.
Augenschein *m* appearance.
augenscheinlich *adj* obvious.
Augenstern *m* pupil.
Augentäuschung *f* optical
illusion.
Augenwimper *f* eyelash.
Augenzeuge *m* eyewitness.
August *m* August.
Auktion *f* auction.
Auktionator(in) *m(f)* auc-
tioneer.
Aula *f* hall, auditorium.
aus *prep* out of, from; made
of:—*adv* finished, over.
ausarbeiten *vt* to work out.
Ausbau *m* extension.
ausbauen *vt* to extend.
Ausbeute *f* profit.
ausbeuten *vt* to exploit.
Ausbeutung *f* exploitation.
ausbezahlen *vt* to pay off.
ausbilden *vt* to train; to
educate.
Ausbildung *f* education,
training.
Ausblick *m* outlook.
ausbrechen *vt* to break out;
to vomit: —*vi* to break
out.
ausbreiten *vt* to expand.
ausbringen *vt* to bring out;
to yield.
Ausbruch *m* outbreak;
breakout; eruption.
Ausdauer *f* endurance.
ausdauern *vi* to endure.
ausdehnen *vt vr* to extend.
Ausdruck *m* expression;
printout.

ausdrucken *vt* to print out.
ausdrücken *vt* to express;
to squeeze; to stub out.
ausdrücklich *adj* express.
auseinander *adv* apart.
auseinandersetzen *vt* to
put asunder; to explain;
to argue; to agree.
Auseinandersetzung *f* disagreement.
auserlesen *adj* selected.
Ausfahrt *f* departure;
excursion; exit.
Ausfall *m* falling out; loss;
shortage; fallout.
ausfallen *vi* to fall out; to
be missing; to be can-
celled; to break down; to
stop.
ausfertigen *vt* to draw up.
Ausfertigung *f* drawing
up.
ausfließen *vi* to flow out.
Ausflucht *f* pretext.
Ausflug *m* excursion.
Ausfluß *m* outflow.
Ausfuhr *f* export(s).
ausführbar *adj* feasible.
ausführen *vt* to take out,
carry out; to export.
ausführlich *adj* detailed:—
adv in detail.
Ausführung *f* execution,
implementation.
ausfüllen *vt* to fill in.
Ausgabe *f* expenditure;
edition, issue.
Ausgang *m* exit.
ausgeben *vt* to spend; to
distribute:—*vr* to pass
oneself off.
ausgebildet *adj* qualified.
ausgefallen *adj* exceptional.
ausgeglichen *adj* balanced.
ausgehen *vi* to go out; to
end:—**davon** ~ to assume.
ausgenommen *prep* except.

ausgeprägt *adj* prominent.

ausgeschlossen *adj* excluded.

ausgesprochen *adj adv* distinct(ly).

ausgezeichnet *adj* excellent.

Ausgleich *m* balance; equalization.

ausgleichen *vt* to reconcile:—*vi* to equalize.

auskleiden *vr* undress.

auskommen *vi* to manage.

auskömmlich *adj* adequate.

Auskunft *f* information.

Ausland *n*:—**im ~** abroad.

Ausländer(in) *m(f)* foreigner.

ausländisch *adj* foreign.

auslassen *vt* to leave out; to let out.

auslegen *vt* to lay out; to put down; to lend; to explain.

Auslegung *f* explanation, interpretation.

Auslese *f* selection.

auslesen *vt* to select.

ausliefern *vt* to hand over.

Auslieferung *f* delivery.

ausmachen *vt* to turn off; to make out, distinguish; to agree; to represent, constitute; to matter.

Ausmaß *n* size, scale.

Ausnahme *f* exception.

ausnahmslos *adv* without exception.

ausnehmen *vt* to take out; to clean out:—*vr* to look.

Auspuff *m* exhaust.

Auspuffrohr *n* exhaust pipe.

Auspufftopf *m* silencer (car).

ausräuchern *vt* to fumigate.

ausräumen *vt* to empty, clear away.

ausrechnen *vt* to calculate, work out.

Ausrede *f* excuse.

ausreden *vt* to dissuade:—*vi* to have one's say.

ausreichen *vi* to suffice.

ausreichend *adj* sufficient.

Ausreise *f* departure.

ausreißen *vt* to tear out:—*vi* to get torn; to run away.

ausrichten *vt* to arrange; to hand over; to line up.

Ausruf *m* cry; announcement.

ausrufen *vt* to call out, proclaim.

Ausrufungszeichen *n* exclamation mark.

ausrüsten *vt* to equip, fit.

Ausrüstung *f* equipment.

Aussage *f* statement.

aussagen *vt vi* to state.

ausschauen *vi* to look out.

ausscheiden *vt* to separate; to excrete; to secrete; to depart.

Ausscheidung *f* separation; excretion; secretion; departure.

ausschlafen *vi* to sleep in.

ausschlagen *vt* to knock out; to reject:—*vi* to kick out; to germinate.

ausschlaggebend *adj* decisive:—**~e Stimme** casting vote.

ausschließen *vt* to exclude.

ausschließlich *adj adv* exclusive(ly): —*prep* excluding.

Ausschluß *m* exclusion.

ausschneiden *vt* to cut out.

Ausschnitt *m* extract; section.

ausschöpfen *vt* to drain; to exhaust.

ausschreiben *vt* to write

out; to advertise.

Ausschreibung *f* announcement; call for tenders.

Ausschuß *m* committee; waste.

aussehen *vi* to look.

Aussehen *n* appearance.

außen *adv* outside.

Außenhandel *m* foreign trade.

Außenminister *m* foreign minister.

Außenministerium *n* foreign ministry.

Außenpolitik *f* foreign policy.

Außenseite *f* outside.

Außenseiter *m* outsider.

außer *prep* out of, except:— **~ sich** beside oneself:— *conj* except.

außerdem *conj* besides, moreover.

äußere(r, s) *adj* outer.

außerehelich *adj* illegitimate; extramarital.

außergerichtlich *adj* extrajudicial.

außergewöhnlich *adj* unusual.

außerhalb *adv prep* outside.

äußerlich *adj* external, outward.

äußern *vt* to utter:—*vr* to express one's opinion.

außerordentlich *adj* unusual.

äußerst *adv* extremely:—*adj* utmost.

Äußerung *f* utterance.

Aussicht *f* view.

aussichtslos *adj* hopeless.

Aussichtspunkt *m* viewpoint.

aussichtsreich *adj* promising.

aussöhnen *vt* to reconcile:—*vr* to be reconciled.

Aussöhnung *f* reconciliation.

Aussprache *f* pronunciation; discussion.

aussprechen *vt* to pronounce:—*vr* to speak; to discuss:—*vi* to finish speaking.

Ausspruch *m* utterance.

ausstatten *vt* to equip.

Ausstattung *f* equipment; outfit.

aussteigen *vi* to get out.

ausstellen *vt* to exhibit.

Ausstellung *f* exhibition.

Aussteuer *f* dowry.

Ausstieg *m* exit.

Austausch *m* exchange.

austauschen *vt* to exchange.

austeilen *vt* to distribute.

Auster *f* oyster.

austoben *vr* to run wild:—*vi* to calm down.

Australien *n* Australia.

Australier(in) *m(f)* Australian.

australienisch *adj* Australian.

austreiben *vt* to drive out.

austreten *vt* to wear out:—*vi* to leave.

Austritt *m* emission; withdrawal.

ausüben *vt* to exercise, perform.

Ausverkauf *m* (clearance) sale.

ausverkaufen *vt* to sell out, sell up.

ausverkauft *adj* sold out.

Auswahl *f* selection.

auswählen *vt* to select.

Auswanderer(in) *m(f)* emigrant.

auswandern *vi* to emigrate.

Auswanderung *f* emigration.

auswärtig *adj* foreign, external.

auswärts *adv* outside; outwards; away.

Ausweg *m* way out.

Ausweis *m* passport, identity card.

ausweisen *vt* to expel:—*vr* to prove one's identity.

ausweiten *vt vr* extend.

auswendig *adv* by heart.

auswirken *vt* to effect:—*vr* to have an effect.

Auswirkung *f* effect.

Auswuchs *m* outgrowth.

Auswurf *m* ejection.

Auszug *m* departure; extract.

Auto *n* car.

Autobahn *f* motorway, freeway.

Autobiographie *m* autobiography.

autobiographisch *adj* autobiographical.

Autobus *m* bus, coach.

Autofähre *f* car ferry.

Autofahrer(in) *m(f)* motorist.

Autogramm *n* autograph.

Autohändler *m* car dealer.

Autokrat *m* autocrat.

Automat *m* vending machine.

automatisch *adj* automatic.

Autor(in) *m(f)* author.

autorisieren *vt* to authorize.

Autorität *f* authority.

Axt *f* axe.

B

Baby *n* baby.
Bach *m* stream.
Backbord *n* port (ship).
backen *vt vi* to bake.
Bäcker *m* baker.
Bäckerei *f* bakery.
Backofen *m* oven.
Backstein *m* brick.
Bad *n* bath; swim.
Badeanzug *m* swimming costume.
baden *vt vi* to bathe, bath.
Badewanne *f* bathtub.
Badezimmer *n* bathroom.
Bahn *f* railway; road; track.
Bahnhof *m* station.
Bahnsteig *m* platform.
Bahre *f* barrow; stretcher.
bald *adv* soon.
Balkon *m* balcony.
Ball *m* ball.
Ballett *n* ballet.
Ballon *m* balloon.
Banane *f* banana.
Band *m* band; tape; volume.
Bandage *f* bandage.
Bande *f* band, team.
Bandit *m* bandit.
Bank *f* bench; bank.
Bankier *m* banker.
Bankkonto *m* bank account.
Banknote *f* banknote.
Bankraub *m* bank robbery.
Bankräuber *m* bank robber.
bankrott *adj* bankrupt.
Bankrott *m* bankruptcy.
Bankwesen *n* banking.
Banner *n* banner.
Bar *f* bar.

Bär *m* bear.
barbarisch *adj* barbaric.
Bargeld *n* cash.
Bariton *m* baritone.
barock *adj* **Barock** *n* baroque.
Barometer *n* barometer.
Baron(esse) *m(f)* baron(ess).
Barrikade *f* barricade.
Bart *m* beard.
Base *f* base; female cousin.
Basel *n* Basle.
basieren *vt* to base:—*vi* to be based.
Basis *f* base, basis.
Baß *m* bass (voice).
basteln *vt* to make:—*vi* to practise a hobby.
Bastler *m* hobbyist.
Batterie *f* battery.
Bau *m* building; structure.
Bauarbeiter *m* construction worker.
Bauch *m* stomach.
Bauchschmerzen *mpl* stomach ache.
bauen *vt vi* to build.
Bauer *m* farmer; peasant.
Bäuerin *f* farmer; farmer's wife.
Bauernhaus *n* farmhouse.
Bauernhof *m* farmyard.
Baum *m* tree.
Baumgarten *m* orchard.
Baumwolle *f* cotton.
Bauplatz *m* building site.
Bayern *n* Bavaria.
bayrisch *adj* Bavarian.
beabsichtigen *vt* to intend.
beachten *vt* to comply with.

beachtlich *adj* considerable.
Beachtung *f* notice, compliance.
Beamte(r) *m* **Beamtin** *f* official, civil servant.
beängstigen *vt* to worry.
beängstigend *adj* worrying.
beanstanden *vt* to complain.
Beanstandung *f* complaint.
bearbeiten *vt* to work on.
Bearbeitung *f* treatment.
beaufsichtigen *vt* to supervise.
Beaufsichtigung *f* supervision.
beauftragen *vt* to order; to entrust.
beben *vi* to shake.
Becher *m* mug.
bedanken *vr* to thank.
Bedarf *m* need, demand:— **bei ~** if necessary.
bedauerlich *adj* regrettable.
bedauern *vt* to regret.
Bedauern *n* regret.
bedenken *vt* to consider.
Bedenken *n* consideration; doubt.
bedenklich *adj* dubious.
bedeuten *vt* to mean.
bedeutend *adj* important.
Bedeutung *f* meaning.
bedeutungslos *adj* insignificant.
bedeutungsvoll *adj* significant.
bedienen *vt* to serve; to operate:—*vr* to help oneself:—**~ Sie sich!** help yourself.

Bedienung *f* service.

Bedingung *f* condition.

bedrohen *vt* to threaten.

bedrohlich *adj* threatening.

Bedrohung *f* threat.

bedürfen *vi* to need.

Bedürfnis *n* need.

beehren *vt* to honour.

beeilen *vr* to hurry.

beendigen *vt* to end.

beerben *vt* to inherit.

Beere *f* berry.

Beet *n* bed (in garden).

befassen *vr* to handle, deal with.

Befehl *m* order.

befehlen *vt* to order:—*vi* to give orders.

befestigen *vt* to fasten; to strengthen.

Befestigung *f* fastening; strengthening.

befinden *vr* to be (located); to feel.

befreien *vt* to release.

Befreiung *f* liberation.

befreunden *vr* to make friends.

befriedigen *vt* to satisfy.

befriedigend *adj* satisfactory.

Befriedigung *f* satisfaction.

befristet *adj* time-limited.

befruchten *vt* to fertilize.

Befruchtung *f* fertilization.

befugen *vt* to authorize.

Befugnis *f* authority.

befugt *adj* authorized.

begabt *adj* gifted.

Begabung *adj* talent.

begegnen *vi* to meet.

Begegnung *f* meeting.

begehen *vt* to go along; to commit; to celebrate.

begehren *vt* to covet.

begehrlich *adj* covetous.

begeistern *vt* to excite.

begeisternd *adj* exciting.

Begeisterung *f* enthusiasm.

Beginn *m* beginning.

beginnen *vt vi* to begin.

beglaubigen *vt* to certify.

beglaubigt *adj* certified.

Beglaubigung *f* certification.

begleiten *vt* to accompany.

Begleiter *m* companion.

Begleitung *f* accompaniment.

begraben *vt* to bury.

Begräbnis *n* burial, funeral.

begreifen *vt* to understand.

begreiflich *adj* understandable.

begrenzen *vt* to limit.

begrenzt *adj* limited.

Begrenzung *f* limitation.

Begriff *m* concept:—**im ~ sein** be about to.

begründen *vt* to justify.

begründet *adj* justified.

begrüßen *vt* to greet.

Begrüßung *f* greeting.

begünstigen *vt* to favour; to promote.

Begünstigung *f* promotion; favour.

behagen *vi* to please.

behaglich *adj* comfortable.

Behaglichkeit *f* comfort.

behalten *vt* to keep.

Behälter *m* container.

behandeln *vt* to handle.

Behandlung *f* handling.

behaupten *vt* to assert:—*vr* to assert oneself.

Behauptung *f* claim.

beheben *vt* to remove.

Behebung *f* removal.

beherrschen *vt* to control; to master.

Beherrschung *f* control.

beherzt *adj* courageous.

Beherztheit *f* courage.

behindern *vt* to hinder.

Behinderte(r) *f(m)* handicapped person.

Behinderung *f* hindrance; handicap.

Behörde *f* official body:—**die Behörden** *pl* the authorities.

behördlich *adj* official.

behüten *vt* to protect:—**Gott behüte!** God forbid.

behutsam *adj* careful.

bei *prep* near; by; at; at the home of; among; in; during.

beibehalten *vt* to keep.

Beibehaltung *f* retention.

beibringen *vt* to bring forward; to provide.

Beichte *f* confession.

beichten *vt vi* to confess.

beide(r, s) *adj* both.

beiderseitig *adj* mutual.

beiderseits *adv* mutually:—*prep* on both sides of.

beidhändig *adj* ambidextrous.

Beifahrer *m* passenger.

Beifall *m* applause.

beifügen *vt* to enclose.

Beifügung *f* enclosure.

Beihilfe *f* assistance; subsidy.

Beil *n* axe.

Beilage *f* enclosure; vegetables; garnish.

beiläufig *adj adv* incidental(ly).

beiliegend *adj* enclosed.

Bein *n* leg; bone.

beinah(e) *adv* nearly.

beinhalten *vt* to contain.

Beirat *m* adviser; supervisory board.

Beispiel *n* example:—**zum ~** for example.

beispielhaft *adj* exemplary.

beispielsweise *adv* for example.

beißen *vt vi* to bite.

Beistand *m* support.

beistehen *vi* to assist.

beistimmen *vi* to agree with.

Beitrag *m* contribution.

beitragen *vt* to contribute.

Beize *f* corrosion.

bejahen *vt* to say yes to.

bejahrt *adj* elderly.

Bejahung *f* affirmation.

bekannt *adj* (well-)known; acquainted.

Bekannte(r) *f(m)* acquaintance.

bekanntgeben *vt* to announce.

bekanntmachen *vt* to announce.

Bekanntmachung *f* announcement.

Bekanntschaft *f* acquaintance.

bekehren *vt vi* to convert.

bekennen *vt* to admit.

Bekenntnis *n* admission; confession.

beklagen *vt* to lament:—*vr* to complain.

Beklagte(r) *f(m)* defendant; respondent.

bekleiden *vt* to clothe.

Bekleidung *f* clothing.

bekommen *vt* to receive.

Belag *m* covering, coating.

belagern *vt* to besiege.

Belagerung *f* siege.

belasten *vt* to burden; to charge.

Belastung *f* load; charge.

beleben *vt* to enliven.

belebend *adj* invigorating.

belebt *adj* busy.

Belebung *f* animation.

Beleg *m* receipt; proof.

belegen *vt* to cover; to prove.

beleidigen *vt* to insult.

Beleidigung *f* insult; libel; slander.

beleuchten *vt* to illuminate.

Beleuchtung *f* illumination.

Belgien *n* Belgium.

Belgier(in) *m(f)* Belgian.

belgisch *adj* Belgian.

Belgrad *n* Belgrade.

belichten *vt* to expose (film).

Belichtung *f* exposure.

Belieben *n*:—**nach ~** as you wish.

beliebt *adj* popular.

Beliebtheit *f* popularity.

beliefern *vt* to supply.

bellen *vi* to bark.

belohnen *vt* to reward.

Belohnung *f* reward.

belüften *vt* to ventilate.

Belüftung *f* ventilation.

bemannen *vt* to staff.

bemerkbar *adj* noticeable.

bemerken *vt* to notice; to remark.

bemerkenswert *adj* remarkable.

Bemerkung *f* remark.

bemessen *vt* to measure; to assess.

bemühen *vr* to endeavour.

Bemühung *f* effort.

benachbart *adj* neighbouring.

benachrichtigen *vt* to notify.

Benachrichtigung *f* notification.

benehmen *vr* to take away; to behave.

Benehmen *n* behaviour.

beneiden *vt* to envy.

beneidenswert *adj* enviable.

benennen *vt* to name.

Benennung *f* naming.

benötigen *vt* to need.

benutzen, benützen *vt* to use.

Benutzer *m* user.

Benutzung *f* use.

Benzin *n* petrol.

beobachten *vt* to watch.

Beobachter *m* observer.

Beobachtung *f* observation.

bequem *adj* comfortable.

Bequemlichkeit *f* convenience, comfort.

beraten *vt* to advise.

Berater *m* adviser.

Beratung *f* advice; consultation.

berechnen *vt* to calculate; to charge.

Berechnung *f* calculation; charge.

berechtigen *vt* to entitle.

berechtigt *adj* justified.

Berechtigung *f* entitlement.

Bereich *m* area.

bereit *adj* ready.

bereiten *vt* to prepare.

Berg *m* mountain, hill.

bergab *adv* downhill.

bergauf *adv* uphill.

Bergbau *m* mining.

bergen *vt* to shelter; to save; to hide.

bergig *adj* mountainous.

Bergmann *m* miner.

Bergsteigen *n* mountaineering.

Bergsteiger(in) *m(f)* mountaineer.

Bergwerk *n* mine.

Bericht *m* report.

berichten *vt vi* to report.

Berichterstatter *m* reporter.

berichtigen *vt* to correct.

Berichtigung *f* correction.

bersten *vi* to burst.

berücksichtigen *vt* to consider.

Berücksichtigung *f* consideration.

Beruf *m* occupation.

berufen *vt* to appoint:—*vr* to appeal.

beruflich *adj* professional.

Berufung *f* calling.

beruhen *vi* to be based.

beruhigen *vt* to calm:—*vr* to calm down.

Beruhigung *f* calming.

berühmt *adj* famous.

Berühmtheit *f* fame.

berühren *vt* to touch; to affect:—*vr* to come into contact.

Berührung *f* contact.

besagen *vt* to mean.

besagt *adj* in question.

Besatzung *f* garrison; crew; occupation.

beschädigen *vt* to damage.

Beschädigung *f* damage.

beschaffen *vt* to obtain.

Bechaffenheit *f* nature.

Beschaffung *f* acquisition.

beschäftigen *vt* to occupy.

beschäftigt *adj* occupied.

Beschäftigung *f* occupation; concern.

beschämen *vt* to shame.

beschämend *adj* shameful, shaming.

beschämt *adj* ashamed.

Bescheid *m* information; directions: —~ **wissen** be well aware.

bescheiden *vr* to make do:—*adj* modest, shy.

bescheinigen *vt* to confirm.

Bescheinigung *f* certificate, confirmation.

beschießen *vt* to fire at.

beschimpfen *vt* to insult.

Beschimpfung *f* abuse.

beschleunigen *vt vi* to accelerate.

Beschleunigung *f* acceleration.

beschränken *vt* to confine.

beschränkt *adj* confined.

Beschränkung *f* limitation.

beschreiben *vt* to describe.

Beschreibung *f* description.

beschuldigen *vt* to accuse.

Beschuldigung *f* accusation.

Beschwerde *f* complaint.

beseitigen *vt* to remove.

Beseitigung *f* removal.

Besen *m* broom.

besetzen *vt* to occupy; to fill.

besetzt *adj* occupied.

Besetzung *f* occupation.

besichtigen *vt* to inspect.

Besichtigung *f* inspection.

Besitz *m* possession.

besitzen *vt* to possess.

Besitzer(in) *m(f)* owner.

besoffen *adj* drunk.

besondere(r, s) *adj* particular, special.

Besonderheit *f* peculiarity.

besonders *adv* particularly.

besonnen *adj* sensible.

besonnt *adj* sunny.

besorgen *vt* to provide, acquire.

Besorgnis *f* concern.

besorgt *adj* concerned.

Besorgtheit *f* concern.

Besorgung *f* acquisition.

besprechen *vt vr* to discuss.

Besprechung *f* discussion, meeting.

besser *adj adv* better.

bessern *vt* to improve.

Besserung *f* improvement.

Bestand *m* durability; stock, supply.

Bestandteil *m* component.

bestärken *vt* to strengthen.

bestätigen *vt* to confirm.

Bestätigung *f* confirmation.

bestatten *vt* to bury, cremate.

Bestatter *m* undertaker.

Bestattung *f* funeral.

beste(r, s) *adj* best.

bestechen *vt* to bribe.

Bestechung *f* bribery.

Besteck *n* cutlery.

bestehen *vi* to exist:—*vt* to pass (exam, etc):—~ **auf** insist on:—~ **aus** consist of.

bestellen *vt* to order; to appoint.

Bestellung *f* order.

bestenfalls *adv* at best.

bestens *adv* very well, best.

bestimmen *vt* to determine; to specify.

bestimmt *adj adv* definite(ly).

Bestimmung *f* determination; destination.

bestrahlen *vt* to shine on; to irradiate.

Bestrahlung *f* irradiation; radiotherapy.

Besuch *m* visit.

besuchen *vt* to visit, attend.

Besucher(in) *m(f)* visitor.

betätigen *vt* to operate, control.

Betätigung *f* activity.

betäuben *vt* to deafen; to stun.

Betäubungsmittel *n* anaesthetic.

Bete *f* beetroot.

beteiligen *vt* to involve:—*vr* to participate.

Beteiligung *f* participation.

beten *vt vi* to pray.

Beton *m* concrete.

betonen *vt* to emphasize.

Betonung *f* emphasis.

Betracht *m* consideration.
betrachten *vt* to consider.
beträchtlich *adj* considerable.
Betrag *m* amount.
betragen *vt* to amount to:—*vr* to behave.
betreffen *vt* to relate, affect.
betreffend *adj* relevant.
betreten *vt* to enter:—~ **verboten** no entry:—*adj* confused, embarrassed.
Betrieb *m* company; factory; operation:—**außer ~** out of order.
Betriebsrat *m* works council.
betrinken *vr* to get drunk.
betroffen *adj* affected; shocked.
betrüben *vt vr* to grieve.
betrübt *adj* grieved.
Betrug *m* deception; fraud.
betrügen *vt* to deceive.
Betrüger(in) *m(f)* cheat.
betrunken *adj* drunk.
Bett *n* bed.
betteln *vi* to beg.
betten *vt* to put to bed; to embed.
Bettflasche *f* hot water bottle.
Bettlaken *n* sheet.
Bettler(in) *m(f)* beggar.
Beuge *f* bend.
beugen *vt* to bend:—*vr* to bow.
Beule *f* bump, lump.
beurteilen *vt* to judge.
Beurteilung *f* judgment.
Beute *f* loot.
Beutel *m* bag; purse.
Bevölkerung *f* population.
bevollmächtigen *vt* to authorize.
Bevollmächtigte(r) *f(m)* authorized representative.

Bevollmächtigung *f* authorization; power of attorney.
bevor *conj* before.
bevorzugen *vt* to prefer.
Bevorzugung *f* preference.
bewachen *vt* to watch.
Bewachung *f* guard.
bewahren *vt* to keep.
bewähren *vt* to prove.
bewährt *adj* tried and tested.
Bewährung *f* probation.
bewaldet *adj* wooded.
bewältigen *vt* to overcome, manage.
Bewältigung *f* conquest.
bewässern *vt* to water.
Bewässerung *f* irrigation.
bewegen *vt vr* to move.
beweglich *adj* movable.
bewegt *adj* rough (sea); moved.
Bewegung *f* movement.
Beweis *m* proof.
beweisen *vt* to prove.
bewohnen *vt* to inhabit.
Bewohner(in) *m(f)* inhabitant.
bewölkt *adj* cloudy.
Bewunderer(in) *m(f)* admirer.
bewußt *adj* conscious; deliberate.
bewußtlos *adj* unconscious.
Bewußtsein *n* consciousness.
bezahlen *vt vi* to pay (for).
Bezahlung *f* payment.
bezeichnen *vt* to describe; to mark; to call; to label.
Bezeichnung *f* description; name.
beziehen *vt vr* to refer.
Beziehung *f* connection, relationship.
beziehungsweise *adv* or; respectively.

Bezirk *m* district.
Bezug *m* covering; purchase; income; reference:—**in ~ auf** with reference to.
bezüglich *prep adj* concerning.
Bezugnahme *f* reference.
bezweifeln *vt* to doubt.
Bibel *f* bible.
Bibliographie *f* bibliography.
Bibliothek *f* library.
Bibliothekar(in) *m(f)* librarian.
biblisch *adj* biblical.
biegen *vt vr* to bend; *vi* to turn (corner).
biegsam *adj* flexible.
Biegung *f* bend.
Biene *f* bee.
Bienenkorb *m* beehive.
Bier *n* beer.
bieten *vt* to offer, bid.
Bieter(in) *m(f)* bidder.
Bigamie *f* bigamy.
Bikini *m* bikini.
Bilanz *f* balance; balance sheet.
Bild *n* picture.
bilden *vt* to form; to educate:—*vr* to develop.
Bildhauer(in) *m(f)* sculptor.
Bildschirm *m* TV screen.
Bildung *f* formation; education.
Billard *n* billiards.
billig *adj* cheap; reasonable.
billigen *vt* to approve.
Billigkeit *f* fairness; cheapness.
Billigung *f* approval.
Binde *f* band, bandage; sanitary towel.
binden *vt* to tie.
Bindestrich *m* hyphen.
Bindfaden *m* string.

Bindung *f* connection; compound.

binnen *prep* within.

Biographie *f* biography.

Biologe *m* biologist.

Biologie *f* biology.

biologisch *adj* biological.

Birke *f* birch.

Birne *f* pear; lightbulb.

bis *prep* until; by; to, as far as; up to: —*conj* to; until.

Bischof *m* bishop.

bisexuell *adj* bisexual.

bisher *adv* hitherto.

bisherig *adj* previous.

bislang *adv* hitherto.

Biskuit *n* biscuit.

Biß *m* bite.

bißchen *adj adv*:—**ein ~** a bit, a little.

bissig *adj* biting.

bisweilen *adv* sometimes.

Bitte *f* request.

bitte *excl* please:—**(wie) bitte?** pardon?:—**bitte (schön)** don't mention it.

bitten *vt vi* to ask.

bitter *adj* bitter.

Bitterkeit *f* bitterness.

blank *adj* bright; bare; broke.

Blase *f* bubble; blister; bladder.

blasen *vt vi* to blow.

Blasphemie *f* blasphemy.

blaß *adj* pale.

Blässe *f* paleness.

Blatt *n* leaf; page; sheet; newspaper.

blättern *vi*:—**~ in** to leaf through.

blau *adj* blue; drunk.

blaumachen *vi* to play truant.

Blech *n* tin; sheet metal.

Blei *n* lead.

bleiben *vi* to remain.

bleifrei *adj* unleaded.

Bleistift *m* pencil.

Blende *f* blind.

blenden *vt* to blind.

Blick *m* look.

blicken *vt* to look.

blind *adj* blind.

Blindheit *f* blindness.

blinken *vi* to flash; to sparkle.

blinzeln *vi* to blink, wink.

Blitz *m* lightning; flash.

blitzschnell *adj adv* quick as a flash.

Block *m* block; notepad.

Blockflöte *f* recorder.

blockieren *vt* to block.

blöd *adj* stupid.

Blödsinn *m* nonsense.

blond *adj* blond(e).

bloß *adj* naked; sheer:—*adv* only.

Blöße *f* bareness.

blühen *vi* to flower; to flourish.

Blume *f* flower; bouquet (wine).

Blumenkohl *m* cauliflower.

Bluse *f* blouse.

Blut *n* blood.

Blüte *n* blossom.

bluten *vi* to bleed.

blutig *adj* bloody.

Bö *f* gust.

Bock *m* buck; ram; support.

Boden *m* ground, floor, soil.

Bogen *m* bow; arch; curve.

Bohle *f* board.

Bohne *f* bean.

bohren *vt* to drill.

Bohrer *m* drill.

Bolzen *m* bolt.

Bombe *f* bomb.

Bonbon *m* sweet.

Boot *n* boat.

Bord *n* shelf; edge:—**an ~** on board.

Bordell *n* brothel.

borgen *vt* to borrow; to lend.

Börse *f* purse; stock exchange.

bös *adj* angry; bad.

bösartig *adj* malicious.

Bösartigkeit *f* malice.

Botanik *f* botany.

Botaniker *m* botanist.

botanisch *adj* botanical.

Bote *m* messenger.

Botschaft *f* message; embassy.

Botschafter(in) *m(f)* ambassador.

boxen *vi* to box.

Boxen *n* boxing.

Boxer *m* boxer.

Branche *f* (sector of) industry.

Brand *m* fire; gangrene.

branden *vi* to surge; to break.

Brandstifter *m* arsonist.

Branntwein *m* brandy, spirits.

braten *vt* to roast; to bake; to fry.

Bratpfanne *f* frying pan.

Bratwurst *f* grilled sausage.

brauchbar *adj* usable.

brauchen *vt* to use; to need.

Braue *f* brow.

brauen *vt* to brew.

Brauerei *f* brewery.

braun *adj* brown.

Bräune *f* brownness; tan.

braunen *vt* to brown.

Braut *f* bride, fiancée.

Brautigam *m* bridegroom, fiancé.

brechen *vt vi* to break; to vomit.

Brei *m* porridge, oatmeal; pulp.

breit *adj* wide.

Breite *f* width; latitude.
breiten *vt* to spread.
Bremse *f* brake.
bremsen *vt vi* to brake.
brennbar *adj* (in)flam-
    mable.
brennen *vr vi* to burn.
Brett *n* board.
Brief *m* letter.
Briefkasten *m* letter box.
Briefmarke *f* stamp.
Briefträger(in) *m(f)* post-
    man.
Brille *f* glasses.
bringen *vt* to bring.
Brombeere *f* blackberry.
Bronze *f* bronze.
Broschüre *f* brochure.
Brot *n* bread; loaf.
Brötchen *n* (bread) roll.
Bruch *m* break.
Brücke *f* bridge.
Bruder *m* brother.
brüderlich *adj* brotherly.
Brunnen *m* well; spring;
    fountain.
Brüssel *n* Brussels.
Brust *f* breast, chest.
brüten *vi vt* to hatch, brood.
Bube *m* lad; jack (cards).
Buch *n* book.
Buche *f* beech.
buchen *vt* to book.
Buchführung *f* bookkeep-
    ing.

Büchse *f* box; can; rifle.
Büchsenöffner *m* can
    opener.
Buchstabe *m* letter;
    character.
buchstabieren *vt* to spell.
Bucht *f* bay.
Buckel *m* hump.
bücken *vt vr* to bend.
Bude *f* booth; stall.
Büffel *m* buffalo; oaf.
Bug *m* bow (ship); nose
    (aircraft).
Bügel *m* clothes hanger;
    stirrup.
Bügelbrett *n* ironing board.
Bügeleisen *n* iron.
bügeln *vt vi* to iron.
Bühne *f* stage, platform.
Bukarest *n* Bucharest.
Bulgarien *n* Bulgaria.
Bulle *m* bull.
Bummel *m* stroll.
bummeln *vi* to stroll, daw-
    dle.
Bund *n* bundle; band:—*m*
    tie; alliance; federation.
Bündel *n* bundle.
bundeln *vt* to bundle.
Bundes- *prefix* federal,
    German.
Bundesrat *m* upper house
    of German parliament.
Bundesrepublik *f* Federal
    Republic (of Germany).

Bundestag *m* lower house
    of German parliament.
Bündnis *n* alliance.
bunt *adj* colourful.
Burg *f* castle.
bürgen *vt* to guarantee.
Bürger(in) *m(f)* citizen.
Bürgerkrieg *m* civil war.
bürgerlich *adj* middle-class;
    civil.
Bürgermeister *m* mayor.
Bürgersteig *m* pavement.
Bürgschaft *f* security, guar-
    antee.
Büro *n* office.
Büroangestellte(r) *f(m)*
    office worker.
Büroklammer *f* paperclip.
Bursche *m* lad; guy;
    servant.
Bürste *f* brush.
bürsten *vt* to brush.
Bus *m* bus.
Busch *m* bush.
Büste *f* bust.
Büstenhalter *m* bra.
Butter *f* butter.
Butterblume *f* buttercup.
Butterbrot *n* bread and
    butter.
Butterbrotpapier *n* grease-
    proof paper.

C

Café *n* café.
Cafeteria *f* cafeteria.
Camp *n* camp.
campen *vi* to camp.
Camper *m* camper.
Caravan *m* caravan.
CD-Spieler *m* CD player.
Cellist *m* cellist.
Cello *n* cello.
Celcius *n* Celsius.
Chamäleon *n* chameleon.
Chance *f* chance, opportunity.
Chaos *n* chaos.
chaotisch *adj* chaotic.
Charakter *m* character.
charakterisieren *vt* to characterize.
charakteristisch *adj* characteristic.
charmant *adj* charming, delightful.
Charme *m* charm.

Chauffeur *m* chauffeur.
Chauvinist *m* chauvinist.
Chef(in) *m(f)* boss, head (of firm).
Chemie *f* chemistry.
Chemikalie *f* chemical.
Chemiker(in) *m(f)* chemist.
chemisch *adj* chemical.
chilenisch *adj* Chilean.
Chinese *m* Chinese.
Chinesin *f* Chinese.
chinesisch *adj* Chinese.
Chirurg *m* surgeon.
Chirurgie surgery.
chirurgisch *adj* surgical.
Chlor *n* chlorine.
Cholera *f* cholera.
cholerisch *adj* choleric.
Chor *m* choir; chorus.
Choral *m* chorale.
Choregraph *m* choreographer.
Christ(in) *m(f)* Christian.

Christbaum *m* Christmas tree.
Christenheit *f* Christianity.
christlich *adj* Christian.
Christus *m* Christ.
Chrom *n* chromium; chrome.
Chronik *f* chronicle.
chronisch *adj* chronic.
Chronologie *f* chronology.
chronologisch *adj* chronological.
Chrysantheme *f* chrysanthemum.
Cocktail *m* cocktail.
Computer *m* computer.
Container *m* container.
Creme *f* cream; polish; (tooth)paste.
cremig *adj* creamy.

D

da *adv* there; here; then; so:—*conj* as.

dabei *adv* in the process.

Dach *n* roof.

Dachs *m* badger.

dadurch *adv* through it; by it:—~ daß because.

dafür *adv* for it.

dagegen *adv* against it; however:—*conj* whereas.

daher *adv* from there; hence.

dahin *adv* there; then; gone.

Dahlie *f* dahlia.

damalig *adj* then:—der ~e Präsident the then president.

damals *adv* at that time.

Dame *f* lady; queen (cards, chess).

damit *adv* with it; by it:—*conj* so that.

dämmern *vi* to dawn; to grow dusky.

Dämmerung *f* dawn; dusk.

Dampf *m* steam; vapour.

dampfen *vi* to steam.

dämpfen *vt* to steam; to dampen.

Dampfer *m* steamer.

danach *adv* after that; accordingly.

daneben *adv* beside it; also.

Däne *m* Dänin *f* Dane.

Dänemark *n* Denmark.

dänisch *adj* Danish.

dank *prep* thanks to.

Dank *m* thanks.

dankbar *adj* grateful.

Dankbarkeit *f* gratitude.

danke (schön) *excl* thank you, thanks.

danken *vt* to thank.

dann *adv* then.

daran *adv* on it; of it; about it.

darauf *adv* on it; to it; afterwards.

daraufhin *adv* afterwards.

daraus *adv* from it.

darin *adv* in there; in it.

darlegen *vt* to explain.

Darlegung *f* explanation.

Darleh(e)n *n* loan.

Darm *m* intestine.

darstellen *vt* to depict.

Darstellung *f* presentation.

darüber *adv* over it; about it:—~ hinaus in addition, furthermore.

darum *adv* around it; therefore.

darunter *adv* under it.

das *def art* the:—*pn* that.

daß *conj* that.

dasselbe *art pn* the same.

datieren *vt* to date.

Dattel *f* date (fruit).

Datum *n* date.

Dauer *f* duration.

dauerhaft *adj* lasting.

dauern *vi* to last.

Daumen *m* thumb.

Daune *f* down.

davon *adv* of that/it; away.

davor *adv* before it, in front of it.

dazu *adv* to that, to it; also.

dazwischen *adv* between (them).

Deck *n* deck.

Decke *f* covering; blanket; ceiling.

Deckel *m* lid.

decken *vt* to cover; to lay (table):—*vr* to cover oneself; to coincide.

Deckung *f* covering.

Defekt *m* defect.

defekt *adj* defective.

definieren *vt* to define.

Definition *f* definition.

definitiv *adj* definit(iv)e.

deftig *adj* heavy; rude.

Degen *m* sword.

dehnen *vt vr* to stretch.

dein(e) *poss adj* your.

deine(r, s) *poss pn* yours.

dekorieren *vt* to decorate.

Delegation *f* delegation.

delegieren *vt* to delegate.

Delegierte(r) *f(m)* delegate.

delikat *adj* delicate; delicious.

Delikt *n* offence.

Delphin *m* dolphin.

demnach *adv* therefore.

demnächst *adv* soon.

Demokratie *f* democracy.

demokratisch *adj* democratic.

demolieren *vt* to demolish.

Demut *f* humility.

demütig *adj* humble.

demüten *vt* to humiliate.

Demütung *f* humiliation.

demzufolge *adv* accordingly.

den *art acc of* der.

denen *pn dat pl of* der, die, das.

denkbar *adj* conceivable.
denken *vt vi vr* to think.
Denkmal *n* monument.
denn *conj* as; than:—*adv* then:—**es sei ~, daß** unless.
dennoch *adv conj* however.
Depot *n* deposit; warehouse.
Depression *f* depression.
deprimieren *vt* to depress.
der *def art* the.
derb *adj* solid.
dergleichen *on* such.
derjenige *pn* he, she, it; the one (who); that (which).
derselbe *art pn* the same.
derzeitig *adj* current.
des *art gen of* **der, das.**
desgleichen *pn* the same.
deshalb *adv* therefore.
dessen *pn gen of* **der, das.**
Dessert *n* dessert.
desto *adv* all the, so much the.
deswegen *conj* therefore.
Detail *n* detail.
Detektiv *m* detective.
deuten *vt* to interpret:—*vi* to point.
deutlich *adj* clear.
Deutlichkeit *f* clarity.
deutsch *adj* German.
Deutsch *n* German (language).
Deutsche(r) *f(m)* German.
Deutschland *n* Germany.
Deutung *f* interpretation.
Devise *f* foreign currency.
Dezember *m* December.
dezent *adj* unobtrusive.
dezimal *adj* decimal.
Diagnose *f* diagnosis.
diagonal *adj* diagonal.
Diagonale *f* diagonal.
Dialekt *m* dialect.
Dialog *m* dialogue.

Diamant *m* diamond.
Diapositiv *n* slide.
Diät *f* diet.
dich *pn acc of* **du** you, yourself.
dicht *adj* tight; dense:—*adv* close.
Dichte *f* density, thickness; tightness.
dichten *vt* to seal.
Dichter(in) *m(f)* poet(ess).
Dichtung *f* poetry.
dick *adj* thick; fat.
Dicke *f* thickness; fatness.
die *def art* the.
Dieb(in) *m(f)* thief.
Diebstahl *m* theft.
dienen *vi* to serve.
Diener(in) *m(f)* servant.
Dienst *m* service; duty.
Dienstag *m* Tuesday.
dies *pn* this; these.
diesbezüglich *adj* relevant.
dieselbe *pn art* the same.
diese(r, s) *pn* this (one).
diesmal *adv* this time.
diesseits *adv prep* on this side.
Diktat *n* dictation.
Diktator *m* dictator.
Diktatur *f* dictatorship.
diktieren *vt* to dictate.
Dilemma *n* dilemma.
Dimension *f* dimension.
Ding *n* thing.
Diplom *n* diploma.
Diplomat *m* diplomat.
Diplomatie *f* diplomacy.
diplomatisch *adj* diplomatic.
dir *pn dat of* **du** (to) you.
direkt *adj* direct.
Direktion *f* management.
Direktor *m* director.
Dirigent *m* conductor.
Dirne *f* prostitute.
Diskette *f* diskette.

Diskothek *f* disco(thèque).
diskret *adj* discreet.
Diskretion *f* discretion.
Diskussion *f* discussion.
diskutieren *vt vi* to discuss.
Dissertation *f* dissertation.
Dissident(in) *m(f)* dissident.
Distanz *f* distance.
Distel *f* thistle.
Disziplin *f* discipline.
Dividende *f* dividend.
dividieren *vt* to divide.
Division *f* division.
doch *conj* however:—*adv* after all, yet.
Dock *n* dock(yard).
Doktor(in) *m(f)* doctor.
Dolch *m* dagger.
Dollar *m* dollar.
dolmetschen *vt vi* to interpret.
Dolomien *pl* (the) Dolomites.
Dometscher(in) *m(f)* interpreter.
Dom *m* cathedral.
dominieren *vt vi* to dominate.
Donau *f* Danube.
Donner *m* thunder.
donnern *vi* to thunder.
Donnerstag *m* Thursday.
doof *adj* dull.
Doppelbett *n* double bed.
doppeln *vt* to double.
Doppelpunkt *m* colon.
doppelt *adj* double.
Dorf *n* village.
Dorn *m* thorn.
dorren *vi* to dry up.
dörren *vt* to dry.
Dorsch *m* cod.
dort *adv* there.
dorther *adv* from there, hence.
dorthin *adv* (to) there.

dorthinaus *adv* out there.

dorthinein *adv* in there.

dortig *adj* there.

dösen *vi* to doze.

Dose *f* box, can.

Dosenöffner *m* can opener.

dosieren *vt* to dose, measure out.

dösig *adj* dozy.

Dosis *f* dose.

Dozent *m* lecturer.

Drache *m* dragon.

Drachen *m* kite.

Draht *m* wire.

Drahtzange *f* pliers.

Drall *m* twist, spin.

Drama *n* drama.

Dramatiker *m* dramatist.

dramatisch *adj adv* dramatic(ally).

Drang *m* pressure; impulse.

drängeln *vi* to jostle.

drängen *vt* to push:—*vi* to be urgent.

dränieren *vt* to drain.

drastisch *adj adv* drastic(ally).

draußen *adv* outside.

Dreck *m* filth.

dreckig *adj* filthy.

drehbar *adj* revolving.

drehen *vt vi* to turn.

Drehung *f* turn.

drei *num* three.

Dreibein *n* tripod.

Dreieck *n* triangle.

dreieckig *adj* triangular.

Dreieinigkeit *f* Trinity.

dreifach *adj adv* triple.

dreißig *num* thirty.

dreizehn *num* thirteen.

drillen *vt* to drill.

dringen *vi* to penetrate; to insist.

dringlich *adj* urgent.

drinnen *adv* inside.

dritte(r, s) *adj* third.

Dritte(r) *m* third (party).

Drittel *n* third.

Droge *f* drug.

Drogerie *f* drugstore.

drohen *vi* to threaten.

Drohung *f* threat.

Drossel *f* thrush; throttle.

drüben *adv* over there.

Druck *m* pressure; printing.

drücken *vt* to press; to oppress:—*vi* to press, touch:—*vr* to get out of.

Drucker *m* printer.

Dschungel *m* jungle.

du *pn nom* you.

Duell *n* duel.

Duett *n* duet.

Duft *m* scent.

duften *vi* to smell (pleasant).

duftig *adj* fragrant.

dulden *vt* to tolerate.

dumm *adj* stupid.

Dummheit *f* stupidity.

Dummkopf *m* idiot.

dunkel *adj* dark.

Dunkelheit *f* darkness.

dunkeln *vi* to darken.

dünn *adj* thin.

Dunst *m* vapour.

Dur *n* (*mus*) major.

durch *prep* through, by.

durchaus *adv* completely.

durchbrechen *vt vi* to break through.

Durchbruch *m* breakthrough.

durchdringen *vi* to penetrate.

Durchdringung *f* penetration.

durcheinander *adv* higgledy-piggledy.

Durcheinander *n* confusion.

Durchfall *m* diarrhoea.

durchfallen *vi* to fall through; to fail.

durchführbar *adj* feasible.

durchführen *vt* to carry through.

Durchführung *f* completion.

Durchgang *m* passage.

durchlässig *adj* permeable.

Durchmesser *m* diameter.

Durchschnitt *m* average.

durchschnittlich *adj* average:—*adv* on average.

durchsehen *vt vi* to look through.

durchsichtig *adj* transparent.

durchweg *adv* throughout.

dürfen *vi* to be allowed.

dürftig *adj* needy.

dürr *adj* arid.

Durst *m* thirst:—~ **haben** to be thirsty.

dürstig *adj* thirsty.

Dusche *f* shower.

duschen *vt vi* to shower.

Düse *f* nozzle; jet.

Düsenflugzeug *n* jet (aircraft).

Düsentriebwerk *n* jet engine.

düster *adj* dark.

Düsterheit, Düsterkeit *f* gloom.

Dutzend *n* dozen.

duzen *vt* to call someone *du*, be familiar.

dynamisch *adj* dynamic.

Dynamit *n* dynamite.

Dynamo *m* dynamo.

E

Ebbe *f* low tide.
eben *adj* level:—*adv* exactly.
Ebene *f* plain.
ebenfalls *adv* also.
ebenso *adv* equally.
Echo *n* echo.
echt *adj* genuine.
Ecke *f* corner; angle.
edel *adj* noble; precious.
Efeu *m* ivy.
effektiv *adj* effective.
egal *adj* equal:—**das ist mir** ~ it's all the same to me.
Egoismus *m* egotism.
Egoist(in) *m(f)* egotist.
egoistisch *adj* selfish.
ehe *conj* before.
Ehe *f* marriage.
Ehebrecher(in) *m(f)* adulterer.
ehebrecherisch *adj* adulterous.
Ehebruch *m* adultery.
Ehefrau *f* wife.
ehelich *adj* matrimonial.
ehemalig *adj* former.
ehemals *adv* formerly.
Ehemann *m* husband.
Ehepaar *n* married couple.
eher *adv* sooner; rather.
Ehering *m* wedding ring.
Ehescheidung *f* divorce.
ehrbar *adj* honourable.
Ehre *f* honour.
ehren *vt* to honour.
Ehrgeiz *m* ambition.
ehrgeizig *adj* ambitious.
ehrlich *adj* honest:—*adv* honestly.

Ehrlichkeit *f* honesty.
ehrlos *adj* dishonourable.
Ei *n* egg.
Eibe *f* yew.
Eiche *f* oak.
Eichel *f* acorn.
eichen *vt* to standardize.
Eichhörnchen *n* squirrel.
Eid *m* oath.
Eidechse *f* lizard.
eidgenössisch *adj* Swiss.
Eidotter *n* egg yolk.
Eierbecher *m* eggcup.
Eierkuchen *m* omelette, pancake.
Eierschale *f* eggshell.
Eierstock *m* ovary.
Eifer *m* enthusiasm.
eifern *vi* to be eager for.
Eifersucht *f* jealousy.
eifersüchtig *adj* jealous.
eiförmig *adj* egg-shaped, oval.
eifrig *adj* eager.
Eigelb *n* egg yolk.
eigen *adj* own; particular; unusual.
Eigenart *f* peculiarity.
eigenartig *adj* peculiar.
Eigenheit *f* peculiarity.
eigens *adv* deliberately.
Eigenschaft *f* characteristic.
eigentlich *adj* actual, real:—*adv* actually, really.
Eigentor *n* own goal.
Eigentum *n* property, ownership.
Eigentümer(in) *m(f)* owner.
eigentümlich *adj* special, particular.

Eigentümlichkeit *f* peculiarity.
eignen *vr* to suit.
Eigner *m* owner.
Eignung *f* suitability.
Eilbote *m* courier.
Eilbrief *m* express letter.
Eile *f* hurry.
eilen *vi vr* to hurry.
eilig *adj* hurried.
Eimer *m* bucket.
ein(e) *num* one:—*indef art* a, an:—*pn* **eine(r, s)** one.
Einblick *m* view; insight.
einbringen *vt* to bring in.
Einbruch *m* break-in; invasion; arrival (night).
eindeutig *adj* clear.
Eindruck *m* impression.
eineinhalb *num* one and a half.
einerseits *adv* on the one hand.
einfach *adj* single; simple:—*adv* simply.
Einfachheit *f* simplicity.
Einfahrt *f* entrance.
Einfall *m* idea; incursion.
einfallen *vi* to raid; to occur; to fall in.
einfließen *vi* to flow in.
Einfluß *m* influence.
Einfuhr *f* import(s).
einführen *vt* to introduce; to import.
Einführung *f* introduction.
Eingabe *f* application.
Eingang *m* entrance; arrival; receipt.

eingenommen *adj* partial, biased.

Eingenommenheit *f* bias.

Eingeweide *pl* entrails.

Einheit *f* unit; unity.

einheitlich *adj* uniform.

Einheitlichkeit *f* uniformity.

einholen *vt vi* to bring in; to catch up.

einig *adj* united; agreed.

einige(r, s) *adj pn* some.

einigen *vt* to unite:—*vr* to agree.

Einigkeit *f* unity.

Einigung *f* agreement; unification.

Einkauf *m* purchase.

einkaufen *vt* to buy:—*vi* to shop.

Einkaufszentrum *n* shopping centre.

Einklang *m* harmony.

einkommen *vi* to apply; to come in.

Einkommen *n* income.

Einkommen(s)steuer *f* income tax.

Einkünfte *fpl* income.

einladen *vt* to invite.

Einladung *f* invitation.

einleiten *vt* to introduce.

Einleitung *f* introduction.

einmal *adv* once; one day; even:—**auf ~** suddenly.

einmalig *adv* unique.

einmütig *adj* unanimous.

Einmütigkeit *f* unanimity.

Einnahme *f* capture; income.

einnehmen *vt* to take (in, up).

Einöde *f* desert.

Einreise *f* entry.

einrichten *vt* to arrange.

Einrichtung *f* furnishings; installation; institution.

eins *num* one.

Eins *f* one.

einsam *adj* lonely.

Einsamkeit *f* loneliness.

Einsatz *m* insert; use; effort.

einschlafen *vi* to fall asleep.

Einschlag *m* impact; hint.

einschlägig *adj* relevant.

einschließen *vt* to lock up; to enclose.

einschließlich *adv* inclusive:—*prep* including.

Einschluß *m* inclusion.

Einschreiben *n* recorded delivery.

Einsicht *f* inspection; insight.

Einspruch *m* objection.

einst *adv* once.

einstig *adj* former.

einstweilen *adv* meanwhile.

einstweilig *adj* temporary.

eintönig *adj* monotonous.

Eintönigkeit *f* monotony.

Eintrag *m* entry.

eintreten *vi* to enter; to join; to occur.

Eintritt *m* entrance.

Eintrittskarte *f* (entrance) ticket.

Einvernehmen *n* agreement.

einverstanden *adj* agreed.

Einverständnis *n* agreement.

Einwand *m* objection.

Einwanderer *m* immigrant.

einwandern *vi* to immigrate.

Einwanderung *f* immigration.

einwandfrei *adj* impeccable:—*adv* absolutely.

einwärts *adv* inward(s).

einwenden *vt* to object.

Einwendung *f* objection.

einwirken *vi* to affect.

Einwirkung *f* effect.

Einwohner(in) *m(f)* inhabitant.

Einwurf *m* throw-in; slot; objection.

Einzelfall *m* individual case.

Einzelhandel *m* retailing.

Einzelhändler *m* retailer.

Einzelheit *f* detail.

einzeln *adj* single:—*adv* individually.

einzig *adj* single; only.

einzigartig *adj* unique.

Einzug *m* entrance.

Eis *n* ice (cream).

Eisbahn *f* skating rink.

Eisbär *m* polar bear.

Eisberg *m* iceberg.

Eisen *n* iron.

Eisenbahn *f* railway, railroad.

eisern *adj* iron.

Eishockey *n* ice hockey.

eisig *adj* icy.

eiskalt *adj* ice-cold.

Eislauf *m* skating.

eislaufen *vi* to skate.

Eisläufer(in) *m(f)* skater.

Eisschrank *m* fridge.

eitel *adj* vain.

Eitelkeit *f* vanity.

Eiweiß *n* egg white; protein.

Ekel *m* disgust.

ekelhaft, ek(e)lig *adj* disgusting.

ekeln *vt* to disgust.

Ekstase *f* ecstasy.

ekstatisch *adj* ecstatic.

elastisch *adj* elastic.

Elefant *m* elephant.

elegant *adj* elegant.

Elektriker *m* electrician.

elektrisch *adj* electrical.

Elektrizität *f* electricity.

Elektronik *f* electronics.

elektronisch *adj* electronic.

Element *n* element.
elementar *adj* elementary.
Elend *n* misery.
elend *adj* miserable.
elf *num* eleven.
Elfenbein *n* ivory.
eliminieren *vt* to eliminate.
Elite *f* elite.
Ellenbogen *m* elbow.
Elsaß *n* Alsace.
Eltern *pl* parents.
Empfang *m* reception; receipt.
empfangen *vt* to receive.
Empfänger *m* recipient.
Empfängnis *f* conception.
Empfängnisverhütung *f* contraception.
empfehlen *vt* to recommend.
Empfehlung *f* recommendation.
empfinden *vt* to feel.
empfindlich *adj* sensitive.
Emfindlichkeit *f* sensitivity.
empfindsam *adj* sentimental.
Emfindsamkeit *f* sentimentality.
Empfindung *f* feeling.
empfindungslos *adj* insensitive.
Ende *n* end.
enden *vi* to end.
endgültig *adj* final.
endlich *adj adv* final(ly).
endlos *adj* endless.
Energie *f* energy.
energisch *adj* energetic.
eng *adj* narrow; close; tight.
Engel *m* angel.
England *n* England.
Engländer *m* Englishman.
Engländerin *f* Englishwoman.
Englisch *n* English (language).

englisch *adj* English.
Enkel *m* grandson.
Enkelin *f* granddaughter.
enorm *adj* enormous.
entarten *vi* to degenerate.
entartet *adj* degenerate.
entbinden *vt* to release.
entdecken *vt* to discover.
Entdeckung *f* discovery.
Ente *f* duck.
entfallen *vi* to fall; to escape.
entfalten *vt* to unfold.
entfernen *vt* to remove.
entfernt *adj* distant.
Entfernung *f* distance.
entführen *vt* to abduct.
Entführer *m* kidnapper.
Entführung *f* abduction.
entgegen *adv prep* against, contrary to.
entgegengesetzt *adj* opposite.
entgehen *vi* to escape.
Entgelt *n* compensation, reward.
entkommen *vi* to escape.
entladen *vt* to unload; to set off:—*vr* to discharge.
entlang *adv prep* along.
entlassen *vt* to dismiss.
Entlassung *f* dismissal.
Entnahme *f* withdrawal.
entnehmen *vt* to remove.
entschädigen *vt* to compensate.
Entschädigung *f* compensation.
entscheiden *vt vi* to decide.
entscheidend *adj* decisive.
Entscheidung *f* decision.
entschlossen *adj* determined.
Entschlossenheit *f* determination.
Entschluß *m* decision.
entschuldigen *vt* to excuse:—*vr* to apologize.

Entschuldigung *f* excuse:— ~! sorry!
entsetzen *vt* to dismiss; to frighten; to appal.
Entsetzen *n* terror; dismay.
entsetzlich *adj* appalling.
Entsetzung *f* dismissal.
entspannen *vt vr* to relax.
Entspannung *f* relaxation.
entsprechen *vi* to correspond.
entsprechend *adj adv* appropriate(ly).
entstehen *vi* to come into being.
enttäuschen *vt* to disappoint.
Enttäuschung *f* disappointment.
entweder *conj*:—~... **oder** either... or.
entwickeln *vt vr* to develop.
Entwicklung *f* development.
Entwurf *m* design.
entzücken *vt* to delight.
entzückend *adj* delightful.
Enzyklopädie *f* encyclopedia.
Epidemie *f* epidemic.
Episode *f* episode.
Epoche *f* epoch.
er *pn nom* he.
erachten *vi* to consider.
Erachten *n* opinion.
Erbarmen *n* pity.
Erbe *m* heir.
erben *vt* to inherit.
Erbin *f* heiress.
erbitten *vt* to ask for.
erblicken *vt* to see.
erbrechen *vt vr* to vomit.
erbringen *vt* to provide.
Erbschaft *f* inheritance, estate.
Erbse *n* pea.
Erdbeben *n* earthquake.

Erdbeere *f* strawberry.

Erde *f* earth.

Erdgas *n* natural gas.

Erdgeschoß *n* ground floor.

Erdkunde *f* geography.

Erdnuß *f* peanut.

ereignen *vr* to occur.

Ereignis *n* event.

erfahren *vt* to experience:—*adj* experienced.

Erfahrung *f* experience.

erfassen *vt* to grasp; to understand.

erfinden *vt* to discover, invent.

Erfinder *m* inventor.

Erfindung *f* invention.

Erfolg *m* result; success:—~ **haben** to succeed.

erfolgen *vi* to result; to happen.

erfolglos *adj* unsuccessful.

erfolgreich *adj* successful.

erforderlich *adj* necessary.

erfordern *vt* to require.

erforschen *vt* to explore; to investigate.

Erforschung *f* exploration; investigation.

erfreuen *vt* to please:—*vr* to enjoy.

erfreulich *adj* pleasing.

Erfrischung *f* refreshment.

erfüllen *vt* to fill; to comply with:—*vr* to be fulfilled.

Erfüllung *f* fulfilment.

ergänzen *vt* to supplement.

ergänzend *adj* additional.

Ergänzung *f* supplement.

Ergebnis *n* result.

ergreifen *vt* to grasp.

erhalten *vt* to receive; to maintain.

erhältlich *adj* available.

Erhaltung *f* maintenance; preservation.

erheben *vt* to raise:—*vr* to rise.

erheblich *adj* considerable:—*adv* considerably.

erhöhen *vt* to raise.

erholen *vr* to recover.

Erholung *f* recovery.

erhören *vt* to hear; to grant.

erinnern *vt* to remind:—*vr* to remember.

Erinnerung *f* memory.

erkälten *vr* to catch cold.

Erkältung *f* cold.

erkennbar *adj* recognizable.

erkennen *vt* to recognize.

erkenntlich *adj* perceptible.

Erkenntnis *f* knowledge; acknowledgment.

Erkennung *f* recognition.

erklären *vt* to explain; to declare.

Erklärung *f* explanation.

erklettern, erklimmen *vt* to climb.

erkundigen *vr* to inquire.

Erkundigung *f* inquiry.

erlangen *vt* to reach.

Erlaß *m* exemption; decree.

erlassen *vt* to issue; to exempt.

erläßlich *adj* allowable.

erlauben *vt* to allow.

Erlaubnis *f* permission.

erlaubt *adj* allowed.

erläutern *vt* to explain.

Erläuterung *f* explanation.

erleben *vt* to experience.

Erlebnis *n* experience.

erledigen *vt* to carry out; to finish.

erledigt *adj* done.

Erledigung *f* settlement; handling.

erleichtern *vt* to relieve.

erleichtert *adj* relieved.

Erleichterung *f* relief.

erleiden *vt* to suffer.

erlernen *vt* to learn.

erlesen *vt* to select:—*adj* select.

Erlös *m* proceeds.

erlöschen *vi* to be extinguished.

ermächtigen *vt* to authorize.

Ermächtigung *f* authorization.

ermitteln *vt* to determine.

Ermitt(e)lung *f* determination.

ermöglichen *vt* to make possible.

ermorden *vt* to murder.

Ermordung *f* murder.

ermüden *vt vi* to tire.

ermunten, ermutigen *vt* to encourage.

ernähren *vt* to feed:—*vr* to earn a living.

Ernährung *f* nutrition.

ernennen *vt* to appoint.

erneuern *vt* to renew.

Erneuerung *f* renewal, renovation.

erneut *adj* renewed:—*adj* again.

Ernst *m* seriousness:—**im ~** in earnest.

ernst *adj* serious.

Ernstfall *m* emergency.

ernsthaft *adj* serious.

ernstlich *adj adv* serious(ly).

Ernte *f* harvest.

ernten *vt vi* to harvest.

Eroberer *m* conqueror.

erobern *vt* to conquer.

Eroberung *f* conquest.

eröffnen *vt* to open.

erörtern *vt* to discuss.

erotisch *adj* erotic.

erreichbar *adj* accessible.

erreichen *vt* to reach.

errichten *vt* to erect.

erringen *vt* to achieve.

Ersatz *m* compensation; alternative, substitute.

Ersatzreifen *m* spare tyre.

Ersatzteil *n* spare part.

erscheinen *vi* to appear.

Erscheinung *f* appearance.

erschießen *vt* to shoot (dead).

Erschießung *f* shooting, execution.

erschöpfen *vt* to exhaust.

erschöpft *adj* exhausted.

Erschöpfung *f* exhaustion.

erschrecken *vt* to frighten:—*vi vr* to be frightened.

erschrocken *adj* frightened.

erschüttern *vt* to shake; to upset.

erschütternd *adj* shocking.

Erschütterung *f* shock.

ersehen *vt* to see, note.

ersetzbar *adj* replaceable.

ersetzen *vt* to replace.

ersichtlich *adj* obvious.

ersparen *vt* to spare, save.

erst *adv* first; only; not until.

erstaunen *vt* to astonish:—*vi* to be astonished.

erstaunlich *adj* astonishing.

erste(r, s) *adj* first.

erstellen *vt* to provide; to construct.

erstens *adv* firstly.

erstklassig *adj* first-class.

erstmals *adv* for the first time.

erstrecken *vr* to extend.

ersuchen *vt* to request.

Ersuchen *n* request.

erteilen *vt* to give, grant.

Ertrag *m* yield, profit.

ertragen *vt* to endure.

erträglich *adj* bearable.

ertrinken *vi* to drown.

erwachen *vi* to awake.

erwachsen *adj* grown-up.

Erwachsene(r) *f(m)*dult.

erwägen *vt* to consider.

Erwägung *f* consideration.

erwähnen *vt* to mention.

Erwähnung *f* mention.

erwärmen *vt* to warm, heat:—*vr* to heat up.

erwarten *vt* to expect.

Erwartung *f* expectation.

erwartungsvoll *adj* expectant:—*adv* expectantly.

erwecken *vt* to wake, stir up.

erweisen *vt* to prove.

erweitern *vt vr* to widen, expand.

Erweiterung *f* expansion.

Erwerb *m* acquisition; occupation.

erwerben *vt* to acquire; to earn.

erwidern *vt* to return; to reply.

Erwiderung *f* reply.

erwünscht *adj* desired.

erwürgen *vt* to strangle.

Erz *n* ore.

erzählen *vt* to tell.

Erzählung *f* story.

Erzbischof *m* archbishop.

erzeugen *vt* to produce.

Erzeugnis *n* product.

Erzeugung *f* production.

erziehen *vt* to bring up; to educate.

Erziehung *f* bringing up; education.

erzielen *vt* to achieve.

erzwingen *vt* to force.

es *pn nom acc* it.

Esche *f* ash (tree).

Esel *m* donkey.

eßbar *adj* edible.

essen *vt vi* to eat.

Essen *n* food; meal.

Essig *m* vinegar.

Estland *n* Estonia.

etablieren *vt vr* to establish.

Etage *f* floor, storey.

ethisch *adj* ethical.

Etikett *n* label.

Etikette *f* etiquette.

etwa *adv* about, approximately; for example.

etwaig *adj* any; possible.

etwas *pn* something; anything:—*adj* some, a little.

euch *pn* (*acc dat of* **ihr**) (to) you; (to) yourselves.

euer *pn* (*gen of* **ihr**) of you:—*poss adj* your.

Eule *f* owl.

eure(r, s) *poss pn* yours.

Europa *n* Europe.

Europäer(in) *m(f)* European.

europäisch *adj* European.

eventuell *adj* possible:—*adv* possibly, if necessary.

ewig *adj* eternal.

Ewigkeit *f* eternity.

Examen *n* examination.

Exemplar *n* sample; copy (of book).

Exil *n* exile.

Existenz *f* existence.

existieren *vi* to exist.

exklusiv *adj* exclusive.

exklusive *adv* excluding.

Exkursion *f* excursion.

exotisch *adj* exotic.

Expansion *f* expansion.

Expedition *f* dispatch; expedition.

Experiment *n* experiment.

experimentell *adj* experimental.

experimentieren *vi* to experiment.

Experte *m* **Expertin** *f* expert.

explodieren *vi* to explode.

Explosion *f* explosion.

explosiv *adj* explosive.

Export *m* export.

Exporteur *m* exporter.

exportieren *vt* to export.

expreß *adv* express(ly).

extensiv *adj* extensive.

extern *adj* external.

extra *adj adv* extra.

extravagant *adj* extravagant.

extrem *adj* extreme.

exzentrisch *adj* eccentric.

Exzeß *m* excess.

F

Fabel *f* fable.
fabelhaft *adj* fabulous.
Fabrik *f* factory.
Fabrikant *m* manufacturer.
Fach *n* compartment; subject.
fächeln *vt* to fan.
Fachhochschule *f* technical university.
fachlich *adj* technical, professional.
Fachmann *m* expert.
fade *adj* dull.
Faden *m* thread.
fähig *adj* capable.
Fähigkeit *f* ability.
Fahne *f* flag.
Fähre *f* ferry.
fahren *vt vi* to travel; to drive.
Fahrer(in) *m(f)* driver.
Fahrgeld *n* fare.
Fahrkarte *f* ticket.
fahrlässig *adj* negligent.
Fahrlässigkeit *f* negligence.
Fahrlehrer(in) *m(f)* driving instructor.
Fahrplan *m* timetable.
Fahrprüfung *f* driving test.
Fahrrad *n* bicycle.
Fahrt *f* journey:—**gute ~** have a good trip.
Fahrzeug *n* vehicle.
faktisch *adj* factual:—*adv* actually, de facto.
Faktor *m* factor.
Falke *m* falcon.
Fall *m* fall; case:—**auf jeden ~, auf alle Fälle** in any case:—**auf keinen ~** by no means.
fallen *vi* to fall:—**~ lassen** to drop.
fällig *adj* due.
falls *conj* in case.
falsch *adj* wrong; false.
fälschen *vt* to falsify.
Falschheit *f* falsity.
fälschlich *adv* falsely.
Fälschung *f* fake.
falten *vt* to fold.
Familie *f* family.
Familienname *m* surname.
Fanatiker *m* fanatic.
fanatisch *adj* fanatic(al).
Fang *m* catch.
fangen *vt* to catch.
Farbe *f* colour; dye; paint.
Farbfernsehen *n* colour television.
farbig *adj* coloured.
farblos *adj* colourless.
Farbstoff *m* dye, colouring.
Faser *f* fibre.
Faß *n* barrel.
fassen *vt* to grasp; to understand.
Fassung *f* frame, mount; version; composure.
fast *adv* nearly.
fasten *vi* to fast.
Fastzeit *f* Lent.
faszinieren *vt* to fascinate.
fatal *adj* fatal; awkward.
faul *adj* rotten; lazy.
faulen *vi* to rot.
Faulheit *f* laziness.
Fäulnis *f* decay.
Faust *f* fist.
Februar *m* February.

fechten *vi* to fence; to fight.
Feder *f* feather; spring; nib.
Fee *f* fairy.
fegen *vt vi* to sweep.
fehlen *vi* to be absent; to lack:—**Ich fehle sie** I miss her.
Fehler *m* mistake; fault.
fehlerfrei *adj* faultless.
fehlerhaft *adj* faulty.
Fehlschlag *m* miss; failure.
fehlschlagen *vi* to fail.
Feier *f* celebration.
feierlich *adj* festive; ceremonious.
feiern *vt* to celebrate.
Feiertag *m* holiday.
feig(e) *adj* cowardly.
Feige *f* fig.
Feigheit *f* cowardice.
Feigling *m* coward.
Feile *f* file.
feilen *vt* to file.
fein *adj* fine.
Feind *m* enemy.
feindlich *adj* hostile.
Feindlichkeit *f* hostility.
Feinheit *f* fineness, refinement.
Feinkost *f* delicatessen.
Feld *n* field.
Feldwebel *m* sergeant.
Fell *n* skin, hide.
Fels *m* rock.
Felsen *m* cliff.
Fenster *n* window.
Ferien *pl* holidays, vacation.
Ferkel *n* piglet.
fern *adj adv* far, distant.

Ferne *f* distance.
ferner *adj* further:—*adv* furthermore.
Fernglas *n* binoculars.
fernhalten *vt* to keep away.
Fernrohr *n* telescope.
Fernsehen *n* television.
fernsehen *vi* to watch television.
Fernseher *m* television (set).
Ferse *f* heel.
fertig *adj* ready; complete.
Fertigkeit *f* skill.
fertigmachen *vt* to complete.
Fertigung *f* production.
fesseln *vt* to bind.
fest *adj* firm; solid; fixed.
Fest *n* festival; party.
festbinden *vt* to fasten.
festhalten *vt* to hold; to arrest.
festigen *vt* to strengthen.
Festigkeit *f* strength.
festlegen *vt* to fix.
festlich *adj* festive.
festmachen *vt* to fix:—*vi* to moor.
Festnahme *f* capture.
festnehmen *vt* to capture, arrest.
feststehen *vi* to be certain.
feststellen *vt* to establish; to state.
Festung *f* fortress.
Fett *n* fat, grease.
fett *adj* fat, greasy.
fetten *vt* to grease.
feucht *adj* damp.
Feuchtigkeit *f* damp, humidity.
Feuer *n* fire:—**haben Sie ~?** have you got a light?
Feueralarm *n* fire alarm.
feuergefährlich *adj* (in)flammable.

Feuerlöscher *m* fire extinguisher.
Feuermann *m* **-frau** *f* fireman, -woman.
feuern *vt vi* to fire.
Feuerversicherung *f* fire insurance.
Feuerwehr *f* fire brigade.
Feuerwehrwagen *n* fire engine.
Feuerwerk *n* fireworks.
Feuerzeug *n* cigarette lighter.
feurig *adj* fiery.
Fichte *f* spruce, pine.
Fieber *n* fever.
fieberhaft *adj* feverish.
Figur *f* figure; chess piece.
Fiktion *f* fiction.
fiktiv *adj* fictitious.
Filiale *f* branch; subsidiary.
Film *m* film.
filmen *vt vi* to film.
Filter *m* filter.
filtern *vt* to filter.
Filz *m* felt.
Filzstift *m* felt-tip (pen).
Finanz *f* finance.
finanziell *adj* financial.
finanzieren *vt* to finance.
Finanzminister *m* finance minister.
Finanzministerium *n* finance ministry.
finden *vt* to find; to think, believe:—*vr* to be (located).
Finger *m* finger.
Fingerabdruck *m* fingerprint.
Fingerhut *m* thimble; foxglove.
Fingernagel *m* fingernail.
Finke *m* finch.
Finne *m* **Finnin** *f* Finn.
finnisch *adj* Finnish.
Finnland *n* Finland.

finster *adj* dark, gloomy.
Finsternis *f* darkness.
Firma *f* company.
Fisch *m* fish.
fischen *vt vi* to fish.
Fischermann *m* fisherman.
Fischfang *m* fishing.
Fischhändler *m* fishmonger.
fischig *adj* fishy.
fix *adj* fixed; clever.
flach *adj* flat; shallow.
Fläche *f* surface; area.
flackern *vi* to flicker; to flare.
Flagge *f* flag.
Flamme *f* flame.
flammen *vi* to blaze.
Flanke *f* flank; wing (football, etc).
Flasche *f* bottle.
Flaschenöffner *m* bottle opener.
flattern *vi* to flutter.
flau *adj* weak.
Flaute *f* calm; recession.
Fleck *m* spot; stain.
Fledermaus *f* bat.
flehen *vi* to implore.
Fleisch *n* flesh; meat.
fleißig *adj* hard-working.
Flieder *m* lilac.
Fliege *f* fly; bow tie.
fliegen *vt vi* to fly.
Fliegenpilz *m* toadstool.
Flieger *m* flier.
fliehen *vt vi* to flee.
Fliese *f* tile.
Fließband *n* conveyor belt.
fließen *vi* to flow.
fließend *adj* flowing; fluent.
flimmern *vi* to glitter.
flink *adj* quick, agile.
Flinte *f* rifle.
Flitterwochen *pl* honeymoon.
Flocke *f* flake.
Floh *m* flea.

Florenz *n* Florence.
Flöte *f* flute.
Fluch *m* curse.
fluchen *vi* to curse, swear.
Flucht *f* flight.
flüchten *vi* to flee.
flüchtig *adj* fugitive; fleeting.
Flüchtling *m* refugee.
Flug *m* flight.
Flugblatt *n* leaflet.
Flügel *m* wing; grand piano.
Fluggast *m* (air) passenger.
Fluggesellschaft *f* airline.
Flughafen *m* airport.
Flugzeug *n* aircraft.
Flugzeugträger *m* aircraft carrier.
Flur *m* hall.
Fluß *m* river; flow.
flüssig *adj* liquid.
Flüssigkeit *f* liquid, fluid.
flüstern *vi vt* to whisper.
Flut *f* flood; high tide.
fluten *vi* to flood.
Folge *f* result; series; sequence.
folgen *vi* to follow.
folglich *adv* consequently.
folgsam *adj* obedient.
Folie *f* foil, film.
Folter *f* torture.
foltern *vt* to torture.
Fön *m* hair drier.
Fonds *m* fund.
Fontäne *f* fountain.
Förderband *n* conveyor belt.
fordern *vt* to demand.
fördern *vt* to promote, encourage.
Forderung *f* demand.
Förderung *f* promotion, encouragement.
Forelle *f* trout.
Form *f* form, shape; mould.

Formalität *f* formality.
Format *n* format; importance.
formatieren *vt* to format.
Formation *f* formation.
Formel *f* formula.
formell *adj* formal.
formen *vt* to form.
förmlich *adj* formal; literal.
formlos *adj* shapeless; informal.
Formular *n* form.
formulieren *vt* to formulate.
forschen *vi* to investigate, research.
Forscher(in) *m(f)* researcher, scientist.
Forschung *f* research.
Forst *m* forest.
fort *adv* away; gone; on(wards).
fortan *adv* from now on.
Fortbestand *m* continuance.
fortbestehen *vi* to continue, survive.
fortbewegen *vt* to move on, away.
Fortbildung *f* further education.
fortdauern *vi* to continue.
fortfahren *vi* to drive on; to leave.
fortgehen *vi* to go away, continue.
fortgeschritten *adj* advanced.
fortleben *vi* to survive.
fortpflanzen *vt vr* to reproduce.
Fortschritt *m* progress.
fortsetzen *vt* to continue.
Fortsetzung *f* continuation.
Foto *n* photo(graph).
Fotoapparat *m* camera.
Fotograf(in) *m(f)* photographer.
Fotografie *f* photograph(y).

fotografieren *vt* to photograph:—*vi* to take photographs.
fotografisch *adj* photographic.
Fotokopie *f* photocopy.
fotokopieren *vt* to photocopy.
Fracht *f* freight.
Frage *f* question.
fragen *vt vi* to ask.
Fragezeichen *n* question mark.
fraglich *adj* questionable, doubtful.
frankieren *vt* to frank.
franko *adv* post-paid.
Frankreich *n* France.
Franzose *m* Frenchman.
Französin *f* Frenchwoman.
französisch *adj* French.
Frau *f* woman; wife; Mrs, Ms.
Fräulein *n* young woman; Miss, Ms.
frech *adj* cheeky.
Frechheit *f* cheek.
frei *adj* free; freelance.
freigebig *adj* generous.
Freihandel *m* free trade.
Freiheit *f* freedom.
freilassen *vt* to release.
Freilassung *f* release.
freilich *adv* certainly.
Freimaurer *m* freemason.
freisprechen *vt* to acquit.
Freispruch *m* acquittal.
freistellen *vt* to exempt.
Freitag *m* Friday.
freiwillig *adj* voluntary:—*adv* voluntarily.
Freiwillige(r) *f(m)* volunteer.
Freizeit *f* free time.
fremd *adj* strange, foreign.
Fremde(r) *f(m)* stranger, foreigner.

Frequenz *f* frequency.
fressen *vt vi* to eat, guzzle.
Freude *f* joy.
freudig *adj* joyful.
freuen *vt* to please:—*vr* to be happy; to look forward.
Freund *m* (boy)friend.
Freundin *f* (girl)friend.
freundlich *adj* friendly.
Freundschaft *f* friendship.
Frieden *m* peace.
Friedhof *m* cemetery.
friedlich *adj* peaceful.
frieren *vt vi* to freeze.
frisch *adj* fresh.
Frische *f* freshness.
Friseur *m* **Friseuse** *f* hairdresser.
Frist *f* period; time limit, deadline.
fristlos *adj* without notice.
froh, fröhlich *adj* happy.
fromm *adj* pious.
Frömmigkeit *f* piety.
Front *f* front.
Frosch *m* frog.
Frost *m* frost.
frostig *adj* frosty.
Frucht *f* fruit; corn.

fruchtbar *adj* fruitful.
fruchtlos *adj* fruitless.
Fruchtsaft *m* fruit juice.
früh *adj adv* early; in the morning.
Frühling *m* spring.
Frühstück *n* breakfast.
frühzeitig *adj* early, premature.
Frustration *f* frustration.
frustrieren *vt* to frustrate.
Fuchs *m* fox.
Füchsin *f* vixen.
fügen *vt* to place; to ordain:—*vr* to comply, adapt.
fügsam *adj* obedient.
fühlbar *adj* tangible.
fühlen *vt vi vr* to feel.
führen *vt vi* to lead; to manage:—*vr* to behave.
Führer *m* leader.
Führerschein *m* driver's licence.
Führung *f* leadership, management.
füllen *vt* to fill.
Fund *m* find.
fünf *num* five.
fünfte(r, s) *adj* fifth.

Fünftel *n* fifth.
fünfzehn *num* fifteen.
fünfzig *num* fifty.
Funk *m* radio.
Funke *m* spark.
funkeln *vi* to sparkle.
Funkgerät *n* radio (set).
Funkstation *f* radio station.
Funktion *f* function.
funktionell *adj* functional.
funktionieren *vi* to function.
für *prep* for:—**was** ~ what kind of.
Furcht *f* fear.
furchtbar *adj* fearful, dreadful.
fürchten *vt* to fear:—*vr* to be afraid.
fürs = **für das**.
Fürsorge *f* care; welfare.
Fürst(in) *m(f)* prince(ss).
Fürstentum *n* principality.
Fusion *f* fusion, merger.
Fuß *m* foot.
Fußball *m* football.
Fußboden *m* floor.
Fußgänger(in) *m(f)* pedestrian.
füttern *vt* to feed.

G

Gabe *f* gift.
Gabel *f* fork.
gähnen *vi* to yawn.
Galerie *f* gallery.
Gang *m* walk; operation; corridor; gangway; aisle; gear.
Gans *f* goose.
Gänseblümchen *n* daisy.
ganz *adj* all; whole:—*adv* very; completely.
gar *adj* well cooked; *adv* absolutely: —~ **nicht** not at all:—~ **nichts** nothing at all.
Garage *f* garage.
Garantie *f* guarantee.
garantieren *vt* to guarantee.
Garderobe *f* wardrobe; cloakroom.
Gardine *f* curtain.
gären *vi* to ferment.
Garten *m* garden.
Gartenarbeit *f* gardening.
Gärtner(in) *m(f)* gardener.
Gärung *f* fermentation.
Gas *n* gas.
Gasse *f* street, alley.
Gast *f* guest.
Gastarbeiter(in) *m(f)* foreign worker.
gastfreundlich *adj* hospitable.
Gastfreundschaft *f* hospitality.
Gastgeber(in) *m(f)* host(ess).
Gaststätte *f* restaurant.
Gastwirt *m* landlord, hotelier.

Gaswerk *n* gasworks.
Gaszähler *m* gas meter.
Gatte *m* **Gattin** *f* spouse.
Gattung *f* type, genus.
gaukeln *vi* to juggle, do tricks.
Gauner *m* swindler.
Gebäck *n* pastry.
Gebärde *f* gesture.
gebärden, gebaren *vr* to behave.
gebären *vt* to give birth to.
Gebärmutter *f* womb.
Gebäude *n* building.
geben *vt* to give:—**es gibt** there is / are.
Gebet *n* prayer.
Gebiet *n* area.
Gebilde *n* object; structure.
gebildet *adj* educated.
Gebinde *n* bundle.
Gebirge *n* mountains.
Gebiß *n* teeth; dentures.
geboren *adj* born; née.
geborgen *adj* safe.
Geborgenheit *f* safety.
Gebot *n* commandment; bid.
Gebrauch *m* use; custom.
gebrauchen *vt* to use.
gebräuchlich *adj* customary.
Gebrauchsanweisung *f* instructions (for use).
gebraucht *adj* used.
gebrochen *adj* broken.
Gebühr *f* fee.
Geburt *f* birth.
Geburtsdatum *n* date of birth.

Geburtsort *m* place of birth.
Geburtstag *m* birthday.
Gedächtnis *n* memory.
Gedanke *m* thought.
gedeihen *vi* to thrive.
Gedicht *n* poem.
gedrängt *adj* crowded, compressed.
gedrückt *adj* depressed.
Geduld *f* patience.
geduldig *adj* patient.
geehrt *adj* honoured:—**sehr geehrter Herr…** Dear Mr…
geeignet *adj* suitable.
Gefahr *f* danger; risk.
gefährden *vt* to endanger.
gefährlich *adj* dangerous.
Gefallen *m* favour, kindness:—*n* pleasure.
gefallen *vi* to please:—**es gefällt mir** I like it.
gefällig *adj* pleasant.
gefangen *adj* captive.
Gefangene(r) *f(m)* prisoner.
Gefängnis *n* prison.
Gefühl *n* feeling.
gegebenenfalls *adv* if necessary.
gegen *prep* towards; against; about; in return for; versus.
Gegend *f* area.
Gegensatz *m* contrast; contrary.
gegensätzlich *adj* contrary.
gegenseitig *adj* mutual.
Gegenspieler *m* opponent.

Gegenstand *m* object.

Gegenteil *n* opposite; to the contrary.

gegenüber *adv* opposite:— *prep* opposite, towards.

Gegenwart *f* present.

gegenwärtig *adj* present.

Gegner *m* opponent.

gegnerisch *adj* opposing.

Gegnerschaft *f* opposition.

Gehalt *m* contents; salary.

geheim *adj* secret.

Geheimnis *n* secret.

gehen *vt vi* to go; to walk:— **wie geht's?** how are you?

Gehirn *n* brain.

Gehör *n* hearing.

gehorchen *vi* to obey.

gehören *vi* to belong to.

gehörig *adj* belonging to; appropriate.

gehorsam *adj* obedient.

Gehorsam *m* obedience.

Geier *m* vulture.

Geige *f* violin.

Geiger(in) *m(f)* violinist.

geil *adj* randy.

Geisel *f* hostage.

Geist *m* spirit, mind; ghost.

geistig *adj* intellectual.

geistlich *adj* spiritual.

Geistliche(r) *f(m)* priest.

Geistlichkeit *f* clergy.

Geiz *m* meanness.

Geizhals *m* miser.

geizig *adj* mean.

gekonnt *adj* clever.

Gelächter *n* laughter.

geladen *adj* loaded; live (wire).

Geländer *n* railings, banisters.

gelangen *vi* to reach.

gelassen *adj* calm.

Gelassenheit *f* calmness.

geläufig *adj* fluent; common.

gelaunt *adj*:—**gut/schlecht** ~ in a good/bad mood.

gelb *adj* yellow.

Geld *n* money.

Geldstück *n* coin.

Gelee *m or n* jelly.

gelegen *adj* located; convenient.

Gelegenheit *f* opportunity; occasion.

gelegentlich *adj adv* occasional(ly).

gelehrt *adj* learned.

Geleit *n* escort.

geleiten *vt* to escort.

Gelenk *n* joint.

gelernt *adj* skilled.

gelingen *vi* to succeed:—**es gelang mir** I succeeded.

geloben *vt* to promise.

Gelöbnis *n* promise.

gelten *vt* to be worth:—*vi* to be valid, apply.

Geltung *f* validity.

gelungen *adj* successful.

Gemälde *n* painting.

gemäß *prep* in accordance with.

gemäßigt *adj* moderate.

gemein *adj* common.

Gemeinde *f* district.

gemeinsam *adj* joint, common.

Gemeinschaft *f* community.

Gemisch *n* mixture.

gemischt *adj* mixed.

Gemüse *n* vegetables.

Gemüt *n* nature, temperament.

gemütlich *adj* cosy, comfortable.

Gemütlichkeit *f* cosiness, comfort.

Gen *n* gene.

genau *adj* exact:—*adv* exactly.

Genauigkeit *f* accuracy.

genauso *adv* just the same.

genehm *adj* acceptable.

genehmigen *vt* to approve, allow.

Genehmigung *f* approval, authorization.

geneigt *adj* inclined.

Generation *f* generation.

Generator *m* generator.

genesen *vi* to recover.

Genf *n* Geneva.

Genick *n* neck.

Genie *n* genius.

genießen *vt* to enjoy; to eat.

Genosse *m* **Genossin** *f* companion.

Genossenschaft *f* cooperative (society).

Genua *n* Genoa.

genug *adj adv* enough.

genügen *vi* to suffice.

Genugtuung *f* satisfaction.

Genuß *m* pleasure; enjoyment.

genußreich *adj* enjoyable.

Geograph *m* geographer.

Geographie *f* geography.

geographisch *adj* geographical.

Geologe *m* geologist.

Geologie *f* geology.

geologisch *adj* geological.

Gepäck *n* baggage.

gepflegt *adj* smart.

Gepflogenheit *f* habit.

gerade *adj* straight:—*adv* exactly; especially; even (number); just (about).

geradeaus *adv* straight on.

geradezu *adv* almost.

Gerät *n* tool, (item of) equipment.

geraten *vi* to turn out.

geräumig *adj* spacious.

Geräusch *n* noise.

geräuschlos *adj* noiseless.

geräuschvoll *adj* noisy.

gerecht *adj* fair.
Gerechtigkeit *f* justice.
Gerede *n* talk.
geregelt *adj* regular.
gereizt *adj* irritated.
Gereiztheit *f* irritation.
Gericht *n* dish, course; court.
gerichtlich *adj* judicial.
Gerichtshof *m* court.
gering *adj* little, slight.
geringfügig *adj* minor, slight.
gern(e) *adv* willingly:—~ **haben, mögen, tun** to like:—**ich schwimme ~** I like swimming.
Gerste *f* barley.
Geruch *m* smell.
Gerücht *n* rumour.
gesamt *adj* whole.
Geschäft *n* business; transaction; shop.
Geschäftsfrau *f* businesswoman.
Geschäftsführer *m* director.
Geschäftsführung *f* management.
Geschäftsmann *m* businessman.
geschehen *vi* to happen.
gescheit *adj* clever.
Geschenk *n* gift.
Geschichte *f* story; history.
geschichtlich *adj* historic(al):—*adv* historically.
Geschick *n* destiny; skill.
geschickt *adj* skilful.
geschieden *adj* divorced.
Geschirr *n* crockery, kitchen utensils; harness.
Geschirrtuch *n* dishcloth.
Geschlecht *n* sex, gender; species.
geschlechtlich *adj* sexual.
geschlossen *adj* closed.

Geschmack *m* taste.
Geschöpf *n* creature.
Geschoß *n* projectile; floor, storey.
Geschrei *n* shouting.
Geschütz *n* gun.
Geschwader *n* squadron.
Geschwindigkeit *f* speed.
Geschwister *pl* brother(s) and sister(s).
Geselle *m* companion.
gesellig *adj* sociable.
Geselligkeit *f* sociability.
Gesellschaft *f* company; society.
Gesetz *n* law.
Gesetzgebung *f* legislation.
gesetzlich *adj* legal, statutory.
gesetzlos *adj* lawless.
gesetzmäßig *adj* legal.
gesetzwidrig *adj* illegal.
Gesicht *n* face.
Gesichtspunkt *m* point of view.
gesinnt *adj* disposed.
Gesinnung *f* disposition.
Gespann *n* team.
gespannt *adj* tight; in suspense.
Gespenst *n* ghost.
gespensterhaft *adj* ghostly.
Gespinst *n* tissue, fabric.
Gespött *n* mockery.
Gespräch *n* talk, conversation.
gesprächig *adj* talkative.
Gesprechspartner *m* interlocutor.
Gestalt *f* shape; figure.
gestalten *vt* to form; to design:—*vr* to turn out.
Gestalter(in) *m(f)* designer.
Gestaltung *f* formation; arrangement.
Geständnis *n* confession.
gestatten *vt* to allow.

Geste *f* gesture.
gestehen *vt vi* to confess.
Gestein *n* rock.
Gestell *n* frame.
gestern *adv* yesterday.
Gestirn *n* star; constellation.
gestrichen *adj* painted; cancelled.
Gesuch *n* request.
gesucht *adj* sought-after.
gesund *adj* healthy.
Gesundheit *f* health.
Gesundung *f* recovery.
Getränk *n* drink.
Getreide *n* corn; grain, cereals.
Getriebe *n* gears, gearbox.
geübt *adj* experienced.
Geübtheit *f* skill, experience.
Gewächs *n* growth; plant.
Gewächshaus *n* greenhouse.
gewagt *adj* daring.
gewählt *adj* selected.
gewahren *vt* to perceive.
Gewähr *f* guarantee.
gewähren *vt* to grant.
gewährleisten *vt* to guarantee.
Gewährleistung *f* guarantee.
Gewahrsam *m / n* safekeeping; custody.
Gewalt *f* power; violence.
gewaltig *adj* huge.
gewalttätig *adj* violent.
gewandt *adj* agile, skilful.
Gewebe *n* fabric, tissue.
Gewehr *n* gun.
Gewerbe *n* occupation; industry.
gewerblich *adj* commercial, industrial.
Gewerkschaft *f* trade union.

Gewicht *n* weight.
gewichtig *adj* heavy.
gewiegt *adj* experienced.
gewillt *adj* willing.
Gewinn *n* profit.
gewinnbringend *adj* profitable.
gewinnen *vt vi* to win.
Gewinner(in) *m(f)* winner.
Gewinnung *f* winning; extraction.
gewiß *adj* certain:—*adv* certainly.
Gewissen *n* conscience.
gewissenhaft *adj* conscientious.
gewissenlos *adj* unscrupulous.
gewissermaßen *adv* as it were; to an extent.
Gewißheit *f* certainty.
Gewitter *n* (thunder)storm.
gewöhnen *vt* to accustom:—*vr* to become used to.
Gewohnheit *f* habit.
gewöhnlich *adj* usual:—*adv* usually.
gewohnt *adj* usual; used to.
gewollt *adj* deliberate.
Gewürz *n* spice.
Gezeiten *pl* tide.
gezielt *adj* deliberate; specific.
Gier *f* greed, eagerness.
gierig *adj* greedy.
gießen *vt vi* to pour.
Gießkanne *f* watering can.
Gift *m* poison.
giftig *adj* poisonous.
Gigant *m* giant.
Gipfel *m* summit.
Gips *m* gypsum; plaster.
gipsen *vt* to plaster.
Gipser *m* plasterer.
Giraffe *f* giraffe.
Giro *n* giro.

Girobank *f* clearing bank.
Girokonto *n* current account.
Gitarre *f* guitar.
Gitter *n* grille, grating.
Glanz *m* brightness; glory.
glänzen *vt* to polish:—*vi* to gleam.
glänzend *adj* brilliant.
Glas *n* glass.
Glaser *m* glazier.
gläsern *adj* glassy.
glatt *adj* smooth:—*adv* smoothly.
Glatteis *n* (black) ice.
Glatze *f* bald patch, bald head.
Glauben *m* belief.
glauben *vt vi* to believe.
glaubhaft *adj* credible.
gläubig *adj* believing.
Gläubiger(in) *m(f)* creditor.
glaublich, glaubwürdig *adj* credible.
gleich *adj* same:—*adv* equally; immediately:—*prep* like.
gleichartig *adj* similar.
gleichen *vi* to be equal to; to resemble.
gleichfalls *adv* also.
Gleichgewicht *n* balance.
Gleichheit *f* equality.
gleichkommen *vi* to equal.
gleichlautend *adj* similar.
gleichmachen *vt* to equalize.
gleichmäßig *adj* proportionate; uniform.
Gleichmäßigkeit *f* uniformity.
gleichmütig *adj* even-tempered.
gleichsam *adv* as it were.
gleichsehen *vi* to resemble.
Gleichstrom *m* direct current.

Gleichung *f* equation.
gleichwertig *adj* equivalent.
gleichzeitig *adj* simultaneous.
Gleis *n* track; platform.
gleiten *vi* to glide; to slide.
Gletscher *m* glacier.
Glied *n* member; limb.
Gliederung *f* structure; classification.
glimmen *vi* to smoulder, glimmer.
Globus *m* globe.
Glocke *f* bell.
Glück *n* luck; happiness:— ~ **haben** to succeed.
glücklich *adj* fortunate; happy:—*adv* fortunately.
glücklicherweise *adv* fortunately.
glückselig *adj* ecstatic.
Glückwunsch *m* best wishes.
Glückwunschkarte *f* greetings card.
Glühbirne *f* light bulb.
glühen *vi* to glow.
glühend *adj* glowing.
Gnade *f* grace, favour; mercy.
gnädig *adj* gracious.
Gold *n* gold.
golden *adj* golden.
Goldfisch *m* goldfish.
Goldschmied *m* goldsmith.
Golf *m* gulf:—*n* golf.
gönnen *vt* to allow.
Gorilla *m* gorilla.
Gott *m* god, God.
Göttin *f* goddess.
göttlich *adj* divine.
Götze *m* idol.
Grab *n* grave.
graben *vt vi* to dig.
Graben *m* ditch.
Grabstein *m* gravestone.
Grad *m* degree.

Graf *m* count; earl.

Gräfin *f* countess.

Gram *m* grief.

grämen *vt vr* to grieve.

Gramm *n* gram.

Grammatik *f* grammar.

grammatisch *adj* grammatical.

Gran *n* grain.

Granate *f* grenade.

Granit *m* granite.

Graphik *f* graphics.

graphisch *adj adv* graphic(ally).

Gras *n* grass.

grasen *vi* to graze.

gräßlich *adj* horrible.

Grat *m* ridge.

Gräte *f* fishbone.

gratulieren *vi* to congratulate.

grau *adj* grey.

grausam *adj* cruel.

Grausamkeit *f* cruelty.

gravieren *vt* to engrave.

Gravitation *f* gravitation.

Gravüre *f* engraving.

greifbar *adj* tangible.

greifen *vt* to grip.

Greis *m* old man.

grell *adj* shrill; garish.

Gremium *n* body, group.

Grenze *f* boundary, frontier.

Greuel *m* horror.

greulich *adj* horrible.

Griecher *m* **Griechin** *f* Greek.

Griechenland *n* Greece.

griechisch *adj* Greek.

Griff *m* grasp, hold; lever; handle.

Grill *m* grill.

Grille *f* cricket; whim.

grillen *vt* to grill.

Grinsen *n* grin.

grinsen *vi* to grin.

Grippe *f* flu.

grob *adj* coarse; gross.

Groll *m* grudge.

grollen *vi* to sulk.

Gros *n* gross; majority.

Groschen *m* ten pfennig coin.

groß *adj* great; large; tall; *adv* greatly, highly.

großartig *adj* great.

Großbritannien *n* (Great) Britain.

Großbuchstabe *m* capital (letter).

Größe *f* size; quantity.

Großeltern *pl* grandparents.

großenteils *adv* largely.

Großhandel *m* wholesale (trade).

Großhändler *m* wholesaler.

Großmut *f* generosity.

großmütig *adj* generous.

Großmutter *f* grandmother.

Großstadt *f* city.

größtenteils *adv* mainly.

großtun *vi* to boast.

Großvater *m* grandfather.

großzügig *adj* large-scale; generous.

Großzügigkeit *f* grandness; generosity.

grotesk *adj* grotesque.

Grube *f* pit, mine.

grün *adj* green.

Grund *m* ground; reason.

Grundbesitz *m* property.

gründen *vt* to establish:— *vr* ~ **auf** to be based on.

Gründer(in) *m(f)* founder.

Grundgesetz *n* constitution.

Grundlage *f* basis.

grundlegend *adj* fundamental.

gründlich *adj* thorough.

grundlos *adj* groundless.

Grundriß *m* ground-plan, layout.

Grundsatz *m* principle.

grundsätzlich *adj* fundamental:—*adv* fundametally.

Grundschule *f* primary school.

Grundstück *n* (piece of) land.

Gründung *f* foundation.

grunzen *vt vi* to grunt.

Gruppe *f* group.

gruppieren *vt* to group.

Gruß *m* greeting; salute:— **mit freundlichen Grüßen** yours sincerely:—**viele Grüße** best wishes.

grüßen *vt* to greet, welcome.

gucken *vi* to look, peep.

gültig *adj* valid.

Gültigkeit *f* validity.

Gummi *m/n* rubber.

Gunst *f* favour.

günstig *adj* favourable.

Gurgel *f* throat.

gurgeln *vt vi* to gurgle, gargle.

Gurke *f* cucumber, gherkin.

Gurt, Gürtel *m* belt.

gut *adj* good:—*adv* well.

Gut *n* good(s); property.

Gutachten *n* assessment, valuation.

gutartig *adj* good-natured.

gutaussehend *adj* good-looking.

Güte *f* goodness.

gutgelaunt *adj* cheerful.

gütig *adj* kind.

gütlich *adj* amicable.

Gymnasium *n* secondary school.

Gymnastik *f* gymnastics.

Gynäkologe *m* gynaecologist.

Gynäkologie *f* gynaecology.

H

Haar *n* hair.
haarig *adj* hairy.
haben *vt v aux* to have.
hacken *vt vi* to chop.
Hafen *m* port, harbour.
Hafer *m* oats.
Haft *f* custody.
haftbar *adj* liable.
haften *vi* to stick, persist; to
 be liable.
Haftung *f* liability.
Hagel *m* hail.
Hahn *m* cock, rooster; tap.
Hähnchen *n* cockerel;
 chicken.
Hai *m* shark.
Hain *m* copse.
Haken *m* hook.
Hakenkreuz *n* swastika.
halb *adj adv* half:—~ **vier**
 half past three.
Halbfinale *n* semi-final.
halbieren *vt* to halve.
Halbinsel *f* peninsula.
Halbkreis *m* semicircle.
Halbkugel *f* hemisphere.
halboffen *adj* half-open,
 ajar.
halbrund *adj* semicircular.
Halbtagsarbeit *f* part-time
 work.
Halbton *m* semitone.
halbwegs *adv* halfway.
Hälfte *f* half.
Halle *f* hall.
hallen *vi* to echo.
Hals *m* neck, throat.
Halskette *f* necklace.
Halt *m* hold; stop.
haltbar *adj* lasting.

Haltbarkeit *f* durability.
halten *vt* to hold; to keep;
 to contain: —~ **für** to
 consider.
Haltestelle *f* stop.
Haltung *f* attitude.
Hammer *m* hammer.
hämmern *vt vi* to hammer.
Hand *f* hand.
Handbremse *f* handbrake.
Handbuch *n* manual.
Handel *m* trade, commerce;
 deal.
handeln *vi* to act; to
 trade:—*vr* **sich ~ um** to
 be a matter of.
Handgelenk *n* wrist.
handhaben *vt* to handle.
Händler(in) *m(f)* dealer;
 shopkeeper.
handlich *adj* handy.
Handlung *f* action; shop.
Handschrift *f* handwriting.
Handschuh *m* glove.
Handtasche *f* handbag.
Handtuch *n* towel.
Hang *m* slope.
hängen *vt vi* to hang.
Hannover *n* Hanover.
Harfe *f* harp.
Harke *f* rake.
harmlos *adj* harmless.
Harmonie *f* harmony.
harmonisch *adj* harmo-
 nious.
Harn *m* urine.
harnen *vi* to urinate.
harren *vi* to wait.
hart *adj* hard.
Härte *f* hardness.

härten *vt vi* to harden.
hartnäckig *adj* obstinate.
Hase *m* hare.
Haß *m* hatred.
hassen *vt* to hate.
häßlich *adj* ugly.
Hast *f* haste.
hasten *vi* to hurry.
hastig *adj adv* hurried(ly).
Haube *f* hood; bonnet.
Hauch *m* breath; trace.
hauchen *vi* to breathe.
hauen *vt* to cut; to thrash.
häufeln *vt vi* to pile (up).
Haufen *m* pile.
häufen *vt vr* to pile (up).
häufig *adj* frequent:—*adv*
 frequently, often.
Häufigkeit *f* frequency.
Haupt *n* head; chief.
Haupt- *in compounds* chief,
 main.
Hauptbahnhof *m* main station.
Hauptmann *m* captain.
hauptsächlich *adj* main:—
 adv mainly.
Hauptschule *f* secondary
 school.
Hauptstadt *f* capital city.
Haus *n* house; building:—
 nach ~e home:—**zu ~e**
 (at) home.
Hausarbeit *f* housework;
 homework.
Hausfrau *f* housewife.
Haushalt *m* household.
häuslich *adj* domestic.
Haustier *n* pet.
Haut *f* skin.

Hebel *m* lever.
heben *vt* to lift.
Hecke *f* hedge.
Heer *n* army.
Hefe *f* yeast.
Heft *n* handle; notebook; issue.
heften *vt* to attach.
heftig *adj* strong, intense.
hegen *vt* to tend; to harbour (grudge).
Heide *f* heath, heather.
heikel *adj* fussy; difficult.
Heil *n* well-being.
heil *adj* safe, uninjured.
heilen *vt* to cure:—*vi* to heal.
heilig *adj* holy.
Heilige(r) *f(m)*saint.
Heilung *f* cure.
Heim *n* home.
heim *adv* home.
Heimat *f* home(land).
heimisch *adj* home, native.
heimlos *adj* homeless.
heimisch *adj* home, native:—**sich ~ fühlen** to feel at home.
Heimweh *n* homesickness.
Heirat *f* marriage.
heiraten *vt vi* to marry.
heiser *adj* hoarse.
Heiserkeit *f* hoarseness.
heiß *adj* hot.
heißen *vt* to call:—*vi* to be called; to mean:—**das heißt** that is (to say).
heiter *adj* bright; cheerful; sunny.
Heiterkeit *f* cheerfulness.
heizen *vt* to heat.
Heizung *f* heating.
hektisch *adj* hectic.
Held(in) *m(f)* hero.
heldenhaft *adj* heroic:—*adv* heroically.
Heldentum *n* heroism.

helfen *vi* to help.
Helfer(in) *m(f)* helper.
Helium *n* helium.
hell *adj* clear; bright; light (colour).
Helle, Helligkeit *f* brightness.
hellwach *adj* wide awake.
Helm *m* helmet; rudder.
Hemd *m* shirt.
Hemisphäre *f* hemisphere.
hemmen *vt* to obstruct.
Henkel *m* handle.
henken *vt* to hand.
Henker *m* hangman.
Henne *f* hen.
her *adv* here; from; ago.
herab *adv* down(wards).
heran *adv* this way; here; near.
herauf *adv* up(wards), up here.
heraus *adv* out(wards); from.
herausfordern *vt* to challenge.
Herausforderung *f* challenge.
herb *adj* bitter.
herbei *adv* here.
Herberge *f* hostel, inn.
Herbst *m* autumn.
Herd *m* cooker.
herein *adv* in (here); into:—**~!** come in!
Hering *m* herring.
herkommen *vi* to approach.
herkömmlich *adj* traditional.
Herkunft *f* origin.
Herr *m* lord; Mr; gentleman.
herrlich *adj* magnificent.
Herrschaft *f* domination; rule.
herrschen *vi* to rule; to prevail.

Herrscher(in) *m(f)* ruler.
herstellen *vt* to produce.
Hersteller(in) *m(f)* manufacturer.
Herstellung *f* production.
herum *adv* around.
herunter *adv* down.
hervor *adv* forth, out.
hervorragend *adj* outstanding.
Herz *n* heart.
Herzanfall *m* heart attack.
herzlich *adj* cordial.
herzlos *adj* heartless.
Herzog *m* duke.
Herzogin *f* duchess.
hetzen *vt* to hunt:—*vi* to hurry.
Heu *n* hay.
Heuchelei *f* hypocrisy.
heucheln *vt* to pretend:—*vi* to be a hypocrite.
heulen *vi* to howl; to hoot; to cry.
heute *adv* today.
heutig *adj* present-day.
heutzutage *adv* nowadays.
Hexagon *m* hexagon.
Hexe *f* witch.
Hexerei *f* witchcraft.
Hieb *m* blow; cut.
hier *adv* here.
hierauf *adv* thereupon.
hieraus *adv* from this.
hierbei *adv* at this, herewith.
hierdurch *adv* through here.
hierfür *adv* for this.
hierher *adv* here.
hierin *adv* in this.
hiermit *adv* herewith.
hiernach *adv* after this.
hierüber *adv* over here; about this.
hierum *adv* about this.
hierunter *adv* under this.
hiervon *adv* of this.

hierzu *adv* to this; moreover.

Hilfe *f* help:—**erste** ~ first aid.

hilflos *adj* helpless.

hilfreich *adj* helpful.

Hilfskraft *f* assistant.

Hilfsmittel *n* aid, means.

Himbeere *f* raspberry.

Himmel *m* sky; heaven.

Himmelfahrt *f* ascension.

hin *adv* there; away; gone:—~ **und zurück** there and back:—~ **und her** to and fro.

hinauf *adv* up(wards).

hinaufsteigen *vi* to climb.

hinaus *adv* out.

Hinblick *m*:—**in** ~ **auf** in view of.

hindern *vt* to hinder.

Hindernis *n* hindrance *f* obstacle.

hindeuten *vi* to point.

hindurch *adv* through.

hinein *adv* in(to).

Hingabe *f* devotion.

hingeben *vr* to devote oneself.

hinken *vi* to limp.

Hinsicht *f* respect, regard.

hinsichtlich *adv* with regard to.

hinten *adv* behind.

hinter *prep* behind.

Hintergrund *m* background.

hinterher *adv* behind; afterwards.

hinterlassen *vt* to leave (behind).

Hintertür *f* back door.

hinüber *adv* across.

hinunter *adv* down.

hinweg *adv* away; off.

Hinweis *m* reference; instruction.

hinweisen *vt* to refer to:— *vi* to point at.

hinzu *adv* there; also.

hinzufügen *vt* to add.

Hirn *n* brain.

Hirsch *m* stag.

Hirt *m* herdsman.

hissen *vt* to hoist.

Historiker *m* historian.

historisch *adj* *adv* historic(ally).

Hitze *f* heat.

Hitzewelle *f* heatwave.

hitzig *adj* hot-headed.

Hobby *n* hobby.

Hobel *m* plane.

hoch *adj* high.

Hochachtung *f* respect.

hochachtungsvoll *adj* yours faithfully.

Hochfrequenz *f* high frequency.

Hochmut *m* pride.

hochmütig *adj* haughty.

Hochschule *f* college.

Hochsprung *m* high jump.

Hochspringer(in) *m(f)* high-jumper.

höchst *adj* highest:—*adv* highly.

höchstens *adv* at most.

hochwertig *adj* high-quality.

Hochzeit *f* wedding.

hochziehen *vt* to raise.

hocken *vi* to crouch.

Hocker *m* stool.

Höcker *m* hump.

Hockey *n* hockey.

Hoden *m* testicle.

Hof *n* court(yard); farm.

hoffen *vt* *vi* to hope.

hoffentlich *adv* hopefully.

Hoffnung *f* hope.

hoffnungslos *adj* hopeless.

hoffnungsvoll *adj* hopeful.

höflich *adj* polite:—*adv* politely.

Höflichkeit *f* politeness.

Höhe *f* height; amount.

Hoheit *f* Highness; sovereignty.

Höhepunkt *m* climax.

höher *adj* *adv* higher.

hohl *adj* hollow.

Höhle *f* cave.

Hohn *m* scorn.

höhnen *vi* to mock.

höhnisch *adj* scornful.

holen *vt* to fetch, get.

Holland *n* Holland; Netherlands.

Holländer(in) *m(f)* Dutchman(woman).

holländisch *adj* Dutch.

Hölle *f* hell.

höllisch *adj* hellish.

holp(e)rig *adj* bumpy.

holpern *vi* to stumble.

Holz *n* wood.

hölzern *adj* wooden.

Holzfäller *m* woodcutter.

holzig *adj* woody.

Holzkohle *f* charcoal.

homosexuell *adj* homosexual.

Honig *m* honey.

Hopfen *m* hop(s).

Hörapparat *m* hearing aid.

hörbar *adj* audible.

horchen *vi* to listen.

hören *vt* *vi* to hear; to listen.

Hörer(in) *m(f)* listener; receiver.

Horizont *m* horizon.

horizontal *adj* horizontal.

Hormon *n* hormone.

Horn *n* horn.

Horoskop *n* horoscope.

Hörsaal *m* lecture hall.

Hörspiel *n* radio play.

horten *vt* to hoard.

Hose *f* trousers.

Hoseträger *m* braces.

Hotel *n* hotel.

hübsch *adj* pretty.
Hubschrauber *m* helicopter.
Huf *m* hoof.
Hufeisen *n* horseshoe.
Hüfte *f* hip.
Hügel *m* hill.
Huhn *n* hen, chicken.
huldigen *vi* to pay homage to.
Hülle *f* covering; wrapping.
hüllen *vt* to wrap.
Hülse *f* husk.
Hummel *f* bumblebee.
Hummer *m* lobster.
Humor *m* humour.
humoristisch, humorvoll *adj* humorous.

Hund *m* dog.
hundert *num* hundred.
hundertprozentig *adj* a hundred per cent.
Hündin *f* bitch.
Hunger *m* hunger:—~ **haben** to be hungry.
hungern *vi* to starve.
hungrig *adj* hungry.
Hupe *f* horn.
hupern *vi* to hoot.
hüpfen *vi* to hop.
Hürde *f* hurdle.
Hure *f* whore.
husten *vi* to cough.
Husten *m* cough.
Hut *m* hat:—*f* care.

hüten *vt* to guard:—*vr* to take care.
Hütte *f* hut; foundry.
Hygiene *f* hygiene.
hygienisch *adj* hygienic:— *adv* hygienically.
Hymne *f* hymn; anthem.
Hypnose *f* hypnosis.
hypnotisch *adj* hypnotic.
Hypothek *f* mortgage.
Hypothese *f* hypothesis.
hypothetisch *adj* hypothetical.
Hysterie *f* hysteria.
hysterisch *adj* hysterical.

I

ich *nom pn* I.
ideal *adj* ideal.
Ideal *n* ideal.
Idee *f* idea.
identifizieren *vt vr* to identify.
Identifizierung *f* identification.
identisch *adj* identical.
Identität *f* identity.
Ideologie *f* ideology.
ideologisch *adj* ideological.
Idiot *m* idiot.
idyllisch *adj* idyllic.
Igel *m* hedgehog.
ihm *dat pn* (to) him, (to) it.
ihn *acc pn* him, it.
ihnen *dat pn* (to) them.
Ihnen *dat pn* (to) you.
ihr *nom pn* you:—*dat* (to) her, (to) it: —*poss adj* her, its, their.
illegal *adj* illegal.
Illusion *f* illusion.
Illustration *f* illustration.
illustrieren *vt* to illustrate.
Illustrierte *f* magazine.
Imbiß *m* snack.
Imitation *f* imitation.
imitieren *vt* to imitate.
immer *adv* always, ever:—**noch ~** still:—**~ wieder** repeatedly.
immerhin *adv* after all.
impfen *vt* to vaccinate.
Import *m* import.
importieren *vt* to import.
Impuls *m* impulse.
impulsiv *adj* impulsive.
in *prep* in, into.

indem *conj* as; while.
Inder(in) *m(f)* Indian.
Indianer(in) *m(f)* (Red) Indian.
indianisch *adj* (Red) Indian.
Indien *n* India.
indirekt *adj* indirect.
indisch *adj* Indian.
individuell *adj* individual.
Indonesien *n* Indonesia.
Industrie *f* industry.
industriell *adj* industrial.
Infektion *f* infection.
infizieren *vt* to infect:—*vr* to become infected.
Inflation *f* inflation.
infolge *prep* due to.
Information *f* information.
informieren *vt* to inform.
Ingenieur *m* engineer.
Inhaber(in) *m(f)* owner.
Inhalt *m* content(s).
Initiative *f* initiative.
Inland *n* home country.
innehaben *vt* to hold.
innehalten *vt* to comply with:—*vi* to pause.
innen *adv* inside.
Innenminister *m* minister of the interior.
inner *adj* inner, interior.
innerhalb *adv prep* within.
innerlich *adj* inner; mental.
innig *adj* warm; sincere.
inoffiziell *adj* unofficial.
Insasse *m* occupant.
insbesondere *adv* in particular.
Inschrift *f* inscription.

Insekt *n* insect.
Insel *f* island.
insgesamt *adv* altogether.
insofern, insoweit *adv* in so far, in this respect:—*conj* if; so.
Inspektion *f* inspection.
Inspiration *f* inspiration.
inspirieren *vt* to inspire.
instandhalten *vt* to maintain, service.
instandsetzen *vt* to repair.
Instanz *f* authority; court.
Instinkt *m* instinct.
instinktiv *adj* instinctive.
Institut *n* institution.
Instrument *n* instrument.
intellektuell *adj* intellectual.
Intellektuelle(r) *f(m)* intellectual.
intelligent *adj* intelligent.
Intelligenz *f* intelligence.
intensiv *adj* intensive.
interessant *adj* interesting.
Interesse *n* interest
interessieren *vt* to interest:—*vr* to be interested.
intern *adj* internal.
international *adj* international.
Interpretation *f* interpretation.
interpretieren *vt* to interpret.
Intervall *n* interval.
Interview *n* interview.
interviewen *vt* to interview.
intim *adj* intimate; cosy.
Intimität *f* intimacy.
Intrige *f* intrigue.

Invasion *f* invasion.
Inventar *n* inventory.
Inventur *f* stocktake.
investieren *vt* to invest.
Investition *f* investment.
inwendig *adv* inward.
inwiefern, inwieweit *adv* to what extent.
inzwischen *adv* meanwhile; since.
Irak *m* Iraq.
Iran *n* Iran.
irdisch *adj* earthly.
Ire *m* Irishman.
irgend *adv* some, any; at all; ever:—**wer** ~ whoever:—~ **etwas** something, anything.

irgendein *adj* some, any.
irgendeiner *pn* somebody.
irgendwann *adv* sometime.
irgendwie *adv* somehow.
irgendwo *adv* somewhere.
irgendwohin *adv* somewhere.
Irin *f* Irishwoman.
Iris *f* iris.
irisch *adj* Irish.
Irland *n* Ireland.
Irländer(in) *m(f)* Irishman, Irishwoman.
Ironie *f* irony.
ironisch *adj* ironic.
irre *adj* mad.
Irre(r) *f(m)* lunatic.
irreführen *vt* to mislead.

irren *vi vr* to get lost; to make a mistake.
irritieren *vt* to irritate.
Irrtum *m* error.
irrtümlich *adj* wrong.
Island *n* Iceland.
islandisch *adj* Icelandic.
Isolation *f* isolation; insulation.
isolieren *vt* to isolate; to insulate.
Israel *n* Israel.
Israeli *m* Israeli.
israelisch *adj* Israeli.
Italien *n* Italy.
Italiener(in) *m(f)* Italian.
italienisch *adj* Italian.

J

ja *adv* yes.
Jacht *f* yacht.
Jacke *f* jacket.
Jagd *f* hunt(ing).
jagen *vt vi* to hunt.
Jäger *m* hunter.
Jahr *n* year.
Jahreszeit *f* season.
Jahrhundert *n* century.
jährlich *adj adv* annual(ly).
Jahrzehnt *n* decade.
Jammer *m* misery.
jämmerlich *adj* lamentable.
jammern *vt* to arouse
  pity:—*vi* to lament.
Januar, Jänner *m* January.
Japaner(in) *m(f)* Japanese
  (person).
japanisch *adj* Japanese.
jawohl *adv* yes (certainly).
Jazz *m* jazz.
je *adv* ever, every; each:—~

größer, desto besser the
  bigger the better.
jede(r, s) *pn* each, every.
jedenfalls *adv* in any case.
jedermann *pn* everyone.
jederzeit *adv* at any time.
jedesmal *adv* every time.
jedoch *adv* however.
jemals *adv* ever.
jemand *pn* somebody, any-
  body.
jene(r, s) *adv* that:—*pn* that
  one.
jetzt *adv* now.
jeweilig *adj* respective.
jeweils *adv* respectively.
Jordanien *n* Jordan.
Journalist(in) *m(f)* journalist.
Jubiläum *n* jubilee;
  anniversary.
jucken *vi* to itch.

Jude *m* **Jüdin** *f* Jew, Jewess.
jüdisch *adj* Jewish.
Jugend *f* youth.
Jugendherberge *f* youth
  hostel.
jugendlich *adj* youthful.
Jugendliche(r) *f(m)* young
  person.
Jugendstil *m* art nouveau.
Juli *m* July.
jung *adj* young.
Junge *m* boy.
Jungfer *f* spinster.
Jungfrau *f* virgin.
Juni *m* June.
Jurist *m* lawyer.
Justiz *f* justice.
Juwel *n* jewel.
Juwelier *m* jeweller.

K

Kabarett *n* cabaret.
Kabel *n* cable.
Kabine *f* cabin; cubicle.
Kabinett *n* cabinet.
Kachel *f* tile.
Käfer *m* beetle.
Kaffee *m* coffee.
Käfig *m* cage.
kahl *adj* bare, bald.
Kai *m* quay.
Kaiser(in) *m(f)* emperor (empress).
Kakao *m* cocoa.
Kaktus *m* cactus.
Kalb *n* calf.
Kalbfleisch *n* veal.
Kalender *m* calendar.
Kalk *m* calcium, chalk.
kalkulieren *vt* to calculate.
kalt *adj* cold:—**mir ist ~** I am cold.
Kälte *f* cold.
Kamel *n* camel.
Kamera *f* camera.
Kamerad(in) *m(f)* comrade.
Kameradschaft *f* comradeship.
Kamin *m* chimney; fireplace.
Kamm *m* comb; crest.
kämmen *vt vi* to comb:—*vr* to comb one's hair.
Kammer *f* chamber.
Kampf *m* fight; battle.
kämpfen *vi* to fight.
Kämpfer *m* fighter.
Kanada *n* Canada.
Kanadier(in) *m(f)* Canadian.
kanadisch *adj* Canadian.
Kanal *m* channel; canal.

Kanalisation *f* drain.
Kanarienvogel *m* canary.
Kandidat(in) *m(f)* candidate.
Känguruh *n* kangaroo.
Kaninchen *n* rabbit.
Kanne *f* can; pot.
Kanone *f* cannon.
Kante *f* edge.
Kantine *f* canteen.
Kanton *m* canton.
Kanu *n* canoe.
Kanzel *f* pulpit.
Kanzler *m* chancellor.
Kap *n* cape.
Kapazität *f* capacity.
Kapelle *f* chapel.
kapieren *vt vi* to understand.
Kapital *n* capital.
Kapitalismus *m* capitalism.
Kapitalist *m* capitalist.
kapitalistisch *adj* capitalist.
Kapitän *m* captain.
Kapitel *n* chapter.
Kappe *f* cap.
Kapsel *f* capsule.
Kapstadt *n* Cape Town.
kaputt *adj* broken.
Karawane *f* caravan.
Karfreitag *m* Good Friday.
karg, kärglich *adj* meagre.
karibisch *adj* Caribbean.
Karneval *m* carnival.
Karo *n* square; diamonds (cards).
Karotte *f* carrot.
Karriere *f* career.
Karte *f* card; chart; map; ticket; menu.

Kartell *n* cartel.
Kartoffel *f* potato.
Karton *m* cardboard.
Karussell *n* roundabout.
Käse *m* cheese.
Kaserne *f* barracks.
Kasino *n* casino.
Kaskade *f* cascade.
Kasse *f* cashbox; booking office.
Kassette *f* cassette; box.
kassieren *vt vi* to collect (money).
Kassierer(in) *m(f)* cashier.
Kastanie *f* chestnut.
Kasten *m* box.
kastrieren *vt* to castrate.
Katalog *m* catalogue.
Katapult *m* catapult.
katastrophal *adj* catastrophic.
Katastrophe *f* catastrophe.
Kategorie *f* category.
kategorisch *adj* categorical.
Kater *m* tom-cat; hangover.
Katholik(in) *m(f)* Catholic.
katholisch *adj* Catholic.
Katze *f* cat.
Katzenjammer *m* hangover.
kauen *vt vi* to chew.
Kauf *m* purchase.
kaufen *vt vi* to buy.
Käufer(in) *m(f)* buyer.
Kaufhaus *n* department store.
Kaufleute *pl* tradespeople.
käuflich *adj* for sale.
Kaufmann *m* businessman.
Kaugummi *m* chewing gum.

kaum *adv* hardly.
Kegel *m* skittle; cone.
Kegelbahn *f* bowling alley.
Kehle *f* throat.
Kehlkopf *m* larynx.
Kehre *f* turn, bend.
kehren *vt vi* to turn; to sweep.
Keil *m* wedge.
Keim *m* germ; bud.
kein(er, e, es) *adj* no, not any.
keinesfalls, keineswegs *adv* not at all.
keinmal *adv* never.
Keks *m*/*n* biscuit.
Keller *m* cellar.
Kellner(in) *m(f)* waiter (waitress).
kennbar *adj* recognizable.
kennen *vt* to know.
kennenlernen *vt* to get to know; to meet.
Kenner(in) *m(f)* connoisseur, expert.
Kenntnis *f* knowledge.
Kennzeichen *n* sign; characteristic.
kennzeichnen *vt* to characterize.
kennzeichnend *adj* characteristic.
Keramik *f* ceramics.
Kerl *m* chap, guy.
Kern *m* kernel; nucleus.
Kernenergie *f* nuclear energy.
Kernkraftwerk *n* nuclear power station.
Kerze *f* candle; spark plug.
Kessel *m* kettle; boiler.
Kette *f* chain.
kichern *vi* to giggle.
Kiefer *m* jaw:—*f* pine.
Kies *m* gravel.
Kiesel(stein) *m* pebble.
Kilogramm *n* kilogram.

Kilometer *m* kilometre.
Kind *n* child.
Kindergarten *m* nursery school.
Kinderwagen *m* pram.
Kindheit *f* childhood.
kindisch *adj* childish.
kindlich *adj* childlike.
Kinn *n* chin.
Kino *n* cinema.
Kiosk *m* kiosk.
Kippe *f* cigarette end.
kippen *vt vi* to tip, tilt.
Kirche *f* church.
Kirchenlied *n* hymn.
Kirchturm *m* steeple.
Kirsche *f* cherry.
Kissen *n* cushion.
Kiste *m* box, chest.
Kitsch *m* kitsch, trash.
kitschig *adj* trashy.
Kitt *m* putty.
kitzeln *vt* to tickle.
Klage *f* complaint; lawsuit.
klagen *vi* to complain.
Kläger(in) *m(f)* plaintiff.
kläglich *adj* lamentable.
Klang *m* sound.
Klappe *f* flap; valve.
klappen *vt vi* to tip:—**das klappt nicht** it doesn't work.
klar *adj* clear.
klären *vt* to clarify.
Klarheit *f* clarity.
Klarinette *f* clarinet.
klarmachen *vt* make clear; to prepare.
Klärung *f* clarification.
Klasse *f* class.
klassifizieren *vt* to classify.
Klassifizierung *f* classification.
Klassiker *m* classic.
klassisch *adj* classical; traditional.

Klatsch *m* clap; smack; gossip.
klatschen *vi* to clap; to smack; to gossip.
Klaue *f* claw.
Klausel *f* clause.
Klavier *n* piano.
Klavierspieler(in) *m(f)* pianist.
kleben *vt vi* to stick.
klebrig *adj* sticky.
Klebestreifen *m* sticky tape.
Kleb(e)stoff *m* glue.
Kleid *n* dress; **Kleider** *pl* clothes.
kleiden *vt* to clothe:—*vr* to dress.
Kleiderschrank *m* wardrobe.
Kleidung *f* clothing.
klein *adj* small.
Kleingeld *n* change.
Kleinigkeit *f* trifle.
klettern *vi* to climb.
Klient(in) *m(f)* client.
Klima *n* climate.
Klimaanlage *f* air conditioning.
klimatisch *adj* climatic.
klimmen *vi* to climb.
Klinge *f* blade, sword.
Klingel *f* bell.
klingeln *vi* to ring.
Klinik *f* clinic.
Klinke *f* handle.
Klippe *f* cliff; reef; obstacle.
klirren *vi* to clink, clatter.
Klo *n* loo.
klopfen *vt vi* to knock.
Kloster *n* monastery; convent.
Klotz *m* log.
Klub *m* club.
Kluft *f* gap; chasm.
klug *adj* clever.
Klugheit *f* cleverness.

Klumpen *m* lump.

knabbern *vt vi* to nibble.

Knabe *m* boy.

knacken *vt vi* to crack.

Knall *m* bang.

knallen *vi* to bang.

knapp *adj* tight; scarce; brief:—*adv* just under.

Knappheit *f* tightness; scarcity; brevity.

knarren *vi* to creak.

Knauf *m* knob.

Kneipe *f* bar.

Knick *m* crack; fold.

knicken *vt vi* to crack.

Knie *n* knee.

knien *vi* to kneel.

knirschen *vi* to grind.

knistern *vi* to crackle.

Knitter *m* crease.

Knoblauch *m* garlic.

Knöchel *m* knuckle; ankle.

Knochen *m* bone.

Knochengerüst *n* skeleton.

Knödel *m* dumpling.

Knolle *f* bulb.

Knopf *m* button.

knöpfen *vt* to button.

Knopfloch *n* buttonhole.

Knospe *f* bud.

Knoten *m* knot; lump.

knüpfen *vt* to tie.

Knüppel *m* club, truncheon.

knusperig *adj* crisp.

Koalition *f* coalition.

Koch *m* (male) cook.

kochen *vt vi* to cook; to boil.

Kocher *m* cooker.

Köchin *f* (female) cook.

Kochtopf *m* saucepan.

Koffer *m* (suit)case.

Kofferraum *m* boot (of vehicle).

Kognak *m* brandy.

Kohl *m* cabbage.

Kohle *f* coal; charcoal; carbon.

Kohlendioxyd *n* **Kohlensäure** *f* carbon dioxide.

Kokosnuß *f* coconut.

Kollege *m* **Kollegin** *f* colleague.

kollektiv *adj* collective.

Köln *n* Cologne.

Kolonie *f* colony.

Kolonne *f* column.

Kolumbien *n* Colombia.

Kolumbus *m* Columbus.

Kombination *f* combination.

kombinieren *vt vi* to combine:—*vi* to deduce.

Kombi(wagen) *m* estate car, station wagon.

Komfort *m* comfort.

Komik *f* comedy.

Komiker(in) *m(f)* comedian.

komisch *adj* funny; strange.

Komma *n* comma; decimal point.

Kommandant *m* commander.

kommandieren *vt vi* to command.

Kommando *n* command; squad.

kommen *vi* to come.

Kommentar *m* commentary.

Kommentator *m* commentator.

kommentieren *vt* to comment upon.

kommerziell *adj* commercial.

Kommissar *m* commissioner; (police) inspector.

Kommission *f* commission; committee.

Kommode *f* chest of drawers.

Kommunikation *f* communication.

Kommunion *f* communion.

Kommunismus *m* communism.

Kommunist(in) *m(f)* communist.

kommunistisch *adj* communist.

kommunizieren *vi* to communicate.

Komödie *f* comedy.

Kompaß *m* compass.

kompensieren *vt* to compensate.

kompetent *adj* competent; responsible.

Kompetenz *f* competence; jurisdiction.

komplett *adj* complete.

Kompliment *n* compliment.

komplimentieren *vt* to compliment.

kompliziert *adj* complicated.

Komponente *f* component.

komponieren *vt* to compose.

Komponist *m* composer.

Komposition *f* composition.

Kompromiß *m* compromise.

Kondensation *f* condensation.

kondensieren *vt* to condense.

Konditorei *f* café; cake shop.

Kondom *n* condom.

Konferenz *f* conference.

Konfession *f* religion; denomination.

Konfirmation *f* confirmation.

konfirmieren *vt* to confirm.

konfiszieren *vt* to confiscate.

Konfiszierung *f* confiscation.

Konfitüre *f* jam.
Konflikt *m* conflict.
konfrontieren *vt* to confront.
Konfusion *f* confusion.
Kongreß *m* congress.
König *m* king.
Königin *f* queen.
königlich *adj* royal.
Königreich *n* kingdom.
Konjunktur *f* (state of the) economy.
konkret *adj* concrete.
Konkurrent(in) *m(f)* competitor.
Konkurrenz *f* competition.
konkurrieren *vi* to compete.
Konkurs *m* bankruptcy.
können *v aux* to be able:—ich kann I can:—ich kann Deutsch I speak German.
Können *n* ability.
konsequent *adj* consistent.
Konsequenz *f* consistency; consequence.
konservativ *adj* conservative.
Konserve(n) *f* tinned food.
konservieren *vt* to preserve.
Konservierung *f* preservation.
konsolidieren *vt vr* to consolidate.
Konsolidierung *f* consolidation.
Konsonant *m* consonant.
konstant *adj* constant.
konstatieren *vt* to state; to establish.
Konstanz *n* Constance.
Konstellation *f* constellation.
konstruieren *vt* to construct.
Konstruktion *f* construction.

Konsul *m* consul.
Konsulat *n* consulate.
konsultieren *vt* to consult.
Konsum *m* consumption.
Konsument(in) *m(f)* consumer.
Kontakt *m* contact.
kontaktarm *adj* unsociable.
kontaktfreudig *adj* sociable.
Kontaktlinsen *pl* contact lenses.
Kontinent *m* continent.
kontinental *adj* continental.
kontinuierlich *adj* continuous.
Konto *n* account.
Kontoauszug *m* statement.
Kontrabaß *m* double bass.
Kontrast *m* contrast.
Kontrolle *f* control; check.
Kontrolleur *m* inspector.
kontrollieren *vt* to check.
Kontroverse *f* controversy.
Konvention *f* convention.
konventionell *adj* conventional.
Konversation *f* conversation.
konvertieren *vt vi* to convert.
Konzentration *f* concentration.
konzentrieren *vt vr* to concentrate.
Konzept *n* draft.
Konzern *m* group (of companies).
Konzert *n* concert; concerto.
Konzertsaal *m* concert hall.
Konzession *f* concession.
Kooperation *f* cooperation.
kooperativ *adj* cooperative.
koordinieren *vt* to coordinate.
Koordinierung *f* coordination.

Kopenhagen *n* Copenhagen.
Kopf *m* head.
Kopfkissen *n* pillow.
Kopfschmerzen *mpl* headache.
Kopftuch *n* headscarf.
Kopfzeile *f* headline.
Kopie *f* copy.
kopieren *vt* to copy.
koppeln *vt* to link.
Korb *m* basket.
Korbball *m* basketball.
Kordel *f* cord.
Kork *m* cork.
Korkenzieher *m* corkscrew.
Korn *n* corn; grain; (gun)sight.
Körper *m* body.
körperlich *adj* physical.
Körperschaft *f* corporation.
korrekt *adj* correct.
Korrektur *f* correction.
Korrespondent(in) *m(f)* correspondent.
Korrespondenz *f* correspondence.
Korridor *m* corridor.
korrigieren *vt* to correct.
Korrosion *f* corrosion.
Korruption *f* corruption.
Kosmetik *f* cosmetics.
kosmetisch *adj* cosmetic.
Kosmos *m* cosmos.
Kost *f* food; accommodation.
kostbar *adj* precious; costly.
Kosten *pl* costs.
kosten *vt vi* to cost; to taste.
kostlos *adj adv* free (of charge).
köstlich *adj* precious; delicious.
Kostüm *n* costume.
Kot *m* excrement.
Kotelett *n* cutlet.
Krabbe *f* shrimp.

krabbeln *vi* to crawl.

Krach *m* crash; noise; argument.

krachen *vi* to crash:—*vr* to have a row.

krächzen *vi* to croak.

Kraft *f* strength, force, power:—**in ~ treten** to come into force.

Kraftfahrer(in) *m(f)* driver.

Kraftfahrzeug *n* motor vehicle.

kräftig *adj* strong:—*adv* strongly.

kräftigen *vt* to strengthen.

kraftlos *adj* powerless.

kraftvoll *adj* strong.

Kraftwagen *m* motor vehicle.

Kraftwerk *n* power station.

Kragen *m* collar.

Krähe *f* crow.

Kralle *f* claw.

Kram *m* stuff, odds and ends.

Krampf *m* cramp; spasm.

Kran *m* crane; tap.

krank *adj* ill.

Kranke(r) *f(m)* sick person, patient.

kranken *vi* to suffer.

kränken *vt* to hurt.

Krankenhaus *n* hospital.

Krankenschwester *f* nurse.

Krankenwagen *m* ambulance.

Krankheit *f* illness, disease.

kränklich *adj* sickly.

Kränkung *f* insult.

Kranz *m* wreath.

kratzen *vt vi* to scratch.

Kratzer *m* scratch.

kraus *adj* curly.

Kraut *n* cabbage; herb; plant.

Krawall *m* uproar.

Krawatte *f* tie.

Krebs *m* crab; cancer.

Kredit *m* credit.

Kreditkarte *f* credit card.

Kreide *f* chalk.

Kreis *m* circle; district.

kreischen *vi* to scream.

Kreisel *m* top; roundabout.

kreisen *vi* to rotate.

kreisförmig *adj* circular.

Kreislauf *m* circulation.

Krematorium *n* crematorium.

kremieren *vt* to cremate.

Kreuz *n* cross; clubs (cards).

kreuzen *vt vi vr* to cross.

Kreuzfahrt *f* cruise.

kreuzigen *vt* to crucify.

Kreuzigung *f* crucifixion.

Kreuzung *f* crossing.

Kreuzweg *m* crossroads.

Kreuzworträtsel *n* crossword.

Kreuzzug *m* crusade.

kriechen *vi* to creep, crawl.

Krieg *m* war.

kriegen *vt* to get, receive.

Krieger *m* warrior.

kriegerisch *adj* warlike.

Krimi *m* thriller.

kriminell *adj* criminal.

Kriminelle(r) *f(m)* criminal.

Krise *f* crisis; recession.

Kristall *m* crystal:—*n* crystal (glass).

Kritik *f* criticism.

Kritiker *m* critic.

kritisch *adj* critical.

kritisieren *vt vi* to criticize.

Krokodil *n* crocodile.

Krone *f* crown.

krönen *vt* to crown.

Kronjuwelen *pl* crown jewels.

Kronleuchter *m* chandelier.

Krönung *f* coronation.

Kröte *f* toad.

Krug *m* jug.

Krümel *m* crumb.

krümeln *vi vr* to crumble.

krumm *adj* crooked.

Krümmung *f* curve.

Krüppel *m* cripple.

Kruste *f* crust; scab.

Küche *f* kitchen.

Kuchen *m* cake.

Kuckuck *m* cuckoo.

Kugel *f* ball; sphere; bullet.

Kugellager *n* ball bearing.

Kugelschreiber *m* ballpoint pen.

Kuh *f* cow.

kühl *adj* cool.

Kühle *f* coolness.

kühlen *vt* to cool.

Kühlschrank *m* refrigertor.

kühn *adj* bold.

kultivieren *vt* to cultivate.

Kultur *f* culture.

kulturell *adj* cultural.

Kunde *f* information:—*m* customer.

kündigen *vt* to terminate, cancel:—*vi* to give notice.

Kündigung *f* notice.

Kundschaft *f* customers.

künftig *adj* future:—*adv* in future.

Kunst *f* art; skill.

Künstler(in) *m(f)* artist.

künstlich *adj* artificial.

kunstvoll *adj* artistic.

Kupfer *n* copper.

Kupplung *f* clutch (car); coupling.

Kur *f* cure; stay in a health resort.

Kurort *m* health resort.

Kurs *m* price; exchange rate.

Kurse, Kursus *m* course (of teaching).

Kurve *f* curve.

kurz *adj adv* short(ly).

kürzen *vt* to shorten, reduce.

kurzfristig *adj* short-term.

kürzlich *adv* recently.

kurtzsichtig *adj* short-sighted.

Kusine *f* cousin.

Kuß *m* kiss.

küssen *vt vr* to kiss.

Küste *f* coast.

Kutsche *f* coach.

L

Labor(atorium) *n* lab(oratory).

lächeln *vi* to smile.

Lächeln *n* smile.

lachen *vi* to laugh.

lächerlich *adj* ridiculous.

Lachs *m* salmon.

Lack *m* varnish; paint.

laden *vt* to load; to charge; to invite.

Laden *m* shop.

Ladentisch *m* counter.

Ladung *f* load; invitation.

Lage *f* position; layer.

Lager *n* camp; warehouse; bearing.

lagern *vt* to store:—*vi* to lie down; to camp.

Lagerraum *m* storeroom.

lahm *adj* lame.

lähmen *vt* to cripple, paralyse.

Lähmung *f* paralysis.

Laib *m* loaf.

Laibach *n* Ljubljana.

Laie *m* layman, lay person.

Laken *n* sheet.

lallen *vt* *vi* to babble.

Lamm *n* lamb.

Lampe *f* lamp.

Lampenschirm *m* lampshade.

Land *n* land; country; countryside; state (of Germany).

Landhaus *n* country house.

landen *vi* to land.

ländlich *adj* rural.

Landschaft *f* countryside; landscape.

Landstraße *f* country road.

Landtag *m* state parliament.

Landung *f* landing.

Landwirt *m* farmer.

Landwirtschaft *f* agriculture.

lang *adj* long; tall

lange *adv* for a long time.

Länge *f* length; height; longitude.

Längegrad *m* (degree of) longitude.

länger *adj* *adv* longer.

Langeweile *f* boredom.

langfristig *adj* long-term.

längs *adv* *prep* along.

langsam *adj* slow.

Langsamkeit *f* slowness.

längst *adv* for a long time; long ago.

langweilen *vt* to bore:—*vr* to be bored.

langweilig *adj* boring.

Langwelle *f* long wave.

langwierig *adj* protracted.

Lanze *f* lance.

Lappen *m* rag; lobe.

Lärm *m* noise.

lärmen *vi* to make a noise.

Laser *m* laser.

lassen *vt* to let; to leave; to stop:—*v aux* to cause to be.

Last *f* load; trouble; tax, charge.

lasten *vi* to burden.

Laster *n* vice.

lästig *adj* burdensome.

Lastkraftwagen *m* lorry.

Latein *n* Latin.

Lateinamerika *n* Latin America.

lateinisch *adj* Latin.

latent *adj* latent.

Laterne *f* lantern.

Laternenpfahl *m* lamppost.

Latte *f* lath, slat.

Lattich *m* lettuce.

Laub *n* foliage.

lauern *vi* to lurk.

Lauf *m* run; race; course.

Laufbahn *f* career.

laufen *vt* *vi* to run; to walk.

Laufen *n* running, walking.

laufend *adj* continuous; current.

Läufer(in) *m(f)* runner.

Laune *f* mood.

lauschen *vi* to eavesdrop.

laut *adj* loud:—*adv* loudly:—*prep* according to.

Laut *m* sound.

lauten *vi* to sound; to say.

läuten *vt* *vi* to ring.

lauter *adj* pure, sheer.

Lautheit *f* loudness.

Lautsprecher *m* loudspeaker.

lauwarm *adj* lukewarm.

Lawine *f* avalanche.

Leben *n* life.

leben *vt* *vi* to live.

lebendig *adj* alive, lively.

Lebensalter *n* age.

Lebensgefahr *f* danger (of death).

Lebenslauf *m* life; curriculum vitae.

Lebensmittel *pl* food.

Lebensraum *m* living space.

Lebenszeit *f* lifetime.
Leber *f* liver.
lebhaft *adj* lively.
leblos *adj* lifeless.
Leck *n* leak.
lecken *vt* to lick:—*vi* to leak.
lecker *adj* delicious.
Leder *n* leather.
ledig *adj* unmarried; empty.
lediglich *adv* only, merely.
leer *adj* empty.
Leere *f* emptiness.
leeren *vt vr* to empty.
legal *adj* legal.
legalisieren *vt* to legalize.
Legalität *f* legality.
legen *vt* to lay, place:—*vr* to lie down, abate.
legendar *adj* legendary.
Legende *f* legend.
legitim *adj* legitimate.
Legitimität *f* legitimacy.
Lehne *f* support; arm(rest), back(rest).
lehnen *vt vr* to lean.
Lehnstuhl *m* armchair.
Lehrbuch *n* textbook.
Lehre *f* teaching.
lehren *vt* to teach,
Lehrer(in) *m(f)* teacher.
Lehrgang *m* course.
Lehrling *m* apprentice.
Leib *m* body.
leiblich *adj* bodily.
Leibwache *f* bodyguard.
Leiche *f* corpse.
Leichenwagen *m* hearse.
Leichnam *m* corpse.
leicht *adj* light; easy.
leid *adj*:—**es tut mir ~** I am sorry.
Leid *n* pain, sorrow.
leiden *vt vi* to suffer.
Leiden *n* suffering.
Leidenschaft *f* passion.
leidenschaftlich *adj* passionate.

leider *adv* unfortunately.
leihen *vt* to lend:—*vr* to borrow.
Leim *m* glue.
Leine *f* cord; leash.
Leinen *n* linen.
Leinwand *f* canvas.
leise *adj* soft, quiet.
Leiste *f* ledge, edge.
leisten *vt* to perform:—*vr* to afford.
Leistung *f* performance; output.
leistungsfähig *adj* efficient.
Leistungsfähigkeit *f* efficiency.
leiten *vt* to lead, manage.
Leiter *m* leader:—*f* ladder.
Leitmotiv *n* leitmotiv, recurring theme.
Leitung *f* management; pipe; cable.
Lektion *f* lesson.
lenken *vt* to steer.
Lenkrad *n* steering wheel.
Leopard *m* leopard.
Lerche *f* lark.
lernen *vt vi* to learn.
lesbar *adj* legible.
Lesbarkeit *f* legibility.
Lesbierin *f* lesbian.
lesbisch *adj* lesbian.
lesen *vt vi* to read; to pick.
Leser(in) *m(f)* reader.
letzte(r,s) *adj* last; latest.
letztens *adv* recently.
letztlich *adv* recently; ultimately.
Leuchte *f* light.
leuchten *vi* to shine.
Leuchtturm *m* lighthouse.
leugnen *vt vi* to deny.
Leute *pl* people.
Leutnant *m* lieutenant.
Libanon *m* Lebanon.
liberal *adj* liberal.
Libyen *n* Libya.

Licht *n* light.
Lid *n* eyelid.
lieb *adj* dear; pleasant.
Liebe *f* love.
lieben *vt vi* to love; to like.
liebenswert *adj* lovable.
liebenswürdig *adj* kind.
lieber *adv* rather.
liebevoll *adj* loving.
liebhaben *vt* to like.
Liebhaber(in) *m(f)* lover.
lieblich *adj* lovely.
Liebling *m* darling; favourite.
Liebschaft *f* love affair.
liebste(r, s) *adj* favourite.
Lied *n* song.
liederlich *adj* careless.
Lieferant *m* supplier.
liefern *vt vi* to deliver, supply.
Lieferung *f* delivery.
liegen *vi* to lie.
Liegestuhl *m* deckchair.
Likör *m* liqueur.
Lilie *f* lily.
Limonade *f* lemonade.
Linde *f* lime (tree).
Linie *f* line.
Linke *f* left (side).
links *adv* (on/to the) left.
linkshändig *adj* left-handed.
Linse *f* lens; lentil.
Lippe *f* lip.
Lippenstift *m* lipstick.
lispeln *vi* to lisp.
Lissabon *n* Lisbon.
List *f* cunning; trick.
Liste *f* list.
listig *adj* cunning.
Litauen *n* Lithuania.
litauisch *adj* Lithuanian.
Liter *m/n* litre.
literarisch *adj* literary.
Literatur *f* literature.
Lizenz *f* licence.

Lob *n* praise.

lobenswert *adj* praiseworthy.

Loch *n* hole.

Locke *f* lock; curl.

locken *vt* to entice; to curl.

locker *adj* loose.

Löffel *m* spoon.

Logik *f* logic.

logisch *adj* logical.

Lohn *m* wages; reward.

lokal *adj* local.

Lokal *n* bar.

Lokomotive *f* locomotive.

Los *n* lot; lottery ticket.

los *adj* loose; separate:—**was ist ~?** what's the matter?

löschen *vt* to extinguish.

Löschpapier *n* blotting paper.

losfahren, losgehen *vi* to leave.

loskommen *vi* to come off, escape.

loslassen *vt* to release.

löslich *adj* soluble.

losmachen *vt* to undo.

Lösung *f* solution.

loswerden *vt* to get rid of.

Lothringen *n* Lorraine.

Löwe *m* lion; (*astrol*) Leo.

Löwenzahn *m* dandelion.

Lücke *f* gap.

Luft *f* air.

luftdicht *adj* airtight.

lüften *vt* to ventilate.

Luftfahrt *f* aviation.

luftig *adj* airy.

Luftkissenfahrzeug *n* hovercraft.

Luftpost *f* airmail.

Lüftung *f* ventilation.

Luftwaffe *f* air force.

Lüge *f* lie.

lügen *vi* to lie, tell lies.

Lügner(in) *m(f)* liar.

Lumpen *m* rag.

Lunge *f* lung.

Lust *f* pleasure; willingness:—**~ haben** to feel like.

lustig *adj* cheerful.

lustlos *adj* listless.

Luxus *m* luxury.

M

machen *vt* to make, do.
Macht *f* power.
mächtig *adj* powerful; huge.
Mädchen *n* girl.
Magazin *n* magazine.
Magen *m* stomach.
mager *adj* meagre, thin.
Magie *f* magic.
Magier *m* magician.
magisch *adj* magical.
Magnet *m* magnet.
magnetisch *adj* magnetic.
mähen *vt vi* to mow.
Mahl *n* meal.
mahlen *vt vi* to grind.
Mahlzeit *f* meal.
Mai *m* May.
Mailand *n* Milan.
Mais *m* maize; corn.
Makler(in) *m(f)* broker.
Mal *n* time, occasion:—
   zum ersten ~ for the first time.
mal *adv* times; once.
malen *vt vi* to paint.
Maler(in) *m(f)* painter.
Malz *n* malt.
man *pn* one.
Manager *m* manager.
Management *n* management.
manche(r, s) *adj* many:—*pn* some.
manchmal *adv* sometimes.
Mangel *m* defect; shortage.
mangelhaft *adj* defective; incomplete.
mangeln *vt* to mangle; *vi* to be missing.

mangels *prep* in the absence of.
Mann *m* man; husband.
männlich *adj* male, masculine.
Mannschaft *f* team.
Manöver *n* manoeuvre.
Mantel *m* coat.
Märchen *n* fairytale.
märchenhaft *adj* fairytale.
Mark *n* marrow; boundary; (deutsch)-mark.
markant *adj* striking.
Marke *f* mark; brand(name).
Markt *m* market.
Marmelade *f* jam.
Marmor *m* marble.
Marokko *n* Morocco.
Marsch *m* march:—*f* marsh.
marschieren *vi* to march.
Marxismus *m* Marxism.
März *m* March.
Masche *f* mesh; stitch.
Maschine *f* machine.
Maschinenbau *m* mechanical engineering.
Maschinengewehr *n* machine gun.
maschineschreiben *vi* to type.
Maschineschreiber(in) *m(f)* typist.
Maske *f* mask.
maskieren *vt* to mask.
Maß *n* measure; extent:—*f* litre (of beer).
Massage *f* massage.
Masse *f* mass.
Maßgabe *f* proportion:—

nach ~ according to.
maßgebend, maßgeblich *adj* authoritative.
mäßig *adj* moderate.
Maßnahme *f* measure.
Mast *m* mast.
Material *n* material.
Materialismus *m* materialism.
materialistisch *adj* materialistic.
materiell *adj* material.
Mathematik *f* mathematics.
Matratze *f* mattress.
Matrose *m* sailor.
matt *adj* matt; dull; mate (chess).
Matte *f* mat.
Mauer *f* wall.
mauern *vt vi* to lay bricks.
Maul *n* mouth.
Maulwurf *m* mole.
Maurer *m* bricklayer.
Maus *f* mouse.
Maximum *n* maximum.
Mechaniker *m* mechanic.
mechanisch *adj* mechanical.
Medaille *f* medal.
Medizin *f* medicine.
Meer *n* sea.
Mehl *n* flour.
mehr *adj adv* more.
Mehrarbeit *f* overtime.
mehrere(r, s) *adj* several.
mehrfach *adj* multiple:—*adv* repeatedly.
Mehrheit *f* majority.
mehrmals *adv* several times.

Mehrwertsteuer *f* value added tax.

Mehrzahl *f* majority.

Meile *f* mile.

mein(e) *poss adj* my.

meine(r, s) *poss pn* mine.

meinen *vt vi* to think, be of the opinion.

Meinung *f* opinion.

meist *adj* most:—*adv* mostly.

meistens *adv* usually, generally.

Meister *m* master; champion.

meisterhaft *adj* masterly.

Meisterschaft *f* mastery; championship.

Meisterwerk *n* masterpiece.

Melancholie *f* melancholy.

melancholisch *adj* melancholic.

melden *vt vi* to report.

Meldung *f* report.

melken *vt vi* to milk.

Melodie *f* melody.

Menge *f* crowd; quantity.

Mensch *m* human being; person.

Menschheit *f* humanity.

menschlich *adj* human.

merkbar *adj* noticeable.

merken *vt* to notice.

merklich *adj* noticeable.

Merkmal *n* characteristic.

Merkur *f* Mercury.

merkwürdig *adj* noteworthy; remarkable.

Messe *f* mass; (trade) fair.

messen *vt* to measure, to compare:—*vr* to compete.

Messer *n* knife.

Messing *n* brass.

Metall *n* metal.

metallisch *adj* metallic.

Meter *m* / *n* metre.

Methode *f* method.

Metzger *m* butcher.

Metzgerei *f* butcher's.

Mexiko *n* Mexico.

mich *pn acc* me, myself.

Miete *f* rental.

mieten *vt* to rent, hire.

Mieter(in) *m(f)* tenant.

Mikrofilm *m* microfilm.

Mikrofon *n* microphone.

Mikroskop *n* microscope.

mikroskopisch *adj* microscopic.

Milch *f* milk.

mild *adj* mild, soft.

militärisch *adj* military.

Milliarde *f* billion.

Millimeter *m* / *n* millimetre.

Million *f* million.

Millionär(in) *m(f)* millionaire(ss).

minder *adj* inferior:—*adv* less.

Minderheit *f* minority.

minderjährig *adj* minor, under age.

mindern *vt vr* to decrease, diminish.

Minderung *f* decrease.

minderwertig *adj* inferior.

Minderwertigkeit *f* inferiority.

mindeste(r, s) *adj* least.

mindestens *adv* at least.

Mine *f* mine; lead; refill.

Mineral *n* mineral.

mineralisch *adj* mineral.

Mineralwasser *n* mineral water.

minimal *adj* minimal.

Minimum *n* minimum.

Minister *m* minister.

Ministerium *n* ministry.

minus *adj* minus.

Minute *f* minute.

Minze *f* mint.

mir *pn dat* (to) me, (to) myself.

mischen *vt vr* to mix.

Mischung *f* mixture.

Mißbrauch *m* misuse, abuse.

mißbrauchen *vt* to misuse, abuse.

missen *vt* to miss.

Mission *f* mission.

Missionar *m* missionary.

mißtrauen *vi* to distrust.

Mißtrauen *n* distrust.

mißtrauisch *adj* distrustful.

Mist *m* manure.

mit *prep* with.

Mitarbeit *f* cooperation.

mitarbeiten *vi* to cooperate.

Mitarbeiter(in) *m(f)* colleague.

Mitglied *n* member.

Mitgliedschaft *f* membership.

mithelfen *vi* to help.

Mithilfe *f* assistance.

Mitleid *n* pity.

Mittag *m* midday.

Mittagessen *n* lunch.

Mitte *f* middle.

mitteilen *vt* to inform.

Mitteilung *f* communication.

Mittel *n* means, resources; average.

Mittelamerika *n* Central America.

mittelbar *adj* direct.

Mitteleuropa *n* central Europe.

mittelfristig *adj* medium-term.

Mittelmeer *n* Mediterranean (Sea).

Mittelwelle *f* medium wave.

Mitternacht *f* midnight.

Mittwoch *m* Wednesday.

mitwirken *vi* to cooperate.

Mitwirkung *f* cooperation.

Möbel *n* (item of) furniture.
Mode *f* fashion.
Modell *n* model.
modern *adj* modern.
modernisieren *vt* to modernize.
Modernisierung *f* modernization.
mögen *v aux* to want, like.
möglich *adj* possible.
möglicherweise *adv* possibly.
Möglichkeit *f* possibility.
Mohn *m* poppy.
Moldau *f* Vltava.
Molekül *n* molecule.
Molkerei *f* dairy.
Moll *n* (*mus*) minor.
Moment *m* moment.
momentan *adj* momentary; present: —*adv* at/for the moment.
Monarchie *f* monarchy.
Monat *m* month.
monatlich *adj* monthly.
Mönch *m* monk.
Mond *m* moon.
Mondlicht *n*, **Mondschein** *m* moonlight.
Monitor *m* monitor.
monogam *adj* monogamous.
Monogamie *f* monogamy.
Monolog *m* monologue.
Monopol *n* monopoly.
monoton *adj* monotonous.
Monotonie *f* monotony.
Monsun *m* monsoon.
Montag *m* Monday.
Montage *f* assembly, installation.

Moor *n* moor(land).
Moos *n* moss.
Moral *f* moral; morality; morale.
Mord *m* murder.
morden *vt vi* to murder.
Mörder(in) *m(f)* murderer.
mörderisch *adj* murderous.
Morgen *m* morning:—
guten ~ good morning.
morgen *adv* tomorrow:—~
früh tomorrow morning.
Morgenrock *m* dressing gown.
morgens *adv* in the morning(s).
Mosaik *n* mosaic.
Moschee *f* mosque.
Mosel *m* Moselle.
Moskau *n* Moscow.
Moskito *m* mosquito.
Moslem *m* Moslem.
Motel *n* motel.
Motiv *n* motif; motive.
motivieren *vt* to motivate.
Motivierung *f* motivation.
Motor *m* motor, engine.
Motte *f* moth.
Motto *n* motto.
Möwe *f* seagull.
Mücke *f* gnat, mosquito.
müde *adj* tired.
Müdigkeit *f* fatigue.
Mühe *f* trouble, effort.
mühelos *adj* easy.
mühevoll *adj* difficult.
Mühle *f* mill.
Mühlstein *m* millstone.
mühsam *adj* troublesome.
Müll *m* rubbish, refuse.

Mülleimer *m* dustbin.
Müllwagen *m* dustcart.
Mumie *f* mummy.
München *n* Munich.
Mund *m* mouth.
mündlich *adj* oral, verbal.
Mündung *f* mouth (of river).
Mundwasser *n* mouthwash.
Munition *f* ammunition.
munter *adj* lively.
Munterkeit *f* liveliness.
Münze *f* coin.
murmeln *vt vi* to murmur.
murren *vi* to grumble.
Muschel *f* mussel; shell(fish); earpiece.
Museum *n* museum.
Musik *f* music.
musikalisch *adj* musical.
Musiker *m* musician.
Muskel *m* muscle.
müssen *vi v aux* to have to.
müßig *adj* idle.
Muster *n* pattern, sample.
Mut *m* courage.
mutig *adj* courageous.
Mutter *f* mother.
mütterlich *adj* motherly, maternal.
Mutterschaft *f* maternity.
Mutti *f* mum(my).
Mütze *f* cap.
mysteriös *adj* mysterious.
Mythe *f* myth.
Mythologie *f* mythology.
mythologisch *adj* mythological.

N

nach *prep* after; to; according to:—**~ und ~** little by little.

nachahmen *vt vi* to imitate.

Nachahmung *f* imitation.

Nachbar(in) *m(f)* neighbour.

Nachbarschaft *f* neighbourhood.

nachdem *adv* afterwards:—*conj* after:—**je ~** it depends.

Nachdruck *m* emphasis.

nachdrücklich *adj* express:—*adv* expressly.

Nachfahr *m* descendant.

Nachfolge *f* succession; emulation.

nachfolgen *vi* to succeed; to emulate.

Nachfolger(in) *m(f)* successor.

Nachfrage *f* inquiry; demand.

nachfragen *vi* to inquire.

nachlässig *adj* negligent.

Nachlässigkeit *f* negligence.

nachmals *adv* afterwards.

Nachmittag *m* afternoon.

nachmittags *adv* in the afternoon.

nachprüfen *adj* to verify.

Nachricht *f* (item of) news, message.

Nachrichten *fpl* news.

Nachruf *m* obituary.

Nachschrift *f* postscript.

Nachsicht *f* tolerance.

nachsichtig *adj* tolerant.

Nachspeise *f* dessert.

nächst *prep* next to.

nächste(r, s) *adj* next; nearest.

nächstens *adv* soon.

Nacht *f* night.

Nachteil *m* disadvantage.

Nachtigall *f* nightingale.

Nachtklub *m* nightclub.

Nachtrag *m* supplement.

nachtragen *vt* to carry; to add.

nachträglich *adj adv* subsequent(ly).

nachts *adv* at night(s).

Nachweis *m* proof, evidence.

nachweisbar *adj* demonstrable.

nachweisen *vt* to prove.

nackt *adj* naked.

Nacktheit *f* nakedness.

Nadel *f* needle; pin; brooch.

Nagel *m* nail.

nageln *vt vi* to nail.

nagen *vt vi* to gnaw.

nah(e) *adj* near(by); close:—*adv* near(by); close; closely:—*prep* near (to), close to.

Nähe *f* nearness, proximity; vicinity: —**in der ~** close by.

nahebei *adv* nearby.

nahekommen *vi* to approach.

naheliegen *vi* to be obvious.

naheliegend *adj* nearby; obvious.

nahen *vi vr* to approach.

nähen *vt vi* to sew.

näher *adj* nearer; more specific.

nähern *vt vr* to approach.

nahestehend *adj* close.

nahezu *adv* nearly.

Nähmaschine *f* sewing machine.

nähren *vt* to feed.

nahrhaft *adj* nutritious.

Nahrung *f* **Nahrungsmittel** *n* food.

Naht *f* seam; stitch.

naiv *adj* naive.

Naivität *f* naivety.

Name *m* name.

namens *adv* called:—*prep* on behalf of.

namentlich *adj adv* by name; in particular.

namhaft *adj* renowned.

nämlich *adv* namely.

Narbe *f* scar.

Narkose *f* anaesthetic.

narkotisch *adj* narcotic.

Narr *m* fool.

Narrheit *f* folly.

närrisch *adj* foolish.

Narzisse *f* daffodil.

naschen *vt vi* to nibble.

Nase *f* nose.

Nasenloch *n* nostril.

Nashorn *n* rhinoceros.

naß *adj* wet.

Nässe *f* wetness.

nässen *vt* to wet.

Nation *f* nation.

national *adj* national.

nationalisieren *vt* to nationalize.

Nationalisierung *f* nationalization.

Nationalismus *m* nationalism.

Nationalist *m* nationalist.

nationalistisch *adj* nationalistic.

Nationalität *f* nationality.

Nativität *f* nativity.

Natrium *n* sodium.

Natron *n* soda, sodium hydroxide.

Natur *f* nature.

Naturalismus *m* naturalism.

Naturalist *m* naturalist.

naturalistisch *adj* naturalistic.

natürlich *adj* natural:—*adv* naturally, of course.

Naturschutz *m* conservation.

Naturwissenschaftler(in) *m(f)* (natural) scientist.

Nazi *m* Nazi.

Nazismus *m* Nazism.

Neapel *n* Naples.

Nebel *m* mist, fog.

neb(e)lig *adj* misty, foggy.

neben *prep* beside.

Nebenprodukt *n* by-product.

nebensächlich *adj* secondary, incidental.

nebst *prep* in addition to.

necken *vt* to tease.

nee *adv* no.

Neffe *m* nephew.

negativ *adj* negative.

Negative *n* negative.

Neger(in) *m(f)* negro.

nehmen *vt* to take.

Neid *m* envy, jealousy.

neidisch *adj* envious, jealous.

neigen *vt* to incline; to bow:—*vi* to tend.

Neigung *f* inclination, tendency; like.

nein *adv* no.

Nektar *m* nectar.

Nelke *f* pink, carnation; clove.

nennen *vt* to name, call.

Nenner *m* denominator.

Neon *n* neon.

Nerv *m* nerve.

nervenkrank *adj* mentally ill.

Nervensystem *n* nervous system.

Nervenzusammenbruch *m* nervous breakdown.

nervös *adj* nervous.

Nessel *f* nettle.

Nest *n* nest.

nett *adj* nice.

netto *adv* net.

Netz *n* net; network.

Netzhaut *f* retina.

neu *adj* new.

Neufundland *n* Newfoundland.

Neugier(de) *f* curiosity.

neugierig *adj* curious.

Neuheit *f* newness.

Neuigkeit *f* news.

Neujahr *n* New Year.

neulich *adv* recently.

Neumond *m* new moon.

neun *num* nine.

neunzehn *num* nineteen.

neunzig *num* ninety.

Neurose *f* neurosis.

neurotisch *adj* neurotic.

Neuseeland *n* New Zealand.

neutral *adj* neutral.

Neutrum *n* neuter.

nicht *adv* not.

Nichte *f* niece.

nichts *pn* nothing.

Nickel *n* nickel.

nicken *vi* to nod.

nie *adv* never.

nieder *adj* low; inferior:—*adv* down.

niederfallen *vi* to fall down.

Niedergang *m* descent, decline.

niedergehen *vi* to go down, descend.

niedergeschlagen *adj* downcast.

Niederlage *f* defeat.

Niederlande *pl* the Netherlands.

Niederländer(in) *m(f)* Dutchman (-woman).

niederländisch *adj* Dutch.

niederlassen *vr* to settle.

Niederlassung *f* settlement; branch (bank, etc).

niederlegen *vt* to put down; to resign.

Niedersachsen *n* Lower Saxony.

niemals *adv* never.

niemand *pn* no one.

Niere *f* kidney.

nieseln *vi* to drizzle.

niesen *vi* to sneeze.

Nikotin *n* nicotine.

nimmer *adv* never.

nirgendwo(hin) *adv* nowhere.

Niveau *n* level.

nivellieren *vt* to level.

noch *adv* yet; still; also; even; else:—**immer ~** still:—**~ nicht** not yet:—**~ besser** even better:—**~ einmal** once again.

nochmals *adv* once again.

Nominativ *m* (*gr*) nominative.

nominieren *vt* to nominate.

Nonne *f* nun.

Nord(en) *m* north.

Nordamerika *n* North America.

Nordeuropa *n* northern Europe.

Nordirland *n* Northern Ireland.

nordisch *adj* northern.

nördlich *adj* northern, northerly.

Nordlicht *n* northern lights, aurora borealis.

Nordost(en) *m* northeast.

Nordpol *m* North Pole.

Nordrhein-Westfalen *n* North Rhine-Westphalia.

Nordsee *f* North Sea.

nordwärts *adv* northwards.

Nordwest(en) *m* northwest.

nörgeln *vt* to nag, carp.

Nörgler *m* faultfinder.

Norm *f* standard, norm.

normal *adj* normal.

normalerweise *adv* normally.

Normandie *f* Normandy.

Norwegen *n* Norway.

Norweger(in) *m(f)* Norwegian.

norwegisch *adj* Norwegian.

Not *f* need; emergency; poverty.

Notar *m* notary.

Notausgang *m* emergency exit.

Note *f* note; mark.

Notfall *m* emergency.

notfalls, nötigenfalls *adv* if necessary.

notieren *vt* to note; to quote:—*vi* to be quoted.

Notierung *f* quotation, price.

nötig *adj* necessary:—~ **haben** to need.

Notiz *f* note, notice.

Notlandung *f* emergency landing.

notleidend *adj* needy.

Notlüge *f* white lie.

notorisch *adj* notorious.

Notstand *m* state of emergency.

Notwehr *f* self-defence.

notwendig *adj* necessary.

Notwendigkeit *f* necessity.

Notzucht *f* rape.

Novelle *f* short novel; amendment.

November *m* November.

nüchtern *adj* sober, sensible.

Nüchternheit *f* sobriety.

Nudel *f* noodle.

Null *f* zero, nought.

null *adj*:—~ **und nichtig** null and void.

numerisch *adj* numerical.

Nummer *f* number.

Nummernschild *n* number plate.

nun *adv* now:—*excl* well.

nur *adv* only.

Nürnberg *n* Nuremberg.

Nuß *f* nut.

Nußbaum *m* walnut tree.

Nußknacker *m* nutcracker.

nutzbar *adj* useful, usable.

Nutzen *m* use; benefit.

nutzen, nützen *vt* to use:—*vi* to be useful.

nützlich *adj* useful.

nutzlos *adj* useless.

Nylon *n* nylon.

O

ob *conj* if, whether.

oben *adv* above; upstairs.

obenerwähnt, obengenannt *adj* above mentioned.

Ober *m* waiter.

Oberarm *m* upper arm.

Oberfläche *f* surface.

oberflächlich *adj* superficial.

oberhalb *adv prep* above.

Oberkellner *m* head waiter.

Oberlicht *n* skylight.

Oberst *m* colonel.

oberste(r, s) *adj* very top, topmost.

obgleich *conj* although.

Objekt *n* objective.

Objektiv *n* lens.

objektiv *adj* objective.

Objektivität *f* objectivity.

obligatorisch *adj* obligatory, mandatory.

Oboe *f* oboe.

obschon *conj* although.

Observatorium *n* observatory.

obskur *adj* obscure; dubious.

Obst *n* fruit.

Obstbaum *m* fruit tree.

Obstgarten *m* orchard.

obszön *adj* obscene.

Obszönität *f* obscenity.

obwohl *conj* although.

Ochse *m* ox.

öd(e) *adj* waste, barren; chill.

Öde *f* desert, waste(land); tedium.

oder *conj* or.

Ofen *m* stove; oven; cooker.

offen *adj* open; frank; vacant.

offenbar *adj* obvious.

offenbleiben *vi* to stay open; to remain open.

offenhalten *vi* to keep open.

Offenheit *f* candour, frankness.

offensichtlich *adj* obvious, evident.

offenstehen *vi* to be open; to be unpaid.

öffentlich *adj* public.

Öffentlichkeit *f npl* the general public.

offiziell *adj* official.

Offizier *m* officer.

öffnen *vt vr* to open.

Öffnung *f* opening.

oft *adv* often.

ohne *prep conj* without:—~ **weiteres** without a second thought.

Ohnmacht *f* faint; impotence:—**in ~ fallen** to faint.

Ohr *n* ear; hearing.

Ohrring *m* earring.

Ökologe *m* **Ökologin** *f* ecologist.

Ökologie *f* ecology.

ökologisch *adj* ecological.

ökonomisch *adj* economical.

Oktan *n* octane.

Oktave *f* octave.

Oktober *m* October.

Öl *n* oil.

ölen *vt* to fuel, lubricate.

Ölfeld *n* oilfield.

ölig *adj* oily.

Ölindustrie *f* oil industry.

Olive *f* olive.

Öltanker *m* oil tanker.

Ölung *f* lubrication; oiling; anointment.

olympisch *adj* Olympic.

Oma *f* granny.

Omelett *n* omelette.

onanieren *vi* to masturbate.

Onkel *m* uncle.

Opa *m* grandpa.

Oper *f* opera; opera house.

Operation *f* operation.

operieren *vt* to operate on:—*vi* to operate.

Opernsänger(in) *m(f)* opera singer.

Opfer *n* sacrifice; victim.

opfern *vt* to sacrifice.

Opposition *f* opposition.

Optik *f* optics.

Optiker *m* optician.

optimal *adj* optimal, optimum.

Optimismus *m* optimism.

Optimist *m* optimist.

optimistisch *adj* optimistic.

Optimum *n* optimum.

optisch *adj* optical.

oral *adj* oral.

Orange *f* orange.

orange *adj* orange.

Orangenmarmelade *f* marmalade.

Orchester *n* orchestra.

ordentlich *adj* decent, respectable; proper:—*adv* properly.

ordinär *adj* common, vulgar.

ordnen *vt* to order, put in order.

Ordner *m* steward; file.

Ordnung *f* order; ordering; tidiness: —**in ~!** okay!

ordnungsgemäß *adj* proper, according to the rules.

Organ *n* organ; voice.

Organisation *f* organization.

organisieren *vt vr* to organize.

Organismus *m* organism.

Organist *m* organist.

Orgel *f* organ.

Orientierung *f* orientation.

original *adj* original.

Original *n* original.

Originalität *f* originality.

originell *adj* original.

Orkan *m* hurricane.

Ornament *n* decoration, ornament.

Ort *m* place:—**an ~ und Stelle** on the spot.

orthodox *adj* orthodox.

örtlich *adj* local.

Osten *m* east.

Osterei *n* Easter egg.

Osterglocke *f* daffodil.

Osterhase *m* Easter bunny.

Ostern *n* Easter.

Österreich *n* Austria,

Österreicher(in) *m(f)* Austrian.

österreichisch *adj* Austrian.

östlich *adj* eastern, easterly.

Ostsee *f* Baltic Sea.

Otter *m* otter:—*f* adder.

Ouvertüre *f* overture.

oval *adj* oval.

Ozean *m* ocean.

P

Paar *n* pair; couple: **eipaar** a few.

Pacht *f* lease.

Pack *m* pack, bundle:—*n* mob, rabble.

packen *vt* to pack; to grasp, seize; to grip.

Packung *f* packet.

Paket *n* parcel; packet.

Pakt *m* pact.

Palast *m* palace.

Palme *f* palm (tree).

Pampelmuse *f* grapefruit.

Panik *f* panic.

panisch *adj* panic-stricken.

Panne *f* breakdown.

Panther *m* panther.

Pantoffel *m* slipper.

Pantomime *f* mime.

Panzer *m* tank; armour.

Papagei *m* parrot.

Papier *n* paper.

Pappel *f* poplar.

Papst *m* pope.

päpstlich *adj* papal.

Paradox *n* paradox.

Paragraph *m* paragraph; section.

parallel *adj* parallel.

Parasit *m* parasite.

Parfüm *n* perfume, scent.

Paris *n* Paris.

Park *m* park, public garden.

parken *vt vi* to park.

Parkplatz *m* car park; parking space.

Parkuhr *f* parking meter.

Parlament *n* parliament.

Parodie *f* parody.

Partei *f* (political) party.

Partie *f* part; game; outing.

Partizip *n* participle.

Partner(in) *m(f)* partner.

Partnerschaft *f* partnership.

Party *f* party.

Paß *m* pass; passport.

Passagier *m* passenger.

passen *vi* to fit; to suit, be convenient.

passieren *vt* to pass; to strain:—*vi* to happen.

Passion *f* passion.

passioniert *adj* passionate, enthusiastic.

passiv *adj* passive.

Passivität *f* passiveness.

Paste *f* paste.

Pastell *n* pastel.

Pastete *f* pie, pastry.

Pate *m* godfather.

Patenkind *n* godchild.

Patent *n* patent.

Patentante *f* godmother.

patentieren *vt* to patent.

Pathologe *m* pathologist.

pathologisch *adj* pathological.

Patient(in) *m(f)* patient.

Patin *f* godmother.

Patina *f* patina.

Patriot *m* patriot.

patriotisch *adj* patriotic.

Patriotismus *m* patriotism.

Pauke *f* kettledrum.

pauschal *adj* inclusive; sweeping.

Pauschalsumme *f* lump sum.

Pause *f* interval; break; pause.

pausen *vt* to trace.

Pavian *m* baboon.

Pazifik *m* Pacific (Ocean).

Pedal *n* pedal.

Pedant *m* pedant.

pedantisch *adj* pedantic.

Pein *f* pain, agony.

peinigen *vi* to torture; to torment.

peinlich *adj* awkward, painful; painstaking.

Peitsche *f* whip.

peitschen *vt* to whip.

Pelikan *m* pelican.

Pelle *f* skin.

pellen *vi* to skin, peel.

Pelz *m* fur.

Pendel *n* pendulum.

Pendler *m* commuter.

Penis *m* penis.

Penner *m* tramp.

Pension *f* pension; retirement; guest-house.

Pensionär(in) *m(f)* pensioner.

pensionieren *vt* to pension off.

pensioniert *adj* retired.

Pensionierung *f* retirement.

per *prep* by, per.

perfekt *adj* perfect.

perforieren *vt* to perforate.

Periode *f* period.

periodisch *adj* periodic; recurring.

Perle *f* pearl.

perlen *vi* to sparkle; to trickle.

Perlmutt *n* mother-of-pearl.

Person *f* person.

Personal *n* personnel, staff.

Personalausweis *m* identity card.

Personenaufzug *m* lift, elevator.

persönlich *adj* personal:— *adv* personally; in person.

Persönlichkeit *f* personality.

Perspektive *f* perspective.

Perücke *f* wig.

Pessimismus *m* pessimism.

Pessimist *m* pessimist.

pessimistisch *adj* pessimistic.

Pest *f* plague.

Petersilie *f* parsley.

Pfad *m* path.

Pfadfinder(in) *m(f)* boy scout (girl guide).

Pfahl *m* post, stake.

Pfand *n* pledge, security.

pfänden *vt* to seize, distrain.

Pfändung *f* seizure, distraint.

Pfanne *f* frying pan.

Pfannkuchen *m* pancake.

Pfarrer *m* vicar; priest.

Pfarrhaus *n* vicarage.

Pfau *m* peacock.

Pfeffer *m* pepper.

Pfefferminz *n* peppermint.

pfeffern *vt* to pepper.

Pfeife *f* whistle.

pfeifen *vi vt* to whistle.

Pfeiler *m* pillar.

Pferd *n* horse.

Pferdestall *m* stable.

Pfirsich *m* peach.

pflanzen *vt* to plant.

Pflanzenwuchs *m* vegetation.

Pflaume *f* plum; prune.

pflegen *vt* to nurse, look after.

Pfleger(in) *m(f)* nurse.

Pflicht *f* duty.

pflücken *vt* to pick, pluck, gather.

Pflug *m* plough.

pflügen *vt* to plough.

Pfote *f* paw.

Pfund *n* pound.

Pfütze *f* puddle.

Phänomen *n* phenomenal.

phänomenal *adj* phenomenal.

Phantasie *f* fancy, imagination.

phantasieren *vi* to fantasize.

phantasievoll *adj* imaginative.

phantastisch *adj* fantastic.

Philippinen *pl* (the) Philippines.

Philologe *m* philologist.

Philologie *f* philology.

Philosoph *m* philosopher.

Philosophie *f* philosophy.

philosophisch *adj* philosophical.

Phonetik *f* phonetics.

phonetisch *adj* phonetic.

Phosphor *m* phosphorus.

Phrase *f* phrase.

Physik *f* physics.

physikalisch *adj* of physics.

Physiker(in) *m(f)* physicist.

Physiologie *f* physiology.

physisch *adj* physical.

Pianist(in) *m(f)* pianist.

picken *vi* to pick, peck.

Picknick *n* picnic.

piepen *vi* to chirp.

piepsen *vi* to chirp.

Pigment *n* pigment.

Pilger(in) *m(f)* pilgrim.

Pilgerfahrt *f* pilgrimage.

Pille *f* pill.

Pilot *m* pilot.

Pilz *m* fungus; mushroom; toadstool.

Pinguin *m* penguin.

Pinie *f* pine.

pinkeln *vi* to pee.

Pinsel *m* paintbrush.

Pirat *m* pirate.

Pistole *f* pistol.

Pizza *f* pizza.

Plage *f* plague; nuisance.

plagen *vt* to torment:—*vr* to toil, slave.

Plakat *n* placard; poster.

Plan *m* plan; map.

planen *vt* to plan; plot.

Planer *m* planner.

Planet *m* planet.

planieren *vt* to plane, level.

Planke *f* plank.

Plankton *n* plankton.

planmäßig *adj* systematic; according to plan.

planschen *vi* to splash.

Plantage *f* plantation.

Planung *f* planning.

Plasma *n* plasma.

Plastik *f* sculpture:—*n* plastic.

Plastiktüte *f* plastic bag.

plastisch *adj* plastic.

Platane *f* plane (tree).

Platin *n* platinum.

platonisch *adj* platonic.

platschen *vi* to splash.

plätschern *vi* to babble.

platschnaß *adj* drenched.

platt *adj* flat.

Platte *f* plate; flag; record; tile.

Plattenspieler *m* record-player.

Platz *m* place; seat; space, room; square:—~ **nehmen** to take a seat.

platzen *vi* to burst; to explode.

Platzkarte *f* seat reservation.

Platzmangel *m* lack of space.

Plauderei *f* chat, conversation.

plaudern *vi* to chat, talk.
plausibel *adj* plausible.
plazieren *vt* to place:—*vr* to be placed.
Pleite *f* bankruptcy.
Plombe *f* lead seal; (tooth) filling.
plombieren *vt* to seal; to fill (tooth).
plötzlich *adj adv* sudden(ly).
plump *adj* clumsy; heavy-looking.
Plunder *m* rubbish.
plündern *vt* to plunder; to sack:—*vi* to plunder.
Plural *m* plural.
Plus *n* plus; advantage; profit.
Plutonium *n* plutonium.
Poesie *f* poetry.
Poet *m* poet.
poetisch *adj* poetic.
Pol *m* pole.
polar *adj* polar.
Polarkreis *m* Arctic circle.
Pole *m* Pole.
Polen *n* Poland.
Police *f* insurance policy.
polieren *vt* to polish.
Polin *f* Pole.
Politik *f* politics; policy.
Politiker(in) *m(f)* politician.
politisch *adj* political.
Politur *f* polish.
Polizei *f* police.
Polizeibeamte(r) *m* police officer.
Polizeiwache *f* police station.
Polizist(in) *m(f)* policeman (-woman).
polnisch *adj* Polish.
poltern *vi* to crash; to rant.
populär *adj* popular.
Popularität *f* popularity.
Pore *f* pore.

Porree *f* leek.
Portefeuille *n* portfolio.
Portemonnaie *n* purse.
Portugal *n* Portugal.
Portugiese *m* **Portugiesin** *f* Portuguese.
portugiesisch *adj* Portuguese.
Posaune *f* trombone.
Pose *f* pose.
Position *f* position.
positiv *adj* positive.
possessiv *adj* possessive.
Post *f* post (office); mail.
Postamt *n* post office.
Poster *n* poster.
Postfach *n* PO box.
Postkarte *f* postcard.
Postleitzahl *f* post code.
Poststempel *m* postmark.
potent *adj* potent.
Potential *n* potential.
potentiell *adj* potential.
Potenz *f* power; potency.
Pracht *f* splendour, magnificence.
prächtig *adj* splendid.
prachtvoll *adj* splendid, magnificent.
Prag *n* Prague.
prägen *vt* to stamp; to mint; to coin; to form.
Prägung *f* minting; forming.
prahlen *vi* to boast, brag.
Prahlerei *f* boasting.
Praktik *f* practice.
praktikabel *adj* practicable.
Praktikant(in) *m(f)* trainee.
praktisch *adj* practical, handy.
praktizieren *vt vi* to practise.
Praline *f* chocolate.
prall *adj* taut; firmly rounded; plump.
prallen *vi* to bounce, rebound; to blaze.

Prämie *f* premium; prize, award.
prämieren *vt* to give an award to.
Präparat *n* preparation; medicine.
Präposition *f* preposition.
Prärie *f* prairie.
Präsens *n* present tense.
präsentieren *vt* to present.
Präsident(in) *m(f)* president.
Präsidentschaft *f* presidency.
Präsidium *n* presidency, chairmanship.
prasseln *vi* to crackle; to drum.
Praxis *f* practice; surgery; office.
präzis *adj* precise.
Präzision *f* precision.
predigen *vt vi* to preach.
Predigt *f* sermon.
Preis *m* prize; price.
preisbewußt *adj* price-conscious.
Preiselbeere *f* cranberry.
preisen *vi* to praise.
preisgeben *vt* to abandon; to sacrifice; to expose.
Preisklasse *f* price range.
Preisliste *f* price list.
prekär *adj* precarious.
prellen *vt* to bump; to cheat, swindle.
Prellung *f* bruise.
Premiere *f* premiere.
Premierminister *m* prime minister.
Presse *f* press, newspapers.
Pressekonferenz *f* press conference.
pressen *vt* to press.
pressieren *vi* to (be in a) hurry.
Preßburg *n* Bratislava.

Preßluft *f* compressed air.
Prestige *n* prestige.
Preuße *m* Prussian.
Preußen *n* Prussia.
preußisch *adj* Prussian.
prickeln *vt vi* to tingle; to tickle.
Priester *m* priest.
prima *adj* excellent, first-class.
primär *adj* primary.
Primel *f* primrose.
primitiv *adj* primitive.
Prinz *m* prince.
Prinzessin *f* princess.
Prinzip *n* principle.
Priorität *f* priority.
Prisma *n* prism.
privat *adj* private.
privatisieren *vt* to privatize.
Privatisierung *f* privatization.
pro *prep* per.
Probe *f* test; sample; rehearsal.
proben *vt* to try; to rehearse.
probieren *vt vi* to try; to taste.
Problem *n* problem.
problematisch *adj* problematical.
Produkt *n* product; produce.
Produktion *f* production; output.
produktiv *adj* productive.
Produktivität *f* productivity.
Produzent(in) *m(f)* manufacturer; producer.
produzieren *vt* to produce.
Professor *m* professor.
Profil *n* profile; image.
Profit *m* profit.
profitieren *vi* to profit.
Prognose *f* prognosis, prediction.

Programm *n* program(me).
Projekt *m* project.
progressiv *adj* progressive.
Projektion *f* projection.
Projektor *m* projector.
proklamieren *vt* to proclaim.
Promenade *f* promenade.
Promotion *f* doctorate.
prompt *adj* prompt.
Pronomen *n* pronoun.
Propaganda *f* propaganda.
Prophet *m* prophet.
prophezieren *vt* to prophesy.
Prophezierung *f* prophecy.
Proportion *f* proportion.
Prosa *f* prose.
prosaisch *adj* prosaic.
Prospekt *m* prospectus; brochure, leaflet.
prost *excl* cheers.
Prostituierte *f* prostitute.
Prostitution *f* prostitution.
Protein *n* protein.
Protest *m* protest.
Protestant(in) *m(f)* Protestant.
protestantisch *adj* Protestant.
protestieren *vi* to protest.
Provinz *f* province.
provinziell *adj* provincial.
Provision *f* commission; bank charges.
provisorisch *adj* provisional.
Provokation *f* provocation.
provozieren *vt* to provoke.
Prozent *n* per cent, percentage.
Prozeß *m* lawsuit, action, trial.
Prozession *f* procession.
prüde *adj* prudish.
Prüderie *f* prudery.
prüfen *vt* to examine, test; to check.

Prüfer *m* examiner.
Prüfung *f* test, examination; checking.
prügeln *vt* to beat:—*vr* to fight.
Psalm *m* psalm.
Psychiater *m* psychiatrist.
psychiatrisch *adj* psychiatric.
psychisch *adj* mental.
Psychoanalyse *f* psychoanalysis.
Psychologe *m* psychologist.
Psychologie *f* psychology.
psychologisch *adj* psychological.
Pubertät *f* puberty.
Publikum *n* crowd; audience.
publizieren *vt* to publish, publicize.
Pudel *m* poodle.
Puder *m* powder.
Puderdose *f* powder compact.
pudern *vt* to powder.
Puffer *m* buffer.
Puls *m* pulse.
Pulsader *f* artery.
pulsieren *vi* to throb, pulsate.
Pult *n* desk.
Pulver *n* powder.
pulverig *adj* powdery.
Pumpe *f* pump.
pumpen *vt* to pump.
Punkt *m* point; dot; full stop.
pünktlich *adj* punctual.
Pünktlichkeit *f* punctuality.
Punktzahl *f* score.
Pupille *f* pupil.
Puppe *f* doll; puppet; chrysalis.
pur *adj* pure; sheer; neat.
purpurn *adj* purple, crimson.

Pute *f* turkey-hen; **Puter** *m* turkey-cock.

Putz *m* plaster, roughcast.

putzen *vt* to clean:—*vr* to clean oneself.

Pyramide *f* pyramid.

Pyrenäen *pl* (the) Pyrenees.

Q

quadratisch *adj* square.

quaken *vi* to croak; to quack.

Qual *f* pain, agony; anguish.

quälen *vt* to torment.

Qualifikation *f* qualification.

qualifizieren *vt vr* to qualify.

Qualität *f* quality.

Qualle *f* jellyfish.

qualvoll *adj* agonising, excruciating.

Quantität *f* quantity.

quantitativ *adj* quantitative.

Quantum *n* quantity, amount.

Quarantäne *f* quarantine.

Quartal *n* quarter (year).

Quartett *n* quartet.

Quatsch *m* nonsense, rubbish.

quatschen *vi* to chat, natter.

Quecksilber *n* mercury.

Quelle *f* spring; source.

quellen *vi* to well up; to stream.

Quellwasser *n* spring water.

quengling *adj* whining *f*.

quer *adv* crosswise; at right angles.

Querschnitt *m* cross-section.

Querstraße *f* intersecting road.

quetschen *vt* to squash, crush; to bruise.

Quetschung *f* bruise.

quietschen *vt* to screech.

Quintett *n* quintet.

quitt *adj* quits, even.

Quitte *f* quince.

quittieren *vt* to give a receipt for.

Quittung *f* receipt.

Quiz *n* quiz.

Quote *f* rate, number.

Quotient *m* quotient.

R

Rabe *f* raven.

Rache *f* revenge.

rächen *vt* to avenge:—*vr* to take (one's) revenge.

Rad *n* wheel; bike.

Radar *m*/*n* radar.

radfahren *vi* to cycle.

Radfahrer(in) *m(f)* cyclist.

radieren *vt* to rub out, erase; to etch.

Radiergummi *m* rubber, eraser.

Radierung *f* etching.

Radieschen *n* radish.

radikal *adj* radical.

Radio *n* radio.

radioaktiv *adj* radioactive.

Radioaktivität *f* radioactivity.

Radius *m* radius.

Radkappe *f* hub cap.

Radrennen *n* cycling race.

Rahm *m* cream.

Rahmkase *m* cream cheese.

Rahmen *m* frame(work):—**im ~ von** within the framework of.

rahmen *vt* to frame.

Rakete *f* rocket.

Rand *m* edge; rim; margin.

Rang *m* rank; standing; quality.

rar *adj* rare.

Rarität *f* rarity; curio.

rasch *adj* quick, swift.

rascheln *vi* to rustle.

Rasen *m* lawn; grass.

rasen *vi* to rave; to race.

rasend *adj* furious.

rasieren *vt vr* to shave.

Rasse *f* race; breed.

Rast *f* rest.

rasten *vi* to rest.

rastlos *adj* tireless; restless.

Rasur *f* shaving.

Rat *m* councillor; counsellor; counsel, advice.

Rate *f* instalment.

raten *vt vi* to guess:—**jdm ~** to advise somebody.

Rathaus *n* town hall.

Ration *f* ration.

rational *adj* rational.

ratsam *adj* advisable.

Ratschlag *m* piece of advice.

Rätsel *n* puzzle; riddle.

rätselhaft *adj* mysterious.

Ratte *f* rat.

Rattenfänger *m* ratcatcher.

Raub *m* robbery.

rauben *vt* to rob; to kidnap, abduct.

Räuber *m* robber.

raubgierig *adj* rapacious.

Raubtier *n* predator.

Raubvogel *m* bird of prey.

Rauch *m* smoke.

rauchen *vt vi* to smoke.

Raucher(in) *m(f)* smoker.

räuchern *vt* to smoke, cure.

rauchig *adj* smoky.

raufen *vt* to pull out (hair):—*vi vr* to fight.

Rauferei *f* brawl.

rauh *adj* rough, coarse; harsh.

Raum *m* room; space.

räumen *vt* to clear; to vacate; to put away.

Raumfähre *f* space shuttle.

Raumfahrt *f* space travel.

räumlich *adj* spatial.

Räumlichkeiten *fpl* premises.

Räumung *f* evacuation; clearing away, vacating.

raunen *vi* to whisper, murmur.

Raupe *f* caterpillar.

Rausch *m* intoxication.

rauschen *vi* to rush; to rustle; to hiss.

rauschend *adj* thunderous; sumptuous.

Rauschgift *n* drug.

Razzia *f* raid.

reagieren *vi* to react.

Reaktion *f* reaction.

Reaktor *m* reactor.

real *adj* real, material.

realisieren *vi* to carry out.

Realismus *m* realism.

realistisch *adj* realistic.

Rebe *f* vine.

rebellieren *vi* to rebel.

Rebellion *f* rebellion.

rebellisch *adj* rebellious.

Rebhuhn *n* partridge.

rebooten *vt* to reboot.

Rechen *m* rake.

rechen *vt vi* to rake.

Rechenfehler *m* miscalculation.

rechnen *vt vi* to calculate.

Rechnen *n* arithmetic.

Rechner *m* calculator; computer.

Rechnung *f* calculation(s); bill, invoice.

Rechnungsprüfer *m* auditor.

Rechnungswesen *n* accountancy.

Recht *n* right, law:—**das ~ verletzen** to break the law.

recht *adj* right:—*adv* really, quite:—**~ haben** to be right.

Rechte *f* right (hand); (*pol*) right.

rechte(r, s) *adj* right; right-wing.

Rechteck *n* right angle.

rechten *vi* to argue, dispute.

rechtfertigen *vt* to justify:—*vr* to justify oneself.

Rechtfertigung *f* justification.

rechtlich *adj* legal.

rechtmäßig *adj* legal, lawful.

rechts *adv* on/to the right.

Rechtsanwalt *m*
Rechtsanwältin *f* lawyer.

rechtzeitig *adj* timely:—*adv* on time.

Redakteur *m* editor.

Redaktion *f* editing; editorial staff.

Rede *f* talk; speech.

redegewandt *adj* eloquent.

reden *vt vi* to say; to talk.

redlich *adj* honest.

Redner(in) *m(f)* orator, speaker.

reduzieren *vt* to reduce.

Reeder *m* shipowner.

Reederei *f* shipping company.

referieren *vi*:—**~ über** +*acc* to speak/talk on.

reflektieren *vt* to reflect.

Reflex *m* reflex.

reflexiv *adj* (*gr*) reflexive.

Reform *f* reform.

Reformation *f* reformation.

reformieren *vt* to reform.

Regal *n* shelves, bookcase; stand, rack.

rege *adj* lively; keen.

Regel *f* rule; (*med*) period:—**in der ~** as a rule.

regelmäßig *adj* regular.

Regelmäßigkeit *f* regularity.

regeln *vt* to regulate, control; settle: —*vr* **sich von selbst ~** to take care of itself.

Regelung *f* regulation; settlement; ruling.

regelwidrig *adj* irregular, against the rules.

regen *vt vr* to move, stir.

Regen *m* rain.

Regenbogen *m* rainbow.

Regenguß *m* shower.

Regenmantel *m* raincoat.

Regenschirm *m* umbrella.

Regenwald *m* rainforest.

Regenwurm *m* earthworm.

Regenzeit *f* rainy season.

regieren *vt* to govern, rule.

Regierung *f* government.

Regiment *n* regiment.

Region *f* region.

Regisseur *m* producer; film director.

Register *n* register; table of contents, index.

registrieren *vt* to register.

Regler *m* regulator, governor.

reglos *adj* motionless.

regnen *vi* to rain.

regnerisch *adj* rainy.

regulär *adj* regular.

regulieren *vt* to regulate; to settle; to adjust.

Regung *f* motion; feeling, impulse.

Reh *n* roe, deer.

Rehbock *m* roebuck.

Rehkitz *n* fawn.

Reibe *f* grater.

reiben *vt* to rub; grate.

Reibung *f* friction.

Reich *n* realm; kingdom, empire:—**das Dritte ~** the Third Reich.

reich *adj* rich.

reichen *vi* to reach; to be enough:—*vt* to hold out; to pass, hand out.

Reichtum *m* wealth, riches.

reif *adj* ripe; mature.

Reif *m* ring, hoop.

Reife *f* ripeness; maturity.

reifen *vi* to ripen; to mature.

Reifen *m* ring, hoop; tyre.

Reihe *f* row; series.

Reihenfolge *f* sequence.

Reiher *m* heron.

Reim *m* rhyme.

reimen *vt* to rhyme.

rein *adj* clean; pure:—*adv* purely.

Reinfall *m* let-down.

Reingewinn *m* net profit.

Reinheit *f* purity; cleanness.

reinigen *vt* to clean, purify.

Reinigung *f* cleaning.

Reinigungsmittel *n* detergent.

Reis *m* rice.

Reise *f* journey; voyage.

Reisebüro *n* travel agency.

Reisebus *m* coach.

Reiseführer *m* guide; guidebook.

Reiseindustrie *f* travel industry.

Reiseleiter *m* courier.

reisen *vi* to travel.

Reisende *m* traveller.

Reisepaß *m* passport.

reißen *vt* to tear; to pull, drag:—*vi* to tear; to pull, drag.

reißend *adj* raging.

Reißnagel *m* drawing pin.

Reißverschluß *m* zip, zip fastener.

reiten *vt vi* to ride (horse).

Reiter(in) *m(f)* rider.

Reiz *m* charm; attraction; stimulus.

reizbar *adj* irritating.

Reizbarkeit *f* irritability.

reizen *vt* to stimulate; to irritate; to appeal to, attract.

reizend *adj* charming.

reizevoll *adj* attractive.

rekeln *vr* to stretch out; to lounge about.

Reklamation *f* complaint.

Reklame *f* advertisement; advertising.

reklamieren *vt* to demand back; to put in a claim.

rekonstruieren *vt* to reconstruct.

Rekord *m* record.

Rektor *m* rector; headteacher.

Rektorat *n* rectorate; headship.

Rekrut *m* recruit, conscript.

Relais *n* relay.

relativ *adj* relative.

Relativität *f* relativity.

relevant *adj* relevant.

Religion *f* religion.

religiös *adj* religious.

Rendezvous *n* rendezvous.

Rendite *f* rate of return.

Rennbahn *f* racecourse; race track.

rennen *vi* to run, race.

Rennen *n* race; running.

Rennfahrer *m* racing driver.

Rennpferd *n* racing horse.

Rennwagen *m* racing car.

renommiert *adj* renowned.

renovieren *vt* to renovate, refurbish.

Renovierung *f* renovation, refurbishment.

rentabel *adj* profitable, lucrative.

Rentabilität *f* profitability.

Rente *f* pension.

Rentier *n* reindeer.

rentieren *vr* to pay, be profitable.

Rentner(in) *m(f)* pensioner.

Reparatur *f* repair; repairing.

reparieren *vt* to repair.

Reportage *f* report; live coverage.

Reporter *m* reporter, commentator.

repräsentativ *adj* representative; impressive.

repräsentieren *vt* to represent; to constitute:—*vi* to perform official duties.

reprivatisieren *vt* to denationalize.

Repravitisierung *f* denationalization.

Reproduktion *f* reproduction.

reproduzieren *vt* to reproduce.

Reptil *n* reptile.

Republik *f* republic.

Republikaner *m* Republican.

republikanisch *adj* republican.

Reservat *n* reservation.

Reserve *f* reserve.

Reserverad *n* spare wheel.

reservieren *vt* to reserve.

Reservoir *n* reservoir.

Reservierung *f* reservation.

Residenz *f* residence, seat.

resignieren *vi* to resign.

resolut *adj* resolute.

Resonanz *f* resonance; response.

Respekt *m* respect.

respektieren *vt* to respect.

respektlos *adj* disrespectful.

respektvoll *adj* respectful.

Ressort *n* departure.

Rest *m* rest, remainder; remains.

Restaurant *n* restaurant.

restaurieren *vt* to restore.

restlich *adj* remaining.

Resultat *n* result.

retten *vt* to save, rescue.

Retter(in) *m(f)* rescuer.

Rettich *m* radish.

Reue *f* remorse; regret.

reuig *adj* penitent.

Revanche *f* revenge.

Revier *n* district; police station; beat.

Revolte *f* revolt.

revoltieren *vi* to rebel.

Revolution *f* revolution.

Revolutionär *m* revolutionary.

revolutionieren *vt* to revolutionize.

Revolver *m* revolver.

rezensieren *vt* to review.

Rezension *f* review.

Rezept *n* recipe; (*med*) prescription.

Rezeption *f* reception.

Rezession *f* recession.

rezitieren *vt* to recite.

Rhabarber *m* rhubarb.

Rhein *m* Rhine.

rhetorisch *adj* rhetorical.

Rheuma *n* rheumatism.

rheumatisch *adj* rheumatic.

Rheumatismus *m* rheumatism.

Rhinozeros *n* rhinoceros.

rhythmisch *adj* rhythmical.

Rhythmus *m* rhythm.

richten *vt* to adjust; to direct; to aim: —*vr* **sich ~ an** +*acc* to direct at.

Richter(in) *m(f)* judge, magistrate.

richterlich *adj* judicial.

Richtlinie *f* guideline.

Richtung *f* direction; tendency.

riechen *vt vi* to smell.

Riese *m* giant.

rieseln *vt* to trickle; to fall gently.

Riesenrad *n* big wheel.

riesig *adj* gigantic.

Riesenschlange *f* boa constrictor.

Riff *n* reef.

Rind *n* ox; cow; cattle; beef.

Rinde *f* bark; crust; rind.

Rindfleisch *n* beef.

Ring *m* ring.

Ringeinatter *f* grass snake.

ringen *vi* to wrestle; to struggle.

Ringen *n* wrestling.

Ringfinger *m* ring finger.

Ringkämpfer *m* wrestler.

ringsherum *adv* round about.

Ringstraße *f* ring road.

Rinne *f* gutter, drain.

rinnen *vi* to run, trickle.

Rippe *f* rib.

Risiko *n* risk; venture.

riskant *adj* risky, hazardous.

riskieren *vt* to risk.

Riß *m* tear; crack; scratch.

rissig *adj* torn; cracked; scratched.

Ritt *m* ride.

Ritter *m* knight.

ritterlich *adj* chivalrous.

Rivale *m* rival.

Rivalität *f* rivalry.

Robbe *f* seal.

Roboter *m* robot.

robust *adj* robust.

Rock *m* skirt; jacket; tunic.

Rodel *m* toboggan.

Rodelbahn *f* toboggan run.

rodeln *vi* to toboggan.

roden *vi* to clear.

Rogen *m* roe, spawn.

Roggen *m* rye.

Roggenbrot *n* rye bread.

roh *adj* raw; coarse, crude.

Rohmaterial *n* raw material.

Rohöl *n* crude oil.

Rohr *n* pipe, tube; cane; reed; barrel.

Röhre *f* tube, pipe; valve; oven.

Rohrleitung *f* pipeline.

Rohrzucker *m* cane sugar.

Rohstoff *m* raw material.

Rokoko *n* rococo.

Rolladen *m* shutter.

Rollbahn *f* runway.

Rolle *f* roll; role; spool:— **keine ~ spielen** not to matter.

rollen *vt vi* to roll; to taxi.

Rollschuh *m* roller skate.

Rollstuhl *m* wheelchair.

Rolltreppe *f* escalator.

Rom *n* Rome.

Roman *m* novel.

Romantik *f* romanticism.

romantisch *adj* romantic.

Romanze *f* romance.

Römer *m* Roman.

römisch *adj* Roman.

römisch-katholisch *adj* Roman Catholic.

röntgen *vt* to X-ray.

Röntgenstrahlen *pl* X-rays.

rosa *adj* pink.

Rose *f* rose.

Rosenholz *n* rosewood.

Rosenkohl *m* Brussels sprouts.

Rosenkranz *m* rosary.

Rosenstock *m* rosebush.

rosig *adj* rosy.

Rosine *f* raisin, currant.

Roß *n* horse, steed.

Roßkastanie *f* horse chestnut.

Rost *m* rust; grill.

rosten *vi* to rust.

rösten *vt* to roast; to toast; to grill.

rostfrei *adj* rust-free; rustproof; stainless.

rostig *adj* rusty.

rot *adj* red.

Rotkehlchen *n* robin.

rötlich *adj* reddish.

Rotwein *m* red wine.

Route *f* route.

Routine *f* experience; routine.

Rube *f* turnip.

Rubin *m* ruby.

Ruck *m* jerk, jolt.

rücken *vt* to move.

Rücken *m* back; ridge.

Rückfahrt *f* return journey.

Rückfall *m* relapse.

rückfällig *adj* relapsing.

Rückgabe *f* return.

Rückgang *m* decline, fall.

Rückhalt *m* backing, support.

Rückkehr *f* return.

rücklings *adv* from behind; backwards.

Rucksack *m* rucksack.

Rücktritt *m* resignation.

rückversichern *vt* to reinsure.

Rückversicherung *f* reinsurance.

rückwärtig *adj* rear.

rückwärts *adv* back, backwards.

Rückweg *m* return journey, way back.

rückwirkend *adj* retroactive.

Rückwirkung *f* retroactive effect.

Rückzahlung *f* repayment.

Rudel *n* pack; herd.

Ruder *n* oar; rudder.

Ruderboot *n* rowing boat.

rudern *vt vi* to row.

Rudersport *m* rowing.

Ruf *m* shout, call; reputation.

rufen *vi vt* to call, cry.

rügen *vt* to rebuke.

Ruhe *f* rest; peace, quiet; calm; silence.

ruhelos *adj* restless.

ruhen *vi* to rest.

Ruhestand *m* retirement:— **in den ~ treten** to retire.

ruhig *adj* quiet; still; steady.

Ruhm *m* glory, fame.

rühmen *vt* to praise:—*vr* to boast.

Ruhr *f* dysentery.

Rührei *n* scrambled eggs.

rühren *vt vr* to stir:—*vr ~ von* to come from.

rührend *adj* moving, touching.

Rührung *f* emotion.

Ruin *m* ruin.

Ruine *f* ruin.

ruinieren *vt* to ruin.

rülpsen *vi* to burp, belch.

Rumäne *m* Romanian.

Rumänien *n* Romania.

Rumänin *f* Romanian.

rumänisch *adj* Romanian.

Rummel *m* hubbub; fair.

Rummelplatz *m* fair, fairground.

Rumpf *m* trunk, torso; fuselage; hull.

rund *adj* round:—*adv* around.

Rundbrief *m* circular.

Runde *f* round; lap; circle.

Rundfahrt *f* round trip.

Rundfunk *m* broadcasting.

Rundfunkgerät *n* wireless set.

Rundfunksender *m* transmitter.

Rundfunksendung *f* broadcast, radio programme.

rundheraus *adv* straight out, bluntly.

rundherum *adv* round about; all round.

rundlich *adj* plump, rounded.

Rundreise *f* round trop.

Rundschreiben *n* circular.

Runzel *f* wrinkle.

runzeln *vt* to wrinkle.

rupfen *vt* to pluck.

Ruß *m* spot.

Russe *m* Russian.

Rüssel *m* snout; (elephant's) trunk.

rußig *adj* sooty.

Russin *f* Russian.

russisch *adj* Russian.

Rußland *n* Russia.

rüsten *vt* to prepare:—*vi* to prepare; to arm:—*vr* to prepare oneself; to arm oneself.

Rüstung *f* preparation; arming; armour; armaments.

Rute *f* rod.

Rutsch *m* slide; landslide.

rutschen *vi* to slide; to slip.

rutschig *adj* slippery.

rütteln *vt vi* to shake, jolt.

S

Saal *m* hall; room.

Saat *f* seed; crop.

Sabotage *f* sabotage.

Sache *f* thing, object; affair, business; matter.

sächlich *adj* neuter.

Sachse *m* Saxon.

Sachsen *n* Saxony.

sächsisch *adj* Saxon.

Sachverständige(r) *f(m)* expert, specialist.

Sack *m* sack.

säen *vt vi* to sow.

Saft *m* juice.

saftig *adj* juicy.

Sage *f* saga.

Säge *f* saw.

Sägemehl *n* sawdust.

sagen *vt vi* to say, tell.

sägen *vt vi* to saw.

Sahne *f* cream.

Saison *f* season.

Saite *f* string, chord.

Saiteninstrument *n* string instrument.

Salat *m* salad; lettuce.

Salz *n* salt.

salzen *vt* to salt.

salzig *adj* salty.

Salzsäure *f* hydrochloric acid.

Salzwasser *n* salt water.

Samen *m* seed; sperm.

sammeln *vt* to collect:—*vr* to assemble, gather.

Sammlung *f* collection; assembly, gathering.

Samstag *m* Saturday.

Samt *m* velvet.

samt *prep* (along) with, together with.

Sand *m* sand.

sanft *adj* gentle, soft.

Sänger(in) *m(f)* singer.

Saphir *m* sapphire.

Sardelle *f* anchovy.

Sardine *f* sardine.

Sardinien *n* Sardinia.

Sarg *m* coffin.

Sarkasmus *m* sarcasm.

Satan *m* Satan, devil.

Satellit *m* satellite.

Satire *f* satire.

satirisch *adj* satirical.

satt *adj* full; rich, deep.

Sattel *m* saddle.

satteln *vt* to saddle.

Satz *m* sentence; clause; (*mus*) movement; set; jump.

Satzlehre *f* syntax.

Satzung *f* by-law, statute.

Satzzeichen *n* punctuation mark.

Sau *f* sow.

sauber *adj* clean.

säubern *vt* to clean.

Säuberung *f* cleaning.

sauer *adj* sour; acid.

Sauerkraut *n* sauerkraut.

Sauerstoff *m* oxygen.

saufen *vt vi* to drink, booze.

saugen *vt vi* to suck; to vacuum.

säugen *vi* to suckle.

Sauger *m* dummy; teat.

Säugetier *n* mammal.

Säugling *m* infant.

Säule *f* pillar, column.

Saum *m* hem; seam.

säumen *vt* to hem; to seam:—*vi* to hesitate, delay.

Sauna *f* sauna.

Saxophon *n* saxophone.

schäbig *adj* shabby.

Schablone *f* stencil; pattern.

Schach *n* chess; check.

schachmatt *adj* checkmate.

Schachspiel *n* game of chess.

Schacht *m* shaft.

Schachtel *f* box.

schade *adj* a pity / shame:— *excl* **(wie)** ~! (what a) pity / shame.

Schädel *m* skull.

Schaden *m* harm, damage; injury.

schaden *vi* +*dat* to hurt.

Schadenersatz *m* damages.

Schadenfreude *f* malicious glee.

schädigen *vt* to damage, harm.

Schaf *n* sheep.

Schafbock *m* ram.

Schäfer(in) *m(f)* shepherd(ess).

Schäferhund *m* sheepdog.

schaffen *vt* to create; to manage.

Schakal *m* jackal.

Schal *m* scarf.

Schale *f* shell, peel, skin, pod, husk.

schälen *vt* to peel; to shell:—*vr* to peel.

Schall *m* sound.

Schalldämpfer *m* silencer.

schalldicht *adj* soundproof.

Schallmauer *f* sound barrier.

Schallplatte *f* record player.

schalten *vt* to switch:—*vi* to change gear.

Schalter *m* ticket office; (bank, etc) counter; switch.

Schaltjahr *n* leap year.

Scham *f* shame; modesty.

schämen *vr* to be ashamed.

schamlos *adj* shameless.

Schande *f* shame, disgrace.

schändlich *adj* shameful, disgraceful.

scharf *adj* sharp.

Schärfe *f* sharpness.

schärfen *vt* to sharpen.

Schatten *m* shadow, shade.

schattig *adj* shady.

Schatz *m* treasure.

schätzen *vt* to estimate; to value.

schauen *vi* to look.

Schaufel *f* shovel; scoop.

Schaukel *f* swing.

Schaum *m* foam; froth.

schäumen *vi* to foam.

schaumig *adj* frothy, foamy.

Schauspiel *n* spectacle; play.

Schauspieler(in) *m(f)* actor (actress).

Schauspielhaus *n* theatre.

Scheck *m* cheque.

Scheckheft *m* chequebook.

Scheckkarte *f* cheque (guarantee) card.

Scheibe *f* pane; disc; slice; target.

Scheibenwischer *m* windscreen wiper.

Scheide *f* sheath; boundary; vagina.

scheiden *vt* to separate; to dissolve:—*vi* to depart; to part.

Scheidung *f* divorce.

Schein *m* light; appearance; bank-note; certificate.

scheinbar *adj* apparent.

scheinen *vi* to shine; to look, seem, appear.

Scheitel *m* top; (hair) parting.

scheiteln *vt* to part.

scheitern *vi* to fail.

Schellfisch *m* haddock.

Schelte *f* scolding.

schelten *vt* to scold.

Schema *n* scheme, plan.

schematisch *adj* schematic.

Schenkel *m* thigh.

schenken *vt* to give.

Schere *f* scissors.

scheren *vt* to cut; to shear.

Scherz *m* joke.

scherzen *vi* to joke.

Scheu *f* shyness.

Scheune *f* barn.

Schicht *f* layer; shift.

schichten *vt* to heap, layer.

schicken *vt* to send.

Schicksal *n* fate, destiny.

schieben *vt vi* to push.

schief *adj* crooked; sloping; leaning.

Schiene *f* rail.

schießen *vt vi* to shoot.

Schiff *m* vessel, boat, ship; nave.

Schikane *f* dirty trick; harassment.

schikanieren *vt* to harass, torment.

Schild *m* shield; sign, nameplate.

schildern *vt* to depict, portray.

Schildkröte *f* tortoise; turtle.

Schilling *m* schilling.

Schimmel *m* mould; white horse.

Schimmer *m* shimmer; glimmer.

schimmern *vi* to shimmer, glimmer.

Schimpanse *f* chimpanzee.

schimpfen *vt* to scold:—*vi* to curse, complain.

Schinken *m* ham.

Schirm *m* umbrella; parasol; screen.

schizophren *adj* schizophrenic.

Schlacht *f* battle.

schlachten *vt* to slaughter, kill.

Schlachter *m* butcher.

Schlachtfeld *n* battlefield.

Schlachthof *m* slaughterhouse, abattoir.

Schlaf *m* sleep, doze.

schlafen *vi* to sleep:—~ **gehen** to go to bed.

schlaflos *adj* sleepless.

Schlaflosigkeit *f* sleeplessness, insomnia.

schläfrig *adj* sleepy.

Schlafwagen *m* sleeping car, sleeper.

schlafwandeln *vi* to sleepwalk.

Schlafzimmer *n* bedroom.

Schlag *m* blow; stroke; beat:—**mit einem** ~ all at once:—~ **auf** ~ in rapid succession.

Schlagader *f* artery.

schlagen *vt vi* to beat; to strike, hit:—*vr* to fight.

Schlager *m* hit.

Schlagsahne *f* whipped cream.

Schlamm *m* mud.

schlammig *adj* muddy.

Schlange *f* snake, serpent; queue.

Schlangengift *n* snake venom.

schlank *adj* slim, slender.

Schlankheit *f* slimness, slenderness.

Schlankheitskur *f* diet.

schlapp *adj* limp.

schlau *adj* sly, cunning.

Schlauheit *f* cunning.

schlecht *adj adv* bad(ly).

Schlechtigkeit *f* badness, wickedness.

schlecken *vt vi* to lick.

schleichen *vi* to crawl, creep.

schleichend *adj* gradual; creeping.

Schleier *m* veil.

Schleim *m* slime.

schleimig *adj* slimy.

schlendern *vi* to stroll.

Schleppe *f* train.

schleppen *vt* to tow; drag; haul.

Schlepper *m* tug; tractor.

Schlesien *n* Silesia.

Schleuse *f* lock; sluice.

schlicht *adj* simple, plain.

schließen *vt vi vr* to close, shut.

schließlich *adv* finally.

schlimm *adj* bad.

schlimmer *adj* worse.

schlimmste(r, s) *adj* worst.

Schlips *m* tie.

Schlitten *m* sledge.

Schlittenfahren *n* tobog-ganing.

schlittern *vi* to slide.

Schlitz *m* slit; slot.

schlitzen *vt* to slit.

Schloß *n* lock; castle.

Schlott *m* chimney; funnel.

schlottern *vi* to shake, tremble.

Schlucht *f* ravine, gorge.

schluchzen *vi* to sob.

Schluck *m* swallow.

Schluckauf *m* hiccups.

schlucken *vt vi* to swallow.

Schluß *m* end, conclusion.

Schlüssel *m* key.

Schlüsselblume *f* cowslip, primrose.

schmal *adj* narrow.

Schmalz *n* dripping, lard.

schmecken *vt vi* to taste.

schmelzen *vi* to melt.

Schmerz *m* pain, grief.

schmerzen *vi* to hurt, be painful, to grieve.

schmerzhaft *adj* painful, sore.

schmerzlich *adj* painful; grievous.

schmerzlos *adj* painless.

Schmetterling *m* butterfly.

Schmied *m* (black)smith.

schmieren *vt* to smear.

Schmuck *m* jewellery; adornment.

schmücken *vt* to decorate.

Schmuggel *m* smuggling.

schmuggeln *vt vi* to smug-gle.

Schmuggler *m* smuggler.

Schmutz *m* filth, dirt.

schmutzig *adj* dirty.

Schnabel *m* bill, beak.

Schnake *f* cranefly; gnat.

Schnaps *m* spirits; schnaps.

Schnauze *f* snout, muzzle; spout.

Schnecke *f* snail.

Schnee *m* snow.

Schneeball *m* snowball.

Schneeflocke *f* snowflake.

Schneeglöckchen *n* snow-drop.

Schneemann *n* snowman.

Schneepflug *m* snow-plough.

schneiden *vt* to cut.

Schneider(in) *m(f)* tailor.

Schneiderei *f* tailor's.

schneien *vi* to snow.

schnell *adj* quick, rapid, fast:—*adv* quickly, fast.

Schnelligkeit *f* speed.

Schnellimbiß *m* snack bar.

schnellstens *adv* as quickly as possible.

Schnellzug *m* express train.

schneuzen *vr* to blow one's nose.

Schnitt *m* cut(ting); (inter)section.

Schnitte *f* slice.

Schnitzel *n* chip; escalope.

schnitzen *vt* to carve.

Schnitzer *m* carver.

schnüffeln *vt* to sniff.

Schnupfen *m* cold.

schnuppern *vt* to sniff.

Schnur *f* string, cord.

schnüren *vt* to tie.

schnurgerade *adj* straight (as a die).

Schnurrbart *m* moustache.

schnurren *vi* to purr; to hum.

Schnursenkel *m* shoelace.

Schock *m* shock.

schockieren *vt* to shock, outrage.

Schokolade *f* chocolate.

schon *adv* already; all right; just.

schön *adj* beautiful; nice.

Schönheit *f* beauty.

schöpfen *vt* to scoop, ladle; to breathe in.

Schöpfer *m* creator; founder.

schöpferisch *adj* creative.

Schöpfung *f* creation; gene-sis.

Schornstein *m* chimney; funnel.

Schornsteinfeger *m* chim-ney sweep.

Schotte *m* Scot(sman).
Schottin *f* Scot(swoman).
schottish *adj* Scottish.
Schottland *n* Scotland.
schräg *adj* slanting.
Schrank *m* cupboard.
Schraube *f* screw.
schrauben *vt* to screw.
Schraubenzieher *m* screwdriver.
Schreck *m* terror; fright.
schrecken *vt* to frighten,
scare.
schrecklich *adj* terrible,
awful.
Schrei *m* shout; scream.
schreiben *vt vi* to write.
Schreibmaschine *f* typewriter.
Schreibtisch *m* desk.
schreien *vt vi* to scream,
cry out.
Schrein *m* shrine.
schreiten *vi* to stride.
Schrift *f* (hand)writing;
script; type-face.
schriftlich *adj* written:—*adv*
in writing.
Schriftsteller(in) *m(f)*
writer, author.
Schritt *m* step; walk; pace.
Schrittmacher *m* pace-
maker.
schroff *adj* steep; brusque.
Schrott *m* scrap metal.
Schrotthaufen *m* scrap
heap.
schrottreif *adj* ready for the
scrap heap.
Schubkarren *m* wheelbarrow.
Schublade *f* drawer.
schüchtern *adj* shy, timid.
Schüchternheit *f* shyness,
timidity.
Schuh *m* shoe.
Schuld *f* guilt, fault:—**~en**

pl debts: —**in ~en gerat-
en** to get into debt.
schuldig *adj* guilty.
Schuldner(in) *m(f)* debtor.
Schule *f* school.
schulen *vt* to train.
Schüler(in) *m(f)* pupil.
Schulter *f* shoulder.
schultern *vt* to shoulder.
Schulung *f* schooling, edu-
cation.
Schuppe *f* (fish) scale:—**~n**
pl dandruff.
Schürze *f* apron.
Schuß *m* shot.
Schüssel *f* dish.
schütteln *vt* to shake.
Schutz *m* shelter; protec-
tion.
Schütze *m* gunman; marks-
man; (*astrol*) Sagittarius.
schützen *vt* to protect.
Schutzmarke *f* trademark.
Schwaben *n* Swabia.
schwach *adj* weak, feeble.
Schwäche *f* weakness.
schwächen *vt* to weaken.
Schwachheit *f* weakness.
Schwager *m* brother-in-
law.
Schwägerin *f* sister-in-law.
Schwalbe *f* swallow.
Schwamm *m* sponge.
Schwan *m* swan.
schwanger *adj* pregnant.
Schwangerschaft *f* pregnancy.
schwanken *vi* to sway; to
fluctuate; to stagger.
Schwankung *f* fluctuation.
Schwanz *m* tail.
schwänzen *vt* to skip,
cut:—*vi* to play truant.
Schwarm *m* swarm.
schwarz *adj* black.
schwärzen *vt* to blacken,
slander.

Schwarzmarkt *m* black
market.
Schwarzwald *m* (the) Black
Forest.
Schwarzweißfilm *m* black
and white film.
schweben *vi* to soar.
Schwede *m* Swede.
Schweden *n* Sweden.
Schwedin *f* Swede.
schwedisch *adj* Swedish.
Schwefel *m* sulphur.
Schwefelsäure *f* sulphuric
acid.
Schweigen *n* silence.
schweigen *vi* to be silent.
schweigsam *adj* silent, taci-
turn.
Schweigsamkeit *f* quietness.
Schwein *n* pig.
Schweinefleisch *n* pork.
Schweinestall *m* pigsty.
Schweiß *m* sweat.
schweißen *vt vi* to weld.
Schweißer *m* welder.
Schweiz *f* Switzerland.
Schweizer(in) *m(f)* Swiss.
schweizerisch *adj* Swiss.
Schwelle *f* threshold.
schwellen *vi* to swell.
schwenken *vt* to swing; to
wave:—*vi* to swivel.
schwer *adj* heavy; difficult,
hard; serious.
Schwere *f* heaviness; gravi-
ty.
Schwergewicht *n* heavy-
weight; emphasis.
Schwerindustrie *f* heavy
industry.
Schwerpunkt *m* centre of
gravity; emphasis.
Schwert *n* sword.
Schwester *f* sister; nurse.
schwesterlich *adj* sisterly.
Schwiegereltern *pl* par-
ents-in-law.

Schwiegermutter *f* mother-in-law.

Schwiegersohn *m* son-in-law.

Schwiegertochter *f* daughter-in-law.

Schwiegervater *m* father-in-law.

schwierig *adj* difficult.

Schwierigkeit *f* difficulty.

Schwimmbad *n* swimming baths.

schwimmen *vi* to swim.

Schwimmveste *f* life jacket.

schwinden *vi* to disappear; to decline.

schwingen *vt vi* to swing.

Schwingung *f* vibration; oscillation.

schwitzen *vi* to sweat.

schwören *vt vi* to swear.

schwül *adj* stuffy, close.

Schwung *m* swing; momentum.

Schwur *m* oath.

schwürzen *vi* to swear.

sechs *num* six.

sechste(r, s) *adj* sixth.

sechzehn *num* sixteen.

sechzig *num* sixty.

See *m* lake:—*f* sea.

Seehund *m* seal.

Seeigel *m* sea urchin.

seekrank *adj* seasick.

Seekrankheit *f* seasickness.

Seelachs *m* rock salmon.

Seele *f* soul.

seelisch *adj* mental.

Seelöwe *m* sea lion.

Seemann *m* sailor, seaman.

Seemöwe *f* seagull.

Seenot *f* distress.

Seepolyp *m* octopus.

Seeräuber *m* pirate.

Seerose *f* water lily.

Seestern *m* starfish.

Seetang *m* seaweed.

seetüchtig *adj* seaworthy.

Seeweg *m* sea route.

Seezunge *f* sole.

Segel *n* sail.

Segelboot *n* yacht.

segeln *vt vi* to sail.

Segelschiff *n* sailing vessel.

Segelsport *m* sailing.

Segen *m* blessing.

Segler *m* sailor, yachtsman.

segnen *vt* to bless.

sehen *vt vi* to see.

sehnen *vr*:—**sich ~ nach** to yearn for.

Sehnsucht *f* longing.

sehr *adv* very.

Seide *f* silk.

seiden *adj* silk.

Seidenraupe *f* silkworm.

Seife *f* soap.

Seil *n* rope, cable.

Seilbahn *f* cable railway.

Seiltänzer(in) *m(f)* tightrope walker.

sein *vi v aux* to be.

sein(e) *poss adj* his; its.

seine(r, s) *poss pn* his; its.

seit *prep conj* since.

seitdem *adv conj* since.

Seite *f* side; page.

seitens *prep* on the part of.

seither *adv conj* since (then).

seitwärts *adv* sidewards.

Sekretär(in) *m(f)* secretary.

Sekretariat *n* secretariat.

Sekt *m* champagne.

Sekunde *f* second.

selber = **selbst**.

Selbst *n* self.

selbst *pn*:—**ich ~** myself, **wir ~** ourselves, etc; alone, on one's own:—*adv* even.

selbständig *adj* independent; self-employed.

Selbständigkeit *f* independence; self-employment.

selbstbewußt *adj* self-confident.

selbstlos *adj* selfless, unselfish.

Selbstmord *m* suicide:—~ **begehen** to commit suicide.

Selbstmörder(in) *m(f)* suicide.

selbstmörderisch *adj* suicidal.

Selbstsucht *f* selfishness.

selbstsüchtig *adj* selfish.

selbstverständlich *adj* obvious:—*adv* naturally.

Selbstverteidigung *f* self-defence.

selig *adj* blessed; deceased, late.

Sellerie *m / f* celery.

selten *adj* rare, scarce:—*adv* seldom, rarely.

Seltenheit *f* rarity.

seltsam *adj* strange.

Seltsamkeit *f* strangeness.

Semikolon *n* semicolon.

senden *vt vi* to send; to transmit, broadcast.

Sender *m* station; transmitter.

Sendung *f* consignment; broadcast, transmission; programme.

Senf *m* mustard.

Senke *f* depression.

senken *vt* to lower:—*vr* to sink.

senkrecht *adj* vertical, perpendicular.

Sensation *f* sensation.

sensationell *adj* sensational.

Sense *f* scythe.

September *m* September.

Serie *f* series.

seriös *adj* serious.

Service *n* set, service:—*m* service.

servieren *vt vi* to serve.
Serviererin *f* waitress.
Serviette *f* serviette, napkin.
Sessel *m* armchair.
Sessellift *m* chairlift.
setzen *vt* to put, set; to plant:—*vr* to settle; to sit down:—*vi* to leap; to bet.
Seuche *f* epidemic.
seufzen *vi* to sigh.
Seufzer *m* sigh.
Sex *m* sex.
Sexualität *f* sexuality.
sexuell *adj* sexual.
Shampoo *n* shampoo.
Sibieren *n* Siberian.
sibirisch *adj* Siberian.
sich *pn* oneself, himself, herself, itself, themselves.
Sichel *f* sickle; crescent.
sicher *adj* safe; certain; secure.
Sicherheit *f* certainty; safety; security.
sicherlich *adv* surely, certainly.
sichern *vt* to protect; secure.
Sicherung *f* fuse; safety catch.
Sicht *f* sight.
sichtbar *adj* visible.
sichtlich *adj* obvious.
sie *pn nom* she, it, they; *acc* her, it, them.
Sie *pn nom acc* you.
Sieb *n* sieve; strainer.
sieben *num* seven:—*vt* to sift; to strain.
siebzehn *num* seventeen.
siebzig *num* seventy.
sieden *vt* to boil, simmer.
Siedler *m* settler.
Siedlung *f* settlement; housing estate.
Sieg *m* victory, triumph.

Siegel *m* seal.
siegen *vi* to win, be victorious.
Sieger *m* victor; winner.
siegreich *adj* victorious.
Signal *n* signal, call.
Silbe *f* syllable.
Silber *n* silver.
silbern *adj* silver.
Silhouette *f* silhouette.
Silvester(abend) *m* New Year's Eve.
Sims *n* mantelpiece; sill.
simulieren *vt* to simulate:—*vi* to feign illness.
simultan *adj* simultaneous.
Sinfonie *f* symphony.
singen *vt vi* to sing.
Singular *m* singular.
sinken *vi* to sink; to fall.
Sinn *m* sense; mind; meaning.
sinnen *vi* to ponder.
sinngemäß *adj* faithful.
sinnlich *adj* sensual; sensory.
Sinnlichkeit *f* sensuality.
sinnlos *adj* senseless; meaningless.
Sinnlosigkeit *f* senselessness; meaninglessness.
sinnvoll *adj* sensible.
Sirene *f* siren.
Sirup *m* syrup.
Sitte *f* custom:—**~n** *pl* morals.
sittlich *adj* moral.
Sittlichkeit *f* morality.
Situation *f* situation.
Sitz *m* seat.
sitzen *vi* to sit.
Sitzung *f* meeting.
Sizilien *n* Sicily.
Skandal *m* scandal.
skandalös *adj* scandalous.
Skandinavien *n* Scandinavia.

Skandinavier(in) *m(f)* Scandinavian.
skandinavisch *adj* Scandinavian.
Skelett *n* skeleton.
Skepsis *f* scepticism.
skeptisch *adj* sceptical.
Ski *m* ski:—**~ laufen** to ski.
Skiläufer *m* skier.
Skilehrer *m* ski instructor.
Skizze *f* sketch.
skizzieren *vt vi* to sketch.
Sklave *m* slave.
Sklaverei *f* slavery.
Sklavin *f* slave.
Skonto *m* discount.
Skorpion *m* scorpion; (*astrol*) Scorpio.
Skulptur *f* (piece of) sculpture.
Smaragd *m* emerald.
Smoking *m* dinner jacket.
so *adv* so; like this:—**~ daß** *conj* so that:—*excl* **so?** really?
Socke *f* sock.
soeben *adv* just (now).
sofern *conj* if, provided (that).
sofort *adv* immediately, at once.
Software *f* software.
sogar *adv* even.
sogenannt *adj* so-called.
sogleich *adv* straight away.
Sohle *f* sole.
Sohn *m* son.
solch *pn* such.
solche(r, s) *adj*:—**ein ~** such a(n).
Soldat *m* soldier.
solidarisch *adj* in solidarity.
Solidarität *f* solidarity.
solid(e) *adj* solid; respectable.
Solist(in) *m(f)* soloist.
Soll *n* debit.

sollen *v aux* to be supposed to, should.

Solo *n* solo.

somit *conj* and so, therefore.

Sommer *m* summer.

Sonate *f* sonata.

Sonde *f* probe.

Sonderangebot *m* special offer.

sonderbar *adj* odd, strange.

Sonderfall *m* special case.

sonderlich *adj* particular; peculiar; remarkable.

sondern *conj* but:—*vt* to separate:—**nicht nur... ~ auch** not only... but also.

Sonnabend *m* Saturday.

Sonne *f* sun.

Sonnenaufgang *m* sunrise.

sonnenbaden *vi* to sunbathe.

Sonnengbrille *f* sunglasses.

Sonnenenergie *f* solar energy.

Sonnenfinsternis *f* solar eclipse.

Sonnenschein *m* sunshine.

Sonnenuntergang *m* sunset.

sonnig *adj* sunny.

Sonntag *m* Sunday.

sonst *adv conj* otherwise.

Sopran *m* soprano.

Sorge *f* care, worry.

sorgen *vi*:—**für jdn ~** to look after somebody:—*vr* **sich ~ (um)** to worry (about).

sorgenfrei *adj* carefree.

sorgenvoll *adj* worried.

Sorgfalt *f* carefulness.

sorgfältig *adj* careful.

sorglos *adj* careless; carefree.

Sorte *f* sort; brand.

sortieren *vt* to sort (out).

Sortiment *n* assortment.

Soße *f* sauce; gravy.

soviel *conj* as far as (I know, etc).

soweit *conj* as far as.

sowenig *conj* as little as.

sowie *conj* as soon as; as well as.

sowohl *conj*:—**~... als auch** both... and.

sozial *adj* social.

Sozialismus *m* socialism.

Sozialist(in) *m(f)* socialist.

sozialistisch *adj* socialist.

sozialogisch *adj* sociological.

Spalte *f* column (in newspaper, etc).

Spanien *n* Spain.

Spanier(in) *m(f)* Spaniard.

spanisch *adj* Spanish.

spannen *vt* to tighten:—*vi* to be tight.

spannend *adj* exciting, gripping.

Spannung *f* tension; voltage; suspense.

sparen *vt vi* to save, economize.

Sparer *m* saver.

Spargel *m* asparagus.

Sparkasse *f* savings bank.

Sparkonto *n* savings account.

sparsam *adj* economical, thrifty.

Sparsamkeit *f* thrift.

Sparschwein *n* piggy bank.

Spaß *m* joke; fun:—**jdm ~ machen** to be fun (for somebody).

spaßen *vi* to joke.

spaßhaft *adj* jocular, funny.

spät *adj adv* late:—**wie ~ ist es?** what time is it?

Spaten *m* spade.

später *adj adv* later.

spätestens *adv* at the latest.

Spatz *m* sparrow.

spazieren *vi* to stroll, walk.

spazierenfahren *vi* to go for a drive.

spazierengehen *vi* to go for a walk.

Spaziergang *m* walk.

Spazierstock *m* walking stick.

Specht *m* woodpecker.

Speck *m* bacon.

Spediteur *m* carrier.

Spedition *f* carriage.

Speer *m* spear; javelin.

Speichel *m* saliva, spit.

Speicher *m* storehouse.

speichern *vt* to store.

speien *vt vi* to spit; to vomit.

Speise *f* food.

speisen *vt* to feed; to eat:— *vi* to dine.

Speisewagen *m* dining car.

Spekulant *m* speculator.

Spekulation *f* speculation.

spekulieren *vi* to speculate.

Spende *f* donation.

spenden *vt* to give, donate.

Spender *m* donor.

Sperling *m* sparrow.

Sperre *f* barrier; ban.

sperren *vt* to block; to bar:—*vr* to baulk.

Spiegel *m* mirror.

Spiegelei *n* fried egg.

Spiel *n* play, game, match.

spielen *vt vi* to play; to gamble.

Spieler(in) *m(f)* player; gambler.

Spielkarte *f* playing card.

Spielzeug *n* toy, plaything.

Spinat *m* spinach.

Spinn(en)gewebe *m* cobweb.

Spinne *f* spider.

spinnen *vt* to spin.

Spion *m* spy.

Spionage *f* espionage.

spitz *adj* acute, pointed.

Spitzen *pl* lace.

sponsern *vt* to sponsor.

Sport *m* sport.

Spott *m* mockery.

Sprache *f* language.

sprechen *vt vi* to speak.

sprengen *vt* to blow up; to sprinkle, water.

Sprengstoff *m* explosive.

Sprichwort *n* proverb, saying.

sprießen *vt* to sprout.

Springbrunnen *m* fountain.

springen *vi* to jump.

spritzen *vt* to squirt.

sprühen *vi* to sparkle.

spucken *vi* to spit.

spülen *vt* to wash up, rinse.

spüren *vt* to perceive.

Staat *m* state.

Staatsanwalt *m* public prosecutor.

Stachel *m* sting, prickle; thorn.

Stachelbeere *f* gooseberry.

Stadt *f* town.

Städter *m* citizen, townsman.

städtlich *adj* urban.

Stadtrat *m* town council(lor).

Stahl *m* steel.

Stamm *m* trunk, stem.

stampfen *vt* to mash, crush.

Stand *m* state, position, situation.

starr *adj* stiff; rigid; staring.

starren *vi* to stare.

Starrsinn *m* obstinacy.

Start *m* start; takeoff.

Startbahn *f* runway.

starten *vt* to start:—*vi* to take off.

Starter *m* starter.

statt *conj prep* instead of.

Stätte *f* place.

stattfinden *vi* to take place.

Statue *f* statue.

Status *m* status.

Staub *m* dust.

staubig *adj* dusty.

Staubsauger *m* vacuum cleaner.

Staubtuch *n* duster.

Staunen *n* astonishment, surprise.

staunen *vi* to be astonished, surprised (**über** at).

stechen *vt* to prick; to stab.

stecken *vt* to put, insert.

Steckrübe *f* turnip.

stehen *vi* to stand; to be.

stehenbleiben *vi* to stop.

stehlen *vt* to steal.

steif *adj* stiff.

Steifheit *f* stiffness.

Steigbügel *m* stirrup.

steigen *vi* to climb; to rise.

steigern *vt* to raise; to compare:—*vi* to bid:—*vr* to increase.

Steigung *f* incline, gradient, rise.

steil *adj* steep.

Stein *m* stone; jewel.

Steinbock *m* (*astrol*) Capricorn.

steinig *adj* stony.

Stelle *f* place; post, job; office.

stellen *vt* to put; to set.

Stellenangebot *n* job offer.

Stellung *f* position.

Stellungnahme *f* comment.

Stempel *m* stamp.

stempeln *vt* to stamp.

Stengel *m* stalk, stem.

Sterbefall *m* death.

Sterbehilfe *f* euthanasia.

sterben *vi* to die.

sterblich *adj* mortal.

Sterblichkeit *f* mortality.

steril *adj* sterile.

Stern *m* star.

Sternbild *n* constellation.

stet *adj* steady.

stetig *adj* constant, continual.

stets *adv* continually, always.

Steuer *f* tax:—*n* helm; rudder; steering wheel.

Steuerberater(in) *m(f)* tax consultant.

Steuerbord *n* (*mar*) starboard.

steuern *vt* to steer; to pilot.

Steuerrad *n* steering wheel.

Steuerzahler *m* taxpayer.

Steward(eß) *m(f)* steward(ess).

Stich *m* sting; stab; stitch; tinge.

Stichprobe *f* spot check.

Stichwort *n* cue; headword; note.

sticken *vt vi* to embroider.

Stickerei *f* embroidery.

stickig *adj* stuffy, close.

Stickstoff *m* nitrogen.

Stiefel *m* boot.

Stiefkind *n* stepchild.

Stiefmutter *f* stepmother.

Stiefmütterchen *n* pansy.

Stiefvater *m* stepfather.

Stier *m* bull; (*astrol*) Taurus.

Stierkampf *m* bullfight.

Stierkampfarena *f* bullring.

Stierkämpfer *m* bullfighter.

Stiftung *f* donation; foundation.

Stil *m* style.

still *adj* quiet; still; secret.

Stille *f* stillness, quietness.

stil(l)legen *vt* to close down.

stillschweigen *vt* to be silent.

Stillschweigen *n* silence.

stillschweigend *adj* (*adv*) silent(ly); tacit(ly).

Stimme *f* voice; vote.

stimmen *vt* to tune:—*vi* to be right.

Stimmung *f* mood.

stinken *vi* to stink.

Stirn *f* forehead; brow.

Stirnhöhle *f* sinus.

Stock *m* (walking) stick; storey, floor.

stocken *vt* to stop, pause.

Stockung *f* stoppage.

Stockwerk *n* storey, floor.

Stoff *m* material, cloth; matter; subject.

Stoffwechsel *m* metabolism.

stöhnen *vi* to groan.

stoisch *adj* stoical.

Stolz *m* pride, arrogance.

stolz *adj* proud.

stoppen *vt vi* to stop.

Stoppuhr *f* stopwatch.

Storch *m* stork.

stören *vt* to disturb; to interfere with.

störend *adj* disturbing, annoying.

Störung *f* disturbance; interference.

Stoß *m* push; blow; knock.

Stoßdämpfer *m* shock absorber.

stoßen *vt* to push, shove; to knock, bump:—*vr* to get a knock:—*vi* ~ **an/auf** +*acc* to bump into; to come across.

stottern *vt vi* to stutter.

strafbar *adj* punishable.

Strafe *f* punishment; penalty; sentence.

strafen *vt* to punish.

Strafgefangene(r) *f*(*m*) prisoner.

Strahl *m* ray, beam; jet.

strahlen *vi* to radiate.

Strahlung *f* radiation.

Strand *m* shore, strand; beach.

Strapaze *f* strain, exertion.

strapazieren *vt* to treat roughly; to wear out.

Straßburg *n* Strasbourg.

Straße *f* street, road.

Straßenbahn *f* tram(way).

Straßenbahnwagen *m* tram car.

Straßenbeleuchtung *f* street lighting.

Straßenkarte *f* street map.

Strategie *f* strategy.

strategisch *adj* strategic.

Strauch *m* shrub, bush.

Strauß *m* ostrich; bouquet, bunch.

streben *vi* to strive, endeavour.

Strecke *f* stretch; distance.

strecken *vt* to stretch.

Streich *m* trick, prank; blow.

streicheln *vt* to stroke.

streichen *vt* to stroke; to spread; to paint; to delete.

Streichholz *n* match.

Streife *f* patrol.

streifen *vt* to brush against; to touch on; to take off:—*vi* to roam.

Streifen *m* strip; stripe; film.

Streik *m* strike.

streiken *vi* to strike.

Streit *m* argument; dispute.

streiten *vi* to argue; to dispute.

streng *adj* strict; severe.

Strenge *f* strictness, severity.

Streß *m* stress.

stressen *vt* to put under stress.

streuen *vt* to strew, scatter.

Strich *m* line; stroke.

Strichkode *m* barcode.

Strichpunkt *m* semicolon.

Stroh *n* straw.

Strohhelm *m* (drinking) straw.

Strom *m* river; (electric) current; stream.

stromabwärts *adv* downstream.

stromaufwärts *adv* upstream.

strömen *vt* to stream, pour.

Stromkreis *m* circuit.

Strömung *f* current.

Strophe *f* verse, stanza.

Struktur *f* structure.

Strumpf *m* stocking.

Strumpfhose *f* (pair of) tights.

Stube *f* room.

Stück *n* play; piece, part.

Student(in) *m*(*f*) student.

Studie *f* study.

studieren *vt vi* to study.

Studio *n* studio.

Stufe *f* step; stage.

Stuhl *m* chair.

stumm *adj* silent; dumb.

stumpf *adj* blunt; dull; obtuse (of angle).

Stunde *f* hour; lesson.

stündlich *adj* hourly.

Sturm *m* storm, gale, tempest; attack, assault.

stürmen *vt vi* to storm.

stürmisch *adj* stormy.

Sturz *m* fall; overthrow.

stürzen *vt* to overthrow:—*vr* to rush: —*vi* to dash; to dive.

Stute *f* mare.

Stütze *f* support; help.
stützen *vt* to support.
Subjekt *n* subject.
subjektiv *adj* subjective.
Substantiv *n* noun, substantive.
Substanz *f* substance.
subtil *adj* subtle.
subtrahieren *vt* to subtract, deduct.
Subtraktion *f* subtraction.
Subvention *f* subsidy.
subventionieren *vt* to subsidize.
Suche *f* search.
suchen *vt vi* to seek.
Sucht *f* mania; addiction, craving.
süchtig *adj* addicted.
Süchtige(r) *f(m)* addict.
Südamerika *n* South America.
Südafrika *n* South Africa.
Süden *m* south.

südlich *adj* southern, southerly.
Südosten *m* southeast.
südöstlich *adj* southeastern.
Südpol *m* South Pole.
südwärts *adv* southwards.
Südwesten *m* southwest.
südwestlich *adj* southwestern.
Sultan(ine) *m(f)* sultan(a).
Summe *f* sum, total.
summen *vt vi* to buzz; to hum.
Sumpf *m* marsh, swamp.
sumpfig *adj* marshy.
Sünde *f* sin.
Sündenbock *m* scapegoat.
Sünder(in) *m(f)* sinner.
sündigen *vi* to sin.
Supermacht *f* superpower.
Supermarkt *m* supermarket.
Suppe *f* soup.

süß *adj* sweet.
Süße *f* sweetness.
süßen *vt* to sweeten.
Süßigkeit *f* sweetness, sweet.
Symbol *n* symbol.
symbolisch *adj* symbolic.
Symmetrie *f* symmetry.
symmetrisch *adj* symmetrical.
Sympathie *f* sympathy, liking.
sympathisch *adj* likeable.
sympathisieren *vi* to sympathize.
Symptom *n* symptom.
Synagoge *f* synagogue.
Synonym *n* synonym.
synonym *adj* synonymous.
synthetisch *adj* synthetic.
Syrien *n* Syria.
System *n* system.
systematisch systematic.
Szene *f* scene.

T

Tabak *m* tobacco.
Tabelle *f* table.
Tablett *n* tray.
Tablette *f* tablet, pill.
Tabu *n* taboo.
tabu *adj* taboo.
tadeln *vt* to scold.
Tafel *f* table; board; blackboard.
Tag *m* day, daylight:—
  guten ~! good
  morning / afternoon.
Tagebuch *n* diary, journal.
tagen *vi* to sit, meet.
Tagesanbruch *m* daybreak.
täglich *adj* daily.
tagsüber *adv* during the
  day.
Tagung *f* conference.
Taille *f* waist.
Takt *m* tact; (*mus*) time.
Taktik *f* tactics.
taktisch *adj* tactical.
taktlos *adj* tactless.
taktvoll *adj* tactful.
Tal *n* valley.
Talent *n* talent.
Talsperre *f* dam.
Tang *m* seaweed.
Tank *m* tank.
tanken *vi* to fill up with
  petrol; to refuel.
Tanker *m* tanker.
Tankstelle *f* service station.
Tanne *f* spruce, fir.
Tannenbaum *m* fir tree.
Tannenzapfen *m* fir cone.
Tante *f* aunt.
Tanz *m* dance.
tanzen *vt vi* to dance.

Tänzer(in) *m(f)* dancer.
Tanzsaal *m* dance hall, ballroom.
Tapete *f* wallpaper.
tapezieren *vt* to wallpaper.
Tapezierer *m* (interior) decorator.
tapfer *adj* gallant, brave.
Tapferkeit *f* courage, bravery.
Tarif *m* tariff, scale of
  charges.
tarnen *vt* to camouflage; to
  disguise.
Tasche *f* pocket; handbag.
Taschenbuch *n* paperback.
Taschendieb *m* pickpocket.
Taschengeld *n* pocket
  money.
Taschenlampe *f* torch.
Taschenmesser *m* penknife.
Taschentuch *n* handkerchief.
Tasse *f* cup.
Tastatur *f* keyboard.
Taste *f* key.
tasten *vt* to feel, touch:—*vi*
  to feel, grope:—*vr* to feel
  one's way.
Tat *f* deed, act, action:—**in
  der ~** as a matter of fact,
  indeed.
tatenlos *adj* inactive.
Täter(in) *m(f)* perpetrator,
  culprit.
tätig *adj* active, busy.
Tätigkeit *f* activity; occupation.
tätlich *adj* violent.
Tätlichkeit *f* violence.

tätowieren *vt* to tattoo.
Tatsache *f* fact.
tatsächlich *adj* actual:—*adv*
  really.
Tatze *f* paw.
Tau *n* rope:—*m* dew.
taub *adj* deaf.
Taube *f* pigeon; dove.
Taubheit *f* deafness.
taubstumm *adj* deaf-and-dumb.
tauchten *vt* to dip:—*vi* to
  dive; to submerge.
tauen *vt vi* to thaw.
Taufbecken *n* font.
Taufe *f* baptism, christening.
taufen *vt* to christen, baptize.
Taufschein *m* certificate of
  baptism.
taugen *vi* to be of use.
Taugenichts *m* good-for-nothing.
tauglich *adj* suitable; (*mil*)
  fit.
Taumel *m* dizziness; frenzy.
taumeln *vi* to reel, stagger.
Tausch *m* exchange.
tauschen *vt* to exchange,
  swap.
täuschen *vt* to deceive:—*vi*
  to be deceptive:—*vr* to be
  wrong.
täuschend *adj* deceptive.
Täuschung *f* deception.
tausend *num* thousand.
Tauwetter *n* thaw.
Taxi *n* taxi.
Taxifahrer(in) *m(f)* taxi driver.

Taxistand *m* taxi rank.

Technik *f* technology; technique.

Techniker *m* technician.

technisch *adj* technical.

Technologie *f* technology.

technologisch *adj* technological.

Tee *m* tea.

Teebeutel *m* tea bag.

Teekanne *f* teapot.

Teelöffel *m* teaspoon.

Teer *m* tar.

teeren *vt* to tar.

Teich *m* pond.

Teig *m* dough.

Teil *m / n* part; share; component:—**zum ~** partly.

teilbar *adj* divisible.

Teilchen *n* (atomic) particle.

teilen *vt vr* to divide; to share.

teilhaben *vi:*—**~ an** +*dat* to share in.

Teilnahme *f* participation.

teilnehmen *vi:*—**~ an** +*dat* to take part in.

teilweise *adv* partially, in part.

Teint *m* complexion.

Telefax *n* fax.

Telefon *n* telephone.

Telefonbuch *n* telephone directory.

Telefonhörer *m* receiver.

telefonieren *vi* to telephone.

Telefonist(in) *m(f)* telephonist.

Telefonkarte *f* phonecard.

Telefonnummer *f* phone number.

Telefonzelle *f* telephone kiosk, callbox.

Telefonzentrale *f* telephone exchange.

Telegraf *m* telegraph.

telegrafieren *vt vi* to telegraph, wire.

Telegramm *n* telegram, cable.

Teleobjektiv *n* telephoto lens.

telepathisch *adj* telepathic.

Teleskop *n* telscope.

Telex *n* telex; telex machine.

Teller *m* plate.

Tempel *m* temple.

Temperament *n* temperament; liveliness.

temperamentvoll *adj* high-spirited, lively.

Temperatur *f* temperature.

Tempo *n* speed, pace; (*mus*) tempo.

Tendenz *f* tendency; intention.

tendieren *vi:*—**~ zu** to show a tendency to, incline towards.

Tennis *n* tennis.

Tennisball *m* tennis ball.

Tennisplatz *m* tennis court.

Tennisschläger *m* tennis racket.

Tennisspieler(in) *m(f)* tennis player.

Tenor *m* tenor.

Teppich *m* carpet.

Termin *m* date; time limit, deadline; appointment.

Termite *f* termite.

Terpentin *n* turpentine, turps.

Terrasse *f* terrace.

Terrine *f* tureen.

Territorium *m* territory.

Terror *m* terror.

terrorisieren *vt* to terrorize.

Terrorismus *m* terrorism.

Terrorist *m* terrorist.

Terz *f* (*mus*) third.

Terzett *n* trio.

Test *m* test.

Testament *n* will; (*rel*) Testament.

testen *vt* to test.

teuer *adj* expensive, dear.

Teufel *m* devil.

Text *m* text.

textil *adj* textile.

Textilien *pl* textiles.

Textverarbeitung *f* word processing.

Theater *n* theatre:—**ins ~ gehen** to go to the theatre.

Theaterbesucher *m* playgoer.

Theaterkasse *f* box office.

Theaterstück *n* (stage-)play.

Thema *n* theme, subject, topic.

Themse *f* Thames.

Theologe *m* theologian.

Theologie *f* theology.

theologisch *adj* theological.

theoretisch *adj* theoretical.

Theorie *f* theory.

Therapie *f* therapy.

Thermometer *m* thermometer.

Thermostat *m* thermostat.

These *f* thesis.

Thrombose *f* thrombosis.

Thron *m* throne.

Thunfisch *m* tuna.

Thymian *m* thyme.

Tick *m* tic; quirk.

ticken *vi* to tick.

tief *adj* deep; profound; low.

Tiefe *f* depth.

Tier *n* animal.

Tierarzt *n* vet, veterinary surgeon.

Tiergarten *m* zoo.

Tierkreis *m* zodiac.

Tierkunde f zoology.

Tiger(in) *m(f)* tiger (tigress).

Tinte *f* ink.

Tintenfisch *m* cuttlefish.

Tip *m* tip.

tippen *vi vt* to touch, tap; to type.

Tirol *n* the Tyrol.

Tiroler(in) *m(f)* Tyrolean.

tirolisch *adj* Tyrolean.

Tisch *m* table.

Tischdecke *f* tablecloth.

Tischler *m* joiner, carpenter.

tischlern *vi* to do carpentry.

Tischtennis *n* table tennis.

Tischtuch *n* tablecloth.

Titel *m* title.

Toast *m* toast.

Toaster *m* toaster.

toben *vi* to rage.

tobsüchtig *adj* maniacal.

Tochter *f* daughter.

Tod *m* death.

Todesanzeige *f* obituary.

Todesstrafe *f* death penalty.

tödlich *adj* fatal, deadly.

Toilette *f* toilet.

Toilettenpapier *n* toilet paper.

tolerant *adj* tolerant.

Toleranz *f* tolerance.

tolerieren *vt* to tolerate.

toll *adj* mad; wild.

tollen *vi* to romp.

Tollkirsche *f* deadly nightshade.

Tollwut *f* rabies.

Tomate *f* tomato.

Tombola *f* tombola.

Ton *m* clay; sound; note; tone; shade.

Tonart *f* (musical) key.

Tonband *n* sound-recording tape.

Tonbandgerät *n* tape recorder.

tönen *vi* to sound:—*vt* to shade; to tint.

tönern *adj* clay.

Tonleiter *f* (*mus*) scale.

Tonne *f* barrel; ton(ne).

Topas *m* topaz.

Topf *m* pot.

Topfblume *f* pot plant.

Töpfer *m* potter.

Tor *m* fool; gate; goal.

Torbogen *m* archway.

Torf *m* peat.

Torheit *f* foolishness.

töricht *adj* foolish.

torkeln *vi* to reel, stagger.

Torpedo *m* torpedo.

Torte *f* tart; cake.

Tortur *f* ordeal.

tosen *vi* to roar.

tot *adj* dead.

total *adj* total.

totalitär *adj* totalitarian.

Tote(r) *f(m)* dead (wo)man.

töten *vt vi* to kill.

Totenkopf *m* skull.

Totschlag *m* manslaughter.

Tötung *f* killing.

Toupet *n* toupee.

Tour *f* tour, excursion; revolution.

Tourist *m* tourist.

Trab *m* trot.

traben *vi* to trot.

Tracht *f* costume, dress.

trachten *vi:*—*~* **(nach)** to strive (for).

trächtig *adj* pregnant.

Tradition *f* tradition.

traditionell *adj* traditional.

Tragbahre *f* stretcher.

tragbar *adj* portable; wearable; bearable.

träge *adj* sluggish; inert.

tragen *vt* to wear; to carry; to bear:—*vi* to be pregnant.

Träger *m* carrier; wearer; bearer.

Trägheit *f* laziness; inertia.

Tragik *f* tragedy.

tragisch *adj* tragic.

Tragödie *f* tragedy.

Tragweite *f* range; scope.

Trainer *m* trainer, coach; (football) manager.

trainieren *vt* to train, coach.

Training *n* training.

Traktor *m* tractor; tractor feed.

Tram *f* tram.

tranchieren *vt* to carve.

Träne *f* tear.

tränen *vi* to water.

Tränengas *n* teargas.

tränken *vi* to water.

transparent *adj* transparent.

Transparent *n* transparency.

Transplantation *f* transplantation; graft.

Transport *m* transport.

transportieren *vt* to transport.

Trapez *n* trapeze.

Traube *f* grape; bunch of grapes.

Traubenzucker *m* glucose.

trauen *vi:*—**jdm/etw ~** to trust somebody / something:—*vr* to dare:—*vt* to marry.

Trauer *f* sorrow; mourning:—**in ~ sein (um)** be in mourning (for).

Trauerfall *m* death, bereavement.

Trauerfeier *f* funeral service.

Trauerkleidung *f* mourning.

trauern *vi* to mourn.

Trauerspiel *n* tragedy.

traulich *adj* cosy, intimate.

Traum *m* dream.

Trauma *n* trauma.

träumen *vt vi* to dream.

Träumer *m* dreamer.

Träumerei *f* dreaming.

träumerisch *adj* dreamy.

traumhaft *adj* dreamlike.

traurig *adj* sad.

Traurigkeit *f* sadness.

Trauring *m* wedding ring.

Trauschein *m* marriage certificate.

Trauung *f* wedding ceremony.

Trecker *m* tractor.

treffen *vt* to meet; to strike, hit:—*vi* to hit:—*vr* to meet.

Treffen *n* meeting.

treffend *adj* pertinent.

Treffpunkt *m* meeting place.

Treibeis *n* drift ice.

treiben *vt* to drive; to do, go in for; to pursue:—*vi* to drift; to sprout.

Treibhaus *n* greenhouse.

trennbar *adj* separable.

trennen *vt* to separate; to divide:—*vr* to separate.

Trennung *f* separation.

Trennungsstrich *m* hyphen.

Trennwand *f* partition wall.

treppab *adv* downstairs.

treppauf *adv* upstairs.

Treppe *f* stairs, staircase.

Treppenabsatz *m* landing.

Treppengeländer *n* banisters.

Tresor *m* safe; bank vault.

Tretboot *n* pedal boat.

treten *vt* to step; to appear:—*vt* to kick; to trample.

treu *adj* faithful, loyal.

Treubruch *m* breach of faith.

Treue *f* faithfulness, loyalty.

Treuhand *f* trust.

treulos *adj* unfaithful, disloyal.

Tribüne *f* grandstand; platform.

Trichter *m* funnel.

triefen *vi* to drip, be dripping.

triftig *adj* good, convincing.

trimmen *vi* to do keep fit exercises.

trinkbar *adj* drinkable.

trinken *vt vi* to drink.

Trinker *m* drinker.

Trinkgeld *n* tip, gratuity.

Trinkwasser *n* drinking water.

Tritt *m* step; kick.

Triumph *m* triumph.

triumphieren *vi* to triumph; to exult.

trocken *adj* dry.

trocknen *vt vi* to dry.

Trommel *f* drum.

Trommelfell *n* eardrum.

trommeln *vt vi* to drum.

Trompete *f* trumpet.

Trompeter *m* trumpeter.

tröpfeln *vi* to drop, trickle.

Tropfen *m* drop.

tropfen *vt vi* to drip.

tropisch *adj* tropical.

Trost *m* comfort, consolation.

trösten *vt* to comfort, console.

trostreich *adj* comforting.

Trott *m* trot; routine.

trotten *vi* to trot.

Trottoir *n* pavement.

trotz *prep* in spite of, despite.

trotzdem *adv* nevertheless, all the same:—*conj* although.

trüb *adj* dull; gloomy; cloudy.

trüben *vt* to cloud:—*vr* to become clouded.

Trübheit *f* dullness; cloudiness; gloom.

Trübsal *f* distress.

Trübsinn *m* depression.

trübsinnig *adj* gloomy, depressed.

trügen *vt* to deceive:—*vi* to be deceptive.

trügerisch *adj* deceptive.

Truhe *f* chest.

Trumpf *m* trump.

trumpfen *vt vi* to trump.

trunken *adj* intoxicated.

Trunkenheit *f* intoxication.

Truthahn *m* turkey.

Tscheche *m* Czech.

Tschechin *f* Czech.

tschechisch *adj* Czech.

tschüs *excl* cheerio.

T-Shirt *n* T-shirt.

Tube *f* tube.

Tuberkulose *f* tuberculosis.

Tuch *n* cloth; scarf; towel.

tüchtig *adj* efficient, able, capable.

Tüchtigkeit *f* efficiency, ability.

Tücke *f* malice; problem.

tückisch *adj* malicious.

Tugend *f* virtue.

tugendhaft *adj* virtuous.

Tüll *m* tulle.

Tüle *f* spout.

Tulpe *f* tulip.

Tumor *m* tumour.

Tümpel *m* pond, pool.

Tumult *m* tumult.

tun *vt* to do:—*vi* to act.

tunken *vt* to dunk.

Tunnel *m* tunnel.

Tupfen *m* dot, spot.

tupfen *vt vi* to dot.

Tür *f* door.

Turban *m* turban.

Turbine *f* turbine.

Türke *m* Turk.

Türkei *f* Turkey.

Türkin *f* Turk.

türkisch *adj* Turkish.

Turm *m* tower; steeple;
 rook, castle (in chess).
türmen *vr* to tower up:—*vi*
 to heap up.
Turnen *n* gymnastics; physical education.
Turner(in) *m(f)* gymnast.

Turnhalle *f* gym, gymnasi-
 um.
Turnier *n* tournament.
Tüte *f* bag.
tuten *vi* to hoot.
Typ *m* type.
Type *f* type.

typisch *adj* typical.
Tyrann *m* tyrant.
Tyrannei *f* tyranny.
tyrannisch *adj* tyrannical.
tyrannisieren *vt* to tyran-
 nize.

U

U-Bahn *f* underground.

übel *adj* bad, wicked.

Übel *n* evil.

Übelkeit *f* nausea.

üben *vt vi* to exercise, practise.

über *prep* over, above; via; about.

überall *adv* everywhere.

Überblick *m* view; overview, survey.

überblicken *vt* to survey.

übereinkommen *vi* to agree.

Übereinkunft *f* agreement.

übereinstimmen *vi* to agree.

Übereinstimmung *f* agreement.

Überfall *m* assault.

überfallen *vt* to attack; to raid.

überfällig *adj* overdue.

Überfluß *m* excess.

überflüssig *adj* superfluous.

Übergewicht *n* excess weight.

überhaupt *adv* at all; in general; especially:—~ **nicht** not at all.

überholen *vt* to overtake; to overhaul.

überholt *adj* obsolete, out-of-date.

überhören *vt* not to hear; to ignore.

überleben *vi* to survive.

Überlebende(r) *f(m)* survivor.

überlegen *vt* to consider:— *adj* superior.

Überlegenheit *f* superiority.

Überlegung *f* consideration, deliberation.

überm = **über dem**.

Übermacht *f* superior force.

übermächtig *adj* superior; overpowering.

Übermaß *m* excess.

übermäßig *adj* excessive.

Übermensch *m* superman.

übermenschlich *adj* superhuman.

übermitteln *vt* to convey.

Übermittlung *f* transmission.

übermorgen *adv* the day after tomorrow.

übernachten *vi*:—**(bei jdm)** ~ to spend the night (at somebody's place).

übernatürlich *adj* supernatural.

überprüfen *vt* to check, examine.

überraschen *vt* to surprise.

Überraschung *f* surprise.

überreden *vt* to persuade.

Überredung *f* persuasion.

übers = **über das**.

Überschallgeschwindigkeit *f* supersonic speed.

Überschrift *f* heading, title.

Überschuß *m* surplus.

übersetzen *vt* to translate:— *vi* to cross.

Übersetzer(in) *m(f)* translator.

Übersetzung *f* translation.

Übersicht *f* overall view.

übersichtlich *adj* clear; open.

Übersichtlichkeit *f* clarity, lucidity.

übertragbar *adj* transferable; (*med*) infectious.

übertragen *vt* to transfer; to broadcast; to transmit (illness):—*vr* to spread.

Übertragung *f* broadcast; transmission.

übertreiben *vt* to exaggerate.

Übertreibung *f* exaggeration.

überwachen *vt* to supervise; to keep under surveillance.

Überwachung *f* supervision; surveillance.

überwältigen *vt* to overpower.

überwältigend *adj* overwhelming.

überweisen *vt* to transfer.

Überweisung *f* transfer.

überzeugen *vt* to convince, persuade.

überzeugend *adj* convincing.

Überzeugung *f* conviction, belief.

üblich *adj* usual.

U-Boot *n* submarine.

übrig *adj* remaining.

übrigbleiben *vi* to remain, be left (over).

übrigens *adv* besides; by the way.

übriglassen *vt* to leave (over).

Übung *f* practice; exercise:—~ **macht den Meister** practice makes perfect.

Ufer *n* bank; shore.

Uhr *f* watch; clock:—**20 ~ 8** o'clock: —**wieviel ~ ist es?** what time is it?

Uhrband *n* watch strap.

Uhrmacher *m* watchmaker.

Uhrwerk *n* clockwork.

Uhu *m* eagle owl.

ulkig *adj* funny.

Ulme *f* elm.

Ultimatum *n* ultimatum.

Ultraschall *m* ultrasound.

ultraviolett *adj* ultraviolet.

um *prep* (a)round; at (of time); by:—*adv* about:— ~... **zu** in order to.

umarmen *vt* to embrace.

umbuchen *vi* to change one's flight / reservation.

umdrehen *vi vr* to turn (round).

Umdrehung *f* revolution; rotation.

Umfang *m* extent; range; area.

umfangreich *adj* extensive; voluminous.

umfassen *vt* to embrace; to surround; to include.

umfassend *adj* comprehensive, extensive.

Umfrage *f* poll.

Umgang *m* company; way of behaving; dealings.

Umgangssprache *f* colloquial language.

umgeben *vt* to surround.

Umgebung *f* surroundings; environment.

umgekehrt *adj* reverse(d); opposite:—*adv* vice versa,

the other way round.

umher *adv* about, around.

umhergehen *vi* to walk about.

Umkreis *m* neighbourhood:—**im ~ von** within a radius of.

Umlauf *m* circulation.

Umlaufbahn *f* orbit.

Umlaut *m* umlaut.

umleiten *vt* to divert.

Umleitung *f* diversion.

umliegend *adj* surrounding.

umrechnen *vt* to convert.

Umrechnung *f* conversion.

Umrechnungskurs *m* rate of exchange.

Umriß *m* outline.

ums = **um das**.

Umsatz *m* turnover.

Umsatzsteuer *f* sales tax.

Umschlag *n* envelope.

umschulen *vt* to retrain.

umsehen *vr* to look around / about.

umseitig *adv* overleaf.

umsichtig *adj* cautious, prudent.

umsonst *adv* for nothing; in vain.

Umstand *m* circumstance.

umständlich *adj* cumbersome; long-winded.

Umstandskleid *n* maternity dress.

umsteigen *vi* to change (train, etc).

umstellen *vt* to rearrange; to convert: —*vr* to adapt (oneself).

Umstellung *f* change; conversion.

umstritten *adj* disputed.

Umsturz *m* overthrow.

Umtausch *m* exchange.

umtauschen *vt* to exchange.

Umweg *m* detour.

Umwelt *f* environment.

Umweltschützer *m* environmentalist.

Umweltverschmutzung *f* environmental pollution.

umziehen *vt vr* to change:—*vi* to move.

Umzug *m* procession; move, removal.

unabhängig *adj* independent.

Unabhängigkeit *f* independence.

Unart *f* bad manners; bad habit.

unartig *adj* badly behaved; naughty.

unbeabsichtigt *adj* unintentional.

unbegrenzt *adj* unlimited.

unbekannt *adj* unknown.

unbequem *adj* uncomfortable; inconvenient.

unbeweglich *adj* motionless.

unbewohnt *adj* unoccupied, vacant.

unbewußt *adj* unconscious.

und *conj* and:—~ **so weiter** and so on.

Undank *m* ingratitude.

undankbar *adj* ungrateful.

undeutich *adj* indistinct.

undicht *adj* leaky.

uneben *adj* uneven.

unendlich *adj* endless, infinite.

unfähig *adj* incapable, incompetent.

unfair *adj* unfair.

Unfall *m* accident.

unfreundlich *adj* unfriendly.

Unfreundlichkeit *f* unfriendliness.

Ungar(in) *m(f)* Hungarian.

ungarisch *adj* Hungarian.
Ungarn *n* Hungary.
Ungeduld *f* impatience.
ungeduldig *adj* impatient.
ungefähr *adj* approximate(ly).
ungeheuer *adj* huge:—*adv* enormously.
Ungeheuer *m* monster.
ungeheuerlich *adj* monstrous.
ungewöhnlich *adj* unusual.
ungläubig *adj* unbelievable.
unglaublich *adj* incredible.
Unglück *n* bad luck; misfortune; calamity; accident.
unglücklich *adj* unhappy; unlucky; unfortunate.
unglücklicherweise *adv* unfortunately.
Unglücksfall *m* accident, calamity.
ungültig *adj* invalid.
Ungültigkeit *f* invalidity.
Unheil *n* evil; misfortune.
unheilbar *adj* incurable.
Uniform *f* uniform.
Universität *f* university.
Universum *n* universe.
Unkraut *n* weed(s).
Unmensch *m* ogre, brute.
unmenschlich *adj* inhuman, brutal; awful.
unmittelbar *adj* immediate.
unmöglich *adj* impossible.
Unmöglichkeit *f* impossibility.
unmoralisch *adj* immoral.
unnötig *adj* unnecessary.
Unordnung *f* disorder.
unpersönlich *adj* impersonal.
unrecht *adj* wrong.
Unrecht *m* wrong.
unregelmäßig *adj* irregular.

Unregelmäßigkeit *f* irregularity.
Unruhe *f* unrest.
unruhig *adj* restless.
uns *pn acc dat* us; ourselves.
Unschuld *m* innocence.
unschuldig *adj* innocent.
unser(e) *poss adj* our.
unsere(r, s) *poss pn* ours.
unsichtbar *adj* invisible.
Unsinn *m* nonsense.
unsterblich *adj* immortal.
untätig *adj* idle.
unteilbar *adj* indivisible.
unten *adv* below; downstairs; at the bottom.
unter *prep* under; underneath, below; among(st).
Unterarm *m* forearm.
Unterbewußtsein *n* subconscious.
unterbrechen *vt* to interrupt.
Unterbrechung *f* interruption.
unterbringen *vt* to stow; to accommodate.
unterdessen *adv* meanwhile.
unterdrücken *vt* to suppress; to oppress.
untere(r, s) *adj* lower.
unterentwickelt *adj* underdeveloped.
unterernährt *adj* underfed, undernourished.
Unterernährung *f* malnutrition.
Untergang *m* downfall, decline; sinking.
untergeben *adj* subordinate.
untergehen *vi* to go down; to set (of the sun); to fall; to perish.
Untergeschoß *n* basement.
Untergewicht *n* underweight.

Untergrund *m* foundation; underground.
Untergrundbahn *f* underground, tube.
unterhalb *prep adv* below.
Unterhalt *m* maintenance.
unterhalten *vt* to maintain; to entertain:—*vt* to talk; to enjoy oneself.
unterhaltend *adj* entertaining, amusing.
Unterhaltung *f* maintenance; talk; amusement, entertainment.
Unterhemd *n* vest.
Unterhose *f* underpants.
Unterkunft *f* accommodation.
Unterlage *f* foundation; document.
unterlassen *vt* to refrain from; to fail to do.
Unterleib *m* abdomen.
unterliegen *vi* to be subject to.
unternehmen *vi* to undertake.
Unternehmen *n* undertaking, enterprise.
Unternehmer *m* businessman, entrepreneur.
Unterricht *m* instruction, lessons.
unterrichten *vt* to instruct; to teach.
untersagen *vt* to forbid.
unterschätzen *vt* to underestimate.
unterscheiden *vt* to distinguish:—*vr* to differ.
Unterscheidung *f* distinction; differentiation.
Unterschied *m* difference.
unterschreiben *vt* to sign.
Unterschrift *f* signature.
unterste(r, s) *adj* lowest, bottom.

unterstützen *vt* to support.

Unterstützung *f* support.

untersuchen *vt* to examine; to investigate.

Untersuchung *f* examination; investigation.

Untertan *m* subject (of a country).

Untertasse *f* saucer.

Untertitel *m* subtitle.

Unterwäsche *f* underwear.

unterwegs *adv* on the way.

unterzeichnen *vt* to sign.

untragbar *adj* intolerable.

untreu *adj* unfaithful.

Untreue *f* unfaithfulness.

unvollkommen *adj* imperfect.

unvollständig *adj* incomplete.

unwahr *adj* untrue.

unwahrscheinlich *adj* improbable, unlikely.

Unwetter *n* thunderstorm.

unwiderruflich *adj* irrevocable.

unwirklich *adj* unreal.

unwohl *adj* unwell, ill.

unwürdig *adj* unworthy.

Unze *f* ounce.

uralt *adj* very old, ancient.

Ural *m* (the) Urals.

Uran *n* uranium.

Urbild *n* original.

Urgroßmutter *f* great-grandmother.

Urgroßvater *m* great-grandfather.

Urin *m* urine.

Urkunde *f* deed, document.

Urlaub *m* holiday(s), leave.

Urlauber *m* holiday-maker.

Urlaubsort *m* holiday resort.

Urne *f* urn.

Ursache *f* cause.

Ursprung *m* origin, source.

ursprünglich *adj* original:—*adv* originally.

Urteil *m* judgment, sentence; opinion.

urteilen *vt* to judge.

Urwald *m* primeval forest; jungle.

Urzeit *f* prehistoric times.

usw (= **und so weiter**) etc.

Utopie *f* illusion, pipedream.

utopisch *adj* utopian.

V

vag(e) *adj* vague.
Vakuum *n* vacuum.
Vampir *m* vampire.
Vanille *f* vanilla.
Variation *f* variation.
variieren *vt vi* to vary.
Vase *f* vase.
Vater *m* father.
Vaterland *n* native country, fatherland.
väterlich *adj* fatherly.
Vaterschaft *f* paternity.
Vati *m* daddy.
Vatikan *m* (the) Vatican.
Vegetarier(in) *m(f)* vegetarian.
Veilchen *n* violet.
Vene *f* vein.
Venedig *n* Venice.
Ventil *n* valve.
verabscheuen *vt* to abhor, detest.
verabschieden *vt* to say goodbye to; to discharge:—*vr* to take one's leave.
Verabschiedung *f* leave-taking; discharge.
verachten *vt* to despise, scorn.
verächtlich *adj* contemptible, despicable.
Verachtung *f* contempt, scorn.
Veranda *f* veranda.
veränderlich *adj* changeable, unsettled.
verändern *vt vr* to change, alter.

Veränderung *f* change, alteration.
veranlassen *vt* to cause.
veranstalten *vt* to arrange, organize.
Veranstaltung *f* organising; function, event.
verantwortlich *adj* responsible.
Verantwortung *f* responsibility.
verarbeiten *vt* to process.
Verarbeitung *f* processing.
verärgern *vt* to annoy.
Verb *n* verb.
Verband *m* association, society; (*med*) bandage.
verbannen *vt* to banish.
Verbannung *f* exile.
verbergen *vt vr*:—**(sich) ~** (**vor** +*dat*) to hide (from).
verbessern *vt vr* to improve.
Verbesserung *f* improvement.
verbeugen *vr* to bow.
Verbeugung *f* bow.
verbiegen *vi* to bend.
verbieten *vt* to forbid, prohibit.
verbinden *vt vr* to combine.
verbindlich *adj* binding.
Verbindung *f* combination; (*chem*) compound.
verblüffen *vt* to amaze.
Verblüffung *f* amazement.
Verbot *n* ban, prohibition.
verboten *adj* forbidden:—**Rauchen ~!** no smoking.
Verbrauch *m* consumption.

verbrauchen *vt* to use up.
Verbraucher *m* consumer.
verbraucht *adj* finished, used up; worn-out.
Verbrechen *n* crime, offence.
verbrechen *vi* to commit a crime.
Verbrecher *m* criminal.
verbrecherisch *adj* criminal.
verbreiten *vt vr* to spread.
verbreitern *vt* to broaden.
verbrennbar *adj* combustible.
verbrennen *vt* to burn; to cremate.
Verbrennung *f* burning; combustion; cremation.
verbringen *vt* to spend (of time).
verbunden *adj* connected.
Verdacht *f* suspicion.
verdächtig *adj* suspicious, suspect.
verdächtigen *vt* to suspect.
verdammen *vt* to damn, condemn.
verdammt *adj adv* damned.
verdampfen *vi* to evaporate, vaporize.
verdanken *vt*:—**jdm etw ~** to owe somebody something.
verdauen *vt* to digest.
verdaulich *adj* digestible.
Verdauung *f* digestion.
Verderben *n* ruin.
verderben *vt* to ruin; to spoil to corrupt:—*vi* to rot.

verderblich *adj* perishable; pernicious.

verdorben *adj* ruined; spoilt; corrupt.

verdrehen *vt* to twist; to roll (one's eyes).

verdrießen *vt* to annoy.

verdrießlich *adj* annoyed.

Verdruß *m* annoyance.

verehren *vt* to venerate, worship.

Verehrer(in) *m(f)* admirer, worshipper.

verehrt *adj* esteemed.

Verehrung *f* respect; worship.

Verein *m* association, club.

vereinbar *adj* compatible.

vereinbaren *vt* to agree upon.

Vereinbarung *f* agreement.

vereinen *vt* to unite; to reconcile.

vereinfachen *vt* to simplify.

vereinigen *vt vr* to unite.

Vereinigte Staaten *mpl* United States.

Vereinigung *f* union.

vereint *adj* united.

Vereinte Nationen *fpl* United Nations.

vererben *vt* to bequeath:— *vr* to be hereditary.

vererblich *adj* hereditary.

Vererbung *f* bequeathing; heredity.

Verfahren *n* procedure; process; (*jur*) proceedings.

Verfall *m* decline; dilapidation; expiry.

verfallen *vi* to decline; to lapse.

verfassen *vt* to prepare, work out.

Verfasser(in) *m(f)* writer, author.

Verfassung *f* constitution.

verfaulen *vi* to rot.

verfilmen *vt* to film.

verfluchen *vt* to curse.

verfolgen *vt* to pursue; to prosecute; to persecute.

Verfolger *m* pursuer.

Verfolgung *f* pursuit; prosecution; persecution.

verfügbar *adj* available.

verfügen *vt* to direct, order:— *vr* to proceed.

Verfügung *f* direction, order:— **zur ~** at one's disposal.

verführen *vt* to tempt; to seduce.

Verführer *m* tempter; seducer.

verführerisch *adj* seductive.

Verführung *f* temptation; seduction.

vergangen *adj* past.

Vergangenheit *f* past.

vergeben *vt* to forgive.

vergebens *adv* in vain.

vergeblich *adv* in vain:— *adj* vain, futile.

Vergebung *f* forgiveness.

Vergehen *n* offence.

vergehen *vi* to pass away:— *vr* to commit an offence.

Vergeltung *f* retaliation, reprisal.

vergessen *vt* to forget.

Vergessenheit *f* oblivion.

vergeßlich *adj* forgetful.

Vergeßlichkeit *f* forgetfulness.

vergeuden *vt* to waste, squander.

vergewaltigen *vt* to rape; to violate.

Vergewaltigung *f* rape.

vergiften *vt* to poison.

Vergiftung *f* poisoning.

Vergißmeinnicht *n* forget-me-not.

Vergleich *m* comparison; (*jur*) settlement.

vergleichbar *adj* comparable.

vergleichen *vt* to compare:— *vr* to reach a settlement.

vergnügen *vt* to enjoy oneself.

Vergnügen *n* pleasure.

vergnügt *adj* cheerful.

Vergnügung *f* pleasure, amusement.

vergrößern *vt* to enlarge; to magnify.

Vergrößerung *f* enlargement; magnification.

Vergrößerungsglas *n* magnifying glass.

Vergütung *f* remuneration.

verhaften *vt* to arrest.

Verhaftung *f* arrest.

Verhalten *n* behaviour.

Verhältnis *n* relationship; proportion, ratio.

Verhandlung *f* negotiation; (*jur*) proceedings, trial.

verhaßt *adj* hateful, odious.

verheiraten *vr* to get married.

verheiratet *adj* married.

verhüten *vt* to prevent, avert.

Verhütung *f* prevention.

Verhütungsmittel *n* contraceptive.

verirren *vr* to go astray.

Verkauf *m* sale.

verkaufen *vt* to sell.

Verkäufer(in) *m(f)* seller; salesman(-woman); shop assistant.

Verkehr *m* traffic; circulation.

Verkehrsampel *pl* traffic lights.

Verkehrsamt *n* tourist office.

Verkehrsmittel *n* means of transport.

Verkehrszeichen *m* traffic sign.

verkehrt *adj* wrong; the wrong way round.

verkleinern *vt* to make smaller.

verkommen *vi* to decay, deteriorate; to come down in the world:—*adj* dissolute, depraved.

verkörpern *vt* to embody, personify.

Verlag *m* publishing house.

verlangen *vt* to demand; to desire.

Verlangen *n* desire.

verlängern *vt* to extend; to lengthen.

Verlängerung *f* extension.

verlangsamen *vi* to decelerate, slow down.

verlassen *vt* to leave:—*vr* **sich ~ auf** +*acc* to depend on:—*adj* desolate; abandoned.

verläßlich *adj* reliable.

verlegen *vt* to move; to mislay; to publish:—*adj* embarrassed.

Verleger *m* publisher.

verleihen *vt* to lend; to confer, bestow; to award.

Verleihung *f* lending; bestowal; award.

verletzen *vt* to injure; to violate (law, etc).

verletzend *adj* hurtful.

verletzlich *adj* vulnerable, sensitive.

Verletzte(r) *f(m)* injured person.

Verletzung *f* injury; infringement, violation.

verleumden *vt* to slander, defame.

Verleumdung *f* slander, libel.

verlieben *vr*:—**sich ~ (in** +*acc*) to fall in love (with).

verliebt *adj* in love.

verlieren *vt vi* to lose:—*vr* to get lost.

Verlierer *m* loser.

verloben *vr* to get engaged (to).

Verlobte(r) *f(m)* fiancé(e).

Verlobung *f* engagement.

verlocken *vt* to entice, lure.

Verlockung *f* attraction, enticement.

verloren *adj* lost; poached (of eggs).

Verlust *m* loss.

vermeiden *vt* to avoid.

vermeintlich *adj* supposed.

Vermerk *m* note; endorsement.

vermerken *vt* to note.

vermessen *vt* to survey:— *adj* presumptuous.

Vermessenheit *f* presumptuousness.

Vermessung *f* surveying.

vermieten *vt* to let, rent (out); to hire (out).

Vermieter(in) *m(f)* landlord(lady).

Vermietung *f* letting, renting (out); hiring (out).

vermindern *vt vr* to decrease, reduce; to diminish.

Verminderung *f* reduction.

vermissen *vt* to miss.

vermitteln *vi* to mediate:— *vt* to connect.

Vermittler *m* agent, mediator.

Vermittlung *f* procurement; agency; mediation.

vermögen *vi* to be capable of.

Vermögen *n* wealth; property; ability.

vermuten *vt* to suppose; to suspect.

vermutlich *adj* supposed, presumed: —*adv* probably.

Vermutung *f* supposition; suspicion.

vernachlässigen *vt* to neglect.

verneinen *vi* to deny; to answer in the negative.

verneinend *adj* negative.

Verneinung *f* negation.

vernichten *vt* to annihilate, destroy.

Vernunft *f* reason, judgement.

vernünftig *adj* reasonable, judicious.

veröffentlichen *vt* to publish.

Veröffentlichung *f* publication.

verordnen *vt* (*med*) to prescribe.

Verordnung *f* order, decree; (*med*) prescription.

verpassen *vt* to miss.

verpflichten *vt* to bind, oblige; to engage:—*vr* to undertake; (*mil*) to sign on:—*vi* to carry obligations.

Verpflichtung *f* duty, obligation.

Verrat *m* treason; treachery.

verraten *vt* to betray:—*vr* to give oneself away.

Verräter *m* traitor.

verringern *vt* to reduce:— *vr* to diminish.

Verringerung f reduction.
verrücken vt to shift, move.
verrückt adj mad, crazy.
Verrückte(r) f(m) lunatic.
Verrücktheit f madness, lunacy.
Vers m verse.
versagen vi to fail.
Versagen n failure.
Versager m failure.
versammeln vt vr to assemble, gather.
Versammlung f meeting, gathering.
Versand m dispatch, forwarding.
versäumen vt to miss; to neglect.
verschärfen vt vr to intensify.
verschieden adj different; various.
Verschleiß m wear and tear.
verschleißen vt to wear out.
verschleudern vt to squander.
verschlingen vt to devour, swallow up.
verschwenden vt to squander.
Verschwender m spendthrift.
verschwinden vi to disappear, vanish.
Verschwinden n disappearance.
versehen vt to supply, provide; to carry out (duty, etc):—vr to make a mistake.
Versehen n oversight:—**aus** ~ by mistake.
versichern vt to assure; to insure.
Versicherung f assurance; insurance.

versöhnen vt to reconcile:—vr to become reconciled.
versöhnlich adj forgiving, conciliatory.
Versöhnung f reconciliation.
versorgen vt to provide, supply; to look after.
Versorgung f provision; assistance, benefit.
verspäten vr to be late.
verspätet adj late; belated.
Verspätung f delay:—~ **haben** to be late.
verspotten vt to mock.
versprechen vt to promise.
Versprechen n promise.
verstaatlichen vt to nationalize.
Verstand m intelligence; mind.
verständlich adj understandable.
Verständlichkeit f intelligibility.
Verständnis n understanding.
verstärken vt vr to intensify.
Verstärker m amplifier.
Verstärkung f strengthening; amplification.
verstecken vt vr to hide:—adj hidden.
verstehen vt to understand.
versteigern vt to auction.
Versteigerung f auction.
verstellbar adj adjustable, variable.
verstellen vt to shift, move; to adjust; to block; to disguise:—vr to pretend.
Verstellung f pretence.
Verstoß m infringement, violation.
verstoßen vt to disown, reject:—vi ~ **gegen** to offend against.

Versuch m attempt.
versuchen vi to try; to tempt.
Versuchung f temptation.
vertagen vt vi to adjourn.
verteidigen vt to defend.
Verteidiger m defender; (jur) defence counsel.
Verteidigung f defence.
verteilen vt to distribute; to assign.
Verteilung f distribution, allotment.
vertiefen vt to deepen.
Vertiefung f depression.
vertikal adj vertical.
Vertrag m contract, agreement; treaty.
vertragen vt to tolerate, stand:—vr to get along.
vertraglich adj contractual.
Vertrauen n trust, confidence.
vertrauen vi:—**jdm** ~ to trust somebody:—~ **auf** +acc to rely on.
vertraulich adj familiar; confidential.
vertraut adj familiar.
Vertrautheit f familiarity.
vertreiben vt to drive away; to expel; to sell.
vertreten vt to represent.
Vertreter m representative.
Vertretung f representation.
Vertrieb m marketing (department).
verursachen vt to cause.
verurteilen vt to sentence, condemn.
Verurteilung f sentence; condemnation.
vervielfachen vt to multiply.
vervielfältigen vt to copy, duplicate.
Vervielfältigung f copying, duplication.

vervollkommen *vt* to perfect.

vervollständigen *vt* to complete.

verwalten *vt* to administer; to manage.

Verwalter *m* manager; trustee.

Verwaltung *f* administration; management.

verwandeln *vt* to change, transform: —*vr* to change; to be transformed.

Verwandlung *f* change, transformation.

verwandt *adj* related.

Verwandte(r) *f(m)* relation.

Verwandtschaft *f* relationship; relations.

verwechseln *vt* to confuse.

Verwechslung *f* confusion.

Verweigerung *f* refusal.

Verweis *m* rebuke, reprimand; reference.

verweisen *vt* to refer.

verwendbar *adj* usable.

verwenden *vt* to use; to spend:—*vr* to intercede.

Verwendung *f* use.

verwirklichen *vt* to realize, put into effect.

Verwirklichung *f* realization.

verwirren *vt* to tangle; to confuse.

Verwirrung *f* confusion.

verwittern *vt* to weather.

verwitwet *adj* widowed.

verwöhnen *vt* to spoil, pamper.

verworfen *adj* depraved.

verwunden *vt* to wound.

Verwundete(r) *f(m)*wounded person, casualty.

Verwundung *f* wound.

verzagen *vi* to despair.

verzählen *vr* to miscount.

verzeichnen *vt* to list; to register.

Verzeichnis *n* list; index.

verzeihen *vt vi* to forgive.

verzeihlich *adj* pardonable.

Verzeihung *f* pardon, forgiveness:—~! excuse me!, sorry!

verzichten *vi*:—~ **auf** +*acc* to give up, forgo.

verzieren *vi* to decorate, ornament.

Verzierung *f* decoration.

verzögern *vt* to delay.

Verzögerung *f* delay.

verzollen *vt* to pay duty on:—**haben Sie etwas zu ~?** do you have anything to declare?

verzückt *adj* enraptured.

Verzug *m* delay.

verzweifeln *vi* to despair.

verzweifelt *adj* desperate.

Verzweiflung *f* despair, desperation.

Veto *n* veto.

Vetter *m* cousin.

vibrieren *vi* to vibrate.

Video *n* video.

Videorecorder *m* video recorder.

Vieh *n* cattle.

viel *adj adv* much, a lot (of).

vieles *pn* a lot.

vielleicht *adv* perhaps, maybe.

vielmal(s) *adv* many times:—**danke vielmals** many thanks.

vielmehr *adv* rather, on the contrary.

vier *num* four.

Viereck *n* quadrilateral; square.

viereckig *adj* four-sided; square.

vierte(r, s) *adj* fourth.

Viertel *n* quarter.

Vierteljahr *n* quarter.

vierteljährlich *adj* quarterly.

vierteln *vt* to divide into four / quarters.

Viertelnote *f* crotchet.

Viertelstunde *f* quarter of an hour.

Vierwaldstätter See *m* Lake Lucerne.

vierzehn *num* fourteen.

vierzehntägig *adj adv* fortnightly.

vierzig *num* forty.

Villa *f* villa.

Violine *f* violin.

Virus *m* / *n* virus.

Visite *f* (*med*) visit.

Visum *n* visa.

vital *adj* lively, vital.

Vitamin *n* vitamin.

Vogel *m* bird.

Vogelbauer *n* birdcage.

Vogelhäuschen *n* bird house.

Vogelperspektive *f* bird's-eye view.

Vogelscheuche *f* scarecrow.

Vokabel *f* word.

Vokabular *n* vocabulary.

Vokal *m* vowel.

Volk *n* people; nation.

Volksentscheid *m* referendum.

Volksfest *n* fair.

Volkslied *n* folksong.

Volkstanz *m* folk dance.

Volkswirtschaft *f* economics.

Volkszählung *f* census.

voll *adj* full:—*adv* fully.

vollauf *adv* amply.

Vollbart *m* full beard.

vollbringen *vt* to accomplish.

vollenden *vt* to finish, complete.

vollendet *adj* completed.

vollends *adv* completely.

Vollendung *f* completion.

voller *adj* fuller.

Volleyball *m* volleyball.

völlig *adj* complete:—*adv* completely.

volljährig *adj* of age.

vollkommen *adj* perfect.

Vollkommenheit *f* perfection.

Vollkornbrot *n* wholemeal bread.

Vollmacht *f* authority, full powers.

Vollmilch *f* full-cream milk.

Vollmond *m* full moon.

Vollpension *f* full board.

vollständig *adj* complete.

vollstrecken *vt* to execute.

vollziehen *vt* to carry out:—*vr* to happen.

Vollzug *m* execution.

Volt *n* volt.

Volumen *n* volume.

vom = von dem.

von *prep* of; from; by; about.

voneinander *adv* from each other.

vor *prep* in front of; before; with:—~ **allem** most of all:—~ **3 Tagen** 3 days ago.

Vorabend *m* eve, evening before.

voran *adv* before, ahead.

vorangehen *vi* to go ahead.

vorankommen *vi* to come along, make progress.

Voranschlag *m* estimate.

Vorarbeiter *m* foreman.

voraus *adv* ahead; in advance.

vorausgehen *vi* to go (on) ahead; to precede.

Voraussage *f* prediction.

voraussagen *vt* to predict.

voraussehen *vt* to foresee.

voraussetzen *vt* to assume:—**vorausgesetzt, daß…** provided that…

Voraussetzung *f* requirement.

Voraussicht *f* foresight.

voraussichtlich *adv* probably.

Vorbehalt *m* reservation, proviso.

vorbereiten *vt* to prepare.

Vorbereitung *f* preparation.

vordere(r, s) *adj* front.

Vordergrund *m* foreground.

voreingenommen *adj* biased.

Voreingenommenheit *f* bias.

Vorfahr *m* ancestor.

Vorfahrt *f* right of way.

Vorfall *m* incident.

vorfallen *vi* to occur.

vorfinden *vt* to find.

vorführen *vt* to show, display.

Vorgang *m* course of events; process.

Vorgänger(in) *m(f)* predecessor.

vorgefertigt *adj* prefabricated.

vorgehen *vi* to go (on) ahead; to proceed; to take precedence.

Vorgesetzte(r) *f(m)* superior.

vorgestern *adv* the day before yesterday.

vorhaben *vt* to intend.

Vorhaben *n* intention.

Vorhalle *f* entrance hall.

vorhalten *vt* to hold up:— *vi* to last.

vorhanden *adj* existing; available.

Vorhang *m* curtain.

Vorhängeschloß *m* padlock.

vorher *adv* before(hand).

vorherstimmen *vt* to preordain.

vorhergehen *vi* to precede.

vorherig *adj* previous.

Vorherrschaft *f* supremacy, predominance.

vorherrschen *vi* to predominate.

Vorhersage *f* forecast.

vorhersagen *vt* to forecast, predict.

vorhersehbar *adj* predictable.

vorhersehen *vt* to foresee.

vorhin *adv* just now, not long ago.

vorig *adv* last, previous.

Vorkämpfer(in) *m(f)* pioneer.

Vorkaufsrecht *n* purchase option.

Vorkehrung *f* precaution.

vorkommen *vi* to come forward; to happen, occur.

Vorkommen *n* occurrence.

Vorladung *f* summons.

Vorlage *f* pattern, model; bill (for a law).

vorlassen *vt* to admit.

vorläufig *adj* temporary, provisional.

vorlaut *adj* cheeky, impertinent.

vorlesen *vt* to read (out).

Vorleser(in) *m(f)* lecturer, reader.

Vorlesung *f* lecture:—**eine ~ halten** to give a lecture.

Vorliebe *f* preference, partiality.

vorliegen *vi* to be (here).

vorliegend *adj* present, at issue.

Vormachtstellung *f* supremacy.

Vormarsch *m* advance.

vormerken *vt* to book.

Vormittag *m* morning.

vormittags *adv* in the morning, before noon.

Vormund *m* guardian.

vorn *adv* in front.

Vorname *m* first/Christian name.

vornehm *adj* refined; distinguished; aristocratic.

vornehmen *vt* to carry out.

Vorort *m* suburb.

Vorrang *m* precedence, priority.

vorranging *adj* of prime importance.

Vorrat *m* stock, supply.

vorrätig *adj* in stock.

Vorratskammer *f* pantry.

Vorrecht *n* privilege.

Vorrichtung *f* device, contrivance.

vorrücken *vi* to advance:—*vt* to move forward.

Vorsatz *m* intention; (*jur*) intent.

vorsätzlich *adj* intentional; (*jur*) premeditated:—*adv* intentionally.

Vorschau *f* (TV, etc) preview;(film) trailer.

Vorschlag *m* suggestion, proposal.

vorschlagen *vi* to suggest, propose.

vorschreiben *vt* to prescribe, specify.

Vorschrift *f* regulation(s); rule(s); instruction(s).

vorschriftsmäßig *adj* as per regulations/instructions.

Vorschuß *m* advance.

vorsehen *vt* to plan, provide for:—*vr* to be careful, take care:—*vi* to be visible.

Vorsehung *f* providence.

Vorsicht *f* caution, care.

vorsichtig *adj* cautious, careful.

vorsichtshalber *adv* just in case.

Vorsilbe *f* prefix.

vorsingen *vt* to sing (to); to audition (for):—*vi* to sing.

Vorsitz *m* chair(manship).

Vorsitzende(r) *f(m)* chairman (-woman).

Vorsorge *f* precaution(s), provision(s).

vorsorgen *vi*:—~ **für** to make pro-vision(s) for.

Vorsorgeuntersuchung *f* check-up.

vorsorglich *adj* as a precaution.

Vorspeise *f* hors d'œuvre.

Vorspiel *n* prelude.

Vorsprung *m* projection; advantage, start.

Vorstadt *f* suburbs.

Vorstand *m* executive committee; board (of directors).

vorstehen *vi* to project.

vorstellbar *adj* conceivable.

vorstellen *vt* to introduce; to represent:—*vr* **sich** *dat* etw ~ to imagine something.

Vorstellung *f* introduction; performance; idea, thought.

Vorteil *m* advantage.

vorteilhaft *adj* advantageous.

Vortrag *m* lecture, talk.

vortragen *vt* to carry forward; to perform (song, etc).

vortreten *vi* to step forward; to protrude.

vorüber *adv* past, over.

Vorurteil *n* prejudice.

Vorwand *m* pretext.

vorwärts *adv* forward.

vorweg *adv* in advance.

vorweisen *vt* to show, produce.

vorwerfen *vi*:—**jdm etw ~** to reproach somebody for something.

vorwiegend *adj* (*adv*) predominant(ly).

Vorwort *n* preface.

Vorwurf *m* reproach.

vorzeigen *vt* to show, produce.

vorzeitig *adj* premature.

vorziehen *vt* to pull forward; to prefer.

Vorzug *m* preference; advantage.

vorzüglich *adj* excellent.

vulgär *adj* vulgar.

Vulkan *m* volcano.

W

Waage *f* scale(s); balance; (*astrol*) Libra.

Wabe *f* honeycomb.

wach *adj* awake.

wachen *vi* to watch; to be awake.

wachhalten *vt* to keep awake.

wachhaltend *adj* on duty.

Wacholder *m* juniper.

Wachposten *m* guard, sentry.

wachrütteln *vt* to rouse; to shake up.

Wachs *n* wax.

wachsam *adj* watchful, on one's guard, vigilant.

wachsen *vi* to grow; to increase.

wachsen *vt* to wax.

wächsern *adj* waxy.

Wachstum *n* growth; increase.

Wachtel *f* quail.

Wächter *m* guard.

Wachtturm *m* watchtower.

wackelig *adj* shaky; loose.

wackeln *vi* to shake; to wobble, be loose.

Wade *f* calf.

Waffe *f* weapon.

Waffel *f* waffle; wafer.

Wagemut *m* daring.

wagen *vt* to dare; to risk.

Wagen *m* car; truck, lorry; cart, wag(g)on, carriage.

wägen *vt* to weigh (one's words, etc).

Waggon *m* wag(g)on.

waghalsig *adj* foolhardy.

Wagnis *n* risk.

Wahl *f* choice; option; selection; election; vote.

wählbar *adj* eligible.

wählen *vt vi* to choose, pick, select; to vote, elect.

Wähler(in) *m(f)* voter.

wählerisch *adj* fastidious, particular.

Wählerschaft *f* electorate.

Wahlgang *m* ballot.

Wahlkabine *f* polling booth.

Wahlkreis *m* constituency.

wahllos *adj* at random.

Wahlspruch *m* motto.

Wahlurne *f* ballot box.

Wahn *m* delusion; folly.

wähnen *vt* to believe (to be).

Wahnsinn *m* madness, insanity.

wahnsinnig *adj* mad, insane:—*adv* incredibly.

wahr *adj* true; real; genuine.

wahren *vt* to keep (secret, etc); to protect (interests, etc).

währen *vi* to last.

während *prep* during:—*conj* while; whereas.

wahrhaft *adv* truly.

wahrhaftig *adj* true, real:—*adv* really.

Wahrheit *f* truth.

wahrlich *adv* really, certainly.

wahrnehmen *vt* to perceive, notice.

Wahrnehmung *f* perception.

wahrsagen *vi* to tell fortunes, prophesy.

Wahrsager(in) *m(f)* fortuneteller.

wahrscheinlich *adj* probable:—*adv* probably.

Wahrscheinlichkeit *f* probability, likelihood.

Wahrung *f* protection; safeguarding.

Währung *f* currency.

Wahrzeichen *n* landmark.

Waise *f* orphan.

Waisenhaus *n* orphanage.

Wal *m* whale.

Wald *m* wood(s), forest.

Walfang *m* whaling.

Wall *m* dam, embankment; rampart.

Wallach *m* gelding.

wallen *vi* to flow.

Wallfahrer(in) *m(f)* pilgrim.

Wallfahrt *f* pilgrimage.

Walnuß *f* walnut.

Walroß *n* walrus.

walten *vi* to rule.

Walze *f* roller; cylinder.

walzen *vt* to roll.

wälzen *vt* to roll; to hunt through:—*vr* to wallow; to roll about.

Walzer *m* waltz.

Wand *f* wall; partition; precipice.

Wandalismus *m* vandalism.

Wandel *m* change.

wandelbar *adj* changeable, variable.

wandeln *vt vr* to change:—*vi* to walk.

Wanderer *m* hiker, rambler.

wandern *vi* to hike; to ramble, roam, wander.

Wandlung *f* change, transformation.

Wandtafel *f* blackboard.

Wandteppich *m* tapestry.

Wange *f* cheek.

wanken *vi* to stagger, reel; to rock; to waver.

wann *inter adv* when, at what time.

Wanne *f* tub; bathtub.

Wanze *f* bedbug.

Wappen *n* (coat of) arms, crest.

Ware *f* goods; article; product.

Warenhaus *n* department store.

Warenlager *n* stock, store.

Warenzeichen *n* trade mark.

warm *adj* warm; hot.

Wärme *f* warmth; heat.

wärmen *vt* to warm (up).

Warmwasserbereiter *m* water heater.

Warmwasserversorgung *f* hot-water supply.

warnen *vt* to warn, caution.

Warnung *f* warning, caution.

Warschau *n* Warsaw.

Warte *f* point of view; level.

warten *vi* to wait; to await:—*vt* to service, maintain.

Wärter *m* attendant; keeper.

Wartesaal *m* waiting room.

Wartung *f* maintenance.

warum *adv* why.

Warze *f* wart.

was *inter pn* what:—*rel pn* what.

waschbar *adj* washable.

Waschbecken *n* washbasin.

Wäsche *f* wash(ing), laundry; linen; underwear.

waschen *vt vr* to wash.

Wäscherei *f* laundry.

Waschmaschine *f* washing machine.

Wasser *n* water.

wasserdicht *adj* waterproof; watertight.

Wasserfall *m* waterfall; falls.

Wassermann *m* (*astrol*) Aquarius.

Wassermelone *f* watermelon.

wassern *vi* to land on water; to splash down.

wässern *vt* to soak; to water:—*vi* to water (of eyes, etc).

Wasserrohr *n* water pipe.

Wasserspiegel *m* water level.

Wasserstoff *m* hydrogen.

Wasserversorgung *f* water supply.

Wasserzeichen *n* watermark.

wäßrig *adj* watery.

waten *vi* to wade.

watscheln *vi* to waddle.

Watt *n* watt.

Watte *f* cotton wool.

wau *excl* woof.

weben *vt* to weave.

Weber *m* weaver.

Weberei *f* weaving mill.

Webstuhl *m* loom.

Wechsel *m* change; bill of exchange.

Wechselgeld *n* change.

wechselhaft *adj* variable.

Wechselkurs *m* rate of exchange.

wechseln *vt vi* to change.

Wechselstrom *m* alternating current.

Wechselwirkung *f* interaction.

wecken *vt* to wake (up).

Wecker *m* alarm clock.

weder *conj*:—~... **noch** neither... nor.

Weg *m* way; path; route.

weg *adv* away, off.

wegbleiben *vi* to stay away.

wegen *prep* because of.

weggehen *vi* to go away; to leave.

wegnehmen *vt* to take away.

wegwerfen *vt* to throw away.

wegwerfend *adj* disparaging.

weh *adj* sore:—~ **tun** to hurt.

wehen *vt vi* to blow.

wehmütig *adj* melancholy.

Wehrdienst *m* military service.

Weib *n* woman, female, wife.

weiblich *adj* female.

weich *adj* soft.

Weichheit *f* softness.

Weide *f* willow; pasture.

weiden *vi* to graze.

weigern *vt* to refuse.

Weigerung *f* refusal.

Weiher *m* pond.

Weihnachten *n* Christmas.

weihnachtlich *adj* Christmas.

Weihnachtsabend *m* Christmas Eve.

Weihnachtslied *n* Christmas carol.

Weinachtsmann *m* Father Christmas, Santa Claus.

Weihnachtstag *m* Christmas Day.

Weihrausch *m* incense.

Weihwasser *n* holy water.

weil *conj* because.

Weile *f* while, short time.

Wein *m* wine; vine.

Weinberg *m* vineyard.

Weinbrand *m* brandy.

weinen *vt vi* to cry.

Weinglas *n* wine glass.

Weinkarte *f* wine list.

Weinlese *f* vintage.

Weinprobe *f* wine-tasting.

Weinrebe *f* vine.

Weinstock *m* vine.

Weintraube *f* grape.

weise *adj* wise.

Weise *m* way, manner; tune:—**auf diese ~** in this way.

weisen *vt* to show.

Weisheit *f* wisdom.

Weisheitszahn *m* wisdom tooth.

weiß *adj* white.

Weißbrot *n* white bread.

weißen *vt* to whitewash.

Weißglut *f* incandescence.

Weißwein *m* white wine.

weit *adj* wide; broad; long.

weitaus *adv* by far.

weitblickend *adj* far-seeing.

Weite *f* width; space; distance.

weiten *vt vi* to widen.

weiter *adj* wider; broader; farther; further:—*adv* further:—**ohne ~es** without further ado.

weiterarbeiten *vi* to go on working.

weiterbilden *vr* to continue one's education.

Weiterfahrt *f* continuation of the journey.

weitergehen *vi* to go on.

weiterkommen *vi* to make progress.

weiterläufig *adj* spacious; lengthy; distant.

weiterleiten *vt* to pass on.

weitermachen *vt vi* to continue.

weitgehend *adj* considerable:—*adv* largely.

weitreichend *adj* long-range; far-reaching.

weitschweifig *adj* long-winded.

weitsichtig *adj* long-sighted; far-sighted.

Weitsprung *m* long jump.

weitverbreitet *adj* widespread.

Weizen *m* wheat.

welche(r, s) *inter pn* which:—*indef pn* some; any:—*rel pn* who; which, that.

Welle *f* wave; shaft.

Wellensittich *m* budgerigar.

Welt *f* world.

Weltall *n* universe,

Weltanschauung *f* philosophy of life.

weltberühmt *adj* world-famous.

Weltkrieg *m* world war.

weltlich *adj* worldly; secular.

Weltmacht *f* world power.

Weltmeister *m* world champion.

Weltraum *m* space.

weltweit *adj* worldwide.

wem *pn* (*dat of* **wer**) to whom.

wen *pn* (*acc of* **wer**) whom.

Wende *f* turn; change.

Wendekreis *m* tropic.

Wendeltreppe *f* spiral staircase.

wenden *vt vi vr* to turn.

Wendepunkt *m* turning point.

Wendung *f* turn; idiom.

wenig *adj* less; fewer:—*adv* less.

wenige *pn pl* few.

wenigste(r, s) *adj* least.

wenigstens *adv* at least.

wenn *conj* if; when.

wer *pn nom* who.

werben *vt* to recruit:—*vi* to advertise.

Werbung *f* advertisement; recruitment.

werden *vi v aux* to become.

werfen *vt* to throw.

Werft *f* shipyard.

Werk *n* work; job; works.

Werkstatt *f* workshop.

Werkzeug *n* tool.

Wert *m* worth; value.

wert *adj* worth; dear; worthy.

werten *vt* to rate.

wertlos *adj* worthless.

Wertpapier *n* security.

wertvoll *adj* valuable.

Wesen *n* being; nature.

wesentlich *adj* significant; considerable.

weshalb *adv* why.

Wespe *f* wasp.

wessen *pn* (*gen of* **wer**) whose.

Weste *f* waistcoat.

Westen *m* west.

Westeuropa *n* western Europe.

Westindien *n* (the) West Indies.

westlich *adj* western:—*adv* to the west.

wett *adj* even.

Wettbewerb *m* competition.

Wette *f* wager, bet.

wetten *vt vi* to bet.

Wetter *n* weather.

Wetterbericht *m* weather report.

Wettervorhersage *f* weather forecast.

Wettkampf *m* contest.

wettmachen *vt* to make good.

wichtig *adj* important.

Wichtigkeit *f* importance.

Widder *m* ram; (*astrol*) Aries.

wider *prep* against.

widerlegen *vt* to refute.

widerlich *adj* repulsive.

widerrechtlich *adj* unlawful.

Widerrede *f* contradiction.

Widerruf *m* retraction.

widerrufen *vt* to retract.

widerspiegeln *vt* to mirror, reflect:—*vr* to be reflected.

widersprechen *vt* to contradict.

Widerspruch *m* contraction.

Widerstand *m* resistance.

widerstandsfähig *adj* resistant.

widerstehen *vi*:—**jdm/etw** ~ to withstand somebody / something.

widmen *vt* to dedicate; to devote:—*vr* to devote oneself.

widrig *adj* adverse.

wie *adv* how:—*conj*:—**so schön** ~ as beautiful as.

wieder *adv* again.

Wiederaufbau *m* rebuilding.

wiederaufnehmen *vt* to resume.

wiederbekommen *vt* to get back.

wiederbringen *vt* to bring back.

wiedererkennen *vt* to recognize.

Wiedergabe *f* reproduction.

wiedergeben *vt* to return; to repeat.

wiedergutmachen *vt* to make up for.

Wiedergutmachung *f* reparation.

wiederherstellen *vt* to restore.

wiederholen *vt* to repeat.

Wiederholung *f* repeat.

Wiederkehr *f* return; recurrence.

wiedersehen *vt* to see again:—**auf Wiedersehen** goodbye.

wiederum *adv* again; on the other hand.

wiedervereinigen to reunite; to reunify.

Wiederwahl *f* re-election.

Wiege *f* cradle.

wiegen *vt* to rock; *vt vi* to weigh.

wiehern *vi* to neigh, whinny.

Wien *n* Vienna.

Wiese *f* meadow.

Wiesel *n* weasel.

wieso *adv* why.

wieviel *adj* how much.

wieweit *adv* to what extent.

wild *adj* wild.

Wild *n* game.

wildern *vi* to poach.

Wildheit *f* wildness.

Wildleder *n* suede.

Wildnis *f* wilderness.

Wildschwein *n* (wild) boar.

Wille *m* will.

willen *prep* +*gen* **um... ~** for the sake of...

willenstark *adj* strong-willed.

willig *adj* willing.

Willkommen *n* welcome.

willkommen *adj* welcome.

willkürlich *adj* arbitrary; voluntary.

wimmeln *vi*:—~ **(von)** to swarm (with).

wimmern *vi* to whimper.

Wind *m* wind.

Winde *f* winch, windlass; bindweed.

Windel *f* nappy.

winden *vi* to be windy:—*vt* to wind; to wave; to twist.

Windhund *m* greyhound.

windig *adj* windy; dubious.

Windmühle *f* windmill.

Windpocken *pl* chickenpox.

Windschutzscheibe *f* windscreen.

Windstärke *f* wind-force.

windstill *adj* still, windless.

Windstille *f* calm.

Windstoß *m* gust of wind.

Wink *m* wave; nod; hint.

Winkel *m* angle; set square; corner.

winkeln *vt vi* to wave.

winseln *vi* to whine.

Winter *m* winter.

winterfest *adj* (*bot*) hardy.

Wintergarten *m* conservatory.

winterlich *adj* wintry.

Winterreifen *m* winter tyre.

Wintersport *m* winter sports.

Winzer *m* vine grower.

winzig *adj* tiny.

Wipfel *m* treetop.

wir *pn nom* we.

Wirbel *m* whirl, swirl; fuss; vertebra.

wirbeln *vi* to whirl, swirl.

Wirbelsäule *f* spine.

wirken *vi* to have an effect; to work; to seem:—*vt* to work.

wirklich *adj* real:—*adv* really.

Wirklichkeit *f* reality.

wirksam *adj* effective.

Wirkung *f* effect.

wirr *adj* confused, wild.

Wirrwarr *m* chaos, disorder.

Wirt(in) *m(f)* landlord (landlady).

Wirtschaft *f* pub; economy.

wirtschaftlich *adj* economical; economic.

Wirtschaftskrise *f* economic crisis.

Wirtshaus *n* inn.

wischen *vt* to wipe.

Wischer *m* wiper.

wispern *vi* to whisper.

wissen *vt* to know.

Wissen *n* knowledge.

Wissenschaft *f* science.

Wissenschaftler(in) *m(f)* scientist.

wissenschaftlich *adj* scientific.

wissenswert *adj* worth knowing.

wissentlich *adj* knowing.

wittern *vt* to scent; to suspect.

Witterung *f* weather; scent.

Witwe *f* widow.

Witwer *m* widower.

Witz *m* joke.

witzig *adj* funny,

wo *adv* where; somewhere.

woanders *adv* elsewhere.

wobei *adv* by / with which.

Woche *f* week.

Wochenende *n* weekend.

wochenlang *adj adv* for weeks.

Wochenschau *f* newsreel.

wöchentlich *adj adv* weekly.

wodurch *adv* through which.

wofür *adv* for which.

wogegen *adv* against which.

woher *adv* where… from.

wohin *adv* where… to.

wohl *adv* well; probably; certainly; perhaps.

Wohl *n* welfare.

Wohlfahrt *f* welfare.

wohlhabend *adj* wealthy.

Wohlstand *m* prosperity.

Wohltat *f* relief; act of charity.

Wohltäter(in) *m(f)* benefactor.

wohltätig *adj* charitable.

Wohltun *vi* to do good.

Wohlwollen *n* goodwill.

wohnen *vi* to live, dwell, reside.

wohnhaft *adj* resident.

Wohnort *m* domicile.

Wohnsitz *m* place of residence.

Wohnung *f* house; flat, apartment.

Wohnzimmer *n* living room.

wölben *vt vr* to curve.

Wölbung *f* curve.

Wolf *m* wolf.

Wolke *f* cloud.

Wolkenkratzer *m* skyscraper.

wolkig *adj* cloudy.

Wolle *f* wool.

wollen *adj* woollen.

wollen *vt vi v aux* to want.

wollüstig *adj* lusty, sensual.

womit *adv* with which.

wonach *adv* after / for which.

woran *adv* on / at which.

worauf *adv* on which.

woraus *adv* from / out of which.

worin *adv* in which.

Wort *n* word.

Wörterbuch *n* dictionary.

Wortlaut *m* wording.

wortlos *adj* mute.

wortreich *adv* wordy, verbose.

Wortschatz *m* vocabulary.

Wortspiel *n* pun.

worüber *adv* over / about which.

worum *adv* about / round which.

worunter *adv* under which.

wovon *adv* from which.

wovor *adv* in front of / before which.

wozu *adv* to / for which.

Wrack *n* wreck.

wringen *vt* to wring.

Wucher *m* profiteering.

Wucherer *m* profiteer.

wuchern *vi* to grow wild.

Wucherung *f* growth, tumour.

Wuchs *m* growth; build.

Wucht *f* force.

wühlen *vi* to scrabble; to root; to burrow:—*vt* to dig.

Wulst *m* bulge; swelling.

wund *adj* sore, raw.

Wunde *f* wound.

Wunder *n* miracle.

wunderbar *adj* wonderful, marvellous.

Wunderkind *n* infant prodigy.

wunderlich *adj* odd, peculiar.

wundern *vr* to be surprised:—*vt* to surprise.

wunderschön *adj* beautiful.

wundervoll *adj* wonderful.

Wunsch *m* wish.

wünschen *vt* to wish, desire.

wünschenswert *adj* desirable.

Würde *f* dignity; honour.

würdevoll *adj* dignified.

würdig *adj* worthy.
würdigen *vt* to appreciate.
Wurf *m* throw; litter.
Würfel *m* dice; cube.
würfeln *vi* to play dice:—*vt* to dice.
würgen *vi vt* to choke.

Wurm *m* worm.
Wurst *f* sausage.
Würze *f* spice.
Würzel *f* root.
würzen *vt* to season, spice.
würzig *adj* spicy.

wüst *adj* untidy, messy; wild; waste.
Wüste *f* desert.
Wut *f* rage, fury.
wüten *vi* to rage.
wütend *adj* furious.

X, Y

xerokopieren *vt* to xerox, photocopy.

x-mal *adv* any number of times:—*n* times.

Xylophon *n* xylophone.

Yacht *f* yacht.

Ypsilon *n* the letter Y.

Z

zaghaft *adj* timid.
Zaghaftigkeit *f* timidity.
zäh *adj* tough; tenacious.
Zähigkeit *f* toughness; tenacity.
Zahl *f* number.
zahlbar *adj* payable.
zahlen *vt vi* to pay:—
  zahlen bitte! the bill please!
zählen *vt vi* to count.
Zähler *m* meter; numerator.
zahllos *adj* countless.
zahlreich *adj* numerous.
Zahlung *f* payment.
zahm *adj* tame.
zähmen *vt* to tame; to curb.
Zahn *m* tooth.
Zahnarzt *m* **Zahnärztin** *f* dentist.
Zahnbürste *f* toothbrush.
Zahnfleisch *n* gums.
Zahnpasta *f* toothpaste.
Zahnrad *n* cog.
Zahnschmerzen *pl* toothache.
Zange *f* pliers; tongs; pincers; forceps.
zanken *vi vr* to quarrel.
zänkisch *adj* quarrelsome.
zart *adj* soft; tender; delicate.
Zartheit *f* softness; tenderness.
zärtlich *adj* tender, affectionate.
Zauber *m* magic; spell.
Zauberei *f* magic.
zauberhaft *adj* magical, enchanting.

Zauberkünstler *m* conjuror.
zaubern *vi* to conjure, practise magic.
zaudern *vi* to hesitate.
Zaum *m* bridle.
Zaun *m* fence.
Zaunkönig *m* wren.
z.B. (= zum Beispiel) e.g.
Zebra *n* zebra.
Zebrastreifen *m* zebra crossing.
Zeche *f* bill; mine.
Zeh *m* toe.
Zehe *f* toe; clove.
zehn *num* ten.
zehnte(r, s) *adj* tenth.
Zeichen *n* sign.
zeichnen *vt vi* to draw; to sign.
Zeichnung *f* drawing.
zeigen *vt* to show:—*vi* to point:—*vr* to show oneself.
Zeiger *m* pointer; hand (of clock).
Zeile *f* line; row.
Zeit *f* time; (*gr*) tense:—**zur ~** at the moment.
Zeitalter *n* age.
Zeitgenosse *m* contemporary.
zeitig *adj* early.
zeitlich *adj* temporal.
Zeitlupe *f* slow motion.
Zeitraum *m* period.
Zeitrechnung *f* time, era:—
  nach/vor unserer ~ AD/BC.
Zeitschrift *f* periodical.
Zeitung *f* newspaper.

Zeitvertreib *m* pastime, diversion.
zeitweilig *adj* temporary.
zeitweise *adv* for a time.
Zeitwort *n* verb.
Zeitzünder *m* time fuse.
Zelle *f* cell; callbox.
Zellstoff *m* cellulose.
Zelt *n* tent.
zelten *vi* to camp.
Zeltplatz *m* campsite.
Zement *m* cement.
zementieren *vt* to cement.
zensieren *vt* to censor.
Zentimeter *m*/*n* centimetre.
Zentner *m* hundredweight.
Zensur *f* censorship.
zentral *adj* central.
Zentrale *f* central office; (telephone) exchange.
Zentralheizung *f* central heating.
Zentrum *n* centre.
zerbrechen *vt vi* to break.
zerbrechlich *adj* fragile.
zerdrücken *vt* to smash, crush; to mash (of potatoes).
Zeremonie *f* ceremony.
Zerfall *m* decay.
zerfallen *vi* to disintegrate, decay.
zergehen *vi* to melt, dissolve.
zerkleinern *vt* to reduce to small pieces.
zerlegbar *adj* able to be dismantled.
zerlegen *vi* to take to pieces; to carve.

zermürben *vt* to wear down.

zerquetschen *vt* to squash.

Zerrbild *n* caricature.

zerreißen *vt* to tear to pieces:—*vi* to tear, rip.

zerren *vt* to drag:—*vi* ~ (**an** +*dat*) to tug (at).

zerrinnen *vi* to melt away.

zerrissen *adj* torn, tattered.

Zerrissenheit *f* tattered state.

Zerrung *f* (*med*) pulled muscle.

zerrütten *vt* to wreck, destroy.

zerrüttet *adj* wrecked, shattered.

zerschlagen *vt* to shatter, smash:—*vr* to fall through.

zerschneiden *vt* to cut up.

zersetzen *vt vr* to decompose.

zerspringen *vi* to shatter, burst.

Zerstäuber *m* atomiser.

zerstören *vt* to destroy.

Zerstörung *f* destruction.

zerstreuen *vt* to scatter, disperse; to dispel:—*vr* to scatter, disperse; to be dispelled.

zerstreut *adj* scattered; absent-minded.

Zerstreutheit *f* absent-mindedness.

Zerstreuung *f* dispersion.

zerteilen *vt* to divide into parts.

Zertifikat *n* certificate.

zertreten *vt* to crush underfoot.

zertrümmern *vt* to demolish, to shatter.

zetern *vi* to shout; to shriek.

Zettel *m* slip of paper; note; form.

Zeug *n* stuff; gear:—**das ~ haben zu** to have the makings of.

Zeuge *m* witness.

Zeugenaussage *f* evidence.

Zeugin *f* witness.

zeugen *vi* to testify, bear witness:—*vt* to father.

Zeugnis *n* certificate; report; evidence, testimony.

Zickzack *m* zigzag.

Ziege *f* goat.

Ziegel *m* brick; tile.

ziehen *vt* to draw; to pull; to move:—*vi* to draw; to move; to drift.

Ziehharmonika *f* concertina; accordion.

Ziehung *f* drawing.

Ziel *n* destination; finish; target; goal.

ziemlich *adj* quite a, fair:—*adv* rather; quite a bit.

zieren *vi* to act coy.

zierlich *adj* dainty.

Ziffer *f* figure, digit.

Zigarette *f* cigarette.

Zigarre *f* cigar.

Zigeuner(in) *m(f)* gypsy.

Zimmer *n* room.

Zimt *m* cinnamon.

Zink *n* zinc.

Zinn *n* tin; pewter.

Zins *m* interest.

zinslos *adj* interest-free.

Zinssatz *m* rate of interest.

zirka *adv* (round) about.

Zirkus *m* circus.

zischen *vi* to hiss.

Zitat *n* quotation, quote.

zitieren *vt* to quote.

Zitrone *f* lemon.

Zitronensaft *m* lemon juice.

zittern *vi* to tremble.

zivil *adj* civil; moderate.

Zivil *n* plain clothes.

Zivilbevölkerung *f* civil population.

Zivilisation *f* civilization.

zivilisieren *vt* to civilize.

Zivilist *m* civilian.

zögern *vi* to hesitate.

Zoll *m* customs; duty.

Zollamt *n* customs office.

Zollbeamte(r) *m* customs officer.

Zollerklärung *f* customs declaration.

zollfrei *adj* duty-free.

Zollkontrolle *f* customs check.

zollpflichtig *adj* liable to duty.

Zone *f* zone.

Zoo *m* zoo.

Zoologe *m* zoologist.

Zoologie *f* zoology.

zoologisch *adj* zoological.

Zorn *m* anger.

zornig *adj* angry.

zu *prep* to; at; with; for; into:—*conj* to:—*adv* too; towards; shut, closed.

zuallererst *adv* first of all.

zuallerletzt *adv* last of all.

Zubehör *n* accessories.

zubereiten *vt* to prepare.

zubilligen *vt* to grant.

zubinden *vt* to tie up.

zubringen *vt* to spend.

Zucchini *pl* courgette.

Zucht *f* breeding; cultivation; breed; discipline.

züchten *vt* to breed; to cultivate; to grow.

Züchter *m* breeder; grower.

Zuchthaus *n* prison.

züchtigen *vt* to chastise.

Züchtung *f* breed; variety.

zucken *vi* to jerk, twitch; to flicker:—*vi* to shrug.

Zucker *m* sugar; (*med*) diabetes.

Zuckerguß *m* icing.

zuckerkrank *adj* diabetic.

Zuckerkrankheit (*med*) diabetes.

zuckern *vt* to sugar.

Zuckerrohr *n* sugar cane.

Zuckerrübe *f* sugar beet.

Zuckung *f* convulsion, spasm; twitch.

zudecken *vt* to cover (up).

zudem *adv* in addition.

zudringlich *adj* forward, pushing, obtrusive.

zudrücken *vt* to close.

zueinander *adv* to one another; together.

zuerkennen *vt* to award.

zuerst *adv* first; at first.

Zufahrt *f* approach.

Zufahrtsstraße *f* approach road; slip road.

Zufall *m* chance; coincidence:—**durch ~** by accident.

zufallen *vi* to close, shut; to fall.

zufällig *adj* chance:—*adv* by chance.

Zuflucht *f* recourse; refuge.

zufolge *prep* judging by; according to.

zufrieden *adj* content(ed), satisfied.

zufriedengeben *vr* to be content/satisfied (with).

zufriedenstellen *vt* to satisfy.

zufrieren *vi* to freeze up.

zufügen *vt* to add.

Zug *m* train; draught; pull; feature; move, stroke; breath; procession.

Zugabe *f* extra; encore.

Zugang *m* access, approach.

zugänglich *adj* accessible; approachable.

zugeben *vt* to add; to admit; to permit.

zugehen *vi* to shut.

Zugehörigkeit *f* membership; belonging (to).

Zügel *m* rein(s); curb.

Zugeständnis *n* concession.

zugestehen *vt* to admit; to concede.

Zugführer *m* guard.

zugig *adj* draughty.

zügig *adj* swift, speedy.

zugreifen *vi* to seize/grab at; to help.

zugrunde *adv*:—**~ gehen** to collapse: —**einer Sache dat etw ~ legen** to base something on something:—**~ richten** to destroy, ruin.

zugunsten *prep* in favour of.

Zugvogel *m* migratory bird.

zuhalten *vt* to keep closed:—*vi* **auf jdn/etw ~** to make a beeline for somebody/something.

Zuhälter *m* pimp.

Zuhause *n* home.

zuhören *vi* to listen.

Zuhörer *m* listener.

zukleben *vi* to paste up.

zukommen *vi* to come up.

Zukunft *f* future.

zukünftig *adj* future:—*adv* in future.

Zulage *f* bonus.

zulassen *vt* to admit; to permit; to license.

zulässig *adj* permissible.

Zulassung *f* authorization; licensing.

zulaufen *vi*:—**~ auf jdn/etw** to run up to somebody or something:—**~ auf** to lead towards.

zuletzt *adv* finally, at last.

zum = **zu dem**.

zumachen *vt* to shut; to do up, fasten:—*vi* to shut; to hurry up.

zumal *conj* especially (as).

zumindest *adv* at least.

zumutbar *adj* reasonable.

zumuten *vt*:—**(jdm) etw ~** to expect/ask something (of somebody).

Zumutung *f* unreasonable expectation, impertinence.

zunächst *adv* first of all.

Zunahme *f* increase.

Zuname *m* surname.

zünden *vi* to light, ignite; to fire.

zündend *adj* fiery.

Zünder *m* fuse; detonator.

Zündholz *n* match.

Zündkerze *f* spark plug.

Zündschlüssel *m* ignition key.

Zündung *f* ignition.

zunehmen *vi* to increase, grow; to put on weight.

Zuneigung *f* affection.

Zunft *f* guild.

zünftig *adj* proper; decent.

Zunge *f* tongue.

zuoberst *adv* at the top.

zupfen *vt* to pull, pick, pluck.

zur = **zu der**.

zurechtweisen *vt* to reprimand.

Zurechtweisung *f* reprimand, rebuff.

zureden *vi*:—**jdm ~** to persuade/urge someone.

Zürich *n* Zurich.

zurück *adv* back.

zurückhaltend *adj* reserved.

Zurückhaltung *f* reserve.

zurückkehren *vi* to return.

Zuruf *f* cry, shout.

Zusage *f* promise; consent.

zusagen *vt* to promise:—*vi* to accept.

zusammen *adv* together.

Zusammenarbeit *f* cooperation.

zusammenarbeiten *vi* to cooperate.

zusammenbrechen *vt* to collapse; to break down.

Zusammenbruch *m* collapse.

zusammenfassen *vt* to summarize; to unite.

Zusammenfassung *f* summary.

Zusammenhang *m* connection.

zusammenkommen *vi* to assemble; to occur at once.

zusammenschließen *vt vi* to join (together).

Zusammenschluß *m* amalgamation.

zusammensetzen *vr* to be composed of; to get together.

Zusammensetzung *f* composition.

Zusammenstoß *m* collision.

zusätzlich *adj* additional:—*adv* in addition.

zuschauen *vt* to look on, watch.

Zuschauer(in) *m(f)* spectator.

Zuschlag *m* extra charge, surcharge.

zuschlagen *vt* to slam; to hit:—*vi* to shut; to hit, punch.

zuschreiben *vt* to ascribe, attribute.

Zuschrift *f* letter, reply.

Zuschluß *m* subsidy, allowance.

zusehen *vi* to watch; to take care.

zusehends *adv* visibly.

zusenden *vt* to forward, send on.

zuspielen *vt vi* to pass.

zuspitzen *vt* to sharpen:—*vr* to become critical.

zusprechen *vt* to award:—*vi* to speak.

Zustand *m* state, condition.

zustande *adv*:—~ **bringen** to bring about:—~ **kommen** to come about.

zuständig *adj* responsible.

Zuständigkeit *f* responsibility.

zustehen *vi*:—**jdm** ~ to be one's right.

zustellen *vt* to send; to block.

zustimmen *vi* to agree.

Zustimmung *f* agreement, consent.

zustoßen *vi* to happen.

zutage *adv*:—~ **bringen** to bring to light:—~ **treten** to come to light.

Zutaten *pl* ingredients.

zuteilen *vt* to designate, assign; to allocate.

zutiefst *adv* deeply.

zutragen *vt* to bring; to tell:—*vr* to happen.

Zutrauen *n* trust.

zutrauen *vt*:—**jdm etw** ~ to credit somebody with something.

zutraulich *adj* trusting, friendly.

zutreffen *vi* to be correct; to apply.

zutreffend *adj* accurate.

Zutritt *m* access, admittance.

Zutun *n* assistance.

zuverlässig *adj* reliable.

Zuverlässigkeit *f* reliability.

zuviel *adv* too much.

zuvor *adv* before, previously.

zuvorkommen *vt* +*dat* to anticipate.

zuvorkommend *adj* courteous, obliging.

Zuwachs *m* growth, increase.

zuwachsen *vi* to become overgrown; to heal (of wound).

zuwenig *adv* too little.

zuweilen *adv* at times, now and then.

zuwenden *vt* (+*dat*) to turn (towards).

zuziehen *vt* to draw, close; to call in (experts, etc):—*vi* to move in.

zuzüglich *prep* plus, with the addition of.

Zwang *m* compulsion, coercion.

zwängen *vt vr* to squeeze.

zwanglos *adj* informal.

zwanzig *num* twenty.

zwar *adv* indeed, to be sure.

Zweck *m* purpose, aim.

zwecklos *adj* pointless.

zwei *num* two.

zweideutig *adj* ambiguous.

zweifach *adj* double.

Zweifel *m* doubt.

zweifelhaft *adj* doubtful.

zweifellos *adj* doubtless.

zweifeln *vi*:—~ (**an etw** *dat*) to doubt (something).

Zweig *m* branch.

zweimal *adv* twice.

zweite(r, s) *adj* second.

Zwerg *m* dwarf.

Zwetsch(g)e *f* plum.

Zwieback *m* rusk.

Zwiebel *f* onion.

Zwilling *m* twin:—~e *pl* (*astrol*) Gemini.

zwingen *vt* to force, compel.

zwingend *adj* compulsive.

zwischen *prep* between.

Zwischenzeit *f* interval:— **in der** ~ meanwhile.

zwitschern *vt vi* to chirp, twitter.

zwo *num* two.

zwölf *num* twelve.

Zyklus *m* cycle.

Zylinder *m* cylinder; top hat.

Zyniker *m* cynic.

zynisch *adj* cynical.

Zypern *n* Cyprus.

Zyste *f* cyst.

English–German Dictionary

A

a *art* ein, eine; per, pro, je.

abandon *vt* auf-, preis-geben; im Stich lassen.

abbey *n* Abtei *f*.

abbot *n* Abt *m*.

abbreviate *vt* (ab)kürz-en.

abbreviation *n* Abkürzung *f*.

abdomen *n* Unterleib *m*, Bauch *m*.

ability *n* Fähigkeit *f*.

able *adj* fähig, tüchtig.

abnormal *adj* abnormal.

abnormality *n* Abnormalität *f*.

aboard *adv* an Bord.

abolish *vt* abschaffen, aufheben.

abolition *n* Abschaffung *f*, Aufhebung *f*.

abominable *adj* abscheulich.

about *prep* über; von; um… herum: —*adv* herum, umher; etwa, ungefähr.

above *prep* über, oberhalb:—*adv* oben, darüber:—~ **all** vor allem:—~ **mentioned** oben erwähnt.

abroad *adv* im Ausland, ~ ins Ausland.

absence *n* Abwesenheit *f*; Mangel *m*.

absent *adj* abwesend; fehlend.

absent-minded *adj* zer-streut.

absolute *adj* uneingeschränkt; vol-lkommen.

absorb *vt* aufsaugen; aufnehmen.

absorption *n* Aufnahme *f*; Vertieftsein *n*.

abstain *vi* sich ent-halten.

abstract *adj* abstrakt:—*n* Auszug *m*; Übersicht *f*.

absurd *adj* absurd; lächer-lich.

absurdity *n* Unsinn *m*; Lächerlichkeit *f*.

abundance *n* Überfluß *m*.

abundant *adj* reichlich.

abuse *vt* mißbrauchen; beleidigen:—*n* Mißbrauch *m*; Mißhandlung *f*.

abyss *n* Abgrund *m*.

academic *adj* akademisch; allgemeinbildend.

academy *n* Akademie *f*; Hochschule *f*.

accelerate *vt* beschleuni-gen.

acceleration *n* Beschleunigung *f*.

accent *n* Akzent *m*; Betonung *f*:—*vt* betonen.

accept *vt* annehmen.

acceptable *adj* annehmbar.

acceptance *n* Annahme *f*; Aufnahme *f*.

access *n* Zugang *m*; Zutritt *m*.

accident *n* Zufall *m*; Unfall *m*.

accidental *adj* zufällig; Unfalls-.

accommodate *vt* anpassen; unterbringen.

accommodation *n* Unterkunft *f*; Beilegung *f*.

accompany *vt* begleiten.

accord *n* Übereinstimmung *f*, Abkommen *n*.

accordance *n*:—**in ~ with** in Übereinstimmung mit, gemäß.

according *prep* gemäß, entsprechend: —~**ly** *adv* demnach, entsprechend.

account *n* Rechnung *f*; Konto *n*:—**on ~ of** wegen.

accountancy *n* Buchhaltung *f*.

accountant *n* Buchhalter(in) *m(f)*.

accuracy *n* Genauigkeit *f*.

accurate *adj* genau.

accuse *vt* anklagen; beschuldigen.

accustomed *adj* gewohnt, üblich; gewöhnt.

ace *n* As *n*.

ache *n* Schmerz *m*:—*vi* schmerzen, weh tun.

achieve *vt* erlangen; erre-ichen.

achievement *n* Leistung *f*; Ausführung *f*; Erreichung *f*.

acid *adj* sauer; scharf:—*n* Säure *f*.

acknowledge *vt* anerken-nen; zugeben; bestätigen.

acknowledgment *n*
Anerkennung *f*;
Bestätigung *f*.

acorn *n* Eichel *f*.

acoustics *n* Akustik *f*.

acquaint *vt* bekannt
machen, vertraut machen.

acquaintance *n*
Bekanntschaft *f*; Be-kan-
nte(r) *f(m)*; Kenntnis *f*.

acquire *vt* erwerben, erlangen.

acquisition *n* Erwerb *m*,
Anschaffung *f*.

across *adv* hinüber; quer-
durch; drüben:—*prep*
über; (mitten) durch.

act *vi* handeln; spielen:—*n*
Tat *f*; Akt *m*.

action *n* Handlung *f*; (*law*)
Klage *f*.

active *adj* aktiv; lebhaft.

activity *n* Aktivität *f*;
Tätigkeit *f*.

actor *n* Schauspieler *m*.

actress *n* Schauspielerin *f*.

actual *adj* tatsächlich.

acute *adj* scharf; heftig;
akut.

ad *n* Anzeige *f*.

adapt *vt* anpassen;
umstellen.

add *vt* hinzufügen.

adder *n* Natter *f*.

addict *n* Süchtige(r) *f(m)*.

addiction *n* Sucht *f*.

addition *n* Zusatz *m*.

additional *adj* zusätzlich.

address *vt* ansprechen;
adressieren: —*n* Anschrift
f; Rede *f*.

adequate *adj* angemessen;
ausreichend.

adjective *n* Adjektiv *n*.

adjust *vt* anpassen; einstellen.

adjustment *n* Anpassung,
Einstellung *f*.

administration *n*
Verwaltung *f*.

administrator *n*
Verwaltungsbeamte(r)
f(m).

admiral *n* Admiral *m*.

admiration *n*
Bewunderung *f*.

admire *vt* bewundern.

admission *n* Eintritt *m*;
Einlaß *m*; Zulassung *f*.

admit *vt* einlassen;
zulassen; zugeben.

adopt *vt* adoptieren;
annehmen.

adoption *n* Adoption *f*;
Annahme *f*.

adore *vt* anbeten; verehren.

adult *adj* erwachsen:—*n*
Erwachse-ne(r) *f(m)*.

adultery *n* Ehebruch *m*.

advance *vt vi* vorrücken:—
n Vorrücken *n*; Fortschritt
m.

advanced *adj* fortgeschritten.

advantage *n* Vorteil *m*.

adventure *n* Abenteuer *n*.

adventurous *adj* abenteuerlich.

adverb *n* Adverb *n*.

advertise *vt* ankündigen;
werben für: —*vi*
inserieren.

advertisement *n* Anzeige *f*.

advertising *n* Werbung *f*.

advice *n* Rat *m*; Nachricht *f*.

advise *vt* (be)raten;
benachrichtigen.

aeroplane *n* Flugzeug *n*.

affair *n* Angelegenheit *f*;
Sache *f*; Affäre *f*.

affection *n* Liebe *f*;
Zuneigung *f*.

affectionate *adj* liebevoll,
zärtlich.

affix *vt* befestigen; hinzufügen:—*n* (*gr*) Affix *n*;
Anhang *m*.

affluence *n* Überfluß *f*;
Wohlstand *m*.

afford *vt* sich leisten; auf-
bringen.

afraid *adj*:—**be ~** Angst
haben, sich fürchten.

after *prep* hinterher; nach:—
adv nachher; darauf.

afternoon *n* Nachmittag *m*.

afterwards *adv* später, hinterher.

again *adv* wieder;
außerdem:—**~ and ~**
immer wieder.

against *prep* gegen.

age *n* Alter *n*; Zeit *f*:—*vi*
altern.

agency *n* Agentur *f*.

agent *n* Agent(in) *m(f)*.

aggression *n* Agression *f*.

aggressive *adj* aggressiv.

agitate *vt* schütteln; aufregen; aufwiegeln.

ago *adv* vor.

agree *vt* vereinbaren:—*vi*
zustimmen.

agreement *n* Vereinbarung
f; Übereinstimmung *f*.

agricultural *adj* land-
wirtschaftlich, Agrar-.

agriculture *n*
Landwirtschaft *f*.

ahead *adv* vorn; voraus.

aid *vt* helfen; fördern:—*n*
Hilfe *f*; Beistand *m*;
Helfer(in) *m(f)*.

aim *vt vi* zielen:—*n* Ziel *n*;
Absicht *f*.

air *n* Luft *f*.

air-conditioned *adj* klima-
tisiert.

air-conditioning *n*
Klimaanlage *f.*
aircraft *n* Flugzeug *n.*
airline *n* Fluggesellschaft *f.*
airport *n* Flughafen *m.*
alarm *n* Alarm *m*; Wecker
m; Alarmanlage *f:—vt*
alarmieren.
alcohol *n* Alkohol *m.*
alcoholic *adj* alkoholisch;
Alkohol-: —*n*
Alkoholiker(in) *m(f).*
alert *adj* wachsam; munter.
alien *adj* fremd; ausländisch:—*n*
Ausländer(in) *m(f).*
alike *adj adv* gleich; ähnlich.
alive *adj* lebendig; am
Leben.
all *adj* all, ganz; jede(r, s);
völlig:—*adv* ganz, völ-
lig:—~ **at once** plötzlich:—
~ **the same** trotzdem:—
not at ~ überhaupt nicht.
allergy *n* Allergie *f.*
alley *n* Gasse *f.*
alliance *n* Bund *m*, Bündnis
n.
alligator *n* Alligator *m.*
allocate *vt* verteilen;
zuweisen.
allocation *n* Verteilung *f*;
Zuweisung *f.*
allow *vt* erlauben; bewilli-
gen; zugeben.
allowance *n* Erlaubnis *f*;
Zuschuß *m.*
ally *n* Verbündete(r) *f(m):—*
vi sich verbünden.
almond *n* Mandel *f.*
almost *adv* fast, beinahe.
alone *adj adv* allein.
along *prep* entlang:—*adv*
vorwärts, weiter.
aloud *adv* laut.

alphabet *n* Alphabet *n.*
already *adv* schon, bereits.
also *adv* auch, außerdem.
altar *n* Altar *m.*
alter *vt* (ver)ändern.
alteration *n* Änderung *f*;
Umbau *m.*
alternative *n* Alternative
f:—adj alternativ; andere(r,
s):—**~ly** *adv* im anderen
Falle, wahlweise.
although *conj* obwohl,
wenn auch.
altogether *adv* insgesamt;
ganz.
aluminium *n* Aluminium
n.
always *adv* immer, jederzeit.
amateur *n* Amateur *m*;
Liebhaber(in) *m(f)*;
Dilettant(in) *m(f).*
amaze *vt* überraschen, in
Staunen versetzen.
amazement *n* (Er)staunen
n; Überraschung *f.*
amazing *adj* erstaunlich;
unglaublich.
ambassador *n* Botschafter
m; Ge-sandte(r) *f(m).*
ambiguity *n* Zwei-,
Vieldeutigkeit *f.*
ambiguous *adj* zwei-,
vieldeutig.
ambition *n* Ehrgeiz *m*; Ziel
n.
ambitious *adj* ehrgeizig.
ambulance *n*
Krankenwagen *m.*
amend *vt* verbessern; abändern, ergänzen.
amendment *n*
(Ver)Besserung *f*;
Ergänzung *f*;
Änderungsantrag *m.*
America *n* Amerika *n.*

American *adj*
amerikanisch.
ammunition *n* Munition *f.*
among *prep* unter, inmitten.
amount *n* Betrag *m*; Menge
f:—vi betragen.
ample *adj* weit, groß,
geräumig; reichlich, genügend.
amplify *vt* erweitern, verstärken.
amuse *vt* amüsieren, unterhalten.
amusement *n* Unterhaltung
f, Vergnügen *n.*
amusing *adj* amüsant.
anaesthetic *n*
Betäubungsmittel *n.*
analogy *n* Entsprechung *f.*
analyse *vt* analysieren;
untersuchen.
analysis *n* Analyse *f*;
Untersuchung *f.*
analyst *n*
(Psycho)Analytiker(in)
m(f).
analytical *adj* analytisch.
anarchic *adj* anarchistisch.
anarchist *n* Anarchist(in)
m(f).
anarchy *n* Anarchie *f.*
anatomy *n* Anatomie *f.*
ancestry *n* Abstammung *f*;
Vorfahren *mpl.*
anchor *n* Anker *m:—vi*
ankern.
anchovy *n* Sardelle *f.*
ancient *adj* (ur)alt.
and *conj* und.
anecdote *n* Anekdote *f.*
anew *adv* von neuem.
angel *n* Engel *m.*
anger *n* Ärger *m*; Wut *f:—vt*
verärgern, erzürnen.
angle *n* Winkel *m*; Ecke *f:—*
vt (ab)-biegen; angeln.

angry *adj* verärgert; stürmisch.

anguish *n* Qual *f;* Schmerz *m.*

animal *n* Tier *n.*

animate *vt* beleben, aufmuntern:—*adj* lebendig, lebhaft.

ankle *n* (Fuß)Knöchel *m;* Fessel *f.*

annex *vt* beifügen, anhängen; annektieren:—*n* Anhang *m;* Anlage *f.*

annihilate *vt* vernichten.

annihilation *n* Vernichtung *f.*

anniversary *n* Jahrestag *m;* Jubiläum *n.*

announce *vt* ankündigen; bekanntgeben.

announcement *n* Ankündigung *f;* Ansage *f.*

annoy *vt* ärgern; belästigen.

annoyance *n* Ärgernis *n;* Belästigung *f.*

annoying *adj* ärgerlich; lästig.

annual *adj* jährlich, Jahres-.

anonymity *n* Anonymität *f.*

anonymous *adj* anonym.

another *adj* ein anderer; noch ein(er, e, es):—**one ~** einander.

answer *vt* (be)antworten; verantworten:—*n* Antwort *f.*

ant *n* Ameise *f.*

Antarctic *adj* antarktisch.

antelope *n* Antilope *f.*

antenna *n* Antenne *f;* Fühler *m.*

anthology *n* Anthologie *f.*

anthropology *n* Anthropologie *f*

antibiotic *n* Antibiotikum *n.*

antibody *n* Antikörper *m.*

anticipate *vt* voraussehen; erwarten.

anticipation *n* (Vor)Ahnung *f;* Vorfreude *f.*

anticlockwise *adv* gegen den Uhrzeigersinn.

antidote *n* Gegengift, Gegenmittel *n.*

antifreeze *n* Frostschutzmittel *n.*

antipathy *n* Abneigung *f.*

antiquated *adj* veraltet.

antique n Antiquität *f:—adj* antik.

antisocial *adj* asozial; ungesellig.

antler *n* Geweih *n.*

anvil *n* Amboß *m.*

anxiety *n* Angst *f;* Beklemmung *f.*

anxious *adj* ängstlich, besorgt; gespannt.

any *adj pn* (irgend)eine(r); (irgend)-welche; jede(r, s); **~body** irgend jemand; jeder(mann):—**~how** irgendwie:—**~thing** etwas; alles.

apart *adv* für sich; getrennt.

apathetic *adj* teilnahmslos.

apathy *n* Teilnahmslosigkeit *f.*

ape *n* (Menschen)Affe *m:—vt* nachäffen.

apiary *n* Bienenhaus *n.*

apologetic *adj* entschuldigend; reumütig.

apologist *n* Verteidiger *m.*

apologize *vu* sich entschuldigen.

apology *n* Entschuldigung *f.*

apostrophe *n* Apostroph *m.*

appal *vt* erschrecken.

appalling *adj* entsetzlich.

apparatus *n* Apparat *m.*

apparent *adj* offensichtlich; scheinbar.

appeal *vi* Berufung einlegen; sich berufen; appellieren:—*n* (*law*) Berufung *f;* Appell *m.*

appear *vi* (er)scheinen.

appearance *n* Erscheinen *n;* Auftreten *n;* Erscheinung *f.*

appendix *n* Blinddarm *m.*

appetite *n* Appetit *m.*

applaud *vt vi* applaudieren.

applause *n* Beifall *m.*

apple *n* Apfel *m.*

apple tree *n* Apfelbaum *m.*

appliance *n* Gerät *n.*

applicable *adj* anwendbar.

application *n* Anwendung *f;* Antrag *m.*

apply *vt* anwenden; auftragen:—*vi* zutreffen; sich anwenden lassen.

appoint *vt* ernennen; bestimmen.

appointment *n* Ernennung *f;* Bestimmung *f.*

appreciate *vt* (ein)schätzen.

appreciation *n* (Ein)Schätzung *f.*

apprentice *n* Lehrling *m.*

approach *vt vi* sich nähern; nahekommen:—*n* Nahen *n;* Annäherung *f.*

appropriate *adj* passend, angemessen.

approval *n* Billigung *f;* Beifall *m.*

approve *vt* billigen; gutheißen.

approximate *vi* sich nähern:—*adj* annähernd.

approximation *n* Annäherung *f.*

apricot *n* Aprikose *f.*

April *n* April *m.*

apron *n* Schürze *f;* Schurz *m.*

apt *adj* passend; geneigt; geschickt.

aquarium *n* Aquarium *n.*

Aquarius *n* (*astrol*) Wassermann *m.*

aquatic *adj* Wasser-.

arch *n* Bogen *m.*

archaeological *adj* archäologisch.

archaeology *n* Archäologie *f.*

archaic *adj* archaisch.

archbishop *n* Erzbischof *m.*

archer *n* Bogenschütze *m.*

archery *n* Bogenschießen *n.*

architect *n* Architekt(in) *m(f).*

architectural *adj* architektonisch.

architecture *n* Architektur *f.*

Arctic *adj* arktisch.

area *n* Fläche *f;* Gebiet *n.*

arena *n* Arena *f;* Schauplatz *m.*

argue *vi* argumentieren; streiten.

argument *n* Auseinandersetzung *f;* Argument *n.*

aria *n* Arie *f.*

Aries *n* (*astrol*) Widder *m.*

arise *vi* entstehen; sich erheben.

aristocracy *n* Aristokratie *f.*

aristocrat *n* Aristokrat(in) *m(f).*

aristocratic *adj* aristokratisch, adlig.

arithmetic *n* Rechnen *n.*

arithmetical *adj* arithmetisch.

ark *n* Arche *f.*

arm *n* Arm *m;* Waffe *f:—vt* sich waffnen.

armchair *n* Sessel *m.*

armed *adj* bewaffnet.

armistice *n* Waffenstillstand *m.*

armour *n* Rüstung *f;* Panzer *m.*

armpit *n* Achselhöhle *f.*

army *n* Armee *f;* Heer *n;* Militär *n.*

aroma *n* Duft *m.*

aromatic *adj* aromatisch.

around *prep* um… herum; etwa:—*adv* (rund)herum.

arouse *vt* (auf)wecken; erregen.

arrange *vt* (ein)richten.

arrangement *n* (An)Ordnung *f.*

arrest *n* Festnahme *f;* Aufhalten *n:—vt* aufhalten; festnehmen.

arrival *n* Ankunft *f.*

arrive *vi* ankommen.

arrogance *n* Überheblichkeit *f.*

arrogant *adj* überheblich.

arrow *n* Pfeil *m.*

arsenic *n* Arsen *n.*

arson *n* Brandstiftung *f.*

art *n* Kunst *f.*

artery *n* Schlagader *f.*

arthritis *n* Arthritis *f.*

artichoke *n* Artischocke *f.*

article *n* Artikel *m.*

artificial *adj* künstlich, Kunst-.

artillery *n* Artillerie *f.*

artist *n* Künstler(in) *m(f).*

artistic *adj* künstlerisch.

as *conj* (so) wie; als; obwohl; weil.

asbestos *n* Asbest *m.*

ascend *vi* (auf)steigen.

ascent *n* Aufstieg *m;* Besteigung *f.*

ash *n* (*bot*) Esche *f*

ashamed *adj* beschämt.

ashtray *n* Aschenbecher *m.*

ask *vt* fragen; bitten; verlangen:—~ **for** bitten um.

asleep *adj* schlafend:—**fall** ~ einschlafen.

asparagus *n* Spargel *m.*

aspect *n* Aspekt *m;* Aussehen *n;* Hinsicht *f.*

ass *n* Esel *m:—***she** ~ Eselin *f.*

assassin *n* Attentäter(in) *m(f).*

assassinate *vt* ermorden.

assassination *n* Attentat.

assault *n* Angriff *m:—vt* angreifen.

assemble *vt* versammeln:— *vi* sich versammeln.

assembly *n* Versammlung *f;* Montage *f.*

assent *n* Zustimmung *f:—vi* zustimmen.

assert *vt* behaupten; durchsetzen.

assertion *n* Behauptung *f.*

assess *vt* festsetzen; (ab)schätzen; besteuern.

assessment *n* (Ab) Schätzung *f;* Beurteilung *f.*

asset *n* Vorzug *m;* Gewinn *m;* Vermög-enswert *m:—* ~**s** *pl* Vermögen *n.*

assign *vt* zuweisen; bestimmen.

assignment *n* Zuweisung *f;* Bestimmung *f;* Aufgabe *f.*

assist *vt* helfen; unterstützen.

assistance *n* Hilfe *f;* Unterstützung *f.*

assistant *n* Assistent(in) *m(f);* Ange-stellte(r) *f(m).*

associate *vt* verbinden; anschließen: —*n* Partner *m*; Genosse *m*.

association *n* Vereinigung *f*; Verein *m*.

assume *vt* annehmen; voraussetzen; übernehmen; sich anmaßen.

assumption *n* Annahme *f*; Voraussetzung *f*; Anmaßung *f*.

assurance *n* Zusicherung *f*; Selbstsicherheit *f*.

assure *vt* (ver)sichern; zusichern; beruhigen.

asthma *n* Asthma *n*.

asthmatic *adj* asthmatisch.

astonish *vt* in Erstaunen setzen; verblüffen.

astonishing *adj* erstaunlich.

astonishment *n* (Er)Staunen *n*.

astound *vt* verblüffen; überraschen.

astrologer *n* Astrologe *m*.

astrological *adj* astrologisch.

astrology *n* Astrologie *f*.

astronaut *n* Astronaut *m*.

astronomer *n* Astronom *m*.

astronomical *adj* astronomisch.

astronomy *n* Astronomie *f*.

astute *adj* scharfsinnig; schlau.

at *prep* in; an; bei; zu; auf; nach; gegen; um; mit.

atheism *n* Atheismus *m*.

atheist *n* Atheist *m*.

athlete *n* (Leicht)Athlet(in) *m(f)*; Sportler(in) *m(f)*.

athletic *adj* Sport-; sportlich; muskulös.

atlas *n* Atlas *m*.

atmosphere *n* Atmosphäre *f*.

atmospheric *adj* Luft-; Wetter-; stimmungsvoll.

atom *n* Atom *n*.

atomic *adj* Atom-.

atrocious *adj* abscheulich; grauenhaft.

atrocity *n* Abscheulichkeit *f*; Greueltat *f*.

attach *vt* befestigen; beifügen; verbinden.

attaché *n* Attaché *m*.

attachment *n* Befestigung *f*; Anhängsel *n*; Zuneigung *f*; Zugehörigkeit *f*.

attack *vt* angreifen; in Angriff nehmen:—*n* Angriff *m*; Anfall *m*.

attacker *n* Angreifer(in) *m(f)*.

attain *vt* erreichen; erlangen.

attainable *adj* erreichbar.

attempt *vt* versuchen:—*n* Versuch *m*.

attend *vt vi* (be)achten; bedienen; teilnehmen an.

attendance *n* Dienst *m*; Bedienung *f*; Pflege *f*; Anwesenheit *f*.

attendant *n* Begleiter(in) *m(f)*; Diener (in) *m(f)*; Wart *m*.

attention *n* Aufmerksamkeit *f*; Beachtung *f*.

attentive *adj* aufmerksam.

attic *n* Dachgeschoß *n*; Mansarde *f*.

attitude *n* Haltung *f*; (Ein)Stellung *f*.

attract *vt* anziehen; gewinnen; erregen.

attraction *n* Anziehungskraft *f*; Attraktion *f*.

attractive *adj* anziehend; attraktiv.

auction *n* Versteigerung *f*.

audience *n* Publikum *n*; Audienz *f*; Gehör *n*.

augment *vt* vermehren; vergrößern: —*vi* zunehmen.

August *n* August *m*.

aunt *n* Tante *f*.

aura *n* Aura *f*.

auspicious *adj* günstig; glücklich.

austere *adj* streng; karg; hart.

austerity *n* Strenge *f*; Kargheit *f*.

authentic *adj* authentisch; echt.

authenticate *vt* beglaubigen; die Echtheit bescheinigen.

authenticity *n* Echtheit *f*; Glaubwürdigkeit *f*.

author(ess) *n* Urheber(in) *m(f)*; Ver-fasser(in) *m(f)*.

authoritarian *adj* autoritär.

authoritative *adj* herrisch; maßgebend.

authority *n* Autorität *f*; Vollmacht *f*.

authorize *vt* ermächtigen; genehmigen.

autograph *n* Autogramm *n*.

automated *adj* vollautomatisiert.

automatic *adj* automatisch.

automaton *n* Roboter *m*.

autonomy *n* Autonomie *f*; Selbständigkeit *f*.

autopsy *n* Autopsie *f*.

autumn *n* Herbst *m*.

auxiliary *adj* Hilfs-.

available *adj* verfügbar; vorhanden.

avalanche *n* Lawine *f*.

avarice *n* Geiz *m*.

avaricious *adj* geizig.

avenge *vt* rächen.

avenue *n* Weg *m*; Allee *f*.

average *vt* durchschnittlich betragen: —*n* Durchschnitt *m*.

aviary *n* Vogelhaus *n*.

avoid *vt* (ver)meiden.

avoidable *adj* vermeidbar.

await *vt* erwarten.

awake *vt* wecken:—*vi* aufwachen; erwachen:—*adj* wach; sich bewußt.

awakening *n* Erwachen *n*; Wecken *n*.

award *vt* zusprechen; verleihen:—*n* Urteil *n*; Zuerkennung *f*.

aware *adj* bewußt.

awareness *n* Bewußtsein *n*.

away *adv* weg; fort; entfernt.

awe *n* (Ehr)Furcht *f*.

awful *adj* furchtbar; schrecklich.

awkward *adj* ungeschickt; unangenehm; unhandlich.

axe *n* Axt *f*.

axiom *n* Axiom *n*.

axis *n* Achse *f*.

axle *n* Achse *f*.

B

baby *n* Baby *n.*

baboon *n* Pavian *m.*

bachelor *n* Bakkalaureus *m* Junggeselle *m.*

back *n* Rücken *m;* Rückseite *f:—adj* Hinter-; Rück-:—*adv* zurück:—*vt* unterstützen.

background *n* Hintergrund *m.*

backward *adj* Rück(wärts)-; rückständig:—**~s** *adv* rückwärts; zurück.

bacon *n* Speck *m.*

bad *adj* schlecht; böse; schlimm.

badge *n* Abzeichen *n.*

badger *n* Dachs *m.*

bag *n* Tasche *f;* Tüte *f.*

baggage *n* Gepäck *n.*

bagpipe *n* Dudelsack *m.*

bake *vt* backen; braten.

bakery *n* Bäckerei *f.*

baker *n* Bäcker *m.*

balance *n* Waage *f;* Gleichgewicht *n;* Kontostand *m:—vt* abwägen; balancieren; ausgleichen.

balance sheet *n* Bilanz *f.*

balcony *n* Balkon *m.*

bald *adj* kahl.

ball *n* Ball *m;* Kugel *f;* Ballen *m.*

ballet *n* Ballett *n.*

balloon *n* Ballon *m.*

ballroom *n* Ballsaal *m.*

bamboo *n* Bambus *m.*

ban *n* Verbot *n;* Sperre *f;*

Ächtung *f:* —*vt* verbieten; sperren.

banana *n* Banane *f.*

band *n* Gruppe *f;* Bande *f.*

bandage *n* Bandage *f.*

bandit *n* Bandit *m;* Räuber *m.*

bang *n* Knall *m:—vt* dröhnend (zu) schlagen; knallen; (an)stoßen.

bank *n* Bank *f;* Ufer *n.*

banker *n* Bankier *m.*

banking *n* Bankwesen n; Bankgeschäft *n.*

bankrupt *adj* bankrott:—*n* Bankrotteur *m.*

bankruptcy *n* Bankrott *m;* Konkurs *m.*

banner *n* Banner *n;* Standarte *f.*

banquet *n* Bankett *n;* Festessen *n.*

baptise *vt* taufen.

baptism *n* Taufe *f.*

bar *n* Stange *f;* Riegel *m:—* *vt* verriegeln; versperren.

barbarian *n* Barbar(in) *m(f):—adj* barbarisch.

barbaric *adj* barbarisch; grausam.

barbecue *n* Grillfest *n;* Grill *m.*

barber *n* (Herren)Friseur *m.*

bar code *n* Strichcode *m.*

bard *n* Barde *m.*

bare *adj* bloß; nackt; kahl.

barefoot *adj* barfuß.

barely *adv* kaum; knapp.

bargain *n* Geschäft *n;*

Sonderangebot *n:—vi* (ver)handeln.

baritone *n* Bariton *m.*

bark *n* Rinde *f;* Bellen *n:—* *vi* bellen.

barley *n* Gerste *f.*

barmaid *n* Bardame *f.*

barman *n* Barmann *m.*

barn *n* Scheune *f;* Stall *m.*

barometer *n* Barometer *n.*

baron(ess) *n* Baron(ess) *m(f).*

barrel *n* Faß *n.*

barren *adj* unfruchtbar; öde.

base *n* Basis *f;* Grundlage *f:—vt* stützen; gründen:— *adj* Grund-; gemein; niedrig; unecht.

basement *n* Keller(geschoß) *m(n).*

basic *adj* grundlegend; Grund-.

basin *n* Becken *n;* Schale *f.*

basis *n* Basis *f;* Grundlage *f.*

basket *n* Korb *m.*

basketball *n* Basketball *m.*

bass *n* (*mus*) Baß *m.*

bassoon *n* Fagott *n.*

bat *n* Fledermaus *f;* Schläger *m.*

bath *n* Bad *n.*

bathe *vt vi* baden.

bathroom *n* Badezimmer *n.*

bathtub *n* Badewanne *f.*

battalion *n* Bataillon *n.*

battery *n* Batterie *f.*

battle *n* Schlacht *f;* Kampf *m:—vi* kämpfen; streiten.

battlefield *n* Schlachtfeld *n*.

battleship *n* Schlachtschiff *n*.

bay *n* Bucht *f*.

bayonet *n* Bajonett *n*.

bazaar *n* Basar *m*.

be *vi* sein.

beach *n* Strand *m*.

beacon *n* Leuchtturm *m*; Leuchtfeuer *n*.

bead *n* Perle *f*; Tropfen *m*.

beak *n* Schnabel *m*.

beaker *n* Becher *m*.

beam *n* Strahl *m*; Balken *m*:—*vi* strahlen.

bean *n* Bohne *f*.

bear *n* Bär *m*:—**she** ~ Bärin *f*:—*vt vi* tragen.

bearable *adj* erträglich.

beard *n* Bart *m*.

beast *n* Tier *n*; Bestie *f*; Vieh *n*.

beat *vt vi* schlagen:—*n* Schlag *m*.

beautiful *adj* schön; wunderbar.

beauty *n* Schönheit *f*.

beaver *n* Biber *m*.

because *conj* weil; da.

become *vt* (an)stehen; sich schicken für:—*vi* werden.

bed *n* Bett *n*; Lager *n*; Beet *n*.

bedroom *n* Schlafzimmer *n*.

bedtime *n* Schlafenszeit *f*.

bee *n* Biene *f*.

beech *n* Buche *f*.

beef *n* Rindfleisch *n*; Mastrind *n*.

beehive *n* Bienenstock *m*.

beer *n* Bier *n*.

beet *n* Bete *f*; Runkelrübe *f*.

beetle *n* Käfer *m*.

before *adv* vorn; vorher:— *prep* vor: —*conj* bevor; ehe.

beg *vt* erbetteln; (er)bitten:—*vi* betteln; bitten.

beggar *n* Bettler(in) *m(f)*.

begin *vt vi* beginnen, anfangen.

beginner *n* Anfänger(in) *m(f)*.

beginning *n* Anfang *m*; Beginn *m*.

behalf *n*:—**on ~ of** im Namen von; im Auftrag von.

behave *vi* sich benehmen; sich verhalten.

behaviour *n* Benehmen *n*; Verhalten *n*.

behind *prep* hinter:—*adv* (nach) hinten; hinterher.

being *n* (Da)Sein *n*; Existenz *f*; Wesen *n*.

belfry *n* Glockenturm *m*.

belief *n* Glaube *m*.

believable *adj* glaubhaft.

believe *vt vi* glauben.

bell *n* Glocke *f*; Klingel *f*; Läuten *n*.

belly *n* Bauch *m*; Magen *m*.

belong *vi* gehören.

beloved *adj* geliebt.

below *adv* unten; hinunter; (dar)unter: —*prep* unter; unterhalb.

belt *n* Gürtel *m*; Gurt *m*; Riemen *m*.

bench *n* Bank *f*; Sitz *m*; Gericht *n*.

bend *vt* biegen; krümmen; beugen:—*vi* sich krümmen; sich (ver)beugen: — *n* Kurve *f*; Krümmung *f*.

beneficial *adj* nützlich; wohltuend; nutznießend.

benefit *n* Vorteil *m*; Nutzen *m*; Unterstützung *f*:—*vt* nützen; zugute kommen:—*vi* Nutzen ziehen.

bent *n* Neigung *f*; Hang *m*; Veranlagung *f*.

berry *n* Beere *f*.

beside(s) *prep* neben; dicht bei; außer(halb):—*adv* außerdem; sonst.

best *adj* beste(r, s); größte(r, s):—*adv* am besten; am meisten:—*n* (der, die, das) Beste *m/f/n*.

bestial *adj* tierisch; bestialisch; gemein.

bestiality *n* Bestialität *f*; Greueltat *f*.

bestow *vt* schenken; verleihen.

bestseller *n* Bestseller *m*.

bet *n* Wette *f*:—*vt* wetten.

betray *vt* verraten; hintergehen.

betrayal *n* Verrat *m*.

better *adj adv* besser:—*vt* verbessern; übertreffen.

between *prep* zwischen.

beware *vi* sich hüten; sich in acht nehmen.

beyond *prep* jenseits; außer; über… hinaus.

Bible *n* Bibel *f*.

biblical *adj* biblisch.

bibliography *n* Bibliographie *f*.

bicycle *n* Fahrrad *n*.

bid *vt* bieten; gebieten:—*n* Gebot *n*.

big *adj* groß.

bilingual *adj* zweisprachig.

bill *n* Schnabel *m*; Rechnung *f*.

billion *n* Milliarde *f*.

bin *n* Kasten *m*; Behälter *m*.

bind *vt* (ver)binden.

biographer *n* Biograph *m*.

biographical *adj* biographisch.

biography *n* Biographie *f*.

biological *adj* biologisch.
biology *n* Biologie *f*.
birch *n* Birke *f*.
bird *n* Vogel *m*.
birth *n* Geburt *f*;
   Abstammung *f*;
   Entstehung *f*.
birthday *n* Geburtstag *m*.
biscuit *n* Keks *m*.
bishop *n* Bischof *m*.
bit *n* Gebiß *n*.
bitch *n* Hündin *f*.
bite *vt* beißen:—*n* Biß *m*;
   Bissen *m*; Schärfe *f*.
bitter *adj* bitter; erbittert;
   scharf.
bitterness *n* Bitterkeit *f*;
   Erbitterung *f*.
bitumen *n* Bitumen *n*;
   Asphalt *m*.
bizarre *adj* bizarr; abson-
   derlich.
black *adj* schwarz; dunkel;
   düster:—*n* Schwarz *n*;
   Schwarze(r) *f(m)*.
blackberry *n* Brombeere *f*.
blackbird *n* Amsel *f*.
blackboard *n* Tafel *f*.
blacken *vt* schwärzen.
blackmail *n* Erpressung
   f:—*vt* erpressen.
black market *n*
   Schwarzmarkt *m*.
black pudding *n* Blutwurst
   f.
blacksmith *n* Schmied *m*.
bladder *n* Blase *f*.
blade *n* Klinge *f*; Blatt *n*;
   Halm *m*.
blame *vt* tadeln; die Schuld
   geben:—*n* Tadel *m*; Schuld
   f.
bland *adj* mild; verbindlich;
   fad; langweilig.
blank *adj* blank; leer;
   Blanko-; verblüfft:—*n*

Leere *f*; Lücke *f*.
blanket *n* Decke *f*.
blare *vi* schmettern; plär-
   ren; dröhnen; grell
   leuchten.
blaspheme *vt* lästern;
   schmähen.
blasphemous *adj*
   (gottes)lästerlich.
blasphemy *n* Blasphemie *f*;
   (Gottes)-Lästerung *f*.
blast *n* Windstoß *m*; Ton *m*;
   Explosion *f*; Sprengung *f*.
blatant *adj* lärmend; auf-
   dringlich; eklatant.
blaze *n* loderndes Feuer
   n:—*vi* lodern.
bleach *vt vi* bleichen:—*n*
   Bleichmittel *n*.
bleak *adj* öde; rauh.
bleat *n* Blöken *n*:—*vi*
   blöken.
bleed *vi* bluten:—*vt* zur
   Ader lassen; abzapfen.
blend *vt* mischen.
bless *vt* segnen.
blessing *n* Segen *m*.
blind *adj* blind:—*vt* (ver)
   blenden:—*n* Rolladen *m*.
blindness *n* Blindheit *f*.
blink *vi* blinzeln; zwinkern.
bliss *n* (Glück)Seligkeit *f*.
blissful *adj* (glück)selig.
blister *n* Blase *f*; Bläschen
   n:—*vi* Blasen werfen.
blitz *n* heftiger
   (Luft)Angriff *m*; Blitzkrieg
   m.
blizzard *n* Schneesturm *m*.
block *n* Block *m*; Klotz *m*;
   Verstopfung *f*:—*vt* sperren; blockieren; ver-
   stopfen.
blond(e) *adj* blond; hell:—*n*
   Blondine *f*.
blood *n* Blut *n*.

bloody *adj* blutig.
bloom, blossom *n* Blüte
   f:—*vi* (er)-blühen.
blow *vt vi* blasen; wehen:—
   ~ **up** sprengen:—*n* Blasen
   n; Schlag *m*.
blue *adj* blau.
bluebell *n* Glockenblume *f*;
   Sternhyazinthe *f*.
bluff *n* Bluff *m*:—*vt*
   bluffen.
blunt *adj* stumpf:—*vt* abs-
   tumpfen.
blur *n* Fleck *m*:—*vt* verwis-
   chen:—*vi* verschwimmen.
blush *n* Erröten *n*; Röte *f*:—
   vi erröten; rot werden.
boa *n* Boa *f*.
boar *n* Eber *m*:—**wild ~**
   Keiler *m*.
board *n* Brett *n*; Tisch *m*;
   Tafel *f*; Bord *m*:—*vt* an
   Bord gehen.
boast *vi* prahlen; sich rühmen:—*n* Prahlerei *f*.
boat *n* Boot *n*; Schiff *n*.
body *n* Körper *m*; Leiche *f*;
   Masse *f*.
bodyguard *n* Leibwächter
   m.
bog *n* Sumpf *m*.
boil *vt vi* kochen.
bold *adj* kühn; mutig.
bolt *n* Bolzen *m*; Riegel *m*.
bomb *n* Bombe *f*.
bond *n* Bund *m*;
   (Ver)Bindung *f*; Anleihe *f*.
bone *n* Knochen *m*.
book *n* Buch *n*.
bookkeeper *n*
   Buchhalter(in) *m(f)*.
bookkeeping *n*
   Buchhaltung *f*;
   Buchführung *f*.
bookshop *n* Buchhandlung
   f.

boost *n* Förderung *f*; Auftrieb *m*:—*vt* nachhelfen; steigern.

boot *n* Stiefel *m*; Kofferraum *m*.

booth *n* Bude *f*; Zelle *f*; Kabine *f*.

border *n* Rand *m*; Grenze *f*:—*vt* säumen; grenzen an.

bore *vt* langweilen; bohren:—*n* Langweiler *m*; Bohrung *f*.

boredom *n* Langeweile *f*.

boring *adj* langweilig.

born *adj* geboren; angeboren.

borrow *vt* borgen; leihen.

boss *n* Boß *m*; Chef *m*; Vorgesetzer *m*.

botanical *adj* botanisch.

botany *n* Botanik *f*.

both *adj* beide(r, s):—*conj* sowohl… als.

bottle *n* Flasche *f*.

bottom *n* Boden *m*; Unterseite *f*; Hintern *m*:—*adj* unterste(r, s); Grund-.

bounce *vi* aufprallen; springen:—*n* Aufprall *m*; Sprung *m*.

bound *n* Grenze *f*; Sprung *m*:—*adj* gebunden; verpflichtet.

boundary *n* Grenze *f*.

bouquet *n* Blumenstrauß *m*.

bovine *adj* Rinder-.

bow *vt* biegen; beugen:—*vi* sich (ver)beugen:—*n* Verbeugung *f*; *n* Bogen *m*.

bowl *n* Schüssel *f*; Schale *f*; Napf *m*, Becken *n*.

bowling *n* Bowling *n*; Kegeln *n*.

box *n* Kiste *f*; Kasten *m*; Dose *f*:—*vi* boxen.

boxer *n* Boxer *m*.

boxing *n* Boxen *n*.

box office *n* Kasse *f*.

boy *n* Junge *m*.

boyfriend *n* Freund *m*.

bra *n* BH *m*.

bracket *n* Klammer *f*.

brain *n* Gehirn *n*; Verstand *m*.

brake *n* Bremse *f*:—*vt vi* bremsen.

branch *n* Zweig *m*; Zweigstelle *f*.

brand *n* Marke *f*; Art *f*; Brand *m*.

brandy *n* Weinbrand *m*.

brass *n* Messing *n*.

brave *adj* mutig; tapfer.

bravery *n* Mut *m*; Tapferkeit *f*.

bread *n* Brot *n*.

breadcrumbs *npl* Paniermehl *n*.

breadth *n* Breite *f*.

break *vt vi* brechen.

breakdown *n* Panne *f*; Zusammenbruch *m*.

breakfast *n* Frühstück *n*.

breast *n* Brust *f*.

breath *n* Atem(zug) *m*.

breathe *vt vi* atmen.

breeze *n* Brise *f*.

brew *vt* brauen:—*n* Gebräu *n*.

brewer *n* Brauer *m*.

brewery *n* Brauerei *f*.

bribe *n* Bestechung *f*:—*vt* bestechen.

bribery *n* Bestechung *f*.

brick *n* Ziegelstein *m*.

bride *n* Braut *f*.

bridegroom *n* Bräutigam *m*.

bridesmaid *n* Brautjungfer *f*.

bridge *n* Brücke *f*.

bridle *n* Zaum *m*:—*vt* zäumen; zügeln.

brief *adj* kurz; knapp.

bright *adj* hell; leuchtend.

brighten *vi* sich aufhellen; aufleuchten.

brightness *n* Helligkeit *f*; Glanz *m*.

brilliant *adj* leuchtend; glänzend.

bring *vt* (mit)bringen.

brink *n* Rand *m*; Ufer *n*.

broad *adj* breit; weit.

broadbean *n* Saubohne *f*.

broadcast *n* Übertragung *f*; Sendung *f*:—*vt vi* senden; übertragen.

broaden *vt vi* verbreitern; erweitern.

broccoli *n* Brokkoli *m*.

brochure *n* Broschüre *f*; Prospekt *m*.

broken *adj* gebrochen; kaputt.

broker *n* Makler *m*; Vermittler *m*.

bronze *n* Bronze *f*:—*vt* bronzieren.

brook *n* Bach *m*.

broom *n* Besen *m*; (Besen)Ginster *m*.

broth *n* Suppe *f*; Brühe *f*.

brothel *n* Bordell *n*.

brother *n* Bruder *m*.

brother-in-law *n* Schwager *m*.

brotherly *adj* brüderlich.

brow *n* Braue *f*; Stirn *f*.

brown *adj* braun.

brush *n* Bürste *f*; Pinsel *m*:—*vt* bürsten.

Brussels sprouts *npl* Rosenkohl *m*.

brutal *adj* brutal; roh.

bubble *n* (Seifen)Blase *f*; Schwindel *m*:—*vi* sprudeln; brodeln.

bucket *n* Eimer *m*; Kübel *m*; Schaufel *f*.

bud *n* Knospe *f*; Auge *n*; Keim *m*:—*vi* knospen; keimen; heranreifen.

Buddhism *n* Buddhismus *m*.

buddy *n* Kumpel *m*; Kamerad *m*.

budge *vi* sich rühren; sich bewegen.

budgerigar *n* Wellensittich *m*.

budget *n* Budget *n*; Etat *m*; Haushaltsplan *m*; Finanzen *pl*.

buffalo *n* Büffel *m*; Bison *m*.

buffer *n* Puffer *m*; Prellbock *m*.

buffoon *n* Possenreißer *m*; Hanswurst *m*.

bug *n* Wanze *f*; Insekt *n*; Bazillus *m*; Fanatiker(in) *m(f)*; Defekt *m*.

build *vt* (er)bauen; errichten; aufbauen.

builder *n* Erbauer *m*; Bauunternehmer *m*; Bauhandwerker *m*.

building *n* Gebäude *n*; (Er)Bauen *n*; Bau *m*.

bulb *n* Knolle *f*; Zwiebel *f*; Kugel *f*; (Glüh)Birne *f*.

bulk *n* Masse *f*; Umfang *m*; Volumen *n*:—**in ~** lose; in großen Mengen.

bull *n* Bulle *m*; Stier *m*.

bulldog *n* Bulldogge *f*.

bulldozer *n* Planierraupe *f*.

bullet *n* Kugel *f*.

bullfight *n* Stierkampf *m*.

bullfighter *n* Stierkämpfer *m*.

bullring *n* Stierkampfarena *f*.

bully *n* Schläger *m*; brutaler Kerl *m*: —*vt* tyrannisieren.

bum *n* Hintern *m*; Herumtreiber *m*; Tippelbruder *m*.

bump *n* heftiger Stoß *m*; Beule *f*.

bun *n* süßes Brötchen; (Haar)Knoten *m*.

bundle *n* Bündel *n*:—*vt* bündeln.

bungalow *n* Bungalow *m*.

bunk *n* Koje *f*.

bunker *n* Bunker *m*.

buoy *n* Boje *f*; Bake *f*.

buoyant *adj* schwimmend; lebhaft.

burden *n* Last *f*; Ladung *f*; Bürde *f*:—*vt* belasten.

bureau *n* Schreibpult *n*; Büro *n*; Amt *n*.

bureaucracy *n* Bürokratie *f*.

bureaucrat *n* Bürokrat *m*.

burglar *n* Einbrecher *m*.

burglary *n* Einbruch *m*.

burial *n* Begräbnis *n*; Beerdigung *f*.

burn *vt vi* (ver)brennen:—*n* Verbrennung *f*; verbrannte Stelle *f*.

burner *n* Brenner *m*.

burning *adj* brennend; glühend.

burrow *n* Bau *m*; Höhle *f*:— *vi* graben; sich vergraben.

bursar *n* Quästor *m*; Finanzverwalter *m*.

burst *vi* bersten; platzen:— *n* Platzen *n*; (Aus)Bruch *m*; Stoß *m*.

bury *vt* vergraben;

begraben; beerdigen.

bus *n* Bus *m*; Omnibus *m*.

bush *n* Busch *m*, Strauch *m*; Gebüsch *n*; Schopf *m*.

business *n* Geschäft *n*; Arbeit *f*; Unternehmen *n*; Sache *f*; Angelegenheit *f*.

businessman *n* Geschäftsmann *m*.

businesswoman *n* Geschäftsfrau *f*.

bus-stop *n* Bushaltestelle *f*.

bust *n* Büste *f*; Busen *m*.

busy *adj* beschäftigt; belebt; arbeitsreich.

but *conj* aber, jedoch; sondern.

butcher *n* Metzger *m*, Fleischer *m*, Schlachter *m*:—*vt* (ab)schlachten.

butcher's *n* Metzgerei *f*.

butler *n* Butler *m*.

butter *n* Butter *f*:—*vt* buttern.

buttercup *n* Butterblume *f*.

butterfly *n* Schmetterling *m*.

button *n* Knopf *m*; Taste *f*:—*vt* (zu)-knöpfen.

buy *vt* (ein)kaufen.

buyer *n* (Ein)Käufer(in) *m(f)*.

buzz *n* Summen *n*; Schwirren *n*:—*vi* summen; schwirren.

by *prep* bei; an; neben; durch; nach; von; mit; um.

by-law *n* Satzung *f*; Ortsstatut.

bypass *n* Umgehungsstraße *f*.

by-product *n* Nebenprodukt *n*.

byte *n* Byte *n*.

C

cab *n* Taxi *n*; Führerhaus *n*.

cabbage *n* Kohl *m*.

cabin *n* Hütte *f*; Kabine *f*.

cabinet *n* Kabinett *n*; Schrank *m*.

cable *n* Kabel *n*; Tau *n*.

cable car *n* Seilbahn *f*.

cactus *n* Kaktus *m*.

café *n* Café *n*.

cafeteria *n* Cafeteria *f*; Kantine *f*.

cage *n* Käfig *m*; Förderkorb *m*.

cake *n* Kuchen *m*, Torte *f*.

calculate *vt* berechnen; kalkulieren.

calculation *n* Berechnung *f*; Kalkulation *f*.

calculator *n* Rechner *m*.

calendar *n* Kalender *m*.

calf *n* Kalb *n*; Wade *f*.

call *vt* (an)rufen; (ein)berufen:—*n* Ruf *m*; Anruf *m*; Berufung *f*.

calm *n* Ruhe *f*; Stille *f*:—*adj* ruhig; still:—*vt* beruhigen; besänftigen.

calorie *n* Kalorie *f*.

camel *n* Kamel *n*.

camera *n* Kamera *f*.

camouflage *n* Tarnung *f*; Verschleierung *f*.

camp *n* Lager *n*:—*vi* kampieren; lagern; zelten.

campaign *n* Kampagne *f*; Wahlkampf *m*.

camping *n* Zelten *n*; Camping *n*.

campsite *n* Lagerplatz *m*; Zeltplatz *m*.

can *v aux* können:—*vt* eindosen:—*n* Kanne *f*; Dose *f*.

canal *n* Kanal *m*.

cancel *vt* kündigen.

cancellation *n* Kündigung *f*.

cancer, Cancer (*astrol*) *n* Krebs *m*.

candidate *n* Kandidat(in) *m(f)*; Be-werber(in) *m(f)*.

candle *n* Kerze *f*.

cane *n* Rohr *n*; (Spazier)Stock *m*.

canine *adj* Hunde-; hündisch.

cannabis *n* Cannabis *m*; Haschisch *n*.

cannibal *n* Kannibale *m*.

cannibalism *n* Kannibalismus *m*.

cannon *n* Kanone *f*; Geschütz *n*.

canoe *n* Kanu *n*.

canon *n* Kanon *m*.

canopy *n* Baldachin *m*.

canteen *n* Kantine *f*; Feldflasche *f*.

canter *n* Arbeitsgalopp *m*.

canvas *n* Segeltuch *n*; (Zelt)Leinwand *f*.

canyon *n* Felsschlucht *f*.

cap *n* Mütze *f*.

capable *adj* fähig; tüchtig; imstande.

capacity *n* Kapazität *f*; Fähigkeit *f*; Leistung *f*.

cape *n* Umhang *m*; Cape *n*; Kap *n*.

capital *adj* kapital; Haupt-; groß(artig): —*n* Hauptstadt *f*; Großbuchstabe *m*; Kapital *n*.

capitalism *n* Kapitalismus *m*.

capitalist *n* Kapitalist *m*.

Capricorn *n* (*astrol*) Steinbock *m*.

captain *n* Kapitän *m*; Hauptmann *m*.

capture *n* Gefangennahme *f*:—*vt* gefangennehmen.

car *n* Auto *n*; Wagen *m*.

caravan *n* Karawane *f*; Wohnwagen *m*.

carbon *n* Kohlenstoff *m*; Kohle *f*; Kohlepapier *n*.

card *n* Karte *f*.

care *n* Sorge *f*; Sorgfalt *f*; Pflege *f*:—*vi* sich sorgen.

career *n* Karriere *f*; Beruf *m*:—*vi* rasen, rennen.

careful *adj* vorsichtig; sorgfältig.

careless *adj* unvorsichtig; sorglos.

caress *n* Liebkosung *f*:—*vt* liebkosen; streicheln.

caretaker *n* Hausmeister(in) *m(f)*.

car-ferry *n* Autofähre *f*.

cargo *n* Fracht *f*; Ladung *f*.

carnation *n* Nelke *f*; Blaßrot *n*.

carnival *n* Karneval *m*; Fasching *m*; Volksfest *n*.

carol *n* Weihnachtslied *n*.

carpenter *n* Zimmermann *m*; Tischler *m*.

carpentry *n* Zimmerei *f*; Zimmerhandwerk *n*.

carpet *n* Teppich *m*.

carriage *n* Wagen *m*; Kutsche *f*; Transport *m*; Fracht *f*.

carrot *n* Karotte *f*; Möhre *f*.

carry *vi vt* tragen:—~ **on** weitermachen; fortsetzen.

cart *n* Karre *f*; Karren *m*; Wagen *m*:—*vt* karren.

carton *n* Karton *m*; Schachtel *f*.

cartoon *n* Cartoon *m*; Zeichentrickfilm *m*.

carve *vt* schnitzen; tranchieren.

case *n* Kiste *f*; Koffer *m*; Behälter *m*; Gehäuse *n*; Fall *m*; Sache *f*; **in ~** im Falle.

cash *n* Bargeld *n*:—*vt* einlösen; zu Geld machen.

casino *n* Kasino *n*.

cassette *n* Kassette *f*.

cast *vt* werfen; gießen:—*n* Wurf *m*; Besetzung *f*; Guß *m*.

castle *n* Schloß *n*; Burg *f*; Turm *m*.

casual *adj* zufällig; gelegentlich.

casualty *n* Unfall *m*; Opfer *n*.

cat *n* Katze *f*.

catalogue *n* Katalog *m*.

catastrophe *n* Katastrophe *f*.

catch *vt* (ein)fangen:—*n* Fang *m*; Fangen *n*.

category *n* Kategorie *f*.

caterpillar *n* Raupe *f*.

cathedral *n* Kathedrale *f*; Dom *m*.

catholic *adj* katholisch:—*n* Katho-lik(in) *m(f)*.

Catholicism *n* Katholizismus *m*.

cattle *n* Vieh *n*.

cauliflower *n* Blumenkohl *m*.

cause *n* Ursache *f*; Grund *m*:—*vt* verursachen.

caution *n* Vorsicht *f*; Verwarnung *f*.

cautious *adj* vorsichtig; achtsam.

cave *n* Höhle *f*.

cavern *n* Höhle *f*.

cease *vt vi* aufhören.

ceasefire *n* Waffenruhe *f*.

cedar *n* Zeder *f*.

cede *vt* abtreten; überlassen.

ceiling *n* Decke *f*.

celebrate *vt* feiern.

celebration *n* Feier *f*; Verherrlichung *f*.

celebrity *n* Berühmtheit *f*; Ruhm *m*.

celery *n* Sellerie *m*.

cell *n* Zelle *f*.

cellar *n* (Wein)Keller *m*.

cello *n* Cello *n*.

cement *n* Zement *m*; Mörtel *m*; Kitt *m*.

cemetery *n* Friedhof *m*.

censor *n* Zensor *m*.

censorship *n* Zensur *f*.

centenary *n* Jahrhundert *n*; hundertjähriges Jubiläum *n*.

centre *n* Zentrum *n*; Mitte *f*; Mittelpunkt *m*; Zentrale *f*.

centigrade *adj* Celsius.

centilitre *n* Zentiliter *m*.

centimetre *n* Zentimeter *m*.

centipede *n* Hundertfüßer *m*.

central *adj* zentral; Haupt-.

century *n* Jahrhundert *n*.

ceramic *adj* keramisch.

ceremony *n* Zeremonie *f*.

certain *adj* sicher; bestimmt; gewiß.

certainty *n* Sicherheit *f*; Bestimmtheit *f*.

certificate *n* Bescheinigung *f*; Urkunde *f*.

certify *vt* bescheinigen; beglaubigen.

chain *n* Kette *f*:—*vt* (an)ketten.

chair *n* Stuhl *m*; Sessel *m*; Vorsitz *m*.

chairman *n* Vorsitzender *m*.

chalk *n* Kreide *f*; Kalk *m*.

challenge *n* Herausforderung *f*:—*vt* herausfordern.

chamber *n* Kammer *f*; Zimmer *n*.

champagne *n* Sekt *m*.

champion *n* Sieger *m*; Meister *m*.

championship *n* Meisterschaft *f*.

chance *n* Chance *f*; Zufall *m*:—**by ~** zufällig.

chancellor *n* Kanzler *m*.

change *vt* (ver)ändern; wechseln:—*vi* sich (ver)ändern; wechseln; sich umziehen:—*n* (Ver)Änderung *f*; Wechsel *m*; Wechselgeld *n*.

channel *n* Kanal *m*; Rinne *f*.

chaos *n* Chaos *n*; Durcheinander *n*.

chaotic *adj* chaotisch.

chapel *n* Kapelle *f*; Gottesdienst *m*.

chapter *n* Kapitel *n*.

character *n* Charakter *m*; Figur *f*; Rolle *f*; Buchstabe *m*.

charge *vt* (be)laden; beauf-tragen; anklagen; belas-ten:—*n* Ladung *f*; Belastung *f*; Angriff *m*; Anklage *f*.

charity *n* Nächstenliebe *f*; Wohltätigkeit *f*.

charm *n* Charme *m*; Zauber *m*; Talis-mann *m*:—*vt* bezaubern; verzaubern.

charming *adj* bezaubernd; charmant.

chart *n* Tabelle *f*; Karte *f*; Schaubild *n*.

charter *n* Urkunde *f*; Freibrief *m*; Charta *f*; Chartern *n*:—*vt* chartern.

chase *vt* jagen; verfolgen:— *n* Jagd *f*; Verfolgung *f*.

chat *vi* plaudern:—*n* Plauderei *f*; Schwätzchen *n*.

chatter *vi* schnattern; klap-pern:—*n* Geschnatter *n*; Klappern *n*.

cheap *adj* billig; preiswert; schäbig; ordinär.

cheapen *vt* verbilligen; her-absetzen.

cheat *vt vi* betrügen:—*n* Betrüger(in) *m(f)*.

check *vt* überprüfen; kon-trollieren; Schach bieten:—*n* Schach *n*; Hindernis *n*; Kontrolle *f*; Karo(muster) *n*.

checkmate *n* Matt *n*.

cheek *n* Wange *f*.

cheekbone *n* Wangenknochen *m*.

cheer *n* Beifall *m*; Aufmunterung *f*:—*vt* Beifall spenden; auf-muntern.

cheerful *adj* fröhlich; fre-undlich.

cheese *n* Käse *m*.

chef *n* Küchenchef *m*.

chemical *adj* chemisch.

chemist *n* Chemiker(in) *m(f)*; Apo-theker(in) *m(f)*; Drogist(in) *m(f)*.

chemistry *n* Chemie *f*.

cheque *n* Scheck *m*.

cherish *vt* (wert)schätzen; in Ehren halten; hegen; zugetan sein.

cherry *n* Kirsche *f*; Kirschrot *n*:—*adj* kirschrot:—~ **tree** *n* Kirschbaum *m*.

chess *n* Schach *n*.

chessboard *n* Schachbrett *n*.

chessman *n* Schachfigur *f*.

chest *n* Truhe *f*; Kiste *f*; Kasten *m*; Brust *f*.

chestnut *n* Kastanie *f*; Kastanienbraun *n*.

chestnut tree *n* Kastanienbaum *m*.

chew *vt* kauen; sinnen.

chewing gum *n* Kaugummi *m*.

chicken *n* Huhn *n*; Hähnchen *n*.

chief *adj* wichtigste(r, s); hauptsächlich; Haupt-; oberste(r, s):—~**ly** *adv* hauptsächlich; vor allem:—*n* Chef *m*; (Ober)Haupt *n*; Häuptling *m*.

child *n* Kind *n*.

childhood *n* Kindheit *f*.

childish *adj* kindisch.

childless *adj* kinderlos.

childlike *adj* kindlich.

chimney *n* Schornstein *m*; Kamin *m*.

chimpanzee *n* Schimpanse *m*.

chin *n* Kinn *n*.

china(ware) *n* Porzellan *n*.

chip *n* Splitter *m*; Schnitzel *n*:—~**s** *npl* Pommes frites *pl*.

chocolate *n* Schokolade *f*; Praline *f*; Schokoladenbraun *n*.

choice *n* (Aus)Wahl *f*; Auslese *f*:—*adj* ausge-sucht; wählerisch.

choir *n* Chor *m*.

choke *vt* (er)würgen; ersticken.

choose *vt* (aus)wählen; aus-suchen; vorziehen.

chop *vt* (zer)hacken:—*n* Hieb *m*; Schlag *m*; Kotelett *n*.

choral *adj* Chor-.

chord *n* Saite *f*; Akkord *m*.

Christ *n* Christus *m*.

christen *vt* taufen.

christening *n* Taufe *f*.

Christian *adj* christlich:—*n* Christ(in) *m(f)*:—~ **name** Vorname *m*.

Christianity *n* Christentum *n*; Christenheit *f*.

Christmas *n* Weihnachten *n*.

Christmas Eve *n* Heiligabend *m*.

chronic *adj* chronisch.

chronicle *n* Chronik *f*.

chronology *n* Chronologie *f*.

church *n* Kirche *f*.

cider *n* Apfelwein *m*; Apfelmost *m*.

cigar *n* Zigarre *f*.

cigarette *n* Zigarette *f*.

cinema *n* Kino *n*.

cinnamon *n* Zimt *m*.

circle *n* Kreis *m*.

circuit *n* Kreislauf *m*; Stromkreis *m*.

circular *adj* kreisförmig; rund:—*n* Rundschreiben *n*.

circulate *vi* im Umlauf sein; kursieren; kreisen.

circulation *n* Zirkulation *f*; Kreislauf *m*; Umlauf *m*.

circumstance *n* Umstand *m*; Sachverhalt *m*:—~s *pl* Verhältnisse *npl*.

circus *n* Zirkus *m*.

citizen *n* Bürger(in) *m(f)*.

city *n* (Groß)Stadt *f*.

civil *adj* staatlich; Bürger-; bürgerlich; zivil(rechtlich).

civilian *n* Zivilist *m*.

civilization *n* Zivilisation *f*.

civilize *vt* zivilisieren.

claim *vt* fordern; beanspruchen; in Anspruch nehmen; behaupten:—*n* Forderung *f*; Anspruch *m*; Behauptung *f*.

clam *n* Muschel *f*.

clamber *vi* klettern.

clap *vt* klatschen; schlagen; klopfen.

clarification *n* Klärung *f*.

clarify *vt* (er)klären; klarstellen.

clarinet *n* Klarinette *f*.

clarity *n* Klarheit *f*.

clash *vi* klirren; zusammen-stoßen:—*n* Geklirr *n*; Zusammenstoß *m*.

class *n* Klasse *f*; Kurs *m*:—*vt* klassifizieren.

classic(al) *adj* klassisch; erstklassig: —*n* Klassiker *m*.

classification *n* Klassifikation *f*.

classify *vt* klassifizieren.

classroom *n* Klassenzimmer *n*.

clause *n* Klausel *f*; Abschnitt *m*; Satz *m*.

claw *n* Klaue *f*; Kralle *f*:—*vt*

(zer)-kratzen; krallen; packen.

clay *n* Lehm *m*; Ton *m*.

clean *adj* sauber; rein:—*vt* reinigen; säubern.

cleaner *n* Reinigung *f*; Reinigungsmittel *n*; Raumpfleger(in) *m(f)*.

clear *adj* klar; hell:—*vt* (auf)klären; (weg)räu-men:—*vi* sich klären; sich aufhellen.

clef *n* (Noten)Schlüssel *m*.

clever *adj* klug.

click *vt* klicken; schnalzen:—*vi* klicken; schnalzen; zuschnappen.

client *n* Kunde *m*, Kundin *f*; Klient(in) *m(f)*.

cliff *n* Klippe *f*; Felswand *f*.

climate *n* Klima *n*.

climax *n* Höhepunkt *m*.

climb *vt* erklettern; besteigen:—*vi* klettern; steigen.

clinic *n* Klinik *f*.

clip *vt* (be)schneiden:—*n* Klammer *f*; Schur *f*.

cloak *n* Umhang *m*; (Deck)Mantel *m*.

cloakroom *n* Garderobe *f*.

clock *n* Uhr *f*.

close *vt vi* schließen:—*adj* dicht; eng: —*adv* nahe.

closed *adj* geschlossen.

cloth *n* Tuch *n*.

clothe *vt* kleiden; einhüllen.

clothing *n* Kleidung *f*.

cloud *n* Wolke *f*.

cloudy *adj* bewölkt; Wolken-.

clover *n* Klee *m*.

clown *n* Clown *m*.

club *n* Keule *f*; Knüppel *m*; Schläger *m*; Klub *m*.

clue *n* Hinweis *m*;

Anhaltspunkt *m*.

clumsy *adj* ungeschickt; unbeholfen.

coach *n* Reisebus *m*; Kutsche *f*; Trainer *m*; Nachhilfelehrer *m*:—*vt* trainieren.

coal *n* Kohle *f*.

coalmine *n* Kohlenbergwerk *n*.

coarse *adj* grob.

coast *n* Küste *f*.

coastal *adj* Küsten-.

coat *n* Mantel *m*; Schicht *f*:—*vt* beschichten.

coax *vt* überreden.

cobweb *n* Spinnwebe *f*.

cock *n* Hahn *m*.

cocktail *n* Cocktail *m*.

cocoa *n* Kakao *m*.

coconut *n* Kokosnuß *f*.

cocoon *n* Kokon *m*.

cod *n* Kabeljau *m*.

coffee *n* Kaffee *m*.

coffeepot *n* Kaffeekanne *f*.

coffin *n* Sarg *m*.

cog *n* Zahnrad *n*.

coil *n* Rolle *f*; Spirale *f*.

coin *n* Münze *f*:—*vt* münzen; prägen.

coincide *vi* zusammen-reffen.

cold *adj* kalt; kühl:—*n* Kälte *f*; Erkältung *f*.

collaborate *vt* zusamme-narbeiten; kollaborieren.

collaboration *n* Zusammenarbeit *f*; Kollaboration *f*.

collapse *vi* zusammen-brechen:—*n* Zusammenbruch *m*.

collar *n* Kragen *m*.

colleague *n* Kollege *m*, Kollegin *f*; Mitarbeiter(in) *m(f)*.

collect *vt* (ein)sammeln;
abholen; versammeln.

collection *n* (An)Sammlung
f; Kollektion *f*.

collide *vi* kollidieren;
zusammenstoßen.

collision *n* Zusammenstoß
m; Kollision *f*.

colloquial *adj*
umgangssprachlich.

colon *n* Doppelpunkt *m*.

colonel *n* Oberst *m*.

colony *n* Kolonie *f*;
Siedlung *f*.

colossal *adj* kolossal; riesig.

colour *n* Farbe *f*.

colourful *adj* farben-
prächtig; bunt.

colt *n* Fohlen *n*.

column *n* Spalte *f*;
Kolonne *f*.

comb *n* Kamm *m*; Wabe *f*;
Striegel *m*: —*vt*
(durch)kämmen; striegeln.

combat *n* Kampf *m*;
Gefecht *n*:—*vt*
(be)kämpfen.

combination *n* Kombination
f; Verbindung *f*;
Vereinigung *f*.

combine *vt* verbinden; kombinieren: —*vi* sich vereinigen; sich verbünden.

come *vi* kommen.

comedy *n* Komödie *f*.

comet *n* Komet *m*.

comfortable *adj* bequem.

comic(al) *adj* komisch.

comma *n* (*gr*) Komma *n*.

command *vt* befehlen
beherrschen:—*n* Befehl *m*;
Beherrschung *f*.

commander *n* Befehlshaber
m; Kommandant *m*.

commemorate *vt* gedenken;
feiern; erinnern an.

commemoration *n*
Gedenkfeier *f*; Geden-
ken *n*.

commence *vt vi* beginnen;
anfangen.

comment *n* Kommentar *m*;
Bemerkung *f*:—*vt*
bemerken:—*vi* kommen-
tieren.

commentary *n* Kommentar
m.

commerce *n* Handel *m*;
Verkehr *m*.

commercial *adj* Handels-;
kommerziell.

commission *n* Auftrag *m*;
Provision *f*: —*vt* beauf-
tragen.

commit *vt* anvertrauen;
verpflichten.

commitment *n*
Verpflichtung *f*; Überant-
wortung *f*.

committee *n* Komitee *n*;
Ausschuß *m*.

common *adj* gemeinsam;
all(gemein): —*n*
Gemeinsamkeit *f*;
Gemeindeland *n*.

communicate *vt* mitteilen;
übertragen:—*vi* kommu-
nizieren.

communication *n*
Kommunikation *f*;
Mitteilung *f*.

communism *n*
Kommunismus *m*.

communist *n*
Kommunist(in) *m(f)*.

community *n*
Gemeinschaft *f*.

compact *adj* kompakt.

compact disc *n* Compact
Disc *f*.

companion *n* Begleiter(in)
m(f).

company *n* Gesellschaft *f*;
Firma *f*.

comparable *adj* vergleichbar.

compare *vt* vergleichen.

comparison *n* Vergleich *m*.

compartment *n* Abteil *n*;
Abteilung *f*.

compassion *n* Mitleid *n*;
Mitgefühl *n*.

compassionate *adj* mitfüh-
lend; mitleidig.

compel *vt* (er)zwingen;
(ab)nötigen.

compensate *vt* entschädigen.

compensation *n*
Entschädigung *f*.

compete *vi* in Wettbewerb
treten; konkurrieren.

competence *n* Kompetenz
f; Fähigkeit *f*.

competent *adj* fähig;
fachkundig; gekonnt.

competition *n* Wettbewerb
m; Konkurrenz *f*.

competitive *adj* konkurri-
erend; Wettbewerbs-.

competitor *n*
Mitbewerber(in) *m(f)*;
Konkurrent(in) *m(f)*.

compile *vt* zusammen-
stellen; kompilieren.

complain *vi* sich beschw-
eren; klagen; beanstanden.

complaint *n* Beschwerde(n)
f(pl); Klage *f*; Reklamation
f.

complete *adj* vollständig;
völlig:—*vt* vollenden.

completion *n* Beendigung
f; Vervollständigung *f*.

complex *adj* komplex;
vielschichtig.

complicate *vt* kompli-
zieren.

complicated *adj* kompliziert.

compliment *n* Kompliment *n*; Lob *n*: —*vt* ein Kompliment machen.

complimentary *adj* Höflichkeits-; Frei-; Gratis-.

compose *vt* zusammensetzen; verfassen.

composer *n* Komponist(in) *m(f)*.

composition *n* Komposition *f*; Zusammensetzung *f*.

comprehensive *adj* umfassend.

compress *vt* zusammenpressen.

compulsion *n* Zwang *m*.

compulsory *adj* Zwangs-; obligatorisch.

computer *n* Computer *m*.

conceal *vt* verbergen.

conceit *n* Einbildung *f*; Selbstgefälligkeit *f*.

conceited *adj* eingebildet; selbstgefällig.

conceive *vt* sich vorstellen; ausdenken:—*vi* schwanger werden; trächtig werden.

concentrate *vt* konzentrieren.

concentration *n* Konzentration *f*.

concept *n* Vorstellung *f*; Begriff *m*.

concern *vt* betreffen; beunruhigen; beschäftigen:—*n* Angelegenheit *f*.

concerning *prep* betreffend; hinsichtlich.

concert *n* Konzert *n*.

concerto *n* Konzert *n*.

concise *adj* kurz; bündig; knapp.

conclude *vt* beenden; (ab)schließen; entscheiden.

conclusion *n* (Ab)Schluß *m*; Ende *n*; Entscheidung *f*.

concrete *n* Beton *m*.

condemn *vt* verurteilen; verdammen; verwerfen.

condense *vt* kondensieren; kürzen; zusammenfassen.

condition *n* Bedingung *f*; Abmachung *f*; Zustand *m*; Lage *f*.

conditional *adj* bedingt; abhängig; konditional.

condom *n* Kondom *n*.

conduct *n* (Durch)Führung *f*:—*vt* (durch)führen.

conductor *n* Schaffner *m*; Dirigent *m*.

cone *n* Kegel *m*; Zapfen *m*.

confer *vi* sich beraten:—*vt* verleihen; erteilen.

conference *n* Konferenz *f*; Besprechung *f*.

confess *vt vi* gestehen; zugeben.

confession *n* Geständnis *n*.

confidence *n* Vertrauen *n*; Selbstbewußtsein *n*.

confident *adj* gewiß; (selbst)sicher; zuversichtlich.

confidential *adj* vertraulich; Vertrauens-.

confine *vt* begrenzen; beschränken; einsperren.

confirm *vt* bestätigen; festigen.

confirmation *n* Bestätigung *f*; Festigung *f*.

conflict *n* Konflikt *m*; Kampf *m*.

conform *vt vi* (sich) anpassen; übereinstimmen.

confuse *vt* verwechseln; verwirren.

confusing *adj* verwirrend.

confusion *n* Verwirrung *f*; Verwechslung *f*.

congested *adj* überfüllt; verstopft.

congestion *n* Stauung *f*; Stockung *f*; Andrang *m*.

congratulate *vt* gratulieren; beglückwünschen.

congratulation *n* Glückwunsch *m*.

congregate *vt* (sich) (ver)sammeln.

congregation *n* Versammlung *f*.

congress *n* Kongreß *m*.

conjugate *vt* (*gr*) konjugieren.

conjugation *n* Konjugation *f*.

conjunction *n* Verbindung *f*; Konjunktion *f*.

connect *vt* verbinden; verknüpfen.

connection *n* Verbindung *f*; Zusammenhang *m*.

connoisseur *n* Kenner *m*.

conquer *vt* erobern; besiegen; unterwerfen; überwinden.

conqueror *n* Eroberer *m*; Sieger *m*.

conquest *n* Eroberung *f*; Überwindung *f*; Bezwingung *f*.

conscience *n* Gewissen *n*.

conscientious *adj* gewissenhaft; Gewissens-.

conscious *adj* bewußt; bei Bewußtsein.

consciousness *n* Bewußtsein *n*.

consent *n* Zustimmung *f*; Einwilligung *f*:—*vi* zustimmen; einwilligen.

consequence *n* Folge *f*; Konsequenz *f*; Bedeutung *f*; Einfluß *m*.

consequent *adj* (nach)folgend; konsequent:—**~ly** *adv* in der Folge; folglich.

conservation *n* Naturschutz *m*; Umweltschutz *m*; Konservieren *n*.

conserve *vt* erhalten; bewahren; einmachen:—*n* Eingemachtes *n*.

consider *vt vi* nachdenken.

considerable *adj* beachtlich; beträchtlich; ansehnlich; erheblich.

considerate *adj* rücksichtsvoll; aufmerksam; taktvoll; besonnen.

consideration *n* Erwägung *f*; Überlegung *f*; Berücksichtigung *f*.

consist *vi* bestehen; vereinbar sein.

consistent *adj* konsequent; übereinstimmend; konsistent.

consolation *n* Trost *m*.

console *vt* trösten.

consolidate *vt vi* (ver)stärken; konsolidieren.

consolidation *n* (Ver)Stärkung *f*; Konsolidierung *f*.

consonant *n* (*gr*) Konsonant *m*.

conspicuous *adj* deutlich sichtbar; auffällig; bemerkenswert.

conspiracy *n* Verschwörung *f*.

conspirator *n* Verschwörer *m*.

conspire *vi* sich verschwören; ein Komplott schmieden.

constant *adj* (be)ständig; standhaft; konstant.

constituency *n* Wählerschaft *f*; Wahlkreis *m*.

constituent *n* Bestandteil *m*; Wähler-(in) *m(f)*.

constitute *vt* ernennen; erlassen; gründen; darstellen.

construct *vt* errichten; bauen; konstruieren.

construction *n* Konstruktion *f*; Bau *m*; Bauwerk *n*; Auslegung *f*.

consul *n* Konsul *m*.

consult *vt* um Rat fragen; konsultieren.

consume *vt* zerstören; verzehren:—*vi* (dahin)schwinden.

consumer *n* Verbraucher(in) *m(f)*.

contact *n* Kontakt *m*; Kontaktperson *f*; Berührung *f*; Verbindung *f*.

contain *vt* enthalten; umfassen; zügeln; in Schach halten; eindämmen.

container *n* Behälter *m*; Container *m*.

contaminate *vt* verunreinigen; infizieren; vergiften; verseuchen.

contemplate *vt* betrachten.

contemplation *n* Betrachtung *f*.

contemporary *adj* zeitgenössisch; gleichzeitig; gleichaltrig.

contempt *n* Verachtung *f*; Mißachtung *f*; Schande *f*.

contemptible *adj* verächtlich; verachtenswert; gemein.

content *adj* zufrieden; bereit:—*n* Zufriedenheit *f*; Inhalt *m*.

contest *vt* kämpfen um; bestreiten:—*n* (Wett)Kampf *m*; (Wett)Streit *m*.

contestant *n* Wettkämpfer(in) *m(f)*.

context *n* Zusammenhang *m*; Umgebung *f*.

continent *n* Kontinent *m*.

continental *adj* kontinental.

continual *adj* fortwährend.

continuation *n* Fortsetzung *f*.

continue *vt* fortsetzen:—*vi* fortfahren.

continuity *n* Kontinuität *f*.

continuous *adj* ununterbrochen; (an)-dauernd; kontinuierlich.

contour *n* Kontur *f*; Umriß *m*.

contraception *n* Empfängnisverhütung *f*.

contraceptive *n* empfängnisverhütendes Mittel *n*:—*adj* empfängnisverhütend.

contract *vt* zusammenziehen:—*vi* sich zusammenziehen; (ein)schrumpfen; einen Vertrag schließen:—*n* Vertrag *m*.

contractor *n* Unternehmer *m*; Lieferant *m*.

contradict *vt* widersprechen.

contradiction *n* Widerspruch *m*.

contradictory *adj* widersprechend.

contrary *adj* widersprechend; gegensätzlich; widrig:—*n* Gegenteil *n*; **on the ~** im Gegenteil.

contrast *n* Kontrast *m*:—*vt* kontrastieren.

contrasting *adj* kontrastierend.

contribute *vt* beitragen.

contribution *n* Beitrag *m*.

control *n* Beherrschung *f*; Kontrolle *f*: —*vt* beherrschen; kontrollieren.

controversial *adj* umstritten; kontrovers.

controversy *n* Kontroverse *f*; Streit *m*.

convenience *n* Bequemlichkeit *f*.

convenient *adj* bequem; praktisch; günstig.

conventional *adj* konventionell.

conversation *n* Unterhaltung *f*; Gespräch *n*.

converse *vi* sich unterhalten; srechen.

conversion *n* Umwandlung *f*; Umbau *m*; Umstellung *f*.

convert *vt* umwandeln:—*n* Bekehrte-(r) *f(m)*; Konvertit(in) *m(f)*.

convertible *adj* umwandelbar.

convict *vt* für schuldig erklären; verurteilen:—*n* Strafgefangene(r) *f(m)*; Verurteilte(r) *f(m)*.

conviction *n* Schuldspruch *m*; Verurteilung *f*; Überzeugung *f*.

convince *vt* überzeugen.

convincing *adj* überzeugend.

cook *n* Koch *m*, Köchin *f*:— *vt vi* kochen.

cooker *n* Herd *m*; Kocher *m*; Kochfrucht *f*.

cookery *n* Kochen *n*; Kochkunst *f*.

cool *adj* kühl; frisch.

cooperate *vi* zusammenarbeiten; mitwirken.

cooperation *n* Zusammenarbeit *f*; Mitarbeit *f*.

coordinate *vt* koordinieren.

coordination *n* Koordination *f*.

cope *vi* fertig werden; gewachsen sein; bewältigen.

copier *n* Kopierer *m*.

copper *n* Kupfer(rot) *n*.

copy *n* Kopie *f*; Abschrift *f*; Exemplar *n*:—*vt* kopieren; abschreiben; nachahmen.

copyright *n* Urheberrecht *n*.

core *n* Kern *m*; Kerngehäuse *n*; Innerste *n*; Herz *n*.

cork *n* Kork(en) *m*.

corkscrew *n* Korkenzieher *m*.

corn *n* Korn *n*.

corner *n* Ecke *f*.

coronation *n* Krönung *f*.

corporation *n* Körperschaft *f*; (Akti-en)Gesellschaft *f*.

corpse *n* Leiche *f*.

correct *vt* korrigieren:—*adj* korrekt; richtig; genau.

correction *n* Korrektur *f*.

correspond *vi* korrespondieren; entsprechen.

correspondence *n* Korrespondenz *f*; Entsprechung *f*.

correspondent *n* Korrespondent(in) *m(f)*.

corridor *n* Flur *m*; Korridor *m*; Gang *m*.

corrupt *vt vi* verderben:— *adj* korrupt; bestechlich; verderbt.

corruption *n* Korruption *f*; Bestechlichkeit *f*; Verderbtheit *f*.

cosmetic *adj* kosmetisch; Schönheits-: —*n* Kosmetik *f*; Schönheitsmittel *n*.

cosmic *adj* kosmisch.

cost *n* Kosten *pl*; Preis *m*:— *vi* kosten.

costly *adj* kostspielig; teuer.

costume *n* Kostüm *n*; Kleidung *f*.

cosy *adj* gemütlich.

cottage *n* kleines Landhaus *n*; Hütte *f*.

cotton *n* Baumwolle *f*.

couch *n* Sofa *n*; Liege *f*.

cough *n* Husten *m*:—*vi* husten.

count *vt* zählen; (be)rechnen:—*n* Graf *m*; Zählung *f*; (Be)Rechnung *f*.

counter *n* Ladentisch *m*; Schalter *m*; Zähler *m*.

countess *n* Gräfin *f*; Komteß *f*.

country *n* Land *n*.

couple *n* Paar *n*; Koppel *f*; Verbindungsglied *n*.

courage *n* Mut *m*; Tapferkeit *f*.

courageous *adj* mutig; beherzt; tapfer.

course *n* Kurs *m*; Lauf *m*; Weg *m*; Richtung *f*:—**of ~** selbstverständlich; natürlich.

court *n* Hof *m*; Gericht *n*.

courteous *adj* höflich.

courtesy *n* Höflichkeit *f*.

courtroom *n* Gerichtssaal *m*.

cousin *n* Cousin(e) *m(f)*, Vetter *m*, Base *f*.

cover *n* Decke *f*:—*vt* bedecken.

cow *n* Kuh *f*.

coward *n* Feigling *m*.

cowardice *n* Feigheit *f*.

cowardly *adj* feig(e).
cowboy *n* Cowboy *m*.
coy *adj* schüchtern; scheu; spröde.
crab *n* Krabbe *f*; Krebs *m*.
crack *n* Knall *m*; Schlag *m*:—*vt vi* knallen; knacken.
cradle *n* Wiege *f*.
craft *n* Gewerbe *n*; Handwerk *n*; Kunst (fertigkeit) *f*; Schiff *n*; Flugzeug *n*.
crafty *adj* schlau; verschlagen.
crane *n* Kran *m*; (*zool*) Kranich *m*.
crash *n* Krach *m*; *vi* (zusammen) krachen .
crass *adj* grob; krass; derb.
crate *n* Kiste *f*; Kasten *m*.
crater *n* Krater *m*.
crawl *vi* kriechen; krabbeln.
crazy *adj* verrückt; wahnsinnig.
creak *vi* knarren; quietschen.
cream *n* Sahne *f*; Creme *f*.
crease *n* Falte *f*; Kniff *m*:—*vt* falten; kniffen.
create *vt* (er)schaffen.
creation *n* Schöpfung *f*; (Er)Schaffung *f*.
creative *adj* schöpferisch; kreativ.
creator *n* Schöpfer *m*.
creature *n* Kreatur *f*; Geschöpf *n*.
credibility *n* Glaubwürdigkeit *f*.
credible *adj* glaubwürdig.
credit *n* Kredit *m*; (Gut)Haben *n*.
creditor *n* Gläubiger *m*.
creep *vi* kriechen; schleichen; kribbeln.

cremate *vt* (Leichen) verbrennen; einäschern.
cremation *n* (Leichen)Verbrennung *f*; Einäscherung *f*.
crematorium *n* Krematorium *n*.
crescent *n* Halbmond *m*; Mondsichel *f*.
cress *n* Kresse *f*.
crest *n* Kamm *m*; Mähne *f*.
crew *n* Mannschaft *f*.
cricket *n* Grille *f*; Kricket *n*.
crime *n* Verbrechen *n*; Straftat *f*; Frevel *m*.
criminal *adj* kriminell; verbrecherisch; strafrechtlich; Straf-:—*n* Kriminelle (r) *f(m)*; Verbrecher(in) *m(f)*.
cripple *n* Krüppel *m*:—*vt* lähmen.
crippled *adj* verkrüppelt; gelähmt.
crisis *n* Krise *f*.
crisp *adj* knusprig; kraus.
criterion *n* Kriterium *n*; Maßstab *m*.
critic *n* Kritiker(in) *m(f)*; Rezensent(in) *m(f)*.
critical *adj* kritisch.
criticism *n* Kritik *f*.
criticize *vt* kritisieren; rezensieren.
croak *vi* quaken; krächzen.
crockery *n* Geschirr *n*; Töpferware *f*.
crocodile *n* Krokodil *n*.
crooked *adj* krumm; gewunden; unehrlich.
crop *n* (Feld)Frucht *f*; Ernte *f*.
cross *n* Kreuz(zeichen) *n*:—*adj* ärgerlich; entgegengesetzt; quer:—*vt* kreuzen; überqueren.
crossing *n* Kreuzung *f*.

crow *n* Krähe *f*; Krähen *n*.
crowd *n* Menge *f*; Masse *f*; Haufen *m*: —*vt* zusammendrängen; hineinstopfen; bevölkern:—*vi* sich drängen.
crown *n* Krone *f*; Kranz *m*; Schei-tel(punkt) *m*; Kopf *m*; Gipfel *m*:—*vt* krönen; überkronen.
crucial *adj* kritisch; entscheidend.
crude *adj* roh; grob.
cruel *adj* grausam.
cruelty *n* Grausamkeit *f*.
cruise *n* Kreuzfahrt *f*.
crumb *n* Krümel *m*; Brösel *m*.
crumble *vt* zerkrümeln; zerbröckeln: —*vi* zerbröckeln; zerfallen.
crusade *n* Kreuzzug *m*.
crush *vt* (zer)quetschen; (zer)drücken: —*n* (zermalmender) Druck *m*; Gedränge *n*; Schwärmerei *f*.
crust *n* Kruste *f*; Rinde *f*.
cry *vt vi* schreien; rufen; weinen:—*n* Schrei *m*; Ruf *m*; Geschrei *n*.
crypt *n* Krypta *f*.
crystal *n* Kristall *m* / *n*.
cub *n* Junge *n*; Bengel *m*; Anfänger *m*.
cube *n* Würfel *m*.
cubic *adj* Kubik-; kubisch.
cuckoo *n* Kuckuck *m*.
cucumber *n* Gurke *f*.
cuddle *vt vi* schmusen:—*n* enge Umarmung *f*.
cult *n* Kult *m*; Sekte *f*.
cultivate *vi* kultivieren.
cultivation *n* Kultivierung *f*.
cultural *adj* kulturell; Kultur-.

culture *n* Kultur *f.*

cunning *adj* geschickt; schlau.

cup *n* Tasse *f.*

cupboard *n* Schrank *m.*

cure *n* Kur *f;* Heilung *f:—vt* heilen; kurieren.

curiosity *n* Neugier *f.*

curious *adj* neugierig.

curl *n* Locke *f:—vi* sich locken.

currant *n* Korinthe *f;* Johannisbeere *f.*

currency *n* Währung *f;* Umlauf *m.*

current *adj* (um)laufend; gegenwärtig; aktuell:—*n* Strom *m;* Strömung *f.*

currently *adv* gegenwärtig; flüssig.

curry *n* Curry *m, n.*

curse *vt* verfluchen:—*vi* fluchen:—*n* Fluch *m.*

curt *adj* kurz (angebunden); knapp; barsch.

curtail *vt* beschneiden; (ab)kürzen; einschränken.

curtain *n* Gardine *f;* Vorhang *m.*

curve *vt* biegen; krümmen:—*n* Kurve *f;* Krümmung *f;* Biegung *f.*

cushion *n* Kissen *n;* Polster *n;* Bande *f.*

custom *n* Brauch *m;* Sitte *f;* Kundschaft *f.*

customary *adj* üblich; gebräuchlich; gewohnt.

customer *n* Kunde *m;* Kundin *f.*

customs *npl* Zoll *m.*

customs officer *n* Zollbeamter *m.*

cut *vt vi* schneiden:—*n* Schnitt *m.*

cutlery *n* Besteck *n.*

cyanide *n* Zyanid *n.*

cycle *n* Zyklus *m;* Kreis(lauf) *m;* Periode *f;* Fahrrad *n:—vi* radfahren.

cyclist *n* Radfahrer(in) *m(f).*

cyclone *n* Zyklon *m.*

cygnet *n* junger Schwan *m.*

cylinder *n* Zylinder *m;* Walze *f;* Trommel *f.*

cylindrical *adj* zylindrisch.

cynical *adj* zynisch.

cynicism *n* Zynismus *m.*

cypress *n* Zypresse *f.*

D

daffodil *n* Narzisse *f;*
Osterglocke *f.*

dagger *n* Dolch *m.*

daily *adj adv* (all)täglich.

dairy *n* Molkerei *f.*

daisy *n* Gänseblümchen *n;*
Margerite *f.*

damage *n* Schaden(ersatz)
m; Verlust *m:—vt*
(be)schädigen.

dame *n* Freifrau *f.*

damn *vt* verdammen.

damp *adj* feucht; klamm.

dampen *vt* befeuchten.

dance *n* Tanz *m:—vi*
tanzen.

dancer *n* Tänzer(in) *m(f).*

dandelion *n* Löwenzahn *m.*

danger *n* Gefahr *f.*

dangerous *adj* gefährlich.

dare *vt vi* wagen.

dark *adj* dunkel; finster.

darken *vt* verdunkeln:—*vi*
sich verdunkeln.

darkness *n* Dunkelheit *f;*
Finsternis *f.*

darling *n* Liebling *m.*

dash *vi* stürmen; stürzen:—
n Schlag *m;* Schuß *m.*

data *n* Daten *pl.*

database *n* Datenbank *f.*

date *n* Datum *n;* Dattel *f.*

daughter *n* Tochter *f.*

daughter-in-law
Schwiegertochter *f.*

dawn *n*
(Morgen)Dämmerung *f;*
(Ta-ges)Anbruch *m.*

day *n* Tag *m.*

daze *vt* betäuben; verwirren.

dazzle *vt* blenden.

dazzling *adj* blendend.

dead *adj* tot.

deadly *adj* tödlich; Todes-.

deaf *adj* taub.

deal *n* Geschäft *n; vi* handeln.

dealer *n* Händler(in) *m(f).*

dear *adj* lieb; teuer.

death *n* Tod *m.*

debate *n* Debatte *f:—vt*
debattieren.

debit *n* Soll *n;*
(Konto)Belastung *f:—vt*
belasten.

debt *n* Schuld *f;*
Forderung *f.*

debtor *n* Schuldner(in)
m(f).

decade *n* Jahrzehnt *n.*

decadence *n* Dekadenz *f;*
Verfall *m.*

decanter *n* Karaffe *f.*

decay *vi* verfallen:—*n*
Verfall *m.*

deceit *n* Betrug *m.*

deceitful *adj* betrügerisch.

deceive *vt* (be)trügen.

December *n* Dezember *m.*

decency *n* Anstand *m;*
Anständigkeit *f.*

decent *adj* anständig.

deceptive *adj*
(be)trügerisch.

decide *vt vi* (sich) entscheiden.

decision *n* Entscheidung *f.*

deck *n* Deck *n;*
(Karten)Spiel *n.*

declaration *n*
(Zoll)Erklärung *f.*

declare *vt* erklären;
verkünden.

decline *vt* neigen:—*vi* sich
neigen:—*n* Abhang *m.*

decor *n* Dekor *n.*

decorate *vt* schmücken.

decoration *n* Verzierung *f;*
Schmuck *m.*

decrease *vt* vermindern:—*n*
Vermin-derung *f.*

dedicate *vt* widmen.

dedication *n* Widmung *f.*

deduce *vt* folgern;
schließen.

deduct *vt* abziehen; abset-
zen.

deduction *n* Abzug *m;*
Subtraktion *f.*

deed *n* Tat *f;* Handlung *f;*
Urkunde *f.*

deep *adj* tief.

deepen *vt* vertiefen.

deer *n* Hirsch *m;* Rotwild *n;*
Reh *n.*

defeat *n* Niederlage *f:—vt*
besiegen; (nieder)schla-
gen.

defect *n* Defekt *m;* Fehler
m; Mangel *m.*

defection *n* Abfall *m;* Über-
laufen *n.*

defence *n* Verteidigung *f;*
Schutz *m.*

defend *vt* verteidigen;
schützen.

defer *vt* verschieben; (ver)zögern.

defiance *n* Trotz *m*; Herausforderung *f*.

defiant *adj* trotzig; herausfordernd.

deficiency *n* Mangel *m*; Unzulän-glichkeit *f*.

deficient *adj* unzulänglich; mangelhaft; fehlend.

deficit *n* Defizit *n*; Mangel *m*; Verlust *m*.

define *vt* definieren; bestimmen.

definite *adj* bestimmt; festgelegt.

definition *n* Definition *f*.

definitive *adj* definitiv; endgültig.

defuse *vt* entschärfen.

defy *n* trotzen; herausfordern.

degree *n* Grad *m*; Rang *m*; Stufe *f*; (Aus)Maß *n*.

deity *n* Gottheit *f*.

delay *vt* verzögern:—*n* Verzögerung *f*.

delegate *vt* delegieren:—*n* Delegier-te(r) *f(m)*.

delegation *n* Delegation *f*.

deliberate *adj* absichtlich.

delicate *adj* zart; fein (fühlig).

delicious *adj* köstlich.

delight *n* Entzücken *n*:—*vt* entzücken.

delighted *adj* entzückt.

delightful *adj* entzückend; köstlich.

deliver *vt* (aus)liefern.

delivery *n* (Aus)Lieferung *f*.

demand *n* (An)Forderung *f*; Verlangen *n*; Nachfrage *f*:—*vt* (er)fordern; verlangen.

democracy *n* Demokratie *f*.

democrat *n* Demokrat(in) *m(f)*.

democratic *adj* demokratisch.

demolish *vt* demolieren.

demolition *n* Demolierung *f*.

demonstrate *vt* beweisen:— *vi* demon-strieren.

demonstration *n* Demonstration *f*.

dense *adj* dicht.

density *n* Dichte *f*.

dental *adj* Zahn-; zahnärztlich.

dentist *n* Zahnarzt *m*, Zahnärztin *f*.

dentistry *n* Zahnmedizin *f*.

deny *vt* (ver)leugnen.

depart *vi* fortgehen; abreisen; abfahren.

department *n* Abteilung *f*.

department store *n* Kaufhaus *n*.

departure *n* Abreise *f*; Abfahrt *f*; Abflug *m*.

depend *vi*:—~ **on** sich verlassen auf.

dependent *adj* abhängig; angewiesen; bedingt; vertrauend.

depict *vt* darstellen.

deposit *vt* (hinter)legen; deponieren: —*n* Anzahlung *f*; Pfand *n*.

depot *n* Depot *n*; Lagerhaus *n*.

depress *vt* deprimieren; (be)drücken.

depressed *adj* deprimiert; nieder-geschlagen.

depression *n* Depression *f*; Niedergeschlagenheit *f*.

depth *n* Tiefe *f*.

derive *vt* herleiten.

descend *vi* herabsteigen; hinuntergehen; niedergehen.

descendant *n* Nachkomme *m*; Deszendent *m*.

descent *n* Abstieg *m*; Niedergang *m*.

describe *vt* beschreiben.

description *n* Beschreibung *f*.

descriptive *adj* beschreibend.

desert *n* Wüste *f*; Ödland *n*.

deserve *vt* verdienen.

design *vt* gestalten:—*n* Design *n*; Gestaltung *f*; Konstruktion *f*.

designer *n* Designer(in) *m(f)*; Konstrukteur *m*.

desire *n* Wunsch *m*:—*vt* wünschen.

desk *n* Schreibtisch *m*; Pult *n*.

despair *n* Verzweiflung *f*:— *vi* verz-weifeln.

desperate *adj* verzweifelt; hoffnungslos.

despise *vt* verachten.

despite *prep* trotz.

dessert *n* Nachtisch *m*; Dessert *n*.

destination *n* Bestimmungsort *m*; Ziel *n*.

destiny *n* Schicksal *n*.

destroy *vt* zerstören; vernichten.

destruction *n* Zerstörung *f*; Vernichtung *f*.

destructive *adj* zerstörend; vernichtend.

detail *n* Detail *n*; Einzelheit *f*:—**in** ~ detailliert.

detective *n* Detektiv(in) *m(f)*.

deter *vt* abschrecken; abhalten.

deteriorate *vt* ver-
  schlechtern; (ver)-mindern.
deterioration *n*
  Verschlechterung *f*;
  Wertminderung *f*.
determination *n*
  Feststellung *f*.
determine *vt* feststellen.
determined *adj*
  entschlossen.
detest *vt* verabscheuen;
  hassen.
detonate *vi* detonieren.
detonation *n* Detonation *f*.
detour *n* Umweg *m*.
develop *vt* entwickeln.
development *n*
  Entwicklung *f*.
deviate *vi* abweichen.
deviation *n* Abweichung *f*.
devil *n* Teufel *m*.
devote *vt* weihen.
devoted *adj* ergeben.
devotion *n* Ergebenheit *f*.
devour *vt* verschlingen;
  vernichten.
devout *adj* fromm;
  andächtig; innig.
dew *n* Tau *m*.
diabetic *n* Diabetiker(in)
  m(f).
diagnosis *n* Diagnose *f*.
diagonal *adj* diagonal:—*n*
  Diagonale *f*.
diagram *n* Diagramm *n*.
dial *n* Zifferblatt *n*;
  Wählscheibe *f*.
dialect *n* Dialekt *m*;
  Mundart *f*.
diameter *n* Durchmesser *m*.
diamond *n* Diamant *m*;
  Karo *n*.
diarrhoea *n* Durchfall *m*.
diary *n* Tagebuch *n*.
dictate *vt* diktieren:—*n*
  Diktat *n*.

dictation *n* Diktat *n*.
dictatorship *n* Diktatur *f*.
dictionary *n* Wörterbuch *n*.
die *vi* sterben:—*n* Würfel *m*.
diesel *n* Diesel *m*.
diet *n* Diät *f*; Ernährung *f*;
  Kost *f*:—*vi* Diät halten.
differ *vi* sich unterscheiden.
difference *n* Unterschied *m*.
different *adj* verschieden;
  anders:—**~ly** *adv* verschieden; unterschiedlich.
differentiate *vt* differen-
  zieren.
difficult *adj* schwierig;
  schwer.
difficulty *n* Schwierigkeit *f*.
diffidence *n*
  Schüchternheit *f*.
diffident *adj* schüchtern.
dig *vt* (ein)graben:—*n*
  (Aus)Grabung *f*.
digest *vt* verdauen.
digestion *n* Verdauung *f*.
digit *n* Finger *m*; Zehe *f*;
  Ziffer *f*.
digital *adj* digital; Finger-.
dignity *n* Würde *f*.
diligent *adj* fleißig.
dim *adj* (halb)dunkel;
  trüb:—*vt* verdunkeln;
  trüben.
diminish *vt* vermindern:—
  vi sich vermindern.
diminution *n*
  (Ver)Minderung *f*.
din *n* Lärm *m*; Getöse *n*.
dine *vi* speisen.
dinner *n* Abendessen *n*.
dinosaur *n* Dinosaurier *m*.
dip *vt* (ein)tauchen;
  (ein)tunken.
diploma *n* Diplom *n*;
  Urkunde *f*.
diplomacy *n* Diplomatie *f*.

diplomat *n* Diplomat *m*.
diplomatic *adj* diplomatisch.
direct *adj* direkt; gerade;
  unmittelbar.
direction *n* Richtung *f*.
director *n* Direktor *m*;
  Regisseur *m*.
dirt *n* Schmutz *m*.
dirty *adj* schmutzig.
disadvantage *n* Nachteil *m*.
disadvantageous *adj*
  nachteilig.
disagreement *n*
  Unstimmigkeit *f*.
disappear *vi* verschwinden.
disappearance *n*
  Verschwinden *n*.
disappoint *vt* enttäuschen.
disappointed *adj* ent-
  täuscht.
disappointing *adj* ent-
  täuschend.
disappointment *n*
  Enttäuschung *f*.
disaster *n* Katastrophe *f*.
disastrous *adj* katastrophal.
discern *vt* erkennen;n.
discipline *n* Disziplin *f*:—*vt*
  disziplinieren.
disco *n* Disko *f*.
discount *n* Preisnachlaß *m*;
  Skonto *n*; Abzug *m*.
discover *vt* entdecken.
discovery *n* Entdeckung *f*.
discreet *adj* diskret.
discriminate *vt* diskrim-
  inieren.
discrimination *n*
  Diskriminierung *f*.
discuss *vt* diskutieren.
discussion *n* Diskussion *f*.
disease *n* Krankheit *f*.
disgrace *n* Schande *f*.
disgraceful *adj* schändlich.
disguise *vt* verkleiden:—*n*
  Verkleidung *f*.

disgust n Ekel m:—vt
(an)ekeln.

disgusting adj ekelhaft.

dish n (Servier)Platte f;
Gericht n.

dishonest adj unehrlich.

dishonesty n Unehrlichkeit
f.

dishonour n Unehre f.

disillusion vt
Ernüchterung f.

disillusioned adj ernüchtert.

disk n Scheibe f;
(Schall)Platte f.

diskette n Diskette f.

dismantle vt demontieren;
abbauen.

dismay n Entsetzen f;
Bestürzung f.

dismiss vt entlassen;
fortschicken.

disorder n Unordnung f;
Durcheinander n.

dispatch vt (ab)senden:—n
(Ab)Sen-dung f.

dispel vt zerstreuen.

display vt ausbreiten;
(her)zeigen:—n
(Her)Zeigen n;
Ausstellung f.

dispute n Streit m:—vt streiten über.

disrupt vt unterbrechen.

disruption n
Unterbrechung f.

dissolve vt (auf)lösen;
schmelzen:—vi sich
auflösen.

distance n Entfernung f.

distant adj entfernt.

distinct adj deutlich.

distinction n Unterschied
m; Unterscheidung f;
Auszeichnung f.

distinctive adj
Unterscheidungs-.

distinguish vt unterscheiden; ausmachen; ausze-
ichnen.

distract vt ablenken.

distraction n Ablenkung f.

distress n Qual f; Elend
n:—vt quälen; bedrücken.

distressing adj quälend;
bedrückend.

distribute vt verteilen; verbreiten.

distribution n Verteilung f;
Verbreitung f.

district n Gegend f.

disturb vt stören;
beunruhigen.

disturbance n Störung f;
Beunruhigung f.

disturbed adj gestört;
beunruhigt.

disturbing adj störend;
beunruhigend.

ditch n Graben m.

dive vi tauchen.

diversion n Umleitung f.

divert vt umleiten.

divide vt (ver)teilen.

dividend n Dividende f;
Gewinnanteil m.

divine adj göttlich.

diving n Tauchen n.

division n (Ver)Teilung f.

divorce n (Ehe)Scheidung
f:—vi sich scheiden lassen.

divorced adj geschieden.

dizzy adj schwindlig.

do vt tun; machen.

dock n Dock n:—vi
(an)docken.

docker n Hafenarbeiter m.

dockyard n Werft f.

doctor n Doktor m; Arzt m,
Ärztin f.

document n Dokument n;
Urkunde f.

dog n Hund m.

dogmatic adj dogmatisch.

doll n Puppe f.

dollar n Dollar m.

dolphin n Delphin m.

domain n Domäne f;
Gebiet n.

dome n Kuppel f; Dom m.

domestic adj häuslich.

dominant adj dominant;
(vor)herr-schend.

dominate vi dominieren;
(vor)herr-schen.

domination n
(Vor)Herrschaft f.

donate vt schenken.

donation n Schenkung f.

donkey n Esel m.

donor n Schenker(in) m(f).

door n Tür f.

dormouse n Schlafmaus f;
Haselmaus f.

dosage n Dosierung f.

dose n Dosis f:—vt
dosieren.

dot n Punkt m; Tupfen m.

double adj (ver)doppelt:—
vt verd-oppeln.

doubt n Zweifel m:—vt
bezweifeln.

doubtful adj zweifelhaft.

doubtless adv zweifellos.

dough n Teig m.

dove n Taube f.

down prep hinunter.

downstairs adv (nach)
unten.

downward(s) adv abwärts;
hinunter.

dozen n Dutzend n.

draft n Entwurf m.

drag vt schleppen.

dragon n Drache(n) m.

dragonfly n Libelle f.

drain n Entwässerungs-
graben m; (Straßen)Rinne
f.

drake *n* Enterich *m*.

drama *n* Drama *n*; Schauspielkunst *f*.

dramatic *adj* dramatisch; Theater-.

dramatist *n* Dramatiker(in) *m(f)*.

drastic *adj* drastisch.

draught *n* Zug *m*; Tiefgang *m*.

draughts *npl* Damespiel *n*.

draughty *adj* zugig.

draw *vt* (an)ziehen; zeichnen.

drawer *n* Schublade *f*; Zeichner *m*.

drawing *n* Zeichnung *f*.

dread *n* Furcht *f*:—*vt* fürchten.

dreadful *adj* furchtbar; schrecklich.

dream *n* Traum *m*:—*vi* träumen.

dress *vt* bekleiden; anziehen:—*vi* sich anziehen:—*n* Kleid *n*; Kleidung *f*.

dried *adj* getrocknet; Dörr-.

drill *n* Bohrer *m*; Bohrmaschine *f*; Drill *m*:—*vt* bohren; drillen.

drink *vt vi* trinken; saufen:—*n* Getränk *m*.

drinking water *n* Trinkwasser *n*.

drip *vi* tropfen:—*n* Tropfen *n*; Tropf *m*.

drive *vt vi* fahren; treiben:—*n* Fahrt *f*; Treiben *n*.

driver *n* Fahrer(in) *m(f)*.

drop *n* Tropfen *m*:—*vt* (herab)tropfen; fallen lassen.

drought *n* Dürre *f*.

drown *vt* ertränken; überschwemmen:—*vi* ertrinken.

drug *n* Droge *f*; Medikament *n*.

drum *n* Trommel *f*:—*vi* trommeln.

drunk *adj* betrunken.

drunkard *n* Trinker(in) *m(f)*; Säufer-(in) *m(f)*.

drunken *adj* betrunken.

dry *adj* trocken:—*vt vi* trocknen.

duck *n* Ente *f*.

due *adj* fällig.

duel *n* Duell *n*.

duet *n* Duett *n*.

dull *adj* stumpf.

dumb *adj* stumm.

dump *n* Schutthaufen *m*.

dumpling *n* Knödel *m*.

durable *adj* dauerhaft.

duration *n* Dauer *f*.

during *prep* während.

dust *n* Staub *m*.

duster *n* Staubtuch *n*.

dusty *adj* staubig.

duty *n* Pflicht *f*.

dwarf *n* Zwerg *m*.

dye *vt* färben:—*n* Farbstoff *m*; Färbung *f*.

dynamic *adj* dynamisch.

dynamics *n* Dynamik *f*.

dynamite *n* Dynamit *n*.

dynamo *n* Dynamo *m*.

dynasty *n* Dynastie *f*.

E

each *pn* jede(r, s):—~ **other**
einander.
eager *adj* eifrig; begierig.
eagle *n* Adler *m*.
ear *n* Ohr *n*.
earache *n* Ohrenschmerzen
mpl.
eardrum *n* Trommelfell *n*.
early *adj adv* früh.
earn *vt* verdienen.
earnest *adj* ernst; ernsthaft.
earring *n* Ohrring *m*.
earth *n* Erde *f*; Boden *m*.
earthquake *n* Erdbeben *n*.
ease *n* Bequemlichkeit *f*;
Ruhe *f*.
east *n* Osten *m*.
Easter *n* Ostern *n*.
Easter egg *n* Osterei *n*.
eastern *adj* östlich; Ost-.
easy *adj* leicht; mühelos;
einfach.
eat *vt vi* essen; fressen;
nagen.
ebb *n* Ebbe *f*:—*vi* zurückge-
hen; abebben.
ebony *n* Ebenholz *n*.
eccentric *adj* exzentrisch.
echo *n* Echo *n*:—*vi*
(wider)hallen.
ecology *n* Ökologie *f*.
economic(al) *adj*
wirtschaftlich; sparsam.
economics *npl*
Volkswirtschaft(slehre) *f*.
economist *n* Volkswirt *m*.
economy *n* Sparsamkeit *f*;
Wirtschaftlichkeit *f*.
edge *n* Rand *m*.

edible *adv* eßbar.
edition *n* Ausgabe *f*;
Auflage *f*.
editor *n* Redakteur(in) *m(f)*.
educate *vt* erziehen; unterrichten; (aus)bilden.
education *n* Erziehung *f*;
(Aus)Bildung *f*.
eel *n* Aal *m*.
effect *n* Effekt *m*;
Wirkung *f*.
effective *adj* effektiv;
(rechts)wirksam.
efficiency *n* Effizienz *f*;
(Leistungs)-Fähigkeit *f*.
efficient *adj* effizient; (leistungs)fähig.
effort *n* Anstrengung *f*;
Mühe *f*.
effortless *adj* mühelos.
effrontery *n*
Unverschämtheit *f*.
egg *n* Ei *n*.
eggcup *n* Eierbecher *m*.
ego(t)ism *n* Egoismus *m*;
Selbstsucht *f*.
ego(t)ist *n* Egoist(in) *m(f)*;
selbstgefälliger Mensch *m*.
eight *num* acht.
eighteen *num* achtzehn.
eighth *adj* achte(r, s).
eighty *num* achtzig.
either *conj* entweder.
elastic *adj* elastisch; dehn-
bar; Gummi-band.
elbow *n* Ell(en)bogen *m*.
elder *adj* ältere(r, s).
eldest *adj* älteste(r, s).
elect *vt* wählen.

election *n* Wahl *f*.
elector *n* Wähler(in) *m(f)*.
electric(al) *adj* elektrisch;
Elektro-.
electrician *n* Elektriker *m*.
electricity *n* Elektrizität *f*.
electron *n* Elektron *n*.
electronic *adj* elektronisch:—~**s** *npl* Elektronik *f*.
elegance *n* Eleganz *f*..
elegant *adj* elegant.
element *n* Element *n*.
elephant *n* Elefant *m*.
eleven *num* elf.
elk *n* Elch *m*; Wapiti *n*.
elm *n* Ulme *f*.
eloquence *n* Beredsamkeit *f*.
eloquent *adj* beredt.
else *adv* sonst; weiter;
andere(r, s).
elsewhere *adv* anderswo;
woanders hin.
embarrass *vt* verlegen
machen; in Verlegenheit
bringen.
embarrassed *adj* verlegen.
embarrassing *adj* unangenehm; peinlich.
embarrassment *n*
Verlegenheit *f*.
embassy *n* Botschaft *f*.
embitter *vt* bitter(er)
machen.
embrace *vt* umarmen;
umfassen:—*n* Umarmung
f.
embroider *vt* (be)sticken.
embroidery *n* Stickerei *f*.
emerald *n* Smaragd *m*.

emerge *vi* auftauchen; sich herausstellen.

emergency *n* Not(lage) *f*; Notfall *m*.

emigrant *n* Emigrant(in) *m(f)*; Auswanderer *m*.

emigrate *vi* auswandern; emigrieren.

emigration *n* Auswanderung *f*; Emigration *f*.

eminence *n* Anhöhe *f*; Eminenz *f*.

eminent *adj* eminent; hervorragend.

emit *vt* ausstoßen; ausstrahlen.

emotion *n* Gefühl *n*; Erregung *f*; Rührung *f*.

emotional *adj* emotionell; gefühlsmäßig.

emperor *n* Kaiser *m*.

emphasis *n* Betonung *f*; Schwerpunkt *m*.

emphasize *vt* betonen; hervorheben.

empire *n* Reich *n*; Imperium *n*.

employ *vt* beschäftigen; einstellen.

employee *n* Arbeitnehmer(in) *m(f)*; Angestellte(r) *f(m)*.

employer *n* Arbeitgeber(in) *m(f)*; Unternehmer(in) *m(f)*.

employment *n* Beschäftigung *f*; Arbeit *f*.

empress *n* Kaiserin *f*.

empty *adj* leer.

enable *vt* ermächtigen; befähigen; ermöglichen.

enact *vt* erlassen; verfügen; aufführen; darstellen.

enclose *vt* einschließen.

enclosure *n* Einfriedung *f*.

encounter *n* Begegnung *f*:—*vt* begegnen.

encourage *vt* ermutigen.

encouragement *n* Ermutigung *f*.

encyclopedia *n* Enzyklopädie *f*.

end *n* Ende *n*; Folge *f*; Zweck *n*; Ziel *n*:—*vt* beenden:—*vi* enden.

endless *adj* endlos; unendlich.

enemy *n* Feind(in) *m(f)*.

energetic *adj* energisch.

energy *n* Energie *f*.

engage *vt* verpflichten; anstellen.

engaged *adj* verlobt; verpflichtet; besetzt.

engagement *n* Verpflichtung *f*; Verlobung *f*.

engine *n* Motor *m*.

engineer *n* Ingenieur *m*.

engineering *n* Ingenieurwesen *n*.

enigma *n* Rätsel *n*.

enjoy *vt* genießen.

enjoyable *adj* genießbar.

enjoyment *n* Genuß *m*.

enlarge *vt* vergrößern.

enlargement *n* Vergrößerung *f*.

enormous *adj* ungeheuer(lich); enorm; riesig.

enough *adv* genug; ausreichend.

enrage *vt* wütend machen.

enrich *vt* bereichern; anreichern.

ensure *vt* sichern; sicherstellen; sorgen für.

enter *vt* eintreten (in).

enterprise *n* Unternehmen *n*; Unternehmung *f*.

entertain *vt* unterhalten.

entertainer *n* Unterhaltungskünstler-(in) *m(f)*.

entertainment *n* Unterhaltung *f*.

enthusiasm *n* Begeisterung *f*.

enthusiastic *adj* begeistert.

entice *vt* (ver)locken.

entire *adj* ganz; vollständig:—**~ly** *adv* völlig; durchaus.

entrance *n* Eintritt *m*; Eingang *m*.

entrant *n* Teilnehmer(in) *m(f)*; Ein-tretende(r) *f(m)*.

entrepreneur *n* Unternehmer *m*.

entrust *vt* anvertrauen; betrauen.

entry *n* Eintritt *m*; Einreise *f*; Auftritt *m*.

envelope *vt* (Brief)Umschlag *m*.

enviable *adj* beneidenswert.

envious *adj* neidisch.

environment *n* Umgebung *f*; Umwelt *f*.

environmental *adj* Umwelt-.

envy *n* Neid *m*:—*vt* beneiden.

epidemic *n* Epidemie *f*; Seuche *f*.

epilogue *n* Epilog *m*; Nachwort *n*.

Epiphany *n* Dreikönigstag *m*.

episode *n* Episode *f*; Ereignis *n*.

epoch *n* Epoche *f*; Zeitalter *n*.

equal *adj* gleich(förmig); gleichberechtigt:—*n* Gleichgestellte(r) *f(m)*: — *vt* gleichen; entsprechen.

equality *n* Gleichheit *f*;
Gleichberechtigung *f*.

equate *vt* gleichmachen;
ausgleichen.

equation *n* Gleichung *f*.

equator *n* Äquator *m*.

equip *vt* ausrüsten; ausstatten.

equipment *n* Ausrüstung *f*;
Ausstattung *f*;
Einrichtung *f*.

equivalent *adj* äquivalent:—*n* Äquivalent *n*.

era *n* Ära *f*; Zeitalter *n*.

eradicate *vt* ausreißen; ausrotten.

eradication *n* Ausrottung *f*;
Entwurzelung *f*.

erase *vt* ausradieren;
(aus)löschen; tilgen.

erect *vt* aufrichten; errichten:—*adj* aufgerichtet;
aufrecht.

erection *n* Errichtung *f*;
Montage *f*; Erektion *f*.

erode *vt* zerfressen;
erodieren.

erotic *adj* erotisch.

err *vi* irren; falsch sein.

errand *n* Auftrag *m*;
(Boten)Gang *m*;
Besorgung *f*.

erratic *adj* (umher)wandernd; regellos.

error *n* Irrtum *m*; Fehler *m*;
Versehen *n*.

erupt *vi* ausbrechen; durchbrechen.

eruption *n* Ausbruch *m*.

escalator *n* Rolltreppe *f*.

escape *vt vi* entkommen:—
n Flucht *f*; Rettung *f*.

escort *n* Eskorte *f*;
Begleitung *f*:—*vt* eskortieren; begleiten.

especially *adv* besonders.

essay *n* Essay *n*; Aufsatz *m*.

essence *n* Essenz *f*; Wesen *n*.

essential *adj* wesentlich:—
~**ly** *adv* im wesentlichen.

establish *vt* festsetzen; einrichten; (be)gründen.

establishment *n*
Festsetzung *f*; Gründung
f; Einrichtung *f*.

estate *n* Vermögen *n*;
Nachlaß *m*.

estimate *vt* (ein)schätzen.

eternal *adj* ewig; unveränderlich.

eternity *n* Ewigkeit *f*.

ethical *adj* ethisch;
moralisch.

ethics *npl* Ethik *f*; Moral *f*;
Ethos *m*.

ethnic *adj* ethnisch.

ethos *n* Ethos *m*.

etiquette *n* Etikette *f*.

evacuate *vt* evakuieren;
entleeren; räumen.

evacuation *n* Evakuierung *f*;
Entleerung *f*; Räumung *f*.

evaporate *vi* verdampfen.

evaporation *n*
Verdampfung *f*.

eve *n* Vorabend *m*;
Vortag *m*.

even *adj* eben; gerade;
glatt:—*adv* sogar; gerade;
eben; ganz.

evening *n* Abend *m*.

event *n* Ereignis *n*;
(Vor)Fall *m*.

eventual *adj* schließlich.

ever *adv* immer (wieder);
je(mals); irgend:—**~ since**
seitdem.

every *adj* jede(r, s):—
~**where** über-all(hin):—
~**thing** alles:—**~one,**
~**body** jeder (einzelne).

evidence *n* Beweis *m*.

evident *adj* offensichtlich;
augen-scheinlich.

evil *adj* böse; übel:—*n* Böse
n; Übel *n*.

evolution *n* Evolution *f*.

ewe *n* Mutterschaf *n*.

exact *adj* exakt.

exaggerate *vt* übertreiben.

exaggeration *n* Übertreibung *f*.

examination *n*
Untersuchung *f*; Prüfung *f*.

examine *vt* untersuchen;
prüfen.

examiner *n* Prüfer(in) *m(f)*.

example *n* Beispiel *n*.

exceed *vt* überschreiten;
übersteigen.

excellent *adj* ausgezeichnet.

except *prep* ausgenommen.

exception *n* Ausnahme *f*.

excerpt *n* Auszug *m*.

excess *n* Übermaß *n*;
Exzeß *m*.

exchange *vt* (aus)tauschen;
(um)-wechseln:—*n*
(Aus)Tausch *m*;
(Um)Wechseln *n*; Börse *f*.

excite *vt* erregen; aufregen;
reizen.

excited *adj* aufgeregt; erregt.

excitement *n* Erregung *f*;
Aufregung *f*; Reizung *f*.

exciting *adj* aufregend;
erregend; spannend.

exclaim *vt* ausrufen; hervorstoßen.

exclamation *n* Ausruf *m*;
(Auf)Schrei *m*.

exclude *vt* ausschließen.

exclusion *n* Ausschluß *m*;
Ausschließung *f*.

exclusive *adj* exklusiv;
ausschließlich.

excursion *n* Exkursion *f*;
Ausflug *m*.

excuse *vt* entschuldigen; verzeihen: —*n* Entschuldigung *f*; Vorwand *m*.

execute *vt* ausführen; hinrichten.

execution *n* Ausführung *f*; Hinrichtung *f*.

executioner *n* Henker *m*; Scharfrichter *m*.

exempt *adj* befreit.

exemption *n* Befreiung *f*.

exercise *n* (Aus)Übung *f*.

exhaust *n* Abgas *n*; Auspuff *m*: —*vt* erschöpfen.

exhausted *adj* erschöpft.

exhaustion *n* Erschöpfung *f*.

exhibit *vt* ausstellen.

exhibition *n* Ausstellung *f*.

exile *n* Exil *n*; Verbannung *f*: —*vt* verbannen.

exist *vi* existieren; bestehen.

existence *n* Existenz *f*; Bestand *m*.

existent *adj* existierend; bestehend.

exit *n* Ausgang *m*; Ausfahrt *f*; Abgang *m*: —*vi* abgehen; abtreten.

exotic *adj* exotisch.

expand *vt* erweitern; ausbreiten.

expansion *n* Ausbreitung *f*; Erweiterung *f*.

expect *vt* erwarten; annehmen.

expectation *n* Erwartung *f*.

expel *vt* vertreiben; hinauswerfen.

expenditure *n* Ausgabe *f*; Aufwand *m*.

expensive *adj* teuer; kostspielig.

experience *n* Erfahrung *f*; Erlebnis *n*: —*vt* erfahren; erleben.

experienced *adj* erfahren; erprobt.

experiment *n* Experiment *n*: —*vi* experimentieren.

expert *adj* Experte *m*, Expertin *f*; Sachverständige(r) *f(m)*.

expertise *n* Expertise *f*; Sachkenntnis *f*.

explain *vt* erklären.

explanation *n* Erklärung *f*.

explode *vi* explodieren; platzen.

exploit *vt* verwerten; ausnutzen.

exploitation *n* Ausnutzung *f*; Verwertung *f*.

exploration *n* Erforschung *f*.

explore *vt* (er)forschen.

explorer *n* Forscher(in) *m(f)*.

explosion *n* Explosion *f*; Ausbruch *m*.

explosive *adj* explosiv; Explosions-: —*n* Sprengstoff *m*.

export *vt* exportieren; ausführen: —*n* Export *m*; Ausfuhr *f*.

exporter *n* Exporteur *m*.

expose *vt* aussetzen; bloßstellen.

exposed *adj* ausgesetzt; ungeschützt.

exposure *n* Aussetzung *f*; Bloßstellung *f*.

express *vt* ausdrücken; äußern:—*adj* ausdrücklich; Expreß-; Eil-:—*n* Schnellzug *m*.

expression *n* Ausdruck *m*.

expressive *adj* ausdrucksvoll; Ausdrucks-.

extend *vt* (aus)dehnen:—*vi* sich ausdehnen.

extension *n* Ausdehnung *f*.

extensive *adj* ausgedehnt; weitläufig.

extent *n* Ausdehnung *f*; Umfang *m*.

exterior *adj* äußerlich.

external *adj* äußere(r, s).

extinct *adj* ausgestorben; erloschen.

extinction *n* Aussterben *n*; (Aus)Lös-chen *n*; Vernichtung *f*.

extinguish *vt* (aus)löschen; vernichten.

extinguisher *n* Feuerlöscher *m*.

extra *adv* extra.

extract *vt* usziehen:—*n* Auszug *m*.

extraordinary *adj* außerordentlich.

extreme *adj* extrem; äußerste(r, s):—**~ly** *adv* äußerst; höchst.

eye *n* Auge *n*.

eyeball *n* Augapfel *m*.

eyebrow *n* Augenbraue *f*.

eyelash *n* Wimper *f*.

eyelid *n* Augenlid *n*.

eyesight *n* Sehkraft *f*.

eyrie *n* Horst *m*.

F

fable *n* Fabel *f*; Sage *f*.

fabric *n* Stoff *m*; Gewebe *n*.

fabulous *adj* sagenhaft; fabelhaft.

facade *n* Fassade *f*.

face *n* Gesicht *n*; Miene *f*.

facial *adj* Gesichts-.

facility *n* Leichtigkeit *f*; Gelassenheit *f*.

fact *n* Tatsache *f*:—**in ~** in der Tat.

factor *n* Faktor *m*; Umstand *m*.

factory *n* Fabrik *f*.

fade *vi* (ver)welken; verblassen; sich auflösen.

fail *vt vi* versagen; durch-fallen.

faint *vi* ohnmächtig wer-den:—*n* Ohnmacht *f*.

fair *adj* schön; hell; blond; fair:—*n* Ausstellung *f*; Messe *f*.

fairly *adv* ziemlich; leidlich.

fairy *n* Fee *f*.

fairy tale *n* Märchen *n*.

faith *n* Treue *f*.

faithful *adj* treu.

fake *n* Fälschung *f*:—*vt* fälschen.

fall *vi* fallen:—*n* Fall *m*.

false *adj* falsch.

falsehood *n* Unwahrheit *f*; Lüge *f*; Falschheit *f*.

fame *n* Ruhm *m*, Berühmtheit *f*.

familiar *adj* vertraut.

family *n* Familie *f*.

famous *adj* berühmt.

fan *n* Fächer *m*; Fan *m*.

fanatic *adj* fanatisch:—*n* Fanatiker(in) *m(f)*.

fancy *n* Laune *f*; Phantasie *f*; Vorliebe *f*.

fantastic *adj* phantastisch.

fantasy *n* Phantasie *f*.

far *adv* weit (entfernt); fern.

fare *n* Fahrpreis *m*; Fahrgast *m*.

farm *n* Bauernhof *m*.

farmer *n* Landwirt(in) *m(f)*; Bauer *m*, Bäuerin *f*.

farmhouse *n* Bauernhaus *n*.

farmyard *n* Hof *m*.

farther *adv* weiter; mehr:— *adj* weiter (weg); entfernter.

fascinate *vt* faszinieren.

fascination *n* Faszination *f*.

fascism *n* Faschismus *m*.

fashion *n* Mode *f*.

fashionable *adj* modisch.

fast *n* Fasten *n*:—*adj* schnell; fest(ge-macht):—*adv* (zu) schnell; rasch; fest.

fasten *vt* befestigen; fest-binden.

fat *adj* dick; fett; beleibt:—*n* Fett *n*.

fatal *adj* tödlich; fatal.

fate *n* Schicksal *n*.

father *n* Vater *m*; Pater *m*.

fatherhood *n* Vaterschaft *f*.

father-in-law *n* Schwiegervater *m*.

fatherland *n* Vaterland *n*.

fatherly *adj* väterlich; Vater-.

fatigue *n* Ermüdung *f*.

fault *n* Fehler *m*; Mangel *m*; Irrtum *m*.

fauna *n* Fauna *f*.

favour *n* Gunst *f*; Begünstigung *f*:—*vt* begünstigen.

favourable *adj* wohlgesin-nt; günstig.

favourite *adj* Lieblings-.

fax *n* Fax *n*:—*vt* faxen.

fear *vi* (sich) fürchten:—*n* Furcht *f*.

fearful *adj* furchtbar.

feast *n* Fest(mahl) *n*; Feiertag *m*.

feather *n* Feder *f*.

feature *n* (Gesichts)Zug *m*.

February *n* Februar *m*.

federal *adj* Bundes-.

federation *n* Föderation *f*; Staatenbund *m*.

fee *n* Gebühr *f*; Honorar *n*.

feed *vt* (ver)füttern; ernähren.

feel *vt vi* fühlen.

feeling *n* Gefühl *n*.

fellow *n* Kerl *m*.

felt *n* Filz *m*.

female, feminine *adj* weib-lich.

feminist *n* Feminist(in) *m(f)*.

fence *n* Zaun *m*:—*vt* einzäunen:—*vi* fechten.

ferry *n* Fähre *f*:—*vt* überset-zen.

fertile *adj* fruchtbar; reich.

fertilizer *n* Dünger *m*; Befruchter *m*.

festival *n* Fest *n*.

fetch *vt* (ab)holen.

fever *n* Fieber *n*.

few *adj* wenige:—**a ~** einige; ein paar.

fiancé(e) *n* Verlobte(r) *f(m)*.

field *n* Feld *n*.

fieldmouse *n* Feldmaus *f*.

fierce *adj* wild; grimmig.

fifteen *num* fünfzehn.

fifth *adj* fünfte(r, s).

fifty *num* fünfzig.

fig *n* Feige *f*.

fight *vt vi* kämpfen:—*n* Kampf *m*.

fighter *n* Kämpfer(in) *m(f)*.

figure *n* Zahl *f*; Ziffer *f*; Figur *f*; Gestalt *f*.

file *n* Ordner *m*; Akte *f*:—*vt* ablegen; (ein)ordnen; zu den Akten nehmen.

fill *vt* (ab)füllen; erfüllen; ausfüllen; besetzen.

film *n* Film *m*; dünne Schicht *f*:—*vt* (ver)filmen:—*vi* einen Film drehen.

filter *n* Filter *m*:—*vt* filtern; filtrieren; (durch)seihen.

filth *n* Schmutz *m*; Dreck *m*; Schweinerei *f*.

filthy *adj* schmutzig; dreckig; schweinisch; scheußlich.

fin *n* Finne *f*; Flosse *f*; Kühlrippe *f*.

final *adj* letzte(r, s); endgültig; End-; Schluß-:—**~ly** *adv* endlich; schließlich; zum Schluß; endgültig.

finale *n* Finale *n*.

finalist *n* Endkampfteilnehmer(in) *m(f)*.

finalize *vt* beenden; abschließen.

finance *n* Finanzwesen *n*; *pl* Finanzen *pl*; Einkünfte *pl*.

financial *adj* finanziell; Finanz-.

financier *n* Finanzier *m*.

find *vt* (heraus)finden; feststellen:—**~ out** entdecken:—*n* Fund *m*; Entdeckung *f*.

fine *adj* fein; schön:—*n* Geldstrafe *f*; Bußgeld *n*:—*vt* zu einer Geldstrafe verurteilen.

finger *n* Finger *m*.

fingernail *n* Fingernagel *m*.

fingerprint *n* Fingerabdruck *m*.

finish *vt* (be)enden.

fir (tree) *n* Tanne *f*.

fire *n* Feuer *n*;Brand *m*:—*vt* (ab)feuern; abschießen:—*vi* feuern.

firearm *n* Schußwaffe *f*.

fireman *n* Feuerwehrmann *m*.

fireplace *n* (offener) Kamin *m*.

fireproof *adj* feuerfest.

fireworks *npl* Feuerwerk *n*.

firm *adj* fest:—*n*Firma *f*; Betrieb *m*.

first *adj* erste(r, s); erstklassig:—*adv* zuerst.

fish *n* Fisch *m*:—*vi* fischen; angeln.

fisherman *n* Fischer *m*; Angler *m*.

fishmonger *n* Fischhändler *m*.

fist *n* Faust *f*.

fit *n* Paßform *f*; Zusammenpassen *n*; Anfall *m*:—*adj* passend; geeignet; tauglich; fähig; gesund:—*vt* (an) passen; ausrüsten.

five *num* fünf.

fix *vt* befestigen; festsetzen; reparieren.

fixture *n* festes Inventar *n*; Installa-tionsteil *n*; Spannvorrichtung *f*.

fizzy *adj* zischend; sprudelnd.

flag *n* Flagge *f*; Fahne *f*.

flake *n* Flocke *f*:—*vi* flocken.

flaky *adj* flockig; blätterig.

flamboyant *adj* extravagant; auffallend.

flame *n* Flamme *f*.

flamingo *n* Flamingo *m*.

flank *n* Flanke *f*; Seite *f*:—*vt* flankieren.

flannel *n* Flanell *m*; Waschlappen *m*.

flap *n* Flattern *n*; Schlag *m*; Klappe *f*.

flash *n* Aufleuchten *n*:—*vt* aufleuchten lassen.

flat *adj* flach; platt; glatt; (*mus*) erniedrigt:—*n* Fläche *f*; Ebene *f*; (*mus*) B *n*.

flatten *vt* (ein)ebnen; flach machen.

flatter *vt* schmeicheln.

flattering *adj* schmeichelhaft.

flattery *n* Schmeichelei *f*.

flavour *n* Geschmack *m*; Aroma *n*; Würze *f*:—*vt* würzen.

flaw *n* Fehler *m*; Mangel *m*; Makel *m*; Defekt *m*.

flax *n* Flachs *m*; Lein *m*.

flea *n* Floh *m*.

flee *vt* fliehen vor; fliehen aus; meiden:—*vi* fliehen; flüchten.

fleet *n* Flotte *f*.

fleeting *adj* flüchtig.

flesh *n* Fleisch *f*.

flesh wound *n*
Fleischwunde *f.*
fleshy *adj* fleischig.
flex *n* Kabel *n;* Schnur *f;*
Beugen *n:—vt* biegen;
beugen; anspannen.
flexibility *n* Flexibilität *f;*
Biegsamkeit *f.*
flexible *adj* flexibel;
biegsam.
flick *n* Klaps *m;* schnelle
Bewegung *f;* Knall *m:—vt*
leicht schlagen; knallen
mit.
flicker *vi* flackern; zucken;
flimmern.
flier *n* Flieger *m;*
Schwungrad *n;* Flugblatt *n.*
flight *n* Flug *m;* Fliegen *n;*
Schwarm *m;* Treppe *f;*
Flucht *f.*
flimsy *adj* dünn; leichtzer-
brechlich.
flinch *vi* zurückschrecken;
(zurück)-zucken.
fling *vt* werfen; schleudern.
flint *n* Flint *m;* Feuerstein *m.*
flip *vt* schnippen; schnellen.
flippant *adj* respektlos;
schnippisch.
flipper *n* Flosse *f.*
flirt *vi* herumsausen;
flirten; liebäugeln:—*n*
Schäker(in) *m(f).*
flirtation *n* Flirten *n;* Flirt
m; Liebäugeln *n.*
flit *vi* flitzen; huschen; flattern.
float *vt* treiben lassen;
flößen:—*vi* schwimmen;
treiben:—*n* Floß *n;*
Prahm *m.*
flock *n* Herde *f;* Schwarm
m; Flocke *f.*
flog *vt* prügeln; auspeitschen; antreiben.

flogging *n* Prügel(strafe) *f;*
Auspeitschen *n.*
flood *n* Flut *f;* Über-
schwemmung *f;* Schwall
m:—vt (über)fluten; überschwemmen.
flooding *n* Überschwem-
mung *f;* Überflutung *f.*
floodlight *n* Flutlicht *n.*
floor *n* (Fuß)Boden *m.*
florist *n* Blumenhändler(in)
m(f).
flour *n* Mehl *n;* Pulver *n.*
flourishing *adj* blühend;
gedeihend.
flout *vt* verspotten;
mißachten.
flow *vi* fließen; strömen;
rinnen; wallen; entsprin-
gen:—*n* Fließen *n;* Fluß *m;*
Schwall *m;* Flut *f.*
flower *n* Blume *f;* Blüte *f:—*
vi blühen.
flowerpot *n* Blumentopf *m.*
flowery *adj* geblümt.
fluctuate *vi* schwanken;
fluktuieren.
fluency *n* Flüssigkeit *f;*
(Rede)Ge-wandtheit *f.*
fluent *adj* flüssig; fließend;
gewandt.
fluff *n* Staubflocke *f;* Fussel
f; Flaum *m.*
fluffy *adj* flaumig; flockig;
locker.
fluid *adj* flüssig:—*n*
Flüssigkeit *f.*
flute *n* Flöte *f;* Riefe *f.*
flutter *vi* flattern; zittern:—
n Flattern *n;* Verwirrung *f.*
fly *vt vi* fliegen:—*n* Fliege *f;*
Flug *m;* Hosenschlitz *m.*
foal *n* Fohlen *n.*
foam *n* Schaum *m:—vi*
schäumen.
foamy *adj* schaumig.

focus *n* Brennpunkt *m;*
Scharfeinstellung *f;* Herd *m.*
fodder *n* Futter *n.*
foe *n* Feind(in) *m(f);*
Widersacher(in) *m(f).*
fog *n* Nebel *m;* Schleier *m.*
foggy *adj* neblig; nebelhaft.
foil *n* Folie *f.*
fold *n* Falte *f:—vt* falten.
folder *n* Mappe *f;*
Schnellhefter *m;*
Faltprospekt *m.*
folio *n* Blatt *n;* Foliant *m.*
folk *n* Leute *pl;* Volk *n;*
Folk *m.*
folklore *n* Folklore *f;*
Volkskunde *f;* Volkstum *n.*
follow *vt vi* (nach)folgen.
folly *n* Torheit *f;*
Verrücktheit *f.*
fond *adj* zärtlich; liebevoll.
fondle *vt* streicheln; spielen
mit.
food *n* Essen *n;* Nahrung *f;*
Verpflegung *f;*
Lebensmittel *pl;* Futter *n.*
fool *n* Narr *m;* Närrin *f;*
Dummkopf *m:—vt* zum
Narren halten; reinlegen;
betrügen.
foolish *adj* dumm; töricht;
albern; unklug; lächerlich.
foot *n* Fuß *m:—***on/by** ~ zu
Fuß.
football *n* Fußball *m.*
footpath *n* Pfad *m;* Fußweg
m.
footprint *n* Fußabdruck *m.*
for *prep* für:—*conj* denn.
forbid *vt* verbieten.
force *n* Kraft *f;* Stärke *f:—vt*
(er)-zwingen.
forearm *n* Unterarm *m.*
foreboding *n* (böse)
Vorahnung *f;* (böses)
Vorzeichen.

forecast *vt* vorhersagen; voraussagen:—*n* Vorhersage *f*; Prognose *f*.

forecourt *n* Vorhof *m*; Vorplatz *m*.

forefather *n* Ahn *m*; Vorfahr *m*.

forefinger *n* Zeigefinger *m*.

forefront *n*:—**in the ~ of** in vorderster Linie.

forego *vt* vorangehen; vorhergehen.

foregone *adj* vorhergehend; früher; von vornherein feststehend.

foreground *n* Vordergrund *m*.

forehead *n* Stirn *f*.

foreign *adj* fremd; ausländisch; Auslands-; Außen-.

foreigner *n* Ausländer(in) *m*.

foresee *vt* vorhersehen; voraussehen.

foresight *n* Weitblick *m*; Voraussicht *f*.

forest *n* Wald *m*; Forst *m*.

foretell *vt* vorhersagen; voraussagen.

forewarn *vt* vorher warnen.

foreword *n* Vorwort *n*.

forfeit *n* (Ein)Buße *f*; Strafe *f*; Verlust *m*; Pfand *n*:—*vt* verwirken; verlieren; einbüßen.

forge *n* Schmiede *f*; Esse *f*; Hammerwerk *n*:—*vt* schmieden; formen; erfinden; fälchen.

forger *n* Fälscher *m*; Schmied *m*.

forgery *n* Fälschung *f*; Fälschen *n*.

forget *vt* vergessen:—*vi* vergessen.

forgetful *adj* vergeßlich; nachlässig.

forget-me-not *n* (*bot*) Vergißmeinnicht *n*.

forgive *vt* vergeben; verzeihen.

fork *n* Gabel *f*.

forlorn *adj* verlassen; einsam; verzweifelt; verloren.

form *n* Form *f*; Gestalt *f*:—*vt* formen; bilden.

formal *adj* förmlich; formell; feierlich.

formality *n* Förmlichkeit *f*; Formalität *f*.

format *n* Format *n*; Gestaltung *f*:—*vt* formatieren.

formation *n* Formation *f*; Bildung *f*; Entstehung *f*; Gründung *f*.

former *adj* früher; ehemalig:—**~ly** *adv* früher; ehemals.

formula *n* Formel *f*; Rezept *n*.

fort *n* Fort *n*; Festung *f*.

forthwith *adj* sofort; umgehend; unverzüglich.

fortification *n* Befestigung *f*; Festung *f*; (Ver)Stärkung *f*; Untermauerung *f*.

fortify *vt* befestigen; (ver)stärken; untermauern.

fortnight *n* vierzehn Tage *mpl*:—**~ly** *adj adv* vierzehntägig; alle 14 Tage.

fortress *n* (*mil*) Festung *f*.

fortunate *adj* glücklich; glückverheißend:—**~ly** *adv* glücklicherweise; zum Glück.

fortune *n* Vermögen *n*; Reichtum *m*; (glücklicher) Zufall; Glück *n*; Schicksal *n*.

forty *num* vierzig.

forum *n* Forum *n*; Gericht *n*.

forward *adj* vorwärts; vordere(r, s); frühreif; fortschrittlich; vorlaut; vorschnell; bereitwillig:—**~s** *adv* vor; nach vorn; vorwärts; voraus; voran:—*vt* beschleunigen; fördern; schicken; (nach)senden.

fossil *n* Fossil *n*; Versteinerung *f*.

foster *vt* aufziehen; in Pflege nehmen/geben; hegen; fördern.

foul *adj* stinkend; widerlich; schlecht; faul; schmutzig:—*vt* beschmutzen; verunreinigen; foulen; kollidieren mit.

found *vt* gründen.

foundation *n* Fundament *n*; Gründung *f*; Stiftung *f*.

fountain *n* Quelle *f*; Fontäne *f*; Springbrunnen *m*.

four *num* vier.

fourteen *num* vierzehn.

fourth *adj* vierte(r, s).

fowl *n* Geflügel *n*; Federvieh *n*.

fox *n* Fuchs *m*.

fraction *n* Fraktion *f*; Bruch(teil) *m*.

fracture *n* Bruch *m*; Fraktur *f*.

fragile *adj* gebrechlich.

fragment *n* Fragment *n*.

fragrance *n* Duft *m*.

fragrant *adj* duftend.

frame *n* Rahmen *m*.

France *n* Frankreich *n*.

frank *adj* offen; aufrichtig; freimütig.

fraud *n* Betrug *m*.

free adj frei:—vt befreien.

freedom n Freiheit f.

freeze vi frieren.

freezing adj eiskalt; Gefrier-.

freight n Fracht f; Ladung f.

freighter n Frachter m; Transport-flugzeug n.

French adj französisch.

frequency n Frequenz f; Häufigkeit f.

frequent adj häufig.

fresh adj frisch.

friction n Reibung f.

Friday n Freitag m:—**Good ~** Karfreitag m.

friend n Freund(in) m(f); Bekannte(r) f(m).

friendly adj freundlich.

friendship n Freundschaft f.

fright n Schreck(en) m; Entsetzen n.

frighten vt erschrecken; Angst einjagen.

frightened adj erschrocken; verängstigt.

frightful adj schrecklich; furchtbar.

frigid adj kalt; frostig; frigid.

fringe n Franse f; Rand m; Ponyfrisur f.

frisk vt wedeln mit; durchsuchen.

frog n Frosch m.

from prep von; aus; seit; von... aus.

front n Vorderseite f; Fassade f; Vorderteil n; Front f:—adj Front-; Vorder-.

frontier n Grenze f; Grenzbereich m.

frost n Frost m; Reif m.

frown vi die Stirn runzeln:—n Stirnrunzeln n.

frozen adj (ein)gefroren.

fruit n Obst n; Frucht f.

frustrate vt vereiteln; frustrieren.

frustrated adj frustriert; vereitelt.

frustration n Frustration f; Vereitelung f.

fry vt braten.

fuchsia n Fuchsie f.

fuel n Brennstoff m.

fulfil vt erfüllen.

fulfilment n Erfüllung f.

full adj voll; weit; rund.

fully adv voll; völlig; ganz.

fun n Spaß m.

function n Funktion f; Feier f; Veranstaltung f.

functional adj funktionell; funktionsfähig.

fund n Kapital n; Fonds m:—vt fundieren; finanzieren.

fundamental adj fundamental; grundlegend; grundsätzlich; Grund-:—**~ly** adv im Grunde; im wesentlichen.

funeral n Beerdigung f; Bestattung f; Begräbnis n.

fungus n Pilz m; Schwamm m; Fungus m.

funnel n Trichter m; Schornstein m.

funny adj komisch.

fur n Fell n; Pelz m.

furious adj wütend; wild; heftig.

furnace n Ofen m; Kessel m; Feuerung f.

furnish vt versorgen; ausstatten; möblieren; liefern.

furniture n Möbel pl; Einrichtung f.

further adj adv weiter:—vt fördern; unterstützen.

furthermore adv ferner; überdies; außerdem.

fury n Wut f; Wildheit f; Heftigkeit f; Furie f.

fuse vt einen Zünder anbringen:—vi durchbrennen:—n Zünder m; Sicherung f.

fusion n Fusion f; Schmelzen n; Verschmelzung f; Vereinigung f.

fuss n Aufregung f; Ärger m; Wirbel m; Theater n.

fussy adj aufgeregt; pedantisch.

futile adj zwecklos.

future adj (zu)künftig; Zukunfts-:—n Zukunft f; Futur n.

G

gain *n* Gewinn *m:*—*vt* verdienen; gewinnen.

galaxy *n* Galaxie *f.*

gale *n* Sturm *m.*

gallery *n* Gallerie *f.*

gallop *n* Galopp *m:*—*vi* galoppieren.

gamble *vi* spielen; spekulieren:—*n* Glücksspiel *n.*

gambler *n* Spieler(in) *m(f).*

gambling *n* Spielen *n.*

game *n* Spiel *n.*

gander *n* Gänserich *m.*

gap *n* Lücke *f.*

garage *n* Garage *f;* Reparaturwerkstatt *f.*

garden *n* Garten *m.*

gardener *n* Gärtner(in) *m(f).*

gardening *n* Gärtnerei *f.*

garlic *n* Knoblauch *m.*

garment *n* Kleidungsstück *n;* Gewand *n.*

gas *n* Gas *n.*

gasp *vi* keuchen:—*n* Keuchen *n.*

gate *n* Tor *n;* Pforte *f.*

gather *vt* versammeln:—*vi* sich versammeln.

gay *adj* fröhlich; bunt; schwul.

gaze *vi* starren:—*n* (starrer) Blick *m.*

gear *n* Getriebe *n;* Gang *m;* Gerät *n;* Ausrüstung *f.*

gem *n* Edelstein *m;* Juwel *n.*

Gemini *n* (*astrol*) Zwillinge *pl.*

gene *n* Gen *n.*

general *adj* allgemein:—**in ~** im allgemeinen:—*n* General *m.*

generate *vt* erzeugen.

generation *n* Generation *f;* (Er)Zeu-gung *f.*

generator *n* Generator *m;* Erzeuger *m.*

generic *adj* Gattungs-; allgemein.

generosity *n* Großzügigkeit *f.*

generous *adj* großzügig.

genetics *npl* Genetik *f.*

genius *n* Genie *n;* Genialität *f;* Geist *m.*

gentle *adj* sanft.

gentleman *n* Ehrenmann *m;* Herr *m.*

gentleness *n* Sanftheit *f.*

genuine *adj* echt; aufrichtig; natürlich; ernsthaft.

geographer *n* Geograph(in) *m(f).*

geographical *adj* geographisch.

geography *n* Geographie *f;* Erdkunde *f.*

geological *adj* geologisch.

geologist *n* Geologe *m;* Geologin *f.*

geology *n* Geologie *f.*

geometric(al) *adj* geometrisch.

geometry *n* Geometrie *f.*

geranium *n* (*bot*) Geranie *f;* Storchschnabel *m.*

germ *n* Keim *m;* Mikrobe *f;* Krankheitserreger *m.*

gesture *n* Geste *f;* Gebärde *f.*

get *vt* bekommen; erhalten; kriegen; holen; beschaffen; erreichen.

ghost *n* Gespenst *n;* Geist *m.*

ghostly *adj* geisterhaft; gespenstisch.

giant *n* Riese *m.*

giddy *adj* schwindlig; schwindelerregend.

gift *n* Geschenk *n;* Spende *f;* Schenkung *f;* Gabe *f;* Talent *n.*

gifted *adj* begabt; talentiert.

gigantic *adj* gigantisch; riesig.

giggle *vi* kichern.

gild *vt* vergolden.

gill *n* Kieme *f;* Lamelle *f.*

gimmick *n* Trick *m;* Masche *f.*

gin *n* Gin *m;* Wacholderschnaps *m.*

ginger *n* Ingwer *m.*

gingerbread *n* Lebkuchen *m.*

gipsy *n* Zigeuner(in) *m(f).*

giraffe *n* Giraffe *f.*

girl *n* Mädchen *n.*

girlfriend *n* Freundin *f.*

give *vt vi* geben:—**~ up** *vi* aufgeben.

glacier *n* Gletscher *m.*

glad *adj* froh; erfreut:—**~ly** *adv* gern; mit Freuden.

glamorous *adj* bezaubernd.

glamour *n* Zauber *m;* Glanz *m.*

glance n (flüchtiger)
Blick:—vi (flüchtig)
blicken.

gland n Drüse f.

glare n greller Schein m;
wütender Blick m:—vi
grell leuchten; wütend
starren.

glass n Glas n; Spiegel m:—
~es pl Brille f:—adj Glas-.

glassware n Glaswaren fpl.

glaze vt verglasen;
glasieren; glasig machen.

glide vi gleiten; schweben;
segelfliegen.

glimmer n Schimmer m;
Glimmer m: —vi glim-
men; schimmern.

glimpse n flüchtiger Blick
m; flüchtiger Eindruck
m:—vt einen flüchtigen
Blick erhaschen von.

glint vi glitzern; glänzen.

global adj global; Welt-;
umfassend.

globe n (Erd)Kugel f; Erde
f; Globus m.

gloomy adj düster; schwer-
mütig; trübsinnig; hoff-
nungslos.

glorious adj ruhmreich;
glorreich; herrlich;
prächtig.

glory n Ruhm m; Ehre f;
Stolz m; Herrlichkeit f;
Pracht f.

gloss n Glanz m; Glosse f.

glossary n Glossar n.

glove n Handschuh m.

glow vi glühen:—n
Glühen n.

glue n Leim m; Klebstoff
m:—vt leimen, kleben.

glut n Übersättigung f;
Überangebot n;
Schwemme f.

gnome n (Garten)Zwerg m;
Gnom m.

go vi (fort)gehen; (ab)fahren.

goal n Ziel n; Tor n.

goalkeeper n Torhüter(in)
m(f).

god n Gott m.

godchild n Patenkind n.

goddaughter n
Patentochter f.

goddess n Göttin f.

godfather n Pate m,
Patenonkel m.

godmother n Patin f,
Patentante f.

godson n Patensohn m.

gold n Gold n; Goldgelb n.

golden adj golden; Gold-.

goldfish n Goldfisch m.

goldsmith n
Goldschmied(in) m(f).

golf n Golf n.

golf ball n Golfball m.

golf club n club de golf m.

golf course n Golfplatz m.

golfer n Golfspieler(in) m(f).

gondolier n Gondoliere m.

gong n Gong m.

good adj gut.

goodbye! excl auf
Wiedersehen! auf
Wiederhören!

Good Friday n Karfreitag m.

goodness n Güte f.

goose n Gans f.

gooseberry n Stachelbeere f.

gorilla n Gorilla m.

gorse n Stechginster m.

gospel n Evangelium n.

gossip n Klatsch m;
Schwatz m:—vi klatschen;
schwatzen.

govern vt regieren.

government n Regierung f.

grab vt ergreifen; packen;
schnappen.

grace n Anmut f; Gnade f.

graceful adj anmutig;
graziös.

gracious adj gnädig.

grade n Grad m; Klasse f;
Stufe f.

gradient n Steigung f;
Gefälle n; Gradient m.

gradual adj allmählich:—
~ly adv nach und nach.

grain n Korn n; Getreide n.

gram n Gramm n.

grammar n Grammatik f.

grammatical adj grammatisch.

granary n Kornkammer f;
Getreidespeicher m.

grand adj groß(artig).

grandchild n Enkelkind n.

granddaughter n
Enkeltochter f, Enkelin f:—
great-~ Urenkelin f.

grandfather n Großvater
m:—**great-**
~ Urgroßvater m.

grandmother n
Großmutter f:—**great-~**
Urgroßmutter f.

grandparents npl
Großeltern pl.

grandson n Enkelsohn m,
Enkel m:—**great-~**
Urenkel m.

granite n Granit m.

granny n Oma f.

grant vt gewähren, bewilli-
gen:—n Bewilligung f.

grape n Weintraube f.

grapefruit n Grapefruit f;
Pampelmuse f.

graph n graphische
Darstellung f; Diagramm
n; Kurve f.

graphic(al) adj anschaulich;
plastisch; graphisch;
Schrift-.

graphics *n* Graphik *f;*
graphische Darstellung *f.*

grasp *vt* packen;
(er)greifen; an sich
reißen:—*n* Griff *m;* Gewalt
f; Auffassungsgabe *f;*
Verständnis *n.*

grass *n* Gras *n;* Rasen *m.*

grasshopper *n* Grashüpfer
m; Heuschrecke *f.*

grate *n* Gitter *n;* Rost *m:*—
vt vergittern; reiben.

grateful *adj* dankbar.

gratitude *n* Dankbarkeit *f.*

grave *n* Grab *n:*—*adj* ernst;
gewichtig.

gravedigger *n* Totengräber
m.

gravel *n* Kies *m;* Schotter *m;*
Geröll *n.*

gravestone *n* Grabstein *m.*

graveyard *n* Friedhof *m.*

gravity *n* Schwere *f;*
Gravitation *f.*

graze *vt vi* weiden.

grease *n* Fett *n;* Schmalz
n:—*vt* (ein) fetten.

greasy *adj* fettig; schmierig;
ölig.

great *adj* groß; großartig.

greed *n* (Hab)Gier *f;*
Gierigkeit *f.*

greedy *adj* (hab)gierig;
gefräßig.

Greek *n* Griechisch *n;*
Grieche *m,* Griechin *f.*

green *adj* grün; unreif.

greengrocer *n* Obst- und
Gemüsehändler *m.*

greenhouse *n* Gewächshaus
n; Treibhaus *n.*

greet *vt* (be)grüßen; empfangen.

greeting *n* Gruß *m;*
Begrüßung *f.*

grenade *n* (*mil*) Granate *f;*
Tränengaspatrone *f.*

grey *adj* grau.

greyhound *n* Windhund *m.*

grid *n* Gitter *n;* Rost *m;*
Netz *n.*

grief *n* Gram *m;* Kummer *m.*

grill *n* Grill *m;* Gegrilltes
n:—*vt* grillen.

grim *adj* grimmig; erbittert.

grime *n* Schmutz *m;* Ruß *m.*

grimy *adj* schmutzig; rußig.

grin *n* Grinsen *n:*—*vi* grinsen; feixen.

grind *vt* schleifen; wetzen.

grip *n* Griff *m;* Halt *m:*—*vt*
ergreifen; packen.

grit *n* (Streu)Sand *m;*
Kies *m.*

groan *vi* (auf)stöhnen;
ächzen:—*n* Stöhnen *n;*
Ächzen *n.*

grocer *n*
Lebensmittelhändler *m.*

groom *n* Pferdepfleger(in)
m(f); Bräutigam *m:*—*vt*
pflegen.

gross *adj* brutto; Gesamt-;
schwer; grob; anstößig;
unfein.

grotesque *adj* grotesk.

ground *n* Grund *m;*
(Erd)Boden *m:*—*vt* niederlegen; auf Grund setzen.

group *n* Gruppe *f;* Konzern
m:—*vt* gruppieren.

grow *vi* wachsen.

growl *vi* knurren;
grollen:—*n* Knurren *n;*
Grollen *n.*

growth *n* Wachstum *n.*

grumble *vi* murren; knurren; grollen.

grumpy *adj* mürrisch; miß-
mutig; verdrießlich.

grunt *vi* grunzen; murren;
ächzen:—*n* Grunzen *n;*
Ächzen *n.*

guarantee *n* Garantie *f;*
Bürgschaft *f;* Sicherheit
f:—*vt* garantieren; (ver)
bürgen für; sichern.

guard *n* Wache *f;* Wächter
m:—*vt* bewachen.

guerrilla *n* Guerilla *f.*

guess *vi* raten.

guest *n* Gast *m.*

guide *vt* (an)leiten;
führen:—*n* Füh-rer(in)
m(f); Leitfaden *m.*

guilt *n* Schuld *f.*

guilty *adj* schuldig.

guitar *n* Gitarre *f.*

gulf *n* Golf *m;* Bucht *f;*
Abgrund *m.*

gull *n* Möwe *f.*

gullible *adj* leichtgläubig.

gum *n* Zahnfleisch *n;*
Gummi *m.*

gun *n* Geschütz
*n;*Feuerwaffe *f.*

gunfire *n* Geschützfeuer *n.*

gunman *n* Revolverheld *m;*
Bewaff-nete(r) *f(m).*

gunpowder *n* Schießpulver
n.

gush *vi* strömen; sich
ergießen.

gust *n* Bö *f;* Windstoß *m;*
Ausbruch *m;* Sturm *m.*

gutter *n* Rinnstein *m;* Gosse
f; (Dach) Rinne *f.*

guy *n* Kerl *m;* Typ *m.*

guzzle *vt* saufen; fressen.

gym(nasium) *n* Turnhalle *f.*

gymnast *n* Turner(in) *m(f).*

gymnastics *npl* Turnen *n;*
Gymnastik *f.*

H

habit *n* (An)Gewohnheit *f*;
Sucht *f*.

habitat *n* Habitat *n*.

habitual *adj* gewohn-
heitsmäßig.

haddock *n* Schellfisch *m*.

hail *n* Hagel *m*:—*vi* hageln.

hair *n* Haar *n*; Haare *pl*.

hairbrush *n* Haarbürste *f*;
Haarpinsel *m*.

haircut *n* Haarschnitt *m*;
Frisur *f*.

hairdresser *n* Friseur *m*,
Friseuse *f*.

hairy *adj* haarig.

half *n* Hälfte *f*:—*adj* halb.

hall *n* Halle *f*; Saal *m*.

halt *vi* anhalten:—*n* Halt *m*.

halve *vt* halbieren.

ham *n* Schinken *m*.

hamburger *n* Hamburger *m*.

hammer *n* Hammer *m*:—*vt*
hämmern.

hand *n* Hand *f*.

handbag *n* Handtasche *f*.

handbrake *n* Handbremse *f*.

handcuff *n* Handschelle *f*.

handicap *n* Handikap *n*;
Behinderung *f*.

handicapped *adj* behindert.

handkerchief *n*
Taschentuch *n*.

handle *n* (Hand)Griff *m*:—
vt anfassen.

handsome *adj* hübsch; stat-
tlich.

hang *vt vi* hängen.

hangman *n* Henker *m*.

hangover *n* Kater *m*.

happen *vi* geschehen;
passieren.

happiness *n* Glück *n*;
Glückseligkeit *f*.

happy *adj* glücklich; froh.

harass *vt* belästigen;
schikanieren.

harbour *n* Hafen *m*.

hard *adj* hart; schwierig.

hardly *adv* kaum; hart;
streng.

hardware *n* Hardware *f*.

hare *n* Hase *m*.

harm *n* Schaden *m*; Unrecht
m; Übel *n*:—*vt* schaden;
verletzen.

harmful *adj* nachteilig;
schädlich.

harmless *adj* harmlos.

harmonious *adj* har-
monisch.

harmony *n* Harmonie *f*.

harness *n* Geschirr *n*:—*vt*
anschirren.

harp *n* Harfe *f*.

harpist *n* Harfenist(in) *m(f)*.

harsh *adj* rauh; grell.

harvest *n* Ernte *f*.

haste *n* Eile *f*.

hasten *vt vi* (sich be)eilen.

hasty *adj* hastig; (vor)eilig;
übereilt.

hat *n* Hut *m*.

hatch *vt* ausbrüten:—*n* Brut
f; Luke *f*; Durchreiche *f*.

hate *n* Haß *m*; Abscheu *f*:—
vt hassen, verabscheuen.

hateful *adj* hassenswert;
abscheulich.

hatred *n* Haß *m*; Abscheu *f*.

have *vt v aux* haben.

hawk *n* Falke *m*; Habicht
m; Mörtelbrett *n*.

hawthorn *n* Weißdorn *m*.

hay *n* Heu *n*.

hazard *n* Gefahr *f*; Risiko
m:—*vt* riskieren; wagen.

hazardous *adj* gewagt;
gefährlich.

haze *n* Dunst(schleier) *m*,
Schleier *m*.

hazel *n* Haselnuß *f*;
Nußbraun *n*:—*adj*
nußbraun.

hazelnut *n* Haselnuß *f*.

hazy *adj* dunstig.

he *pn* er.

head *n* Kopf *m*; Haupt *n*.

headache *n* Kopfschmerzen
mpl.

headlight *n* Scheinwerfer *m*.

headline *n* Schlagzeile *f*;
Überschrift *f*.

headmaster *n* Direktor *m*;
Rektor *m*.

headquarters *npl*
Hauptquartier *n*.

heal *vt vi* heilen.

health *n* Gesundheit *f*.

healthy *adj* gesund.

heap *n* Haufen *m*:—*vt*
(über)häufen.

hear *vt vi* hören.

hearse *n* Leichenwagen *m*.

heart *n* Herz *n*:—**by ~**
auswendig.

heat *n* Hitze *f*.

heater *n* Heizgerät *n*.

heating *n* Heizung *f*.
heatwave *n* Hitzewelle *f*.
heaven *n* Himmel *m*.
heavenly *adj* himmlisch.
heavy *adj* schwer; heftig.
hectic *adj* hektisch.
hedge *n* Hecke *f*.
hedgehog *n* Igel *m*.
heel *n* Ferse *f*.
heifer *n* Färse *f*.
height *n* Höhe *f*; Größe *f*.
heighten *vt* erhöhen; hervorheben.
heir *n* Erbe *m*:—~ **apparent** rechtmäßiger Erbe *m*.
heiress *n* Erbin *f*.
heirloom *n* Erbstück *n*.
helicopter *n* Hubschrauber *m*.
hell *n* Hölle *f*.
helm *n* (*mar*) Helm *m*; Ruder *n*.
helmet *n* Helm *m*.
help *vt vi* helfen:—*n* Hilfe *f*.
helper *n* Helfer(in) *m(f)*.
helpful *adj* hilfsbereit; hilfreich.
helpless *adj* hilflos; unbeholfen.
hem *n* Saum *m*; Rand *m*:—*vt* säumen.
hemisphere *n* Hemisphäre *f*; Halbkugel *f*.
hen *n* Henne *f*; Huhn *f*; Weibchen *n*.
her *poss adj* ihr, ihre.
herb *n* Kraut *n*:—~**s** *pl* Kräuter *pl*.
herd *n* Herde *f*; Rudel *n*; Hirt(in) *m(f)*.
here *adv* hier; hierher.
heritage *n* Erbe *n*.
hermit *n* Einsiedler *m*; Eremit *m*.
hero *n* Held *m*; Heros *m*; Halbgott *m*.

heroic *adj* heroisch; heldenhaft; Helden-; grandios.
heroine *n* Heldin *f*; Halbgöttin *f*.
heron *n* Reiher *m*.
herring *n* Hering *m*.
hers *poss pn* (der, die, das) ihrige.
herself *pn* sie selbst; ihr selbst; sich (selbst).
hesitant *adj* zögernd.
hesitate *vi* zögern.
hesitation *n* Zögern *n*.
heterosexual *adj* heterosexuell:—*n* Heterosexuelle(r) *f(m)*.
hibernate *vi* überwintern; Winterschlaf halten.
hiccup *n* Schluckauf *m*:—*vi* den Schluckauf haben.
hide *vt* verbergen; verstecken.
hideous *adj* scheußlich; gräßlich.
hierarchy *n* Hierarchie *f*.
high *adj* hoch.
hijack *vt* entführen; überfallen.
hijacker *n* (Flugzeug)Entführer *m*; Räuber *m*.
hike *vi* wandern; marschieren.
hilarious *adj* lustig; vergnügt.
hill *n* Hügel *m*; Anhöhe *f*; Haufen *m*.
hilt *n* Heft *n*; Griff *m*.
him *pn* ihn; ihm.
himself *pn* sich (selbst); selbst.
hinder *vt* aufhalten; (be)hindern.
hindrance *n* Behinderung *f*; Hindernis *n*.
hinge *n* Scharnier *n*; Angel *f*.

hint *n* Wink *m*; Andeutung *f*:—*vt* andeuten.
hip *n* Hüfte *f*; Hagebutte *f*.
hippopotamus *n* Flußpferd *n*.
hire *vt* (ver)mieten; engagieren:—*n* Miete *f*; Lohn *m*.
his *poss adj* sein, seine:— *poss pn* (der, die, das) seine.
hiss *vt vi* zischen.
historian *n* Historiker(in) *m(f)*.
historic(al) *adj* historisch; geschichtlich.
history *n* Geschichte *f*.
hit *vt* schlagen:—*n* Schlag *m*.
hitch *vt* ankoppeln; per Anhalter fahren:—*n* Knoten *m*; Problem *n*.
hive *n* Bienenstock *m*; Bienenschwarm *n*.
hoard *n* Hort *m*:—*vt* horten.
hoarse *adj* heiser.
hobby *n* Steckenpferd *n*; Hobby *n*; Liebhaberei *f*.
hockey *n* Hockey *n*.
hoe *n* Hacke *f*:—*vt* hacken.
hog *n* (Haus)Schwein *n*.
hold *vt* (fest)halten:—*n* Halt *m*; Griff *m*.
hole *n* Loch *n*.
holiday *n* Feiertag *m*; freier Tag *m*:—~**s** *pl* Ferien *pl*.
hollow *adj* hohl:—*n* Höhle *f*.
holly *n* Stechpalme *f*.
hollyhock *n* Stockrose *f*.
holocaust *n* Holocaust *m*; Katastrophe *f*.
holster *n* Halfter *n*.
holy *adj* heilig; geweiht.
homage *n* Huldigung *f*; Homage *f*.

home *n* Heim *n*; Zuhause
n; Heimat *f*.

homeless *adj* obdachlos.

home-made *adj* haus-
gemacht.

homesick *adj*
heimwehkrank.

homeward *adj* Heim-;
Rück-:—*adv* heimwärts;
nach Hause.

homosexual *adj* homosexuell:—*n* Homosexuelle(r)
f(m).

honest *adj* ehrlich.

honesty *n* Ehrlichkeit *f*.

honey *n* Honig *m*.

honeycomb *n* Honigwabe *f*.

honeymoon *n*
Flitterwochen *fpl*.

honeysuckle *n* Geißblatt *n*.

honour *n* Ehre *f*:—*vt* ehren.

honourable *adj* ehrenwert.

hood *n* Kapuze *f*; Kappe *f*.

hoof *n* Huf *m*.

hook *n* (Angel)Haken *m*:—
vt (zu)haken.

hooligan *n* Rowdy *m*.

hoop *n* Reif(en) *m*; Ring *m*;
Bügel *m*.

hop *n* (*bot*) Hopfen *m*;
Sprung *m*:—*vi* hüpfen;
springen.

hope *n* Hoffnung *f*;
Aussicht *f*:—*vi* (er)
hoffen.

hopeful *adj* hoff-
nungsvoll:—**~ly** *adv* hoffentlich.

hopeless *adj* hoffnungslos.

horizon *n* Horizont *m*.

horizontal *adj* horizontal.

horn *n* Horn *n*; Hupe *f*;
Schalltrichter *m*;
Sattelknopf *m*.

hornet *n* Hornisse *f*.

horoscope *n* Horoskop *n*.

horrible *adj* schrecklich;
furchtbar.

horrific *adj* schrecklich;
entsetzlich.

horrify *vt* entsetzen; mit
Schrecken erfüllen.

horror *n* Entsetzen *n*;
Schrecken *m*.

horse *n* Pferd *n*; Bock *m*.

horse chestnut *n*
Roßkastanie *f*.

horsefly *n* (Pferde)Bremse *f*.

horsepower *n* Pferdestärke
f.

horseradish *n* Meerrettich
m.

horseshoe *n* Hufeisen *n*.

hospitable *adj* gastfreundlich; gastlich.

hospital *n* Krankenhaus *n*.

hospitality *n*
Gastfreundschaft *f*;
Gastlichkeit *f*.

host *n* Gastgeber(in) *m(f)*;
(Gast)Wirt *m*;
Moderator(in) *m(f)*.

hostage *n* Geisel *f*.

hostess *n* Gastgeberin *f*;
(Gast)Wirtin *f*; Hostess *f*.

hostile *adj* feindlich;
feindselig.

hostility *n* Feindschaft *f*;
Feindseligkeit *f*.

hot *adj* heiß; warm.

hotel *n* Hotel *n*.

hound *n* Jagdhund *m*.

hour *n* Stunde *f*.

hourly *adv* stündlich.

house *n* Haus *n*:—*vt* unterbringen.

household *n* Haushalt *m*.

housekeeper *n*
Haushälter(in) *m(f)*.

houskeeping *n*
Haushaltsführung *f*.

housewife *n* Hausfrau *f*.

housework *n* Hausarbeit *f*.

housing *n* Unterbringung *f*.

hover *vi* schweben; sich
herumtreiben; schwanken.

how *adv* wie.

however *adv* wie auch
(immer):—*conj* dennoch;
(je)doch; aber.

howl *vi* heulen; brüllen:—*n*
Heulen *n*; Schrei *m*;
Brüllen *n*.

hub *n* (Rad)Nabe *f*.

hubcap *n* Radkappe *f*.

hug *vt* umarmen:—*n*
Umarmung *f*.

huge *adj* riesig; gewaltig;
mächtig.

hull *n* Rumpf *m*.

hum *vi* summen; brummen.

human *adj* menschlich;
Menschen-.

humanity *n* Menschheit *f*;
Humanität *f*;
Menschlichkeit *f*.

humble *adj* bescheiden;
demütig:—*vt* demütigen;
erniedrigen.

humid *adj* feucht; humid.

humidity *n* Feuchtigkeit *f*.

humiliate *vt* demütigen.

humiliation *n* Demütigung
f.

humility *n* Demut *f*;
Bescheidenheit *f*.

humour *n* Humor *m*.

humorous *adj* humorvoll.

hump *n* Buckel *m*; Höcker
m; (kleiner) Hügel *m*.

hundred *num* hundert.

hundredth *adj* hun-
dertste(r, s).

hunger *n* Hunger *m*:—*vi*
Hunger haben; hungern.

hungry *adj* hungrig.

hunt *vt vi* jagen:—*n* Jagd *f*.

hunter *n* Jäger *m*.

hurdle *n* Hürde *f*;
Hindernis *n*; Geflecht *n*.
hurricane *n* Hurrikan *m*;
Wirbelsturm *m*; Orkan *m*.
hurry *vi* eilen; hasten; sich
beeilen:—*n* Hast *f*; Eile *f*.
hurt *vt* verletzen; verwunden:—*n* Schmerz *m*;
Verletzung *f*; Wunde *f*.
hurtful *adj* verletzend;
schmerzlich; schädlich.
husband *n* Ehemann *m*;
Gatte *m*.

hut *n* Hütte *f*; Baracke *f*.
hyacinth *n* Hyazinthe *f*.
hydraulic *adj* hydraulisch.
hydrogen *n* Wasser-
stoff *m*.
hydrophobia *n* Tollwut *f*;
Hydro-phobie *f*.
hyena *n* Hyäne *f*.
hygiene *n* Hygiene *f*;
Gesundheitspflege *f*.
hygienic *adj* hygienisch.
hyphen *n* (*gr*) Bindestrich
m; Trennungszeichen *n*.

hypocrisy *n* Heuchelei *f*;
Scheinheiligkeit *f*.
hypocrite *n* Heuchler(in)
m(f).
hypocritical *adj* heuch-
lerisch; scheinheilig.
hypothesis *n* Hypothese *f*.
hypothetical *adj* hypothetisch.
hysteria *n* Hysterie *f*.
hysterical *adj* hysterisch.

I

I *pn* ich.
ice *n* Eis *n*.
iceberg *n* Eisberg *m*.
ice cream *n* Eis *n*;
Eiscreme *f*.
ice rink *n* Eisbahn *f*.
ice skating *n* Eislauf *m*;
Eislaufen *n*.
icicle *n* Eiszapfen *m*.
icy *adj* eisig; vereist; eiskalt.
idea *n* Idee *f*.
ideal *adj* ideal.
identical *adj* identisch.
identification *n*
Identifizierung *f*.
identify *vt* identifizieren.
identity *n* Identität *f*.
idiom *n* Idiom *n*;
Redewendung *f*.
idiomatic *adj* idiomatisch.
idiot *n* Idiot *m*; Trottel *m*.
idiotic *adj* idiotisch; blöd.
idle *adj* untätig; müßig;
faul.
idleness *n* Untätigkeit *f*;
Faulheit *f*.
idol *n* Idol *n*; Götze *m*.
if *conj* wenn (auch); falls;
ob:—~ **not** wenn nicht.
igloo *n* Iglu *n*.
ignite *vt* (ent)zünden.
ignition *n* (*chem*) Erhitzung
f; Entzünden *n*; Zündung *f*.
ignorance *n* Unwissenheit *f*;
Unkenntnis *f*;
Ignoranz *f*.
ignorant *adj* unwissentlich.
ignore *vt* ignorieren; nicht
beachten.

ill *adj* schlimm; schlecht;
übel; widrig; unheilvoll;
krank:—*n* Übel *n*.
illegal *adj* illegal; verboten;
gesetzwidrig; regelwidrig.
illegality *n*
Ungesetzlichkeit *f*;
Gesetzwidrigkeit *f*;
Illegalität *f*.
illegible *adj* unleserlich.
illegitimate *adj* unehelich;
inkorrekt; illegal; gesetzwidrig.
illicit *adj* unzulässig; gesetzwidrig.
illiterate *adj* analpha-
betisch; ungebildet.
illness *n* Krankheit *f*.
illogical *adj* unlogisch.
illusion *n* Illusion *f*;
Sinnestäuschung *f*;
Einbildung *f*; Wahn *m*.
illustrate *vt* erläutern; ver-
anschaulichen; illustrieren.
illustration *n* Illustration *f*;
Erläuterung *f*;
Veranschaulichung *f*.
illustrative *adj* erläuternd;
veranschaulichend; illus-
trativ.
illustrious *adj* glanzvoll;
erlaucht; berühmt.
ill-will *n* Übelwollen *n*;
böse Absicht *f*.
image *n* Bild(nis) *n*;
Ebenbild *n*; Bildsäule *f*;
Symbol *n*; Metapher *f*.
imaginable *adj* vorstellbar;
denkbar.

imaginary *adj* imaginär;
eingebildet; Phantasie-.
imagination *n*
Einbildung(skraft) *f*;
Vorstellung *f*.
imaginative *adj* einfallsre-
ich; phantasievoll; phan-
tastisch.
imagine *vt* sich vorstellen;
sich (aus) denken; sich
einbilden.
imbalance *n*
Unausgewogenheit *f*;
Ungleichgewicht *n*.
imbue *vt* durchtränken; tief
färben.
imitate *vt* nachahmen;
nachbilden.
imitation *n* Nachahmung *f*;
Nachbildung *f*.
immature *adj* unreif;
unausgereift.
immediate *adj* unmittelbar;
unverzüglich; sofortig:—
~ly *adv* unmittelbar;
sofort; unverzüglich.
immense *adj* riesig; enorm;
immens.
immigrant *n* Einwanderer
m, Einwanderin *f*;
Immigrant(in) *m(f)*.
immigration *n*
Einwanderung *f*;
Immigration *f*.
imminent *adj* drohend.
immoral *adj* unmoralisch;
unsittlich.
immortal *adj* unsterblich.

immortality *n*
Unsterblichkeit *f*;
Unvergänglichkeit *f*.

immune *adj* immun;
unempfänglich.

impact *n* Aufprall *m*;
Einschlag *m*; Impakt *m*.

impatience *n* Ungeduld *f*.

impatient *adj* ungeduldig;
unduldsam; in-
tolerant.

impersonal *adj* unpersönlich.

impetus *n* Antrieb *m*;
Anstoß *m*.

implicit *adj* impliziert; vor-
behaltlos.

imply *vt* implizieren.

impolite *adj* unhöflich.

import *vt* importieren; einführen;—*n* Import *m*;
Einfuhr *f*.

importance *n* Wichtigkeit *f*.

important *adj* wichtig.

importer *n* Importeur *m*.

impose *vt* auferlegen; aufdrängen.

impossibility *n*
Unmöglichkeit *f*.

impossible *adj* unmöglich.

impractical *adj* unprak-
tisch; unklug; undurch-
führbar.

imprecise *adj* ungenau.

impress *vt* beeindrucken;
imponieren; durchdrin-
gen; tief einprägen; (auf)
drücken; einprägen.

impression *n* Eindruck *m*;
Nachahmung *f*;
(Ab)Druck *m*; Aufdruck
m; Vertiefung *f*; Abzug *m*;
Auflage *f*.

impressive *adj* ein-
drucksvoll; imposant;
wirkungsvoll.

imprison *vt* inhaftieren;
einsperren; einschließen.

imprisonment *n*
Freiheitsstrafe *f*; Haft *f*;
Inhaftierung *f*.

improbable *adj*
unwahrscheinlich.

improve *vt* verbessern:—*vi*
sich (ver) bessern.

improvement *n*
(Ver)Besserung *f*;
Veredelung *f*;
Steigerung *f*.

impulse *n* Impuls *m*;
Antrieb *m*; (An)-Stoß *m*.

impulsive *adj* impulsiv;
spontan; Trieb-.

impure *adj* unrein; verun-
reinigt; verfälscht.

in *prep* in; innerhalb; an;
auf; bei; mit.

inability *n* Unfähigkeit *f*;
Unvermögen *n*.

inaccuracy *n*
Ungenauigkeit *f*.

inaccurate *adj* ungenau;
unrichtig.

inactive *adj* untäig; träge;
lustlos; inaktiv.

inactivity *n* Untätigkeit *f*;
Inaktivität *f*.

inadequate *adj*
unzulänglich;
unangemessen.

inadmissible *adj* unzulässig; unstatthaft.

inane *adj* leer; albern.

inaudible *adj* unhörbar.

inauspicious *adj* ungünstig;
unheilvoll.

incapable *adj* unfähig; hilflos; ungeeignet;
untauglich.

incapacity *n*
(Erwerbs)Unfähigkeit *f*;
Untauglichkeit *f*.

inch *n* Zoll *m*:—~ **by** ~
Zentimeter um
Zentimeter.

incidence *n* Vorkommen *n*;
Häufigkeit *f*.

incident *n* Vorfall *m*;
Zwischenfall.

incinerator *n*
Verbrennungsanlage *f*.

incite *vt* anregen; anspornen.

inclination *n* Neigung *f*;
(Ab)Hang *m*.

incline *vt vi* neigen.

include *vt* einschließen;
umfassen.

including *prep* ein-
schließlich.

inclusion *n* Einschluß *m*;
Einbeziehung *f*.

inclusive *adj* einschließlich;
inklusive.

income *n* Einkommen *n*.

incomparable *adj* unvergle-
ichbar.

incompatibility *n*
Unvereinbarkeit *f*;
Unverträglichkeit *f*.

incompatible *adj* unvereinbar; unverträglich.

incompetence *n*
Unfähigkeit *f*;
Inkompetenz *f*.

incompetent *adj* unfähig;
unqualifiziert.

incomplete *adj* unvollständig; unvollendet.

incomprehensible *adj*
unbegreiflich; unver-
ständlich.

inconclusive *adj* nicht
überzeugend; ergebnislos.

inconsistent *adj* inkonse-
quent; unbeständig;
unvereinbar; wider-
sprüchlich.

inconvenience *n* Unbequemlichkeit *f*; Ungelegenheit *f*; Unannehmlichkeit *f*:—*vt* stören; zur Last fallen; Unannehmlichkeiten bereiten.

inconvenient *adj* unbequem; ungelegen; lästig.

incorporate *vt* vereinigen; einverleiben; aufnehmen; enthalten; einbauen; verkörpern; *vi* sich vereinigen; (*law*) eine Gesellschaft gründen.

incorporation *n* Vereinigung *f*; Einverleibung *f*; Eintragung *f*.

incorrect *adj* unrichtig; fehlerhaft; inkorrekt.

increase *vt* vergrößern; vermehren; steigern; erhöhen:—*vi* zunehmen; sich vermehren:—*n* Vergrößerung *f*; Zunahme *f*; Steigerung *f*; Erhöhung *f*; Vermehrung *f*.

incredible *adj* unglaublich; unglaubwürdig.

incur *vt* sich zuziehen; sich aussetzen; geraten in.

incurable *adj* unheilbar.

indeed *adv* in der Tat; tatsächlich; wirklich; freilich.

indefinite *adj* unbestimmt; unbegrenzt.

independence *n* Unabhängigkeit *f*; Selbständigkeit *f*.

independent *adj* unabhängig; selbständig.

indescribable *adj* unbeschreiblich.

indeterminate *adj* unbestimmt; ungewiß; unentschieden.

index *n* Index *m*; (Inhalts)Verzeichnis *n*; Register *n*.

indicate *vt* zeigen auf; hinweisen auf; andeuten; anzeigen.

indication *n* Zeigen *n*; (An)Zeichen *n*; Hinweis *m*; Andeutung *f*; Indikation *f*.

indifferent *adj* gleichgültig; mittelmäßig; indifferent.

indigenous *adj* einheimisch.

indigent *adj* arm; bedürftig; mittellos.

indigestible *adj* unverdaulich.

indigestion *n* Verdauungsstörung *f*; Magenverstimmung *f*.

indignant *adj* entrüstet; empört.

indignation *n* Entrüstung *f*; Empörung *f*.

indigo *n* Indigo *m*.

indirect *adj* indirekt; mittelbar.

indiscreet *adj* unbesonnen; indiskret.

indiscretion *n* Unbedachtheit *f*; Indiskretion *f*.

indiscriminate *adj* nicht wählerisch; wahllos.

indistinct *adj* undeutlich.

individual *adj* einzeln; Einzel-; individuell.

indoors *adv* im Haus; drinnen; ins Haus.

industrial *adj* industriell; Industrie-.

industrialist *n* Industrielle(r) *f(m)*.

industrious *adj* fleißig.

industry *n* Industrie *f*; Gewerbe *n*; Arbeit *f*; Fleiß *m*.

inefficient *adj* ineffizient; (leistungs)-unfähig.

inequality *n* Ungleichheit *f*; Verschiedenheit *f*.

inert *adj* träge; inert.

inertia *n* Trägheit *f*.

inevitable *adj* unvermeidlich.

inexcusable *adj* unentschuldbar; unverzeihlich.

inexpensive *adj* billig; nicht teuer.

inexperience *n* Unerfahrenheit *f*.

inexperienced *adj* unerfahren.

inexplicable *adj* unerklärlich.

infant *n* Säugling *m*; Kleinkind *n*.

infantry *n* Infanterie *f*.

infatuated *adj* betört; vernarrt.

infatuation *n* Vernarrtheit *f*; Schwarm *m*.

infect *vt* infizieren; anstecken; befallen.

infection *n* Infektion(skrankheit) *f*; Ansteckung *f*; Befall *m*.

infectious *adj* ansteckend; infektiös.

infer *vt* schließen; folgern; andeuten.

inference *n* (Schluß)Folgerung *f*; (Rück)Schluß *m*.

inferior *adj* untergeordnet; niedriger; minderwertig; Unter-:—*n* Untergebene(r) *f(m)*; Unterlegene(r) *f(m)*.

inferiority *n* Unterlegenheit *f*; Minderwertigkeit *f*.

infiltrate *vt* einsickern in;
infiltrieren.

infinite *adj* unendlich;
grenzenlos; endlos.

infinity *n* Unendlichkeit *f*;
Grenzenlosigkeit *f*.

infirm *adj* schwach;
gebrechlich; fragwürdig.

inflate *vt* aufblasen; aufpumpen; aufblähen.

inflation *n* Inflation *f*;
Aufgeblasenheit *f*;
Aufpumpen *n*.

influence *n* Einfluß *m*:—*vt*
beeinflussen; bewegen.

influential *adj* einflußreich;
maßgeblich.

influenza *n* Grippe *f*.

inform *vt* informieren; mitteilen.

informal *adj* zwanglos;
inoffiziell.

informality *n*
Zwanglosigkeit *f*.

information *n* Information
f; Auskunft *f*.

infrastructure *n*
Infrastruktur *f*.

infuriate *vt* wütend
machen.

ingot *n* Barren *m*.

ingratitude *n*
Undankbarkeit *f*.

ingredient *n* Bestandteil *m*;
Zutat *f*.

inhabit *vt* bewohnen; leben
in.

inhabitant *n* Bewohner(in)
m(f); Ein-wohner(in) *m(f)*.

inhale *vt* einatmen;
inhalieren.

inherit *vt* (er)erben; beerben.

inheritance *n* Erbschaft *f*;
Erbgut *n*.

initial *adj* anfänglich;

Ausgangs-; er-ste(r, s):—*n*
Initiale *f*.

initiate *vt* initiieren.

initiation *n* Initiation *f*.

initiative *n* Initiative *f*.

inject *vt* injizieren; ein-
spritzen.

injection *n* Injektion *f*;
Spritze *f*; Einspritzung *f*.

injure *vt* verletzen.

injury *n* Verletzung *f*.

injustice *n* Ungerechtigkeit
f; Unrecht *n*.

ink *n* Tinte *f*; Tusche *f*;
Druckfarbe *f*.

inland *adj* inländisch;
Binnen-; einheimisch:—
adv landeinwärts.

inn *n* Gasthaus *n*;
Wirtshaus *n*.

innate *adj* angeboren;
innewohnen.

inner *adj* Innen-; innere(r, s).

innkeeper *n* (Gast)Wirt(in)
m(f).

innocence *n* Unschuld *f*;
Unwissenheit *f*.

innocent *adj* unschuldig.

inoculate *vt* (ein)impfen.

inoculation *n* (Ein)Impfung
f.

inoffensive *adj* harmlos;
friedfertig.

inorganic *adj* unorganisch.

inquire *vi* (nach)fragen;
sich erkundigen; nach-
forschen.

inquiry *n* Erkundigung *f*;
(An)Frage *f*.

inquisitive *adj* wißbegierig;
neugierig.

insane *adj* wahnsinnig.

insanity *n* Wahnsinn *m*.

insect *n* Insekt *n*.

insecure *adj* unsicher;
ungesichert.

insecurity *n* Unsicherheit *f*.

insert *vt* einführen; einwer-
fen.

insertion *n* Einführung *f*;
Einwurf *m*.

inside *adv* (dr)innen; innerhalb; hinein; herein.

insight *n* Einblick *m*;
Einsicht *f*.

insignificant *adj* bedeutungslos; unwichtig.

insincere *adj* unaufrichtig;
falsch.

insinuate *vt* andeuten;
anspielen auf.

insinuation *n* Andeutung *f*;
Anspielung *f*.

insist *vi* bestehen.

insistence *n* Bestehen *n*.

insistent *adj* beharrlich.

insomnia *n* Schlaflosigkeit *f*.

inspect *vt* untersuchen;
prüfen.

inspection *n* Untersuchung
f; Prüfung *f*.

inspector *n* Inspektor *m*;
Aufsichtsbe-amte(r) *f(m)*;
Prüfer(in) *m(f)*.

inspiration *n* Inspiration *f*.

inspire *vt* inspirieren.

install *vt* installieren; einbauen; einsetzen.

installation *n* Installation *f*;
Einbau *m*; Einrichtung *f*;
Einsetzung *f*.

instalment *n* Rate *f*.

instance *n* Beispiel *n*; Fall
m; Instanz *f*:—**for ~** zum
Beispiel.

instant *n* Moment *m*;
Augenblick *m*.

instead (of) *prep* (an)statt.

instinct *n* Instinkt *m*.

instinctive *adj* instinktiv.

institute *n* Institut *n*;
Anstalt *f*.

institution *n* Institution *f*.
instruct *vt* unterrichten.
instruction *n* Unterricht *m*.
instrument *n* Instrument *n*.
insulate *vt* isolieren.
insulation *n* Isolierung *f*.
insult *vt* beleidigen:—*n* Beleidigung *f*.
insulting *adj* beleidigend; unverschämt.
insurance *n* Versicherung *f*; (Ab)Si-cherung *f*.
insure *vt* versichern.
intact *adj* intakt.
integrate *vt* integrieren.
integration *n* Integration *f*.
integrity *n* Integrität *f*.
intellect *n* Intellekt *m*; Verstand *m*.
intellectual *adj* intellek-tuell; geistig.
intelligence *n* Intelligenz *f*.
intelligent *adj* intelligent.
intend *vi* beabsichtigen; vorhaben.
intense *adj* intensiv.
intensity *n* Intensität *f*; Stärke *f*.
intensive *adj* intensiv; stark; heftig; gründlich.
intent *n* Absicht *f*; Vorsatz *m*; Ziel *n*; Zweck *m*.
intention *n* Absicht *f*; Vorhaben *n*; Vorsatz *m*; Zweck *m*; Ziel *n*.
interest *vt* interessieren:—*n* Interesse *n*; Zinsen *pl*.
interesting *adj* interessant.
interfere *vi* stören; ein-greifen; sich einmischen.
interference *n* Störung *f*; Einmischung *f*.
interior *adj* innere(r, s); Innen-; inländisch; intern.
internal *adj* innere(r, s); innerlich.

international *adj* interna-tional.
interpret *vt* auslegen; inter-pretieren; dolmetschen.
interpreter *n* Dometscher(in) *m(f)*.
interrogate *vt* verhören.
interrogation *n* Verhör *n*.
interrupt *vt* unterbrechen; aufhalten.
interruption *n* Unterbrechung *f*; Störung *f*.
interval *n* Abstand *m*; Intervall *n*; Pause *f*.
interview *n* Interview *n*.
interviewer *n* Interviewer(in) *m(f)*.
intimate *n* Vertraute(r) *f(m)*:—*adj* vertraut.
intimidate *vt* ein-schüchtern.
into *prep* in.
intoxicate *vt* berauschen.
intoxication *n* Rausch *m*.
intricate *adj* verschlungen.
introduce *vt* einführen; vorstellen; einleiten.
introduction *n* Einführung *f*; Vorstellung *f*; Einleitung *f*.
introvert *n* introvertierter Mensch *m*.
intrude *vi* sich eindrängen; sich aufdrängen; stören.
intruder *n* Eindringling *m*; Störenfried *m*.
intuition *n* Intuition *f*.
intuitive *adj* intuitiv.
invade *vt* einfallen in.
invalid *adj* ungültig:—*n* Invalide *m*; Kranke(r) *f(m)*.
invalidate *vt* entkräften.
invaluable *adj* unschätzbar.
invariable *adj* unveränder-lich.

invasion *n* Einfall *m*.
invent *vt* erfinden.
invention *n* Erfindung *f*.
inventive *adj* erfinderisch.
inventor *n* Erfinder(in) *m(f)*.
inverse *adj* umgekehrt.
inversion *n* Umkehrung *f*.
invert *vt* umkehren.
invest *vt* investieren; anle-gen.
investigate *vt* untersuchen.
investigation *n* Untersuchung *f*.
investment *n* Investition *f*; Anlage *f*.
invisible *adj* unsichtbar.
invitation *n* Einladung *f*.
invite *vt* einladen.
invoice *n* Rechnung *f*.
involve *vt* verwickeln.
involved *adj* verwickelt.
involvement *n* Verwicklung *f*.
iris *n* Iris *f*.
iron *n* Eisen *n*; Bügeleisen *n*:—*adj* eisern; Eisen-:—*vt* bügeln.
ironic *adj* ironisch.
irony *n* Ironie *f*.
irrational *adj* irrational.
irrelevant *adj* irrelevant.
irritate *vt* reizen; (ver)ärg-ern; irritieren.
irritating *adj* ärgerlich; irri-tierend; Reiz-.
irritation *n* Ärger *m*; Verärgerung *f*; Reizung *f*; Irritation *f*.
Islam *n* Islam *m*.
island *n* Insel *f*.
isolate *vt* isolieren.
isolation *n* Isolation *f*.
issue *n* Ausgabe *f*; Erteilung *f*:—*vt* (her)aus-geben; erteilen.
it *pn* es; er; ihn; sie.

italic *n* Kursivschrift *f.*
itch *n* Jucken *n*; Juckreiz
  m:—*vi* jucken; kratzen.
item *n* Gegenstand *m*;
  Posten *m.*

itinerary *n* Reiseweg *m*;
  Reisebericht *m*;
  Reiseführer *m.*
its *poss adj* sein, seine; ihr,
  ihre.

itself *pn* sich; sich selbst;
  selbst.
ivory *n* Elfenbein *n.*
ivy *n* Efeu *m.*

J

jack *n* Wagenheber *m*; Bube *m*.

jackal *n* Schakal *m*.

jacket *n* Jacke *f*; Jackett *n*.

jade *n* Jade *f*.

jaguar *n* Jaguar *m*.

jail *n* Gefängnis *n*.

jailer *n* Gefängniswärter *m*.

jam *n* Gedränge *n*; Verstopfung *f*; Marmelade *f*.

January *n* Januar *m*, Jänner *m*.

jar *n* Krug *m*.

javelin *n* Wurfspieß *m*; Speer *m*.

jaw *n* Kiefer *m*.

jay *n* Eichelhäher *m*.

jazz *n* Jazz *m*.

jealous *adj* eifersüchtig.

jealousy *n* Eifersucht *f*.

jeer *vi* höhnisch lachen:—*n* Hohngelächter *n*.

jelly *n* Gallerte *f*; Gelee *n*; Aspik *m*; Götterspeise *f*.

jellyfish *n* Qualle *f*.

jeopardize *vt* gefährden.

jet *n* Düsenflugzeug *n*; Strahl *m*; Düse *f*; Jett *m*.

jettison *vt* über Bord werfen; abwerfen.

jetty *n* Mole *f*; Pier *m*.

Jew *n* Jude *m*.

jewel *n* Juwel *n*; Edelstein *m*.

jeweller *n* Juwelier *m*.

jewellery *n* Juwelen *pl*; Schmuck *m*.

Jewish *adj* jüdisch.

jig *n* Gigue *f*; Einspannvorrichtung *f*.

jigsaw *n* Puzzle *n*; Dekupiersäge *f*.

job *n* Arbeit *f*; Beschäftigung *f*; Stelle *f*; Arbeitsplatz *m*.

jockey *n* Jockey *m*.

jog *vi* trottenn; joggen.

join *vt* verbinden; vereinigen.

joint *n* Verbindung(sstelle) *f*; Gelenk *n*:—*adj* gemeinsam; gemeinschaftlich; vereint.

joke *n* Witz *m*; Scherz *m*; Spaß *m*:—*vi* scherzen; Witze machen.

joker *n* Spaßvogel *m*; Joker *m*.

jolly *adj* lustig; fröhlich; vergnügt.

journal *n* Tagebuch *n*; Journal *n*.

journalism *n* Journalismus *m*.

journalist *n* Journalist(in) *m(f)*.

journey *n* Reise *f*:—*vt* reisen.

joy *n* Freude *f*.

jubilation *n* Jubel *m*.

jubilee *n* Jubiläum *n*.

judge *n* Richter(in) *m(f)*:—*vt* richten; beurteilen.

judgment *n* Urteil *n*; Beurteilung *f*.

jug *n* Krug *m*.

juggle *vi* jonglieren.

juggler *n* Jongleur *m*; Schwindler *m*.

juice *n* Saft *m*.

juicy *adj* saftig.

July *n* Juli *m*.

jumble *vt* durcheinanderwerfen:—*n* Durcheinander *n*; Ramsch *m*.

jump *vi* (über)springen:—*n* (Ab)-Sprung *m*.

jumper *n* Pullover *m*.

June *n* Juni *m*.

jungle *n* Dschungel *m*.

junior *adj* junior; jünger; Unter-.

juniper *n* Wacholder *m*.

junk *n* Plunder *m*; Schrott *m*.

junta *n* Junta *f*.

jurisdiction *n* Rechtssprechung *f*; Gerichtsbarkeit *f*.

jury *n* Jury *f*; Preisgericht *n*.

just *adj* gerecht; rechtmäßig; berechtigt; richtig:—*adv* gerade; (so)eben.

justice *n* Gerechtigkeit *f*; Rechtmäßigkeit *f*.

justify *vt* rechtfertigen.

K

kangaroo *n* Känguruh *n*.

karate *n* Karate *n*.

keen *adj* scharf; fein; heftig; begeistert.

keep *vt* (be)halten; erhalten.

keeper *n* Wächter *m*; Verwalter *m*; Inhaber *m*; Halter *m*.

kennel *n* Hundehütte *f*.

kerb *n* Bordstein *m*.

kernel *n* Kern *m*; Korn *n*.

kettle *n* Kessel *m*.

key *n* Schlüssel *m*; (*mus*) Tonart *f*; Taste *f*.

keyboard *n* Tastatur *f*; Klaviatur *f*.

kick *vt* treten; (mit dem Fuß) stoßen: —*n* (Fuß)Tritt *m*; (Rück)Stoß *m*.

kid *n* Zicklein *n*; Kitz *n*.

kidnap *vt* kidnappen; entführen.

kidney *n* Niere *f*.

kill *vt* (ab)töten; umbringen; ermorden; totschlagen.

killer *n* Mörder *m*; Schlächter *m*.

kilo *n* Kilo *n*.

kilobyte *n* Kilobyte *n*.

kilogram *n* Kilogramm *n*.

kilometre *n* Kilometer *m*.

kilt *n* Kilt *m*; Schottenrock *m*.

kind *adj* freundlich; liebenswürdig: —*n* Art *f*; Sorte *f*.

kindergarten *n* Kindergarten *m*.

king *n* König *m*.

kingdom *n* Königreich *n*; Reich *n*.

kingfisher *n* Eisvogel *m*.

kiosk *n* Kiosk *m*; Telefonzelle *f*.

kipper *n* Räucherhering *m*.

kiss *n* Kuß *m*:—*vt* küssen.

kissing *n* Küssen *n*.

kit *n* Ausrüstung *f*; Montur *f*; Arbeitsgerät *n*.

kitchen *n* Küche *f*.

kite *n* Drachen *m*; Gabelweihe *f*.

kitten *n* Kätzchen *n*.

knack *n* Trick *m*; Kniff *m*; Geschick *n*; Talent *n*.

knave *n* Bube *m*; Schurke *m*.

knead *vt* kneten.

knee *n* Knie(stück) *n*.

kneel *vi* (sich hin)knien.

knell *n* Totengeläut *n*.

knife *n* Messer *n*.

knight *n* Ritter *m*; (*Schach*) Springer *m*; Pferd *n*.

knit *vt vi* tejer, stricken.

knob *n* Knauf *m*; Griff *m*; Höcker *m*; Stück(chen) *n*; Knorren *m*.

knock *vt vi* schlagen; klopfen:—*n* Schlag *m*; Klopfen *n*.

knot *n* Knoten *m*; Schleife *f*:—*vt* (ver)knoten; verheddern.

know *vt* wissen; können; (er)kennen: —*vi* wissen.

know-how *n* Know-how *n*.

knowledge *n* Wissen *n*; Kenntnis *f*.

knuckle *n* Knöchel *m*.

L

label *n* Etikett *n*.

laboratory *n* Labor(atorium) *n*.

labour *n* Arbeit *f*; Mühe *f*.

labyrinth *n* Labyrinth *n*.

lace *n* Spitze *f*.

lack *vi* fehlen:—*n* Mangel *m*.

lad *n* junger Kerl *m*; Junge *m*.

ladder *n* Leiter *f*; Laufmasche *f*.

ladle *n* (Schöpf)Kelle *f*.

lady *n* Dame *f*; Herrin *f*.

ladybird *n* Marienkäfer *m*.

lager *n* Lagerbier *n*.

lagoon *n* Lagune *f*.

lake *n* See *m*.

lamb *n* Lamm *n*:—*vi* lammen.

lame *adj* lahm.

lamp *n* Lampe *f*; Laterne *f*; Leuchte *f*.

lampshade *n* Lampenschirm *m*.

land *n* Land *n*; Boden *m*:—*vt vi* landen.

landlady *n* Vermieterin *f*; Wirtin *f*.

landlord *n* Vermieter *m*; Wirt *m*.

landmark *n* Grenzstein *m*; Landmarke *f*.

landowner *n* Grundbesitzer(in) *m(f)*.

landscape *n* Landschaft *f*.

landslide *n* Erdrutsch *m*.

lane *n* Weg *m*; Gasse *f*.

language *n* Sprache *f*.

lantern *n* Laterne *f*.

larch *n* Lärche *f*.

larder *n* Speisekammer *f*.

large *adj* groß.

lark *n* Lerche *f*.

last *adj* letzte(r, s):—**at ~** *adv* zuletzt: —*vi* (an)dauern.

late *adj* spät; verspätet.

laugh *vi* lachen:—*n* Lachen *n*.

laughter *n* Gelächter *n*.

launder *vt* waschen.

laundry *n* Wäsche *f*; Wäscherei *f*.

lava *n* Lava *f*.

lavatory *n* Toilette *f*.

lavender *n* Lavendel *m*.

law *n* Gesetz *n*; Recht *n*; Rechtswissenschaft *f*.

lawn *n* Rasen *m*.

lawyer *n* Rechtsanwalt *m*, Rechtsanwältin *f*.

lay *vt vi* legen.

layer *n* Schicht *f*; Lage *f*.

layman *n* Laie *m*.

lazy *adj* faul.

lead *n* Blei *n*; Führung *f*:—*vt vi* führen.

leader *n* Führer(in) *m(f)*.

leaf *n* Blatt *n*; Flügel *m*.

leaflet *n* Flugblatt *n*; Prospekt *m*.

leak *n* Leck *n*:—*vi* lecken.

lean *vt* neigen; lehnen:—*vi* sich neigen; sich lehnen:—*adj* mager.

leap *vi* springen:—*n* Sprung *m*.

learn *vt vi* lernen.

least *adj* wenigste(r, s):—**at ~** wenigstens.

leather *n* Leder *n*.

leave *vt* verlassen; weggehen; abreisen.

lecture *n* Vortrag *m*; Vorlesung *f*.

lecturer *n* Vortragende(r) *f(m)*.

leek *n* Porree *m*.

left *adj* linke(r, s); Links-:—**on the ~** links.

left-handed *adj* linkshändig.

leg *n* Bein *n*.

legal *adj* gesetzlich.

legality *n* Gesetzlichkeit *f*.

legend *n* Legende *f*.

legendary *adj* legendär.

legible *adj* leserlich.

legion *n* Legion *f*.

legislation *n* Gesetzgebung *f*.

legitimate *adj* legitim.

leisure *n* Freizeit *f*.

lemon *n* Zitrone *f*.

lemon tree *n* Zitronenbaum *m*.

lend *vt* (ver)leihen.

length *n* Länge *f*.

lengthen *vt* verlängern:—*vi* sich verlängern.

lens *n* Linse *f*; Objektiv *n*.

Lent *n* Fastenzeit *f*.

lentil *n* Linse *f*.

leopard *n* Leopard *m*.

lesbian *n* Lesbierin *f*.

less *adj adv* weniger.

lessen *vt* vermindern:—*vi* sich vermindern.

lesson *n* (Unterrichts)Stunde *f*.

let *vt* lassen; erlauben; vermieten, verpachten.

letter *n* Brief *m*; Buchstabe *m*.

lettuce *n* Salat *m*.

level *adj* eben; waagerecht:—*n* Wasserwaage *f*; Ebene *f*.

lever *n* Hebel *m*.

liability *n* Verantwortlichkeit *f*; Haftung *f*.

liable *adj* verantwortlich; haftpflichtig.

liar *n* Lügner(in) *m(f)*.

liberal *adj* liberal.

liberate *vt* befreien.

liberation *n* Befreiung *f*.

liberty *n* Freiheit *f*.

Libra *n* (*astrol*) Waage *f*.

library *n* Bibliothek *f*.

licence *n* Erlaubnis *f*; Lizenz *f*.

lick *vt* (ab)lecken.

lid *n* Deckel *n*.

lie *n* Lüge *f*:—*vi* lügen; liegen.

lieutenant *n* Leutnant *m*.

life *n* Leben *n*.

lifeboat *n* Rettungsboot *n*.

lift *vt* (hoch)heben; erheben.

light *n* Licht *n*; Helligkeit *f*; Beleuchtung *f*:—*adj* hell; leicht:—*vt* anzünden; (er)leuchten.

lighthouse *n* Leuchtturm *m*.

lighting *n* Beleuchtung *f*.

lightning *n* Blitz *m*.

like *adj* gleich; wie; ähnlich:—*adv* (so) wie:—*vt* gern haben; mögen.

likely *adj* wahrscheinlich; voraussichtlich.

lily *n* Lilie *f*.

lime *n* Kalk *m*; Linde *f*; Limone *f*.

limit *n* Grenze *f*; Beschränkung *f*:—*vt* beschränken; begrenzen.

limp *vi* hinken; humpeln.

line *n* Linie *f*:—*vt* linieren.

linen *n* Leinen *n*; Wäsche *f*.

link *n* Verbindung *f*:—*vt* verbinden.

lion *n* Löwe *m*.

lioness *n* Löwin *f*.

lip *n* Lippe *f*.

lipstick *n* Lippenstift *m*.

liqueur *n* Likör *m*.

liquid *adj* flüssig:—*n* Flüssigkeit *f*.

lisp *vi* lispeln.

list *n* Liste *f*; Verzeichnis *n*:—*vt* verzeichnen.

listen *vi* (zu)hören.

litre *n* Liter *n*.

literature *n* Literatur *f*.

little *adj* klein; wenig.

live *vi* leben; wohnen.

lively *adj* lebendig.

liver *n* Leber *f*.

lizard *n* Eidechse *f*.

load *vt* (be)laden:—*n* Ladung *f*; Last *f*.

loaf *n* Laib *m*; Brot *n*.

loan *n* (Ver)Leihen *n*.

lobe *n* Lappen *m*.

lobster *n* Hummer *m*.

local *adj* lokal; örtlich.

location *n* Stelle *f*; Lage *f*.

lock *n* Schloß *n*:—*vt* verschließen.

loft *n* Dachboden *m*.

logic *n* Logik *f*.

logical *adj* logisch.

loneliness *n* Einsamkeit *f*.

lonely *adj* einsam.

long *adj* lang.

longing *n* Sehnsucht *f*.

long-term *adj* langfristig.

long wave *n* Langwelle *f*.

look *vi* (aus)schauen; aussehen:—*n* Blick *m*; Miene *f*.

loose *adj* lose; locker.

loosen *vt* lösen; lockern.

lose *vt vi* verlieren.

loss *n* Verlust *m*.

lot *n* Los *n*; Anteil *m*; Menge *f*; **a ~** viel.

lottery *n* Lotterie *f*.

loud *adj* laut.

lounge *n* Wohnzimmer *n*; Salon *m*.

louse *n* (*pl* **lice**) Laus *f*.

love *n* Liebe *f*:—**fall in ~** sich verlieben:—*vt* lieben.

lovely *adj* (wunder)schön; reizend.

lover *n* Liebhaber(in) *m(f)*; Geliebte(r) *f(m)*.

low *adj* niedrig.

loyal *adj* loyal; treu.

loyalty *n* Loyalität *f*; Treue *f*.

luck *n* Glück *n*.

lucky *adj* glücklich.

luggage *n* Gepäck *n*.

lullaby *n* Wiegenlied *n*.

lump *n* Klumpen *m*; Brocken *m*.

lunar *adj* lunar; Mond-.

lunch *n* Mittagessen *n*.

lungs *npl* Lunge *f*.

lure *vt* (ver)locken; verführen; ködern.

lust *n* Lust *f*; Wollust *f*.

lute *n* Laute *f*; Kitt *m*.

luxurious *adj* luxuriös.

luxury *n* Luxus *m*.

lymph *n* Lymphe *f*.

lynch *vt* lynchen.

lynx *n* Luchs *m*.

lyrical *adj* lyrisch.

lyrics *npl* (Lied)Text *m*.

M

machine *n* Maschine *f*.
mackerel *n* Makrele *f*.
mad *adj* verrückt.
magazine *n* Zeitschrift *f*, Illustrierte *f*.
magic *n* Zauber *m:—adj* zauberhaft, magisch.
magician *n* Zauberkünstler *m*.
magnet *n* Magnet *n*.
magnetic *adj* magnetisch.
magnetism *n* Magnetismus *m*.
magnificent *adj* herrlich.
magnify *vt* vergrößern.
magpie *n* Elster *f*.
mahogany *n* Mahagoni *n*.
maid *n* Dienstmädchen *n*.
maiden *n* Maid *f*.
mail *n* Post *f*.
main *adj* Haupt-.
mainly *adv* hauptsächlich, größtenteils.
maintain *vt* aufrechterhalten; instand halten; warten.
maintenance *n* Instandhaltung *f*; Wartung *f*.
maize *n* Mais *m*.
majestic *adj* majestätisch.
majesty *n* Majestät *f*.
majority *n* Mehrheit *f*.
make *vt* machen:—*n* Marke *f*.
make-up *n* Make-up *n*.
malaria *n* Malaria *f*.
male *adj* männlich.
malfunction *n* Funktionsstörung *f*.

malice *n* Bosheit *f*.
malicious *adj* böswillig, boshaft.
malt *n* Malz *n*.
mammal *n* Säugetier *n*.
man *n* Mann *m*.
manage *vt vi* führen, leiten; schaffen.
manageable *adj* handlich, fügsam.
management *n* Leitung *f*, Geschäftsführung *f*.
manager *n* Leiter(in) *m(f)*, Manager *m*.
mania *n* Manie *f*.
maniac *n* Verrückte(r) *f(m)*.
manic *adj* hektisch.
manner *n* Weise *f*; Art *f*.
manslaughter *n* Totschlag *m*.
mantelpiece *n* Kaminsims *m*.
manual *adj* manuell; Hand-:—*n* Handbuch *n*.
manufacture *n* Herstellung *f*:—*vt* herstellen.
manufacturer *n* Hersteller *m*.
manure *n* Dünger *m*, Mist *m*.
manuscript *n* Manuskript *n*.
many *adj* viel(e):—~ **a** manche(r, s):—**how ~?** wie viele?
map *n* Landkarte *f*; Stadtplan *m*.
maple *n* Ahorn *m*.
mar *vt* verderben.
marathon *n* Marathonlauf *m*.

marble *n* Marmor *m*, Murmel *f*.
March *n* März *m*.
march *n* Marsch *m:—vi* marschieren.
mare *n* Stute *f*.
margin *n* Rand *m*.
marigold *n* Ringelblume *f*.
mark *n* Sput *f*; Zeichen *n*; Note *f:—vt* markieren; benoten.
market *n* Markt *m*.
marketing *n* Marketing *n*.
marmalade *n* Orangenmarmelade *f*.
marriage *n* Ehe *f*; Trauung *f*; Heirat *f*.
married *adj* verheiratet.
marrow *n* Knochenmark *m*; Speisekürbis *m*.
marry *vt vi* heiraten.
marsh *n* Sumpf *m*.
marshal *n* Marschall *m*.
martial *adj* Kriegs-.
martyr *n* Martyrer(in) *m(f)*.
marvel *n* Wunder *n:—vi* sich wundern.
marvellous *adj* wunderbar, fabelhaft.
masculine *adj* männlich.
mash *vt* zu Brei zerdrücken.
mask *n* Maske *f:—vt* maskieren.
mass *n* Messe *f*; Masse *f*.
massacre *n* Massaker *n:—vt* massakrieren.
massage *n* Massage *f*; *vt* massieren.
massive *adj* massiv.

mast *n* Mast *m.*

master *n* Meister *m:—vt* meistern; beherrschen.

masterpiece *n* Meisterwerk *n.*

mat *n* Matte *f*; Abtreter *m.*

match *n* Streichholz *n*, Spiel *n:—vt* passen zu.

matchbox *n* Streichholzschachtel *f.*

mate *n* Gehilfe *m*; Kumpel *m:—vt* sich paaren.

material *adj* materiell:—*n* Stoff *m*, Material *n.*

maternal *adj* mütterlich.

maternity *n* Mutterschaft *f.*

mathematical *adj* mathematisch.

mathematician *n* Mathematiker *m.*

mathematics *npl* Mathematik *f.*

matrimonial *adj* ehelich, Ehe-.

matt *adj* matt.

matter *n* Materie *f*; Sache *f*; Angelegenheit *f:—***what's the ~?** was ist los?:—*vi* von Bedeutung sein.

mattress *n* Matratze *f.*

mature *adj* reif:—*vt vi* reifen.

maturity *n* Reife *f.*

mauve *adj* lila.

maxim *n* Maxime *f.*

maximum *n* Maxmium *n:—adj* maximal.

may *v aux* können:—**~be** vielleicht.

May *n* Mai *m.*

mayor *n* Bürgermeister(in) *m(f).*

maze *n* Irrgarten *m*; Labyrinth *n.*

me *pn* mich; mir.

meadow *n* Wiese *f.*

meal *n* Mahlzeit *f.*

mean *adj* gemein; geizig:—*vt vi* meinen.

meaning *n* Bedeutung *f.*

meantime, meanwhile *adv* inzwischen.

measure *n* Maß *n*; Maßnahme *f:—vt* messen.

measurement *n* Messung *f.*

meat *n* Fleisch *n.*

mechanic *n* Mechaniker *m.*

mechanical *adj* mechanisch.

mechanics *npl* Mechanik *f.*

mechanism *n* Mechanismus *m.*

medal *n* Medaille *f.*

media *npl* die Medien *pl.*

medical *adj* medizinisch; ärztlich.

medicine *n* Medizin *f.*

medieval *adj* mittelalterlich.

mediocre *adj* mittelmäßig.

Mediterranean *adj:—***the ~ (Sea)** das Mittelmeer.

medium *n* Mittel *n:—adj* Mittel-.

meet *vt* treffen; begegnen:—*vi* sich treffen.

meeting *n* Begegnung *f.*

melody *n* Melodie *f.*

melon *n* Melone *f.*

melt *vi* schmelzen.

member *n* Mitglied *n.*

membership *n* Mitgliedschaft *f.*

memorable *adj* denkwürdig.

memorandum *n* Mitteilung *f.*

memorial *n* Denkmal *n.*

memory *n* Gedächtnis *n*; Erinnerung *f.*

menace *n* Drohung *f:—vt* drohen.

mend *vt* reparieren.

mental *adj* geistig.

mentality *n* Mentalität *f.*

mention *n* Erwähnung *f:—vt* erwähnen.

menu *n* Speisekarte *f.*

merchant *n* Kaufmann *m.*

merciful *adj* barmherzig.

merciless *adj* erbarmungslos.

mercury *n* Quecksilber *n.*

mercy *n* Barmherzigkeit *f.*

mere(ly) *adj* (*adv*) bloß.

merge *vt* verbinden; fusionieren.

merger *n* Fusion *f.*

merit *n* Verdienst *m*; Wert *m:—vt* verdienen.

mermaid *n* Meerjungfrau *f.*

merry *adj* fröhlich.

mesh *n* Masche *f.*

mess *n* Unordnung *f.*

message *n* Botschaft *f.*

messenger *n* Bote *m.*

metal *n* Metall *n.*

metallic *adj* metallisch.

metaphor *n* Metapher *f.*

metaphorical *adj* metaphorisch.

meteor *n* Meteor *m.*

meter *n* Meßgerät *n.*

method *n* Methode *f.*

methodical *adj* systematisch.

Methodist *n* Methodist(in) *m(f).*

metre *n* Meter *m / n.*

metric *adj* metrisch.

mew *vi* miauen.

microbe *n* Mikrobe *f.*

microphone *n* Mikrofon *n.*

microscope *n* Mikroskop *n.*

microscopic *adj* mikroskopisch.

midday *n* Mittag *m.*

middle *adj* Mittel-:—*n* Mitte *f.*

midnight *n* Mitternacht *f.*

midsummer *n* Hochsommer *m.*

might *n* Kraft *f,* Macht *f.*

mighty *adj* mächtig, gewaltig.

migrate *vi* abwandern.

migration *n* Abwanderung *f.*

Milan *n* Mailand.

mild *adj* mild, leicht.

mile *n* Meile *f.*

mileage *n* Meilenzahl *f.*

militant *adj* militant.

military *adj* militärisch, Militär-.

milk *n* Milch *f:—vt* melken.

milky *adj* milchig.

Milky Way *n* Milchstraße *f.*

mill *n* Mühle *f:—vt* mahlen.

millennium *n* Jahrtausend *n.*

miller *n* Müller *m.*

millet *n* Hirse *f.*

milligram *n* Milligramm *n.*

millilitre *n* Milliliter *m.*

millimetre *n* Millimeter *m/n.*

million *n* Million *f.*

millionaire *n* Millionär(in) *m(f).*

mimic *vt* nachäffen.

mince *vt* durchdrehen.

mind *n* Sinn *m;* Geist *m:— vi* sich kümmern.

mine *poss pn* meiner, meine, mein(e)s: —*n* Bergwerk *n;* Mine *f.*

miner *n* Bergarbeiter *m.*

mineral *n* Mineral *n.*

mineral water *n* Mineralwasser *n.*

minimal *adj* minimal.

minimize *vt* auf ein Minimum beschränken.

minimum *n* Minimum *n.*

mining *n* Bergbau *m.*

minister *n* Minister *m;* Pastor *m.*

ministry Ministerium *n.*

minor *adj* klein:—*n* Minderjährige(r) *(f)m.*

minority *n* Minderheit *f.*

mint *n* (*bot*) Minze *f;* Münzanstalt *f: —vt* prägen.

minus *adv* minus.

minute *adj* winzig:—*n* Minute *f.*

miracle *n* Wunder *n.*

mirror *n* Spiegel *m.*

miscellaneous *adj* verschieden.

mischief *n* Unfug *m.*

mischievous *adj* durchtrieben.

miser *n* Geizhals *m.*

miserable *adj* elend, trübsinnig.

misery *n* Elend *n.*

misfortune *n* Unglück *n.*

mishap *n* Mißgeschick *n.*

mislead *vt* irreführen.

Miss *n* Fräulein *n.*

miss *vt* verfehlen; verpassen.

missile *n* Geschoß *n.*

missing *adj* fehlend; vermißt.

mission *n* Aufgabe *f;* Mission *f.*

mist *n* Dunst *m,* Nebel *m.*

mistake *vt* verwechseln:—*n* Fehler *m.*

Mister *n* Herr *m.*

mistress *n* Herrin *f;* Geliebte *f.*

mistrust *vt* mißtrauen:—*n* Mißtrauen *n.*

misty *adj* neblig, dunstig.

misunderstand *vt* mißverstehen.

misuse *n* Mißbrauch *m:—vt* mißbrauchen.

mix *vt* mischen.

mixture *n* Mischung *f,* Gemisch *n.*

moan *vi* ächzen, stöhnen.

mobile *adj* beweglich, fahrbar.

mock *vt vi* verspotten.

mockery *n* Spott *m.*

mode *n* Weise *f.*

model *n* Modell *n:—vt* modellieren.

moderate *adj* mäßig, gemäßigt:—*vt* mäßigen.

moderation *n* Mäßigung *f.*

modern *adj* modern.

modernize *vt* modernisieren.

modest *adj* bescheiden.

modesty *n* Bescheidenheit *f.*

modification *n* Änderung *f.*

modify *vt* ändern.

moist *adj* feucht.

moisten *vt* befeuchten.

moisture *n* Feuchtigkeit *f.*

mole *n* Leberfleck *m;* Maulwurf *m.*

molecule *n* Molekul *n.*

moment *n* Moment *m,* Augenblick *m.*

monarch *n* Monarch *m.*

monarchy *n* Monarchie *f.*

monastery *n* Kloster *n.*

monastic *adj* mönchisch.

Monday *n* Montag *m.*

money *n* Geld *n.*

monk *n* Monch *m.*

monkey *n* Affe *m.*

monopoly *n* Monopol *n.*

monotony *n* Monotonie *f;* Eintönigkeit *f.*

monster *n* Ungeheuer *n.*

monstrous *adj* unerhört.

month *n* Monat *m.*

monthly *adj* monatlich.

monument *n* Denkmal *n.*

moo *vi* muhen.

mood *n* Stimmung *f*; Laune *f*.

moon *n* Mond *m*.

moonlight *n* Mondlicht *n*.

moor *n* Heide *f*:—*vt* festmachen.

moose *n* Elch *m*.

moral *adj* moralisch.

morale *n* Moral *f*.

morality *n* Sittlichkeit *f*.

morbid *adj* krankhaft.

more *adj adv* mehr:—~ **and** ~ immer mehr.

moreover *adv* außerdem.

morning *n* Morgen *m*:— **good** ~ guten Morgen.

mortal *adj* sterblich.

mortality *n* Sterblichkeit *f*.

mortar *n* Mörser *m*.

mortgage *n* Hypothek *f*:— *vt* mit einer Hypothek belasten.

mosaic *n* Mosaik *n*.

Moscow *n* Moskau *n*.

mosque *n* Moschee *f*.

mosquito *n* Moskito *m*.

moss *n* Moos *n*.

most *adj* meist:—*adv* am meisten:—**for the ~ part** zum größten Teil.

mostly *adv* meistens.

moth *n* Nachtfalter *m*.

mother *n* Mutter *f*.

motherhood *n* Mutterschaft *f*.

mother-in-law *n* Schwiegermutter *f*.

motherly *adj* mütterlich.

mother tongue *n* Muttersprache *f*.

motion *n* Bewegung *f*.

motivated *adj* motiviert.

motive *n* Motiv *n*.

motor *n* Motor *m*.

motto *n* Motto *n*.

mould *n* Form *f*:—*vt* formen.

mouldy *adj* schimm(e)lig.

mound *n* Erdhügel *m*.

mount *vt* besteigen.

mountain *n* Berg *m*.

mountaineer *n* Bergsteiger *m*.

mountaineering *n* Bergsteigen *n*.

mountainous *adj* gebirgig.

mourn *vt* betrauern.

mourner *n* Trauernde(r) (*f*)*m*.

mournful *adj* trauervoll.

mourning *n* Trauer *f*.

mouse *n* (*pl* mice) Maus *f*.

mousse *n* Creme *f*.

moustache *n* Schnurrbart *m*.

mouth *n* Mund *m*; Maul *n*.

movable *adj* beweglich.

move *vt* bewegen:—*vi* sich bewegen: —*n* Bewegung *f*; Zug *m*.

movement *n* Bewegung *f*.

mow *vt* mähen.

mower *n* Rasenmäher *m*.

Mrs *n* Frau *f*.

much *adj adv* viel.

muck *n* Mist *m*; Dreck *m*.

mud *n* Schlamm *m*.

muddy *adj* schlammig.

muffle *vt* dämpfen.

mug *n* Becher *m*.

mule *n* Maultier *n*.

multiple *adj* vielfach.

multiplication *n* Multiplikation *f*.

multiply *vt* multiplizieren.

mumble *vt vi* undeutlich sprechen.

mummy *n* Mumie *f*; Mutti *f*.

munch *vt vi* mampfen.

Munich *n* München.

murder *n* Mord *m*:—*vt* ermorden.

murderer *n* Mörder *m*.

murderess *n* Mörderin *f*.

murmur *n* Gemurmel *n*:— *vi* murmeln.

muscle *n* Muskel *m*.

museum *n* Museum *n*.

mushroom *n* Pilz *m*.

music *n* Musik *f*.

musical *adj* musikalisch.

musician *n* Musiker(in) *m*(*f*).

mussel *n* Muschel *f*.

must *v aux* müssen.

mustard *n* Senf *m*.

mutter *vt vi* murmeln.

mutton *n* Hammelfleisch *n*.

mutual *adj* gegenseitig.

my *poss adj* meine(r, s).

myself *pn* selbst; mich (selbst).

mysterious *adj* geheimnisvoll, rätselhaft.

mystery *n* Geheimnis *n*, Rätsel *n*.

myth *n* Mythos *m*.

mythology *n* Mythologie *f*.

N

nail *n* Nagel *m.*
naive *adj* naiv.
naked *adj* nackt.
name *n* Name *m:—vt* nennen.
namely *adv* nämlich.
nap *n* Nickerchen *n.*
napkin *n* Serviette *f.*
nappy *n* Windel *f.*
narcissus *n* Narzisse *f.*
narcotic *n* Betäubungsmittel *n.*
narrate *vt* erzählen.
narrative *n* Erzählung *f.*
narrow *adj* eng.
nasal *adj* nasal.
nasty *adj* ekelhaft, fies.
nation *n* Nation *f.*
national *adj* National-.
nationalism *n* Nationalismus *m.*
nationalist *n* Nationalist *m.*
nationality *n* Staatsangehörigkeit *f.*
nationalize *vt* verstaatlichen.
native *adj* einheimisch:—*n* Einhei-mische(r) *f(m).*
natural *adj* natürlich.
nature *n* Natur *f.*
naughty *adj* unartig.
nausea *n* Ekel *m.*
nauseate *vt* anekeln.
nautical, naval *adj* nautisch, See-.
navigate *vi* navigieren.

navigation *n* Navigation *f.*
navy *n* Marine *f.*
Nazi *n* Nazi *m.*
near *prep* nahe, in der Nähe:—*adv* nah(e):—*vt* sich nähern.
nearby *adj* nahegelegen.
nearly *adv* fast, beinahe.
neat *adj* pur; ordentlich; gepflegt.
necessary *adj* notwendig.
necessitate *vt* benötigen.
necessity *n* Notwendigkeit *f.*
neck *n* Hals *m.*
necklace *n* Halskette *f.*
need *n* Notwendigkeit *f,* Bedarf *m:—vt* brauchen.
needle *n* Nadel *f.*
negative *adj* negativ.
neglect *vt* vernachlässigen:—*n* Vernachlässigung *f.*
negligence *n* Nachlässigkeit *f,* Fahrlässigkeit *m.*
negligent *adj* nachlässig, fahrlässig.
negotiate *vi* verhandeln.
negotiation *n* Verhandlung *f.*
neigh *vi* wiehern.
neighbour *n* Nachbar(in) *m(f).*
neighbouring *adj* benachbart, Nachbar-.

neither *conj:—~… nor* weder… noch.
nephew *n* Neffe *m.*
nerve *n* Nerv *m.*
nervous *adj* nervös.
nest *n* Nest *n.*
net *n* Netz *n.*
Netherlands *npl:—the ~* die Niederlande *pl.*
nettle *n* Nessel *f.*
network *n* Netz *n.*
neuter *adj* sächlich:—*n* Neutrum *n.*
neutral *adj* neutral.
neutrality *n* Neutralität *f.*
never *adv* nie, niemals, nimmer.
nevertheless *adv* trotzdem.
new *adj* neu.
news *npl* Nachrichten *pl.*
newspaper *n* Zeitung *f.*
New Year *n* das Neue Jahr *n.*
New Year's Eve Silvester *n.*
New Zealand *n* Neuseeland *n.*
next *adj* nächste(r, s).
nibble *vt* knabbern.
nice *adj* nett; sympathisch.
nickel *n* Nickel *n.*
nickname *n* Spitzname *m.*
niece *n* Nichte *f.*
night *n* Nacht *f:—good ~* gute Nacht.
nightclub *n* Nachtklub *m.*
nightingale *n* Nachtigall *f.*

nightly adj nächtlich:—adv jede Nacht.

nightmare n Alptraum m.

nimble adj beweglich.

nine num neun.

nineteen num neunzehn.

ninety num neunzig.

ninth adj neunte(r, s).

nitrogen n Stickstoff m.

no adv nein:—adj kein (er, e, es).

noble adj adlig, edel.

nobody pn niemand.

nod n Nicken n:—vi nicken.

noise n Lärm m, Geräusch m.

noisy adj laut.

nominal adj nominell.

nominate vt ernennen, aufstellen.

none pn keiner, keine, kein(e)s.

nonetheless adv nichtsdestoweniger.

nonexistent adj nicht vorhanden.

non-fiction n Sachliteratur f.

nonsense n Unsinn m, Quatsch m.

non-smoker n Nichtraucher m.

nonstop adv ununterbrochen.

noon n Mittag m.

noose n Schlinge m.

nor conj:—**neither... ~** weder... noch.

norm n Norm m.

normal adj normal.

normally adv normalerweise.

north n Norden m.

North Africa n Nordafrika n.

North America n Nordamerika n.

northeast n Nortosten m.

northern adj nördlich, Nord-.

Northern Ireland n Nordirland n.

North Pole n Nordpol m.

North Sea n Nordsee f.

northwards adv nach Norden.

northwest n Nordwesten m.

Norway n Norvegen n.

Norwegian adj norwegisch:—n Norweger(in) m(f); Norwegisch n.

nose n Nase f.

nostalgia n Nostalgie f, Sehnsucht f.

nostril n Nasenloch f.

not adv nicht.

notable adj bemerkenswert, bedeutend.

notary n Notar m.

notch n Kerbe f.

note n Note f; Ton m; Anmerkung f:—vt zur Kenntnis nehmen; aufschreiben.

noted adj bekannt.

nothing n nichts.

notice n Anzeige f, Anschlag m:—vt bemerken.

noticeable adj bemerkbar.

notify vt benachrichtigen.

notion n Idee f.

notorious adj berüchtigt.

notwithstanding adv trozdem.

nought n Null f.

noun n (gr) Substantiv m.

nourish vt ernähren, nähren.

nourishing adj nahrhaft.

nourishment n Nahrung m.

novel n Roman m.

novelist n Romanschriftsteller m.

novelty n Neuheit f.

November n November m.

novice n Neuling m.

now adv jetzt, nun:—**~ and then** hin und wieder.

nowadays adv heutzutage.

nowhere adv nirgends.

nuclear adj nuklear, Kern-.

nucleus n Kern m.

nude adj nackt.

nudist n Nudist(in) m(f).

nudity n Nacktheit f.

nuisance n lästiger Mensch m, Quälgeist m.

null adj nichtig.

nullify vt für nichtig erklären.

numb adj gefühllos:—vt betaüben.

number n Zahl f, Anzahl f:—vt numerieren.

numeral n Ziffer f.

numerical adj numerisch.

numerous adj zahlreich.

nun n Nonne f.

nurse n Krankenschwester f:—vt pflegen.

nursery n Kinderzimmer n; Gärtnerei f.

nursery school n Vorschule f.

nurture vt nähren.

nut n Nuß f.

nutritious adj nahrhaft.

nylon n Nylon n.

nymph n Nymphe f.

O

oak *n* Eiche *f*:—*adj* Eichen(holz)-.

oar *n* Ruder *n*.

oasis *n* Oase *f*.

oath *n* Eid *m*, Schwur *m*; Fluch *m*.

oatmeal *n* Haferschrot *m*.

oats *npl* Hafer *m*.

obedience *n* Gehorsam *m*.

obedient *adj* gehorsam.

obey *vt vi* gehorchen.

obituary *n* Nachruf *m*.

object *n* Gegenstand *m*; Object *n*; Ziel *n*:—*vi* dagegen sein.

objection *n* Einwand *m*, Einspruch *m*.

objective *n* Ziel *n*:—*adj* objektiv.

obligation *n* Verpflichtung *f*.

obligatory *adj* verpflichtend, verbindlich.

oblige *vt* zwingen; einen Gefallen tun.

oblique *adj* schräg, schief:—*n* Schrägstrich *m*.

oblivion *n* Vergessenheit *f*.

oblivious *adj* nichr bewußt.

oboe *n* Oboe *f*.

obscene *adj* obszön.

obscenity *n* Obszönität *f*.

obscure *adj* unklar; undeutlich; unbekannt, obskur; düster.

obscurity *n* Unklarheit *f*; Dunkelheit *f*.

observant *adj* aufmerksam.

observation *n* Bemerkung *f*; Beobachtung *f*.

observatory *n* Sternwarte *f*, Observatorium n.

observe *vt* beobachen; bemerken.

observer *n* Beobachter(in) *m(f)*.

obsess *vt* verfolgen, quälen.

obsession *n* Besessenheit *f*, Wahn *m*.

obsessive *adj* krankhaft.

obsolete *adj* überholt, verlaltet.

obstacle *n* Hindernis *n*.

obstinate *adj* hartnäckig, stur.

obstruct *vt* versperren; verstopfen; hemmen.

obstruction *n* Versperrung *f*; Verstopfung *f*; Hindernis *n*.

obtain *vt* erhalten, bekommen; erzielen.

obtainable *adj* erhältlich.

obvious *adj* offenbar, offensichtlich.

occasion *n* Gelegenheit *f*; Ereignis *n*; Anlaß *m*.

occasional *adj* gelegentlich.

occupant *n* Inhaber(in) *m(f)*; Bewoh-ner(in) *m(f)*.

occupation *n* Tâtigkeit *f*; Beruf *m*; Beschäftigung *f*.

occupier *n* Bewohner(in) *m(f)*.

occupy *vt* besetzen; belegen; bewohnen.

occur *vi* vorkommen.

occurrence *n* Ereignis *n*.

ocean *n* Ozean *m*; Meer *n*.

octagonal *adj* achteckig.

octane *n* Oktan *n*.

octave *n* Oktave *f*.

October *n* Oktober *m*.

octopus *n* Krake *f*.

odd *adj* sonderbar; ungerade; einzeln.

odious *adj* verhaßt; abscheulich.

odour *n* Geruch *m*.

of *prep* von; aus.

off *adv* weg, fort; aus, ab:—*prep* von.

offence *n* Vorgehen *n*, Straftat *f*; Beleidigung *f*.

offend *vt* beleidigen.

offer * *n* Angebot *f*:—*vt* anbieten.

office *n* Büro *n*; Amt *n*.

officer *n* Offizier *m*; Beamte(r) *m*.

official *adj* offiziell, amtlich:—*n* Beamte(r) *m*.

offshore *adj* küstennah, Küsten-.

oil *n* Öl *n*:—*vt* ölen.

oilfield *n* Ölfeld *n*.

oil painting *n* Ölgemälde n.

oil tanker *n* Öltanker *m*.

ointment *n* Salbe *f*.

old *adj* alt.

olive *n* Olive *f*.

omelette *n* Omelett *n*.

omen *n* Omen *n*.

ominous *adj* bedrohlich.

omission *n* Auslassung *f*; Versäumnis *n*.

omit *vt* auslassen; versäumen.

on *prep* auf; an; über:—*adv* an; weiters:—*adj* an; aufgedreht.

once *adv* einmal:—**at ~** sofort:—**~ more** noch einmal:—**~ upon a time** es war einmal.

one *num* eins; ein / eine; *adj* einzige(r, s); *pn* eine(r, s):—**~ by ~** einzeln:—**~ another** einander.

oneself *pn* sich; sich selbst / selber; selbst.

onion *n* Zwiebel *f*.

only *adv* nur, bloß.

open *adj* offen; aufgeschlossen:—*vt* öffnen, aufmachen; eröffnen.

opera *n* Oper *f*.

operate *vt* bedienen; betätigen:—*vi* laufen, in Betrieb sein.

operation *n* Betrieb *m*; Operation *f*.

opinion *n* Meinung *f*; Ansicht *f*.

opponent *n* Gegner *m*.

opportunity *n* Gelegenheit *f*.

oppose *vt* entgegentreten; ablehnen.

opposite *prep* gegenüber:— *n* Gegenteil *n*.

opposition *n* Widerstand *m*; Opposition *f*; Gegensatz *m*.

oppress *vt* unterdrücken.

optical *adj* optisch.

optician *n* Optiker *m*.

optimist *n* Optimist *m*.

optimistic *adj* optimistisch.

option *n* Wahl *f*; Option *f*.

optional *adj* freiwillig; wahlfrei.

or *conj* oder.

oracle *n* Orakel *n*.

oral *adj* mündlich.

orange *n* Apfelsine *f*, Orange *f*:—*adj* orange.

orator *n* Redner(in) *m(f)*.

orbit *n* Umlaufbahn *f*.

orchard *n* Obstgarten *m*.

orchestra *n* Orchester *n*.

orchid *n* Orchidee *f*.

order *n* Ordnung *f*; Befehl *m*; Auftrag *m*; Bestellung *f*:—*vt* befehlen; bestellen.

ordinary *adj* normal, gewöhnlich.

ordnance *n* Artillerie *f*.

ore *n* Erz *n*.

organ *n* Orgel *f*; Organ *n*.

organic *adj* organisch.

organism *n* Organismus *m*.

organist *n* Organist *m*.

organization *n* Organisation *f*.

organize *vt* organisieren.

orgasm *n* Orgasmus *m*.

orgy *n* Orgie *f*.

origin *n* Ursprung *m*, Quelle *f*; Herkunft *f*.

original *adj* ursprünglich, original; originell.

originality *n* Originalität *f*.

originate *vi* entstehen; stammen.

ornament *n* Schmuck *m*.

ornamental *adj* Zier-.

orphan *n* Waise *f*.

orthodox *adj* orthodox.

oscillate *vi* schwingen; schwanken.

osprey *n* Fischadler *m*.

ostrich *n* Strauß *m*.

other *adj pn* andere(r, s):—**~ than** anders als.

otherwise *adv* anders; sonst.

otter *n* Otter *m*.

ought *v aux* sollen.

ounce *n* Unze *f*.

our *poss adj* unser(er, e, es)

ourselves *pn* uns (selbst).

out *adv* hinaus / heraus; draußen:—**~ of** *prep* aus; außerhalb.

outbreak *n* Ausbruch *m*.

outcast *n* Ausgestoßene(r) *f(m)*.

outcome *n* Ergebnis *n*.

outcry *n* Protest *m*.

outdo *vt* übertrumpfen.

outdoors *adv* im Freien.

outer *adj* äußere(r, s).

outfit *n* Kleidung *f*.

outlay *n* Auslage *f*.

outline *n* Umriß *m*.

outlook *n* Aussicht *f*; Einstellung *f*.

outmoded *adj* veraltet.

output *n* Leistung *f*, Produktion *f*.

outrage *n* Ausschreitung *f*; Skandal *m*:—*vt* verstoßen gegen; empören.

outrageous *adj* unerhöht.

outshine *vt* überstrahlen.

outside *n* Außenseite *f*:— *adj* äußere(r, s), Außen-:— *adv* außen: —*prep* außerhalb.

outstanding *adj* hervorragend; ausstehend.

outstretched *adj* ausgestreckt.

outward *adj* äußere(r, s); Hin-; ausgehend:—*adv* nach außen.

outweigh *vt* überwiegen.

oval *n* Oval *n*:—*adj* oval.

ovary *n* Eierstock *m*.

oven *n* Backofen *m*.

over *adv* hinüber / herüber; vorbei; *prep* über.

overall *adj* allgemein; Gesamt-:—*adv* insgesamt.

overawe *vt* einschüchtern;
überwältigen.

overcast *adj* bedeckt.

overcoat *n* Mantel *m.*

overcome *vt* überwinden.

overcrowded *adj* überfüllt.

overdose *n* Überdosis *f.*

overdraft *n* Überziehung *f.*

overdrawn *adj* überzogen.

overdue *adj* überfällig.

overestimate *vt* über-
schätzen.

overgrown *adj* verwildert.

overhaul *vt* überholen;
überprüfen:—
n Überholung *f.*

overhead *adv* oben:—*adj*

Hoch-; überirdisch,
Decken-.

overjoyed *adj* überglücklich.

overleaf *adv* umseitig.

overload *vt* überladen.

overlook *vt* überblicken;
übersehen.

overriding *adj*
vorherrschend.

overseas *adv* nach/in
Übersee:—*adj* Übersee-,
überseeisch.

oversee *vt* beaufsichtigen.

overshadow *vt* über-
schatten.

oversight *n* Versehen *n.*

oversleep *vi* verschlafen.

overt *adj* offen(kundig).

overtake *vt vi* überholen.

overtime *n* Überstunden *fpl.*

overture *n* Ouvertüre *f.*

overwhelm *vt* überwalti-
gen.

overwhelming *adj* über-
waltigend.

owe *vt* schulden.

owing to *prep* wegen.

owl *n* Eule *f.*

own *vt* besitzen:—*adj* eigen.

owner *n* Besitzer(in) *m(f).*

ownership *n* Besitz *m.*

ox *n* Ochse *f.*

oxygen *n* Sauerstoff *m.*

oyster *n* Auster *f.*

P

pace *n* Schritt *m*; Gang *m*; Tempo *n*.

pack *n* Packung *f*; Meute *f*:—*vt* packen.

package *n* Paket *n*.

packet *n* Päckchen *n*.

pad *n* Block *m*; Polster *n*:—*vt* polstern.

padding *n* Polsterung *f*.

paddock *n* Koppel *f*.

page *n* Seite *f*.

pail *n* Eimer *m*.

pain *n* Schmerz *m*.

painful *adj* schmerzhaft; peinlich.

painstaking *adj* gewissenhaft.

paint *n* Farbe *f*:—*vt* anstreichen; malen.

paintbrush *n* Pinsel *m*.

painter *n* Maler *m*.

painting *n* Malerei *f*; Gemälde *n*.

pair *n* Paar *n*.

pal *n* Kumpel *m*.

palace *n* Schloß *n*.

palate *n* Gaumen *m*.

pale *adj* blaß, bleich.

palm *n* Handfläche *f*; Palme *f*.

pamphlet *n* Broschüre *f*.

pan *n* Pfanne *f*:—*vi* schwenken.

pancake *n* Pfannkuchen *m*.

pane *n* Fensterscheibe *f*.

panel *n* Tafel *f*.

panic *n* Panik *f*:—*vi* in Panik geraten.

pansy *n* Stiefmütterchen *n*.

pant *vi* keuchen; hecheln.

panther *n* Panther *m*.

pantry *n* Vorratskammer *f*.

pants *npl* Schlüpfer *m*; Unterhose *f*.

paper *n* Papier *n*:—*adj* Papier-, aus Papier.

paperback *n* Taschenbuch *n*.

parachute *n* Fallschirm *m*:—*vi* (mit dem Fallschirm) abspringen.

parade *n* Parade *f*:—*vt* aufmaschieren lassen; zur Schau stellen:—*vi* paradieren, vorbeimarschieren.

paradise *n* Paradies *n*.

paradox *n* Paradox *n*.

paragraph *n* Absatz *m*.

parallel *adj* parallel:—*n* Parallele *f*.

paralyse *vt* lähmen, paralysieren; lahmlagen.

paralysis *n* Lähmung *f*.

paranoid *adj* paranoid.

parasite *n* Schmarotzer *m*, Parasit *m*.

parasol *n* Sonnenschirm *m*.

parcel *n* Paket *n*.

pardon *n* Verzeihung *f*:—*vt* begnadigen.

parent *n* Elternteil *m*:—*~s* *pl* Eltern *pl*.

parental *adj* elterlich, Eltern-.

parish *n* Gemeinde *f*.

park *n* Park *m*:—*vt vi* parken.

parking *n* Parken *n*.

parliament *n* Parlament *n*.

parliamentary *adj* parlamentarisch, Parlaments-.

parody *n* Parodie *f*:—*vt* parodieren.

parrot *n* Papagei *m*.

parsley *n* Petersilie *m*.

parsnip *n* Pastinake *f*.

part *n* Teil *m*; Rolle *f*; Teil *n*:—*vt* trennen; scheiteln:—*vi* sich trennen.

participant *n* Teilnehmer(in) *m(f)*.

participate *vi* teilnehmen (**in** an).

participation *n* Teilname *f*; Beteiligung *f*.

particle *n* Teilchen *n*; (*gr*) Partikel *m*.

particular *adj* bestimmt; genau; eigen:—**in ~** besonders.

partition *n* Trennwand *f*; Teilung *f*:—*vt* aufteilen.

partly *adv* zum Teil, teilweise.

partner *n* Partner *m*.

partnership *n* Partnerschaft *f*.

partridge *n* Rebhuhn *n*.

party *n* Partei *f*; Party *f*.

pass *vt* vorbeigehen an +*dat*; vorbeifahren an +*dat*; weitergeben; verbringen:—*vi* vorbeigehen; vorbeifahren; vergehen:—*n* Paß *m*; Passierschein *m*.

passage *n* Gang *m*; Textstelle *f*; Überfahrt *f*.

passenger *n* Passagier *m*.
passion *n* Leidenschaft *f*.
passionate *adj* leidenschaftlich.
passive *adj* passiv; pas-
  sivisch.
passport *n* Reisepaß *m*.
password *n* Parole *f*,
  Kennwort *n*.
past *adj* vergangen; ehemalig:—*n* Vergangenheit *f*:—
  prep an +*dat* vorbei;
  hinter +*dat*.
pasta *n* Teigwaren *pl*.
paste *n* Paste *f*:—*vt* kleben.
pastor *n* Pfarrer *m*.
pastry *n* Blätterteig *m*.
pasture *n* Weide *f*.
pat *vt* tätscheln.
patch *n* Fleck *m*:—*vt* flicken.
patent *adj* offenkundig:—*n*
  Patent *n*: —*vt* patentieren.
paternal *adj* väterlich.
paternity *n* Vaterschaft *f*.
path *n* Pfad *m*; Weg *m*.
pathetic *adj* kläglich.
pathological *adj* pathologisch.
pathology *n* Pathologie *f*.
pathos *n* Rührseligkeit *f*.
patience *n* Geduld *f*.
patient *adj* geduldig:—*n*
  Patient(in) *m(f)*.
patriotic *adj* patriotisch.
patrol *n* Patrouille *f*; Streife
  f:—*vi* patrouillieren.
patron *n* Kunde *m*; Gast *m*;
  Förderer *m*.
patronage *n*
  Schirmherrschaft *f*.
patronize *vt* unterstützen;
  besuchen; von oben herab
  behandeln.
patter *n* Trappeln *n*;
  Prasseln *n*:—*vi* trappeln;
  prasseln.

pattern *n* Muster *n*.
pause *n* Pause *f*:—*vi*
  innehalten.
pavement *n* Bürgersteig *m*.
paw *n* Tatze *f*.
pawn *n* Pfand *n*; Bauer
  m:—*vt* verpfänden.
pay *n* Bezahlung *f*, Lohn
  m:—*vt* zahlen.
payment *n* paga *f*;
  Bezahlung *f*.
pea *n* Erbse *f*.
peace *n* Friede(n) *m*.
peaceful *adj* friedlich, ruhig.
peach *n* Pfirsich *m*.
peacock *n* Pfau *m*.
peak *n* Spitze *f*; Gipfel *m*.
peanut *n* Erdnuß *f*.
pear *n* Birne *f*.
pearl *n* Perle *f*.
peasant *n* Bauer *m*.
peat *n* Torf *m*.
pebble *n* Kiesel *m*.
peck *n* Schnabelhieb *m*:—*vt*
  vi picken.
peculiar *adj* seltsam.
peculiarity *n* Besonderheit
  f; Eigenartigkeit *f*.
pedal *n* Pedal *n*.
pedestrian *n* Fußgänger *m*.
peek *vi* gucken.
peel *vt* schälen:—*vi* abblät-
  tern:—*n* Schale *f*.
peer *n* Peer *m*;
  Ebenbürtige(r) *f(m)*:—*vi*
  gucken; starren.
peg *n* Pflock *m*;
  Wäschenklammer *f*.
pelican *n* Pelikan *m*.
pellet *n* Kügelchen *n*.
pelt *n* Pelz *m*, Fell *n*:—*vt*
  bewerfen:—*vi* schüttern.
pen *n* Fedelhalter *m*; Kuli
  m; Pferch *m*.
penalty *n* Strafe *f*; Elfmeter
  m.

pencil *n* Bleistift *m*.
pendant *n* Anhänger *m*.
pending *adj* noch offen.
pendulum *n* Pendel *n*.
penetrate *vt* durchdringen.
penguin *n* Pinguin *m*.
penicillin *n* Penizillin *n*.
peninsula *n* Halbinsel *f*.
penis *n* Penis *m*.
penitence *n* Reue *f*.
penitent *adj* reuig.
penknife *n* Federmesser *n*.
penniless *adj* mittellos.
penny *n* Penny *m*.
pension *n* Rente *f*.
pensioner *n* Rentner(in)
  m(f).
pension fund *n*
  Rentenfonds *m*.
people *n* Volk *n*:—*npl*
  Leute *pl*; Bevölkerung *f*:—
  vt besiedeln.
pepper *n* Pfeffer *m*;
  Paprika *m*.
peppermint *n* Pfefferminz *n*.
per *prep* pro.
perceive *vt* wahrnehmen;
  verstehen.
per cent *n* Prozent *n*.
perception *n* Wahrnehmung
  f; Einsicht *f*.
perfect *adj* vollkommen;
  perfekt:—*n* (*gr*) Perfekt
  n:—*vt* vervollkommen.
perfection *n*
  Vollkommenheit *f*.
perforate *vt* durchlöchern.
perforation *n* Perforation *f*.
perform *vt* durchführen;
  verrichten; spielen:—*vi*
  auftreten.
performance *n*
  Durchführung *f*; Leistung
  f; Vorstellung *f*.
performer *n* Künstler(in)
  m(f).

perfume n Duft m;
　Parfüm n.

perhaps adv vielleicht.

peril n Gefahr f.

period n Periode f;
　Punkt m.

periodic adj periodisch.

periodical n Zeitschrift f.

peripheral adj Rand-:—n
　Peripheriegerät n.

perish vi umkommen;
　verderben.

perm n Dauerwelle f.

permanent adj dauernd,
　ständig.

permeate vt vi durch-
　dringen.

permissible adj zulässig.

permission n Erlaubnis f.

permissive adj nachgiebig.

permit vt erlauben,
　zulassen:—n Zulassung f.

perpendicular adj
　senkrecht.

perpetrate vt begehen.

perpetual adj dauernd,
　ständig.

perpetuate vt verewigen.

perplex vt verblüffen.

persecute vt verfolgen.

persecution n Verfolgung f.

perseverance n Ausdauer f.

persevere vi durchhalten.

Persian adj persisch:—n
　Perser(in) m(f).

persist vi bleiben;
　andauern.

persistence adj
　Beharrlichkeit f.

persistent adj beharrlich;
　ständig.

person n Person f.

personal adj persönlich;
　privat.

personality n
　Persönlichkeit f.

personify vt verkörpern.

personnel n Personal n.

perspective n Perspektive f.

perspiration n
　Transpiration f.

perspire vi transpirieren.

persuade vt überreden;
　überzeugen.

persuasion n Überredung f;
　Überzeugung f.

persuasive adj überzeugend.

pertinent adj relevant.

perturb vt beunruhigen.

pervade vt erfüllen.

perverse adj pervers;
　eigensinnig.

pervert n perverser Mensch
　m:—vt verdrehen;
　verderben.

pessimist n Pessimist m.

pessimistic adj pes-
　simistisch.

pet n Haustier n.

petal n Blütenblatt n.

petition n Bittschrift f.

petroleum n Petroleum n.

petticoat n Unterrock m.

petty adj unbedeutend;
　kleinlich.

pew n Kirchenbank f.

pewter n Zinn n.

phantom n Phantom n.

pharmacist n Pharmazeut
　m; Apotheker m.

pharmacy n Pharmazie f;
　Apotheke f.

phase n Phase f.

pheasant n Fasan m.

phenomenon n Phänomen
　n.

philanthropist n
　Philanthrop m.

philosopher n Philosopher
　m.

philosophical adj
　philosophisch.

philosophy n Philosophie f.

phlegm n Schleim m.

phlegmatic adj gelassen.

phobia n Phobie f.

phone n Telefon n:—vt vi
　telefonieren, anrufen.

phone call n Telefonanruf
　m.

phosphorus n Phosphor m.

photocopier n Kopiergerät
　n.

photocopy n Fotokopie f:—
　vt fotokopieren.

photograph n Fotografie f,
　Aufnahme f:—vt
　fotografieren.

photographer n Fotograf m.

photographic adj
　fotografisch.

photography n Fotografie f.

phrase n Satz m; Ausdruck
　m:—vt ausdrücken, for-
　mulieren.

physical adj physikalisch;
　körperlich, physisch.

physician n Arzt m.

physicist n Physiker(in)
　m(f).

physiotherapy n
　Heilgymnastik f,
　Physiotherapie f.

physique n Körperbau m.

pianist n Pianist(in) m(f).

piano n Klavier n.

pick n Pickel m; Auswahl
　f:—vt pflücken; aus-
　suchen.

picnic n Picknick n.

picture n Bild n:—vt sich
　dat vorstellen.

picturesque adj malerisch.

pie n Pastete f; Torte f.

piece n Stück n.

pier n Pier m, Mole f.

pierce vt durchstechen.

piety n Frömmigkeit f.

pig *n* Schwein *n*.
pigeon *n* Taube *f*.
pigsty *n* Schweinestall *m*.
pike *n* Hecht *m*.
pile *n* Pfahl *m*, Haufen *m*, Stapel *m*:—*vt* aufschichten, stapeln.
pilgrim *n* Pilger *m*.
pilgrimage *n* Pilgerfahrt *f*.
pill *n* Pille *f*:—**be on the ~** die Pille nehmen.
pillar *n* Pfeiler *m*, Säule *f*.
pillow *n* Kopfkissen *n*.
pilot *n* Pilot *m*, Pilotin *f*; (*mar*) Lotse:—*vt* führen; (*mar*) lotsen.
pimple *n* Pickel *m*.
pin *n* Nadel *f*.
pinch *vt* zwicken:—*n* Zwicken *n*.
pine *n* Kiefer *f*:—*vi*:—**~ for** sich sehnen nach.
pineapple *n* Ananas *f*.
pink *n* Rosa *n*:—*adj* rosa *inv*.
pinnacle *n* Spitze *f*.
pint *n* Pint *n*.
pioneer *n* Pionier *m*.
pious *adj* fromm.
pip *n* Kern *m*.
pipe *n* Pfeife *f*; Rohr *n*; Rohrleitung *f*; **~s** Dudelsack *m*.
piper *n* Pfeifer *m*; Dudelsackbläser *m*.
piracy *n* Piraterie *f*; Seeräuberei *f*.
pirate *n* Pirat *m*; Seeräuber *m*.
Pisces *n* (*astrol*) Fische *pl*.
piss *vi* pissen.
pistol *n* Pistole *f*.
piston *n* Kolben *m*.
pit *n* Grube *f*; Miete *f*.
pitch *n* Pech *n*; Tonhöhe *f*.
pitiful *adj* bedauenswert; jämmerlich.

pity *n* Mitleid *n*:—*vt* Mitleid haben mit.
pizza *n* Pizza *f*.
place *n* Platz *m*; Stelle *f*; Ort *m*:—*vt* setzen, stellen, legen.
plague *n* Pest *f*; Plage *f*:—*vt* plagen.
plaice *n* Scholle *f*.
plain *adj* klar, deutlich:—*n* Ebene *f*.
plan *n* Plan *m*:—*vt vi* planen.
plane *n* Ebene *f*; Flugzeug *n*; Hobel *m*; Platane *f*.
planet *n* Planet *m*.
plank *n* Brett *n*.
plant *n* Pflanze *f*; Anlage *f*:—*vt* pflanzen.
plaster *n* Gips *m*; Verputz *m*; Pflaster *n*.
plastic *n* Plastik *n*/*f*:—*adj* Plastik-.
plate *n* Teller *m*.
platform *n* Plattform *f*; Bahnsteig *m*.
platinum *n* Platin *n*.
plausible *adj* plausibel.
play *n* Spiel *n*; Theaterstück *n*:—*vt vi* spielen.
player *n* Spieler(in) *m(f)*.
plea *n* Bitte *f*; Plädoyer *n*.
pleasant *adj* angenehm.
please *vt* gefallen +*dat*; **~!** bitte!
pleased *adj* zufrieden.
pleasure *n* Freude *f*.
pledge *n* Pfand *n*; Versprechen *n*:—*vt* verpfänden; versprechen.
plenty *n* Fülle *f*.
plight *n* Notlage *f*.
plot *n* Komplott *n*; Handlung *f*; Grundstück *n*:—*vi* sich verschwören.

plough *n* Pflug *m*:—*vt* pflügen.
pluck *vt* pflücken:—*n* Mut *m*.
plug *n* Stöpsel *m*; Stecker *m*; Zündkerze *f*:—*vt* stopfen.
plum *n* Pflaume *f*, Zwetsch(g)e *f*.
plumber *n* Klempner *m*, Installateur *m*.
plume *n* Feder *f*; Fahne *f*.
plump *adj* ründlich, füllig.
plunder *n* Plünderung *f*; Beute *f*:—*vt* plündern.
plunge *vt* stoßen:—*vi* (sich) stürzen.
plural *n* Plural *m*, Mehrzahl *f*.
plus *n* Plus(zeichen) *n*:—*prep* plus, und.
ply *vt* betreiben:—*vi* verkehren.
pneumatic *adj* pneumatisch; Luft-.
pneumonia *n* Lüngenentzündung *f*.
poach *vt* pochieren; stehlen:—*vi* wildern.
poached *adj* (**egg**) verloren.
poacher *n* Wilddieb *m*.
pocket *n* Tasche *f*.
pocket money *n* Taschengeld *n*.
pod *n* Hülse *f*.
poem *n* Gedicht *n*.
poet *n* Dichter *m*, Poet *m*.
poetic *adj* poetisch.
poetry *n* Poesie *f*.
point *n* Punkt *m*; Spitze *f*; Zweck *m*:—*vt* zeigen mit; richten:—*vi* zeigen.
pointed *adj* spitz, scharf.
poison *n* Gift *n*:—*vt* vergiften.
poisoning *n* Vergiftung *f*.

poisonous *adj* Gift-, giftig.

poke *vt* stecken; schüren.

poker *n* Schürhaken *m*; Poker *n*.

Poland *n* Polen *n*.

polar *adj* Polar-, polar.

Pole *n* Pole *n*, Polin *f*.

pole *n* Stange *f*, Pfosten *m*; Mast *m*; Pol *m*.

police *n* Polizei *f*.

policeman *n* Polizist *m*.

police station *n* Polizeirevier *n*, Wache *f*.

policewoman *n* Polizistin *f*.

policy *n* Politik *f*, Versicherungspolice *f*.

polio *n* Polio *f*.

Polish *adj* polnisch:—*n* Polnisch *n*.

polish *n* Politur *f*; Wachs *n*; Creme *f*:—*vt* polieren; putzen.

polite *adj* höflich.

politeness *n* Höflichkeit *f*.

political *adj* politisch.

politician *n* Politiker *m*.

politics *npl* Politik *f*.

poll *n* Abstimmung *f*; Wahl *f*; Umfrage *f*.

pollen *n* (*bot*) Blütenstaub *m*, Pollen *m*.

pollute *vt* verschmutzen, verunreinigen.

pollution *n* Verschmutzung *f*.

polo *n* Polo *n*.

polytechnic *n* technische Hochschule *f*.

pomegranate *n* Granatapfel *m*.

pompous *adj* aufgeblasen.

pond *n* Teich *m*.

ponder *vt* nachdenken über +*acc*.

pony *n* Pony *n*.

ponytail *n* Pferdeschwanz *m*.

pool *n* Schwimmbad *n*; Lache *f*:—*vt* zusammenlegen.

poor *adj* arm; schlecht.

pop *n* Knall *m*; Popmusik *f*; Limo *f*.

pope *n* Papst *m*.

poplar *n* Pappel *f*.

poppy *n* Mohn *m*.

popular *adj* beliebt, populär; volkstümlich.

popularity *n* Beliebtheit *f*, Popularität *f*.

populate *vt* bevölkern.

population *n* Bevölkerung *f*.

populous *adj* dicht besiedelt.

porcelain *n* Porzellan *n*.

porch *n* Vorbau *m*, Veranda *f*.

porcupine *n* Stachelschwein *n*.

pore *n* Pore *f*:—*vi* ~ **over** *vt* brüten über.

pork *n* Schweinefleisch *n*.

pornography *n* Pornographie *f*.

porpoise *n* Tümmler *m*.

porridge *n* Haferbrei *m*.

port *n* Hafen *m*; (*mar*) Backbord *n*; Portwein *m*.

porter *n* Pförtner(in) *m*(*f*); Gepäckträger *m*.

portion *n* Teil *m*, Stück *n*.

portrait *n* Porträt *n*.

portray *vt* darstellen.

Portugal *n* Portugal *n*.

Portuguese *adj* potugiesisch:—*n* Portugiese *m* Portugiesin *f*; Portugiesisch *n*.

pose *n* Stellung *f*, Pose *f*:— *vi* posieren:—*vt* stellen.

position *n* Stellung *f*; Lage *f*; Stelle *f*:—*vt* aufstellen.

positive *adj* positiv.

possess *vt* besitzen.

possession *n* Besitz *m*.

possessive *adj* besitzergreifend.

possibility *n* Möglichkeit *f*.

possible *adj* möglich.

post *n* Post *f*; Pfosten *m*; Stelle *f*:—*vt* anschlagen; aufgeben; aufstellen.

postage *n* Porto *n*.

postcard *n* Postkarte *f*.

poster *n* Plakat *n*.

postman *n* Briefträger *m*.

post office *n* Postamt *n*; Post *f*.

postpone *vt* verschieben.

postwar *adj* Nachkriegs-.

pot *n* Topf *m*; Kanne *f*.

potato *n* Kartoffel *f*.

potent *adj* stark; zwingend.

potential *adj* potentiell:—*n* Potential *n*.

pottery *n* Töpferei *f*.

pouch *n* Beutel *m*.

poultry *n* Geflügel *n*.

pound *n* Pfund *n*.

pour *vt* gießen.

poverty *n* Armut *f*.

powder *n* Pulver *n*, Puder *m*:—*vt* sich pudern.

power *n* Macht *f*; Fähigkeit *f*; Stärke *f*:—*vt* antreiben.

powerful *adj* mächtig.

powerless *adj* machtlos.

power station *n* Kraftwerk *n*.

practical *adj* praktisch.

practice *n* Übung *f*; Praxis *f*.

practise *vt vi* üben.

pragmatic *adj* pragmatisch.

praise *n* Lob *n*:—*vt* loben.

praiseworthy *adj* lobenswert.

prawn *n* Garnele *f*.
pray *vi* beten.
prayer *n* Gebet *n*.
preach *vi* predigen.
precede *vt vi* vorausgehen.
precious *adj* wertvoll;
  preziös.
precise *adj* genau, präzis.
precision *n* Präzision *f*.
predict *vt* voraussagen.
predictable *adj* vorhersag-
  bar.
prediction *n* Voraussage *f*.
preface *n* Vorwort *n*.
prefer *vt* vorziehen, lieber
  mögen.
preferable *adj*
  vorzugsweise, am
  liebsten.
preference *n* Vorzug *m*.
preferential *adj* Vorzugs-.
prefix *n* Präfix *n*.
pregnancy *n*
  Schwangerschaft *f*.
pregnant *adj* schwanger.
prejudice *n* Vorurteil *n*;
  Voreingenom-menheit *f*:—
  vt beeinträchtigen.
prejudiced *adj* voreingenommen.
prelude *n* Vorspiel *n*.
premature *adj* vorzeitig;
  Früh-.
premier *n* Premier *m*.
premiere *n* Premiere *f*.
premium *n* Prämie *f*.
preparation *n* Vorbereitung
  f.
prepare *vt* vorbereiten:—*vi*
  sich vorbereiten.
preposition *n* Präposition *f*,
  Verhältniswort *n*.
prescribe *vi* vorschreiben;
  (*med*) verschreiben.
prescription *n* (*med*) Rezept
  n.

presence *n* Gegenwart *f*.
present *adj* anwesend;
  gegenwärtig: —*n*
  Gegenwart *f*; Geschenk
  n:—*vt* vorlegen;
  vorstellen; zeigen.
preservation *n* Erhaltung *f*.
preservative *n*
  Konservierungsmittel *n*.
preserve *vt* erhalten; einmachen.
president *n* Präsident *m*.
press *n* Presse *f*; Druckerei
  f:—*vt* drücken; drängen:—
  vi drücken.
press conference *n*
  Pressekonferenz *f*.
pressing *adj* dringend.
pressure *n* Druck *m*.
prestige *n* Prestige *n*.
presume *vt* annehmen.
presumption *n* Annahme *f*.
pretend *vi* so tun.
pretentious *adj* angeberisch.
pretty *adj* hübsch:—*adv*
  ganz schön.
prevent *vt* verhindern, verhüten.
prevention *n* Verhütung *f*.
preview *n* Vorschau *f*.
previous *adj* früher,
  vorherig.
prewar *adj* Vorkriegs-.
prey *n* Beute *f*.
price *n* Preis *m*.
priceless *adj* unbezahlbar.
prick n Stich *m*:—*vt vi*
  stechen.
prickle *n* Stachel *m*, Dorn *m*.
pride *n* Stolz *m*.
priest(ess) *n* Priester(in)
  m(f).
priesthood *n* Priesteramt *n*.
primary *adj* Haupt-.
prime minister *n*
  Premierminister *m*.

primitive *adj* primitiv.
primrose *n* (*bot*) Primel *f*.
prince *n* Prinz *m*; Fürst *m*.
princess *n* Prinzessin *f*;
  Fürstin *f*.
principal *adj* Haupt-:—*n*
  Direktor *m*.
principle *n* Grundsatz *m*;
  Prinzip *n*.
print *n* Druck *m*; Abdruck
  m; Abzug *m*:—*vt* drucken.
printer *n* Drucker *m*.
priority *n* Priorität *f*.
prison *n* Gefängnis *n*.
prisoner *n* Gefangene(r)
  (*f*)*m*.
privacy *n* Ungestörtheit *f*;
  Privatleben *n*.
private *adj* privat, Privat-.
privilege *n* Privileg *n*.
prize *n* Preis *m*:—*vt*
  (hoch)schätzen.
prizewinner *n*
  Preisträger(in) *m(f)*.
probability *n*
  Wahrscheinlichkeit *f*.
probable *adj* wahrscheinlich.
probation *n* Probe *f*.
probe *n* Sonde *f*;
  Untersuchung *f*:—*vt vi*
  erforschen.
problem *n* Problem *n*.
problematic *adj* problematisch.
procedure *n* Verfahren *n*.
proceed *vi* vorrücken; fortfahren:—~**s** *npl* Erlös *m*.
proceedings *n* Verfahren *n*.
process *n* Prozeß *m*;
  Verfahren *n*.
procession *n* Prozession *f*.
proclaim *vt* verkünden.
proclamation *n*
  Verkündung *f*.
procure *vt* beschaffen.

prodigy *n* Wünder *n*.

produce *n* Produkte *pl*; Erzeugnis *n*: —*vt* herstellen, produzieren; erzeugen.

producer *n* Hersteller *m*, Produzent *m*; Erzeuger *m*.

product *n* Produkt *n*; Erzeugnis *n*.

production *n* Produktion *f*, Herstellung *f*.

productive *adj* produktiv.

productivity *n* Produktivität *f*.

profess *vt* zeigen; vorgeben.

profession *n* Beruf *m*.

professional *adj* Berufs-.

professor *n* Professor *m*.

profile *n* Profil *n*.

profit *n* Gewinn *m*.

profitability *n* Rentabilität *f*.

profitable *adj* rentabel.

profound *adj* tief.

program(me) *n* Program *n*:—*vt* planen; programmieren.

programmer *n* Programmierer(in) *m(f)*.

programming *n* Programmieren *n*.

progress *n* Fortschritt *m*:—*vi* fort-schreiten, weitergehen.

progression *n* Folge *f*.

progressive *adj* fortschritlich, progressiv.

prohibit *vt* verbieten.

prohibition *n* Verbot *n*.

project *n* Projekt *n*:—*vt* vorausplanen; projizieren.

projection *n* Projektion *f*.

projector *n* Projektor *m*.

prolific *adj* produktiv.

prologue *n* Prolog *m*; Vorspiel *n*.

prolong *vt* verlängern.

promenade *n* Promenade *f*.

prominence *n* (große) Bedeutung *f*.

prominent *adj* prominent; bedeutend; auffallend.

promiscuous *adj* lose.

promise *n* Versprechen *n*:—*vt vi* versprechen.

promising *adj* vielversprechend.

promote *vt* befördern; fördern, unterstützen.

promotion *n* Beförderung *f*; Förderung *f*; Werbung *f*.

prompt *adj* prompt, schnell.

pronoun *n* Fürwort *n*.

pronounce *vt* aussprechen.

pronounced *adj* ausgesprochen.

pronouncement *n* Erklärung *f*.

pronunciation *n* Aussprache *f*.

proof *n* Beweis *f*; Korrekturfahne *f*; Alkoholgehalt *m*:—*adj* sicher.

prop *n* Stütze *f*; Requisit *n*:—*vt* (ab)-stützen.

propaganda *n* Propaganda *f*.

propel *vt* (an)treiben.

propeller *n* Propeller *m*.

proper *adj* richtig; schicklich.

property *n* Eigentum *n*.

prophet *n* Prophet *m*.

proportion *n* Verhältnis *n*; Teil *m*.

proportional *adj* proportional.

proportionate *adj* verhältnismäßig.

proposal *n* Vorshlag *m*.

propose *vt* vorschlagen.

proposition *n* Angebot *n*.

proprietor *n* Besitzer *m*, Eigentümer *m*.

prose *n* Prosa *f*.

prosecute *vt* (strafrechtlich) verfolgen.

prosecution *n* strafrechtliche Verfolgung *f*; Anklage *f*.

prosecutor *n* Vertreter *m* der Anklage.

prospect *n* Aussicht *f*.

prospectus *n* Prospekt *m*.

prosper *vi* blühen, gedeihen; erfolgreich sein.

prosperity *n* Wohlstand *m*.

prosperous *adj* reich, wohlhabend.

prostitute *n* Prostituierte *f*, Dirne *f*.

protect *vt* (be)schützen.

protection *n* Schutz *m*.

protective *adj* Schutz-, (be)schützend.

protector *n* Schützer *m*.

protégé *n* Schützling *m*.

protein *n* Protein *n*.

protest *n* Protest *m*:—*vi* protestieren.

Protestant *adj* protestantisch:—*n* Protestant(in) *m(f)*.

protester *n* Demonstrant(in) *m(f)*.

protrude *vi* (her)vorstehen.

proud *adj* stolz.

prove *vt* beweisen.

proverb *n* Sprichwort *n*.

provide *vt* versehen:—~ **for** *vt* sorgen für.

provided *conj*:—~ **that** vorausgesetzt, daß.

province *n* Provinz *f*.

provincial *adj* provinziell.

provision *n* Vorkehrung *f*; Bestimmung *f*.

provisional *adj* provisorisch.

proviso *n* Bedingung *f.*

provocation *n* Herausforderung *f.*

provocative *adj* herausfordernd.

provoke *vt* provozieren; hervorrufen.

proximity *n* Nähe *f.*

prudence *n* Umsicht *f.*

prudent *adj* klug, umsichtig.

prudish *adj* prüde.

prune *n* Backpflaume *f:—vt* ausputzen.

pry *vi:—~* **into** seine Nase stecken (in *+acc*).

pseudonym *n* Pseudonym *n*, Deckname *m.*

psychiatric *adj* psychiatrisch.

psychiatrist *n* Psychiater *m.*

psychiatry *n* Psychiatrie *f.*

psychological *adj* psychologisch.

psychologist *n* Psychologe *m*, Psychologin *f.*

psychology *n* Psychologie *f.*

pub *n* Kneipe *f.*

puberty *n* Pubertät *f.*

public *adj* öffentlich:—*n* Öffentlichkeit *f.*

publican *n* Wirt *m.*

publication *n* Veröffentlichung *f.*

publicity *n* Publicity *f*, Werbung *f.*

publicize *vt* bekannt machen; Publicity machen für.

public opinion *n* öffentliche Meinung *f.*

publish *vt* veröffentlichen.

publisher *n* Verleger *m.*

publishing *n* Verlagswesen *n.*

pudding *n* Nachtisch *m*; Pudding *m.*

puddle *n* Pfütze *m.*

puff *n* Stoß *m*; Puderquaste *f:—vt vi* paffen.

pull *n* Ruck *m*; Beziehung *f:—vt vi* ziehen.

pulley *n* Rolle *f*, Flaschenzug *m.*

pullover *n* Pullover *m.*

pulp *n* Brei *m*; Fruchtfleisch *n.*

pulse *n* Puls *m.*

pump *n* Pumpe *f:—vt* pumpen.

pumpkin *n* Kürbis *m.*

pun *n* Wortspiel *n.*

punch *n* Locher *m*; Faustschlag *m*; Punsche *m*, Bowle *f:—vt* lochen; schlagen, boxen.

punctual *adj* pünktlich.

punctuate *vt* mit Satzzeichen versehen; unterbrechen.

punctuation *n* Zeichensetzung *f.*

punish *vt* bestrafen.

punishment *n* Strafe *f*; Bestrafung *f.*

pupil *n* Schüler(in) *m(f)*; Pupille *f.*

puppet *n* Puppe *f*; Marionette *f.*

puppy *n* junger Hund *m.*

purchase *n* Kauf *m:—vt* kaufen.

purchaser *n* Käufer(in) *m(f).*

pure *adj* rein.

purify *vt* reinigen.

purity *n* Reinheit *f.*

purple *adj* violett; dunkelrot.

purpose *n* Zweck *m*, Ziel *n:—on ~* absichtlich.

purr *vi* schnurren.

purse *n* Portemonnaie *n*, Geldbeutel *m.*

pursue *vi* verfolgen.

pursuit *n* Verfolgung *f*; Beschäftigung *f.*

push *n* Stoß *m*, Schub *m*; Vorstoß *m:—vt* stoßen, schieben.

put *vt* setzen, stellen, legen.

puzzle *n* Rätsel *m*; Verwirrung *f.*

pyjamas *npl* Schlafanzug *m*, Pyjama *m.*

pylon *n* Mast *m.*

pyramid *n* Pyramide *f.*

python *n* Pythonschlange *m.*

Q

quack *vi* quaken:—*n* Quaken *n*.

quadrangle *n* Hof *m*; Viereck *n*.

quadruple *adj* vierfach.

quadruplet *n* Vierling *m*.

quagmire *n* Morass *m*.

quail *n* Wachtel *f*.

quaint *adj* malerisch, kuriös.

quake *vi* beben; zittern.

qualification *n* Qualifikation *f*.

qualified *adj* qualifiziert.

qualify *vt* befähigen:—*vi* qualifizieren.

quality *n* Qualität *f*.

qualm *n* Bedenken *n*.

quandary *n* Verlegenheit *f*.

quantity *n* Quantität *f*, Menge *f*, Anzahl *f*.

quarantine *n* Quarantän *f*.

quarrel *n* Streit *m*:—*vi* sich streiten.

quarrelsome *adj* streitsüchtig.

quarry *n* Steinbruch *m*; Wild *n*.

quarter *n* Viertel n; Quartal *n*.

quartet *n* Quartett *n*.

quartz *n* Quarz *m*.

quay *n* Kai *m*.

queen *n* Königin *f*; Dame *f*.

queer *adj* seltsam.

quell *vt* unterdrucken.

quench *vt* löschen.

quest *n* Suche *f*.

question *n* Frage *f*:—*vt* befragen.

questionable *adj* fragwürdig, zweifelhaft.

question mark *n* Fragezeichen *n*.

questionnaire *n* Fragebogen *m*.

quick *adj* schnell.

quicken *vt* beschleunigen:—*vi* sich beschleunigen.

quiet *adj* leise:—*n* Ruhe *f*.

quintet *n* Quintett *n*.

quit *vt* verlassen:—*vi* aufhören.

quite *adv* ganz, ziemlich; völlig.

quits *adj* quitt.

quiver *vi* zittern:—*n* Köcher *m*.

quiz *n* Quiz *n*:—*vt* prüfen, ausfragen.

quota *n* Quote *f*.

quotation *n* Zitat *n*.

quote *vt* zitieren.

R

rabbit *n* Kaninchen *n*.
rabies *n* Tollwut *f*.
race *n* Rasse *f*; Rennen *n*:—
vi rennen.
radiant *adj* strahlend.
radiate *vt vi* ausstrahlen.
radiation *n* Strahlung *f*.
radiator *n* Heizkörper *m*.
radical *adj* radikal.
radio *n* Radio *n*.
radioactive *adj* radioactiv.
radish *n* Rettich *m*.
raft *n* Floß *n*.
rag *n* Fetzen *m*.
rage *n* Wut *f*:—*vi* toben.
raid *n* Razzia *f*.
rail *n* Schiene *f*; Gelände *n*;
Reling *f*.
railway *n* Eisenbahn *f*.
rain *n* Regen *m*:—*vt vi* regnen.
rainbow *n* Regebogen *m*.
rainy *adj* regnerisch.
raise *vt* heben; erhohen.
raisin *n* Rasine *f*.
rake *n* Harke *f*:—*vt* harken.
ram *n* Widder *m*; Ramme
f:—*vt* rammen.
ramp *n* Rampe *f*.
random *adj* ziellos,
wahllos.
range *n* Reihe *f*; Sortiment
n:—*vt* anordnen, auf-
stellen,
rank *n* Reihe *f*; Rang *m*;
Stand *m*.
ransom *n* Lösegeld *n*.
rape *n* Vergewaltigung *f*:—
vt vergewaltigen.

rapid *adj* schnell, rasch.
rapist *n* Vergewaltiger *m*.
rare *adj* selten, rar.
rarity *n* Seltenheit *f*.
raspberry *n* Himbeere *f*.
rat *n* Ratte *f*.
rate *n* Rate *f*, Tarif *m*;
Tempo *n*:—*vt*
(ein)schätzen.
rather *adv* lieber, eher;
ziemlich.
ratio *n* Verhältnis *n*.
ration *n* Ration *f*.
rational *adj* rational.
rattle *n* Rasseln *n*; Rassel
f:—*vt vi* ratteln.
rattlesnake *n*
Klapperschlange *f*.
rave *vi* toben.
raven *n* Rabe *m*.
raw *adj* roh.
ray *n* Strahl *m*.
razor *n* Rasierapparat *m*.
reach *vt* (er)reichen.
react *vi* reagieren.
reaction *n* Reaktion *f*.
read *vt vi* lesen.
ready *adj* bereit.
real *adj* wirklich; eigentlich;
echt.
reality *n* Wirklichkeit *f*.
realize *vt* begreifen; verwirklichen.
realm *n* Reich *n*.
reap *vt* ernten.
rear *n* Rückseite *f*; Schluß
m:—*vt* aufziehen.
reason *n* Grund *m*;
Verstand *m*.

reasonable *adj* vernünftig.
reassure *vt* beruhigen.
rebel *n* Rebell *m*:—*vi* rebellieren.
rebellion *n* Rebellion *f*,
Aufstand *m*.
rebellious *adj* rebellisch.
receipt *n* Quittung *f*;
Empfang *m*.
receive *vt* erhalten; empfangen.
recently *adv* neulich.
reception *n* Empfang *m*.
recession *n* Rezession *f*.
recipe *n* Rezept *n*.
recital *n* Vortrag *m*.
recite *vt* vortragen.
reckon *vt* rechnen,
berechnen.
reclaim *vt* zurückverlangen.
recline *vi* sich zurück-
lehnen.
recognition *n* Erkennen *n*;
Anerkennung *f*.
recognize *vt* erkennen;
anerkennen.
recommend *vt* empfehlen.
recommendation *n*
Empfehlung *f*.
record *n* Aufzeichnung *f*;
Schallplatte *f*; Rekord *m*:—
vt aufzeichen; aufnehmen.
recount *vt* berichten.
recover *vi* erholen.
recovery *n* Erholung *f*.
recruit *n* Rekrut *m*:—*vt*
rekrutieren.
recruitment *n* Rekrutierung
f.

rectangle *n* Rechteck *n*.

red *adj* rot.

reduce *vt* vermindern.

reduction *n* Verminderung *f*.

redundancy *n* Entlassung *f*.

redundant *adj* überflüssig.

reed *n* Schilf *n*.

reel *n* Spule *f*, Rolle *f*:—*vi* taumeln.

refer *vi*:—~ **to** nachschlagen in +*dat*.

referee *n* Schiedsrichter *m*.

reference *n* Referenz *f*; Verweis *m*.

reflect *vt* reflektieren; spiegeln:—*vi* nachdenken.

reflection *n* Reflexion *f*; Spiegelbild *n*.

reform *n* Reform *f*:—*vt* bessern.

refresh *vt* erfrischen.

refrigerator *n* Kühlschrank *m*.

refuge *n* Zuflucht *f*.

refugee *n* Flüchtling *m*.

refund *n* Rückvergütung *f*:—*vt* zurückerstatten.

refuse *vt* abschlagen:—*vi* sich weigern:—*n* Abfall *n*.

regain *vt* wiedergewinnen.

regard *n* Achtung *f*:—*vt* ansehen.

region *n* Region *f*.

register *n* Register *n*:—*vt* registrieren; eintragen.

registration *n* Registrierung *f*.

regret *n* Bedauern *n*:—*vt* bedauern.

regular *adj* regelmäßig.

regulate *vt* regeln, regulieren.

regulation *n* Vorschrift *f*; Regulierung *f*.

rehearsal *n* Probe *f*.

rehearse *vt* proben.

reign *n* Herrschaft *f*:—*vi* herrschen.

rein *n* Zügel *m*.

reindeer *n* Ren *n*.

reinforce *vt* verstärken.

reject *vt* ablehnen.

rejection *n* Zurückweisung *f*.

relate *vt* erzählen; verbinden.

related *adj* verwandt.

relationship *n* Verhältnis *n*.

relative *n* Verwandte(r) *f(m)*:—*adj* relativ.

relax *vi* sich entspannen.

relaxation *n* Entspannung *f*.

relay *n* Staffel *f*:—*vt* weiterleiten.

release *n* Entlassung *f*:—*vt* befreien; entlassen.

relevant *adj* relevant.

reliable *adj* zuverlässig.

relief *n* Erleichterung *f*; Hilfe *f*.

religion *n* Religion *f*.

religious *adj* religiös.

reluctance *n* Widerstreben *n*.

reluctant *adj* widerwillig.

remain *vi* bleiben; übrigbleiben.

remainder *n* Rest *m*.

remark *n* Bemerkung *f*:—*vt* bemerken.

remarkable *adj* bemerkenswert.

remedy *n* Mittel *n*:—*vt* abhelfen +*dat*.

remember *vt* sich erinnern an +*acc*.

remembrance *n* Erinnerung *f*; Gedenken *n*.

reminder *n* Mahnung *f*.

remote *adj* abgelegen.

removable *adj* entfernbar.

removal *n* Beseitigung *f*; Umzug *m*.

remove *vt* beseitigen, entfernen.

remuneration *n* Vergütung *f*.

render *vt* machen; übersetzen.

renew *vt* erneuern.

renewal *n* Erneuerung *f*.

renounce *vt* verzichten auf +*acc*.

renovate *vt* renovieren.

renown *n* Ruf *m*.

rent *n* Miete *f*:—*vt* mieten.

rental *n* Miete *f*.

reorganize *vt* reorganisieren.

repair *n* Reparatur *f*:—*vt* reparieren; wiedergutmachen.

repay *vt* zurückzahlen.

repayment *n* Rückzahlung *f*.

repeat *vt* wiederholen.

repetition *n* Wiederholung *f*.

replace *vt* ersetzen; zurückstellen.

reply *n* Antwort *f*:—*vi* antworten.

report *n* Bericht *m*:—*vt* berichten; melden; anzeigen:—*vi* Bericht erstatten.

reporter *n* Reporter *m*.

represent *vt* darstellen; vertreten.

representation *n* Darstellung *f*; Vertretung *f*.

representative *n* Vertreter *m*.

repress *vt* unterdrücken.

repression *n* Unterdrückung *f*.

reproach *n* Vorwurf *m*:—*vt* Vorwürfe machen +*dat*.

reproduce *vt* reproduzieren.

reproduction *n* Reproduktion *f*.

reptile *n* Reptil *n*.
republic *n* Republik *f*.
repudiate *vt* zurückweisen.
repugnant *adj* widerlich.
repulse *vt* zurückschlagen.
repulsive *adj* abstoßend.
reputation *n* Ruf *m*.
repute *n* hohes Ansehen *n*.
request *n* Bitte *f*:—*vt* erbitten.
require *vt* brauchen; erfordern.
requirement *n* Bedarf *m*; Anforderung *f*.
rescue *n* Rettung *f*:—*vi* retten.
research *n* Forschung *f*:—*vi* forschen:—*vt* erforschen.
resemblance *n* Ähnlichkeit *f*.
resemble *vt* ähneln +*dat*.
reservation *n* Reservierung *f*; Vorbestellung *f*; Vorbehalt *m*.
reserve *n* Vorrat *m*; Reserve *f*:—*vt* reservieren.
reside *vi* wohnen.
residence *n* Wohnsitz *m*.
resident *n* Bewohner *m*; Einwohner *m*.
resign *vt vi* zurücktreten.
resignation *n* Kündigung *f*; Rucktritt *m*.
resist *vt* widerstehen +*dat*.
resistance *n* Widerstand *m*.
resolute *adj* resolut, entschlossen.
resolution *n* Entschlossenheit *f*.
resolve *vt* beschliessen:—*vi* sich lösen.
resort *n* Erholungsort *m*; Zuflucht *f*.
respect *n* Hinsicht *f*; Achtung *f*:—**with ~ to** hinsichtlich:—*vt* respektieren.

respectable *adj* solide.
respectful *adj* ehrerbietig, respektvoll.
respective *adj* jeweilig.
respiration *n* Atmung *f*.
respite *n* Atempause *f*, Ruhepause *f*.
respond *vi* antworten; reagieren.
response *n* Antwort *f*; Reaktion *f*.
responsibility *n* Verantwortung *f*.
responsible *adj* verantwortlich.
rest *n* Ruhe *f*, Ruhepause *f*; Pause *f*; Stütze *f*:—*vi* ruhen, sich ausruhen.
restful *adj* erholsam, ruhig, friedlich.
restive *adj* unruhig, nervös.
restless *adj* ruhelos, unruhig.
restoration *n* Rückerstattung *f*; Restaurierung *f*.
restore *vt* wiedergeben; restaurieren.
restrain *vt* zurückhalten, unterdrücken.
restraint *n* Zurückhaltung *f*.
restrict *vt* einschränken.
restriction *n* Einschränkung *f*.
restrictive *adj* einschränkend.
result *n* Ergebnis *n*.
resume *vt* fortsetzen; wieder einnehmen.
resurrection *n* Auferstehung *f*.
retail *n* Einzelhandel *m*.
retain *vt* behalten.
retire *vi* in den Ruhestand treten; sich zurückziehen.

retired *adj* im Ruhestand, pensioniert.
retirement *n* Ruhestand *m*.
retrace *vt* zurückverfolgen.
retract *vt* zurücknehmen.
retrain *vt* umschulen.
retreat *n* Rückzug *m*:—*vi* sich zurückziehen.
retrieve *vt* wiederbekommen.
return *n* Rückkehr *f*; Ertrag *m*:—*adj* Rück-:—*vi* zurückkommen, zurückkehren:—*vt* zurückgeben, zurücksenden.
reunion *n* Wiedervereinigung *f*.
reunite *vt* wiedervereinigen.
reveal *vt* enthülen.
revelation *n* Offenbarung *f*.
revelry *n* Rummel *m*.
revenge *n* Rache *f*.
revenue *n* Einnahmen *pl*.
reverse *n* Rückseite *f*; Rückwärtsgang *m*:—*adj* entgegengesetzt:—*vt* umkehren:—*vi* rückwärts fahren.
review *n* Rezension *f*; Zeitschrift *f*:—*vt* rezensieren.
revise *vt* revidieren; überarbeiten.
revision *n* Wiederholung *f*; Prüfung *f*.
revival *n* Wiederbelebung *f*; Wiederaufnahme *f*.
revive *vt* wiederbeleben:—*vi* wiedererwachen.
revolt *n* Aufstand *m*:—*vi* sich auflehnen.
revolting *adj* widerlich.
revolution *n* Umdrehung *f*; Revolution *f*.
revolutionary *adj* revolutionär.

revolve vi kreisen; sich drehen.

revolver n Revolver m.

revolving door n Drehtür f.

revulsion n Ekel m.

reward n Belohnung f:—vt belohnen.

rheumatism n Rheumatismus m.

rhinoceros n Nashorn n.

rhubarb n Rhabarber m.

rhyme n Reim m.

rhythm n Rhythmus m.

rib n Rippe f.

ribbon n Band n.

rice n Reis m.

rich adj reich.

rid vt befreien.

riddle n Rätsel n.

ride n Fahrt f; Ritt m:—vt vi reiten, fahren.

ridge n Kamm m; Spott m.

ridicule n Spott m:—vt lächerlich machen.

ridiculous adj lächerlich.

rifle n Gewehr n:—vt berauben.

right adj richtig, recht; rechte(r, s):—n Recht n; Rechte f:—adj rechts; nach rechts; richtig, recht.

rigid adj starr, steif.

rigidity n Starrheit f.

rigorous adj streng.

rigour n Strenge f.

rim n Rand m.

ring n Ring m; Kreis m; Klingeln n:—vt vi läuten; anrufen.ʼ

rinse n Spülen n:—vt spülen.

riot n Aufruhr m:—vi randalieren.

rip n Riß m:—vt vi rreißen.

ripe adj reif.

rise n Steigung f; Erhöhung f:—vi aufgehen; aufsteigen; steigen.

risk n Risiko n:—vt riskieren.

risky adj riskant.

rival n Rivale m:—vt rivalisieren mit.

rivalry n Rivalität f.

river n Fluß m; Strom m.

road n Straße f.

roam vi umherstreifen.

roar n Brüllen n:—vi brüllen.

roast vt braten.

rob vt bestehlen, berauben.

robber n Räuber m.

robbery n Raub m.

robe n Gewand n; Robe f.

robin n Rotkehlchen m.

rock n Felsen m:—vt vi wiegen, schaukeln.

rocket n Rakete f.

rod n Stange f; Rute f.

rodent n Nagtier n.

roe n Reh n; Rogen m.

roll n Rolle f; Brötchen n; Liste f:—vt rollen, wälzen:—vi schlingern.

roller n Rolle f, Walze f.

Roman adj römisch:—n Römer(in) m(f).

Roman Catholic adj römisch-katholisch:—n Katholik(in) m(f).

romance n Romanze f; Liebesroman m.

romantic adj romantisch.

roof n Dach n.

rook n Saatkräke f; Turm m.

room n Zummer n, Raum m; Platz m; Spielraum m.

rooster n Hahn m.

root n Wurzel f.

rope n Seil n.

rose n Rose f.

rosebud n Rosenknospe m.

rosemary n Rosmarin m.

rot n Fäulnis n; Quatsch m:—vi verfaulen.

rotate vi rotieren.

rotation n Umdrehung f.

rotten adj faul; schlecht, gemein.

rough adj rauh; uneben; grob.

roughen vt aufrauhen.

round adj rund; aufgerundet:—adv um… herum.

rouse vt wecken; aufrütteln; erregen.

route n Route f, Weg m; Strecke f.

row n Lärm f; Streit f; n Reihe f:—vi sich streiten:—vt vi rudern.

royal adj königlich, Königs-.

rub vt reiben.

rubber n Gummi m; Radiergummi m.

rubbish n Abfall m; Quatsch m.

rubbish bin n Mülleimer m.

ruby n Rubin m:—adj rubinrot.

rude adj unverschämt; hart; unsanft; grob.

rudiment n Grundlage f.

rug n Brücke f; Bettvorleger m.

ruin n Ruine f; Ruin m:—vt ruinieren.

rule n Regel f; Regierung f:—vt regieren; linieren:—vi herrschen.

ruler n Lineal n; Herrscher m.

rum n Rum m.

rumour n Gerücht n.

run vi laufen, rennen.

runaway adj flüchtig; ausgebrochen.

rung n Sprosse f.

runner *n* Läufer(in) *m(f)*; Kufe *f*.

runner-bean *n* Stangenbohne *f*.

runway *n* Startbahn *f*.

rupture *n* Bruch *m*.

rush *n* Eile *f*, Hetze *f*:—*vi* eilen.

Russia *n* Rußland *n*.

Russian *adj* russisch:—*n* Russe *m*, Russin *f*; Russisch *f*.

rust *n* Rost *m*:—*vi* rosten.

rusty *adj* rostig.

rye *n* Roggen *m*.

S

sack *n* Sack *m:*—*vt* hinauswerfen; plündern.
sacrifice *n* Opfer *n:*—*vt*
opfern.
sad *adj* traurig.
saddle *n* Sattel *m.*
sadness *n* Traurigkeit *f.*
safe *adj* sicher; vorsichtig:—*n* Safe *m.*
safety *n* Sicherheit *f.*
sage *n* (*bot*) Salbei *f;*
Weise(r) *f(m).*
Sagittarius *n* (*astrol*)
Schütze *m.*
sail *n* Segel *n:*—*vt* segeln:—
vi segeln; auslaufen.
sailing *n* Segeln *n.*
sailor *n* Matrose *m,*
Seemann *m.*
saint *n* Heilige(r) *f(m).*
sake *n:*—**for the ~ of** um…
willen.
salad *n* Salat *m.*
salami *n* Salami *f.*
salary *n* Gehalt *n.*
sale *n* Verkauf *m.*
saliva *n* Speichel *m.*
salmon *n* Lachs *m.*
saloon *n* Salon *m.*
salt *n* Salz *n.*
salty *adj* salzig.
salute *n* Gruß *m:*—*vt* salu-
tieren.
same *adj pn* gleiche(r, s);
derselbe / dieselbe /
dasselbe.
sample *n* Probe *f:*—*vt* probieren.
sanction *n* Sanktion *f.*

sand *n* Sand *m.*
sandal *n* Sandale *f.*
sandwich *n* Sandwich *m / n.*
sane *adj* geistig gesund.
sanity *n* geistige
Gesundheit *f.*
sapphire *n* Saphir *m.*
sarcasm *n* Sarkasmus *m.*
sarcastic *adj* sarkastisch.
sardine *n* Sardine *f.*
satisfaction *n* Befriedigung
f.
satisfactory *adj* zufrieden-
stellend.
satisfy *vt* befriedigen,
zufriedenstellen.
Saturday *n* Samstag *m,*
Sonnabend *m.*
sauce *n* Soße *f,* Sauce *f.*
saucepan *n* Kassrolle *f.*
saucer *n* Untertasse *f.*
saucy *adj* frech, keck.
saunter *vi* schlendern.
sausage *n* Wurst *f.*
savage *adj* wild:—*n*
Wilde(r) *f(m).*
save *vt* retten; sparen:—
prep conj außer,
ausgenommen.
saving *n* Sparen *n,*
Ersparnis *f.*
savings account *n*
Sparkonto *n.*
savings bank *n* Sparkasse *f.*
saviour *n* Erlöser *m.*
savour *vt* schmecken.
savoury *adj* würzig, pikant.
saw *n* Sage *f:*—*vt vi* sägen.
sawdust *n* Sägemehl *n.*

say *vt vi* sagen.
scab *n* Schorf *m.*
scaffold *n* Schafott *n.*
scaffolding *n* Baugerüst *n.*
scald *vt* verbrühen.
scale *n* Schuppe *f;* Tonleiter
f; Maßstab *m:*—*vt* erklimmen.
scan *vt* genau prüfen;
absuchen; skandieren.
scandal *n* Skandal *m.*
Scandinavia *n*
Skandinavien *n.*
Scandinavian *adj* skandinavisch:—*n*
Skandinavier(in) *m(f).*
scapegoat *n* Sünden-
bock *m.*
scar *n* Narbe *f.*
scarce *adj* selten, rar.
scarcely *adv* kaum.
scarcity *n* Mangel *m.*
scare *n* Schrecken *m:*—*vt*
erschrecken.
scarecrow *n* Vogel-
scheuche *f.*
scarf *n* Schal *m.*
scatter *vt* streuen; zerstreuen:—*vi* sich zer-
streuen.
scenario *n* Szenario *n.*
scene *n* Ort *m;* Szene *f.*
scenery *n* Bühnenbild *n;*
Landschaft *f.*
scent *n* Parfüm *n;* Duft
m:—*vt* parfümieren.
sceptical *adj* skeptisch.
schedule *n* Liste *f;*
Programm *n;* Zeitplan *m.*

scheme *n* Schema *n*; Intrige
f; Plan *m*:—*vt* planen:—*vi*
intrigieren.

school *n* Schule *f*.

science *n* Wissenschaft *f*.

scientific *adj* wis-
senschaftlich.

scientist *n*
Wissenschaftler(in) *m(f)*.

scissors *npl* Schere *f*.

scope *n* Ausmaß *n*;
Spielraum *m*.

scorch *n* Brandstelle *f*:—*vt*
versengen.

score *n* Punktzahl *f*;
Spielergebnis *n*; Partitur
f:—*vi* Punkte zählen.

scorn *n* Verachtung *f*:—*vt*
verhöhnen.

Scorpio *n* (*astrol*)
Skorpion *m*.

Scot *n* Schotte *m*, Schottin *f*.

Scotch *n* Scotch *m*.

Scotland *n* Schottland *n*.

Scotsman *n* Schotte *m*.

Scotswoman *n* Schottin *f*.

Scottish *adj* schottisch.

scour *vt* absuchen;
schrubben.

scourge *n* Geißel *f*;
Qual *f*.

scout *n* Pfadfinder *m*.

scrap *n* Stückchen *n*;
Kellerei *f*; Schrott *m*:—*vt*
verwerfen.

scrape *n* Kratzen *n*;
Klemme *f*:—*vt vi* kratzen.

scratch *n* Kratzer *m*,
Schramme *f*:—*vt* kratzen.

scream *n* Schrei *m*:—*vi*
schreien.

screen *n* Schutzschirm *m*;
Leinwand *f*; Bildschirm *m*.

screw *n* Schraube *f*.

screwdriver *n*
Schraubenzieher *m*.

script *n* Handschrift *f*;
Manuskript *n*.

scrub *n* Schrubben *n*;
Gestrüpp *n*:—*vt*
schrubben.

sculptor *n* Bildhauer(in)
m(f).

sculpture *n* Bildhauerei *f*.

sea *n* Meer *n*, See *f*.

seagull *n* Möwe *f*.

seal *n* Seehund *m*; Siegel
n:—*vt* versiegeln.

seam *n* Saum *m*.

search *n* Suche *f*;
Durchsuchung *f*:—*vi*
suchen:—*vt* durchsuchen.

seashore *n* Meeresküste *f*.

seasick *adj* seekrank.

season *n* Jahreszeit *f*;
Saison *f*:—*vt* würzen.

seasonal *adj* Saison-.

seat *n* Sitz *m*, Platz *m*;
Gesäß *n*:—*vt* setzen.

seaweed *n* Seetang *m*.

seaworthy *adj* seetüchtig.

second *adj* zweite(r, s); *adv*
an zweiter Stelle:—*n*
Sekunde *f*.

secondhand *adj* gebraucht.

secrecy *n* Geheimhaltung *f*.

secret *adj* geheim:—*n*
Geheimnis *n*.

secretary *n* Sekretär(in) *m(f)*.

section *n* Teil *m*;
Abschnitt *m*.

sector *n* Sektor *m*.

secular *adj* weltlich,
profan.

secure *adj* sicher; fest:—*vt*
sichern.

security *n* Sicherheit *f*;
Pfand *n*; Wertpapier *n*.

seduce *vt* verführen.

seduction *n* Verführung *f*.

seductive *adj* verführerisch.

see *vt vi* sehen.

seed *n* Samen *m*:—*vt*
plazieren.

seek *vt* suchen.

seem *vi* scheinen.

seesaw *n* Wippe *f*.

seize *vt* greifen, ergreifen,
packen.

seizure *n* Anfall *m*.

seldom *adv* selten.

select *adj* ausgewählt:—*vt*
auswählen.

selection *n* Auswahl *f*.

selfish *adj* selbstsüchtig.

selfishness *n* Selbstsucht *f*.

sell *vt vi* verkaufen.

seller *n* Verkäufer *m*.

semicolon *n* Semikolon *n*.

send *vt* senden, schicken.

senior *adj* älter; Ober-.

sensation *n* Gefühl *n*;
Sensation *f*.

sense *n* Sinn *m*; Verstand
m; Gefühl *n*.

senseless *adj* sinnlos.

sensible *adj* vernünftig.

sensitive *adj* empfindlich.

sensual *adj* sinnlich.

sentence *n* Satz *m*; Strafe *f*;
Urteil *n*.

sentiment *n* Gefühl *n*;
Gedenke *m*.

sentimental *adj* sentimental.

separate *adj* getrennt, sepa-
rat:—*vt* trennen:—*vi* sich
trennen.

separation *n* Trennung *f*.

September *n* September *m*.

sequel *n* Folge *f*.

sequence *n* Reihenfolge *f*.

Serbia *n* Serbien *n*.

serene *adj* heiter.

series *n* Serie *f*.

serious *adj* ernst; schwer.

sermon *n* Predigt *f*.

servant *n* Diener(in) *m(f)*.

serve *vt vi* dienen.

service *n* Dienst *m*; Service *m*, Bedienung *f*:—*vt* warten, überholen.

session *n* Sitzung *f*.

set *n* Satz *m*; Apparat *m*:—*adj* festgelegt; bereit:—*vt* setzen, stellen, legen:—*vi* untergehen; fest werden.

settle *vt* beruhigen; bezahlen; regeln: —*vi* sich einleben; sich setzen.

settlement *n* Regelung *f*; Begleichung *f*; Siedlung *f*.

seven *num* sieben.

seventeen *num* siebzehn.

seventh *adj* siebte(r, s).

seventy *num* siebzig.

several *adj* mehrere(r, s).

severe *adj* streng; schwer.

sew *vt vi* nähen.

sex *n* Sex *m*; Geschlecht *n*.

sexual *adj* sexuell.

sexy *adj* sexy.

shade *n* Schatten *m*; Schirm *m*:—*vt* beschatten; abschirmen.

shadow *n* Schatten *m*.

shake *vt* schütteln:—*vi* schwanken; zittern.

shallow *adj* seicht.

shame *n* Scham *m*; Schande *f*:—*vt* beschämen.

shameful *adj* schändlich.

shameless *adj* schamlos.

shampoo *n* Shampoo *n*.

shamrock *n* Kleeblatt *n*.

shape *n* Form *f*:—*vt* formen, gestalten.

share *n* Anteil *m*; (*fin*) Aktie *f*:—*vt* teilen.

shareholder *n* Aktionär(in) *m(f)*.

shark *n* Hai *m*.

sharp *adj* scharf; spitz; (*mus*) erhöht: —*n* Kreuz *n*.

sharpen *vt* schärfen.

shatter *vt* zerschmettern:—*vi* zerspringen.

shave *n* Rasur *f*:—*vt* rasieren:—*vi* sich rasieren.

shaver *n* Rasierapparat *m*.

she *pn* sie.

shed *n* Schuppen *m*; Stall *m*.

sheep *n* Schaf *n*.

sheer *adj* bloß, rein; steil.

sheet *n* Bettuch *n*; Blatt *n*.

shelf *n* Regal *n*.

shell *n* Schale *f*; Muschel *f*; Granate *f*.

shellfish *n* Schalentier *n*.

shelter *n* Schutz *m*; Bunker *m*:—*vt* schützen:—*vi* sich unterstellen.

shepherd *n* Schäfer *m*.

shield *n* Schild *m*; Schirm *m*:—*vt* schirmen.

shift *n* Verschiebung *f*; Schicht *f*:—*vt* rücken, verschieben.

shine *n* Glanz *m*, Schein *m*:—*vi* scheinen.

shiny *adj* glänzend.

ship *n* Schiff *n*.

shirt *n* Hemd *n*.

shiver *vi* zittern.

shock *n* Erschütterung *f*; Schock *m*; Schlag *m*:—*vt* erschüttern; schockieren.

shoe *n* Schuh *m*; Hufeisen *n*:—*vt* beschlagen.

shoot *vt* schießen.

shop *n* Laden *m*, Geschäft *n*.

shopping *n* Einkaufen *n*.

shopping centre *n* Einkaufszentrum *n*.

shore *n* Strand *m*.

short *adj* kurz.

shorten *vt* abkürzen.

short-sighted *adj* kurzsichtig.

shot *n* Schuß *m*.

shoulder *n* Schulter *f*.

shout *n* Schrei *m*:—*vi* schreien.

shove *n* Stoß *m*:—*vt* schieben, stoßen.

show *n* Schau *f*; Ausstellung *f*; Vorstellung *f*:—*vt* zeigen.

shower *n* Schauer *m*; Dusche *f*.

shred *n* Fetzen *m*:—*vt* zerfetzen.

shrewd *adj* clever.

shriek *n* Schrei *m*:—*vi* schreien.

shrimp *n* Garnele *f*.

shrink *vi* schrumpfen.

shroud *n* Leichentuch *n*.

Shrove Tuesday *n* Fastnachtsdienstag *m*.

shrub *n* Strauch *m*.

shun *vt* scheuen.

shut *vt* schließen, zumachen:—*vi* sich schließen.

shutter *n* Fensterladen *m*.

shy *adj* schüchtern.

sick *adj* krank; makaber.

sicken *vt* krankmachen:—*vi* krank werden.

sickle *n* Sichel *f*.

sickness *n* Krankheit *f*.

side *n* Seite *m*.

siege *n* Belagerung *f*.

sieve *n* Sieb *n*:—*vt* sieben.

sift *vt* sieben.

sigh *n* Seufzer *m*:—*vi* seufzen.

sight *n* Sehvermögen *n*; Blick *m*; Anblick *m*.

sign *n* Zeichen *n*; Schild *n*:—*vt* unterschreiben.

signal *n* Signal *n*.

signature *n* Unterschrift *f*.

significance *n* Bedeutung *f*.

significant *adj* bedeutend.

signify *vt* bedeuten.

signpost *n* Wegweiser *m*.

silence *n* Stille *f*; Schweigen *n*.

silent *adj* still; schweigsam.

silk *n* Seide *f*.

silky *adj* seidig.

silly *adj* dumm, albern.

silver *n* Silber *n*:—*adj* Silber-.

similar *adj* ähnlich.

similarity *n* Ähnlichkeit *f*.

simmer *vi* sieden.

simple *adj* einfach.

simplicity *n* Einfachheit *f*; Einfältigkeit *f*.

simplify *vt* vereinfachen.

simultaneous *adj* gleich- zeitig.

sin *n* Sünde *f*:—*vi* sündigen.

since *adv* seither:—*prep conj* seit.

sincere *adj* aufrichtig.

sincerity *n* Aufrichtigkeit *f*.

sing *vt vi* singen.

Singapore *n* Singapur *n*.

singer *n* Sänger(in) *m(f)*.

single *adj* einzig; Einzel-.

singular *adj* (*gr*) Singular-; merkwürdig.

sinister *adj* böse; unheim- lich.

sink *n* Spülbecken *n*:—*vt* versenken: —*vi* sinken.

sinner *n* Sünder(in) *m(f)*.

sister *n* Schwester *f*.

sister-in-law *n* Schwägerin *f*.

sit *vi* sitzen; tagen:—~ **down** *vi* sich hinsetzen.

site *n* Platz *m*; Baustelle *f*.

sitting *n* Sitzung *f*.

sitting room *n* Wohnzimmer *n*.

situation *n* Lage *f*.

six *num* sechs.

sixteen *num* sechzehn.

sixth *adj* sechste(r, s).

sixty *num* sechzig.

size *n* Größe *f*; Umfang *m*.

skate *n* Schlittschuh *m*; Rochen *m*:—*vi* Schlittschuh laufen.

skating *n* Eislauf *m*.

skating rink *n* Eisbahn *f*.

skeleton *n* Skelett *n*.

sketch *n* Skizze *f*:—*vt* skizzieren.

ski *n* Schi *m*:—*vi* Schi laufen.

skid *n* Schleudern *n*:—*vi* schleudern.

skier *n* Schiläufer(in) *m(f)*.

skiing *n* Schilaufen *n*.

skilful *adj* geschickt.

skill *n* Können *n*.

skin *n* Haut *f*; Schale *f*.

skirt *n* Rock *m*.

skull *n* Schädel *m*.

sky *n* Himmel *m*.

skyscraper *n* Wolkenkratzer *m*.

slab *n* Platte *f*.

slack *adj* locker; nachlässig.

slam *vt vi* zuschlagen.

slander *n* Verleumdung *f*:—*vt* verleumden.

slate *n* Schiefer *m*; Dachziegel:—*vt* verreißen.

slaughter *n* Schlachten *n*:— *vt* schlachten.

Slav *adj* slawisch.

slave *n* Sklave *m*, Sklavin *f*.

slavery *n* Sklaverei *f*.

sledge *n* Schlitten *m*.

sleep *n* Schlaf *m*:—*vi* schlafen.

sleeper *n* Schläfer *m*; Schlafwagen *m*.

sleepless *adj* schlaflos.

sleepwalker *n* Schlafwandler(in) *m(f)*.

sleepy *adj* schläfrig.

sleet *n* Schneeregen *m*.

sleeve *n* Ärmel *m*.

slice *n* Scheibe *f*.

slide *n* Rutschbahn *f*; Diapositiv *n*:—*vt* schieben:—*vi* gleiten, rutschen.

slight *adj* zierlich; ger- ingfügig; gering.

slightly *adv* etwas, ein bißchen.

slim *adj* schlank; dünn:—*vi* eine Schlankheitskur machen.

slip *n* Flüchtigkeitsfehler *m*; Zettel *m*:—*vi* aus- rutschen; gleiten.

slipper *n* Hausschuh *m*.

slogan *n* Schlagwort *n*; Werbespruch *m*.

slope *n* Neigung *f*; Abhang *m*:—*vi* ~ **down** sich senken:—~ **up** ansteigen.

slow *adj* langsam.

slug *n* Nachtschnecke *f*.

slum *n* Elendsquartier *n*.

sly *adj* schlau.

smack *n* Klaps *m*:—*vt* einen Klaps geben + *dat*.

small *adj* klein.

smart *adj* elegant, schick.

smash *n* Zusammenstoß *m*:—*vt* zerschmettern:—*vi* zersplittern.

smell *n* Geruch *m*; Geruchssinn *m*:—*vt vi* riechen.

smile *n* Lächeln *n*:—*vi* lächeln.

smith *n* Schmied *m*.

smoke *n* Rauch *m*:—*vt vi* rauchen.

smoker *n* Raucher(in) *m(f)*.

smooth *adj* glatt.

smug *adj* selbstgefällig.

smuggle *vt* schmuggeln.

smuggler *n* Schmuggler *m*.

snack *n* Imbiß *m*.

snag *n* Haken *m*.

snail *n* Schnecke *m*.

snake *n* Schlange *f*.

snap *n* Schnappen *n*:—*adj* schnell:—*vt* zerbrechen:— *vi* brechen.

snatch *vt* schnappen.

sneeze *vi* niesen.

sniff *vt* schnuppern:—*vi* schnüffeln.

snip *n* Schnippel *m*:—*vt* schnippeln.

snore *vi* schnarchen.

snow *n* Schnee *m*:—*vi* schneien.

snowball *n* Schneeball *m*.

snowdrop *n* Schneeglöckchen *n*.

snowman *n* Schneemann *m*.

snub *vt* schroff abferti- gen:—*n* Verweis *m*.

so *adv* so; auch; so viele; also.

soak *vt* durchnassen:—*vi* weichen.

soap *n* Seife *f*.

soar *vi* aufsteigen.

sob *n* Schluchzen *n*:—*vi* schluchzen.

sober *adj* nüchtern.

soccer *n* Fußball *m*.

sociable *adj* gesellig.

social *adj* sozial.

socialism *n* Sozialismus *m*.

socialist *n* Socialist(in) *m(f)*.

society *n* Gesellschaft *f*.

sociology *n* Soziologie *f*.

sock *n* Socke *f*.

socket *n* Steckdose *f*.

sod *n* Rasenstück *n*.

soda *n* Soda *f*.

sodium *n* Natrium *n*.

sofa *n* Sofa *n*.

soft *adj* weich; leise.

soften *vt* weich machen:—

vi weich werden.

softness *n* Weichheit *f*.

software *n* Software *f*.

soil *n* Erde *f*:—*vt* beschmutzen.

solar *adj* Sonnen-.

soldier *n* Soldat *m*.

sole *n* Sohle *f*; Seezunge *f*:—*adj* alleinig, Allein-.

solicitor *n* Rechtsanwalt *m*, Rechtsanwältin *f*.

solid *adj* fest; massiv; solide.

solidarity *n* Solidarität *f*.

solitary *adj* einsam.

solitude *n* Einsamkeit *f*.

solo *n* Solo *n*.

solution *n* Lösung *f*.

solve *vt* lösen.

some *adj pn* einige; etwas.

somehow *adv* irgendwie.

someone *pn* jemand; *acc* jemand(en); *dat* jemandem.

something *pn* etwas.

sometimes *adv* manchmal.

somewhat *adv* etwas.

somewhere *adv* irgendwo; irgendwohin.

son *n* Sohn *m*.

song *n* Lied *n*.

son-in-law *n* Schwiegersohn *m*.

soon *adv* bald.

soot *n* Ruß *m*.

soothe *vt* beruhigen; lin- dern.

sophisticated *adj* kultiviert.

sordid *adj* erbärmlich.

sore *adj* schmerzend; wund.

sorrow *n* Kummer *m*, Leid *n*.

sorry *adj* traurig, erbärm- lich:—~! Entschuldigung!

sort *n* Art *f*; Sorte *f*:—*vt* sortieren; sichten, in Ordnung bringen.

soul *n* Seele *f*; (*mus*) Soul *m*.

sound *adj* gesund; sicher:— *n* Geräusch *n*, Laut *m*:—*vt* erschallen lassen; abhorchen:—*vi* schallen, tönen; klingen.

soup *n* Suppe *f*.

sour *adj* sauer.

source *n* Quelle *f*.

south *n* Süden *m*.

South Africa *n* Südafrika *n*.

South African *adj* südafrikanisch:—*n* Südafrikaner(in) *m(f)*.

South America *n* Südamerika *n*.

South American *adj* südamerikanisch:—*n* Südamerikaner(in) *m(f)*.

southeast *n* Südosten *m*.

southern *adj* südlich, Süd-.

South Pole *n* Südpol *m*.

southwest *n* Südwesten *m*.

souvenir *n* Souvenir *n*.

sow *n* Sau *f*:—*vt* säen.

soya bean *n* Sojabohne *f*.

space *n* Raum *m*; Platz *m*.

spacecraft *n* Raumfahrzeug *n*.

spacious *adj* geräumig.

spade *n* Spaten *m*; Pik *n*:— **king of ~s** Pik-König *m*.

Spain *n* Spanien *n*.

span *n* Spanne *f*:—*vt* umspannen, überspannen.

Spaniard *n* Spanier(in) *m(f)*.

Spanish *adj* spanisch:—*n* Spanisch *n*.

spare *adj* Ersatz-:—*vt* ver- schonen; ersparen.

spark *n* Funken *m*.

sparkle *n* Funkeln *n*:—*vi* funkeln.

spark plug *n* Zündkerze *f*.

sparrow *n* Spatz *m*.

sparse *adj* spärlich.

speak *vt vi* sprechen.
speaker *n* Sprecher(in) *m(f)*.
spear *n* Speer *m:—vt* aufspießen.
special *adj* besondere(r, s).
speciality *n* Spezialität *f*.
specific *adj* spezifisch.
specimen *n* Probe *f*.
speck *n* Fleckchen *n*.
spectacle *n* Schauspiel *n*.
spectator *n* Zuschauer(in) *m(f)*.
spectre *n* Geist *m*, Gespenst *n*.
speculate *vi* spekulieren.
speculation *n* Nachdenken *n*; Grübeln *n*; Spekulation *f*.
speech *n* Rede *f*, Sprache *f*; Reden *n*, Sprechen *n*.
speed *n* Geschwindigkeit *f*, Eile *f:—vi* eilen, schnell fahren.
speedy *adj* schnell, rasch.
spell *n* Weile *f*; Zauber *m:—vt* buchstabieren.
spend *vt* verwenden; ausgeben; verbringen; verbrauchen.
sperm *n* Sperma *n*.
sphere *n* Kugel *f*, Sphäre *f*; Bereich *m*.
spherical *adj* kugelförmig, sphärisch.
spice *n* Gewürz *n:—vt* würzen.
spider *n* Spinne *f*.
spill *vt* verschütten:—*vi* sich ergießen.
spin *vt* spinnen; herumwirbeln.
spinach *n* Spinat *m*.
spine *n* Rückgrat *n*.
spinster *n* unverheiratete Frau *f*.
spiral *n* Spirale *f*.
spire *n* Turm *m*.

spirit *n* Geist *m*; Stimmung *f*; Alkohol *m:—~s npl* Spirituosen *pl*.
spirited *adj* beherzt.
spit *n* Bratspieß *m*; Spucke *f:—vi* spucken.
spite *n* Gehässigkeit *f:—in ~ of* trotz.
splash *n* Spritzer *m:—vt* bespritzen: —*vi* spritzen.
splendid *adj* glänzend.
splendour *n* Pracht *f*.
split *n* Spalte *f*; Trennung *f:—vt* spalten:—*vi* reißen.
spoil *vt* verderben; verwöhnen.
spokesman *n* Sprecher *m*.
spokeswoman *n* Sprecherin *f*.
sponge *n* Schwamm *m:—vt* abwaschen.
sponsor *n* Sponsor *m:—vt* fördern.
spontaneous *adj* spontan.
spoon *n* Löffel *m*.
sport *n* Sport *m*.
sportsman *n* Sportler *m*.
sportswear *n* Sportkleidung *f*.
sportswoman *n* Sportlerin *f*.
spot *n* Punkt *m*; Fleck *m*; Stelle *f:—vt* erspähen.
spotless *adj* fleckenlos.
spotlight *n* Scheinwerferlicht *n*.
spotted *adj* gefleckt.
spouse *n* Gatte *m*, Gattin *f*.
spray *n* Gischt *f*, Spray *m/n*; Sprühdose *f:—vi* sprühen:—*vt* zerstäuben, spritzen.
spread *n* Verbreitung *f:—vt* ausbreiten; verbreiten:—*vi* sich ausbreiten.
spring *n* Sprung *m*; Feder *f*; Frühling *m:—vi* springen.

sprinkle *vt* streuen; sprenkeln.
sprout *vi* sprießen:—*~s npl* Rosenkohl *m*.
spur *n* Sporn *m*; Ansporn *m:—vt* anspornen.
spy *n* Spion(in) *m(f):—vi* spionieren.
squander *vt* verschwenden.
square *n* Quadrat *n*; Platz *m:—adj* viereckig.
squash *n* Squash *n:—vt* zerquetschen.
squawk *vi* kreischen.
squeak *vi* quieksen; quietschen.
squeeze *vt* pressen, drücken.
squid *n* Tintenfisch *m*.
squint *vi* schielen.
squirrel *n* Eichhörnchen *n*.
stab *n* Stich *m:—vt* erstechen.
stabilize *vt* stabilisieren:—*vi* sich stabilisieren.
stable *n* Stall *m:—adj* stabil.
stack *n* Stapel *m:—vt* stapeln.
stadium *n* Stadion *n*.
staff *n* Stab *m*; Personal *n*.
stag *n* Hirsch *m*.
stage *n* Bühne *f*; Etappe *f*; Stufe *m:—vt* aufführen.
stagger *vi* wanken, taumeln.
stagnant *adj* stagnierend.
stain *n* Fleck *m:—vt* beflecken.
stair *n* Stufe *f*.
staircase *n* Treppenhaus *n*, Treppe *f*.
stale *adj* alt; altbacken.
stalk *n* Stengel *m*, Stiel *m*.
stammer *n* Stottern *n:—vt vi* stottern.

stamp *n* Briefmarke *f*;
Stempel *m*:—*vi*
stampfen:—*vt* stempeln.

stand *vi* stehen.

standard *n* Norm *f*; Fahne
f:—*adj* Normal-.

staple *n* Heftklamme *f*:—
adj Haupt-, Grund-:—*vt*
klammern.

stapler *n* Heftmaschine *f*.

star *n* Stern *m*; Star *m*.

stare *vi*:—~ **at** starren auf,
anstarren: —*n* starrer
Blick *m*.

starling *n* Star *m*.

start *n* Anfang *m*; Start *m*:—
vt in Gang setzen;
anlassen:—*vi* anfangen;
aufbrechen; starten.

startle *vt* erschrecken.

startling *adj* erschreckend.

state *n* Zustand *m*; Staat
m:—*vt* erklären.

statement *n* Aussage *f*.

static *n*
Reibungselektrizität *f*.

station *n* Bahnhof *m*.

stationary *adj* stillstehend.

stationery *n* Schreib-
waren *pl*.

statistics *n* Statistik *f*.

statue *n* Statue *f*.

stay *n* Aufenthalt *m*:—*vi*
bleiben; wohnen.

steady *adj* fest, stabil.

steak *n* Steak *n*; Filet *n*.

steal *vt vi* stehlen.

steam *n* Dampf *m*:—*vi*
dämpfen.

steamer *n* Dämpfer *m*.

steel *n* Stahl *m*:—*adj* Stahl-.

steep *adj* steil.

steeple *n* Kirchturm *m*.

steer *vt vi* steuern;
lenken.

steering *n* Steuerung *f*.

steering wheel *n* Lenkrad,
Steuerrad *n*.

step *n* Schritt *m*; Stufe *f*:—*vi*
treten, schreiten.

stepbrother *n* Stiefbruder *m*.

stepdaughter *n* Stieftochter
f.

stepfather *n* Stiefvater *m*.

stepmother *n* Stiefmutter *f*.

stepsister *n* Stiefschwester *f*.

stepson *n* Stiefsohn *m*.

stereo *n* Stereoanlage *f*.

sterile *adj* steril; unfruchtbar.

stern *adj* streng:—*n* Heck *n*.

stew *n* Eintopf *m*.

steward(ess) *n* Steward(eß)
m(f).

stick *n* Stock *m*; Stück *n*:—
vt stechen, stecken;
kleben.

sticky *adj* klebrig.

stiff *adj* steif; dick; stark.

stiffen *vt vi* versteifen.

still *adj* still:—*adv* (immer)
noch; immerhin.

stimulate *vt* anregen, stim-
ulieren.

stimulus *n* Anregung *f*.

sting *n* Stich *m*:—*vt vi*
stechen.

stingy *adj* geizig.

stink *n* Gestank *m*:—*vi*
stinken.

stir *n* Bewegung *f*; Ruhren
n:—*vt* rühren:—*vi* sich
rühren.

stitch *n* Stich *m*; (*med*)
Faden *m*:—*vt* nähen.

stock *n* Vorrat *m*; Lager *n*;
Vieh *n*; Grundkapital *n*:—
vt führen.

stockbroker *n*
Börsenmakler *m*.

stock exchange *n* Börse *f*.

stocking *n* Strumpf *m*.

stomach *n* Bauch *m*;
Magen *m*.

stone *n* Stein *m*.

stony *adj* steinig.

stool *n* Hocker *m*.

stop *n* Halt *m*; Haltestelle *f*;
Punkt *m*: —*vt* anhalten:—
vi aufhören; stehen-
bleiben; bleiben.

store *n* Vorrat *m*; Lager *n*;
Warenhaus *n*, Kaufhaus
n:—*vt* lagern.

stork *n* Storch *m*.

storm *n* Sturm *m*:—*vt vi*
stürmen.

stormy *adj* stürmisch.

story *n* Geschichte *f*;
Märchen *n*.

stout *adj* tapfer; beleibt:—*n*
Starkbier *n*.

stove *n* Herd *m*; Ofen *m*.

straight *adj* gerade; offen;
pur:—*adv* direkt, ger-
adewegs.

straightaway *adv* sofort.

straighten *vt* gerade
machen.

strain *n* Belastung *f*:—*vt*
überanstrengen; anspan-
nen:—*vi* sich anstrengen.

strange *adj* fremd; seltsam.

stranger *n* Fremde(r) *f(m)*.

strangle *vt* erwürgen.

strap *n* Riemen *m*; Träger
m:—*vt* festschnallen.

strategic *adj* strategisch.

strategy *n* Strategie *f*.

straw *n* Stroh *n*;
Strohhalm *m*.

strawberry *n* Erdbeere *f*.

stray *vi* herumstreunen:—
adj verirrt; zufällig.

stream *n* Bach *m*; Strom
m:—*vi* strömen.

street *n* Straße *f*.

strength *n* Stärke *f*; Kraft *f*.

strengthen *vt* verstärken.

stress *n* Druck *m*; Streß *m*; (*gr*) Betonung *f*:—*vt* betonen.

stretch *n* Strecke *f*:—*vt* ausdehnen, strecken:—*vi* sich strecken.

stretcher *n* Tragbahre *f*.

strict *adj* streng; genau.

stride *n* langer Schritt *m*:—*vi* schreiten.

strike *n* Streik *m*; Schlag *m*:—*vt* schlagen:—*vi* streiken.

striker *n* Streikende(r) *f(m)*.

string *n* Schnur *f*; Saite *f*.

strip *n* Streifen *m*:—*vt* abstreifen, abziehen; ausziehen:—*vi* sich ausziehen.

stripe *n* Streifen *m*.

stroke *n* Schlag *m*; Stoß *m*; (*med*) Schlaganfall *m*; Streicheln *n*:—*vt* streicheln.

stroll *n* Spaziergang *m*:—*vi* schlendern.

strong *adj* stark; fest.

structure *n* Struktur *f*; Aufbau *m*.

struggle *n* Kampf *m*:—*vi* kämpfen.

stubborn *adj* hartnäckig.

student *n* Student(in) *m(f)*:—*adj* Studenten-.

studio *n* Studio *n*; Atelier *n*.

study *n* Studium *n*; Studie *f*:—*vt vi* studieren.

stuff *n* Zeug *n*:—*vt* stopfen; füllen; ausstopfen.

stumble *vi* stolpern.

stun *vt* betäuben.

stunt *n* Kunststück *n*, Trick *m*.

stupid *adj* dumm.

stupidity *n* Dummheit *f*.

sturdy *adj* robust, kräftig.

stutter *vi* stottern.

sty *n* Schweinestall *m*.

style *n* Stil *m*; Mode *f*.

subject *n* Untertan *m*; Thema *n*; Fach *n*; (*gr*) Subjekt *n*:—**be ~ to** unterworfen sein + *dat*.

subjective *adj* subjektiv.

submarine *n* Unterseeboot *n*, U-Boot *n*.

submit *vt* behaupten; unterbreiten:—*vi* sich ergeben.

subscriber *n* Abonnent *m*.

subscription *n* Abonnement *n*.

subsequent *adj* später, folgend.

subsidiary *adj* Neben-:—*n* Tochtergesellschaft *f*.

subsidy *n* Subvention *f*.

substance *n* Substanz *f*.

substantial *adj* wesentlich; fest, kräftig.

substitute *n* Ersatz *m*:—*vt* ersetzen.

substitution *n* Ersetzung *f*.

subtle *adj* fein.

subtract *vt* abziehen.

suburb *n* Vorort *m*.

succeed *vi* erfolgreich sein, Erfolg haben; gelingen:—*vt* (nach)folgen + *dat*.

success *n* Erfolg *m*.

successful *adj* erfolgreich.

such *adj* solche(r, s).

suck *vt* saugen.

suction *n* Saugkraft *f*.

sudden(ly) *adj* (*adv*) plötzlich.

sue *vt* verklagen

suffer *vt vi* leiden.

suffering *n* Leiden *n*.

suffice *vi* genügen.

sufficient *adj* ausreichend.

sugar *n* Zucker *m*.

suggest *vt* vorschlagen.

suggestion *n* Vorschlag *m*.

suicide *n* Selbstmord *m*:—**commit ~** Selbstmord begehen.

suit *n* Anzug *m*; Farbe *f*:—*vt* passen + *dat*.

suitable *adj* passend, geeignet.

suitcase *n* Koffer *m*.

suite *n* Zimmerflucht *f*; Einrichtung *f*; (*mus*) Suite *f*.

sulk *vi* schmollen.

sulphur *n* Schwefel *m*.

sum *n* Summe *f*; Betrag *m*; Rechenaufgabe *f*:—**~ up** *vt vi* zusammenfassen.

summary *n* Zusammenfassung *f*.

summer *n* Sommer *m*.

summit *n* Gipfel *m*.

sun *n* Sonne *m*.

sunbathe *vi* sich sonnen.

sunburn *n* Sonnenbrand *m*.

Sunday *n* Sonntag *m*.

sunflower *n* Sonnenblume *f*.

sunglasses *npl* Sonnenbrille *f*.

sunlight *n* Sonnenlicht *n*.

sunny *adj* sonnig.

sunrise *n* Sonnenaufgang *m*.

sunset *n* Sonnenuntergang *m*.

sunshade *n* Sonnenschirm *m*.

sunshine *n* Sonnenschein *m*.

sunstroke *n* Hitzschlag *m*.

super *adj* prima, klasse.

superior *adj* überlegen:—*n* Vorge-setzte(r) *f(m)*.

superiority *n* Überlegenheit *f*.

supermarket *n* Supermarkt *m*.

supernatural *n* übernatürlich.

superpower *n* Weltmacht *f.*

supersonic *adj* Überschall-.

superstition *n* Aberglaube *m.*

superstitious *adj* abergläubisch.

supervise *vt* beaufsichtigen.

supervision *n* Aufsicht *f.*

supplement *n* Ergänzung *f.*

supplementary *adj*
ergänzend.

supplier *n* Lieferant *m.*

supply *vt* liefern:—*n* Vorrat
m; Lieferung *f.*

support *n* Unterstützung
f:—*vt* stützen; unter-
stützen.

supporter *n* Aufhänger(in)
m(f).

suppose *vt vi* annehmen.

suppress *vt* unterdrücken.

suppression *n*
Unterdrückung *f.*

sure *adj* sicher, gewiß.

surface *n* Oberfläche *f.*

surgeon *n* Chirurg(in) *m(f).*

surgery *n* Chirurgie *f.*

surgical *adj* chirurgisch.

surname *n* Zuname *m.*

surpass *vt* übertreffen.

surplus *n* Überschuß *m*:—
adj überschüssig.

surprise *n* Überraschung
f:—*vt* überreaschen.

surprising *adj* über-
raschend.

surrender *n* Kapitulation
f:—*vi* sich ergeben.

surround *vt* umgeben.

survey *n* Übersicht *f*:—*vt*
überblicken; vermessen.

survival *n* Überleben *n.*

survive *vt vi* überleben.

survivor *n* Überlebende(r)
f(m).

suspect *n* Verdächtige(r)
f(m):—*adj* verdachtig:—*vt*
verdächtigen.

suspend *vt* verschieben;
aufhängen; suspendieren.

suspense *n* Spannung *f.*

suspension *n* Federung *f*;
Suspendierung *f.*

suspicion *n* Verdacht *m.*

suspicious *adj* verdachtig.

sustain *vt* aufrechterhalten;
bestätigen.

swallow *n* Schwalbe *f*;
Schluck *m*:—*vt* schlucken.

swan *n* Schwan *m.*

swastika *n* Hakenkreuz *n.*

sway *vi* schwanken;
schaukeln, sich wiegen:—
vt schwenken.

swear *vi* schwören; fluchen.

sweat *n* Schweiß *m*:—*vi*
schwitzen.

sweater *n* Pullover *m.*

Swede *n* Schwede *m*,
Schwedin *f.*

Sweden *n* Schweden *n.*

Swedish *adj* schwedisch:—
n Schwedisch *n.*

sweep *n* Schornsteinfeger
m:—*vt* fegen, kehren:—*vi*
rauschen.

sweet *n* Nachtisch *m*;
Bonbon *n*:—*adj* süß.

sweeten *vt* süßen.

sweetness *n* Süße *f.*

swell *n* Seegang *n*:—*vt* vermehren:—*vi* schwellen.

swift *n* Mauersegler *m*:—
adj geschwind, schnell,
rasch.

swim *vt vi* schwimmen.

swimming *n* Schwimmen *n.*

swimming pool *n*
Schwimmenbecken *n.*

swimsuit *n* Badeanzug *m.*

swine *n* Schwein *n.*

swing *n* Schaukel *f*;
Schwung *n*:—*vt vi*
schwingen.

Swiss *adj* Schweizer,
schweizerisch:—*n*
Schweizer(in) *m(f).*

switch *n* Schalter *m*;
Wechsel *m*:—*vt* schalten;
wechseln:—~ **off** *vt* auss-
chalten:—~ **on** *vt* einschal-
ten.

Switzerland *n* Schweiz *f.*

sword *n* Schwert *n.*

sycamore *n* Bergahorn *m.*

syllable *n* Silbe *f.*

syllabus *n* Lehrplan *m.*

symbol *n* Symbol *n.*

symbolic *adj* symbolisch.

symmetry *n* Symmetrie *f.*

sympathetic *adj* mitfüh-
lend.

sympathize *vi* mitfühlen.

sympathy *n* Mitleid *n*,
Mitgefühl *n*; Beileid *n.*

symphony *n* Sinfonie *f.*

symptom *n* Sympton *n.*

synagogue *n* Synagoge *f.*

synonym *n* Synonym *n.*

system *n* System *n.*

T

table *n* Tisch *m*.

tablecloth *n* Tischtuch *n*.

tablet *n* Tablette *f*; Täfelchen *n*.

table tennis *n* Tischtennis *n*.

tact *n* Takt *m*.

tactful *adj* taktvoll.

tactical *adj* taktisch.

tactless *adj* taktlos.

tactics *npl* Taktik *f*.

tag *n* Schild *n*, Anhänger *m*.

tail *n* Schwanz *m*:—*vt* folgen +*dat*.

tailor *n* Schneider *m*.

take *vt* nehmen.

takeover *n* Übernahme *f*.

tale *n* Geschichte *f*, Erzählung *f*.

talent *n* Talent *n*.

talk *n* Gespräch *n*; Gerede *n*; Vortrag *m*:—*vi* sprechen, reden.

tall *adj* groß; hoch.

tame *adj* zahm.

tan *n* Sonnenbräune *f*:—*vt* bräunen:—*vi* braun werden.

tangible *adj* greifbar.

tank *n* Tank *m*; Panzer *m*.

tap *n* Hahn *m*; Klopfen *n*:—*vt* klopfen.

tape *n* Band *n*:—*vt* aufnehmen.

tapestry *n* Wandteppich *m*.

tar *n* Teer *m*.

target *n* Ziel *n*.

tariff *n* Tarif *m*.

tart *n* Torte *f*.

task *n* Aufgabe *f*.

taste *n* Geschmack *m*; Geschmackssinn *m*; Vorliebe *f*:—*vt vi* schmecken.

taunt *vt* verhöhnen.

Taurus *n* (*astrol*) Stier *m*.

taut *adj* straff.

tax *n* Steuer *f*:—*vt* besteuern.

taxation *n* Besteuerung *f*.

tax-free *adj* steuerfrei.

taxi *n* Taxi *n*:—*vi* rollen.

taxpayer *n* Steuerzahler *m*.

tea *n* Tee *m*.

teach *vt vi* lehren, unterrichten.

teacher *n* Lehrer(in) *m(f)*.

teacup *n* Teetasse *f*.

team *n* Team *n*; Mannschaft *f*.

teapot *n* Teekanne *f*.

tear *n* Träne *f*; Riß *m*:—*vt vi* zerreißen.

tease *vt* necken.

teaspoon *n* Teelöffel *m*.

technical *adj* technisch; Fach-.

technician *n* Techniker *m*.

technique *n* Technik *f*.

technological *adj* technologisch.

technology *n* Technologie *f*.

teddy (bear) *n* Teddybär *m*.

teenage *adj* Teenager-, jugendlich.

teenager *n* Teenager *m*, Jugendliche(r) *f(m)*.

teething troubles *npl* Kinderkrankheiten *fpl*.

telecommunications *npl* Fernmelde-wesen *n*.

telephone *n* Telefon *n*.

telephone call *n* Telefongespräch *n*.

telephone directory *n* Telefonbuch *n*.

telephone number *n* Telefonnummer *m*.

telescope *n* Teleskop *n*.

television *n* Fernsehen *n*.

television set *n* Fernseher *m*.

tell *vt* erzählen; sagen; erkennen; wissen.

temper *n* Temperament *n*:—*vt* mildern.

temperament *n* Temperament *n*.

temperature *n* Temperatur *f*.

temple *n* Tempel *m*; Schläfe *f*.

temporary *adj* vorläufig; provisorisch.

tempt *vt* verleiten; locken.

temptation *n* Versuchung *f*.

tempting *adj* verlockend.

ten *num* zehn.

tenant *n* Mieter *m*; Pächter *m*.

tend *vt* sich kümmern um.

tendency *n* Tendenz *f*.

tender *adj* zart; zärtlich:—*n* Kostenanschlag *m*:—*vt* (an)bieten.

tenderness *n* Zartheit *f*; Zärtlichkeit *f*.

tennis *n* Tennis *n*.

tennis court *n* Tennisplatz *m*.

tennis player *n* Tennisspieler(in) *m(f)*.

tenor *n* Tenor *m*.

tense *adj* angespannt:—*n* Zeitform *f*.

tension *n* Spannung *f*.

tent *n* Zelt *n*.

tenth *adj* zehnte(r, s).

term *n* Zeitraum *m*; Frist *f*; Bedingung *f*; Ausdruck *m*.

terminal *adj* Schluß-; unheilbar:—*n* Endstation *f*; Terminal *m*.

terminate *vt* beenden:—*vi* enden, aufhören.

terminus *n* Endstation *f*.

terrible *adj* schrecklich.

terrific *adj* fantastisch.

terrify *vt* erschrecken.

territory *n* Gebiet *n*.

terror *n* Schrecken *m*; Terror *m*.

terrorize *vt* terrorisieren.

terrorism *n* Terrorismus *m*.

terrorist *n* Terrorist(in) *m(f)*.

test *n* Probe *f*; Prüfung *f*:—*vt* prüfen.

testicle *n* Hoden *m*.

testify *vi* aussagen.

testimony *n* Zeugenaussage *f*.

text *n* Text *m*.

texture *n* Beschaffenheit *f*.

than *prep* als.

thank *vt* danken +*dat*.

thankful *adj* dankbar.

thankless *adj* undankbar.

thanks *npl* danke.

that *pn* das; jene(r, s):—*rel pn* der, die, das:—*conj* daß:—**so ~** so daß.

the *art* der, die, das.

theatre *n* Theater *n*.

theft *n* Diebstahl *m*.

their *poss adj* ihr(e):—**~s** *poss pn* ihre(r, s).

them *pn acc* sie, *dat* ihnen.

theme *n* Thema *n*.

themselves *pn* sich; selbst.

then *adv* dann; danach:— **now and ~** dann und wann.

theology *n* Theologie *f*.

theoretical *adj* theoretisch.

theory *n* Theorie *f*.

there *adv* da, dort; dahin, dorthin.

therefore *adv* also.

thermometer *n* Thermometer *n*.

these *pn adj* diese.

they *pn* sie; man.

thick *adj* dick; dumm.

thickness *n* Dicke *f*; Dichte *f*.

thief *n* Dieb(in) *m(f)*.

thigh *n* Oberschenkel *m*.

thimble *n* Fingerhut *m*.

thin *adj* dünn, mager.

thing *n* Ding *n*; Sache *f*.

think *vt vi* denken.

third *adj* dritte(r, s).

thirst *n* Durst *f*.

thirsty *adj* durstig:—**be ~** Durst haben.

thirteen *num* dreizehn.

thirty *num* dreißig.

this *adj* diese(r, s):—*pn* dies, das.

thistle *n* Distel *f*.

thorn *n* Dorn *m*.

thorough *adj* gründlich.

those *pl pxn* die (da), jene:—*adj* die, jene.

though *conj* obwohl:—*adv* trotzdem.

thought *n* Gedanke *m*; Denken *n*.

thoughtful *adj* gedankenvoll, nachdenklich.

thousand *num* tausend.

thread *n* Faden *m*, Garn *n*.

threat *n* Dröhung *f*.

threaten *vt* bedrohen:—*vi* drohen.

three *num* drei.

threshold *n* Schwelle *f*.

thrive *vi* gedeihen.

throat *n* Hals *m*, Kehle *f*.

through *prep* durch.

throughout *prep* überall in +*dat*; während:—*adv* überall.

throw *vt* werfen.

thrush *n* Drossel *f*.

thumb *n* Daumen *m*.

thunder *n* Donner *m*.

thunderstorm *n* Gewitter *n*.

Thursday *n* Donnertag *m*.

thus *adv* so; somit, also.

thyme *n* Thymian *m*.

tick *vi* ticken.

ticket *n* Fahrkarte *f*; Eintrittskarte *f*.

ticket office *n* Kasse *f*.

tickle *vt* kitzeln.

ticklish *adj* kitzlig.

tide *n* Gezeiten *pl*.

tidy *adj* ordentlich.

tie *n* Kravatte *f*, Schlips *m*; Unentschieden *n*:—*vt* binden:—*vi* unentschieden spielen.

tier *n* Rang *m*.

tiger *n* Tiger *m*.

tight *adj* eng, knapp; gedrängt; fest: —*adv* fest.

tighten *vt* anziehen, anspannen:—*vi* sich spannen.

tights *npl* Strümpfhose *f*.

tigress *n* Tigerin *f*.

tile *n* Dachziegel *m*; Fliese *f*.

till *n* Kasse *f*:—*vt* bestellen:—*prep conj* bis.

tilt *vt* kippen, neigen:—*vi* sich neigen.

timber *n* Holz *n*; Baumbestand *m*.

time *n* Zeit *f*; Mal *n*; (*mus*) Takt *m*.

timid *adj* ängstlich, schüchtern.

tin *n* Blech *n*; Dose *f*.

tiny *adj* winzig.

tip *n* Spitze *f*; Trinkgeld *n*; Wink *m*, Tip *m*:—*vt* kippen; antippen; ein Trinkgeld geben.

tire *vt vi* ermüden, müde machen/werden.

tireless *adj* unermüdlich.

tiring *adj* ermüdend.

tissue *n* Gewebe *n*; Papiertaschentuch *n*.

title *n* Titel *m*.

to *prep* zu, nach; bis; vor; für.

toad *n* Kröte *m*.

toadstool *n* Giftpilz *n*.

toast *n* Toast *m*; Trinkspruch *m*:—*vt* trinken auf +*acc*; toasten.

toaster *n* Toaster *m*.

tobacco *n* Tabak *m*.

tobacconist *n* Tabakhändler *m*.

tobacconist's *n* Tabakladen *m*.

toboggan *n* Schlitten *m*.

today *adv* heute; heutzutage.

toe *n* Zehe *f*; Spitze *f*.

together *adv* zusammen; gleichzeitig.

toil *n* harte Arbeit *f*; Plackerei *f*:—vi sich abmühen, sich plagen.

toilet *n* Toilette *f*:—*adj* Toiletten-.

toilet paper *n*

Toilettenpapier *n*.

token *n* Zeichen *n*; Gutschein *m*.

Tokyo *n* Tokio *n*.

tolerable *adj* erträglich; leidlich.

tolerance *n* Toleranz *f*.

tolerant *adj* tolerant.

tolerate *vt* dulden; ertragen.

toll *n* Gebühr *f*:—*vi* läuten.

tomato *n* Tomate *f*.

tomb *n* Grab(mal) *n*.

tombstone *n* Grabstein *m*.

tomcat *n* Kater *m*.

tomorrow *adv* morgen.

ton *n* Tonne *f*.

tone *n* Ton *m*:—~ **down** *vt* mäßigen.

tongue *n* Zunge *f*.

tonight *adv* heute abend.

tonsil *n* Mandel *f*.

too *adv* auch.

tool *n* Werkzeug *n*.

tooth *n* Zahn *m*.

toothache *n* Zahnschmerzen *mpl*.

toothbrush *n* Zahnbürste *f*.

toothpaste *n* Zahnpasta *f*.

top *n* Spitze *f*; Gipfel *m*; Wipfel *m*; Kreisel *m*:—*adj* oberste(r, s).

topic *n* Thema *n*.

topical *adj* aktuell.

torch *n* Taschenlampe *f*.

torment *n* Qual *f*:—*vt* quälen.

tortoise *n* Schildkröte *f*.

torture *n* Folter *f*:—*vt* foltern.

toss *vt* schleudern.

total *n* Gesamtheit *f*:—*adj* Gesamt-, total.

totalitarian *adj* totalitär.

touch *n* Berührung *f*; Tastsinn *m*:—*vt* berühren; leicht anstoßen; rühren.

tough *adj* zäh; schwierig.

tour *n* Tour *f*.

tourism *n* Tourismus *m*.

tourist *n* Tourist(in) *m(f)*.

tourist office *n* Verkehrsamt *n*.

tournament *n* Tournier *n*.

tow *vt* schleppen.

towards *prep* gegen; nach.

towel *n* Handtuch *n*.

tower *n* Turm *m*.

town *n* Stadt *f*.

town hall *n* Rathaus *n*.

toy *n* Spielzeug *n*.

trace *n* Spur *f*:—*vt* nachziehen, durchpausen, aufspüren.

track *n* Spur *f*, Weg *m*; Gleis *n*:—*vt* verfolgen.

tractor *n* Traktor *m*.

trade *n* Handel *m*, Gewerbe *f*:—*vi* handeln.

trade fair *n* Messe *f*.

trade mark *n* Warenzeichen *n*.

trader *n* Händler *m*.

tradesman *n* Händler *m*.

trade union *n* Gewerkschaft *f*.

tradition *n* Tradition *f*, Brauch *m*.

traditional *adj* traditionell.

traffic *n* Handel *m*, Verkehr *m*.

traffic lights *npl* Ampel *f*.

tragedy *n* Tragödie *f*.

tragic *adj* tragisch.

trail Spur *f*; Pfad *m*, Weg *m*:—*vt* verfolgen; folgen +*dat*:—*vi* schleifen.

train *n* Zug *m*; Schleppe *f*; Folge *f*:—*vt* ausbilden; abrichten:—*vi* trainieren.

trainee *n* Lehrling *m*.

trainer *n* Trainer *m*; Ausbilder *m*.

traitor *n* Verräter *m*.

tramp *n* Landstreicher *m*:— *vi* stampfen.

tranquil *adj* ruhig, friedlich.

tranquillizer *n* Beruhigungsmittel *n*.

transfer *n* Übertragung *f*; Umzug *m*; Transfer *m*:—*vt* verlegen; versetzen; über- tragen; überweisen.

transit *n* Durchgang *m*.

translate *vt* übersetzen.

translation *n* Übersetzung *f*.

translator *n* Übersetzer(in) *m(f)*.

transmission *n* Übertra- gung *f*.

transmit *vt* übertragen.

transparent *adj* durch- sichtig.

transport *n* Transport *m*:— *vt* transportieren.

trap *n* Falle *f*:—*vt* in einer Falle locken.

travel *n* Reisen *n*:—*vi* reisen.

travel agency *n* Reisebüro *n*.

traveller *n* Reisende(r) *f(m)*.

tray *n* Tablett *n*.

treacherous *adj* verräter- isch.

treachery *n* Verrat *m*.

tread *n* Schritt *m*, Tritt *m*:— *vi* treten.

treason *n* Verrat *m*.

treasure *n* Schatz *m*:—*vt* schätzen.

treat *n* besonderer Freude *f*:—*vt* behandeln; spendieren.

treatment *n* Behandlung *f*.

treaty *n* Vertrag *m*.

treble *adj* dreifach:—*vt* ver- dreifachen.

tree *n* Baum *m*.

tremble *vi* zittern; beben.

tremendous *adj* gewaltig, kolossal; prima.

tremor *n* Zittern *n*; Beben *n*.

trench *n* Graben *m*; (*mil*) Schützengraben *m*.

trend *n* Tendenz *f*.

trendy *adj* modisch.

trial *n* Prozeß *m*; Versuch *m*, Probe *f*.

triangle *n* Dreieck *n*; (*mus*) Triangel *f*.

triangular *adj* dreieckig.

tribal *adj* Stammes-.

tribe *n* Stamm *m*.

tribute *n* Zeichen *n* der Hochachtung.

trick *n* Trick *m*; Stich *m*:—*vt* überlisten, beschwindeln.

trigger *n* Drücker *m*.

trim *adj* gepflegt; schlank.

Trinity *n* Dreieinigkeit *f*.

trip *n* (kurze) Reise *f*; Ausflug *m*; Stolpern *n*:—*vi* trippeln; stolpern.

triple *adj* dreifach.

tripod *n* Stativ *n*.

triumph *n* Triumph *m*:—*vi* triumphieren.

triumphant *adj* trium- phierend.

trolley *n* Handwagen *m*.

trombone *n* Posaune *f*.

trophy *n* Trophäe *f*.

tropical *adj* tropisch.

trot *n* Trott *m*:—*vi* trotten.

trouble *n* Ärger *m*; Sorge *f*; Mühe *f*; Unruhen *pl*:—*vt* stören.

trough *n* Trog *m*; Rinne *f*, Kanal *m*.

trousers *npl* Hose *f*.

trout *n* Forelle *f*.

truck *n* Lastwagen *m*; offener Güterwagen *m*.

true *adj* wahr; echt; treu.

truffle *n* Trüffel *f/m*.

trump *n* Trumpf *m*.

trumpet *n* Trompete *f*.

trunk *n* Stamm *m*; Rumpf *m*; Truhe *f*; Rüssel *m*.

trust *n* Vertrauen *n*; Treuhandvermögen *n*:—*vt* vertrauen.

trustworthy *adj* ver- trauenswürdig.

truth *n* Wahrheit *f*.

truthful *adj* ehrlich.

try *n* Versuch *m*:—*vt* ver- suchen; probieren.

T-shirt *n* T-Shirt *n*.

tub *n* Wanne *f*.

tube *n* Röhre *f*, Rohr *n*; Tube *f*.

Tuesday *n* Dienstag *m*.

tug *n* Schleppendampfer *m*:—*vt vi* schleppen.

tuition *n* Unterricht *m*.

tulip *n* Tulpe *f*.

tumble *n* Sturz *m*:—*vi* fall- en, stürzen.

tummy *n* Bauch *m*.

tuna *n* Thunfisch *m*.

tune *n* Melodie *f*:—*vt* (*mus*) stimmen.

tunnel *n* Tunnel *m*.

Turk *n* Türke *m*, Türkin *f*.

Turkey *n* Türkei *f*.

turkey *n* Puter *m*, Truthahn *m*.

Turkish *adj* türkisch:—*n* Türkisch *n*.

turmoil *n* Aufruhr *m*; Tumult *m*.

turn *n* Umdrehung *f*; Nummer *f*; Schock *m*:—*vi* drehen; umdrehen, wen- den; umblättern.

turnip *n* Steckrübe *f*.

turnover *n* Umsatz *m*.

turntable *n* Plattenteller *m*.

turtle *n* Schildkröte *f*.

tusk *n* Stoßzahn *m*.

tutor *n* Privatlehrer *m*; Tutor *m*.

twelfth *adj* zwölfte(r, s).

twelve *num* zwölf.

twentieth *adj* zwanzigste (r, s).

twenty *num* zwanzig.

twice *adv* zweimal.

twin *n* Zwilling *m*.

twist *n* Drehung *f*:—*vt* drehen; verdrehen:—*vi* sich drehen.

two *num* zwei.

type *n* Typ *m*; Art *f*; Type *f*:—*vt vi* machineschreiben, tippen.

typewriter *n* Schreibmaschine *f*.

typical *adj* typisch.

typist *n* Maschinenschreiber(in) *m*(*f*).

tyre *n* Reifen *m*.

U

ugly *adj* häßlich; böse, schlimm.

ulcer *n* Geschwür *n*.

ultimate *adj* äußerste(r, s), endgültig.

umbrella *n* Schirm *m*.

umpire *n* Schiedsrichter *m*.

umpteenth *num* zig:—**for the ~ time** zum X-ten Mal.

unanimous *adj* einmütig; einstimmig.

unauthorized *adj* unbefugt.

unavoidable *adj* unvermeidlich.

unbearable *adj* unerträglich.

unbelievable *adj* unglaublich.

uncanny *adj* unheimlich.

uncertain *adj* unsicher; ungewiß.

uncertainty *n* Ungewißheit *f*.

uncivilized *adj* unzivilisiert.

uncle *n* Onkel *m*.

uncomfortable *adj* unbequem, ungemütlich.

uncommon *adj* ungewöhnlich.

uncompromising *adj* kompromißlos, unnachgiebig.

unconditional *adj* bedingungslos.

unconscious *adj* bewußtlos; unbeabsichtigt.

unconventional *adj* unkonventionell.

uncover *vt* aufdecken.

under *prep* under:—*adv* darunter.

underestimate *vt* unterschätzen.

undergo *vt* durch machen; sich unterziehen + *dat*.

underground *adj* Untergrund-.

underline *vt* unterstreichen; betonen.

undermine *vt* untergraben.

underneath *adv* darunter:—*prep* unter.

undershirt *n* Unterhemd *n*.

understand *vt vi* verstehen.

understandable *adj* verständlich.

understanding *n* Verständnis *n*:—*adj* verständnisvoll.

understatement *n* Untertreibung *f*.

undertake *vt* unternehmen:—*vi* ~ **to do sth** sich verpflichten, etw zu tun.

undertaking *n* Unternehmen *n*; Verpflichtung *f*.

underwater *adj* Unterwasser-:—*adv* unter Wasser.

underwear *n* Unterwäsche *f*.

underworld *n* Unterwelt *f*.

underwriter *n* Assekurant *m*.

undo *vt* öffnen, aufmachen.

undress *vt* ausziehen:—*vi* sich ausziehen.

unemployed *adj* arbeitslos.

unemployment *n* Arbeitslosigkeit *f*.

uneven *adj* uneben; ungleichmäßig.

unexpected *adj* unerwartet.

unfair *adj* ungerecht, unfair.

unfaithful *adj* untreu.

unfashionable *adj* nicht in Mode.

unfasten *vt* öffnen, aufmachen.

unfavourable *adj* ungünstig.

unfinished *adj* unvollendet.

unfit *adj* ungeeignet; nicht fit.

unfold *vt* entfalten; auseinanderfalten:—*vi* sich entfalten.

unforgettable *adj* unvergeßlich.

unfortunate *adj* unglücklich, bedauerlich.

unfortunately *adv* leider.

unfriendly *adj* unfreundlich.

ungrateful *adj* undankbar.

unhappy *adj* unglücklich.

uniform *n* Uniform *f*:—*adj* einheitlich.

unify *vt* vereinigen.

unintentional *adj* unabsichtlich.

union *n* Vereinigung *f*; Bund *m*, Union *f*; Gewerkschaft *f*.

unique *adj* einzig(artig).

unit *n* Einheit *f*.

unite *vt* vereinigen:—*vi* sich vereinigen.

United Kingdom *n* Vereinigtes Königreich *n*.

United Nations (Organization) *n* Vereinte Nationen *fpl*.

United States (of America) *npl* Vereinigte Staaten *mpl* (von Amerika).

unity *n* Einheit *f*; Einigkeit *f*.

universal *adj* allgemein.

universe *n* Weltall *n*.

university *n* Universität *f*.

unknown *adj* unbekannt.

unless *conj* es sei denn.

unlike *adj* verschieden.

unlikely *adj* unwahrscheinlich.

unlimited *adj* unbegrenzt, unbeschränkt.

unload *vt* entladen.

unlock *vt* aufschließen.

unlucky *adj* unglücklich, unglückbrin-gend.

unmarried *adj* unverheiratet.

unnatural *adj* unnatürlich.

unnecessary *adj* unnötig.

unpack *vt* auspacken.

unpleasant *adj* unangenehm.

unpredictable *adj*

unvorhersehbar; unberechenbar.

unreal *adj* unwirklich.

unrealistic *adj* unrealistisch.

unreasonable *adj* unvernünftig; übertrieben.

unrelated *adj* ohne Beziehung; nicht verwandt.

unreliable *adj* unzuverlässig.

unrest *n* Unruhe *f*; Unruhen *fpl*.

unsafe *adj* nicht sicher.

unsavoury *adj* widerwärtig.

unscrew *vt* aufschrauben.

unskilled *adj* ungelernt.

unstable *adj* instabil.

unsteady *adj* unsicher; unregelmäßig.

unsuccessful *adj* erfolglos.

unsuitable *adj* unpassend.

unsure *adj* unsicher.

untidy *adj* unordentlich.

untie *vt* aufschnüren.

until *prep conj* bis:—~ **now** bis jetzt.

unusual *adj* ungewöhnlich.

unwind *vt* abwickeln:—*vi* sich entspannen.

unwise *adj* unklug.

up *adv* oben.

update *vt* auf den neuesten Stand bringen.

upheaval *n* Umbruch *m*.

uphill *adj* ansteigend; mühsam:—*adv* bergauf.

uphold *vt* unterstützen.

upholstery *n* Polster *n*; Polsterung *f*.

upkeep *n* Instandhaltung *f*.

upon *prep* auf.

upper-class *adj* vornehm.

upright *adj* aufrecht.

uprising *n* Aufstand *m*.

uproar *n* Aufruhr *m*.

uproot *vt* ausreißen.

upstairs *adv* (nach) oben.

upwards *adv* aufwärts.

urban *adj* städtisch, Stadt-.

urge *n* Drang *m*:—*vt* ~ **somebody to do something** jdn (dazu) drängen, etw zu tun.

urgency *n* Dringlichkeit *f*.

urgent *adj* dringend.

us *pn* uns.

usage *n* Gebrauch *m*.

use *n* Gebrauch *m*; Zweck *m*:—*vt* gebrauchen.

used *adj* Gebrauch-.

useful *adj* nützlich.

useless *adj* nützlos, unnütz.

user *n* Benutzer *m*.

usual *adj* gewöhnlich, üblich:—**as** ~ wie üblich.

usually *adv* gewöhnlich.

utter *vt* äußern, aussprechen.

utterance *n* Äußerung *f*.

V

vacancy *n* offene Stelle *f;*
freies Zimmer.
vacant *adj* leer, frei.
vacate *vt* aufgeben, räumen.
vaccinate *vt* impfen.
vaccination *n*
Schutzimpfung *f.*
vaccine *n* Impstoff *m.*
vacuum *n* Vakuum *n.*
vagina *n* Scheide *f.*
vague *adj* vag(e), unklar.
vain *adj* vergeblich, eitel.
valid *adj* gültig.
valley *n* Tal *n.*
valuable *adj* wertvoll.
valuation *n* Bewertung *f.*
value *n* Wert *m:—vt*
schätzen.
value-added tax
Mehrwertsteuer *f.*
valve *n* Ventil *n;* Hahn *m;*
Klappe *f.*
van *n* Lieferwagen *m.*
vanish *vi* verschwinden.
vanity *n* Eitelkeit *f.*
vapour *n* Dampf *m.*
variable *adj* veränderlich,
wechselhaft.
variation *n* Schwankung *f.*
varied *adj* verschiedenartig.
variety *n* Abwechslung *f.*
various *adj* verschieden.
varnish *n* Lack *m:—vt* lack-
ieren.
vary *vt* abändern; *vi*
schwanken.
vase *n* Vase *f.*
vast *adj* riesig.

vat *n* Bottich *f,* Faß *n.*
veal *n* Kalbfleisch *n.*
vegetable *n* Gemüse *n.*
vegetarian *adj* vege-
tarisch:—*n* Vege-tarier(in)
m(f).
vehicle *n* Fahrzeug *n.*
veil *n* Schleier *m.*
vein *n* Vene *f.*
velvet *n* Samt *m.*
vendor *n* Verkäufer *m.*
ventilation *n* Lüftung *f.*
verb *n* Verb *n.*
verbal *adj* verbal,
mündlich, wörtlich.
verdict *n* Urteil *n.*
verify *vt* überprüfen.
versatile *adj* vielseitig.
verse *n* Strophe *f;* Vers *m.*
version *n* Fassung *f.*
versus *prep* gegen.
vertical *adj* senkrecht, vertikal.
vertigo *n* Schwindel *m.*
very *adv* sehr.
vest *n* Unterhemd *n.*
vet *n* Tierarzt *m.*
veterinary *adj* tierärztlich.
veto *n* Veto *n:—vt* verbieten; durch ein Veto
zurückweisen.
via *prep* über.
viable *adj* lebensfähig;
durchführbar.
vibrate *vi* vibrieren,
schwingen, beben.
vibration *n* Vibration *f,*
Schwingung *f.*
vicar *n* Pfarrer *m.*

vicarage Pfarrhaus *n.*
vice *n* Laster *n;*
Schraubstock *m.*
vice versa *adv* umgekehrt.
vicinity *n* Nähe *f.*
vicious *adj* bösartig,
gemein.
victim *n* Opfer *n.*
victor *n* Sieger *m.*
victorious *adj* siegreich.
victory *n* Sieg *m.*
video recorder *n*
Videorecorder *m.*
vie *vi* wetteifern.
Vienna *n* Wien *n.*
view *n* Besichtigung *f;*
Aussicht *f;* Ansicht *m:—vt*
ansehen; betrachten.
vigil *n* Wache *f.*
vigilance *n* Wachsamkeit *f.*
vigilant *adj* wachsam.
vigorous *adj* energisch.
vigour *n* Energie *f,* Vitalität
f.
villa *n* Villa *f.*
village *n* Dorf *n.*
vine *n* Weinstock *m.*
vinegar *n* Essig *m.*
vineyard *n* Weinberg *m;*
Weingarten *m.*
vintage *n* Weinlese *f.*
viola *n* Bratsche *f.*
violate *vt* verletzen;
übertreten.
violation *n* Verletzung *f;*
Übertretung *f.*
violence *n* Gewalt *f.*
violent *adj* gewaltsam.
violet *n* (*bot*) Veilchen *n.*

violin *n* Violine *f*, Geige *f*.

violinist *n* Geiger *m*, Geigerin *f*.

violoncello *n* Cello *n*.

virgin *n* Jungfrau *f*:—*adj* jungfräulich.

virginity *n* Jungfräulichkeit *f*.

Virgo *n* (*astrol*) Jungfrau *f*.

virtual *adj* eigentlich, praktisch.

virtue *n* Tugend *f*.

virtuous *adj* tugendhaft.

virus *n* Virus *m*.

visa *n* Visum *n*.

viscous *adj* zähflüssig.

visibility *n* Sichtbarkeit *f*.

visible *adj* sichtbar.

vision *n* Sehkraft *f*; Vision *f*.

visit *vt* besuchen:—*n* Besuch *m*.

visitor *n* Besucher *m*, Gast *m*.

visual *adj* visuell.

vital *adj* lebenswichtig, vital.

vitality *n* Vitalität *f*.

vitamin *n* Vitamin *n*.

vivid *adj* hell, leuchtend.

vocabulary *n* Wortschatz *m*.

vocal *adj* Stimm-, Gesang-.

vocation *n* Berufung *f*; Begabung *f*; Beruf *m*.

vodka *n* Wodka *m*.

voice *n* Stimme *f*.

void *adj* leer:—*n* Leere *f*.

volatile *adj* flüchtig, überschäumend.

volcanic *adj* vulkanisch.

volcano *n* Vulkan *m*.

volt *n* Volt *n*.

voltage *n* Spannung *f*.

volume *n* Band *m*; Volumen *n*; Lautstärke *f*.

voluntary *adj* freiwillig.

volunteer *n* Freiwillige(r) *f(m)*.

vomit *vt* erbrechen; *vi* sich übergehen.

voracious *adj* gierig.

vote *n* Abstimmung *f*, Stimme *f*:—*vt vi* wählen.

voter *n* Wähler *m*.

voucher *n* Gutschein *m*.

vow *n* Gelübde *f*:—*vt* geloben.

vowel *n* Vokal *m*.

voyage *n* Seereise *f*.

vulgar *adj* vulgar, ordinär.

vulnerable *adj* verletzbar, anfällig.

vulture *n* Geier *m*.

W

wage *n* Lohn *m*.

wag(g)on *n* Fuhrwerk *n*;
Wagen *m*; Waggon *m*.

waist *n* Taille *f*.

waistcoat *n* Weste *f*.

wait *n* Wartezeit *f*:—*vi*
warten.

waiter *n* Kellner *m*.

waiting room *n*
Wartezimmer *n*.

waitress *n* Kellnerin *f*.

waive *vt* verzichten auf.

wake *vt* wecken:—*vt*
aufwachen:—*n*
Totenwache *f*; Kienwasser
n.

waken *vt* aufwecken.

Wales *n* Wales *n*.

walk *n* Spaziergang *m*;
Gang *m*; Weg *m*:—*vi*
gehen; spazierengehen;
wandern.

wall *n* Wand *f*; Mauer *f*.

wallet *n* Brieftasche *f*.

wallflower *n* Goldlack *m*.

wallpaper *n* Tapete *f*.

walnut *n* Walnuß *f*.

walrus *n* Walroß *n*.

waltz *n* Walzer *m*:—*vi*
Walzer tanzen.

wand *n* Zauberstab *m*.

wander *vi* (herum)wandern.

want *v aux vt* wollen.

war *n* Krieg *m*.

wardrobe *n* Kleiderschrank
m.

warehouse *n* Lagerhaus *n*.

warm *adj* warm:—*vt vi*
wärmen.

warmth *n* Wärme *f*.

warn *vt* warnen.

warning *n* Warnung *f*.

warrant *n* Haftbefehl *m*.

warranty *n* Garantie *f*.

warrior *n* Krieger *m*.

Warsaw *n* Warschau *n*.

wash *n* Wäsche *f*:—*vt vi*
waschen.

wasp *n* Wespe *f*.

wastage *n* Verlust *m*.

waste *n* Verschwendung *f*;
Abfall *m*: —*vt* ver-
schwenden; vergeuden.

watch *n* Wache *f*; Uhr *f*:—*vt*
ansehen; beobachten:—*vi*
zusehen.

water *n* Wasser *n*.

watercolour *n* Aquarell *n*.

waterfall *n* Wasserfall *m*.

watermelon *n*
Wassermelone *f*.

watertight *adj* wasserdicht.

watt *n* Watt *n*.

wave *n* Welle *f*; Winken
n:—*vi* winken.

wavelength *n* Wellenlänge *f*.

wax *n* Wachs *n*.

way *n* Weg *m*; Art und
Weise *f*; Richtung *f*.

we *pn* wir.

weak *adj* schwach.

weakness *n* Schwäche *f*.

wealth *n* Reichtum *m*.

wealthy *adj* reich.

weapon *n* Waffe *f*.

wear *vt* tragen; haben;
abnutzen:—*vi* halten;
(sich) verschleißen.

weasel *n* Wiesel *n*.

weather *n* Wetter *n*.

weave *vt* weben.

weaver *n* Weber(in) *m(f)*.

web *n* Netz *n*;
Schwimmhaut *f*.

wed *vt* heiraten.

wedding *n* Hochzeit *f*.

Wednesday *n* Mittwoch *m*.

weed *n* Unkraut *f*.

week *n* Woche *f*.

weekend *n* Wochenende *n*.

weekly *adj* wochentlich.

weep *vi* weinen.

weeping willow *n*
Trauerweide *f*.

weigh *vt vi* wiegen.

weight *n* Gewicht *n*.

welcome *n* Willkommen
n:—*vt* begrüßen.

weld *vt* schweißen.

welder *n* Schweißer(in) *m(f)*.

well *n* Brünnen *m*; Quelle
f:—*adj* gesund:—*adv*
gut:—**as ~** auch.

well-known *adj* bekannt.

Welsh *adj* walisisch:—*n*
Walisisch *n*.

Welshman *n* Waliser *m*.

Welshwoman *n* Waliserin *f*.

west *n* Westen *m*.

western *adj* westlich, West-.

wet *adj* naß.

whale *n* Wal *m*.

what *adj* welche(r, s); was
für ein(e): —*pn* was:—
excl wie, was.

whatever *pn* was (immer
auch).

wheat n Weizen m.
wheel n Rad n.
wheelbarrow n Schubkarren m.
wheelchair n Rollstuhl m.
when adv wann:—conj wenn; als.
whenever adv wann (auch) immer; jedesmal wenn:—conj wenn.
where adv wo; wohin:—~ **from** woher.
wherever adv wo (immer).
whether conj ob.
which adj pn welche(r, s); wer; rel pn der, die, das; was.
while conj während.
whip n Peitsche f:—vt peitschen.
whipped cream n Schlagsahne f.
whirlwind n Wirbelwind m.
whiskers npl Barthaare pl.
whisky n Whisky m.
whisper n Flüstern n:—vt vi flüstern.
whistle n Pfeife f:—vt vi pfeifen.
white adj weiß.
whiting n Weißfisch m.
Whitsun n Pfingsten n.
who pn nom wer, acc wen, dat wem: —rel pn der / die / das.
whoever pn wer / wen / wem auch immer.
whole adj ganz:—n Ganze(s) n.
wholemeal adj Vollkorn-.
wholesale n Großhandel m:—adj Großhandels-.
whom pn acc wen, dat wem:—rel pn acc den / die / das, dat dem / der / dem.

whore n Hure f.
why adv conj warum, weshalb.
wicked adj böse.
wide adj breit; weit.
widen vt erweitern.
widespread adj weitverbreitet.
widow n Witwe f.
widowed adj verwitwet.
widower n Witwer m.
width n Breite f, Weite f.
wife n Frau f, Ehefrau f, Gattin f.
wig n Perücke f.
wild adj wild; heftig; verrückt.
wilderness n Wildnis f, Wüste f.
wildlife n Tierwelt f.
will v aux werden:—vt wollen:—Wille f; Testament n.
willing adj gewillt, bereit.
willow n Weide f.
willpower n Willenskraft f.
wilt vi welken.
win n Sieg m:—vt vi gewinnen.
wince n Zusammenzucken n:—vi zusammenzucken.
winch n Winde f.
wind n Wind m:—vt winden; wickeln:—vi sich winden:—~ **up** vt aufziehen.
windfall n unverhoffte(r) Glücksfall m.
windmill n Windmühle f.
window n Fenster n.
windpipe n Luftrohre f.
windscreen n Windschutzscheibe f.
wine n Wein m.
wing n Flügel m.

wink n Zwinkern n:—vi zwinkern, blinzeln.
winner n Gewinner m; Sieger m.
winter n Winter m.
wipe vt wischen.
wire n Draht m.
wisdom n Weisheit f.
wise adj weise.
wish n Wunsch m:—vt wünschen.
witch n Hexe f.
witchcraft n Hexerei f.
with prep mit.
withdraw vt zurückziehen; zurück-nehmen:—vi sich zurückziehen.
withdrawal n Zurückziehung f; Zurücknahme f.
within prep innerhalb:—adv innen.
without prep ohne.
withstand vt aushalten, widerstehen.
witness n Zeuge m, Zeugin f:—vt beglaubigen.
witty adj witzig, geistreich.
wizard n Zauberer m.
wobble vi wackeln, schwanken.
woe n Leid n, Kummer m.
wolf n Wolf m:—**she ~** Wölfin f.
woman n Frau f.
womb n Gebärmutter f.
wonder n Wunder m, Erstaunen n:—vi sich wundern.
wonderful adj wunderbar.
woo vt den Hof machen, umwerben.
wood n Wald m; Holz n.
wooded adj bewaldet.
wooden adj hölzern.
woodpecker n Specht m.

woodworm *n* Holzwurm *m*.
wool *n* Wolle *f*.
woollen *adj* Woll-.
word *n* Word *n*.
work *n* Arbeit *f*; Werk *n*:—
vi arbeiten.
worker *n* Arbeiter(in) *m(f)*.
world *n* Welt *f*.
worldwide *adj* weltweit.
worm *n* Wurm *m*.
worried *adj* besorgt, beunruhigt.
worry *n* Sorge *f*:—*vt* beunruhigen:—*vi* sich sorgen.
worrying *adj* beunruhigend.
worse *adj* schlechtere(r, s),
schlimmere (r, s).

worship *vt* anbeten.
worst *adj* schlimmste(r, s),
schlechte-ste(r, s).
worth *n* Wert *m*.
worthless *adj* wertlos.
wound *n* Wunde *f*:—*vt* verwunden.
wrap *vt* entwickeln.
wrath *n* Zorn *m*.
wreath *n* Kranz *m*.
wreck *n* Wrack *n*; Ruine
f:—*vt* zerstören.
wren *n* Zaunkönig *m*.
wrestle *vi* ringen.
wrestler *n* Ringer(in) *m(f)*.
wretched *adj* elend;
verflixt.

wrist *n* Handgelenk *n*.
writ *n* gerichtlicher Befehl
m.
write *vt vi* schreiben.
writer *n* Schriftsteller *m*.
writing *n* Schreiben *n*;
Schift *f*:—**in** ~ schriftlich.
wrong *adj* falsch;
unrecht:—*n* Unrecht *n*:—
vt Unrecht tun.
wrongful *adj* unrecht-
mäßig.
wrongly *adv* falsch; zu
Unrecht.
wry *adj* ironisch.

X,Y,Z

Xmas *n* Weihnachten *fpl.*

X-ray *n* Röntgenstrahl *m:*—
vt röntgen.

xylophone *n* Xylophon *n.*

yacht *n* Jacht *f.*

yachting *n* Segelsport *m.*

Yank, Yankee *n* Ami *m.*

yard *n* Hof *m;* Yard *n.*

yarn *n* Garn *n.*

yawn *vi* gähnen:—*n*
Gähnen *n.*

year *n* Jahr *n.*

yearly *adj* jährlich.

yearn *vi* sehnen.

yeast *n* Hefe *f.*

yell *vt vi* schreien:—*n*
Schrei *m.*

yellow *adj* gelb:—*n* Gelb *n.*

yes *adv* ja.

yesterday *adv* gestern:—**the
day before ~** vorgestern.

yet *conj* dennoch:—*adv*
noch.

yew *n* Eibe *f.*

yield *vt* liefern; abwer-
fen:—*vi* nachgeben:—*n*
Ertrag *m;* Ernte *f;*
Zinsertrag *m.*

yoga *n* Joga *n.*

yoghurt *n* Joghurt *m.*

yolk *n* Eidotter *n,* Eigelb *n.*

you *pn* Sie; du, ihr; dich,
dir, euch; Ihnen.

young *adj* jung.

your *poss adj* Ihr; dein, euer.

yours *poss pn* Ihre(r, s);
deine(r, s), eure(r, s).

youth *n* Jugend *f.*

youthful *adj* jugendlich.

yule *n* Weinachte.

zeal *n* Eifer *m.*

zealous *adj* eifrig.

zebra *n* Zebra *n.*

zenith *n* Zenit *m;*
Höhepunkt *m.*

zero *n* Null *f.*

zest *n* Begeisterung *f.*

zigzag *n* Zickzack *m.*

zinc *n* Zink *n.*

zip, zipper *n* Reißverschluß
m.

zither *n* Zither *f.*

zodiac *n* Tierkreis *m.*

zone *n* Zone *f.*

zoo *n* Zoo *m.*

zoological *adj* zoologisch.

zoologist *n* Zoologe *m,*
Zoologin *f.*

zoology *n* Zoologie *f.*

zoom lens *n* Zoom(objektiv) *n.*

German Verbs

Verb Forms

Auxilliary
Auxiliary verbs are used to form compound tenses of verbs, eg *have* in *I have seen*. The auxiliary verbs in German are *haben*, *sein* and *werden*.

Compound
Compound tenses are verb tenses consisting of more than one element. In German, compound tenses are formed by an *auxiliary* verb and the *past participle* or infinitive, eg *er hat gefunden – he has found, wir werden fahren – we will travel*.

Conditional
The conditional is introduced in English by the auxiliary *would*, eg *I would come if I had the time*. In German, this comprises the imperfect subjunctive of *werden* and the infinitive, eg *ich würde machen*.

Imperative
The imperative is used for giving orders, eg *sei gut – be good*, or making suggestions, eg *gehen wir – let's go*.

Imperfect indicative
In German, this tense describes past habitual or continuous action or, in writing, completed past action, eg *ich ging – I was going*.

Indicative
The normal form of a verb, as in *ich mag – I like, er ist gekommen – he has come, ich laufe – I am running*.

Past participle
This is the form used after the auxiliary *have* in English, eg *gegessen – eaten* in *ich habe gegessen – I have eaten*.

Perfect indicative
In German this is the standard past tense of conversation, comprising the *present indicative* of *haben* or *sein* and the *past participle*, eg *ich habe gegeben – I have given, du bist gewesen – you have been*.

Pluperfect indicative
In German and English, this tense expresses an action which happened in the past before another past action. In German, this comprises the *imperfect indicative* of *haben* or *sein* and the *past participle*, eg *he hatte getan – he had done, sie waren angekommen – they had arrived*.

Present participle
This is the form which ends in *-ing* in English, eg *gehend – going*.

Subjunctive
This is rarely used in English. It survives in expressions such as *if I were you*, and *God save the Queen*. In German, the subjunctive is used to convey reported speech.

ankommen *to arrive*

Present participle *ankommend*
Past participle *angekommen*

Present indicative	**Imperfect subjunctive**
ich komme an	ich käme an
du kommst an	du kämest an
er kommt an	er käme an
wir kommen an	wir kämen an
ihr kommt an	ihr kämet an
sie kommen an	sie kämen an

Imperfect indicative	**Future indicative**
ich kam an	ich werde ankommen
du kamst an	du wirst ankommen
er kam an	er wird ankommen
wir kamen an	wir werden ankommen
ihr kamt an	ihr werdet ankommen
sie kamen an	sie werden ankommen

Perfect indicative	**Conditional**
ich bin angekommen	ich würde ankommen
du bist angekommen	du würdest ankommen
er ist angekommen	er würde ankommen
wir sind angekommen	wir würden ankommen
ihr seid angekommen	ihr würdet ankommen
sie sind angekommen	sie würden ankommen

Pluperfect indicative	**Imperative**
ich war angekommen	komm(e) an!
du warst angekommen	kommen wir an!
er war angekommen	kommt an!
wir waren angekommen	kommen Sie an!
ihr wart angekommen	
sie waren angekommen	

Present subjunctive

ich komme an
du kommest an
er komme an
wir kommen an
ihr kommet an
sie kommen an

arbeiten *to work*

Present participle *arbeitend*
Past participle *gearbeitet*

Present indicative	**Imperfect subjunctive**
ich arbeite	ich arbeitete
du arbeitest	du arbeitetest
er arbeitet	er arbeitete
wir arbeiten	wir arbeiteten
ihr arbeitet	ihr arbeitetet
sie arbeiten	sie arbeiteten

Imperfect indicative	**Future indicative**
ich arbeitete	ich werde arbeiten
du arbeitetest	du wirst arbeiten
er arbeitete	er wird arbeiten
wir arbeiteten	wir werden arbeiten
ihr arbeitetet	ihr werdet arbeiten
sie arbeiteten	sie werden arbeiten

Perfect indicative	**Conditional**
ich habe gearbeitet	ich würde arbeiten
du hast gearbeitet	du würdest arbeiten
er hat gearbeitet	er würde arbeiten
wir haben gearbeitet	wir würden arbeiten
ihr habt gearbeitet	ihr würdet arbeiten
sie haben gearbeitet	sie würden arbeiten

Pluperfect indicative	**Imperative**
ich hatte gearbeitet	arbeite!
du hattest gearbeitet	arbeiten wir!
er hatte gearbeitet	arbeitet!
wir hatten gearbeitet	arbeiten Sie!
ihr hattet gearbeitet	
sie hatten gearbeitet	

Present subjunctive

ich arbeite
du arbeitest
er arbeite
wir arbeiten
ihr arbeitet
sie arbeiten

atmen *to breathe*

Present participle *atmend*
Past participle *geatmet*

Present indicative	Imperfect subjunctive
ich atme	ich atmete
du atmest	du atmetest
er atmet	er atmete
wir atmen	wir atmeten
ihr atmet	ihr atmetet
sie atmen	sie atmeten

Imperfect indicative	Future indicative
ich atmete	ich werde atmen
du atmetest	du wirst atmen
er atmete	er wird atmen
wir atmeten	wir werden atmen
ihr atmetet	ihr werdet atmen
sie atmeten	sie werden atmen

Perfect indicative	Conditional
ich habe geatmet	ich würde atmen
du hast geatmet	du würdest atmen
er hat geatmet	er würde atmen
wir haben geatmet	wir würden atmen
ihr habt geatmet	ihr würdet atmen
sie haben geatmet	sie würden atmen

Pluperfect indicative	Imperative
ich hatte geatmet	atme!
du hattest geatmet	atmen wir!
er hatte geatmet	atmet!
wir hatten geatmet	atmen Sie!
ihr hattet geatmet	
sie hatten geatmet	

Present subjunctive

ich atme
du atmest
er atme
wir atmen
ihr atmet
sie atmen

backen *to bake*

Present participle *backend*
Past participle *gebacken*

Present indicative	Imperfect subjunctive
ich backe	ich backte
du bˇckst	du backtest
er bˇckt	er backte
wir backen	wir backten
ihr backt	ihr backtet
sie backen	sie backten

Imperfect indicative	Future indicative
ich backte	ich werde backen
du backtest	du wirst backen
er backte	er wird backen
wir backten	wir werden backen
ihr backtet	ihr werdet backen
sie backten	sie werden backen

Perfect indicative	Conditional
ich habe gebacken	ich würde backen
du hast gebacken	du würdest backen
er hat gebacken	er würde backen
wir haben gebacken	wir würden backen
ihr habt gebacken	ihr würdet backen
sie haben gebacken	sie würden backen

Pluperfect indicative	Imperative
ich hatte gebacken	back(e)!
du hattest gebacken	backen wir!
er hatte gebacken	backt!
wir hatten gebacken	backen Sie!
ihr hattet gebacken	
sie hatten gebacken	

Present subjunctive

ich backe
du backest
er backe
wir backen
ihr backet
sie backen

befehlen *to command*

Present participle *befehlend*
Past participle *befohlen*

Present indicative	**Imperfect subjunctive**
ich befehle	ich bef´hle
du befiehlst	du bef´hlest
er befiehlt	er bef´hle
wir befehlen	wir bef´hlen
ihr befehlt	ihr bef´hlet
sie befehlen	sie bef´hlen

Imperfect indicative	**Future indicative**
ich befahl	ich werde befehlen
du befahlst	du wirst befehlen
er befahl	er wird befehlen
wir befahlen	wir werden befehlen
ihr befahlt	ihr werdet befehlen
sie befahlen	sie werden befehlen

Perfect indicative	**Conditional**
ich habe befohlen	ich würde befehlen
du hast befohlen	du würdest befehlen
er hat befohlen	er würde befehlen
wir haben befohlen	wir würden befehlen
ihr habt befohlen	ihr würdet befehlen
sie haben befohlen	sie würden befehlen

Pluperfect indicative	**Imperative**
ich hatte befohlen	befiehl!
du hattest befohlen	befehlen wir!
er hatte befohlen	befehlt!
wir hatten befohlen	befehlen Sie!
ihr hattet befohlen	
sie hatten befohlen	

Present subjunctive
ich befehle
du befehlest
er befehle
wir befehlen
ihr befehlet
sie befehlen

beginnen *to begin*

Present participle *beginnend*
Past participle *begonnen*

Present indicative	**Imperfect subjunctive**
ich beginne	ich begänne
du beginnst	du begännest
er beginnt	er begänne
wir beginnen	wir begännen
ihr beginnt	ihr begännet
sie beginnen	sie begännen

Imperfect indicative	**Future indicative**
ich begann	ich werde beginnen
du begannst	du wirst beginnen
er begann	er wird beginnen
wir begannen	wir werden beginnen
ihr begannt	ihr werdet beginnen
sie begannen	sie werden beginnen

Perfect indicative	**Conditional**
ich habe begonnen	ich würde beginnen
du hast begonnen	du würdest beginnen
er hat begonnen	er würde beginnen
wir haben begonnen	wir würden beginnen
ihr habt begonnen	ihr würdet beginnen
sie haben begonnen	sie würden beginnen

Pluperfect indicative	**Imperative**
ich hatte begonnen	beginn(e)!
du hattest begonnen	beginnen wir!
er hatte begonnen	beginnt!
wir hatten begonnen	beginnen Sie!
ihr hattet begonnen	
sie hatten begonnen	

Present subjunctive
ich beginne
du beginnest
er beginne
wir beginnen
ihr beginnet
sie beginnen

beißen *to bite*

Present participle *beißend*
Past participle *gebissen*

Present indicative	**Imperfect subjunctive**
ich beißea	ich bisse
du beißt	du bissest
er beißt	er bisse
wir beißen	wir bissen
ihr beißt	ihr bisset
sie beißen	sie bissen

Imperfect indicative	**Future indicative**
ich biß	ich werde beißen
du bissest	du wirst beißen
er biß	er wird beißen
wir bissen	wir werden beißen
ihr bißt	ihr werdet beißen
sie bissen	sie werden beißen

Perfect indicative	**Conditional**
ich habe gebissen	ich würde beißen
du hast gebissen	du würdest beißen
er hat gebissen	er würde beißen
wir haben gebissen	wir würden beißen
ihr habt gebissen	ihr würdet beißen
sie haben gebissen	sie würden beißen

Pluperfect indicative	**Imperative**
ich hatte gebissen	beiß(e)!
du hattest gebissen	beißen wir!
er hatte gebissen	beißt!
wir hatten gebissen	beißen Sie!
ihr hattet gebissen	
sie hatten gebissen	

Present subjunctive

ich beiße
du beißest
er beiße
wir beißen
ihr beißet
sie beißen

bergen *to rescue; to hide*

Present participle *bergend*
Past participle *geborgen*

Present indicative	**Imperfect subjunctive**
ich berge	ich bärge
du birgst	du bärgest
er birgt	er bärge
wir bergen	wir bärgen
ihr bergt	ihr bärget
sie bergen	sie bärgen

Imperfect indicative	**Future indicative**
ich barg	ich werde bergen
du bargst	du wirst bergen
er barg	er wird bergen
wir bargen	wir werden bergen
ihr bargt	ihr werdet bergen
sie bargen	sie werden bergen

Perfect indicative	**Conditional**
ich habe geborgen	ich würde bergen
du hast geborgen	du würdest bergen
er hat geborgen	er würde bergen
wir haben geborgen	wir würden bergen
ihr habt geborgen	ihr würdet bergen
sie haben geborgen	sie würden bergen

Pluperfect indicative	**Imperative**
ich hatte geborgen	birg!
du hattest geborgen	bergen wir!
er hatte geborgen	bergt!
wir hatten geborgen	bergen Sie!
ihr hattet geborgen	
sie hatten geborgen	

Present subjunctive

ich berge
du bergest
er berge
wir bergen
ihr berget
sie bergen

bersten *to burst*

Present participle *berstend*
Past participle *geborsten*

Present indicative	**Imperfect subjunctive**
ich berste	ich bärste
du birst	du bärstest
er birst	er bärste
wir birsten	wir bärsten
ihr birst	ihr bärstet
sie bersten	sie bärsten

Imperfect indicative	**Future indicative**
ich barst	ich werde bersten
du barstest	du wirst bersten
er barst	er wird bersten
wir barsten	wir werden bersten
ihr barstet	ihr werdet bersten
sie barsten	sie werden bersten

Perfect indicative	**Conditional**
ich bin geborsten	ich würde bersten
du bist geborsten	du würdest bersten
er ist geborsten	er würde bersten
wir sind geborsten	wir würden bersten
ihr seid geborsten	ihr würdet bersten
sie sind geborsten	sie würden bersten

Pluperfect indicative	**Imperative**
ich war geborsten	birst!
du warst geborsten	bersten wir!
er war geborsten	berstet!
wir waren geborsten	bersten Sie!
ihr wart geborsten	
sie waren geborsten	

Present subjunctive

ich berste
du berstest
er berste
wir bersten
ihr berstet
sie bersten

biegen *to bend, turn*

Present participle *biegend*
Past participle *gebogen*

Present indicative	**Present subjunctive**
ich biege	ich biege
du biegst	du biegest
er biegt	er biege
wir biegen	wir biegen
ihr biegt	ihr bieget
sie biegen	sie biegen

Imperfect indicative	**Imperfect subjunctive**
ich bog	ich böge
du bogst	du bögest
er bog	er böge
wir bogen	wir bögen
ihr bogt	ihr böget
sie bogen	sie bögen

Perfect indicative	**Future indicative**
ich bin/habe gebogen	ich werde biegen
du bist/hast gebogen	du wirst biegen
er ist/hat gebogen	er wird biegen
wir sind/haben gebogen	wir werden biegen
ihr seid/habt gebogen	ihr werdet biegen
sie sind/haben gebogen	sie werden biegen

Pluperfect indicative	**Conditional**
ich war/hatte gebogen	ich würde biegen
du warst/hattest gebogen	du würdest biegen
er war/hatte gebogen	er würde biegen
wir waren/hatten gebogen	wir würden biegen
ihr wart/hattet gebogen	ihr würdet biegen
sie waren/hatten gebogen	sie würden biegen

Imperative

bieg(e)!
biegen wir!
biegt!
biegen Sie!

bieten *to offer*

Present participle *bietend*
Past participle *geboten*

Present indicative	Imperfect subjunctive
ich biete	ich böte
du bietest	du bötest
er bietet	er böte
wir bieten	wir böten
ihr bietet	ihr bötet
sie bieten	sie böten

Imperfect indicative	Future indicative
ich bot	ich werde bieten
du bot(e)st	du wirst bieten
er bot	er wird bieten
wir boten	wir werden bieten
ihr botet	ihr werdet bieten
sie boten	sie werden bieten

Perfect indicative	Conditional
ich habe geboten	ich würde bieten
du hast geboten	du würdest bieten
er hat geboten	er würde bieten
wir haben geboten	wir würden bieten
ihr habt geboten	ihr würdet bieten
sie haben geboten	sie würden bieten

Pluperfect indicative	Imperative
ich hatte geboten	biet(e)!
du hattest geboten	bieten wir!
er hatte geboten	bietet!
wir hatten geboten	bieten Sie!
ihr hattet geboten	
sie hatten geboten	

Present subjunctive

ich biete
du bietest
er biete
wir bieten
ihr bietet
sie bieten

binden *to tie*

Present participle *bindend*
Past participle *gebunden*

Present indicative	Imperfect subjunctive
ich binde	ich bände
du bindest	du bändest
er bindet	er bände
wir binden	wir bänden
ihr bindet	ihr bändet
sie binden	sie bänden

Imperfect indicative	Future indicative
ich band	ich werde binden
du band(e)st	du wirst binden
er band	er wird binden
wir banden	wir werden binden
ihr bandet	ihr werdet binden
sie banden	sie werden binden

Perfect indicative	Conditional
ich habe gebunden	ich würde binden
du hast gebunden	du würdest binden
er hat gebunden	er würde binden
wir haben gebunden	wir würden binden
ihr habt gebunden	ihr würdet binden
sie haben gebunden	sie würden binden

Pluperfect indicative	Imperative
ich hatte gebunden	bind(e)!
du hattest gebunden	binden wir!
er hatte gebunden	bindet!
wir hatten gebunden	binden Sie!
ihr hattet gebunden	
sie hatten gebunden	

Present subjunctive

ich binde
du bindest
er binde
wir binden
ihr bindet
sie binden

bitten *to request*

Present participle *bittend*
Past participle *gebeten*

Present indicative	**Imperfect subjunctive**
ich bitte	ich bäte
du bittest	du bätest
er bittet	er bäte
wir bitten	wir bäten
ihr bittet	ihr bätet
sie bitten	sie bäten

Imperfect indicative	**Future indicative**
ich bat	ich werde bitten
du bat(e)st	du wirst bitten
er bat	er wird bitten
wir baten	wir werden bitten
ihr batet	ihr werdet bitten
sie baten	sie werden bitten

Perfect indicative	**Conditional**
ich habe gebeten	ich würde bitten
du hast gebeten	du würdest bitten
er hat gebeten	er würde bitten
wir haben gebeten	wir würden bitten
ihr habt gebeten	ihr würdet bitten
sie haben gebeten	sie würden bitten

Pluperfect indicative	**Imperative**
ich hatte gebeten	bitt(e)!
du hattest gebeten	bitten wir!
er hatte gebeten	bittet!
wir hatten gebeten	bitten Sie!
ihr hattet gebeten	
sie hatten gebeten	

Present subjunctive

ich bitte
du bittest
er bitte
wir bitten
ihr bittet
sie bitten

blasen *to blow*

Present participle *blasend*
Past participle *geblasen*

Present indicative	**Imperfect subjunctive**
ich blase	ich bliese
du bläst	du bliesest
er bläst	er bliese
wir blasen	wir bliesen
ihr blast	ihr blieset
sie blasen	sie bliesen

Imperfect indicative	**Future indicative**
ich blies	ich werde blasen
du bliesest	du wirst blasen
er blies	er wird blasen
wir bliesen	wir werden blasen
ihr bliest	ihr werdet blasen
sie bliesen	sie werden blasen

Perfect indicative	**Conditional**
ich habe geblasen	ich würde blasen
du hast geblasen	du würdest blasen
er hat geblasen	er würde blasen
wir haben geblasen	wir würden blasen
ihr habt geblasen	ihr würdet blasen
sie haben geblasen	sie würden blasen

Pluperfect indicative	**Imperative**
ich hatte geblasen	blas(e)!
du hattest geblasen	blasen wir!
er hatte geblasen	blast!
wir hatten geblasen	blasen Sie!
ihr hattet geblasen	
sie hatten geblasen	

Present subjunctive

ich blase
du blasest
er blase
wir blasen
ihr blaset
sie blasen

bleiben *to remain*

Present participle *bleibend*
Past participle *geblieben*

Present indicative	**Imperfect subjunctive**
ich bleibe	ich bliebe
du bleibst	du bliebest
er bleibt	er bliebe
wir bleiben	wir blieben
ihr bleibt	ihr bliebet
sie bleiben	sie blieben

Imperfect indicative	**Future indicative**
ich blieb	ich werde bleiben
du bliebst	du wirst bleiben
er blieb	er wird bleiben
wir blieben	wir werden bleiben
ihr bliebt	ihr werdet bleiben
sie blieben	sie werden bleiben

Perfect indicative	**Conditional**
ich bin geblieben	ich würde bleiben
du bist geblieben	du würdest bleiben
er ist geblieben	er würde bleiben
wir sind geblieben	wir würden bleiben
ihr seid geblieben	ihr würdet bleiben
sie sind geblieben	sie würden bleiben

Pluperfect indicative	**Imperative**
ich war geblieben	bleib(e)!
du warst geblieben	bleiben wir!
er war geblieben	bleibt!
wir waren geblieben	bleiben Sie!
ihr wart geblieben	
sie waren geblieben	

Present subjunctive

ich bleibe
du bleibest
er bleibe
wir bleiben
ihr bleibet
sie bleiben

braten *to fry, roast*

Present participle *bratend*
Past participle *gebraten*

Present indicative	**Imperfect subjunctive**
ich brate	ich briete
du brätst	du brietest
er brät	er briete
wir braten	wir brieten
ihr bratet	ihr brietet
sie braten	sie brieten

Imperfect indicative	**Future indicative**
ich briet	ich werde braten
du briet(e)st	du wirst braten
er briet	er wird braten
wir brieten	wir werden braten
ihr brietet	ihr werdet braten
sie brieten	sie werden braten

Perfect indicative	**Conditional**
ich habe gebraten	ich würde braten
du hast gebraten	du würdest braten
er hat gebraten	er würde braten
wir haben gebraten	wir würden braten
ihr habt gebraten	ihr würdet braten
sie haben gebraten	sie würden braten

Pluperfect indicative	**Imperative**
ich hatte gebraten	brat(e)!
du hattest gebraten	braten wir!
er hatte gebraten	bratet!
wir hatten gebraten	braten Sie!
ihr hattet gebraten	
sie hatten gebraten	

Present subjunctive

ich brate
du bratest
er brate
wir braten
ihr bratet
sie braten

brechen *to break*

Present participle *brechend*
Past participle *gebrochen*

Present indicative	**Imperfect subjunctive**
ich breche	ich bräche
du brichst	du brächest
er bricht	er bräche
wir brechen	wir brächen
ihr brecht	ihr brächet
sie brechen	sie brächen

Imperfect indicative	**Future indicative**
ich brach	ich werde brechen
du brachst	du wirst brechen
er brach	er wird brechen
wir brachen	wir werden brechen
ihr bracht	ihr werdet brechen
sie brachen	sie werden brechen

Perfect indicative	**Conditional**
ich habe gebrochen	ich würde brechen
du hast gebrochen	du würdest brechen
er hat gebrochen	er würde brechen
wir haben gebrochen	wir würden brechen
ihr habt gebrochen	ihr würdet brechen
sie haben gebrochen	sie würden brechen

Pluperfect indicative	**Imperative**
ich hatte gebrochen	brich!
du hattest gebrochen	brechen wir!
er hatte gebrochen	brecht!
wir hatten gebrochen	brechen Sie!
ihr hattet gebrochen	
sie hatten gebrochen	

Present subjunctive

ich breche
du brechest
er breche
wir brechen
ihr brechet
sie brechen

brennen *to burn*

Present participle *brennend*
Past participle *gebrannt*

Present indicative	**Imperfect subjunctive**
ich brenne	ich brennte
du brennst	du brenntest
er brennt	er brennte
wir brennen	wir brennten
ihr brennt	ihr brenntet
sie brennen	sie brennten

Imperfect indicative	**Future indicative**
ich brannte	ich werde brennen
du branntest	du wirst brennen
er brannte	er wird brennen
wir brannten	wir werden brennen
ihr branntet	ihr werdet brennen
sie brannten	sie werden brennen

Perfect indicative	**Conditional**
ich habe gebrannt	ich würde brennen
du hast gebrannt	du würdest brennen
er hat gebrannt	er würde brennen
wir haben gebrannt	wir würden brennen
ihr habt gebrannt	ihr würdet brennen
sie haben gebrannt	sie würden brennen

Pluperfect indicative	**Imperative**
ich hatte gebrannt	brenn(e)!
du hattest gebrannt	brennen wir!
er hatte gebrannt	brennt!
wir hatten gebrannt	brennen Sie!
ihr hattet gebrannt	
sie hatten gebrannt	

Present subjunctive

ich brenne
du brennest
er brenne
wir brennen
ihr brennet
sie brennen

bringen *to bring*

Present participle *bringend*
Past participle *gebracht*

Present indicative	**Imperfect subjunctive**
ich bringe	ich brächte
du bringst	du brächtest
er bringt	er brächte
wir bringen	wir brächten
ihr bringt	ihr brächtet
sie bringen	sie brächten

Imperfect indicative	**Future indicative**
ich brachte	ich werde bringen
du brachtest	du wirst bringen
er brachte	er wird bringen
wir brachten	wir werden bringen
ihr brachtet	ihr werdet bringen
sie brachten	sie werden bringen

Perfect indicative	**Conditional**
ich habe gebracht	ich würde bringen
du hast gebracht	du würdest bringen
er hat gebracht	er würde bringen
wir haben gebracht	wir würden bringen
ihr habt gebracht	ihr würdet bringen
sie haben gebracht	sie würden bringen

Pluperfect indicative	**Imperative**
ich hatte gebracht	bring(e)!
du hattest gebracht	bringen wir!
er hatte gebracht	bringt!
wir hatten gebracht	bringen Sie!
ihr hattet gebracht	
sie hatten gebracht	

Present subjunctive

ich bringe
du bringest
er bringe
wir bringen
ihr bringet
sie bringen

denken *to think*

Present participle *denkend*
Past participle *gedacht*

Present indicative	**Imperfect subjunctive**
ich denke	ich dächte
du denkst	du dächtest
er denkt	er dächte
wir denken	wir dächten
ihr denkt	ihr dächtet
sie denken	sie dächten

Imperfect indicative	**Future indicative**
ich dachte	ich werde denken
du dachtest	du wirst denken
er dachte	er wird denken
wir dachten	wir werden denken
ihr dachtet	ihr werdet denken
sie dachten	sie werden denken

Perfect indicative	**Conditional**
ich habe gedacht	ich würde denken
du hast gedacht	du würdest denken
er hat gedacht	er würde denken
wir haben gedacht	wir würden denken
ihr habt gedacht	ihr würdet denken
sie haben gedacht	sie würden denken

Pluperfect indicative	**Imperative**
ich hatte gedacht	denk(e)!
du hattest gedacht	denken wir!
er hatte gedacht	denkt!
wir hatten gedacht	denken Sie!
ihr hattet gedacht	
sie hatten gedacht	

Present subjunctive

ich denke
du denkest
er denke
wir denken
ihr denket
sie denken

dreschen *to thresh*

Present participle *dreschend*
Past participle *gedroschen*

Present indicative	**Imperfect subjunctive**
ich dresche	ich drösche
du drischst	du dröschest
er drischt	er drösche
wir dreschen	wir dröschen
ihr drescht	ihr dröschet
sie dreschen	sie dröschen

Imperfect indicative	**Future indicative**
ich drosch	ich werde dreschen
du drosch(e)st	du wirst dreschen
er drosch	er wird dreschen
wir droschen	wir werden dreschen
ihr droscht	ihr werdet dreschen
sie droschen	sie werden dreschen

Perfect indicative	**Conditional**
ich habe gedroschen	ich würde dreschen
du hast gedroschen	du würdest dreschen
er hat gedroschen	er würde dreschen
wir haben gedroschen	wir würden dreschen
ihr habt gedroschen	ihr würdet dreschen
sie haben gedroschen	sie würden dreschen

Pluperfect indicative	**Imperative**
ich hatte gedroschen	drisch!
du hattest gedroschen	dreschen wir!
er hatte gedroschen	drescht!
wir hatten gedroschen	dreschen Sie!
ihr hattet gedroschen	
sie hatten gedroschen	

Present subjunctive

ich dresche
du dreschest
er dresche
wir dreschen
ihr dreschet
sie dreschen

dringen *to penetrate*

Present participle *dringend*
Past participle *gedrungen*

Present indicative	**Imperfect subjunctive**
ich dringe	ich dränge
du dringst	du drängest
er dringt	er dränge
wir dringen	wir drängen
ihr dringt	ihr dränget
sie dringen	sie drängen

Imperfect indicative	**Future indicative**
ich drang	ich werde dringen
du drangst	du wirst dringen
er drang	er wird dringen
wir drangen	wir werden dringen
ihr drangt	ihr werdet dringen
sie drangen	sie werden dringen

Perfect indicative	**Conditional**
ich bin gedrungen	ich würde dringen
du bist gedrungen	du würdest dringen
er ist gedrungen	er würde dringen
wir sind gedrungen	wir würden dringen
ihr seid gedrungen	ihr würdet dringen
sie sind gedrungen	sie würden dringen

Pluperfect indicative	**Imperative**
ich war gedrungen	dring(e)!
du warst gedrungen	dringen wir!
er war gedrungen	dringt!
wir waren gedrungen	dringen Sie!
ihr wart gedrungen	
sie waren gedrungen	

Present subjunctive

ich dringe
du dringest
er dringe
wir dringen
ihr dringet
sie dringen

dürfen *to be allowed to*

Present participle *dürfend*
Past participle *gedurft/dürfen**

Present indicative	Present subjunctive
ich darf	ich dürfe
du darfst	du dürfest
er darf	er dürfe
wir dürfen	wir dürfen
ihr dürft	ihr dürfet
sie dürfen	sie dürfen

Imperfect indicative	Imperfect subjunctive
ich durfte	ich dürfte
du durftest	du dürftest
er durfte	er dürfte
wir durften	wir dürften
ihr durftet	ihr dürftet
sie durften	sie dürften

Perfect indicative	Future indicative
ich habe gedurft	ich werde dürfen
du hast gedurft	du wirst dürfen
er hat gedurft	er wird dürfen
wir haben gedurft	wir werden dürfen
ihr habt gedurft	ihr werdet dürfen
sie haben gedurft	sie werden dürfen

Pluperfect indicative	Conditional
ich hatte gedurft	ich würde dürfen
du hattest gedurft	du würdest dürfen
er hatte gedurft	er würde dürfen
wir hatten gedurft	wir würden dürfen
ihr hattet gedurft	ihr würdet dürfen
sie hatten gedurft	sie würden dürfen

*dürfen *is used when preceded by an infinitive*

empfehlen *to recommend*

Present participle *empfehlend*
Past participle *empfohlen*

Present indicative	Imperfect subjunctive
ich empfehle	ich empföhle
du empfiehlst	du empföhlest
er empfiehlt	er empföhle
wir empfehlen	wir empföhlen
ihr empfehlt	ihr empföhlet
sie empfehlen	sie empföhlen

Imperfect indicative	Future indicative
ich empfahl	ich werde empfehlen
du empfahlst	du wirst empfehlen
er empfahl	er wird empfehlen
wir empfahlen	wir werden empfehlen
ihr empfahlt	ihr werdet empfehlen
sie empfahlen	sie werden empfehlen

Perfect indicative	Conditional
ich habe empfohlen	ich würde empfehlen
du hast empfohlen	du würdest empfehlen
er hat empfohlen	er würde empfehlen
wir haben empfohlen	wir würden empfehlen
ihr habt empfohlen	ihr würdet empfehlen
sie haben empfohlen	sie würden empfehlen

Pluperfect indicative	Imperative
ich hatte empfohlen	
du hattest empfohlen	empfiehl!
er hatte empfohlen	empfehlen wir!
wir hatten empfohlen	empfehlt!
ihr hattet empfohlen	empfehlen Sie!
sie hatten empfohlen	

Present subjunctive
ich empfehle
du empfehlest
er empfehle
wir empfehlen
ihr empfehlet
sie empfehlen

erlöschen *to go out (of lights)* erzählen *to tell, narrate*

Present participle *erlöschend*
Past participle *erloschen*

Present participle *erzählend*
Past participle *erzählt*

Present indicative	**Imperfect subjunctive**	**Present indicative**	**Imperfect subjunctive**
ich erlösche	ich erlösche	ich erzähle	ich erzählte
du erlischst	du erlöschest	du erzählst	du erzähltest
er erlischt	er erlösche	er erzählt	er erzählte
wir erlöschen	wir erlöschen	wir erzählen	wir erzählten
ihr erlöscht	ihr erlöschet	ihr erzählt	ihr erzähltet
sie erlöschen	sie erlöschen	sie erzählen	sie erzählten

Imperfect indicative	**Future indicative**	**Imperfect indicative**	**Future indicative**
ich erlosch	ich werde erlöschen	ich erzählte	ich werde erzählen
du erlosch(e)st	du wirst erlöschen	du erzähltest	du wirst erzählen
er erlosch	er wird erlöschen	er erzählte	er wird erzählen
wir erloschen	wir werden erlöschen	wir erzählten	wir werden erzählen
ihr erloscht	ihr werdet erlöschen	ihr erzähltet	ihr werdet erzählen
sie erloschen	sie werden erlöschen	sie erzählten	sie werden erzählen

Perfect indicative	**Conditional**	**Perfect indicative**	**Conditional**
ich bin erloschen	ich würde erlöschen	ich habe erzählt	ich würde erzählen
du bist erloschen	du würdest erlöschen	du hast erzählt	du würdest erzählen
er ist erloschen	er würde erlöschen	er hat erzählt	er würde erzählen
wir sind erloschen	wir würden erlöschen	wir haben erzählt	wir würden erzählen
ihr seid erloschen	ihr würdet erlöschen	ihr habt erzählt	ihr würdet erzählen
sie sind erloschen	sie würden erlöschen	sie haben erzählt	sie würden erzählen

Pluperfect indicative	**Imperative**	**Pluperfect indicative**	**Imperative**
ich war erloschen	erlisch!	ich hatte erzählt	erzähl(e)!
du warst erloschen	erlöschen wir!	du hattest erzählt	erzählen wir!
er war erloschen	erlöscht!	er hatte erzählt	erzählt!
wir waren erloschen	erlöschen Sie!	wir hatten erzählt	erzählen Sie!
ihr wart erloschen		ihr hattet erzählt	
sie waren erloschen		sie hatten erzählt	

Present subjunctive		**Present subjunctive**	
ich erlösche		ich erzähle	
du erlöschest		du erzählest	
er erlösche		er erzähle	
wir erlöschen		wir erzählen	
ihr erlöschet		ihr erzählet	
sie erlöschen		sie erzählen	

essen *to eat*

Present participle *essend*
Past participle *gegessen*

Present indicative	Imperfect subjunctive
ich esse	ich äße
du ißt	du äßest
er ißt	er äße
wir essen	wir äßen
ihr eßt	ihr äßet
sie essen	sie äßen

Imperfect indicative	Future indicative
ich aß	ich werde essen
du aßest	du wirst essen
er aß	er wird essen
wir aßen	wir werden essen
ihr aßt	ihr werdet essen
sie aßen	sie werden essen

Perfect indicative	Conditional
ich habe gegessen	ich würde essen
du hast gegessen	du würdest essen
er hat gegessen	er würde essen
wir haben gegessen	wir würden essen
ihr habt gegessen	ihr würdet essen
sie haben gegessen	sie würden essen

Pluperfect indicative	Imperative
ich hatte gegessen	iß!
du hattest gegessen	essen wir!
er hatte gegessen	eßt!
wir hatten gegessen	essen Sie!
ihr hattet gegessen	
sie hatten gegessen	

Present subjunctive

ich esse
du essest
er esse
wir essen
ihr esset
sie essen

fahren *to go, travel, drive*

Present participle *fahrend*
Past participle *gefahren*

Present indicative	Present subjunctive
ich fahre	ich fahre
du fährst	du fahrest
er fährt	er fahre
wir fahren	wir fahren
ihr fahrt	ihr fahret
sie fahren	sie fahren

Imperfect indicative	Imperfect subjunctive
ich fuhr	ich führe
du fuhrst	du führest
er fuhr	er führe
wir fuhren	wir führen
ihr fuhrt	ihr führet
sie fuhren	sie führen

Perfect indicative	Future indicative
ich bin/habe gefahren	ich werde fahren
du bist/hast gefahren	du wirst fahren
er ist/hat gefahren	er wird fahren
wir sind/haben gefahren	wir werden fahren
ihr seid/habt gefahren	ihr werdet fahren
sie sind/haben gefahren	sie werden fahren

Pluperfect indicative	Conditional
ich war/hatte gefahren	ich würde fahren
du warst/hattest gefahren	du würdest fahren
er war/hatte gefahren	er würde fahren
wir waren/hatten gefahren	wir würden fahren
ihr wart/hattet gefahren	ihr würdet fahren
sie waren/hatten gefahren	sie würden fahren

Imperative

fahr(e)!
fahren wir!
fahrt!
fahren Sie!

fallen *to fall*

Present participle *fallend*
Past participle *gefallen*

Present indicative	Imperfect subjunctive
ich falle	ich fiele
du fällst	du fielest
er fällt	er fiele
wir fallen	wir fielen
ihr fallt	ihr fielet
sie fallen	sie fielen

Imperfect indicative	Future indicative
ich fiel	ich werde fallen
du fielst	du wirst fallen
er fiel	er wird fallen
wir fielen	wir werden fallen
ihr fielt	ihr werdet fallen
sie fielen	sie werden fallen

Perfect indicative	Conditional
ich bin gefallen	ich würde fallen
du bist gefallen	du würdest fallen
er ist gefallen	er würde fallen
wir sind gefallen	wir würden fallen
ihr seid gefallen	ihr würdet fallen
sie sind gefallen	sie würden fallen

Pluperfect indicative	Imperative
ich war gefallen	fall(e)!
du warst gefallen	fallen wir!
er war gefallen	fallt!
wir waren gefallen	fallen Sie!
ihr wart gefallen	
sie waren gefallen	

Present subjunctive
ich falle
du fallest
er falle
wir fallen
ihr fallet
sie fallen

fangen *to catch*

Present participle *fangend*
Past participle *gefangen*

Present indicative	Imperfect subjunctive
ich fange	ich finge
du fängst	du fingest
er fängt	er finge
wir fangen	wir fingen
ihr fangt	ihr finget
sie fangen	sie fingen

Imperfect indicative	Future indicative
ich fing	ich werde fangen
du fingst	du wirst fangen
er fing	er wird fangen
wir fingen	wir werden fangen
ihr fingt	ihr werdet fangen
sie fingen	sie werden fangen

Perfect indicative	Conditional
ich habe gefangen	ich würde fangen
du hast gefangen	du würdest fangen
er hat gefangen	er würde fangen
wir haben gefangen	wir würden fangen
ihr habt gefangen	ihr würdet fangen
sie haben gefangen	sie würden fangen

Pluperfect indicative	Imperative
ich hatte gefangen	fang(e)!
du hattest gefangen	fangen wir!
er hatte gefangen	fangt!
wir hatten gefangen	fangen Sie!
ihr hattet gefangen	
sie hatten gefangen	

Present subjunctive
ich fange
du fangest
er fange
wir fangen
ihr fanget
sie fangen

fechten *to fence*

Present participle *fechtend*
Past participle *gefochten*

Present indicative	Imperfect subjunctive
ich fechte	ich föchte
du fichtst	du föchtest
er ficht	er föchte
wir fechten	wir föchten
ihr fechtet	ihr föchtet
sie fechten	sie föchten

Imperfect indicative	Future indicative
ich focht	ich werde fechten
du fochtest	du wirst fechten
er focht	er wird fechten
wir fochten	wir werden fechten
ihr fochtet	ihr werdet fechten
sie fochten	sie werden fechten

Perfect indicative	Conditional
ich habe gefochten	ich würde fechten
du hast gefochten	du würdest fechten
er hat gefochten	er würde fechten
wir haben gefochten	wir würden fechten
ihr habt gefochten	ihr würdet fechten
sie haben gefochten	sie würden fechten

Pluperfect indicative	Imperative
ich hatte gefochten	ficht!
du hattest gefochten	fechten wir!
er hatte gefochten	fechtet!
wir hatten gefochten	fechten Sie!
ihr hattet gefochten	
sie hatten gefochten	

Present subjunctive

ich fechte
du fechtest
er fechte
wir fechten
ihr fechtet
sie fechten

finden *to find*

Present participle *findend*
Past participle *gefunden*

Present indicative	Imperfect subjunctive
ich finde	ich fände
du findest	du fändest
er findet	er fände
wir finden	wir fänden
ihr findet	ihr fändet
sie finden	sie fänden

Imperfect indicative	Future indicative
ich fand	ich werde finden
du fand(e)st	du wirst finden
er fand	er wird finden
wir fanden	wir werden finden
ihr fandet	ihr werdet finden
sie fanden	sie werden finden

Perfect indicative	Conditional
ich habe gefunden	ich würde finden
du hast gefunden	du würdest finden
er hat gefunden	er würde finden
wir haben gefunden	wir würden finden
ihr habt gefunden	ihr würdet finden
sie haben gefunden	sie würden finden

Pluperfect indicative	Imperative
ich hatte gefunden	find(e)!
du hattest gefunden	finden wir!
er hatte gefunden	findet!
wir hatten gefunden	finden Sie!
ihr hattet gefunden	
sie hatten gefunden	

Present subjunctive

ich finde
du findest
er finde
wir finden
ihr findet
sie finden

fliegen *to fly*

Present participle *fliegend*
Past participle *geflogen*

Present indicative	**Present subjunctive**
ich fliege	ich fliege
du fliegst	du fliegest
er fliegt	er fliege
wir fliegen	wir fliegen
ihr fliegt	ihr flieget
sie fliegen	sie fliegen

Imperfect indicative	**Imperfect subjunctive**
ich flog	ich flöge
du flogst	du flögest
er flog	er flöge
wir flogen	wir flögen
ihr flogt	ihr flöget
sie flogen	sie flögen

Perfect indicative

ich bin/habe geflogen
du bist/hast geflogen
er ist/hat geflogen
wir sind/haben
　geflogen
ihr seid/habt geflogen
sie sind/haben
　geflogen

Pluperfect indicative

ich war/hatte geflogen
du warst/hattest
　geflogen
er war/hatte geflogen
wir waren/hatten
　geflogen
ihr wart/hattet
　geflogen
sie waren/hatten
　geflogen

Future indicative

ich werde fliegen
du wirst fliegen
er wird fliegen
wir werden fliegen
ihr werdet fliegen
sie werden fliegen

Conditional

ich würde fliegen
du würdest fliegen
er würde fliegen
wir würden fliegen
ihr würdet fliegen
sie würden fliegen

Imperative

flieg(e)!
fliegen wir!
fliegt!
fliegen Sie

fliehen *to flee*

Present participle *fliehend*
Past participle *geflohen*

Present indicative	**Present subjunctive**
ich fliehe	ich fliehe
du fliehst	du fliehest
er flieht	er fliehe
wir fliehen	wir fliehen
ihr flieht	ihr fliehet
sie fliehen	sie fliehen

Imperfect indicative	**Imperfect subjunctive**
ich floh	ich flöhe
du flohst	du flöhest
er floh	er flöhe
wir flohen	wir flöhen
ihr floht	ihr flöhet
sie flohen	sie flöhen

Perfect indicative

ich bin/habe geflohen
du bist/hast geflohen
er ist/hat geflohen
wir sind/haben
　geflohen
ihr seid/habt
　geflohen
sie sind/haben
　geflohen

Pluperfect indicative

ich war/hatte
　geflohen
du warst/hattest
　geflohen
er war/hatte geflohen
wir waren/hatten
　geflohen
ihr wart/hattet
　geflohen
sie waren/hatten
　geflohen

Future indicative

ich werde fliehen
du wirst fliehen
er wird fliehen
wir werden fliehen
ihr werdet fliehen
sie werden fliehen

Conditional

ich würde fliehen
du würdest fliehen
er würde fliehen
wir würden fliehen
ihr würdet fliehen
sie würden fliehen

Imperative

flieh(e)!
fliehen wir!
flieht!
fliehen Sie!

fließen *to flow*

Present participle *fließend*
Past participle *geflossen*

Present indicative	**Imperfect subjunctive**
ich fließe	ich flösse
du fließt	du flössest
er fließt	er flösse
wir fließen	wir flössen
ihr fließt	ihr flösset
sie fließen	sie flössen

Imperfect indicative	**Future indicative**
ich floß	ich werde fließen
du flossest	du wirst fließen
er floß	er wird fließen
wir floßen	wir werden fließen
ihr floßt	ihr werdet fließen
sie floßen	sie werden fließen

Perfect indicative	**Conditional**
ich bin geflossen	ich würde fließen
du bist geflossen	du würdest fließen
er ist geflossen	er würde fließen
wir sind geflossen	wir würden fließen
ihr seid geflossen	ihr würdet fließen
sie sind geflossen	sie würden fließen

Pluperfect indicative	**Imperative**
ich war geflossen	fließ(e)!
du warst geflossen	fließen wir!
er war geflossen	fließt!
wir waren geflossen	fließen Sie!
ihr wart geflossen	
sie waren geflossen	

Present subjunctive

ich fließe
du fließest
er fließe
wir fließen
ihr fließet
sie fließen

fragen *to ask*

Present participle *fragend*
Past participle *gefragt*

Present indicative	**Imperfect subjunctive**
ich frage	ich fragte
du fragst	du fragtest
er fragt	er fragte
wir fragen	wir fragten
ihr fragt	ihr fragtet
sie fragen	sie fragten

Imperfect indicative	**Future indicative**
ich fragte	ich werde fragen
du fragtest	du wirst fragen
er fragte	er wird fragen
wir fragten	wir werden fragen
ihr fragtet	ihr werdet fragen
sie fragten	sie werden fragen

Perfect indicative	**Conditional**
ich habe gefragt	ich würde fragen
du hast gefragt	du würdest fragen
er hat gefragt	er würde fragen
wir haben gefragt	wir würden fragen
ihr habt gefragt	ihr würdet fragen
sie haben gefragt	sie würden fragen

Pluperfect indicative	**Imperative**
ich hatte gefragt	frag(e)!
du hattest gefragt	fragen wir!
er hatte gefragt	fragt!
wir hatten gefragt	fragen Sie!
ihr hattet gefragt	
sie hatten gefragt	

Present subjunctive

ich frage
du fragest
er frage
wir fragen
ihr fraget
sie fragen

fressen *to eat (of animals)*

Present participle *fressend*
Past participle *gefressen*

Present indicative	**Imperfect subjunctive**
ich fresse	ich fräße
du frißt	du fräßest
er frißt	er fräße
wir fressen	wir fräßen
ihr freßt	ihr fräßet
sie fressen	sie fräßen

Imperfect indicative	**Future indicative**
ich fraß	ich werde fressen
du fraßest	du wirst fressen
er fraß	er wird fressen
wir fraßen	wir werden fressen
ihr fraßt	ihr werdet fressen
sie fraßen	sie werden fressen

Perfect indicative	**Conditional**
ich habe gefressen	ich würde fressen
du hast gefressen	du würdest fressen
er hat gefressen	er würde fressen
wir haben gefressen	wir würden fressen
ihr habt gefressen	ihr würdet fressen
sie haben gefressen	sie würden fressen

Pluperfect indicative	**Imperative**
ich hatte gefressen	friß!
du hattest gefressen	fressen wir!
er hatte gefressen	freßt!
wir hatten gefressen	fressen Sie!
ihr hattet gefressen	
sie hatten gefressen	

Present subjunctive

ich fresse
du fressest
er fresse
wir fressen
ihr fresset
sie fressen

sich freuen *to be pleased*

Present participle *freuend*
Past participle *gefreut*

Present indicative	**Imperfect subjunctive**
ich freue mich	ich freute mich
du freust dich	du freutest dich
er freut sich	er freute sich
wir freuen uns	wir freuten uns
ihr freut euch	ihr freutet euch
sie freuen sich	sie freuten sich

Imperfect indicative	**Future indicative**
ich freute mich	ich werde mich freuen
du freutest dich	du wirst dich freuen
er freute sich	er wird sich freuen
wir freuten uns	wir werden uns freuen
ihr freutet euch	ihr werdet euch freuen
sie freuten sich	sie werden sich freuen

Perfect indicative	**Conditional**
ich habe mich gefreut	ich würde mich freuen
du hast dich gefreut	du würdest dich freuen
er hat sich gefreut	er würde sich freuen
wir haben uns gefreut	wir würden uns freuen
ihr habt euch gefreut	ihr würdet euch freuen
sie haben sich gefreut	sie würden sich freuen

Pluperfect indicative	**Imperative**
ich hatte mich gefreut	freue dich!
du hattest dich gefreut	freuen wir uns!
er hatte sich gefreut	freut euch!
wir hatten uns gefreut	freuen Sie sich!
ihr hattet euch gefreut	
sie hatten sich gefreut	

Present subjunctive

ich freue mich
du freuest dich
er freue sich
wir freuen uns
ihr freuet euch
sie freuen sich

frieren *to freeze*

Present participle *frierend*
Past participle *gefroren*

Present indicative	**Present subjunctive**
ich friere	ich friere
du frierst	du frierest
er friert	er friere
wir frieren	wir frieren
ihr friert	ihr frieret
sie frieren	sie frieren

Imperfect indicative	**Imperfect subjunctive**
ich fror	ich fröre
du frorst	du frörest
er fror	er fröre
wir froren	wir frören
ihr frort	ihr fröret
sie froren	sie frören

Perfect indicative	**Future indicative**
ich bin/habe gefroren	ich werde frieren
du bist/hast gefroren	du wirst frieren
er ist/hat gefroren	er wird frieren
wir sind/haben gefroren	wir werden frieren
ihr seid/habt gefroren	ihr werdet frieren
sie sind/haben gefroren	sie werden frieren

Pluperfect indicative	**Conditional**
ich war/hatte gefroren	ich würde frieren
du warst/hattest gefroren	du würdest frieren
er war/hatte gefroren	er würde frieren
wir waren/hatten gefroren	wir würden frieren
ihr wart/hattet gefroren	ihr würdet frieren
sie waren/hatten gefroren	sie würden frieren

Imperative

frier(e)!
frieren wir!
friert!
frieren Sie!

führen *to lead*

Present participle *führend*
Past participle *geführt*

Present indicative	**Imperfect subjunctive**
ich führe	ich führte
du führst	du führtest
er führt	er führte
wir führen	wir führten
ihr führt	ihr führtet
sie führen	sie führten

Imperfect indicative	**Future indicative**
ich führte	ich werde führen
du führtest	du wirst führen
er führte	er wird führen
wir führten	wir werden führen
ihr führtet	ihr werdet führen
sie führten	sie werden führen

Perfect indicative	**Conditional**
ich habe geführt	ich würde führen
du hast geführt	du würdest führen
er hat geführt	er würde führen
wir haben geführt	wir würden führen
ihr habt geführt	ihr würdet führen
sie haben geführt	sie würden führen

Pluperfect indicative	**Imperative**
ich hatte geführt	führ(e)!
du hattest geführt	führen wir!
er hatte geführt	führt!
wir hatten geführt	führen Sie!
ihr hattet geführt	
sie hatten geführt	

Present subjunctive

ich führe
du führest
er führe
wir führen
ihr führet
sie führen

gebären *to give birth*

Present participle *gebärend*
Past participle *geboren*

Present indicative	**Imperfect subjunctive**
ich gebäre	ich gebäre
du gebierst	du gebärest
er gebiert	er gebäre
wir gebären	wir gebären
ihr gebärt	ihr gebäret
sie gebären	sie gebären

Imperfect indicative	**Future indicative**
ich gebar	ich werde gebären
du gebarst	du wirst gebären
er gebar	er wird gebären
wir gebaren	wir werden gebären
ihr gebart	ihr werdet gebären
sie gebaren	sie werden gebären

Perfect indicative	**Conditional**
ich habe geboren	ich würde gebären
du hast geboren	du würdest gebären
er hat geboren	er würde gebären
wir haben geboren	wir würden gebären
ihr habt geboren	ihr würdet gebären
sie haben geboren	sie würden gebären

Pluperfect indicative	**Imperative**
ich hatte geboren	gebier!
du hattest geboren	gebären wir!
er hatte geboren	gebärt!
wir hatten geboren	gebären Sie!
ihr hattet geboren	
sie hatten geboren	

Present subjunctive

ich gebäre
du gebärest
er gebäre
wir gebären
ihr gebäret
sie gebären

geben *to give*

Present participle *gebend*
Past participle *gegeben*

Present indicative	**Imperfect subjunctive**
ich gebe	ich gäbe
du gibst	du gäbest
er gibt	er gäbe
wir geben	wir gäben
ihr gebt	ihr gäbet
sie geben	sie gäben

Imperfect indicative	**Future indicative**
ich gab	ich werde geben
du gabst	du wirst geben
er gab	er wird geben
wir gaben	wir werden geben
ihr gabt	ihr werdet geben
sie gaben	sie werden geben

Perfect indicative	**Conditional**
ich habe gegeben	ich würde geben
du hast gegeben	du würdest geben
er hat gegeben	er würde geben
wir haben gegeben	wir würden geben
ihr habt gegeben	ihr würdet geben
sie haben gegeben	sie würden geben

Pluperfect indicative	**Imperative**
ich hatte gegeben	gib!
du hattest gegeben	geben wir!
er hatte gegeben	gebt!
wir hatten gegeben	geben Sie!
ihr hattet gegeben	
sie hatten gegeben	

Present subjunctive

ich gebe
du gebest
er gebe
wir geben
ihr gebet
sie geben

gedeihen *to thrive*

Present participle *gedeihend*
Past participle *gediehen*

Present indicative	Imperfect subjunctive
ich gedeihe	ich gediehe
du gedeihst	du gediehest
er gedeiht	er gediehe
wir gedeihen	wir gediehen
ihr gedeiht	ihr gediehet
sie gedeihen	sie gediehen

Imperfect indicative	Future indicative
ich gedieh	ich werde gedeihen
du gediehst	du wirst gedeihen
er gedieh	er wird gedeihen
wir gediehen	wir werden gedeihen
ihr gedieht	ihr werdet gedeihen
sie gediehen	sie werden gedeihen

Perfect indicative	Conditional
ich bin gediehen	ich würde gedeihen
du bist gediehen	du würdest gedeihen
er ist gediehen	er würde gedeihen
wir sind gediehen	wir würden gedeihen
ihr seid gediehen	ihr würdet gedeihen
sie sind gediehen	sie würden gedeihen

Pluperfect indicative	Imperative
ich war gediehen	gedeih(e)!
du warst gediehen	gedeihen wir!
er war gediehen	gedeiht!
wir waren gediehen	gedeihen Sie!
ihr wart gediehen	
sie waren gediehen	

Present subjunctive

ich gedeihe
du gedeihest
er gedeihe
wir gedeihen
ihr gedeihet
sie gedeihen

gehen *to go*

Present participle *gehend*
Past participle *gegangen*

Present indicative	Imperfect subjunctive
ich gehe	ich ginge
du gehst	du gingest
er geht	er ginge
wir gehen	wir gingen
ihr geht	ihr ginget
sie gehen	sie gingen

Imperfect indicative	Future indicative
ich ging	ich werde gehen
du gingst	du wirst gehen
er ging	er wird gehen
wir gingen	wir werden gehen
ihr gingt	ihr werdet gehen
sie gingen	sie werden gehen

Perfect indicative	Conditional
ich bin gegangen	ich würde gehen
du bist gegangen	du würdest gehen
er ist gegangen	er würde gehen
wir sind gegangen	wir würden gehen
ihr seid gegangen	ihr würdet gehen
sie sind gegangen	sie würden gehen

Pluperfect indicative	Imperative
ich war gegangen	geh(e)!
du warst gegangen	gehen wir!
er war gegangen	geht!
wir waren gegangen	gehen Sie!
ihr wart gegangen	
sie waren gegangen	

Present subjunctive

ich gehe
du gehest
er gehe
wir gehen
ihr gehet
sie gehen

gelten *to be valid*

Present participle *geltend*
Past participle *gegolten*

Present indicative	**Imperfect subjunctive**
ich gelte	ich gälte
du giltst	du gältest
er gilt	er gälte
wir gelten	wir gälten
ihr geltet	ihr gältet
sie gelten	sie gälten

Imperfect indicative	**Future indicative**
ich galt	ich werde gelten
du galt(e)st	du wirst gelten
er galt	er wird gelten
wir galten	wir werden gelten
ihr galtet	ihr werdet gelten
sie galten	sie werden gelten

Perfect indicative	**Conditional**
ich habe gegolten	ich würde gelten
du hast gegolten	du würdest gelten
er hat gegolten	er würde gelten
wir haben gegolten	wir würden gelten
ihr habt gegolten	ihr würdet gelten
sie haben gegolten	sie würden gelten

Pluperfect indicative	**Imperative**
ich hatte gegolten	gilt!
du hattest gegolten	gelten wir!
er hatte gegolten	geltet!
wir hatten gegolten	gelten Sie!
ihr hattet gegolten	
sie hatten gegolten	

Present subjunctive
ich gelte
du geltest
er gelte
wir gelten
ihr geltet
sie gelten

genesen *to recover*

Present participle *genesend*
Past participle *genesen*

Present indicative	**Imperfect subjunctive**
ich genese	ich genäse
du genest	du genäsest
er genest	er genäse
wir genesen	wir genäsen
ihr genest	ihr genäset
sie genesen	sie genäsen

Imperfect indicative	**Future indicative**
ich genas	ich werde genesen
du genasest	du wirst genesen
er genas	er wird genesen
wir genasen	wir werden genesen
ihr genast	ihr werdet genesen
sie genasen	sie werden genesen

Perfect indicative	**Conditional**
ich bin genesen	ich würde genesen
du bist genesen	du würdest genesen
er ist genesen	er würde genesen
wir sind genesen	wir würden genesen
ihr seid genesen	ihr würdet genesen
sie sind genesen	sie würden genesen

Pluperfect indicative	**Imperative**
ich war genesen	genese!
du warst genesen	genesen wir!
er war genesen	genest!
wir waren genesen	genesen Sie!
ihr wart genesen	
sie waren genesen	

Present subjunctive
ich genese
du genesest
er genese
wir genesen
ihr geneset
sie genesen

genießen *to enjoy*

Present participle *genießend*
Past participle *genossen*

Present indicative	**Imperfect subjunctive**
ich genieße	ich genösse
du genießest	du genössest
er genießet	er genösse
wir genießen	wir genössen
ihr genießet	ihr genösset
sie genießen	sie genössen

Imperfect indicative	**Future indicative**
ich genoß	ich werde genießen
du genossest	du wirst genießen
er genoß	er wird genießen
wir genossen	wir werden genießen
ihr genoßt	ihr werdet genießen
sie genossen	sie werden genießen

Perfect indicative	**Conditional**
ich habe genossen	ich würde genießen
du hast genossen	du würdest genießen
er hat genossen	er würde genießen
wir haben genossen	wir würden genießen
ihr habt genossen	ihr würdet genießen
sie haben genossen	sie würden genießen

Pluperfect indicative	**Imperative**
ich hatte genossen	genieß(e)!
du hattest genossen	genießen wir!
er hatte genossen	genießt!
wir hatten genossen	genießen Sie!
ihr hattet genossen	
sie hatten genossen	

Present subjunctive

ich genieße
du genießest
er genieße
wir genießen
ihr genießet
sie genießen

geraten *to get (into debt, etc); turn out*

Present participle *geratend*
Past participle *geraten*

Present indicative	**Present subjunctive**
ich gerate	ich gerate
du gerätst	du geratest
er gerät	er gerate
wir geraten	wir geraten
ihr geratet	ihr geratet
sie geraten	sie geraten

Imperfect indicative	**Imperfect subjunctive**
ich geriet	ich geriete
du geriet(e)st	du gerietest
er geriet	er geriete
wir gerieten	wir gerieten
ihr gerietet	ihr gerietet
sie gerieten	sie gerieten

Perfect indicative	**Future indicative**
ich bin geraten	ich werde geraten
du bist geraten	du wirst geraten
er ist geraten	er wird geraten
wir sind geraten	wir werden geraten
ihr seid geraten	ihr werdet geraten
sie sind geraten	sie werden geraten

Pluperfect indicative	**Conditional**
ich war geraten	ich würde geraten
du warst geraten	du würdest geraten
er war geraten	er würde geraten
wir waren geraten	wir würden geraten
ihr wart geraten	ihr würdet geraten
sie waren geraten	sie würden geraten

Imperative

gerat(e)!
geraten wir!
geratet!
geraten Sie!

gewinnen *to win*

Present participle *gewinnend*
Past participle *gewonnen*

Present indicative	**Imperfect subjunctive**
ich gewinne	ich gewönne
du gewinnst	du gewönnest
er gewinnt	er gewönne
wir gewinnen	wir gewönnen
ihr gewinnt	ihr gewönnet
sie gewinnen	sie gewönnen

Imperfect indicative	**Future indicative**
ich gewann	ich werde gewinnen
du gewannst	du wirst gewinnen
er gewann	er wird gewinnen
wir gewannen	wir werden gewinnen
ihr gewannt	ihr werdet gewinnen
sie gewannen	sie werden gewinnen

Perfect indicative	**Conditional**
ich habe gewonnen	ich würde gewinnen
du hast gewonnen	du würdest gewinnen
er hat gewonnen	er würde gewinnen
wir haben gewonnen	wir würden gewinnen
ihr habt gewonnen	ihr würdet gewinnen
sie haben gewonnen	sie würden gewinnen

Pluperfect indicative	**Imperative**
ich hatte gewonnen	gewinn(e)!
du hattest gewonnen	gewinnen wir!
er hatte gewonnen	gewinnt!
wir hatten gewonnen	gewinnen Sie!
ihr hattet gewonnen	
sie hatten gewonnen	

Present subjunctive

ich gewinne
du gewinnest
er gewinne
wir gewinnen
ihr gewinnet
sie gewinnen

gießen *to pour*

Present participle *gießend*
Past participle *gegossen*

Present indicative	**Imperfect subjunctive**
ich gieße	ich gösse
du gießt	du gössest
er gießt	er gösse
wir gießen	wir gössen
ihr gießt	ihr gösset
sie gießen	sie gössen

Imperfect indicative	**Future indicative**
ich goß	ich werde gießen
du gossest	du wirst gießen
er goß	er wird gießen
wir gossen	wir werden gießen
ihr goßt	ihr werdet gießen
sie gossen	sie werden gießen

Perfect indicative	**Conditional**
ich habe gegossen	ich würde gießen
du hast gegossen	du würdest gießen
er hat gegossen	er würde gießen
wir haben gegossen	wir würden gießen
ihr habt gegossen	ihr würdet gießen
sie haben gegossen	sie würden gießen

Pluperfect indicative	**Imperative**
ich hatte gegossen	gieß(e)!
du hattest gegossen	gießen wir!
er hatte gegossen	gießt!
wir hatten gegossen	gießen Sie!
ihr hattet gegossen	
sie hatten gegossen	

Present subjunctive

ich gieße
du gießest
er gieße
wir gießen
ihr gießet
sie gießen

gleichen *to resemble*

Present participle *gleichend*
Past participle *geglichen*

Present indicative	**Imperfect subjunctive**
ich gleiche	ich gliche
du gleichst	du glichest
er gleicht	er gliche
wir gleichen	wir glichen
ihr gleicht	ihr glichet
sie gleichen	sie glichen

Imperfect indicative	**Future indicative**
ich glich	ich werde gleichen
du glichst	du wirst gleichen
er glich	er wird gleichen
wir glichen	wir werden gleichen
ihr glicht	ihr werdet gleichen
sie glichen	sie werden gleichen

Perfect indicative	**Conditional**
ich habe geglichen	ich würde gleichen
du hast geglichen	du würdest gleichen
er hat geglichen	er würde gleichen
wir haben geglichen	wir würden gleichen
ihr habt geglichen	ihr würdet gleichen
sie haben geglichen	sie würden gleichen

Pluperfect indicative	**Imperative**
ich hatte geglichen	gleich(e)!
du hattest geglichen	gleichen wir!
er hatte geglichen	gleicht!
wir hatten geglichen	gleichen Sie!
ihr hattet geglichen	
sie hatten geglichen	

Present subjunctive

ich gleiche
du gleichest
er gleiche
wir gleichen
ihr gleichet
sie gleichen

gleiten *to glide, slide*

Present participle *gleitend*
Past participle *geglitten*

Present indicative	**Imperfect subjunctive**
ich gleite	ich glitte
du gleitest	du glittest
er gleitet	er glitte
wir gleiten	wir glitten
ihr gleitet	ihr glittet
sie gleiten	sie glitten

Imperfect indicative	**Future indicative**
ich glitt	ich werde gleiten
du glitt(e)st	du wirst gleiten
er glitt	er wird gleiten
wir glitten	wir werden gleiten
ihr glittet	ihr werdet gleiten
sie glitten	sie werden gleiten

Perfect indicative	**Conditional**
ich bin geglitten	ich würde gleiten
du bist geglitten	du würdest gleiten
er ist geglitten	er würde gleiten
wir sind geglitten	wir würden gleiten
ihr seid geglitten	ihr würdet gleiten
sie sind geglitten	sie würden gleiten

Pluperfect indicative	**Imperative**
ich war geglitten	gleit(e)!
du warst geglitten	gleiten wir!
er war geglitten	gleitet!
wir waren geglitten	gleiten Sie!
ihr wart geglitten	
sie waren geglitten	

Present subjunctive

ich gleite
du gleitest
er gleite
wir gleiten
ihr gleitet
sie gleiten

graben *to dig*

Present participle *grabend*
Past participle *gegraben*

Present indicative	**Imperfect subjunctive**
ich grabe	ich grübe
du gräbst	du grübest
er gräbt	er grübe
wir graben	wir grüben
ihr grabt	ihr grübet
sie graben	sie grüben

Imperfect indicative	**Future indicative**
ich grub	ich werde graben
du grubst	du wirst graben
er grub	er wird graben
wir gruben	wir werden graben
ihr grubt	ihr werdet graben
sie gruben	sie werden graben

Perfect indicative	**Conditional**
ich habe gegraben	ich würde graben
du hast gegraben	du würdest graben
er hat gegraben	er würde graben
wir haben gegraben	wir würden graben
ihr habt gegraben	ihr würdet graben
sie haben gegraben	sie würden graben

Pluperfect indicative	**Imperative**
ich hatte gegraben	grab(e)!
du hattest gegraben	graben wir!
er hatte gegraben	grabt!
wir hatten gegraben	graben Sie!
ihr hattet gegraben	
sie hatten gegraben	

Present subjunctive

ich grabe
du grabest
er grabe
wir graben
ihr grabet
sie graben

greifen *to grab, sieze*

Present participle *greifend*
Past participle *gegriffen*

Present indicative	**Imperfect subjunctive**
ich greife	ich griffe
du greifst	du griffest
er greift	er griffe
wir greifen	wir griffen
ihr greift	ihr griffet
sie greifen	sie griffen

Imperfect indicative	**Future indicative**
ich griff	ich werde greifen
du griffst	du wirst greifen
er griff	er wird greifen
wir griffen	wir werden greifen
ihr grifft	ihr werdet greifen
sie griffen	sie werden greifen

Perfect indicative	**Conditional**
ich habe gegriffen	ich würde greifen
du hast gegriffen	du würdest greifen
er hat gegriffen	er würde greifen
wir haben gegriffen	wir würden greifen
ihr habt gegriffen	ihr würdet greifen
sie haben gegriffen	sie würden greifen

Pluperfect indicative	**Imperative**
ich hatte gegriffen	greif(e)!
du hattest gegriffen	greifen wir!
er hatte gegriffen	greift!
wir hatten gegriffen	greifen Sie!
ihr hattet gegriffen	
sie hatten gegriffen	

Present subjunctive

ich greife
du greifest
er greife
wir greifen
ihr greifet
sie greifen

haben *to have*

Present participle *habend*
Past participle *gehabt*

Present indicative	**Imperfect subjunctive**
ich habe	ich hätte
du hast	du hättest
er hat	er hätte
wir haben	wir hätten
ihr habt	ihr hättet
sie haben	sie hätten

Imperfect indicative	**Future indicative**
ich hatte	ich werde haben
du hattest	du wirst haben
er hatte	er wird haben
wir hatten	wir werden haben
ihr hattet	ihr werdet haben
sie hatten	sie werden haben

Perfect indicative	**Conditional**
ich habe gehabt	ich würde haben
du hast gehabt	du würdest haben
er hat gehabt	er würde haben
wir haben gehabt	wir würden haben
ihr habt gehabt	ihr würdet haben
sie haben gehabt	sie würden haben

Pluperfect indicative	**Imperative**
ich hatte gehabt	habe!
du hattest gehabt	haben wir!
er hatte gehabt	habt!
wir hatten gehabt	haben Sie!
ihr hattet gehabt	
sie hatten gehabt	

Present subjunctive

ich habe
du habest
er habe
wir haben
ihr habet
sie haben

halten *to hold*

Present participle *haltend*
Past participle *gehalten*

Present indicative	**Imperfect subjunctive**
ich halte	ich hielte
du hältst	du hieltest
er hält	er hielte
wir halten	wir hielten
ihr haltet	ihr hieltet
sie halten	sie hielten

Imperfect indicative	**Future indicative**
ich hielt	ich werde halten
du hielt(e)st	du wirst halten
er hielt	er wird halten
wir hielten	wir werden halten
ihr hieltet	ihr werdet halten
sie hielten	sie werden halten

Perfect indicative	**Conditional**
ich habe gehalten	ich würde halten
du hast gehalten	du würdest halten
er hat gehalten	er würde halten
wir haben gehalten	wir würden halten
ihr habt gehalten	ihr würdet halten
sie haben gehalten	sie würden halten

Pluperfect indicative	**Imperative**
ich hatte gehalten	halt(e)!
du hattest gehalten	halten wir!
er hatte gehalten	haltet!
wir hatten gehalten	halten Sie!
ihr hattet gehalten	
sie hatten gehalten	

Present subjunctive

ich halte
du haltest
er halte
wir halten
ihr haltet
sie halten

hängen *to hang*

Present participle *hängend*
Past participle *gehangen*

Present indicative	Imperfect subjunctive
ich hänge	ich hinge
du hängst	du hingest
er hängt	er hinge
wir hängen	wir hingen
ihr hängt	ihr hinget
sie hängen	sie hingen

Imperfect indicative	Future indicative
ich hing	ich werde hängen
du hingst	du wirst hängen
er hing	er wird hängen
wir hingen	wir werden hängen
ihr hingt	ihr werdet hängen
sie hingen	sie werden hängen

Perfect indicative	Conditional
ich habe gehangen	ich würde hängen
du hast gehangen	du würdest hängen
er hat gehangen	er würde hängen
wir haben gehangen	wir würden hängen
ihr habt gehangen	ihr würdet hängen
sie haben gehangen	sie würden hängen

Pluperfect indicative	Imperative
ich hatte gehangen	häng(e)!
du hattest gehangen	hängen wir!
er hatte gehangen	hängt!
wir hatten gehangen	hängen Sie!
ihr hattet gehangen	
sie hatten gehangen	

Present subjunctive

ich hänge
du hängest
er hänge
wir hängen
ihr hänget
sie hängen

hauen *to hew, cut*

Present participle *hauend*
Past participle *gehauen*

Present indicative	Imperfect subjunctive
ich haue	ich hiebe
du haust	du hiebest
er haut	er hiebe
wir hauen	wir hieben
ihr haut	ihr hiebet
sie hauen	sie hieben

Imperfect indicative	Future indicative
ich hieb	ich werde hauen
du hiebst	du wirst hauen
er hieb	er wird hauen
wir hieben	wir werden hauen
ihr hiebt	ihr werdet hauen
sie hieben	sie werden hauen

Perfect indicative	Conditional
ich habe gehauen	ich würde hauen
du hast gehauen	du würdest hauen
er hat gehauen	er würde hauen
wir haben gehauen	wir würden hauen
ihr habt gehauen	ihr würdet hauen
sie haben gehauen	sie würden hauen

Pluperfect indicative	Imperative
ich hatte gehauen	hau(e)!
du hattest gehauen	hauen wir!
er hatte gehauen	haut!
wir hatten gehauen	hauen Sie!
ihr hattet gehauen	
sie hatten gehauen	

Present subjunctive

ich haue
du hauest
er haue
wir hauen
ihr hauet
sie hauen

heben *to lift*

Present participle *hebend*
Past participle *gehoben*

Present indicative	**Imperfect subjunctive**
ich hebe	ich höbe
du hebst	du höbest
er hebt	er höbe
wir heben	wir höben
ihr hebt	ihr höbet
sie heben	sie höben

Imperfect indicative	**Future indicative**
ich hob	ich werde heben
du hobst	du wirst heben
er hob	er wird heben
wir hoben	wir werden heben
ihr hobt	ihr werdet heben
sie hoben	sie werden heben

Perfect indicative	**Conditional**
ich habe gehoben	ich würde heben
du hast gehoben	du würdest heben
er hat gehoben	er würde heben
wir haben gehoben	wir würden heben
ihr habt gehoben	ihr würdet heben
sie haben gehoben	sie würden heben

Pluperfect indicative	**Imperative**
ich hatte gehoben	heb(e)!
du hattest gehoben	heben wir!
er hatte gehoben	hebt!
wir hatten gehoben	heben Sie!
ihr hattet gehoben	
sie hatten gehoben	

Present subjunctive

ich hebe
du hebest
er hebe
wir heben
ihr hebet
sie heben

heißen *to be called*

Present participle *heißend*
Past participle *geheißen*

Present indicative	**Imperfect subjunctive**
ich heiße	ich hieße
du heißt	du hießest
er heißt	er hieße
wir heißen	wir hießen
ihr heißt	ihr hießet
sie heißen	sie hießen

Imperfect indicative	**Future indicative**
ich hieß	ich werde heißen
du hießest	du wirst heißen
er hieß	er wird heißen
wir hießen	wir werden heißen
ihr hießt	ihr werdet heißen
sie hießen	sie werden heißen

Perfect indicative	**Conditional**
ich habe geheißen	ich würde heißen
du hast geheißen	du würdest heißen
er hat geheißen	er würde heißen
wir haben geheißen	wir würden heißen
ihr habt geheißen	ihr würdet heißen
sie haben geheißen	sie würden heißen

Pluperfect indicative	**Imperative**
ich hatte geheißen	heiß(e)!
du hattest geheißen	heißen wir!
er hatte geheißen	heißt!
wir hatten geheißen	heißen Sie!
ihr hattet geheißen	
sie hatten geheißen	

Present subjunctive

ich heiße
du heißest
er heiße
wir heißen
ihr heißet
sie heißen

helfen *to help*

Present participle *helfend*
Past participle *geholfen*

Present indicative	**Imperfect subjunctive**
ich helfe	ich hülfe
du hilfst	du hülfest
er hilft	er hülfe
wir helfen	wir hülfen
ihr helft	ihr hülfet
sie helfen	sie hülfen

Imperfect indicative	**Future indicative**
ich half	ich werde helfen
du halfst	du wirst helfen
er half	er wird helfen
wir halfen	wir werden helfen
ihr halft	ihr werdet helfen
sie halfen	sie werden helfen

Perfect indicative	**Conditional**
ich habe geholfen	ich würde helfen
du hast geholfen	du würdest helfen
er hat geholfen	er würde helfen
wir haben geholfen	wir würden helfen
ihr habt geholfen	ihr würdet helfen
sie haben geholfen	sie würden helfen

Pluperfect indicative	**Imperative**
ich hatte geholfen	hilf!
du hattest geholfen	helfen wir!
er hatte geholfen	helft!
wir hatten geholfen	helfen Sie!
ihr hattet geholfen	
sie hatten geholfen	

Present subjunctive

ich helfe
du helfest
er helfe
wir helfen
ihr helfet
sie helfen

holen *to fetch*

Present participle *holend*
Past participle *geholt*

Present indicative	**Imperfect subjunctive**
ich hole	ich holte
du holst	du holtest
er holt	er holte
wir holen	wir holten
ihr holt	ihr holtet
sie holen	sie holten

Imperfect indicative	**Future indicative**
ich holte	ich werde holen
du holtest	du wirst holen
er holte	er wird holen
wir holten	wir werden holen
ihr holtet	ihr werdet holen
sie holten	sie werden holen

Perfect indicative	**Conditional**
ich habe geholt	ich würde holen
du hast geholt	du würdest holen
er hat geholt	er würde holen
wir haben geholt	wir würden holen
ihr habt geholt	ihr würdet holen
sie haben geholt	sie würden holen

Pluperfect indicative	**Imperative**
ich hatte geholt	hol(e)!
du hattest geholt	holen wir!
er hatte geholt	holt!
wir hatten geholt	holen Sie!
ihr hattet geholt	
sie hatten geholt	

Present subjunctive

ich hole
du holest
er hole
wir holen
ihr holet
sie holen

kennen *to know* (*by acquaintance*)

Present participle *kennend*
Past participle *gekannt*

Present indicative	Present subjunctive
ich kenne	ich kenne
du kennst	du kennest
er kennt	er kenne
wir kennen	wir kennen
ihr kennt	ihr kennet
sie kennen	sie kennen

Imperfect indicative	Imperfect subjunctive
ich kannte	ich kennte
du kanntest	du kenntest
er kannte	er kennte
wir kannten	wir kennten
ihr kanntet	ihr kenntet
sie kannten	sie kennten

Perfect indicative	Future indicative
ich habe gekannt	ich werde kennen
du hast gekannt	du wirst kennen
er hat gekannt	er wird kennen
wir haben gekannt	wir werden kennen
ihr habt gekannt	ihr werdet kennen
sie haben gekannt	sie werden kennen

Pluperfect indicative	Conditional
ich hatte gekannt	ich würde kennen
du hattest gekannt	du würdest kennen
er hatte gekannt	er würde kennen
wir hatten gekannt	wir würden kennen
ihr hattet gekannt	ihr würdet kennen
sie hatten gekannt	sie würden kennen

Imperative

kenn(e)!
kennen wir!
kennt!
kennen Sie!

klimmen *to climb*

Present participle *klimmend*
Past participle *geklommen*

Present indicative	Present subjunctive
ich klimme	ich klimme
du klimmst	du klimmest
er klimmt	er klimme
wir klimmen	wir klimmen
ihr klimmt	ihr klimmet
sie klimmen	sie klimmen

Imperfect indicative	Imperfect subjunctive
ich klomm	ich klömme
du klommst	du klömmest
er klomm	er klömme
wir klommen	wir klömmen
ihr klommt	ihr klömmet
sie klommen	sie klömmen

Perfect indicative	Future indicative
ich bin geklommen	ich werde klimmen
du bist geklommen	du wirst klimmen
er ist geklommen	er wird klimmen
wir sind geklommen	wir werden klimmen
ihr seid geklommen	ihr werdet klimmen
sie sind geklommen	sie werden klimmen

Pluperfect indicative	Conditional
ich war geklommen	ich würde klimmen
du warst geklommen	du würdest klimmen
er war geklommen	er würde klimmen
wir waren geklommen	wir würden klimmen
ihr wart geklommen	ihr würdet klimmen
sie waren geklommen	sie würden klimmen

Imperative

klimm(e)!
klimmen wir!
klimmt!
klimmen Sie!

klingen *to sound*

Present participle *klingend*
Past participle *beklungen*

Present indicative	**Imperfect subjunctive**
ich klinge	ich klänge
du klingst	du klängest
er klingt	er klänge
wir klingen	wir klängen
ihr klingt	ihr klänget
sie klingen	sie klängen

Imperfect indicative	**Future indicative**
ich klang	ich werde klingen
du klangst	du wirst klingen
er klang	er wird klingen
wir klangen	wir werden klingen
ihr klangt	ihr werdet klingen
sie klangen	sie werden klingen

Perfect indicative	**Conditional**
ich habe geklungen	ich würde klingen
du hast geklungen	du würdest klingen
er hat geklungen	er würde klingen
wir haben geklungen	wir würden klingen
ihr habt geklungen	ihr würdet klingen
sie haben geklungen	sie würden klingen

Pluperfect indicative	**Imperative**
ich hatte geklungen	kling(e)!
du hattest geklungen	klingen wir!
er hatte geklungen	klingt!
wir hatten geklungen	klingen Sie!
ihr hattet geklungen	
sie hatten geklungen	

Present subjunctive

ich klinge
du klingest
er klinge
wir klingen
ihr klinget
sie kling en

kneifen *to pinch*

Present participle *kneifend*
Past participle *gekniffen*

Present indicative	**Imperfect subjunctive**
ich kneife	ich kniffe
du kneifst	du kniffest
er kneift	er kniffe
wir kneifen	wir kniffen
ihr kneift	ihr kniffet
sie kneifen	sie kniffen

Imperfect indicative	**Future indicative**
ich kniff	ich werde kneifen
du kniffst	du wirst kneifen
er kniff	er wird kneifen
wir kniffen	wir werden kneifen
ihr knifft	ihr werdet kneifen
sie kniffen	sie werden kneifen

Perfect indicative	**Conditional**
ich habe gekniffen	ich würde kneifen
du hast gekniffen	du würdest kneifen
er hat gekniffen	er würde kneifen
wir haben gekniffen	wir würden kneifen
ihr habt gekniffen	ihr würdet kneifen
sie haben gekniffen	sie würden kneifen

Pluperfect indicative	**Imperative**
ich hatte gekniffen	kneif(e)!
du hattest gekniffen	kneifen wir!
er hatte gekniffen	kneift!
wir hatten gekniffen	kneifen Sie!
ihr hattet gekniffen	
sie hatten gekniffen	

Present subjunctive

ich kneife
du kneifest
er kneife
wir kneifen
ihr kneifet
sie kneifen

kommen *to come*

Present participle *kommend*
Past participle *gekommen*

Present indicative	**Imperfect subjunctive**
ich komme	ich käme
du kommst	du kämest
er kommt	er käme
wir kommen	wir kämen
ihr kommt	ihr kämet
sie kommen	sie kämen

Imperfect indicative	**Future indicative**
ich kam	ich werde kommen
du kamst	du wirst kommen
er kam	er wird kommen
wir kamen	wir werden kommen
ihr kamt	ihr werdet kommen
sie kamen	sie werden kommen

Perfect indicative	**Conditional**
ich bin gekommen	ich würde kommen
du bist gekommen	du würdest kommen
er ist gekommen	er würde kommen
wir sind gekommen	wir würden kommen
ihr seid gekommen	ihr würdet kommen
sie sind gekommen	sie würden kommen

Pluperfect indicative	**Imperative**
ich war gekommen	komm(e)!
du warst gekommen	kommen wir!
er war gekommen	kommt!
wir waren gekommen	kommen Sie!
ihr wart gekommen	
sie waren gekommen	

Present subjunctive

ich komme
du kommest
er komme
wir kommen
ihr kommet
sie kommen

können *to be able to, can, may*

Present participle *könnend*
Past participle *gekonnt/können**

Present indicative	**Present subjunctive**
ich kann	ich könne
du kannst	du könnest
er kann	er könne
wir können	wir können
ihr könnt	ihr könnet
sie können	sie können

Imperfect indicative	**Imperfect subjunctive**
ich konnte	ich könnte
du konntest	du könntest
er konnte	er könnte
wir konnten	wir könnten
ihr konntet	ihr könntet
sie konnten	sie könnten

Perfect indicative	**Future indicative**
ich habe gekonnt	ich werde können
du hast gekonnt	du wirst können
er hat gekonnt	er wird können
wir haben gekonnt	wir werden können
ihr habt gekonnt	ihr werdet können
sie haben gekonnt	sie werden können

Pluperfect indicative	**Conditional**
ich hatte gekonnt	ich würde können
du hattest gekonnt	du würdest können
er hatte gekonnt	er würde können
wir hatten gekonnt	wir würden können
ihr hattet gekonnt	ihr würdet können
sie hatten gekonnt	sie würden können

*können *is used when preceded by an infinitive*

kriechen *to creep, crawl*

Present participle *kriechend*
Past participle *gekrochen*

Present indicative	Imperfect subjunctive
ich krieche	ich kröche
du kriechst	du kröchest
er kriecht	er kröche
wir kriechen	wir kröchen
ihr kriecht	ihr kröchet
sie kriechen	sie kröchen

Imperfect indicative	Future indicative
ich kroch	ich werde kriechen
du krochst	du wirst kriechen
er kroch	er wird kriechen
wir krochen	wir werden kriechen
ihr krocht	ihr werdet kriechen
sie krochen	sie werden kriechen

Perfect indicative	Conditional
ich bin gekrochen	
du bist gekrochen	ich würde kriechen
er ist gekrochen	du würdest kriechen
wir sind gekrochen	er würde kriechen
ihr seid gekrochen	wir würden kriechen
sie sind gekrochen	ihr würdet kriechen
	sie würden kriechen

Pluperfect indicative	Imperative
ich war gekrochen	
du warst gekrochen	kriech!
er war gekrochen	kriechen wir!
wir waren gekrochen	kriecht!
ihr wart gekrochen	kriechen Sie!
sie waren gekrochen	

Present subjunctive

ich krieche
du kriechest
er krieche
wir kriechen
ihr kriechet
sie kriechen

lächeln *to smile*

Present participle *lächelnd*
Past participle *gelächelt*

Present indicative	Imperfect subjunctive
ich lächle	ich lächelte
du lächelst	du lächeltest
er lächelt	er lächelte
wir lächeln	wir lächelten
ihr lächelt	ihr lächeltet
sie lächeln	sie lächelten

Imperfect indicative	Future indicative
ich lächelte	ich werde lächeln
du lächeltest	du wirst lächeln
er lächelte	er wird lächeln
wir lächelten	wir werden lächeln
ihr lächeltet	ihr werdet lächeln
sie lächelten	sie werden lächeln

Perfect indicative	Conditional
ich habe gelächelt	ich würde lächeln
du hast gelächelt	du würdest lächeln
er hat gelächelt	er würde lächeln
wir haben gelächelt	wir würden lächeln
ihr habt gelächelt	ihr würdet lächeln
sie haben gelächelt	sie würden lächeln

Pluperfect indicative	Imperative
ich hatte gelächelt	lächle!
du hattest gelächelt	lächeln wir!
er hatte gelächelt	lächelt!
wir hatten gelächelt	lächeln Sie!
ihr hattet gelächelt	
sie hatten gelächelt	

Present subjunctive

ich lächle
du lächlest
er lächle
wir lächeln
ihr lächlet
sie lächeln

laden *to load*

Present participle *ladend*
Past participle *geladen*

Present indicative	**Imperfect subjunctive**
ich lade	ich lüde
du lädst	du lüdest
er lädt	er lüde
wir laden	wir lüden
ihr ladet	ihr lüdet
sie laden	sie lüden

Imperfect indicative	**Future indicative**
ich lud	ich werde laden
du lud(e)st	du wirst laden
er lud	er wird laden
wir luden	wir werden laden
ihr ludet	ihr werdet laden
sie luden	sie werden laden

Perfect indicative	**Conditional**
ich habe geladen	ich würde laden
du hast geladen	du würdest laden
er hat geladen	er würde laden
wir haben geladen	wir würden laden
ihr habt geladen	ihr würdet laden
sie haben geladen	sie würden laden

Pluperfect indicative	**Imperative**
ich hatte geladen	lad(e)!
du hattest geladen	laden wir!
er hatte geladen	ladet!
wir hatten geladen	laden Sie!
ihr hattet geladen	
sie hatten geladen	

Present subjunctive

ich lade
du ladest
er lade
wir laden
ihr ladet
sie laden

lassen *to let; to leave*

Present participle *lassend*
Past participle *gelassen*

Present indicative	**Imperfect subjunctive**
ich lasse	ich ließe
du läßt	du ließest
er läßt	er ließe
wir lassen	wir ließen
ihr laßt	ihr ließet
sie lassen	sie ließen

Imperfect indicative	**Future indicative**
ich ließ	ich werde lassen
du ließest	du wirst lassen
er ließ	er wird lassen
wir ließen	wir werden lassen
ihr ließt	ihr werdet lassen
sie ließen	sie werden lassen

Perfect indicative	**Conditional**
ich habe gelassen	ich würde lassen
du hast gelassen	du würdest lassen
er hat gelassen	er würde lassen
wir haben gelassen	wir würden lassen
ihr habt gelassen	ihr würdet lassen
sie haben gelassen	sie würden lassen

Pluperfect indicative	**Imperative**
ich hatte gelassen	laß!
du hattest gelassen	lassen wir!
er hatte gelassen	laßt!
wir hatten gelassen	lassen Sie!
ihr hattet gelassen	
sie hatten gelassen	

Present subjunctive

ich lasse
du lassest
er lasse
wir lassen
ihr lasset
sie lassen

laufen *to run*

Present participle *laufend*
Past participle *gelaufen*

Present indicative	**Imperfect subjunctive**
ich laufe	ich liefe
du läufst	du liefest
er läuft	er liefe
wir laufen	wir liefen
ihr lauft	ihr liefet
sie laufen	sie liefen

Imperfect indicative	**Future indicative**
ich lief	ich werde laufen
du liefst	du wirst laufen
er lief	er wird laufen
wir liefen	wir werden laufen
ihr lieft	ihr werdet laufen
sie liefen	sie werden laufen

Perfect indicative	**Conditional**
ich bin gelaufen	ich würde laufen
du bist gelaufen	du würdest laufen
er ist gelaufen	er würde laufen
wir sind gelaufen	wir würden laufen
ihr seid gelaufen	ihr würdet laufen
sie sind gelaufen	sie würden laufen

Pluperfect indicative	**Imperative**
ich war gelaufen	lauf(e)!
du warst gelaufen	laufen wir!
er war gelaufen	lauft!
wir waren gelaufen	laufen Sie!
ihr wart gelaufen	
sie waren gelaufen	

Present subjunctive

ich laufe
du laufest
er laufe
wir laufen
ihr laufet
sie laufen

leiden *to suffer*

Present participle *leidend*
Past participle *gelitten*

Present indicative	**Imperfect subjunctive**
ich leide	ich litte
du leidest	du littest
er leidet	er litte
wir leiden	wir litten
ihr leidet	ihr littet
sie leiden	sie litten

Imperfect indicative	**Future indicative**
ich litt	ich werde leiden
du litt(e)st	du wirst leiden
er litt	er wird leiden
wir litten	wir werden leiden
ihr littet	ihr werdet leiden
sie litten	sie werden leiden

Perfect indicative	**Conditional**
ich habe gelitten	ich würde leiden
du hast gelitten	du würdest leiden
er hat gelitten	er würde leiden
wir haben gelitten	wir würden leiden
ihr habt gelitten	ihr würdet leiden
sie haben gelitten	sie würden leiden

Pluperfect indicative	**Imperative**
ich hatte gelitten	leid(e)!
du hattest gelitten	leiden wir!
er hatte gelitten	leidet!
wir hatten gelitten	leiden Sie!
ihr hattet gelitten	
sie hatten gelitten	

Present subjunctive

ich leide
du leidest
er leide
wir leiden
ihr leidet
sie leiden

leihen *to lend*

Present participle *leihend*
Past participle *geliehen*

Present indicative	**Imperfect subjunctive**
ich leihe	ich liehe
du leihst	du liehest
er leiht	er liehe
wir leihen	wir liehen
ihr leiht	ihr liehet
sie leihen	sie liehen

Imperfect indicative	**Future indicative**
ich lieh	ich werde leihen
du liehst	du wirst leihen
er lieh	er wird leihen
wir liehen	wir werden leihen
ihr lieht	ihr werdet leihen
sie liehen	sie werden leihen

Perfect indicative	**Conditional**
ich habe geliehen	ich würde leihen
du hast geliehen	du würdest leihen
er hat geliehen	er würde leihen
wir haben geliehen	wir würden leihen
ihr habt geliehen	ihr würdet leihen
sie haben geliehen	sie würden leihen

Pluperfect indicative	**Imperative**
ich hatte geliehen	leih(e)!
du hattest geliehen	leihen wir!
er hatte geliehen	leiht!
wir hatten geliehen	leihen Sie!
ihr hattet geliehen	
sie hatten geliehen	

Present subjunctive

ich leihe
du leihest
er leihe
wir leihen
ihr leihet
sie leihen

lesen *to read*

Present participle *lesend*
Past participle *gelesen*

Present indicative	**Imperfect subjunctive**
ich lese	ich läse
du liest	du läsest
er liest	er läse
wir lesen	wir läsen
ihr lest	ihr läset
sie lesen	sie läsen

Imperfect indicative	**Future indicative**
ich las	ich werde lesen
du lasest	du wirst lesen
er las	er wird lesen
wir lasen	wir werden lesen
ihr last	ihr werdet lesen
sie lasen	sie werden lesen

Perfect indicative	**Conditional**
ich habe gelesen	ich würde lesen
du hast gelesen	du würdest lesen
er hat gelesen	er würde lesen
wir haben gelesen	wir würden lesen
ihr habt gelesen	ihr würdet lesen
sie haben gelesen	sie würden lesen

Pluperfect indicative	**Imperative**
ich hatte gelesen	lies(e)!
du hattest gelesen	lesen wir!
er hatte gelesen	lest!
wir hatten gelesen	lesen Sie!
ihr hattet gelesen	
sie hatten gelesen	

Present subjunctive

ich lese
du lesest
er lese
wir lesen
ihr leset
sie lesen

lieben *to love*

Present participle *liebend*
Past participle *geliebt*

Present indicative	**Imperfect subjunctive**
ich liebe	ich liebte
du liebst	du liebtest
er liebt	er liebte
wir lieben	wir liebten
ihr liebt	ihr liebtet
sie lieben	sie liebten

Imperfect indicative	**Future indicative**
ich liebte	ich werde lieben
du liebtest	du wirst lieben
er liebte	er wird lieben
wir liebten	wir werden lieben
ihr liebtet	ihr werdet lieben
sie liebten	sie werden lieben

Perfect indicative	**Conditional**
ich habe geliebt	ich würde lieben
du hast geliebt	du würdest lieben
er hat geliebt	er würde lieben
wir haben geliebt	wir würden lieben
ihr habt geliebt	ihr würdet lieben
sie haben geliebt	sie würden lieben

Pluperfect indicative	**Imperative**
ich hatte geliebt	lieb(e)!
du hattest geliebt	lieben wir!
er hatte geliebt	liebt!
wir hatten geliebt	lieben Sie!
ihr hattet geliebt	
sie hatten geliebt	

Present subjunctive

ich liebe
du liebest
er liebe
wir lieben
ihr liebet
sie lieben

liegen *to lie; to be situated*

Present participle *liegend*
Past participle *gelegen*

Present indicative	**Imperfect subjunctive**
ich liege	ich läge
du liegst	du lägest
er liegt	er läge
wir liegen	wir lägen
ihr liegt	ihr läget
sie liegen	sie lägen

Imperfect indicative	**Future indicative**
ich lag	ich werde liegen
du lagst	du wirst liegen
er lag	er wird liegen
wir lagen	wir werden liegen
ihr lagt	ihr werdet liegen
sie lagen	sie werden liegen

Perfect indicative	**Conditional**
ich habe gelegen	ich würde liegen
du hast gelegen	du würdest liegen
er hat gelegen	er würde liegen
wir haben gelegen	wir würden liegen
ihr habt gelegen	ihr würdet liegen
sie haben gelegen	sie würden liegen

Pluperfect indicative	**Imperative**
ich hatte gelegen	lieg(e)!
du hattest gelegen	liegen wir!
er hatte gelegen	liegt!
wir hatten gelegen	liegen Sie!
ihr hattet gelegen	
sie hatten gelegen	

Present subjunctive

ich liege
du liegest
er liege
wir liegen
ihr lieget
sie liegen

lügen *to (tell a) lie*

Present participle *lügend*
Past participle *gelogen*

Present indicative	**Imperfect subjunctive**
ich lüge	ich löge
du lügst	du lögest
er lügt	er löge
wir lügen	wir lögen
ihr lügt	ihr löget
sie lügen	sie lögen

Imperfect indicative	**Future indicative**
ich log	ich werde lügen
du logst	du wirst lügen
er log	er wird lügen
wir logen	wir werden lügen
ihr logt	ihr werdet lügen
sie logen	sie werden lügen

Perfect indicative	**Conditional**
ich habe gelogen	ich würde lügen
du hast gelogen	du würdest lügen
er hat gelogen	er würde lügen
wir haben gelogen	wir würden lügen
ihr habt gelogen	ihr würdet lügen
sie haben gelogen	sie würden lügen

Pluperfect indicative	**Imperative**
ich hatte gelogen	lüg(e)!
du hattest gelogen	lügen wir!
er hatte gelogen	lügt!
wir hatten gelogen	lügen Sie!
ihr hattet gelogen	
sie hatten gelogen	

Present subjunctive

ich lüge
du lügest
er lüge
wir lügen
ihr lüget
sie lügen

machen *to make; to do*

Present participle *machend*
Past participle *gemacht*

Present indicative	**Imperfect subjunctive**
ich mache	ich machte
du machst	du machtest
er macht	er machte
wir machen	wir machten
ihr macht	ihr machtet
sie machen	sie machten

Imperfect indicative	**Future indicative**
ich machte	ich werde machen
du machtest	du wirst machen
er machte	er wird machen
wir machten	wir werden machen
ihr machtet	ihr werdet machen
sie machten	sie werden machen

Perfect indicative	**Conditional**
ich habe gemacht	ich würde machen
du hast gemacht	du würdest machen
er hat gemacht	er würde machen
wir haben gemacht	wir würden machen
ihr habt gemacht	ihr würdet machen
sie haben gemacht	sie würden machen

Pluperfect indicative	**Imperative**
ich hatte gemacht	mach(e)!
du hattest gemacht	machen wir!
er hatte gemacht	macht!
wir hatten gemacht	machen Sie!
ihr hattet gemacht	
sie hatten gemacht	

Present subjunctive

ich mache
du machest
er mache
wir machen
ihr machet
sie machen

mahlen *to grind*

Present participle *mahlend*
Past participle *gemahlen*

Present indicative	Imperfect subjunctive
ich mahle	ich mahlte
du mahlst	du mahltest
er mahlt	er mahlte
wir mahlen	wir mahlten
ihr mahlt	ihr mahltet
sie mahlen	sie mahlten

Imperfect indicative	Future indicative
ich mahlte	ich werde mahlen
du mahltest	du wirst mahlen
er mahlte	er wird mahlen
wir mahlten	wir werden mahlen
ihr mahltet	ihr werdet mahlen
sie mahlten	sie werden mahlen

Perfect indicative	Conditional
ich habe gemahlen	ich würde mahlen
du hast gemahlen	du würdest mahlen
er hat gemahlen	er würde mahlen
wir haben gemahlen	wir würden mahlen
ihr habt gemahlen	ihr würdet mahlen
sie haben gemahlen	sie würden mahlen

Pluperfect indicative	Imperative
ich hatte gemahlen	mahl(e)!
du hattest gemahlen	mahlen wir!
er hatte gemahlen	mahlt!
wir hatten gemahlen	mahlen Sie!
ihr hattet gemahlen	
sie hatten gemahlen	

Present subjunctive

ich mahle
du mahlest
er mahle
wir mahlen
ihr mahlet
sie mahlen

meiden *to avoid*

Present participle *meidend*
Past participle *gemieden*

Present indicative	Imperfect subjunctive
ich meide	ich miede
du meidest	du miedest
er meidet	er miede
wir meiden	wir mieden
ihr meidet	ihr miedet
sie meiden	sie mieden

Imperfect indicative	Future indicative
ich mied	ich werde meiden
du mied(e)st	du wirst meiden
er mied	er wird meiden
wir mieden	wir werden meiden
ihr miedet	ihr werdet meiden
sie mieden	sie werden meiden

Perfect indicative	Conditional
ich habe gemieden	ich würde meiden
du hast gemieden	du würdest meiden
er hat gemieden	er würde meiden
wir haben gemieden	wir würden meiden
ihr habt gemieden	ihr würdet meiden
sie haben gemieden	sie würden meiden

Pluperfect indicative	Imperative
ich hatte gemieden	meid(e)!
du hattest gemieden	meiden wir!
er hatte gemieden	meidet!
wir hatten gemieden	meiden Sie!
ihr hattet gemieden	
sie hatten gemieden	

Present subjunctive

ich meide
du meidest
er meide
wir meiden
ihr meidet
sie meiden

messen *to measure*

Present participle *messend*
Past participle *gemessen*

Present indicative	**Imperfect subjunctive**
ich messe	ich mäße
du mißt	du mäßest
er mißt	er mäße
wir messen	wir mäßen
ihr meßt	ihr mäßet
sie messen	sie mäßen

Imperfect indicative	**Future indicative**
ich maß	ich werde messen
du maßest	du wirst messen
er maß	er wird messen
wir maßen	wir werden messen
ihr maßt	ihr werdet messen
sie maßen	sie werden messen

Perfect indicative	**Conditional**
ich habe gemessen	ich würde messen
du hast gemessen	du würdest messen
er hat gemessen	er würde messen
wir haben gemessen	wir würden messen
ihr habt gemessen	ihr würdet messen
sie haben gemessen	sie würden messen

Pluperfect indicative	**Imperative**
ich hatte gemessen	miß!
du hattest gemessen	messen wir!
er hatte gemessen	meßt!
wir hatten gemessen	messen Sie!
ihr hattet gemessen	
sie hatten gemessen	

Present subjunctive

ich messe
du messest
er messe
wir messen
ihr messet
sie messen

mögen *to like*

Present participle *mögend*
Past participle *gemocht/mögen**

Present indicative	**Present subjunctive**
ich mag	ich möge
du magst	du mögest
er mag	er möge
wir mögen	wir mögen
ihr mögt	ihr möget
sie mögen	sie mögen

Imperfect indicative	**Imperfect subjunctive**
ich mochte	ich möchte
du mochtest	du möchtest
er mochte	er möchte
wir mochten	wir möchten
ihr mochtet	ihr möchtet
sie mochten	sie möchten

Perfect indicative	**Future indicative**
ich habe gemocht	ich werde mögen
du hast gemocht	du wirst mögen
er hat gemocht	er wird mögen
wir haben gemocht	wir werden mögen
ihr habt gemocht	ihr werdet mögen
sie haben gemocht	sie werden mögen

Pluperfect indicative	**Conditional**
ich hatte gemocht	ich würde mögen
du hattest gemocht	du würdest mögen
er hatte gemocht	er würde mögen
wir hatten gemocht	wir würden mögen
ihr hattet gemocht	ihr würdet mögen
sie hatten gemocht	sie würden mögen

* mögen *is used when preceded by an infinitive*

265

müssen *to have to, must*

Present participle *müssend*
Past participle *gemußt/müssen**

Present indicative	**Present subjunctive**
ich muß	ich müsse
du mußt	du müssest
er muß	er müsse
wir müssen	wir müssen
ihr mußt	ihr müsset
sie müssen	sie müssen

Imperfect indicative	**Imperfect subjunctive**
ich mußte	ich müßte
du mußtest	du müßtest
er mußte	er müßte
wir mußten	wir müßten
ihr mußtet	ihr müßtet
sie mußten	sie müßten

Perfect indicative	**Future indicative**
ich habe gemußt	ich werde müssen
du hast gemußt	du wirst müssen
er hat gemußt	er wird müssen
wir haben gemußt	wir werden müssen
ihr habt gemußt	ihr werdet müssen
sie haben gemußt	sie werden müssen

Pluperfect indicative	**Conditional**
ich hatte gemußt	ich würde müssen
du hattest gemußt	du würdest müssen
er hatte gemußt	er würde müssen
wir hatten gemußt	wir würden müssen
ihr hattet gemußt	ihr würdet müssen
sie hatten gemußt	sie würden müssen

*müssen *is used when preceded by an infinitive*

nehmen *to take*

Present participle *nehmend*
Past participle *genommen*

Present indicative	**Imperfect subjunctive**
ich nehme	ich nähme
du nimmst	du nähmest
er nimmt	er nähme
wir nehmen	wir nähmen
ihr nehmt	ihr nähmet
sie nehmen	sie nähmen

Imperfect indicative	**Future indicative**
ich nahm	ich werde nehmen
du nahmst	du wirst nehmen
er nahm	er wird nehmen
wir nahmen	wir werden nehmen
ihr nahmt	ihr werdet nehmen
sie nahmen	sie werden nehmen

Perfect indicative	**Conditional**
ich habe genommen	ich würde nehmen
du hast genommen	du würdest nehmen
er hat genommen	er würde nehmen
wir haben genommen	wir würden nehmen
ihr habt genommen	ihr würdet nehmen
sie haben genommen	sie würden nehmen

Pluperfect indicative	**Imperative**
ich hatte genommen	nimm(e)!
du hattest genommen	nehmen wir!
er hatte genommen	nehmt!
wir hatten genommen	nehmen Sie!
ihr hattet genommen	
sie hatten genommen	

Present subjunctive
ich nehme
du nehmest
er nehme
wir nehmen
ihr nehmet
sie nehmen

nennen *to name, call*

Present participle *nennend*
Past participle *genannt*

Present indicative	**Imperfect subjunctive**
ich nenne	ich nennte
du nennst	du nenntest
er nennt	er nennte
wir nennen	wir nennten
ihr nennt	ihr nenntet
sie nennen	sie nennten

Imperfect indicative	**Future indicative**
ich nannte	ich werde nennen
du nanntest	du wirst nennen
er nannte	er wird nennen
wir nannten	wir werden nennen
ihr nanntet	ihr werdet nennen
sie nannten	sie werden nennen

Perfect indicative	**Conditional**
ich habe genannt	ich würde nennen
du hast genannt	du würdest nennen
er hat genannt	er würde nennen
wir haben genannt	wir würden nennen
ihr habt genannt	ihr würdet nennen
sie haben genannt	sie würden nennen

Pluperfect indicative	**Imperative**
ich hatte genannt	nenn(e)!
du hattest genannt	nennen wir!
er hatte genannt	nennt!
wir hatten genannt	nennen Sie!
ihr hattet genannt	
sie hatten genannt	

Present subjunctive

ich nenne
du nennest
er nenne
wir nennen
ihr nennet
sie nennen

pfeifen *to whistle*

Present participle *pfeifend*
Past participle *gepfiffen*

Present indicative	**Imperfect subjunctive**
ich pfeife	ich pfiffe
du pfeifst	du pfiffest
er pfeift	er pfiffe
wir pfeifen	wir pfiffen
ihr pfeift	ihr pfiffet
sie pfeifen	sie pfiffen

Imperfect indicative	**Future indicative**
ich pfiff	ich werde pfeifen
du pfiffst	du wirst pfeifen
er pfiff	er wird pfeifen
wir pfiffen	wir werden pfeifen
ihr pfifft	ihr werdet pfeifen
sie pfiffen	sie werden pfeifen

Perfect indicative	**Conditional**
ich habe gepfiffen	ich würde pfeifen
du hast gepfiffen	du würdest pfeifen
er hat gepfiffen	er würde pfeifen
wir haben gepfiffen	wir würden pfeifen
ihr habt gepfiffen	ihr würdet pfeifen
sie haben gepfiffen	sie würden pfeifen

Pluperfect indicative	**Imperative**
ich hatte gepfiffen	pfeif(e)!
du hattest gepfiffen	pfeifen wir!
er hatte gepfiffen	pfeift!
wir hatten gepfiffen	pfeifen Sie!
ihr hattet gepfiffen	
sie hatten gepfiffen	

Present subjunctive

ich pfeife
du pfeifest
er pfeife
wir pfeifen
ihr pfeifet
sie pfeifen

preisen *to praise*

Present participle *preisend*
Past participle *gepriesen*

Present indicative	Imperfect subjunctive
ich preise	ich priese
du preist	du priesest
er preist	er priese
wir preisen	wir priesen
ihr preist	ihr prieset
sie preisen	sie priesen

Imperfect indicative	Future indicative
ich pries	ich werde preisen
du priesest	du wirst preisen
er pries	er wird preisen
wir priesen	wir werden preisen
ihr priest	ihr werdet preisen
sie priesen	sie werden preisen

Perfect indicative	Conditional
ich habe gepriesen	ich würde preisen
du hast gepriesen	du würdest preisen
er hat gepriesen	er würde preisen
wir haben gepriesen	wir würden preisen
ihr habt gepriesen	ihr würdet preisen
sie haben gepriesen	sie würden preisen

Pluperfect indicative	Imperative
ich hatte gepriesen	preis(e)!
du hattest gepriesen	preisen wir!
er hatte gepriesen	preist!
wir hatten gepriesen	preisen Sie!
ihr hattet gepriesen	
sie hatten gepriesen	

Present subjunctive

ich preise
du preisest
er preise
wir preisen
ihr preiset
sie preisen

quellen *to gush, well up*

Present participle *quellend*
Past participle *gequollen*

Present indicative	Imperfect subjunctive
ich quelle	ich quölle
du quillst	du quöllest
er quillt	er quölle
wir quellen	wir quöllen
ihr quellt	ihr quöllet
sie quellen	sie quöllen

Imperfect indicative	Future indicative
ich quoll	ich werde quellen
du quollst	du wirst quellen
er quoll	er wird quellen
wir quollen	wir werden quellen
ihr quollt	ihr werdet quellen
sie quollen	sie werden quellen

Perfect indicative	Conditional
ich bin gequollen	ich würde quellen
du bist gequollen	du würdest quellen
er ist gequollen	er würde quellen
wir sind gequollen	wir würden quellen
ihr seid gequollen	ihr würdet quellen
sie sind gequollen	sie würden quellen

Pluperfect indicative	Imperative
ich war gequollen	quill!
du warst gequollen	quellen wir!
er war gequollen	quellt!
wir waren gequollen	quellen Sie!
ihr wart gequollen	
sie waren gequollen	

Present subjunctive

ich quelle
du quellest
er quelle
wir quellen
ihr quellet
sie quellen

raten *to guess; to advise*

Present participle *ratend*
Past participle *geraten*

Present indicative	**Imperfect subjunctive**
ich rate	ich riete
du rätst	du rietest
er rät	er riete
wir raten	wir rieten
ihr ratet	ihr rietet
sie raten	sie rieten

Imperfect indicative	**Future indicative**
ich riet	ich werde raten
du riet(e)st	du wirst raten
er riet	er wird raten
wir rieten	wir werden raten
ihr rietet	ihr werdet raten
sie rieten	sie werden raten

Perfect indicative	**Conditional**
ich habe geraten	ich würde raten
du hast geraten	du würdest raten
er hat geraten	er würde raten
wir haben geraten	wir würden raten
ihr habt geraten	ihr würdet raten
sie haben geraten	sie würden raten

Pluperfect indicative	**Imperative**
ich hatte geraten	rat(e)!
du hattest geraten	raten wir!
er hatte geraten	ratet!
wir hatten geraten	raten Sie!
ihr hattet geraten	
sie hatten geraten	

Present subjunctive

ich rate
du ratest
er rate
wir raten
ihr ratet
sie raten

reden *to talk*

Present participle *redend*
Past participle *geredet*

Present indicative	**Imperfect subjunctive**
ich rede	ich redete
du redest	du redetest
er redet	er redete
wir reden	wir redeten
ihr redet	ihr redetet
sie reden	sie redeten

Imperfect indicative	**Future indicative**
ich redete	ich werde reden
du redetest	du wirst reden
er redete	er wird reden
wir redeten	wir werden reden
ihr redetet	ihr werdet reden
sie redeten	sie werden reden

Perfect indicative	**Conditional**
ich habe geredet	ich würde reden
du hast geredet	du würdest reden
er hat geredet	er würde reden
wir haben geredet	wir würden reden
ihr habt geredet	ihr würdet reden
sie haben geredet	sie würden reden

Pluperfect indicative	**Imperative**
ich hatte geredet	rede!
du hattest geredet	reden wir!
er hatte geredet	redet!
wir hatten geredet	reden Sie!
ihr hattet geredet	
sie hatten geredet	

Present subjunctive

ich rede
du redest
er rede
wir reden
ihr redet
sie reden

reiben *to rub*

Present participle *reibend*
Past participle *gerieben*

Present indicative	**Imperfect subjunctive**
ich reibe	ich riebe
du reibst	du riebest
er reibt	er riebe
wir reiben	wir rieben
ihr reibt	ihr riebet
sie reiben	sie rieben

Imperfect indicative	**Future indicative**
ich rieb	ich werde reiben
du riebst	du wirst reiben
er rieb	er wird reiben
wir rieben	wir werden reiben
ihr riebt	ihr werdet reiben
sie rieben	sie werden reiben

Perfect indicative	**Conditional**
ich habe gerieben	ich würde reiben
du hast gerieben	du würdest reiben
er hat gerieben	er würde reiben
wir haben gerieben	wir würden reiben
ihr habt gerieben	ihr würdet reiben
sie haben gerieben	sie würden reiben

Pluperfect indicative	**Imperative**
ich hatte gerieben	reib(e)!
du hattest gerieben	reiben wir!
er hatte gerieben	reibt!
wir hatten gerieben	reiben Sie!
ihr hattet gerieben	
sie hatten gerieben	

Present subjunctive

ich reibe
du reibest
er reibe
wir reiben
ihr reibet
sie reiben

reißen *to tear*

Present participle *reißend*
Past participle *gerissen*

Present indicative	**Present subjunctive**
ich reiße	ich reiße
du reißt	du reißest
er reißt	er reiße
wir reißen	wir reißen
ihr reißt	ihr reißet
sie reißen	sie reißen

Imperfect indicative	**Imperfect subjunctive**
ich riß	ich risse
du rissest	du rissest
er riß	er risse
wir rißen	wir rissen
ihr rißt	ihr risset
sie rißen	sie rissen

Perfect indicative	**Future indicative**
ich bin/habe gerissen	ich werde reißen
du bist/hast gerissen	du wirst reißen
er ist/hat gerissen	er wird reißen
wir sind/haben gerissen	wir werden reißen
ihr seid/habt gerissen	ihr werdet reißen
sie sind/haben gerissen	sie werden reißen

Pluperfect indicative	**Conditional**
ich war/hatte gerissen	ich würde reißen
du warst/hattest gerissen	du würdest reißen
er war/hatte gerissen	er würde reißen
wir waren/hatten gerissen	wir würden reißen
ihr wart/hattet gerissen	ihr würdet reißen
sie waren/hatten gerissen	sie würden reißen

Imperative

reiß(e)!
reißen wir!
reißt!
reißen Sie!

reiten *to ride (a horse)*

Present participle *reitend*
Past participle *geritten*

Present indicative	**Present subjunctive**
ich reite	ich reite
du reitest	du reitest
er reitet	er reite
wir reiten	wir reiten
ihr reitet	ihr reitet
sie reiten	sie reiten

Imperfect indicative	**Imperfect subjunctive**
ich ritt	ich ritte
du ritt(e)st	du rittest
er ritt	er ritte
wir ritten	wir ritten
ihr rittet	ihr rittet
sie ritten	sie ritten

Perfect indicative	**Future indicative**
ich bin/habe geritten	ich werde reiten
du bist/hast geritten	du wirst reiten
er ist/hat geritten	er wird reiten
wir sind/haben geritten	wir werden reiten
ihr seid/habt geritten	ihr werdet reiten
sie sind/haben geritten	sie werden reiten

Pluperfect indicative

ich war/hatte geritten
du warst/hattest geritten
er war/hatte geritten
wir waren/hatten geritten
ihr wart/hattet geritten
sie waren/hatten geritten

Conditional

ich würde reiten
du würdest reiten
er würde reiten
wir würden reiten
ihr würdet reiten
sie würden reiten

Imperative

reit(e)!
reiten wir!
reitet!
reiten Sie!

rennen *to run*

Present participle *rennend*
Past participle *gerannt*

Present indicative	**Imperfect subjunctive**
ich renne	ich rennte
du rennst	du renntest
er rennt	er rennte
wir rennen	wir rennten
ihr rennt	ihr renntet
sie rennen	sie rennten

Imperfect indicative	**Future indicative**
ich rannte	ich werde rennen
du ranntest	du wirst rennen
er rannte	er wird rennen
wir rannten	wir werden rennen
ihr ranntet	ihr werdet rennen
sie rannten	sie werden rennen

Perfect indicative	**Conditional**
ich bin gerannt	ich würde rennen
du bist gerannt	du würdest rennen
er ist gerannt	er würde rennen
wir sind gerannt	wir würden rennen
ihr seid gerannt	ihr würdet rennen
sie sind gerannt	sie würden rennen

Pluperfect indicative	**Imperative**
ich war gerannt	renn(e)!
du warst gerannt	rennen wir!
er war gerannt	rennt!
wir waren gerannt	rennen Sie!
ihr wart gerannt	
sie waren gerannt	

Present subjunctive

ich renne
du rennest
er renne
wir rennen
ihr rennet
sie rennen

riechen *to smell*

Present participle *riechend*
Past participle *gerochen*

Present indicative	Imperfect subjunctive
ich rieche	ich röche
du riechst	du röchest
er riecht	er röche
wir riechen	wir röchen
ihr riecht	ihr röchet
sie riechen	sie röchen

Imperfect indicative	Future indicative
ich roch	ich werde riechen
du rochst	du wirst riechen
er roch	er wird riechen
wir rochen	wir werden riechen
ihr rocht	ihr werdet riechen
sie rochen	sie werden riechen

Perfect indicative	Conditional
ich habe gerochen	ich würde riechen
du hast gerochen	du würdest riechen
er hat gerochen	er würde riechen
wir haben gerochen	wir würden riechen
ihr habt gerochen	ihr würdet riechen
sie haben gerochen	sie würden riechen

Pluperfect indicative	Imperative
ich hatte gerochen	riech(e)!
du hattest gerochen	riechen wir!
er hatte gerochen	riecht!
wir hatten gerochen	riechen Sie!
ihr hattet gerochen	
sie hatten gerochen	

Present subjunctive
ich rieche
du riechest
er rieche
wir riechen
ihr riechet
sie riechen

ringen *to struggle*

Present participle *ringend*
Past participle *berungen*

Present indicative	Imperfect subjunctive
ich ringe	ich ränge
du ringst	du rängest
er ringt	er ränge
wir ringen	wir rängen
ihr ringt	ihr ränget
sie ringen	sie rängen

Imperfect indicative	Future indicative
ich rang	ich werde ringen
du rangst	du wirst ringen
er rang	er wird ringen
wir rangen	wir werden ringen
ihr rangt	ihr werdet ringen
sie rangen	sie werden ringen

Perfect indicative	Conditional
ich habe gerungen	ich würde ringen
du hast gerungen	du würdest ringen
er hat gerungen	er würde ringen
wir haben gerungen	wir würden ringen
ihr habt gerungen	ihr würdet ringen
sie haben gerungen	sie würden ringen

Pluperfect indicative	Imperative
ich hatte gerungen	ring(e)!
du hattest gerungen	ringen wir!
er hatte gerungen	ringt!
wir hatten gerungen	ringen Sie!
ihr hattet gerungen	
sie hatten gerungen	

Present subjunctive
ich ringe
du ringest
er ringe
wir ringen
ihr ringet
sie ring en

rinnen *to flow, trickle*

Present participle *rinnend*
Past participle *geronnen*

Present indicative	**Imperfect subjunctive**
ich rinne	ich ränne
du rinnst	du rännest
er rinnt	er ränne
wir rinnen	wir rännen
ihr rinnt	ihr rännet
sie rinnen	sie rännen

Imperfect indicative	**Future indicative**
ich rann	ich werde rinnen
du rannst	du wirst rinnen
er rann	er wird rinnen
wir rannen	wir werden rinnen
ihr rannt	ihr werdet rinnen
sie rannen	sie werden rinnen

Perfect indicative	**Conditional**
ich bin geronnen	ich würde rinnen
du bist geronnen	du würdest rinnen
er ist geronnen	er würde rinnen
wir sind geronnen	wir würden rinnen
ihr seid geronnen	ihr würdet rinnen
sie sind geronnen	sie würden rinnen

Pluperfect indicative	**Imperative**
ich war geronnen	rinn!
du warst geronnen	rinnen wir!
er war geronnen	rinnt!
wir waren geronnen	rinnen Sie!
ihr wart geronnen	
sie waren geronnen	

Present subjunctive

ich rinne
du rinnest
er rinne
wir rinnen
ihr rinnet
sie rinnen

rufen *to call, shout*

Present participle *rufend*
Past participle *gerufen*

Present indicative	**Imperfect subjunctive**
ich rufe	ich riefe
du rufst	du riefest
er ruft	er riefe
wir rufen	wir riefen
ihr ruft	ihr riefet
sie rufen	sie riefen

Imperfect indicative	**Future indicative**
ich rief	ich werde rufen
du riefst	du wirst rufen
er rief	er wird rufen
wir riefen	wir werden rufen
ihr rieft	ihr werdet rufen
sie riefen	sie werden rufen

Perfect indicative	**Conditional**
ich habe gerufen	ich würde rufen
du hast gerufen	du würdest rufen
er hat gerufen	er würde rufen
wir haben gerufen	wir würden rufen
ihr habt gerufen	ihr würdet rufen
sie haben gerufen	sie würden rufen

Pluperfect indicative	**Imperative**
ich hatte gerufen	ruf(e)!
du hattest gerufen	rufen wir!
er hatte gerufen	ruft!
wir hatten gerufen	rufen Sie!
ihr hattet gerufen	
sie hatten gerufen	

Present subjunctive

ich rufe
du rufest
er rufe
wir rufen
ihr rufet
sie rufen

saufen *to drink (of animals), booze*

Present participle *saufend*
Past participle *gesoffen*

Present indicative	Present subjunctive
ich saufe	ich saufe
du säufst	du saufest
er säuft	er saufe
wir saufen	wir saufen
ihr sauft	ihr saufet
sie saufen	sie saufen

Imperfect indicative	Imperfect subjunctive
ich soff	ich söffe
du soffst	du söffest
er soff	er söffe
wir soffen	wir söffen
ihr sofft	ihr söffet
sie soffen	sie söffen

Perfect indicative	Future indicative
ich habe gesoffen	ich werde saufen
du hast gesoffen	du wirst saufen
er hat gesoffen	er wird saufen
wir haben gesoffen	wir werden saufen
ihr habt gesoffen	ihr werdet saufen
sie haben gesoffen	sie werden saufen

Pluperfect indicative	Conditional
ich hatte gesoffen	ich würde saufen
du hattest gesoffen	du würdest saufen
er hatte gesoffen	er würde saufen
wir hatten gesoffen	wir würden saufen
ihr hattet gesoffen	ihr würdet saufen
sie hatten gesoffen	sie würden saufen

Imperative

sauf(e)!
saufen wir!
sauft!
saufen Sie!

saugen *to suck*

Present participle *saugend*
Past participle *gesogen*

Present indicative	Imperfect subjunctive
ich sauge	ich söge
du saugst	du sögest
er saugt	er söge
wir saugen	wir sögen
ihr saugt	ihr söget
sie saugen	sie sögen

Imperfect indicative	Future indicative
ich sog	ich werde saugen
du sogst	du wirst saugen
er sog	er wird saugen
wir sogen	wir werden saugen
ihr sogt	ihr werdet saugen
sie sogen	sie werden saugen

Perfect indicative	Conditional
ich habe gesogen	ich würde saugen
du hast gesogen	du würdest saugen
er hat gesogen	er würde saugen
wir haben gesogen	wir würden saugen
ihr habt gesogen	ihr würdet saugen
sie haben gesogen	sie würden saugen

Pluperfect indicative	Imperative
ich hatte gesogen	saug(e)!
du hattest gesogen	saugen wir!
er hatte gesogen	saugt!
wir hatten gesogen	saugen Sie!
ihr hattet gesogen	
sie hatten gesogen	

Present subjunctive

ich sauge
du saugest
er sauge
wir saugen
ihr sauget
sie saugen

schaffen *to create*

Present participle *schaffen*
Past participle *geschaffen*

Present indicative	**Imperfect subjunctive**
ich schaffe	ich schüfe
du schaffst	du schüfest
er schafft	er schüfe
wir schaffen	wir schüfen
ihr schafft	ihr schüfet
sie schaffen	sie schüfen

Imperfect indicative	**Future indicative**
ich schuf	ich werde schaffen
du schufst	du wirst schaffen
er schuf	er wird schaffen
wir schufen	wir werden schaffen
ihr schuft	ihr werdet schaffen
sie schufen	sie werden schaffen

Perfect indicative	**Conditional**
ich habe geschaffen	ich würde schaffen
du hast geschaffen	du würdest schaffen
er hat geschaffen	er würde schaffen
wir haben geschaffen	wir würden schaffen
ihr habt geschaffen	ihr würdet schaffen
sie haben geschaffen	sie würden schaffen

Pluperfect indicative	**Imperative**
ich hatte geschaffen	schaff(e)!
du hattest geschaffen	schaffen wir!
er hatte geschaffen	schafft!
wir hatten geschaffen	schaffen Sie!
ihr hattet geschaffen	
sie hatten geschaffen	

Present subjunctive

ich schaffe
du schaffest
er schaffe
wir schaffen
ihr schaffet
sie schaffen

scheiden *to separate, part*

Present participle *scheidend*
Past participle *geschieden*

Present indicative

ich scheide
du scheidest
er scheidet
wir scheiden
ihr scheidet
sie scheiden

Imperfect indicative

ich schied
du schied(e)st
er schied
wir schieden
ihr schiedet
sie schieden

Perfect indicative

ich bin/habe
   geschieden
du bist/hast
   geschieden
er ist/hat geschieden
wir sind/haben
   geschieden
ihr seid/habt
   geschieden
sie sind/haben
   geschieden

Pluperfect indicative

ich war/hatte
   geschieden
du warst/hattest
   geschieden
er war/hatte
   geschieden
wir waren/hatten
   geschieden
ihr wart/hattet
   geschieden

sie waren/hatten
   geschieden

Present subjunctive

ich scheide
du scheidest
er scheide
wir scheiden
ihr scheidet
sie scheiden

Imperfect subjunctive

ich schiede
du schiedest
er schiede
wir schieden
ihr schiedet
sie schieden

Future indicative

ich werde scheiden
du wirst scheiden
er wird scheiden
wir werden scheiden
ihr werdet scheiden
sie werden scheiden

Conditional

ich würde scheiden
du würdest scheiden
er würde scheiden
wir würden scheiden
ihr würdet scheiden
sie würden scheiden

Imperative

scheid(e)!
scheiden wir!
scheidet!
scheiden Sie!

scheinen *to shine; to seem*

Present participle *scheinend*
Past participle *geschienen*

Present indicative	**Imperfect subjunctive**
ich schiene	ich schiene
du scheinst	du schienest
er scheint	er schiene
wir scheinen	wir schienen
ihr scheint	ihr schienet
sie scheinen	sie schienen

Imperfect indicative	**Future indicative**
ich schien	ich werde scheinen
du schienst	du wirst scheinen
er schien	er wird scheinen
wir schienen	wir werden scheinen
ihr schient	ihr werdet scheinen
sie schienen	sie werden scheinen

Perfect indicative	**Conditional**
ich habe geschienen	ich würde scheinen
du hast geschienen	du würdest scheinen
er hat geschienen	er würde scheinen
wir haben geschienen	wir würden scheinen
ihr habt geschienen	ihr würdet scheinen
sie haben geschienen	sie würden scheinen

Pluperfect indicative	**Imperative**
ich hatte geschienen	schein(e)!
du hattest geschienen	scheinen wir!
er hatte geschienen	scheint!
wir hatten geschienen	scheinen Sie!
ihr hattet geschienen	
sie hatten geschienen	

Present subjunctive

ich schiene
du schienest
er schiene
wir scheinen
ihr schienet
sie scheinen

shelten *to scold*

Present participle *scheltend*
Past participle *gescholten*

Present indicative	**Imperfect subjunctive**
ich schelte	ich schölte
du schiltst	du schöltest
er schilt	er schölte
wir schelten	wir schölten
ihr scheltet	ihr schöltet
sie schelten	sie schölten

Imperfect indicative	**Future indicative**
ich schalt	ich werde schelten
du schalt(e)st	du wirst schelten
er schalt	er wird schelten
wir schalten	wir werden schelten
ihr schaltet	ihr werdet schelten
sie schalten	sie werden schelten

Perfect indicative	**Conditional**
ich habe gescholten	ich würde schelten
du hast gescholten	du würdest schelten
er hat gescholten	er würde schelten
wir haben gescholten	wir würden schelten
ihr habt gescholten	ihr würdet schelten
sie haben gescholten	sie würden schelten

Pluperfect indicative	**Imperative**
ich hatte gescholten	schilt!
du hattest gescholten	schelten wir!
er hatte gescholten	scheltet!
wir hatten gescholten	schelten Sie!
ihr hattet gescholten	
sie hatten gescholten	

Present subjunctive

ich schelte
du scheltest
er schelte
wir schelten
ihr scheltet
sie schelten

scheren *to shear, clip*

Present participle *scherend*
Past participle *geschoren*

Present indicative	**Imperfect subjunctive**
ich schere	ich schöre
du scherst	du schörest
er schert	er schöre
wir scheren	wir schören
ihr schert	ihr schöret
sie scheren	sie schören

Imperfect indicative	**Future indicative**
ich schor	ich werde scheren
du schorst	du wirst scheren
er schor	er wird scheren
wir schoren	wir werden scheren
ihr schort	ihr werdet scheren
sie schoren	sie werden scheren

Perfect indicative	**Conditional**
ich habe geschoren	ich würde scheren
du hast geschoren	du würdest scheren
er hat geschoren	er würde scheren
wir haben geschoren	wir würden scheren
ihr habt geschoren	ihr würdet scheren
sie haben geschoren	sie würden scheren

Pluperfect indicative	**Imperative**
ich hatte geschoren	scher(e)!
du hattest geschoren	scheren wir!
er hatte geschoren	schert!
wir hatten geschoren	scheren Sie!
ihr hattet geschoren	
sie hatten geschoren	

Present subjunctive

ich schere
du scherest
er schere
wir scheren
ihr scheret
sie scheren

schieben *to push*

Present participle *schiebend*
Past participle *geschoben*

Present indicative	**Imperfect subjunctive**
ich schiebe	ich schöbe
du schiebst	du schöbest
er schiebt	er schöbe
wir schieben	wir schöben
ihr schiebt	ihr schöbet
sie schieben	sie schöben

Imperfect indicative	**Future indicative**
ich schob	ich werde schieben
du schobst	du wirst schieben
er schob	er wird schieben
wir schoben	wir werden schieben
ihr schobt	ihr werdet schieben
sie schoben	sie werden schieben

Perfect indicative	**Conditional**
ich habe geschoben	ich würde schieben
du hast geschoben	du würdest schieben
er hat geschoben	er würde schieben
wir haben geschoben	wir würden schieben
ihr habt geschoben	ihr würdet schieben
sie haben geschoben	sie würden schieben

Pluperfect indicative	**Imperative**
ich hatte geschoben	schieb(e)!
du hattest geschoben	schieben wir!
er hatte geschoben	schiebt!
wir hatten geschoben	schieben Sie!
ihr hattet geschoben	
sie hatten geschoben	

Present subjunctive

ich schiebe
du schiebest
er schiebe
wir schieben
ihr schiebet
sie schieben

schießen *to shoot*

Present participle *schießend*
Past participle *geschossen*

Present indicative	**Imperfect subjunctive**
ich schieße	ich schösse
du schießt	du schössest
er schießt	er schösse
wir schießen	wir schössen
ihr schießt	ihr schösset
sie schießen	sie schössen

Imperfect indicative	**Future indicative**
ich schoß	ich werde schießen
du schossest	du wirst schießen
er schoß	er wird schießen
wir schossen	wir werden schießen
ihr schoßt	ihr werdet schießen
sie schossen	sie werden schießen

Perfect indicative	**Conditional**
ich habe geschossen	ich würde schießen
du hast geschossen	du würdest schießen
er hat geschossen	er würde schießen
wir haben geschossen	wir würden schießen
ihr habt geschossen	ihr würdet schießen
sie haben geschossen	sie würden schießen

Pluperfect indicative	**Imperative**
ich hatte geschossen	schieß(e)!
du hattest geschossen	schießen wir!
er hatte geschossen	schießt!
wir hatten geschossen	schießen Sie!
ihr hattet geschossen	
sie hatten geschossen	

Present subjunctive

ich schieße
du schießest
er schieße
wir schießen
ihr schießet
sie schießen

schlafen *to sleep*

Present participle *schlafend*
Past participle *geschlafen*

Present indicative	**Imperfect subjunctive**
ich schlafe	ich schliefe
du schläfst	du schliefest
er schläft	er schliefe
wir schlafen	wir schliefen
ihr schlaft	ihr schliefet
sie schlafen	sie schliefen

Imperfect indicative	**Future indicative**
ich schlief	ich werde schlafen
du schliefst	du wirst schlafen
er schlief	er wird schlafen
wir schliefen	wir werden schlafen
ihr schlieft	ihr werdet schlafen
sie schliefen	sie werden schlafen

Perfect indicative	**Conditional**
ich habe geschlafen	ich würde schlafen
du hast geschlafen	du würdest schlafen
er hat geschlafen	er würde schlafen
wir haben geschlafen	wir würden schlafen
ihr habt geschlafen	ihr würdet schlafen
sie haben geschlafen	sie würden schlafen

Pluperfect indicative	**Imperative**
ich hatte geschlafen	schlaf(e)!
du hattest geschlafen	schlafen wir!
er hatte geschlafen	schlaft!
wir hatten geschlafen	schlafen Sie!
ihr hattet geschlafen	
sie hatten geschlafen	

Present subjunctive

ich schlafe
du schlafest
er schlafe
wir schlafen
ihr schlafet
sie schlafen

schlagen *to hit*

Present participle *schlagend*
Past participle *geschlagen*

Present indicative	**Imperfect subjunctive**
ich schlage	ich schlüge
du schlägst	du schlügest
er schlägt	er schlüge
wir schlagen	wir schlügen
ihr schlagt	ihr schlüget
sie schlagen	sie schlügen

Imperfect indicative	**Future indicative**
ich schlug	ich werde schlagen
du schlugst	du wirst schlagen
er schlug	er wird schlagen
wir schlugen	wir werden schlagen
ihr schlugt	ihr werdet schlagen
sie schlugen	sie werden schlagen

Perfect indicative	**Conditional**
ich habe geschlagen	ich würde schlagen
du hast geschlagen	du würdest schlagen
er hat geschlagen	er würde schlagen
wir haben geschlagen	wir würden schlagen
ihr habt geschlagen	ihr würdet schlagen
sie haben geschlagen	sie würden schlagen

Pluperfect indicative	**Imperative**
ich hatte geschlagen	schlag(e)!
du hattest geschlagen	schlagen wir!
er hatte geschlagen	schlagt!
wir hatten geschlagen	schlagen Sie!
ihr hattet geschlagen	
sie hatten geschlagen	

Present subjunctive

ich schlage
du schlagest
er schlage
wir schlagen
ihr schlaget
sie schlagen

schleichen *to creep*

Present participle *schleichend*
Past participle *geschlichen*

Present indicative	**Imperfect subjunctive**
ich schleiche	ich schliche
du schleichst	du schlichest
er schleicht	er schliche
wir schleichen	wir schlichen
ihr schleicht	ihr schlichet
sie schleichen	sie schlichen

Imperfect indicative	**Future indicative**
ich schlich	ich werde schleichen
du schlichst	du wirst schleichen
er schlich	er wird schleichen
wir schlichen	wir werden schleichen
ihr schlicht	ihr werdet schleichen
sie schlichen	sie werden schleichen

Perfect indicative	**Conditional**
ich bin geschlichen	ich würde schleichen
du bist geschlichen	du würdest schleichen
er ist geschlichen	er würde schleichen
wir sind geschlichen	wir würden schle-ichen
ihr seid geschlichen	ihr würdet schleichen
sie sind geschlichen	sie würden schleichen

Pluperfect indicative	**Imperative**
ich war geschlichen	
du warst geschlichen	schleich!
er war geschlichen	schleichen wir!
wir waren geschlichen	schleicht!
ihr wart geschlichen	schleichen Sie!
sie waren geschlichen	sleifen missing

Present subjunctive

ich schleiche
du schleichest
er schleiche
wir schleichen
ihr schleichet
sie schleichen

schleifen *to drag*

Present participle *schleifend*
Past participle *geschliffen*

Present indicative	**Imperfect subjunctive**
ich schleife	ich schliffe
du schleifst	du schliffest
er schleift	er schliffe
wir schleifen	wir schliffen
ihr schleift	ihr schliffet
sie schliefen	sie schliffen

Imperfect indicative	**Future indicative**
ich schliff	ich werde schleifen
du schliffst	du wirst schleifen
er schliff	er wird schleifen
wir schliffen	wir werden schleifen
ihr schlifft	ihr werdet schleifen
sie schliffen	sie werden schleifen

Perfect indicative	**Conditional**
ich habe geschliffen	ich würde schleifen
du hast geschliffen	du würdest schleifen
er hat geschliffen	er würde schleifen
wir haben geschliffen	wir würden schleifen
ihr habt geschliffen	ihr würdet schleifen
sie haben geschliffen	sie würden schleifen

Pluperfect indicative	**Imperative**
ich hatte geschliffen	schleif(e)!
du hattest gesliffen	schleifen wir!
er hatte geschliffen	schleift!
wir hatten geschliffen	schleifen Sie!
ihr hattet geschliffen	
sie hatten geschliffen	

Present subjunctive

ich schleife
du schleifest
er schleife
wir schleifen
ihr schleifet
sie schleifen

schlingen *to wind, wrap*

Present participle *schlingend*
Past participle *geschlungen*

Present indicative	**Present subjunctive**
ich schlinge	ich schlinge
du schlingst	du schlingest
er schlingt	er schlinge
wir schlingen	wir schlingen
ihr schlingt	ihr schlinget
sie schlingen	sie schlingen

Imperfect indicative	**Imperfect subjunctive**
ich schlang	ich schlänge
du schlangst	du schlängest
er schlang	er schlänge
wir schlangen	wir schlängen
ihr schlangt	ihr schlänget
sie schlangen	sie schlängen

Perfect indicative	**Future indicative**
ich habe geschlungen	ich werde schlingen
du hast geschlungen	du wirst schlingen
er hat geschlungen	er wird schlingen
wir haben geschlungen	wir werden schlingen
ihr habt geschlungen	ihr werdet schlingen
sie haben geschlungen	sie werden schlingen

Pluperfect indicative	**Conditional**
ich hatte geschlungen	ich würde schlingen
du hattest geschlungen	du würdest schlingen
er hatte geschlungen	er würde schlingen
wir hatten geschlungen	wir würden schlingen
ihr hattet geschlungen	ihr würdet schlingen
sie hatten geschlungen	sie würden schlingen

Imperative

schling(e)!
schlingen wir!
schlingt!
schlingen Sie!

schmelzen *to melt*

Present participle *schmelzend*
Past participle *geschmolzen*

Present indicative	**Present subjunctive**
ich schmelze	ich schmelze
du schmilzt	du schmelzest
er schmilzt	er schmelze
wir schmelzen	wir schmelzen
ihr schmelzt	ihr schmelzet
sie schmelzen	sie schmelzen

Imperfect indicative	**Imperfect subjunctive**
ich schmolz	ich schmölze
du schmolzest	du schmölzest
er schmolz	er schmölze
wir schmolzen	wir schmölzen
ihr schmolzt	ihr schmölzet
sie schmolzen	sie schmölzen

Perfect indicative	**Future indicative**
ich habe geschmolzen	ich werde schmelzen
du hast geschmolzen	du wirst schmelzen
er hat geschmolzen	er wird schmelzen
wir haben geschmolzen	wir werden schmelzen
ihr habt geschmolzen	ihr werdet schmelzen
sie haben geschmolzen	sie werden schmelzen

Pluperfect indicative	**Conditional**
ich hatte geschmolzen	ich würde schmelzen
du hattest geschmolzen	du würdest schmelzen
er hatte geschmolzen	er würde schmelzen
wir hatten geschmolzen	wir würden schmelzen
ihr hattet geschmolzen	ihr würdet schmelzen
sie hatten geschmolzen	sie würden schmelzen

Imperative

schmilz!
schmelzen wir!
schmelzt!
schmelzen Sie!

schneiden *to cut*

Present participle *schneidend*
Past participle *geschnitten*

Present indicative	**Imperfect subjunctive**
ich schneide	ich schnitte
du schneidest	du schnittest
er schneidet	er schnitte
wir schneiden	wir schnitten
ihr schneidet	ihr schnittet
sie schneiden	sie schnitten

Imperfect indicative	**Future indicative**
ich schnitt	ich werde schneiden
du schnittst	du wirst schneiden
er schnitt	er wird schneiden
wir schnitten	wir werden schneiden
ihr schnittet	ihr werdet schneiden
sie schnitten	sie werden schneiden

Perfect indicative	**Conditional**
ich habe geschnitten	ich würde schneiden
du hast geschnitten	du würdest schneiden
er hat geschnitten	er würde schneiden
wir haben geschnitten	wir würden schneiden
ihr habt geschnitten	ihr würdet schneiden
sie haben geschnitten	sie würden schneiden

Pluperfect indicative	**Imperative**
ich hatte geschnitten	schneid(e)!
du hattest geschnitten	schneiden wir!
er hatte geschnitten	schneidet!
wir hatten geschnitten	schneiden Sie!
ihr hattet geschnitten	
sie hatten geschnitten	

Present subjunctive

ich schneide
du schneidest
er schneide
wir schneiden
ihr schneidet
sie schneiden

schreien *to shout*

Present participle *schreiend*
Past participle *geschrie(e)n*

Present indicative	**Present subjunctive**
ich schreie	ich schreie
du schreist	du schreiest
er schreit	er schreie
wir schreien	wir schreien
ihr schreit	ihr schreiet
sie schreien	sie schreien

Imperfect indicative	**Imperfect subjunctive**
ich schrie	ich schriee
du schriest	du schrieest
er schrie	er schriee
wir schrieen	wir schrieen
ihr schriet	ihr schrieet
sie schrieen	sie schrieen

Perfect indicative	**Future indicative**
ich habe geschrie(e)n	ich werde schreien
du hast geschrie(e)n	du wirst schreien
er hat geschrie(e)n	er wird schreien
wir haben geschrie(e)n	wir werden schreien
ihr habt geschrie(e)n	ihr werdet schreien
sie haben geschrie(e)n	sie werden schreien

Pluperfect indicative	**Conditional**
ich hatte geschrie(e)n	ich würde schreien
du hattest geschrie(e)n	du würdest schreien
er hatte geschrie(e)n	er würde schreien
wir hatten geschrie(e)n	wir würden schreien
ihr hattet geschrie(e)n	ihr würdet schreien
sie hatten geschrie(e)n	sie würden schreien

Imperative

schrei(e)!
schreien wir!
schreit!
schreien Sie!

schreiten *to stride*

Present participle *schreitend*
Past participle *geschritten*

Present indicative	**Imperfect subjunctive**
ich schreite	ich schritte
du schreitest	du schrittest
er schreitet	er schritte
wir schreiten	wir schritten
ihr schreitet	ihr schrittet
sie schreiten	sie schritten

Imperfect indicative	**Future indicative**
ich schritt	ich werde schreiten
du schritt(e)st	du wirst schreiten
er schritt	er wird schreiten
wir schritten	wir werden schreiten
ihr schrittet	ihr werdet schreiten
sie schritten	sie werden schreiten

Perfect indicative	**Conditional**
ich bin geschritten	ich würde schreiten
du bist geschritten	du würdest schreiten
er ist geschritten	er würde schreiten
wir sind geschritten	wir würden schreiten
ihr seid geschritten	ihr würdet schreiten
sie sind geschritten	sie würden schreiten

Pluperfect indicative	**Imperative**
ich war geschritten	schreit(e)!
du warst geschritten	schreiten wir!
er war geschritten	schreitet!
wir waren geschritten	schreiten Sie!
ihr wart geschritten	
sie waren geschritten	

Present subjunctive

ich schreite
du schreitest
er schreite
wir schreiten
ihr schreitet
sie schreiten

schwellen *to swell*

Present participle *schwellend*
Past participle *geschwollen*

Present indicative	**Present subjunctive**
ich schwelle	ich schwelle
du schwillst	du schwellest
er schwillt	er schwelle
wir schwellen	wir schwellen
ihr schwellt	ihr schwellet
sie schwellen	sie schwellen

Imperfect indicative	**Imperfect subjunctive**
ich schwoll	ich schwölle
du schwollst	du schwöllest
er schwoll	er schwölle
wir schwollen	wir schwöllen
ihr schwollt	ihr schwöllet
sie schwollen	sie schwöllen

Perfect indicative	**Future indicative**
ich bin geschwollen	ich werde schwellen
du bist geschwollen	du wirst schwellen
er ist geschwollen	er wird schwellen
wir sind geschwollen	wir werden schwellen
ihr seid geschwollen	ihr werdet schwellen
sie sind geschwollen	sie werden schwellen

Pluperfect indicative	**Conditional**
ich war geschwollen	ich würde schwellen
du warst geschwollen	du würdest schwellen
er war geschwollen	er würde schwellen
wir waren geschwollen	wir würden schwellen
ihr wart geschwollen	ihr würdet schwellen
sie waren geschwollen	sie würden schwellen

Imperative

schwill!
schwellen wir!
schwellt!
schwellen Sie!

schwimmen *to swim*

Present participle *schwimmend*
Past participle *geschwommen*

Present indicative	**Present subjunctive**
ich schwimme	ich schwimme
du schwimmst	du schwimmest
er schwimmt	er schwimme
wir schwimmen	wir schwimmen
ihr schwimmt	ihr schwimmet
sie schwimmen	sie schwimmen

Imperfect indicative	**Imperfect subjunctive**
ich schwamm	ich schwömme
du schwammst	du schwömmest
er schwamm	er schwömme
wir schwammen	wir schwömmen
ihr schwammt	ihr schwömmet
sie schwammen	sie schwömmen

Perfect indicative	**Future indicative**
ich bin geschwommen	ich werde schwimmen
du bist geschwommen	du wirst schwimmen
er ist geschwommen	er wird schwimmen
wir sind geschwommen	wir werden schwimmen
ihr seid geschwommen	ihr werdet schwimmen
sie sind geschwommen	sie werden schwimmen

Pluperfect indicative	**Conditional**
ich war geschwommen	ich würde schwimmen
du warst geschwommen	du würdest schwimmen
er war geschwommen	er würde schwimmen
wir waren geschwommen	wir würden schwimmen
ihr wart geschwommen	ihr würdet schwimmen
sie waren geschwommen	sie würden schwimmen

Imperative

schwimm(e)!
schwimmen wir!
schwimmt!
schwimmen Sie!

schwingen *to swing*

Present participle *schwingen*
Past participle *beschwungen*

Present indicative	**Present subjunctive**
ich schwinge	ich schwinge
du schwingst	du schwingest
er schwingt	er schwinge
wir schwingen	wir schwingen
ihr schwingt	ihr schwinget
sie schwingen	sie schwing en

Imperfect indicative	**Imperfect subjunctive**
ich schwang	ich schwänge
du schwangst	du schwängest
er schwang	er schwänge
wir schwangen	wir schwängen
ihr schwangt	ihr schwänget
sie schwangen	sie schwängen

Perfect indicative	**Future indicative**
ich habe geschwungen	ich werde schwingen
du hast geschwungen	du wirst schwingen
er hat geschwungen	er wird schwingen
wir haben geschwungen	wir werden schwingen
ihr habt geschwungen	ihr werdet schwingen
sie haben geschwungen	sie werden schwingen

Conditional

Pluperfect indicative	
ich hatte geschwungen	ich würde schwingen
du hattest geschwungen	du würdest schwingen
er hatte geschwungen	er würde schwingen
wir hatten geschwungen	wir würden schwingen
ihr hattet geschwungen	ihr würdet schwingen
sie hatten geschwungen	sie würden schwingen

Imperative

schwing(e)!
schwingen wir!
schwingt!
schwingen Sie!

schwören *to swear, vow*

Present participle *schwörend*
Past participle *geschworen*

Present indicative	**Present subjunctive**
ich schwöre	ich schwöre
du schwörst	du schwörest
er schwört	er schwöre
wir schwören	wir schwören
ihr schwört	ihr schwöret
sie schwören	sie schwören

Imperfect indicative	**Imperfect subjunctive**
ich schwor	ich schwüre
du schworst	du schwürest
er schwor	er schwüre
wir schworen	wir schwüren
ihr schwort	ihr schwüret
sie schworen	sie schwüren

Perfect indicative	**Future indicative**
ich habe geschworen	ich werde schwören
du hast geschworen	du wirst schwören
er hat geschworen	er wird schwören
wir haben geschworen	wir werden schwören
ihr habt geschworen	ihr werdet schwören
sie haben geschworen	sie werden schwören

Conditional

Pluperfect indicative	
ich hatte geschworen	ich würde schwören
du hattest geschworen	du würdest schwören
er hatte geschworen	er würde schwören
wir hatten geschworen	wir würden schwören
ihr hattet geschworen	ihr würdet schwören
sie hatten geschworen	sie würden schwören

Imperative

schwör(e)!
schwören wir!
schwört!
schwören Sie!

sehen *to see*

Present participle *sehend*
Past participle *gesehen*

Present indicative	**Imperfect subjunctive**
ich sehe	ich sähe
du siehst	du sähest
er sieht	er sähe
wir sehen	wir sähen
ihr seht	ihr sähet
sie sehen	sie sähen

Imperfect indicative	**Future indicative**
ich sah	ich werde sehen
du sahst	du wirst sehen
er sah	er wird sehen
wir sahen	wir werden sehen
ihr saht	ihr werdet sehen
sie sahen	sie werden sehen

Perfect indicative	**Conditional**
ich habe gesehen	ich würde sehen
du hast gesehen	du würdest sehen
er hat gesehen	er würde sehen
wir haben gesehen	wir würden sehen
ihr habt gesehen	ihr würdet sehen
sie haben gesehen	sie würden sehen

Pluperfect indicative	**Imperative**
ich hatte gesehen	sieh(e)!
du hattest gesehen	sehen wir!
er hatte gesehen	seht!
wir hatten gesehen	sehen Sie!
ihr hattet gesehen	
sie hatten gesehen	

Present subjunctive

ich sehe
du sehest
er sehe
wir sehen
ihr sehet
sie sehen

sein *to be*

Present participle *seiend*
Past participle *gewesen*

Present indicative	**Imperfect subjunctive**
ich bin	ich wäre
du bist	du wärest
er ist	er wäre
wir sind	wir wären
ihr seid	ihr wäret
sie sind	sie wären

Imperfect indicative	**Future indicative**
ich war	ich werde sein
du warst	du wirst sein
er war	er wird sein
wir waren	wir werden sein
ihr wart	ihr werdet sein
sie waren	sie werden sein

Perfect indicative	**Conditional**
ich bin gewesen	ich würde sein
du bist gewesen	du würdest sein
er ist gewesen	er würde sein
wir sind gewesen	wir würden sein
ihr seid gewesen	ihr würdet sein
sie sind gewesen	sie würden sein

Pluperfect indicative	**Imperative**
ich war gewesen	sei!
du warst gewesen	seien wir!
er war gewesen	seid!
wir waren gewesen	seien Sie!
ihr wart gewesen	
sie waren gewesen	

Present subjunctive

ich sei
du seist
er sei
wir seien
ihr seiet
sie seien

senden *to send*

Present participle *sendend*
Past participle *gesandt*

Present indicative	**Imperfect subjunctive**
ich sende	ich sendete
du sendest	du sendetest
er sendet	er sendete
wir senden	wir sendeten
ihr sendet	ihr sendetet
sie senden	sie sendeten

Imperfect indicative	**Future indicative**
ich sandte	ich werde senden
du sandtest	du wirst senden
er sandte	er wird senden
wir sandten	wir werden senden
ihr sandtet	ihr werdet senden
sie sandten	sie werden senden

Perfect indicative	**Conditional**
ich habe gesandt	ich würde senden
du hast gesandt	du würdest senden
er hat gesandt	er würde senden
wir haben gesandt	wir würden senden
ihr habt gesandt	ihr würdet senden
sie haben gesandt	sie würden senden

Pluperfect indicative	**Imperative**
ich hatte gesandt	send(e)!
du hattest gesandt	senden wir!
er hatte gesandt	sendet!
wir hatten gesandt	senden Sie!
ihr hattet gesandt	
sie hatten gesandt	

Present subjunctive

ich sende
du sendest
er sende
wir senden
ihr sendet
sie senden

singen *to sing*

Present participle *singend*
Past participle *gesungen*

Present indicative	**Imperfect subjunctive**
ich singe	ich sänge
du singst	du sängest
er singt	er sänge
wir singen	wir sängen
ihr singt	ihr sänget
sie singen	sie sängen

Imperfect indicative	**Future indicative**
ich sang	ich werde singen
du sangst	du wirst singen
er sang	er wird singen
wir sangen	wir werden singen
ihr sangt	ihr werdet singen
sie sangen	sie werden singen

Perfect indicative	**Conditional**
ich habe gesungen	ich würde singen
du hast gesungen	du würdest singen
er hat gesungen	er würde singen
wir haben gesungen	wir würden singen
ihr habt gesungen	ihr würdet singen
sie haben gesungen	sie würden singen

Pluperfect indicative	**Imperative**
ich hatte gesungen	sing(e)!
du hattest gesungen	singen wir!
er hatte gesungen	singt!
wir hatten gesungen	singen Sie!
ihr hattet gesungen	
sie hatten gesungen	

Present subjunctive

ich singe
du singest
er singe
wir singen
ihr singet
sie singen

sinken *to sink*

Present participle *sinkend*
Past participle *gesunken*

Present indicative	**Imperfect subjunctive**
ich sinke	ich sänke
du sinkst	du sänkest
er sinkt	er sänke
wir sinken	wir sänken
ihr sinkt	ihr sänket
sie sinken	sie sänken

Imperfect indicative	**Future indicative**
ich sank	ich werde sinken
du sankst	du wirst sinken
er sank	er wird sinken
wir sanken	wir werden sinken
ihr sankt	ihr werdet sinken
sie sanken	sie werden sinken

Perfect indicative	**Conditional**
ich bin gesunken	ich würde sinken
du bist gesunken	du würdest sinken
er ist gesunken	er würde sinken
wir sind gesunken	wir würden sinken
ihr seid gesunken	ihr würdet sinken
sie sind gesunken	sie würden sinken

Pluperfect indicative	**Imperative**
ich war gesunken	sink(e)!
du warst gesunken	sinken wir!
er war gesunken	sinkt!
wir waren gesunken	sinken Sie!
ihr wart gesunken	
sie waren gesunken	

Present subjunctive

ich sinke
du sinkest
er sinke
wir sinken
ihr sinket
sie sinken

sinnen *to meditate*

Present participle *sinnend*
Past participle *gesonnen*

Present indicative	**Imperfect subjunctive**
ich sinne	ich sänne
du sinnst	du sännest
er sinnt	er sänne
wir sinnen	wir sännen
ihr sinnt	ihr sännet
sie sinnen	sie sännen

Imperfect indicative	**Future indicative**
ich sann	ich werde gesinnen
du sannst	du wirst gesinnen
er sann	er wird gesinnen
wir sannen	wir werden gesinnen
ihr sannt	ihr werdet gesinnen
sie sannen	sie werden gesinnen

Perfect indicative	**Conditional**
ich habe gesonnen	ich würde gesinnen
du hast gesonnen	du würdest gesinnen
er hat gesonnen	er würde gesinnen
wir haben gesonnen	wir würden gesinnen
ihr habt gesonnen	ihr würdet gesinnen
sie haben gesonnen	sie würden gesinnen

Pluperfect indicative	**Imperative**
ich hatte gesonnen	sinn(e)!
du hattest gesonnen	sinnen wir!
er hatte gesonnen	sinnt!
wir hatten gesonnen	sinnen Sie!
ihr hattet gesonnen	
sie hatten gesonnen	

Present subjunctive

ich sinne
du sinnest
er sinne
wir sinnen
ihr sinnet
sie sinnen

sitzen *to sit*

Present participle *sitzend*
Past participle *gesessen*

Present indicative	Imperfect subjunctive
ich sitze	ich säße
du sitzt	du säßest
er sitzt	er säße
wir sitzen	wir säßen
ihr sitzt	ihr säßet
sie sitzen	sie säßen

Imperfect indicative	Future indicative
ich saß	ich werde sitzen
du saßest	du wirst sitzen
er saß	er wird sitzen
wir saßen	wir werden sitzen
ihr saßt	ihr werdet sitzen
sie saßen	sie werden sitzen

Perfect indicative	Conditional
ich habe gesessen	ich würde sitzen
du hast gesessen	du würdest sitzen
er hat gesessen	er würde sitzen
wir haben gesessen	wir würden sitzen
ihr habt gesessen	ihr würdet sitzen
sie haben gesessen	sie würden sitzen

Pluperfect indicative	Imperative
ich hatte gesessen	sitz(e)!
du hattest gesessen	sitzen wir!
er hatte gesessen	sitzt!
wir hatten gesessen	sitzen Sie!
ihr hattet gesessen	
sie hatten gesessen	

Present subjunctive

ich sitze
du sitzest
er sitze
wir sitzen
ihr sitzet
sie sitzen

sollen *to be to*

Present participle *sollend*
Past participle *gesollt/sollen**

Present indicative	Present subjunctive
ich soll	ich solle
du sollst	du sollest
er soll	er solle
wir sollen	wir sollen
ihr sollt	ihr sollet
sie sollen	sie sollen

Imperfect indicative	Imperfect subjunctive
ich sollte	ich sollte
du solltest	du solltest
er sollte	er sollte
wir sollten	wir sollten
ihr solltet	ihr solltet
sie sollten	sie sollten

Perfect indicative	Future indicative
ich habe gesollt	ich werde sollen
du hast gesollt	du wirst sollen
er hat gesollt	er wird sollen
wir haben gesollt	wir werden sollen
ihr habt gesollt	ihr werdet sollen
sie haben gesollt	sie werden sollen

Pluperfect indicative	Conditional
ich hatte gesollt	ich würde sollen
du hattest gesollt	du würdest sollen
er hatte gesollt	er würde sollen
wir hatten gesollt	wir würden sollen
ihr hattet gesollt	ihr würdet sollen
sie hatten gesollt	sie würden sollen

* sollen *is used when preceded by an infinitive*

speien *to spew*

Present participle *speiend*
Past participle *gespie(e)n*

Present indicative	Imperfect subjunctive
ich speie	ich spiee
du speist	du spieest
er speit	er spiee
wir speien	wir spieen
ihr speit	ihr spieet
sie speien	sie spieen

Imperfect indicative	Future indicative
ich spie	ich werde speien
du spiest	du wirst speien
er spie	er wird speien
wir spieen	wir werden speien
ihr spiet	ihr werdet speien
sie spieen	sie werden speien

Perfect indicative	Conditional
ich habe gespie(e)n	ich würde speien
du hast gespie(e)n	du würdest speien
er hat gespie(e)n	er würde speien
wir haben gespie(e)n	wir würden speien
ihr habt gespie(e)n	ihr würdet speien
sie haben gespie(e)n	sie würden speien

Pluperfect indicative	Imperative
ich hatte gespie(e)n	spei(e)!
du hattest gespie(e)n	speien wir!
er hatte gespie(e)n	speit!
wir hatten gespie(e)n	speien Sie!
ihr hattet gespie(e)n	
sie hatten gespie(e)n	

Present subjunctive

ich speie
du speiest
er speie
wir speien
ihr speiet
sie speien

spielen *to play*

Present participle *spielend*
Past participle *gespielt*

Present indicative	Imperfect subjunctive
ich spiele	ich spielte
du spielst	du spieltest
er spielt	er spielte
wir spielen	wir spielten
ihr spielt	ihr spieltet
sie spielen	sie spielten

Imperfect indicative	Future indicative
ich spielte	ich werde spielen
du spieltest	du wirst spielen
er spielte	er wird spielen
wir spielten	wir werden spielen
ihr spieltet	ihr werdet spielen
sie spielten	sie werden spielen

Perfect indicative	Conditional
ich habe gespielt	ich würde spielen
du hast gespielt	du würdest spielen
er hat gespielt	er würde spielen
wir haben gespielt	wir würden spielen
ihr habt gespielt	ihr würdet spielen
sie haben gespielt	sie würden spielen

Pluperfect indicative	Imperative
ich hatte gespielt	spiel(e)!
du hattest gespielt	spielen wir!
er hatte gespielt	spielt!
wir hatten gespielt	spielen Sie!
ihr hattet gespielt	
sie hatten gespielt	

Present subjunctive

ich spiele
du spielest
er spiele
wir spielen
ihr spielet
sie spielen

spinnen *to spin*

Present participle *spinnend*
Past participle *gesponnen*

Present indicative	**Imperfect subjunctive**
ich spinne	ich spönne
du spinnst	du spönnest
er spinnt	er spönne
wir spinnen	wir spönnen
ihr spinnt	ihr spönnet
sie spinnen	sie spönnen

Imperfect indicative	**Future indicative**
ich spann	ich werde gespinnen
du spannst	du wirst gespinnen
er spann	er wird gespinnen
wir spannen	wir werden gespinnen
ihr spannt	ihr werdet gespinnen
sie spannen	sie werden gespinnen

Perfect indicative	**Conditional**
ich habe gesponnen	ich würde gespinnen
du hast gesponnen	du würdest gespinnen
er hat gesponnen	er würde gespinnen
wir haben gesponnen	wir würden gespinnen
ihr habt gesponnen	ihr würdet gespinnen
sie haben gesponnen	sie würden gespinnen

Pluperfect indicative	**Imperative**
ich hatte gesponnen	spinn(e)!
du hattest gesponnen	spinnen wir!
er hatte gesponnen	spinnt!
wir hatten gesponnen	spinnen Sie!
ihr hattet gesponnen	
sie hatten gesponnen	

Present subjunctive

ich spinne
du spinnest
er spinne
wir spinnen
ihr spinnet
sie spinnen

sprechen *to speak*

Present participle *sprechend*
Past participle *gesprochen*

Present indicative	**Imperfect subjunctive**
ich spreche	ich spräche
du sprichst	du sprächest
er spricht	er spräche
wir sprechen	wir sprächen
ihr sprecht	ihr sprächet
sie sprechen	sie sprächen

Imperfect indicative	**Future indicative**
ich sprach	ich werde sprechen
du sprachst	du wirst sprechen
er sprach	er wird sprechen
wir sprachen	wir werden sprechen
ihr spracht	ihr werdet sprechen
sie sprachen	sie werden sprechen

Perfect indicative	**Conditional**
ich habe gesprochen	ich würde sprechen
du hast gesprochen	du würdest sprechen
er hat gesprochen	er würde sprechen
wir haben gesprochen	wir würden sprechen
ihr habt gesprochen	ihr würdet sprechen
sie haben gesprochen	sie würden sprechen

Pluperfect indicative	**Imperative**
ich hatte gesprochen	sprich!
du hattest gesprochen	sprechen wir!
er hatte gesprochen	sprecht!
wir hatten gesprochen	sprechen Sie!
ihr hattet gesprochen	
sie hatten gesprochen	

Present subjunctive

ich spreche
du sprechest
er spreche
wir sprechen
ihr sprechet
sie sprechen

sprießen *to sprout*

Present participle *sprießend*
Past participle *gesprossen*

Present indicative	Imperfect subjunctive
ich sprieße	ich sprösse
du sprießt	du sprössest
er sprießt	er sprösse
wir sprießen	wir sprössen
ihr sprießt	ihr sprösset
sie sprießen	sie sprössen

Imperfect indicative	Future indicative
ich sproß	ich werde sprießen
du sprossest	du wirst sprießen
er sproß	er wird sprießen
wir sprossen	wir werden sprießen
ihr sproßt	ihr werdet sprießen
sie sprossen	sie werden sprießen

Perfect indicative	Conditional
ich bin gesprossen	ich würde sprießen
du bist gesprossen	du würdest sprießen
er ist gesprossen	er würde sprießen
wir sind gesprossen	wir würden sprießen
ihr seid gesprossen	ihr würdet sprießen
sie sind gesprossen	sie würden sprießen

Pluperfect indicative	Imperative
ich war gesprossen	sprieß(e)!
du warst gesprossen	sprießen wir!
er war gesprossen	sprießt!
wir waren gesprossen	sprießen Sie!
ihr wart gesprossen	
sie waren gesprossen	

Present subjunctive

ich sprieße
du sprießest
er sprieße
wir sprießen
ihr sprießet
sie sprießen

springen *to jump*

Present participle *springend*
Past participle *gesprungen*

Present indicative	Imperfect subjunctive
ich springe	ich spränge
du springst	du sprängest
er springt	er spränge
wir springen	wir sprängen
ihr springt	ihr spränget
sie springen	sie sprängen

Imperfect indicative	Future indicative
ich sprang	ich werde springen
du sprangst	du wirst springen
er sprang	er wird springen
wir sprangen	wir werden springen
ihr sprangt	ihr werdet springen
sie sprangen	sie werden springen

Perfect indicative	Conditional
ich bin gesprungen	ich würde springen
du bist gesprungen	du würdest springen
er ist gesprungen	er würde springen
wir sind gesprungen	wir würden springen
ihr seid gesprungen	ihr würdet springen
sie sind gesprungen	sie würden springen

Pluperfect indicative	Imperative
ich war gesprungen	spring(e)!
du warst gesprungen	springen wir!
er war gesprungen	springt!
wir waren gesprungen	springen Sie!
ihr wart gesprungen	
sie waren gesprungen	

Present subjunctive

ich springe
du springest
er springe
wir springen
ihr springet
sie springen

stechen *to sting, prick*

Present participle *stechend*
Past participle *gestochen*

Present indicative	**Imperfect subjunctive**
ich steche	ich stäche
du stichst	du stächest
er sticht	er stäche
wir stechen	wir stächen
ihr stecht	ihr stächet
sie stechen	sie stächen

Imperfect indicative	**Future indicative**
ich stach	ich werde stechen
du stachst	du wirst stechen
er stach	er wird stechen
wir stachen	wir werden stechen
ihr stacht	ihr werdet stechen
sie stachen	sie werden stechen

Perfect indicative	**Conditional**
ich habe gestochen	ich würde stechen
du hast gestochen	du würdest stechen
er hat gestochen	er würde stechen
wir haben gestochen	wir würden stechen
ihr habt gestochen	ihr würdet stechen
sie haben gestochen	sie würden stechen

Pluperfect indicative	**Imperative**
ich hatte gestochen	stich!
du hattest gestochen	stechen wir!
er hatte gestochen	stecht!
wir hatten gestochen	stechen Sie!
ihr hattet gestochen	
sie hatten gestochen	

Present subjunctive
ich steche
du stechest
er steche
wir stechen
ihr stechet
sie stechen

stehen *to stand*

Present participle *stehend*
Past participle *gestanden*

Present indicative	**Imperfect subjunctive**
ich stehe	ich stünde
du stehst	du stündest
er steht	er stünde
wir stehen	wir stünden
ihr steht	ihr stündet
sie stehen	sie stünden

Imperfect indicative	**Future indicative**
ich stand	ich werde stehen
du stand(e)st	du wirst stehen
er stand	er wird stehen
wir standen	wir werden stehen
ihr standet	ihr werdet stehen
sie standen	sie werden stehen

Perfect indicative	**Conditional**
ich habe gestanden	ich würde stehen
du hast gestanden	du würdest stehen
er hat gestanden	er würde stehen
wir haben gestanden	wir würden stehen
ihr habt gestanden	ihr würdet stehen
sie haben gestanden	sie würden stehen

Pluperfect indicative	**Imperative**
ich hatte gestanden	steh(e)!
du hattest gestanden	stehen wir!
er hatte gestanden	steht!
wir hatten gestanden	stehen Sie!
ihr hattet gestanden	
sie hatten gestanden	

Present subjunctive
ich stehe
du stehest
er stehe
wir stehen
ihr stehet
sie stehen

stehlen *to steal*

Present participle *stehlend*
Past participle *gestohlen*

Present indicative	Imperfect subjunctive
ich stehle	ich stähle
du stiehlst	du stählest
er stiehlt	er stähle
wir stehlen	wir stählen
ihr stehlt	ihr stählet
sie stehlen	sie stählen

Imperfect indicative	Future indicative
ich stahl	ich werde stehlen
du stahlst	du wirst stehlen
er stahl	er wird stehlen
wir stahlen	wir werden stehlen
ihr stahlt	ihr werdet stehlen
sie stahlen	sie werden stehlen

Perfect indicative	Conditional
ich habe gestohlen	ich würde stehlen
du hast gestohlen	du würdest stehlen
er hat gestohlen	er würde stehlen
wir haben gestohlen	wir würden stehlen
ihr habt gestohlen	ihr würdet stehlen
sie haben gestohlen	sie würden stehlen

Pluperfect indicative	Imperative
ich hatte gestohlen	stiehl!
du hattest gestohlen	stehlen wir!
er hatte gestohlen	stehlt!
wir hatten gestohlen	stehlen Sie!
ihr hattet gestohlen	
sie hatten gestohlen	

Present subjunctive
ich stehle
du stehlest
er stehle
wir stehlen
ihr stehlet
sie stehlen

steigen *to climb*

Present participle *steigend*
Past participle *gestiegen*

Present indicative	Imperfect subjunctive
ich steige	ich stiege
du steigst	du stiegest
er steigt	er stiege
wir steigen	wir stiegen
ihr steigt	ihr stieget
sie steigen	sie stiegen

Imperfect indicative	Future indicative
ich stieg	ich werde steigen
du stiegst	du wirst steigen
er stieg	er wird steigen
wir stiegen	wir werden steigen
ihr stiegt	ihr werdet steigen
sie stiegen	sie werden steigen

Perfect indicative	Conditional
ich bin gestiegen	ich würde steigen
du bist gestiegen	du würdest steigen
er ist gestiegen	er würde steigen
wir sind gestiegen	wir würden steigen
ihr seid gestiegen	ihr würdet steigen
sie sind gestiegen	sie würden steigen

Pluperfect indicative	Imperative
ich war gestiegen	steig(e)!
du warst gestiegen	steigen wir!
er war gestiegen	steigt!
wir waren gestiegen	steigen Sie!
ihr wart gestiegen	
sie waren gestiegen	

Present subjunctive
ich steige
du steigest
er steige
wir steigen
ihr steiget
sie steigen

sterben *to die*

Present participle *sterbend*
Past participle *gestorben*

Present indicative	Imperfect subjunctive
ich sterbe	ich stürbe
du stirbst	du stürbest
er stirbt	er stürbe
wir sterben	wir stürben
ihr sterbt	ihr stürbet
sie sterben	sie stürben

Imperfect indicative	Future indicative
ich starb	ich werde sterben
du starbst	du wirst sterben
er starb	er wird sterben
wir starben	wir werden sterben
ihr starbt	ihr werdet sterben
sie starben	sie werden sterben

Perfect indicative	Conditional
ich bin gestorben	ich würde sterben
du bist gestorben	du würdest sterben
er ist gestorben	er würde sterben
wir sind gestorben	wir würden sterben
ihr seid gestorben	ihr würdet sterben
sie sind gestorben	sie würden sterben

Pluperfect indicative	Imperative
ich war gestorben	stirb!
du warst gestorben	sterben wir!
er war gestorben	sterbt!
wir waren gestorben	sterben Sie!
ihr wart gestorben	
sie waren gestorben	

Present subjunctive

ich sterbe
du sterbest
er sterbe
wir sterben
ihr sterbet
sie sterben

stinken *to stink*

Present participle *stinkend*
Past participle *gestunken*

Present indicative	Imperfect subjunctive
ich stinke	ich stänke
du stinkst	du stänkest
er stinkt	er stänke
wir stinken	wir stänken
ihr stinkt	ihr stänket
sie stinken	sie stänken

Imperfect indicative	Future indicative
ich stank	ich werde stinken
du stankst	du wirst stinken
er stank	er wird stinken
wir stanken	wir werden stinken
ihr stankt	ihr werdet stinken
sie stanken	sie werden stinken

Perfect indicative	Conditional
ich habe gestunken	ich würde stinken
du hast gestunken	du würdest stinken
er hat gestunken	er würde stinken
wir haben gestunken	wir würden stinken
ihr habt gestunken	ihr würdet stinken
sie haben gestunken	sie würden stinken

Pluperfect indicative	Imperative
ich hatte gestunken	stink(e)!
du hattest gestunken	stinken wir!
er hatte gestunken	stinkt!
wir hatten gestunken	stinken Sie!
ihr hattet gestunken	
sie hatten gestunken	

Present subjunctive

ich stinke
du stinkest
er stinke
wir stinken
ihr stinket
sie stinken

stoßen *to push*

Present participle *stoßend*
Past participle *gestoßen*

Present indicative	**Imperfect subjunctive**
ich stoße	ich stieße
du stößt	du stießest
er stößt	er stieße
wir stoßen	wir stießen
ihr stoßt	ihr stießet
sie stoßen	sie stießen

Imperfect indicative	**Future indicative**
ich stieß	ich werde stoßen
du stießest	du wirst stoßen
er stieß	er wird stoßen
wir stießen	wir werden stoßen
ihr stießt	ihr werdet stoßen
sie stießen	sie werden stoßen

Perfect indicative	**Conditional**
ich habe gestoßen	ich würde stoßen
du hast gestoßen	du würdest stoßen
er hat gestoßen	er würde stoßen
wir haben gestoßen	wir würden stoßen
ihr habt gestoßen	ihr würdet stoßen
sie haben gestoßen	sie würden stoßen

Pluperfect indicative	**Imperative**
ich hatte gestoßen	stoß(e)!
du hattest gestoßen	stoßen wir!
er hatte gestoßen	stoßt!
wir hatten gestoßen	stoßen Sie!
ihr hattet gestoßen	
sie hatten gestoßen	

Present subjunctive

ich stoße
du stoßest
er stoße
wir stoßen
ihr stoßet
sie stoßen

streichen *to stroke*

Present participle *streichend*
Past participle *gestrichen*

Present indicative	**Imperfect subjunctive**
ich streiche	ich striche
du streichst	du strichest
er streicht	er striche
wir streichen	wir strichen
ihr streicht	ihr strichet
sie streichen	sie strichen

Imperfect indicative	**Future indicative**
ich strich	ich werde streichen
du strichst	du wirst streichen
er strich	er wird streichen
wir strichen	wir werden streichen
ihr stricht	ihr werdet streichen
sie strichen	sie werden streichen

Perfect indicative	**Conditional**
ich habe gestrichen	ich würde streichen
du hast gestrichen	du würdest streichen
er hat gestrichen	er würde streichen
wir haben gestrichen	wir würden streichen
ihr habt gestrichen	ihr würdet streichen
sie haben gestrichen	sie würden streichen

Pluperfect indicative	**Imperative**
ich hatte gestrichen	streich(e)!
du hattest gestrichen	streichen wir!
er hatte gestrichen	streicht!
wir hatten gestrichen	streichen Sie!
ihr hattet gestrichen	
sie hatten gestrichen	

Present subjunctive

ich streiche
du streichest
er streiche
wir streichen
ihr streichet
sie streichen

streiten *to quarrel*

Present participle *streitend*
Past participle *gestritten*

Present indicative	**Imperfect subjunctive**
ich streite	ich stritte
du streitest	du strittest
er streitet	er stritte
wir streiten	wir stritten
ihr streitet	ihr strittet
sie streiten	sie stritten

Imperfect indicative	**Future indicative**
ich stritt	ich werde streiten
du stritt(e)st	du wirst streiten
er stritt	er wird streiten
wir stritten	wir werden streiten
ihr strittet	ihr werdet streiten
sie stritten	sie werden streiten

Perfect indicative	**Conditional**
ich habe gestritten	ich würde streiten
du hast gestritten	du würdest streiten
er hat gestritten	er würde streiten
wir haben gestritten	wir würden streiten
ihr habt gestritten	ihr würdet streiten
sie haben gestritten	sie würden streiten

Pluperfect indicative	**Imperative**
ich hatte gestritten	streit(e)!
du hattest gestritten	streiten wir!
er hatte gestritten	streitet!
wir hatten gestritten	streiten Sie!
ihr hattet gestritten	
sie hatten gestritten	

Present subjunctive

ich streite
du streitest
er streite
wir streiten
ihr streitet
sie streiten

studieren *to study*

Present participle *studierend*
Past participle *studiert*

Present indicative	**Imperfect subjunctive**
ich studiere	ich studierte
du studierst	du studiertest
er studiert	er studierte
wir studieren	wir studierten
ihr studiert	ihr studiertet
sie studieren	sie studierten

Imperfect indicative	**Future indicative**
ich studierte	ich werde studieren
du studiertest	du wirst studieren
er studierte	er wird studieren
wir studierten	wir werden studieren
ihr studiertet	ihr werdet studieren
sie studierten	sie werden studieren

Perfect indicative	**Conditional**
ich habe studiert	ich würde studieren
du hast studiert	du würdest studieren
er hat studiert	er würde studieren
wir haben studiert	wir würden studieren
ihr habt studiert	ihr würdet studieren
sie haben studiert	sie würden studieren

Pluperfect indicative	**Imperative**
ich hatte studiert	studiere!
du hattest studiert	studieren wir!
er hatte studiert	studiert!
wir hatten studiert	studieren Sie!
ihr hattet studiert	
sie hatten studiert	

Present subjunctive

ich studiere
du studierest
er studiere
wir studieren
ihr studieret
sie studieren

tragen *to wear; to carry*

Present participle *tragend*
Past participle *getragen*

Present indicative	Imperfect subjunctive
ich trage	ich trüge
du trägst	du trügest
er trägt	er trüge
wir tragen	wir trügen
ihr tragt	ihr trüget
sie tragen	sie trügen

Imperfect indicative	Future indicative
ich trug	ich werde tragen
du trugst	du wirst tragen
er trug	er wird tragen
wir trugen	wir werden tragen
ihr trugt	ihr werdet tragen
sie trugen	sie werden tragen

Perfect indicative	Conditional
ich habe getragen	ich würde tragen
du hast getragen	du würdest tragen
er hat getragen	er würde tragen
wir haben getragen	wir würden tragen
ihr habt getragen	ihr würdet tragen
sie haben getragen	sie würden tragen

Pluperfect indicative	Imperative
ich hatte getragen	trag(e)!
du hattest getragen	tragen wir!
er hatte getragen	tragt!
wir hatten getragen	tragen Sie!
ihr hattet getragen	
sie hatten getragen	

Present subjunctive

ich trage
du tragest
er trage
wir tragen
ihr traget
sie tragen

treffen *to meet*

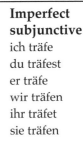

Present participle *treffend*
Past participle *getroffen*

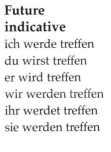

Present indicative	Imperfect subjunctive
ich treffe	ich träfe
du triffst	du träfest
er trifft	er träfe
wir treffen	wir träfen
ihr trefft	ihr träfet
sie treffen	sie träfen

Imperfect indicative	Future indicative
ich traf	ich werde treffen
du trafst	du wirst treffen
er traf	er wird treffen
wir trafen	wir werden treffen
ihr traft	ihr werdet treffen
sie trafen	sie werden treffen

Perfect indicative	Conditional
ich habe getroffen	ich würde treffen
du hast getroffen	du würdest treffen
er hat getroffen	er würde treffen
wir haben getroffen	wir würden treffen
ihr habt getroffen	ihr würdet treffen
sie haben getroffen	sie würden treffen

Pluperfect indicative	Imperative
ich hatte getroffen	triff!
du hattest getroffen	treffen wir!
er hatte getroffen	trefft!
wir hatten getroffen	treffen Sie!
ihr hattet getroffen	
sie hatten getroffen	

Present subjunctive

ich treffe
du treffest
er treffe
wir treffen
ihr treffet
sie treffen

treiben *to drive*

Present participle *treibend*
Past participle *getrieben*

Present indicative	**Imperfect subjunctive**
ich treibe	ich triebe
du treibst	du triebest
er treibt	er triebe
wir treiben	wir trieben
ihr treibt	ihr triebet
sie treiben	sie trieben

Imperfect indicative	**Future indicative**
ich trieb	ich werde treiben
du triebst	du wirst treiben
er trieb	er wird treiben
wir trieben	wir werden treiben
ihr triebt	ihr werdet treiben
sie trieben	sie werden treiben

Perfect indicative	**Conditional**
ich habe getrieben	ich würde treiben
du hast getrieben	du würdest treiben
er hat getrieben	er würde treiben
wir haben getrieben	wir würden treiben
ihr habt getrieben	ihr würdet treiben
sie haben getrieben	sie würden treiben

Pluperfect indicative	**Imperative**
ich hatte getrieben	treib(e)!
du hattest getrieben	treiben wir!
er hatte getrieben	treibt!
wir hatten getrieben	treiben Sie!
ihr hattet getrieben	
sie hatten getrieben	

Present subjunctive

ich treibe
du treibest
er treibe
wir treiben
ihr treibet
sie treiben

treten *to step*

Present participle *tretend*
Past participle *getreten*

Present indicative	**Present subjunctive**
ich trete	ich trete
du trittst	du tretest
er tritt	er trete
wir treten	wir treten
ihr tretet	ihr tretet
sie treten	sie treten

Imperfect indicative	**Imperfect subjunctive**
ich trat	ich träte
du trat(e)st	du trätest
er trat	er träte
wir traten	wir träten
ihr tratet	ihr trätet
sie traten	sie träten

Perfect indicative	**Future indicative**
ich bin/habe getreten	ich werde treten
du bist/hast getreten	du wirst treten
er ist/hat getreten	er wird treten
wir sind/haben getreten	wir werden treten
ihr seid/habt getreten	ihr werdet treten
sie sind/haben getreten	sie werden treten

Pluperfect indicative	**Conditional**
ich war/hatte getreten	ich würde treten
du warst/hattest getreten	du würdest treten
er war/hatte getreten	er würde treten
wir waren/hatten getreten	wir würden treten
ihr wart/hattet getreten	ihr würdet treten
sie waren/hatten getreten	sie würden treten

Imperative

tritt(e)!
treten wir!
tretet!
treten Sie!

trinken *to drink*

Present participle *trinkend*
Past participle *getrunken*

Present indicative	**Imperfect subjunctive**
ich trinke	ich tränke
du trinkst	du tränkest
er trinkt	er tränke
wir trinken	wir tränken
ihr trinkt	ihr tränket
sie trinken	sie tränken

Imperfect indicative	**Future indicative**
ich trank	ich werde trinken
du trankst	du wirst trinken
er trank	er wird trinken
wir tranken	wir werden trinken
ihr trankt	ihr werdet trinken
sie tranken	sie werden trinken

Perfect indicative	**Conditional**
ich habe getrunken	ich würde trinken
du hast getrunken	du würdest trinken
er hat getrunken	er würde trinken
wir haben getrunken	wir würden trinken
ihr habt getrunken	ihr würdet trinken
sie haben getrunken	sie würden trinken

Pluperfect indicative	**Imperative**
ich hatte getrunken	trink(e)!
du hattest getrunken	trinken wir!
er hatte getrunken	trinkt!
wir hatten getrunken	trinken Sie!
ihr hattet getrunken	
sie hatten getrunken	

Present subjunctive

ich trinke
du trinkest
er trinke
wir trinken
ihr trinket
sie trinken

trügen *to deceive*

Present participle *trügend*
Past participle *getrogen*

Present indicative	**Imperfect subjunctive**
ich trüge	ich tröge
du trügst	du trögest
er trügt	er tröge
wir trügen	wir trögen
ihr trügt	ihr tröget
sie trügen	sie trögen

Imperfect indicative	**Future indicative**
ich trog	ich werde trügen
du trogst	du wirst trügen
er trog	er wird trügen
wir trogen	wir werden trügen
ihr trogt	ihr werdet trügen
sie trogen	sie werden trügen

Perfect indicative	**Conditional**
ich habe getrogen	ich würde trügen
du hast getrogen	du würdest trügen
er hat getrogen	er würde trügen
wir haben getrogen	wir würden trügen
ihr habt getrogen	ihr würdet trügen
sie haben getrogen	sie würden trügen

Pluperfect indicative	**Imperative**
ich hatte getrogen	trüg(e)!
du hattest getrogen	trügen wir!
er hatte getrogen	trügt!
wir hatten getrogen	trügen Sie!
ihr hattet getrogen	
sie hatten getrogen	

Present subjunctive

ich trüge
du trügest
er trüge
wir trügen
ihr trüget
sie trügen

tun *to do*

Present participle *tuend*
Past participle *getan*

Present indicative	**Imperfect subjunctive**
ich tue	ich täte
du tust	du tätest
er tut	er täte
wir tun	wir täten
ihr tut	ihr tätet
sie tun	sie täten

Imperfect indicative	**Future indicative**
ich tat	ich werde tun
du tat(e)st	du wirst tun
er tat	er wird tun
wir taten	wir werden tun
ihr tatet	ihr werdet tun
sie taten	sie werden tun

Perfect indicative	**Conditional**
ich habe getan	ich würde tun
du hast getan	du würdest tun
er hat getan	er würde tun
wir haben getan	wir würden tun
ihr habt getan	ihr würdet tun
sie haben getan	sie würden tun

Pluperfect indicative	**Imperative**
ich hatte getan	tu(e)!
du hattest getan	tun wir!
er hatte getan	tut!
wir hatten getan	tun Sie!
ihr hattet getan	
sie hatten getan	

Present subjunctive

ich tue
du tuest
er tue
wir tuen
ihr tuet
sie tuen

verderben *to spoil*

Present participle *verderbend*
Past participle *verdorben*

Present indicative	
ich verderbe	
du verdirbst	
er verdirbt	
wir verderben	
ihr verderbt	
sie verderben	

Imperfect indicative	
ich verdarb	
du verdarbst	
er verdarb	
wir verdarben	
ihr verdarbt	
sie verdarben	

Perfect indicative

ich bin/habe verdorben
du bist/hast verdorben
er ist/hat verdorben
wir sind/haben verdorben
ihr seid/habt verdorben
sie sind/haben verdorben

Pluperfect indicative

ich war/hatte verdorben
du warst/hattest verdorben
er war/hatte verdorben
wir waren/hatten verdorben
ihr wart/hattet verdorben
sie waren/hatten verdorben

Present subjunctive

ich verderbe
du verderbest
er verderbe
wir verderben
ihr verderbet
sie verderben

Imperfect subjunctive

ich verdürbe
du verdürbest
er verdürbe
wir verdürben
ihr verdürbet
sie verdürben

Future indicative

ich werde verderben
du wirst verderben
er wird verderben
wir werden verderben
ihr werdet verderben
sie werden verderben

Conditional

ich würde verderben
du würdest verderben
er würde verderben
wir würden verderben
ihr würdet verderben
sie würden verderben

Imperative

verdirb!
verderben wir!
verderbt!
verderben Sie!

verdrießen *to vex*

Present participle *verdrießend*
Past participle *verdrießen*

Present indicative	**Imperfect subjunctive**
ich verdrieße	ich verdrösse
du verdrießt	du verdrössest
er verdrießt	er verdrösse
wir verdrießen	wir verdrössen
ihr verdrießt	ihr verdrösset
sie verdrießen	sie verdrössen

Imperfect indicative	**Future indicative**
ich verdroß	ich werde verdrießen
du verdrossest	du wirst verdrießen
er verdroß	er wird verdrießen
wir verdrossen	wir werden verdrießen
ihr verdroßt	ihr werdet verdrießen
sie verdrossen	sie werden verdrießen

Perfect indicative	**Conditional**
ich habe verdrossen	
du hast verdrossen	ich würde verdrießen
er hat verdrossen	du würdest verdrießen
wir haben verdrossen	er würde verdrießen
ihr habt verdrossen	wir würden
sie haben verdrossen	verdrießen
	ihr würdet verdrießen

Pluperfect indicative	sie würden verdrießen
ich hatte verdrossen	**Imperative**
du hattest verdrossen	
er hatte verdrossen	verdrieß!
wir hatten verdrossen	verdrießen wir!
ihr hattet verdrossen	verdrießt!
sie hatten verdrossen	verdrießen Sie!

**Present
subjunctive**

ich verdrieße
du verdrießest
er verdrieße
wir verdrießen
ihr verdrießet
sie verdrießen

vergessen *to forget*

Present participle *vergessend*
Past participle *vergessen*

Present indicative	**Imperfect subjunctive**
ich vergesse	ich vergäße
du vergißt	du vergäßest
er vergißt	er vergäße
wir vergessen	wir vergäßen
ihr vergeßt	ihr vergäßet
sie vergessen	sie vergäßen

Imperfect indicative	**Future indicative**
ich vergaß	ich werde vergessen
du vergaßest	du wirst vergessen
er vergaß	er wird vergessen
wir vergaßen	wir werden vergessen
ihr vergaßt	ihr werdet vergessen
sie vergaßen	sie werden vergessen

Perfect indicative	**Conditional**
ich habe vergessen	ich würde vergessen
du hast vergessen	du würdest vergessen
er hat vergessen	er würde vergessen
wir haben vergessen	wir würden vergessen
ihr habt vergessen	ihr würdet vergessen
sie haben vergessen	sie würden vergessen

Pluperfect indicative	**Imperative**
ich hatte vergessen	vergiß!
du hattest vergessen	vergessen wir!
er hatte vergessen	vergeßt!
wir hatten vergessen	vergessen Sie!
ihr hattet vergessen	
sie hatten vergessen	

**Present
subjunctive**

ich vergesse
du vergessest
er vergesse
wir vergvergessen
ihr vergesset
sie vergvergessen

verlieren *to lose*

Present participle *verlierend*
Past participle *verloren*

Present indicative	Imperfect subjunctive
ich verliere	ich verlöre
du verlierst	du verlörest
er verliert	er verlöre
wir verlieren	wir verlören
ihr verliert	ihr verlöret
sie verlieren	sie verlören

Imperfect indicative	Future indicative
ich verlor	ich werde verlieren
du verlorst	du wirst verlieren
er verlor	er wird verlieren
wir verloren	wir werden verlieren
ihr verlort	ihr werdet verlieren
sie verloren	sie werden verlieren

Perfect indicative	Conditional
ich habe verloren	ich würde verlieren
du hast verloren	du würdest verlieren
er hat verloren	er würde verlieren
wir haben verloren	wir würden verlieren
ihr habt verloren	ihr würdet verlieren
sie haben verloren	sie würden verlieren

Pluperfect indicative	Imperative
ich hatte verloren	verlier(e)!
du hattest verloren	verlieren wir!
er hatte verloren	verliert!
wir hatten verloren	verlieren Sie!
ihr hattet verloren	
sie hatten verloren	

Present subjunctive

ich verliere
du verlierest
er verliere
wir verlieren
ihr verlieret
sie verlieren

verschwinden *to disappear*

Present participle *verschwindend*
Past participle *verschwunden*

Present indicative	Imperfect subjunctive
ich verschwinde	ich verschwände
du verschwindest	du verschwändest
er verschwindet	er verschwände
wir verschwinden	wir verschwänden
ihr verschwindet	ihr verschwändet
sie verschwinden	sie verschwänden

Imperfect indicative	Future indicative
ich verschwand	ich werde verschwinden
du verschwand(e)st	du wirst verschwinden
er verschwand	er wird verschwinden
wir verschwanden	wir werden verschwinden
ihr verschwandet	ihr werdet ver- schwinden
sie verschwanden	sie werden verschwinden

Perfect indicative	
ich bin verschwunden	
du bist verschwunden	
er ist verschwunden	**Conditional**
wir sind verschwunden	ich würde verschwinden
ihr seid verschwunden	du würdest verschwinden
sie sind verschwunden	er würde verschwinden

Pluperfect indicative	
ich war verschwunden	wir würden verschwinden
du warst verschwunden	ihr würdet verschwinden
er war verschwunden	sie würden verschwinden
wir waren verschwunden	
ihr wart verschwunden	**Imperative**
sie waren verschwunden	

Present subjunctive

ich verschwinde	verschwind(e)!
du verschwindest	verschwinden wir!
er verschwinde	verschwindet!
wir verschwinden	verschwinden Sie!
ihr verschwindet	
sie verschwinden	

verzeihen *to excuse, pardon*

Present participle *verzeihend*
Past participle *verziehen*

Present indicative	**Imperfect subjunctive**
ich verzeihe	ich verziehe
du verzeihst	du verziehest
er verzeiht	er verziehe
wir verzeihen	wir verziehen
ihr verzeiht	ihr verziehet
sie verzeihen	sie verziehen

Imperfect indicative	**Future indicative**
ich verzieh	ich werde verzeihen
du verziehst	du wirst verzeihen
er verzieh	er wird verzeihen
wir verziehen	wir werden verzeihen
ihr verzieht	ihr werdet verzeihen
sie verziehen	sie werden verzeihen

Perfect indicative	**Conditional**
ich habe verziehen	ich würde verzeihen
du hast verziehen	du würdest verzeihen
er hat verziehen	er würde verzeihen
wir haben verziehen	wir würden verzeihen
ihr habt verziehen	ihr würdet verzeihen
sie haben verziehen	sie würden verzeihen

Pluperfect indicative	**Imperative**
ich hatte verziehen	verzeih(e)!
du hattest verziehen	verzeihen wir!
er hatte verziehen	verzeiht!
wir hatten verziehen	verzeihen Sie!
ihr hattet verziehen	
sie hatten verziehen	

Present subjunctive

ich verzeihe
du verzeihest
er verzeihe
wir verzeihen
ihr verzeihet
sie verzeihen

wachsen *to grow*

Present participle *wachsend*
Past participle *gewachsen*

Present indicative	**Imperfect subjunctive**
ich wachse	ich wüchse
du wächst	du wüchsest
er wächs	er wüchse
wir wachsen	wir wüchsen
ihr wachst	ihr wüchset
sie wachsen	sie wüchsen

Imperfect indicative	**Future indicative**
ich wuchs	ich werde wachsen
du wuchsest	du wirst wachsen
er wuchs	er wird wachsen
wir wuchsen	wir werden wachsen
ihr wuchset	ihr werdet wachsen
sie wuchsen	sie werden wachsen

Perfect indicative	**Conditional**
ich habe gewachsen	ich würde wachsen
du hast gewachsen	du würdest wachsen
er hat gewachsen	er würde wachsen
wir haben gewachsen	wir würden wachsen
ihr habt gewachsen	ihr würdet wachsen
sie haben gewachsen	sie würden wachsen

Pluperfect indicative	**Imperative**
ich hatte gewachsen	wachs(e)!
du hattest gewachsen	wachsen wir!
er hatte gewachsen	wachst!
wir hatten gewachsen	wachsen Sie!
ihr hattet gewachsen	
sie hatten gewachsen	

Present subjunctive

ich wachse
du wachsest
er wachse
wir wachsen
ihr wachset
sie wachsen

wägen *to ponder*

Present participle *wägend*
Past participle *gewogen*

Present indicative	**Imperfect subjunctive**
ich wäge	ich wöge
du wägst	du wögest
er wägt	er wöge
wir wägen	wir wögen
ihr wägt	ihr wöget
sie wägen	sie wögen

Imperfect indicative	**Future indicative**
ich wog	ich werde wägen
du wogst	du wirst wägen
er wog	er wird wägen
wir wogen	wir werden wägen
ihr wogt	ihr werdet wägen
sie wogen	sie werden wägen

Perfect indicative	**Conditional**
ich habe gewogen	ich würde wägen
du hast gewogen	du würdest wägen
er hat gewogen	er würde wägen
wir haben gewogen	wir würden wägen
ihr habt gewogen	ihr würdet wägen
sie haben gewogen	sie würden wägen

Pluperfect indicative	**Imperative**
ich hatte gewogen	wäg(e)!
du hattest gewogen	wägen wir!
er hatte gewogen	wägt!
wir hatten gewogen	wägen Sie!
ihr hattet gewogen	
sie hatten gewogen	

Present subjunctive

ich wäge
du wägest
er wäge
wir wägen
ihr wäget
sie wägen

wandern *to roam*

Present participle *wandernd*
Past participle *gewandert*

Present indicative	**Imperfect subjunctive**
ich wand(e)re	ich wanderte
du wanderst	du wandertest
er wandert	er wanderte
wir wandern	wir wanderten
ihr wandert	ihr wandertet
sie wandern	sie wanderten

Imperfect indicative	**Future indicative**
ich wanderte	ich werde wandern
du wandertest	du wirst wandern
er wanderte	er wird wandern
wir wanderten	wir werden wandern
ihr wandertet	ihr werdet wandern
sie wanderten	sie werden wandern

Perfect indicative	**Conditional**
ich habe gewandert	ich würde wandern
du hast gewandert	du würdest wandern
er hat gewandert	er würde wandern
wir haben gewandert	wir würden wandern
ihr habt gewandert	ihr würdet wandern
sie haben gewandert	sie würden wandern

Pluperfect indicative	**Imperative**
ich hatte gewandert	wandre!
du hattest gewandert	wandern wir!
er hatte gewandert	wandert!
wir hatten gewandert	wandern Sie!
ihr hattet gewandert	
sie hatten gewandert	

Present subjunctive

ich wand(e)re
du wandrest
er wand(e)re
wir wandern
ihr wandert
sie wandern

waschen *to wash*

Present participle *waschend*
Past participle *gewaschen*

Present indicative	Imperfect subjunctive
ich wasche	ich wüsche
du wäschst	du wüschest
er wäsch	er wüsche
wir waschen	wir wüschen
ihr wascht	ihr wüschet
sie waschen	sie wüschen

Imperfect indicative	Future indicative
ich wusch	ich werde waschen
du wuschest	du wirst waschen
er wusch	er wird waschen
wir wuschen	wir werden waschen
ihr wuschet	ihr werdet waschen
sie wuschen	sie werden waschen

Perfect indicative	Conditional
ich habe gewaschen	ich würde waschen
du hast gewaschen	du würdest waschen
er hat gewaschen	er würde waschen
wir haben gewaschen	wir würden waschen
ihr habt gewaschen	ihr würdet waschen
sie haben gewaschen	sie würden waschen

Pluperfect indicative	Imperative
ich hatte gewaschen	wasch(e)!
du hattest gewaschen	waschen wir!
er hatte gewaschen	wascht!
wir hatten gewaschen	waschen Sie!
ihr hattet gewaschen	
sie hatten gewaschen	

Present subjunctive

ich wasche
du waschest
er wasche
wir waschen
ihr waschet
sie waschen

weben *to weave*

Present participle *webend*
Past participle *gewoben*

Present indicative	Imperfect subjunctive
ich webe	ich wöbe
du webst	du wöbest
er webt	er wöbe
wir weben	wir wöben
ihr webt	ihr wöbet
sie weben	sie wöben

Imperfect indicative	Future indicative
ich wob	ich werde weben
du wob(e)st	du wirst weben
er wob	er wird weben
wir woben	wir werden weben
ihr wobt	ihr werdet weben
sie woben	sie werden weben

Perfect indicative	Conditional
ich habe gewoben	ich würde weben
du hast gewoben	du würdest weben
er hat gewoben	er würde weben
wir haben gewoben	wir würden weben
ihr habt gewoben	ihr würdet weben
sie haben gewoben	sie würden weben

Pluperfect indicative	Imperative
ich hatte gewoben	web(e)!
du hattest gewoben	weben wir!
er hatte gewoben	webt!
wir hatten gewoben	weben Sie!
ihr hattet gewoben	
sie hatten gewoben	

Present subjunctive

ich webe
du webest
er webe
wir weben
ihr webet
sie weben

weichen *to yield, give way*

Present participle *weichend*
Past participle *gewichen*

Present indicative	**Imperfect subjunctive**
ich weiche	ich wiche
du weichst	du wichest
er weicht	er wiche
wir weichen	wir wichen
ihr weicht	ihr wichet
sie weichen	sie wichen

Imperfect indicative	**Future indicative**
ich wich	ich werde weichen
du wichst	du wirst weichen
er wich	er wird weichen
wir wichen	wir werden weichen
ihr wicht	ihr werdet weichen
sie wichen	sie werden weichen

Perfect indicative	**Conditional**
ich bin gewichen	ich würde weichen
du bist gewichen	du würdest weichen
er ist gewichen	er würde weichen
wir sind gewichen	wir würden weichen
ihr seid gewichen	ihr würdet weichen
sie sind gewichen	sie würden weichen

Pluperfect indicative	**Imperative**
ich war gewichen	weich(e)!
du warst gewichen	weichen wir!
er war gewichen	weicht!
wir waren gewichen	weichen Sie!
ihr wart gewichen	
sie waren gewichen	

Present subjunctive

ich weiche
du weichest
er weiche
wir weichen
ihr weichet
sie weichen

weisen *to show*

Present participle *weisend*
Past participle *gewiesen*

Present indicative	**Imperfect subjunctive**
ich weise	ich wiese
du weist	du wiesest
er weist	er wiese
wir weisen	wir wiesen
ihr weist	ihr wieset
sie weisen	sie wiesen

Imperfect indicative	**Future indicative**
ich wies	ich werde weisen
du wiesest	du wirst weisen
er wies	er wird weisen
wir wiesen	wir werden weisen
ihr wiest	ihr werdet weisen
sie wiesen	sie werden weisen

Perfect indicative	**Conditional**
ich habe gewiesen	ich würde weisen
du hast gewiesen	du würdest weisen
er hat gewiesen	er würde weisen
wir haben gewiesen	wir würden weisen
ihr habt gewiesen	ihr würdet weisen
sie haben gewiesen	sie würden weisen

Pluperfect indicative	**Imperative**
ich hatte gewiesen	weis(e)!
du hattest gewiesen	weisen wir!
er hatte gewiesen	weist!
wir hatten gewiesen	weisen Sie!
ihr hattet gewiesen	
sie hatten gewiesen	

Present subjunctive

ich weise
du weisest
er weise
wir weisen
ihr weiset
sie weisen

wenden *to turn*

Present participle *wendend*
Past participle *gewandt*

Present indicative	**Imperfect subjunctive**
ich wende	ich wendete
du wendest	du wendetest
er wendet	er wendete
wir wenden	wir wendeten
ihr wendet	ihr wendetet
sie wenden	sie wendeten

Imperfect indicative	**Future indicative**
ich wandte	ich werde wenden
du wandtest	du wirst wenden
er wandte	er wird wenden
wir wandten	wir werden wenden
ihr wandtet	ihr werdet wenden
sie wandten	sie werden wenden

Perfect indicative	**Conditional**
ich habe gewandt	ich würde wenden
du hast gewandt	du würdest wenden
er hat gewandt	er würde wenden
wir haben gewandt	wir würden wenden
ihr habt gewandt	ihr würdet wenden
sie haben gewandt	sie würden wenden

Pluperfect indicative	**Imperative**
ich hatte gewandt	wend(e)!
du hattest gewandt	wenden wir!
er hatte gewandt	wendet!
wir hatten gewandt	wenden Sie!
ihr hattet gewandt	
sie hatten gewandt	

Present subjunctive

ich wende
du wendest
er wende
wir wenden
ihr wendet
sie wenden

werben *to recruit, advertise*

Present participle *werbend*
Past participle *geworben*

Present indicative	**Present subjunctive**
ich werbe	ich werbe
du wirbst	du werbest
er wirbt	er werbe
wir werben	wir werben
ihr werbt	ihr werbet
sie werben	sie werben

Imperfect indicative	**Imperfect subjunctive**
ich warb	ich würbe
du warbst	du würbest
er warb	er würbe
wir warben	wir würben
ihr warbt	ihr würbet
sie warben	sie würben

Perfect indicative	**Future indicative**
ich bin/habe geworben	ich werde werben
du bist/hast geworben	du wirst werben
er ist/hat geworben	er wird werben
wir sind/haben geworben	wir werden werben
ihr seid/habt geworben	ihr werdet werben
sie sind/haben geworben	sie werden werben

Pluperfect indicative	**Conditional**
ich war/hatte geworben	ich würde werben
du warst/hattest geworben	du würdest werben
er war/hatte geworben	er würde werben
wir waren/hatten geworben	wir würden werben
ihr wart/hattet geworben	ihr würdet werben
sie waren/hatten geworben	sie würden werben

Imperative

wirb!
werben wir!
werbt!
werben Sie!

werden *to become*

Present participle *werdend*
Past participle *geworden/worden*

Present indicative	**Imperfect subjunctive**
ich wird	ich würde
du wirst	du würdest
er wird	er würde
wir werden	wir würden
ihr werdet	ihr würdet
sie werden	sie würden

Imperfect indicative	**Future indicative**
ich wurde	ich werde werden
du wurdest	du wirst werden
er wurde	er wird werden
wir wurden	wir werden werden
ihr wurdet	ihr werdet werden
sie wurden	sie werden werden

Perfect indicative	**Conditional**
ich bin geworden	ich würde werden
du bist geworden	du würdest werden
er ist geworden	er würde werden
wir sind geworden	wir würden werden
ihr seid geworden	ihr würdet werden
sie sind geworden	sie würden werden

Pluperfect indicative	**Imperative**
ich war geworden	werde!
du warst geworden	werden wir!
er war geworden	werdet!
wir waren geworden	werden Sie!
ihr wart geworden	
sie waren geworden	

Present subjunctive

ich werde
du werdest
er werde
wir werden
ihr werdet
sie werden

werfen *to throw*

Present participle *werfend*
Past participle *geworfen*

Present indicative	**Imperfect subjunctive**
ich werfe	ich würfe
du wirfst	du würfest
er wirft	er würfe
wir werfen	wir würfen
ihr werft	ihr würfet
sie werfen	sie würfen

Imperfect indicative	**Future indicative**
ich warf	ich werde werfen
du warfst	du wirst werfen
er warf	er wird werfen
wir warfen	wir werden werfen
ihr warft	ihr werdet werfen
sie warfen	sie werden werfen

Perfect indicative	**Conditional**
ich habe geworfen	ich würde werfen
du hast geworfen	du würdest werfen
er hat geworfen	er würde werfen
wir haben geworfen	wir würden werfen
ihr habt geworfen	ihr würdet werfen
sie haben geworfen	sie würden werfen

Pluperfect indicative	**Imperative**
ich hatte geworfen	wirf!
du hattest geworfen	werfen wir!
er hatte geworfen	werft!
wir hatten geworfen	werfen Sie!
ihr hattet geworfen	
sie hatten geworfen	

Present subjunctive

ich werfe
du werfest
er werfe
wir werfen
ihr werfet
sie werfen

wiegen *to weigh*

Present participle *wiegend*
Past participle *gewogen*

Present indicative	Imperfect subjunctive
ich wiege	ich wöge
du wiegst	du wögest
er wiegt	er wöge
wir wiegen	wir wögen
ihr wiegt	ihr wöget
sie wiegen	sie wögen

Imperfect indicative	Future indicative
ich wog	ich werde wiegen
du wogst	du wirst wiegen
er wog	er wird wiegen
wir wogen	wir werden wiegen
ihr wogt	ihr werdet wiegen
sie wogen	sie werden wiegen

Perfect indicative	Conditional
ich habe gewogen	ich würde wiegen
du hast gewogen	du würdest wiegen
er hat gewogen	er würde wiegen
wir haben gewogen	wir würden wiegen
ihr habt gewogen	ihr würdet wiegen
sie haben gewogen	sie würden wiegen

Pluperfect indicative	Imperative
ich hatte gewogen	wieg(e)!
du hattest gewogen	wiegen wir!
er hatte gewogen	wiegt!
wir hatten gewogen	wiegen Sie!
ihr hattet gewogen	
sie hatten gewogen	

Present subjunctive

ich wiege
du wiegest
er wiege
wir wiegen
ihr wieget
sie wiegen

winden *to wind*

Present participle *windend*
Past participle *gewunden*

Present indicative	Imperfect subjunctive
ich winde	ich wände
du windest	du wändest
er windet	er wände
wir winden	wir wänden
ihr windet	ihr wändet
sie winden	sie wänden

Imperfect indicative	Future indicative
ich wand	ich werde winden
du wandest	du wirst winden
er wand	er wird winden
wir wanden	wir werden winden
ihr wandet	ihr werdet winden
sie wanden	sie werden winden

Perfect indicative	Conditional
ich habe gewunden	ich würde winden
du hast gewunden	du würdest winden
er hat gewunden	er würde winden
wir haben gewunden	wir würden winden
ihr habt gewunden	ihr würdet winden
sie haben gewunden	sie würden winden

Pluperfect indicative	Imperative
ich hatte gewunden	wind(e)!
du hattest gewunden	winden wir!
er hatte gewunden	windet!
wir hatten gewunden	winden Sie!
ihr hattet gewunden	
sie hatten gewunden	

Present subjunctive

ich winde
du windest
er winde
wir winden
ihr windet
sie winden

wissen *to know*

Present participle *wissend*
Past participle *gewußt*

Present indicative	Imperfect subjunctive
ich weiß	ich wüßte
du weißt	du wüßtest
er weiß	er wüßte
wir wissen	wir wüßten
ihr wißt	ihr wüßtet
sie wissen	sie wüßten

Imperfect indicative	Future indicative
ich wußte	ich werde wissen
du wußtest	du wirst wissen
er wußte	er wird wissen
wir wußten	wir werden wissen
ihr wußtet	ihr werdet wissen
sie wußten	sie werden wissen

Perfect indicative	Conditional
ich habe gewußt	ich würde wissen
du hast gewußt	du würdest wissen
er hat gewußt	er würde wissen
wir haben gewußt	wir würden wissen
ihr habt gewußt	ihr würdet wissen
sie haben gewußt	sie würden wissen

Pluperfect indicative	Imperative
ich hatte gewußt	wisse!
du hattest gewußt	wissen wir!
er hatte gewußt	wisset!
wir hatten gewußt	wissen Sie!
ihr hattet gewußt	
sie hatten gewußt	

Present subjunctive

ich wisse
du wissest
er wisse
wir wissen
ihr wisset
sie wissen

wollen *to want*

Present participle *wollend*
Past participle *gewollt/wollen*

Present indicative	Imperfect subjunctive
ich will	ich wollte
du willst	du wolltest
er will	er wollte
wir wollen	wir wollten
ihr wollt	ihr wolltet
sie wollen	sie wollten

Imperfect indicative	Future indicative
ich wollte	ich werde wollen
du wolltest	du wirst wollen
er wollte	er wird wollen
wir wollten	wir werden wollen
ihr wolltet	ihr werdet wollen
sie wollten	sie werden wollen

Perfect indicative	Conditional
ich habe gewollt	
du hast gewollt	ich würde wollen
er hat gewollt	du würdest wollen
wir haben gewollt	er würde wollen
ihr habt gewollt	wir würden wollen
sie haben gewollt	ihr würdet wollen
	sie würden wollen

Pluperfect indicative	Imperative
ich hatte gewollt	
du hattest gewollt	wolle!
er hatte gewollt	wollen wir!
wir hatten gewollt	wollt!
ihr hattet gewollt	wollen Sie!
sie hatten gewollt	

Present subjunctive

ich wolle
du wollest
er wolle
wir wollen
ihr wollet
sie wollen

wringen *to wring*

Present participle *wringend*
Past participle *gewrungen*

Present indicative	Imperfect subjunctive
ich wringe	ich wränge
du wringst	du wrängest
er wringt	er wränge
wir wringen	wir wrängen
ihr wringt	ihr wränget
sie wringen	sie wrängen

Imperfect indicative	Future indicative
ich wrang	ich werde wringen
du wrangst	du wirst wringen
er wrang	er wird wringen
wir wrangen	wir werden wringen
ihr wrangt	ihr werdet wringen
sie wrangen	sie werden wringen

Perfect indicative	Conditional
ich habe gewrungen	ich würde wringen
du hast gewrungen	du würdest wringen
er hat gewrungen	er würde wringen
wir haben gewrungen	wir würden wringen
ihr habt gewrungen	ihr würdet wringen
sie haben gewrungen	sie würden wringen

Pluperfect indicative	Imperative
ich hatte gewrungen	wring(e)!
du hattest gewrungen	wringen wir!
er hatte gewrungen	wringt!
wir hatten gewrungen	wringen Sie!
ihr hattet gewrungen	
sie hatten gewrungen	

Present subjunctive

ich wringe
du wringest
er wringe
wir wringen
ihr wringet
sie wringen

zerstören *to destroy*

Present participle *zerstörend*
Past participle *zerstört*

Present indicative	Imperfect subjunctive
ich zerstöre	ich zerstörte
du zerstörst	du zerstörtest
er zerstört	er zerstörte
wir zerstören	wir zerstörten
ihr zerstört	ihr zerstörtet
sie zerstören	sie zerstörten

Imperfect indicative	Future indicative
ich zerstörte	ich werde zerstören
du zerstörtest	du wirst zerstören
er zerstörte	er wird zerstören
wir zerstörten	wir werden zerstören
ihr zerstörtet	ihr werdet zerstören
sie zerstörten	sie werden zerstören

Perfect indicative	Conditional
ich habe zerstört	ich würde zerstören
du hast zerstört	du würdest zerstören
er hat zerstört	er würde zerstören
wir haben zerstört	wir würden zerstören
ihr habt zerstört	ihr würdet zerstören
sie haben zerstört	sie würden zerstören

Pluperfect indicative	Imperative
ich hatte zerstört	zerstör(e)!
du hattest zerstört	zerstören wir!
er hatte zerstört	zerstört!
wir hatten zerstört	zerstören Sie!
ihr hattet zerstört	
sie hatten zerstört	

Present subjunctive

ich zerstöre
du zerstörest
er zerstöre
wir zerstören
ihr zerstöret
sie zerstören

ziehen *to draw, pull*

Present participle *ziehend*
Past participle *gezogen*

Present indicative	**Present subjunctive**
ich ziehe	ich ziehe
du ziehst	du ziehest
er zieht	er ziehe
wir ziehen	wir ziehen
ihr zieht	ihr ziehet
sie ziehen	sie ziehen

Imperfect indicative	**Imperfect subjunctive**
ich zog	ich zöge
du zogst	du zögest
er zog	er zöge
wir zogen	wir zögen
ihr zogt	ihr zöget
sie zogen	sie zögen

Perfect indicative

ich bin/habe gezogen
du bist/hast gezogen
er ist/hat gezogen
wir sind/haben
  gezogen
ihr seid/habt gezogen
sie sind/haben
  gezogen

Future indicative

ich werde ziehen
du wirst ziehen
er wird ziehen
wir werden ziehen
ihr werdet ziehen
sie werden ziehen

Conditional

ich würde ziehen
du würdest ziehen
er würde ziehen
wir würden ziehen
ihr würdet ziehen
sie würden ziehen

Pluperfect indicative

ich war/hatte gezogen
du warst/hattest
  gezogen
er war/hatte gezogen
wir waren/hatten
  gezogen
ihr wart/hattet
  gezogen
sie waren/hatten
  gezogen

Imperative

zieh(e)!
ziehen wir!
zieht!
ziehen Sie!

zwingen *to compel, force*

Present participle *zwingend*
Past participle *gezwungen*

Present indicative	**Present subjunctive**
ich zwinge	ich zwinge
du zwingst	du zwingest
er zwingt	er zwinge
wir zwingen	wir zwingen
ihr zwingt	ihr zwinget
sie zwingen	sie zwingen

Imperfect indicative	**Imperfect subjunctive**
ich zwang	ich zwänge
du zwangst	du zwängest
er zwang	er zwänge
wir zwangen	wir zwängen
ihr zwangt	ihr zwänget
sie zwangen	sie zwängen

Perfect indicative

ich habe gezwungen
du hast gezwungen
er hat gezwungen
wir haben gezwungen
ihr habt gezwungen
sie haben gezwungen

Future indicative

ich werde zwingen
du wirst zwingen
er wird zwingen
wir werden zwingen
ihr werdet zwingen
sie werden zwingen

Pluperfect indicative

ich hatte gezwungen
du hattest gezwungen
er hatte gezwungen
wir hatten
  gezwungen
ihr hattet gezwungen
sie hatten gezwungen

Conditional

ich würde zwingen
du würdest zwingen
er würde zwingen
wir würden zwingen
ihr würdet zwingen
sie würden zwingen

Imperative

zwing(e)!
zwingen wir!
zwingt!
zwingen Sie!

German Vocabulary

The Body   Der Körper

1

head	der Kopf
hair	das Haar, die Haare *pl*
dark	dunkel
fair	hell
bald	glatzköpfig
brown (hair)	braun
smooth	glatt
curly	gelockt
grey hair	graue Haare *pl*
scalp	die Kopfhaut

2

face	das Gesicht
features	die Mine
forehead	die Stirn
cheek	die Wange
wrinkle	die Falte
dimple	das Grübchen
chin	das Kinn
beautiful	schön
handsome	gut aussehend
pretty	hübsch

3

ugly	häßlich
ugliness	die Häßlichkeit
beauty	die Schönheit
beauty spot	der Schönheitsflecken
freckle	die Sommersprosse
freckled	sommersprossig
ear	das Ohr
hearing	das Gehör
to hear	hören
listen	zuhören

4

listener	der Zuhörer
earlobe	das Ohrläppchen
deaf	taub
mute	stumm
deaf-mute	taubstumm
deafness	die Taubheit
to deafen	betäuben
deafening	ohrenbetäubend
eardrum	das Trommelfell
sound	der Ton

5

noise	der Lärm
eye	das Auge
sense	der Sinn
eyesight	der Gesichtssinn
tear	die Träne
eyebrow	die Augenbraue

to frown	die Stirn runzeln
eyelid	das Augenlid
eyelash	die Wimper
pupil	die Pupille

6

retina	die Netzhaut
iris	die Iris
glance	der flüchtige Blick
to see	sehen
to look	schauen
look	der Blick
visible	sichtbar
invisible	unsichtbar
blind	blind
blindness	Blindheit

7

to blind	blenden, blind machen
blind spot	der tote Winkel
one-eyed	einäugig
cross-eyed	schielend
to observe	beobachten
to notice	bemerken
expression	der Ausdruck
to smile	lächeln
smile	das Lächeln
to laugh	lachen

8

laugh	das Lachen
laughing *adj*	lachend
mouth	der Mund
tongue	die Zunge
lip	die Lippe
tooth	der Zahn
eyetooth	der Eckzahn
gum	das Zahnfleisch
palate	der Gaumen
to say	sagen

9

saying	der Ausdruck
to speak	sprechen
to shout	schreien
to be quiet	schweigen
touch (sense)	der Tastsinn
to touch	berühren
to feel	fühlen
tactile	taktil, tastend
nose	die Nase
nostril	das Nasenloch

10

bridge (nose)	der Nasenrücken
smell (sense)	der Geruchssinn
smell	der Geruch

The Body

to smell (of)	riechen (nach)
to taste (of)	schmecken (nach)
to taste	schmecken, probieren
taste (sense)	der Geschmack
taste bud	die Geschmacksknospe
tasty	schmackhaft
tasting	die Probe

11

moustache	der Schnurrbart
beard	der Bart
facial hair	die Gesichtsbehaarung
sideburns	der Backenbart
dandruff	die Schuppen *pl*
plait	der Zopf
curl	die Locke
to shave	sich rasieren
to grow a beard	sich einen Bart stehen lassen
bearded	bärtig

12

clean-shaven	rasiert
jaw	der Kiefer
throat	die Kehle, der Hals
neck	der Hals
shoulder	die Schulter
back	der Rücken
chest	der Brustkasten
breast	die Brust
to breathe	atmen
breath	der Atem

13

breathing	die Atmung
lung	die Lunge
windpipe	die Luftröhre
heart	das Herz
heartbeat	der Herzschlag
rib	die Rippe
side	die Seite
limb	das Glied, die Gliedmaßen *pl*
leg	das Bein
lame	gehbehindert

14

to limp	hinken
thigh	der Oberschenkel
calf	der Unterschenkel
tendon	die Sehne
groin	die Leistengegend
muscle	der Muskel
knee	das Knie
kneecap	die Kniescheibe
to kneel	knien
foot	der Fuß

15

heel	die Ferse
toe	die Zehe
sole	die Sohle
ankle	das Fußgelenk
instep	der Spann
arm	der Arm
forearm	der Vorderarm
right-handed	rechtshändig
left-handed	rechtshändig
right	rechts

16

left	links
hand	die Hand
to handle	hantieren
handshake	das Händeschütteln
handful	die Handvoll
finger	der Finger
index finger	der Zeigefinger
thumb	der Daumen
palm	die Handfläche
nail	der Nagel

17

wrist	das Handgelenk
elbow	der Ellbogen
fist	die Faust
knuckle	der Knöchel
bone	der Knochen
spine	das Rückgrat
dorsal skeleton	das Skelett
skull	der Schädel
blood	das Blut
vein	die Vene

18

artery	die Arterie
capillary	das Blutgefäß
liver	die Leber
skin	die Haut
pore	die Pore
sweat	der Schweiß
to sweat	schwitzen
scar	die Narbe
wart	die Warze
complexion	der Teint

19

brain	das Gehirn
kidney	die Niere
bladder	die Blase
spleen	die Milz
gland	die Drüse
larynx	der Kehlkopf
ligament	das Band
cartilage	der Knorpel

Clothes

womb	der Mutterleib
ovary	der Eileiter

20

height	die Größe
big	groß, dick
small	klein
tall	groß
short	klein
fat	dick
thin	dünn
strong	stark
strength	die Stärke
weak	schwach

21

knock-kneed	mit X-Beinen
bow-legged	mit O-Beinen
to stand	stehen
to stand up	aufstehen
to raise	heben
to lie down	sich hinlegen
to sleep	schlafen
sleep	der Schlaf
to be sleepy	müde sein
to dream	träume

22

to doze	vor sich hindösen
to fall asleep	einschlafen
asleep	schlafend
to be awake	wach sein
to wake up	aufwachen
drowsy	schläfrig
dream	der Traum
nightmare	der Alptraum
conscious	bei Bewußtsein
unconscious	bewußtlos

Clothes   Die Kleider

23

jacket	die Jacke
trousers	die Hose *sing*
jeans	die Jeans *pl*
dungarees	die Latzhose *sing*
overalls	das Overall
braces	die Hosenträger *pl*
sweater	der Pullover
sock	die Socke
to darn	stopfen
raincoat	der Regenmantel

24

overcoat	der Mantel

to shelter	bergen
to protect	schützen
hat	der Hut
brim	der Rand
shadow	der Schatten
cap	die Kappe, Mütze
glasses	die Brille
earmuffs	die Ohrenwärmer
walking stick	der Gehstock

25

umbrella	der Regenschirm
cloth	der Stoff
fine	fein
thick	dick
coarse	grob
shirt	das Hemd
T-shirt	das T-Shirt
tie	die Krawatte
handkerchief	das Taschentuch
suit (men)	der Anzug
suit (women)	das Kostüm

26

waistcoat	die Weste
skirt	der Rock
miniskirt	der Minirock
blouse	die Bluse
stockings	die (langen) Strümpfe *pl*
veil	der Schleier
beret	die Baskenmütze
collar	der Kragen
gloves	die Handschuhe *pl*
belt	der Gürtel

27

scarf	der Schal
handkerchief	das Taschentuch
button	der Knopf
to button	zuknöpfen
to unbutton	aufknöpfen
new	neu
second-hand	aus zweiter Hand
graceful	anmutig
narrow	eng
broad	breit

28

ready-made	fertig, Konfektion
to make	machen
to get made	machen lassen
to wear	tragen
to use	verwenden
worn out	abgetragen
useful	nützlich
useless	nutzlos
practical	praktisch

Clothes

29

housecoat	das Hauskleid
nightdress	das Nachthemd
pyjamas	der Schlafanzug
underpants,	
knickers	die Unterhose *sing*
petticoat	der Unterrock
slip	das Unterkleid
bra	der Büstenhalter
leotard	der Gymnastikanzug

30

coat hanger	der Kleiderbügel
zip	der Reißverschluß
wristband	die Manschette
sweatshirt	das Sweatshirt
shorts	die kurze Hose *sing*,
	die Shorts *pl*
tracksuit	der Jogginganzug
dress	das Kleid
to dress	kleiden
to dress oneself	sich anziehen
to take off	ausziehen

31

to remove	entfernen
to undress	sich ausziehen
naked	nackt
to put	aufsetzen
to put on	anziehen
sash	die Schärpe
apron	die Schürze
shawl	der Schal
sleeve	der Ärmel
to sew	nähen

32

seam	der Saum
seamstress	die Näherin
thread	der Faden
needle	die Nadel
hole	das Loch
scissors	die Schere
ribbon	das Band
linen	das Leinen
lace	die Spitze
velcro	der Klettverschluß

33

fur	der Pelz
furry	aus Pelz
silk	die Seide
silky	seidig
velvet	der Samt
cotton	die Baumwolle
nylon	der Nylon
fan	der Fächer

in fashion	modisch
out of fashion	unmodern

34

dressmaker	der Schneider,
	die Schneiderin
pocket	die Hosentasche,
	die Rocktasche
bag	die Tasche
pin	die Stecknadel
to tie	zubinden
to untie	aufmachen
to loosen	lösen
sandal	die Sandale
slipper	der Hausschuh
pair	das Paar

35

lace	der Schnürriemen
shoe	der Schuh
sole	die Sohle
heel	der Absatz
to polish	putzen
shoe polish	die Schuhcreme
shoehorn	der Schuhlöffel
boot	der Stiefel
leather	das Leder
rubber	der Gummi

36

suede	das Wildleder
barefoot	barfuß
to put on	
one's shoes	sich die Schuhe anziehen
to take off	
one's shoes	sich die Schuhe ausziehen
footwear	die Fußmoden *pl*
shoemaker	der Schuhmacher
ring	der Ring
diamond	der Diamant
necklace	das Halsband
bracelet	das Armband

Family and Relationships
Familie und Beziehungen

37

father	der Vater
mother	die Mutter
parents	die Eltern *pl*
son	der Sohn
daughter	die Tochter
children	die Kinder *pl*
brother	der Bruder
sister	die Schwester

Family and Relationships

brotherhood	die Brüderschaft
brotherly	brüderlich

38

elder	älter
younger	jünger
husband	der Ehemann
wife	die Ehefrau
uncle	der Onkel
aunt	die Tante
nephew	der Neffe
niece	die Nichte
grandfather	der Großvater
grandmother	die Großmutter

39

grandparents	die Großeltern
grandson	der Enkel
granddaughter	die Enkelin
boy	der Junge
girl	das Mädchen
cousin (male)	der Cousin, der Vetter
cousin (female)	die Cousine, die Base
twin	der Zwilling
baby	das Baby, der Säugling
child	das Kind
to be born	geboren werden

40

to grow up	aufwachsen
name	der Name
surname	der Nachname
birthday	der Geburtstag
age	das Alter
old	alt
to get old	alt werden
old man	der alte Mann
old woman	die alte Frau
youth	die Jugend

41

young	jung
young man	der junge Mann
young woman	die junge Frau
father-in-law	der Schwiegervater
mother-in-law	die Schwiegermutter
son-in-law	der Schwiegerson
daughter-in-law	die Schwiegertochter
brother-in-law	der Schwager
sister-in-law	die Schwägern
orphan	der Waise, die Waise

42

stepfather	der Stiefvater
stepmother	die Stiefmutter
stepson	der Stiefsohn
stepdaughter	die Stieftocher

stepbrother	der Stiefbruder
stepsister	die Stiefschwester
bachelor	der ledige Mann
spinster	die ledige Frau
widower	der Witwer
widow	die Witwe

43

ancestor	der Vorfahre
descendant	der Nachkomme
boyfriend	der Freund
girlfriend	die Freundin
couple	das Paar
love	die Liebe
to fall in love	sich verlieben
to marry	heiraten
wedding	die Hochzeit
honeymoon	die Flitterwochen

44

maternity	die Mutterschaft
paternity	die Vaterschaft
to be pregnant	schwanger sein
to give birth	gebähren
childbirth	die Geburt
nurse	die Amme
child minder	das Kindermädchen
to baby-sit	babysitten
baby-sitter	der Babysitter
godmother	die Patin

45

godfather	der Pate
baptism	die Taufe
to baptise	taufen
creche	das Kinderbett
to breastfeed	stillen
infancy	die frühe Kindheit
to spoil (child)	verderben
spoiled	verdorben
divorce	die Scheidung
separation	die Trennung

46

family planning	die Familienplanung
contraception	die Empfängnisverhütung
contraceptive	das Verhütungsmittel
contraceptive pill	die Anti-Baby-Pille
condom	das Kondom
abortion	die Abtreibung
to have an abortion	abtreiben lassen
period	die Periode, die Regel
to menstruate	menstruieren
to conceive	schwanger werden

47

middle-aged	mittleren Alters

Health

menopause	die Wechseljahre *pl*
to retire	in den Ruhestand gehen
pensioner	der Rentner, die Rentnerin
the aging process	der Alterungsprozeß
old age	das Alter
death	der Tod
to die	sterben
dying	sterbend
deathbed	das Totenbett

48

dead man	der Tote
dead woman	die Tote
death certificate	die Sterbeurkunde
mourning	die Trauer
burial	die Beerdigung
to bury	beerdigen
grave	das Grab
cemetery	der Friedhof
wake	die Totenwache
coffin	der Sarg

49

deceased, late	verstorben
to console	trösten
to weep	weinen
to wear mourning	Schwarz tragen
to survive	überleben
survivor	der Überlebende, die Überlebende
crematorium	das Krematorium
cremation	die Einäscherung
to cremate	einäschern
ashes	die Asche *sing*

Health   Die Gesundheit

50

sickness	die Krankheit
nurse	die Krankenschwester, der Krankenbruder
infirmary	das Krankenhaus
sick	krank
hospital	das Krankenhaus
patient	der Patient, die Patientin
cough	der Husten
to cough	husten
to injure	verletzen
injury	die Verletzung

51

cramp	der Krampf
to cut oneself	sich schneiden
to dislocate	ausrenken
faint	schwach
to be ill	krank sein

to become ill	krank werden
to look after	sorgen für
care	die Sorge
careful	sorgsam

52

carelessness	die Sorglosigkeit
careless	sorglos
negligent	nachlässig
doctor	der Arzt, die Ärztin
medicine	die Medizin
prescription	das Rezept
pharmacist	der Apotheker, die Apotheker
pharmacy	die Apotheke
cure	die Heilung
curable	heilbar

53

incurable	unheilbar
to cure	heilen
to get well	gesund werden
healthy	gesund
unhealthy	ungesund
to recover	sich erholen
pain	der Schmerz
painful	schmerzhaft
to suffer	leiden

54

diet	die Diät
obesity	die Fettleibigkeit
obese	fettleibig
anorexic	magersüchtig
anorexia	die Magersucht
obsession	die Besessenheit
to get fat	dick werden
headache	der Kopfschmerz
aspirin	das Aspirin
migraine	die Migräne

55

toothache	der Zahnschmerz
stomach upset	die Magenverstimmung
indigestion	die Verdauungsstörung
food poisoning	die Lebensmittelvergiftung
sore throat	der Halsschmerz
hoarse	heiser
pale	blaß
to turn pale	erblassen
to faint	ohnmächtig werden
cold (illness)	die Erkältung

56

to catch a cold	sich erkälten
wound	die Wunde
surgeon	der Chirurg

Health

to heat	heizen
hot	heiß
temperature	die Temperatur
perspiration	der Schweiß, das Schwitzen
sweaty	verschwitzt
fever	das Fieber
germ	der Keim

57

microbe	die Mikrobe
contagious	ansteckend
vaccine	der Impfstoff
to shiver	zittern
madness	die Verrücktheit
mad	verrückt
drug	die Droge
pill	die Pille
to scar	vernarben
stitches	die Stiche

58

to relieve	lindern
swollen	geschwollen
boil	der Furunkel
to bleed	bluten
to clot	ein Gerinnsel bilden
blood cell	die Blutzelle
blood group	die Blutgruppe
blood pressure	der Blutdruck
blood test	die Blutuntersuchung
check up	der Test

59

epidemic	die Epidemie
plague	die Pest
allergy	die Allergie
allergic	allergisch
angina	die Angina
tonsillitis	die Mandelentzündung
fracture	der Bruch
cast	der Gips
crutches	die Krücken
wheelchair	der Rollstuhl

60

haemophiliac	der Bluter
haemophilia	die Bluterkrankheit
cholesterol	das Cholesterin
vitamin	das Vitamin
calorie	die Kalorie
handicapped person	der Behinderte, die Behinderte
handicap	die Behinderung
pneumonia	die Lungenentzündugn
heart attack	der Herzanfall
bypass operation	die Bypass-Operation

Health

61

heart surgery	die Operation am Herzen
microsurgery	die Mikrochirurgie
pacemaker	der Herzschrittmacher
heart transplant	die Herztransplantation
smallpox	die schwarzen Pocken *pl*
stroke	der Schlaganfall
tumour	der Tumor
HIV positive	HIV-postiv
AIDS	(das) AIDS
cancer	der Krebs

62

breast cancer	der Brustkrebs
chemotherapy	die Chemotherapie
screening	die Reihenuntersuchung
diagnosis	die Diagnose
antibody	der Antikörper
antibiotic	das Antibiotikum
depression	die Depression
depressed	depressiv
to depress	deprimieren
to undergo an operation	sich operieren lassen

63

painkiller	das Schmerzmittel
treatment	die Behandlung
anaesthetic	die Narkose
anaesthetist	der Narkosearzt, die Narkoseärztin
donor	der Spender, die Spenderin
genetic engineering	die Genmanipulation
test-tube baby	das Baby aus dem Reagenzglas
surrogate mother	die Leihmutter
infertile	unfruchtbar
hormone	das Hormon

64

psychologist	der Psychologe, die Psychologin
psychology	die Psychologie
psychoanalyst	der Psychoanalytiker, die Psychoanalytikerin
psychoanalysis	die Psychoanalyse
psychosomatic	psychosomatisch
hypochondriac	der Hypochonder
plastic surgery	die plastische Chirurgie
face-lift	das Lifting
implant	das Implantat
self-esteem	das Selbstbewußtsein

65

to smoke	rauchen
passive smoking	das passive Rauchen
to inhale	inhalieren

321

Nature   Nature

withdrawal		earth	die Erde
syndrome	die Entzugserscheinung	Mercury	der Merkur
alcohol	der Alkohol	Venus	die Venus
hangover	der Kater	Mars	der Mars
alcoholic	der Alkoholiker,	Jupiter	der Jupiter
	die Alkoholikerin	Saturn	der Saturn
drug addict	der Drogenabhängige	Neptune	der Neptun
drug addiction	die Drogenabhängigkeit		
drugs traffic	der Drogenhandel	**70**	
		Uranus	der Uranus
66		Pluto	der Pluto
heroin	das Heroin	orbit	die Umlaufbahn
cocaine	das Kokain	to orbit	umkreisen
drugs trafficker	der Drogenhändler	gravity	die Schwerkraft
to launder money	Geld waschen	satellite	der Satellit
syringe	die Spritze	moon	der Mond
to inject	injizieren	eclipse	die Sonnenfinsternis
to take drugs	Drogen nehmen	sun	die Sonne
clinic	die Klinik	sunspot	der Sonnenflecken
outpatient	der Patient in		
	ambulanter Behandlung	**71**	
therapy	die Behandlung	ray	der Strahl
		to radiate	strahlen
		radiant	strahlend

Nature **Die Natur**

		to shine	leuchten
		shining	leuchtend
67		brilliancy	die Leuchtkraft
world	die Welt	sunrise	der Sonnenaufgang
natural	natürlich	to rise	aufgehen
creation	die Schöpfung	sunset	der Sonnenuntergang
the Big Bang theory	die Big-Bang-Theorie	to set (sun)	untergehen
supernatural	übernatürlich		
to create	schaffen	**72**	
sky	der Himmel	dawn	die Morgendämmerung
galaxy	die Galaxie	dusk	die Abenddämmerung
the Milky Way	die Milchstraße	to grow dark	dunkel werden
the Plough	der große Wagen,	earthquake	das Erdbeben
	der große Bär	volcano	der Vulkan
		eruption	der Ausbruch
		deserted	verlassen
68		desert	die Wüste
astronomer	der Astronom,	plain	die Ebene
	der Sternenkundige		
astronomy	die Astronomie	**73**	
telescope	das Teleskop	flat	flach
UFO	das UFO	level	eben
	(unbekannte Flugobjekt)	valley	das Tal
light year	das Lichtjahr	hill	der Hügel, der Berg
asteroid	der Asteroid	mountain	der Berg
meteor	der Meteorit	mountainous	bergig
comet	der Komet	peak	die Spitze, der Gipfel
star	der Stern	summit	der Gipfel
starry	sternenübersäht	range of mountains	die Bergkette
		crag	die Felsspitze
69			
to twinkle	funkeln	**74**	
to shine	leuchten	rock	der Felsen
planet	der Planet		

Nature

steep	steil
slope	der Abhang
coast	die Küste
coastal	Küsten-
shore	das Ufer
beach	der Strand
cliff	das Kliff
sea	die See, das Meer
tides	die Gezeiten *pl*

75

high tide	die Flut
low tide	die Ebbe
ebb tide	die Ebbe
flood tide	die Flut
wave	die Welle
foam	die Gischt
tempest	der Sturm
hurricane	der Hurrikan
gulf	der Meerbusen
bay	die Bucht

76

cape	das Kap
straits	die Meerenge *sing*
island	die Insel
spring,	die Quelle
fountain	die Quelle
waterfall	der Wasserfall
stream	das Flüßchen
river	der Fluß
current	die Strömung
draught	der Luftzug

77

glacier	der Gletscher
iceberg	der Eisberg
ice cap	die Eiskappe
icefloe	die Eisscholle
to flood	überfluten
flood	die Flut
border	die Grenze
lake	der See
pond	der Teich
marsh	das Marschland

78

deep	tief
depth	die Tiefe
weather	das Wetter
fine, fair	schön
climate	das Klima
barometer	das Barometer
thermometer	das Thermometer
degree	der Grad
air	die Luft
breeze	die Brise

79

cool, fresh	kühl, frisch
wind	der Wind
windy	windig
dampness	die Feuchtigkeit
damp	feucht
to wet	befeuchten
wet	naß
storm	der Sturm
stormy	stürmig
dry	trocken

80

drought	die Trockenheit
to dry	austrocknen
rainbow	der Regenbogen
rain	der Regen
rainy	regnerisch
to rain	regnen
drop	der Tropfen
shower	der Schauer
cloud	die Wolke
cloudy	wolkig

81

to cloud over	sich bewölken
to clear up	sich aufklären
lightning	der Blitz
lightning conductor	der Blitzableiter
to flash (lightning)	blitzen
sheet lightning	der Flächenblitz
fork lightning	der gegabelte Blitz
harmful	schädlich
to harm	schaden
thunder	der Donner

82

to thunder	donnern
fog	der Nebel
mist	der Dunst, der Nebelschleier
foggy	neblig
misty	dunstig
snow	der Schnee
to snow	schneien
snowstorm	der Schneesturm
snowfall	der Schneefall
hailstone	der Hagel

83

to hail	hageln
to freeze	frieren
frozen	gefroren
icicle	der Eiszapfen
frost	der Frost
to thaw	tauen
ice	das Eis
thaw	das Tauwetter

heatwave	die Hitzewelle
sultry	schwül

Minerals   Minerale

84

metal	das Metall
mine	die Mine
forge	die Schmiede,
	das Hüttenwerk
to forge	schmieden
steel	das Stahl
iron	das Eisen
iron *adj*	eisern
bronze	die Bronze
brass	das Messing

85

copper	das Kupfer
tin	das Zinn
lead	das Blei
zinc	das Zink
nickel	das Nickel
aluminium	das Aluminium
silver	das Silber
gold	das Gold
platinum	das Platin
mould	die Form

86

to extract	gewinnen
to exploit	abbauen
miner	der Grubenarbeiter
to melt, smelt	schmelzen
to mould	formen
rust	der Rost
rusty	rostig
to solder	schweißen
to alloy	legieren
alloy	die Legierung

87

stone	der Stein
stony	steinig
quarry	der Steinbruch
granite	der Granit
to polish	polieren
polished	poliert
smooth	glatt
marble	der Marmmor
lime	der Kalk
chalk	die Kreide

88

clay	der Ton
sulphur	der Schwefel

jewel	der Edelstein
pearl	die Perle
diamond	der Diamant
ruby	der Rubin
emerald	der Smaragd
mother-of-pearl	der Perlmutt
enamel	das Email
sapphire	der Saphir

89

agate	der Agat
opal	der Opal
lapis-lazuli	der Lapislazuli
obsidian	der Obsidian
garnet	der Granat
alkali	das Alkali
acid	die Säure
acidity	der Säuregrad
plutonium	das Plutonium
radium	das Radium

Animals   Tiere

90

domestic animal	das Haustier
tame	zahm
cat	die Katze
kitten	das Kätzchen
to mew	miauen
feline	zur Familie der
	Katzen gehörend
claw	die Klaue
dog	der Hund
bitch	die Hündin
puppy	die Welpe

91

to bark	bellen
canine	zur Familie der
	Hunde gehörend
watchful	wachsam
watchdog	der Wachhund
guardian	der Wächter
pet	das Haustier
breed	die Rasse
greyhound	der Windhund
alsatian	der Schäferhund
terrapin	die Dosenschildkröte
tropical fish	die tropischen Fische *pl*

92

aquarium	Aquarium
aquatic horse	Seepferdchen
to neigh	wiehern
stallion	der Hengst
mare	die Stute

Animals

colt	das Fohlen
donkey	der Esel
to bray	iahen
mule	der Maulesel

93

male	das männliche Tier
female	das weibliche Tier
livestock	der Tierbestand
horn	das Horn, das Geweih
paw	die Pfote
hoof	das Huf
tail	der Schwanz
flock	die Herde
cow	die Kuh
ox	der Ochse

94

to low	muhen
bull	der Stier
calf	das Kalb
heifer	die Jungkuh
lamb	das Lamm
sheep	das Schaf
sheepdog	der Schäferhund
ram	der Widder
ewe	das Mutterschaf
goat	die Ziege
pig	das Schwein

95

to grunt	grunzen
to fatten	mästen
wild, savage	wild
carnivorous	fleischfressend
herbivorous	pflanzenfressend
omnivorous	allesfressend
quadruped	der Vierbeiner
biped	der Zweibeiner
mammal	das Säugetier
warm-blooded	warmblütig

96

predator	das Raubtier
prey	die Beute
lion	der Löwe
lioness	die Löwin
cub	das Löwenjunge
to roar	brüllen
mane	die Mähne
tiger	der Tiger
tigress	die Tigerin
cheetah	der Cheetah

97

leopard	der Leopard
lynx	der Luchs

mountain lion	der Berglöwe
hyena	die Hyäne
jackal	der Schakal
scavenger	der Aasfresser
to scavenge	Aas fressen
carrion	das Aas
jaguar	der Jaguar
tapir	der Tapir

98

buffalo	der Büffel
mongoose	der Mungo
porcupine	das Stachelschwein
armadillo	das Gürteltiel
skunk	das Stinktier
sloth	das Faultier
rhinoceros	das Nashorn
hippopotamus	das Nilpferd, Flußpferd
wolf	der Wolf
pack	das Rudel

99

bear	der Bär
to hibernate	überwintern
zebra	das Zebra
stripe (of the zebra)	der Streifen
bison	das Bison
to graze	grasen
pasture	die Weide
wild boar	das (männliche) Wildschwein
ferocious	wild
bristle	brüchig

100

elephant	der Elefant
trunk	der Rüssel
camel	das Kamel
hump	der Höcker
dromedary	das Dromedar
llama	das Lama
deer	das Wild
doe	das Reh
stag	der Hirsch
elk	der Elch

101

moose	der Amerikanische Elch
antler	Geweih
fox	der Fuchs
cunning	schlau
craft, cunning	die Schlauheit
hare	der Feldhase
badger	der Dachs
otter	der Otter
dormouse	die Haselmaus
shrew	die Spitzmaus

Animals

Animals

102
hedgehog	der Igel
weasel	das Wiesel
mink	der Nerz
mink coat	der Nerzmantel
beaver	der Biber
dam	der Damm
mole	der Maulwurf
molehill	der Maulwurfhügel
mouse	die Maus
mousetrap	die Mausefalle

103
rabbit	das Kaninchen
(rabbit) hutch	der (Kaninchen)stall
rat	die Ratte
bat	die Fledermaus
nocturnal	Nacht-
primates	die Menschenaffen *pl*
gorilla	der Gorilla
monkey	das Äffchen
orang-utan	der Orang Utan
baboon	der Pavian

104
gibbon	der Gibbon
marsupial	das Beuteltier
kangaroo	das Känguruh
koala	der Koalabär
giant panda	der Riesenpanda
invertebrate	wirbellos
exoskeleton	Außenskelett
insect	das Insekt
to hum	summen
humming	das Summen

105
antenna	der Fühler
worm	der Wurm
to worm	sich schlängeln
earthworm	der Regenwurm
tapeworm	der Bandwurm
parasite	der Parasit
beetle	der Käfer
stag beetle	der Hirschkäfer
silkworm	der Seidenwurm
caterpillar	die Raupe

106
chrysalis	die Puppe
metamorphosis	die Verpuppung
to metamorphose	sich verpuppen
butterfly	der Schmetterling
moth	die Motte, der Nachtfalter
fly	die Fliege
bluebottle	die Schmeißfliege
spider	die Spinne

web	das Netz
to spin	spinnen

107
wasp	die Wespe
hornet	die Hornisse
to sting	stechen
sting	der Stich
bee	die Biene
worker (bee, ant)	die Arbeiterin
bumblebee	die Hummel
queen bee	die Bienenkönigin
beehive	der Bienenstock
apiary	das Bienenhaus

108
apiarist	der Bienenzüchter
drone	die Drone
honey	der Honig
honeycomb	die Bienenwabe
grasshopper	der Grashüpfer
locust	die Heuschrecke
to infest	befallen
cricket	die Grille
glow-worm	das Glühwürmchen
ant	die Ameise

109
anthill	der Ameisenhügel
colony	die Kolonie
to itch	jucken
itch	der Juckreiz
termite	die Termit
troublesome	lästig
to molest	belästigen
mosquito	die Stechmücke
net	das Netz
malaria	die Malaria

110
flea	der Floh
earwig	der Ohrwurm
praying mantis	die Gottesanbeterin
scorpion	der Skorpion
snail	die Hausschnecke
slug	die Nacktschnecke
louse	die Laus
lousy	verlaust
centipede	der Tausendfüßler
millipede	der Tausendfüßler, die Landassel

111
reptile	das Reptil
cold-blooded animal	der Kaltblüter
tortoise	die Landschildkröte

Animals   Animals

turtle	die Wasserschildkröte
crocodile	das Krokodil
alligator	der Alligator
serpent	die Giftschlange
snake	die Schlange
slowworm	die Blindschleiche
harmless	harmlos

112

crawl	kriechen
viper	die Viper
fang	der Giftzahn
python	die Python
anaconda	die Anakonda
rattlesnake	die Klapperschlange
cobra	die Kobra
poison	das Gift
antidote	das Antidot
poisonous	giftig

113

bird	der Vogel
aviary	das Vogelhaus
ostrich	der Strauß
beak, bill	der Schnabel
wing	der Flügel
to fly	fliegen
flight	der Flug
flightless	flugunfähig
to lay (eggs)	(Eier) legen
to nest	nisten

114

budgerigar, budgie	der Wellensittich
canary	der Kanarienvogel
robin redbreast	das Rotkehlchen
chaffinch	der Buchfink
nightingale	die Nachtigall
sparrow	der Spatz
swallow	die Schwalbe
lark	die Lerche
cuckoo	der Kuckuck
magpie	die Elster

115

blackbird	die Amsel
crow	die Krähe
to caw	krächzen
seagull	die Möve
albatross	der Albatros
cormorant	der Kormoran
partridge	das Rebhuhn
pheasant	der Fasan
stork	der Storch
owl	die Eule

116

rooster	der Hahn
cockcrow	der Hahnenschrei
to crow	krähen
cock-a-doodle-do	kikeriki
hen	das Huhn, die Henne
feather	die Feder
to pluck	rupfen
chicken	das Hühnchen
to brood	brüten
to breed	züchten

117

pigeon	die Taube
duck	die Ente
goose	die Gans
swan	der Schwan
parrot	der Papagei
toucan	der Tukan
turkey	der Truthahn
peacock	der Pfau
hummingbird	der Kolibri
bird of paradise	der Paradiesvogel

118

rapacious	gefräßig
bird of prey	der Raubvogel
eagle	der Adler
vulture	der Geier
peregrine falcon	der Wanderfalke
to swoop	sich herabstürzen
hawk	der Habicht
to hover (hawk)	schweben
falcon	der Falke
condor	der Kondor

119

amphibious	amphibisch
amphibians	die Amphibien *pl only*
frog	der Frosch
bullfrog	der Ochsenfrosch
tadpole	die Kaulquappe
toad	die Kröte
salamander	der Salamander
crustacean	das Krustentier
crab	der Krebs
prawn	die (Stein-)Garnele

120

fish	der Fisch
goldfish	der Goldfisch
piranha	der Piranha
voracious	gefräßig
carp	der Karpfen
sturgeon	der Stör
caviar	der Kaviar
trout	die Forelle

Animals

hake	der Hecht
herring	der Hering

121

sardine	die Sardine
skate	der Glattrochen
cod	der Kabeljau
eel	der Aal
electric eel	der Zitteraal
elver	der Jungaal
salmon	der Lachs
tuna fish	der Thunfisch
school (of fish)	der Schwarm
coral reef	das Korallenriff

122

flipper, fin	die Flosse
gills	die Kiemen *pl*
shell	die Schale
seashell	die Muschel
scale	die Schuppe
squid	der Kalmar
octopus	der Oktopus
tentacle	der Fangarm
cuttlefish	der Tintenfisch
crayfish	der Flußkrebs

123

lobster	der Hummer
sea urchin	der Seeigel
sea horse	das Seepferdchen
starfish	der Seestern
shellfish	das Schalentier
oyster	die Auster
shark	der Hai
whale	der Wal
killer whale	der Mörderwal
dolphin	der Delphin

124

seal	der Seehund
sea lion	der Seelöwe
walrus	das Walroß
natural selection	die natürliche Auswahl
survival of the fittest	die natürliche Zuchtwahl
evolution	die Evolution
to evolve	sich entwickeln
zoology	die Zoologie
zoologist	der Zoologe
zoo	der Zoo, der Tiergarten

125

habitat	der Lebensraum
extinct	ausgestorben
dinosaur	der Dinosaurier
mammoth	der Mammut

dodo	die Dronte
yeti	der Yeti
mythical	sagenhaft, sagenumwoben
myth	die Sage, der Mythos
unicorn	das Einhorn
dragon	der Drache

Plants — Die Pflanzen

126

to plant	pflanzen
to transplant	umpflanzen
root	die Wurzel
to root (pig, etc)	schnüffeln nach
to take root	Wurzeln schlagen
to uproot	entwurzeln
radical	radikal
tendril	die Ranke
stalk	der Stiel
sap	der Saft

127

foliage	das Laub
leaf	das Blatt
leafy	belaubt
to shed leaves	die Blätter verlieren
deciduous	Laub-, jährlich die Blätter abwerfend
evergreen	Immergrün-
perennial	mehrjährig
thorn	der Dorn
thorn tree	der Dornenbusch
thorny	dornig

128

weed	das Unkraut
to weed	Unkraut jäten
to thin	ausdünnen
thistle	die Distel
nettle	die Brennessel
briar	die Heckenrose
hemlock	der Schierling
deadly nightshade	die Tollkirsche
Venus flytrap	die Venus-Fliegenfalle
rush	die Binse

129

reed	das Schilf
epiphyte	die Schmarotzerpflanze
moss	das Moos
spider plant	die Tradescantie
bud	die Knospe
to bud	Knospen treiben
flower	die Blume
to flower	blühen

Plants

blooming	blühend
petal	das Blütenblatt

130

to wither	verdorren
withered	verdorrt
garland	die Girlande
scent	der Duft
garden	der Garten
gardener	der Gärtner
to water	bewässern
watering can	die Gießkanne
irrigation	die Bewässerung

131

herb	das Kraut
thyme	der Thymian
rosemary	der Rosmarin
sage	der Salbei
parsley	die Petersilie
mint	die Minze
tarragon	der Estragon
coriander	der Koriander
dill	der Dill
watercress	die Brunnenkresse

132

balsam	das Rührmichnichtan
chicory	der Chicorée
chives	der Schnittlauch
mustard	der Senf
balm	die Melisse
clover	der Klee
grass	das Gras
shrub	der Strauch
myrtle	die Heidelbeerre
gorse	der (Stech-)Ginster

133

flowerbed	das Blumenbeet
pansy	das Stiefmütterchen
primrose	die Primel
daisy	das Gänseblümchen
anemone	die Anemone
tulip	die Tulpe
hyacinth	die Hyazinthe
lily	die Lilie
lily of the valley	das Maiglöckchen
mignonette	die Reseda

134

snowdrop	das Schneeglöckchen
crocus	der Krokus
carnation	die Nelke
bluebell	die Glockenblume
poppy	der Mohn
cornflower	die Kornblume

Plants

buttercup	die Butterblume
daffodil	die Osterglocke
forget-me-not	das Vergißmeinnicht

135

foxglove	der Fingerhut
sunflower	die Sonnenblume
dandelion	der Löwenzahn
snapdragon	das Löwenmaul
marigold	die Ringelblume
orchid	die Orchidee
bush	der Busch
magnolia	die Magnolie
fuchsia	die Fuchsie
rhododendron	der Rhododendrom

136

shrub	der Strauch
heather	das Heidekraut
undergrowth	das Unterholz
scrub	das Buschwerk
broom	der Ginster
mallow	die Malve
laurel	der Lorbeer
privet hedge	die Ligusterhecke
to enclose	einfassen

137

vegetables	das Gemüse *sing*
kitchen garden	der Küchengarten
mushroom	der Champignon
fungus	der Pilz
harmful	schädlich, giftig
leek	der Lauch
radish	das Radieschen
lettuce	der Salat
celery	der Staudensellerie
rhubarb	der Rhabarber

138

chard	der innere Blattstiel
	der Artischoke
spinach	der Spinat
turnip	die weiße Rübe
potato	die Kartoffel
to peel	schälen
to scrape	abkratzen
husk	die Hülse
to husk	enthülsen
cabbage	der Kohl
hedge	die Hecke

139

fruit	das Obst
fruit tree	der Obstbaum
to graft	aufpfropfen
graft	der Pfropfreis

Plants

to shake	schütteln
to prune	ausschneiden
pear tree	der Birnenbaum
pear	die Birne
apple tree	der Apfelbaum
cherry tree	der Kirschbaum

140

cherry	die Kirsche
plum	die Pflaume
plum tree	der Pflaumenbaum
prune	die Trockenpflaume
stone	der Stein
to stone	entsteinen
almond	die Mandel
almond tree	der Mandelbaum
peach	der Pfirsich
peach tree	der Pfirsichbaum

141

apricot	die Aprikose
apricot tree	der Aprikosenbaum
walnut	die Walnuß
walnut tree	der Walnußbaum
chestnut	die (Eß-)Kastanie
chestnut tree	der (Eß-)Kastanienbaum
hazelnut	die Haselnuß
hazelnut tree	der Haselstrauch
lemon	die Zitrone
lemon tree	der Zitronenbaum

142

orange tree	der Orangenbaum
olive	die Olive
olive tree	der Olivenbaum
date	die Dattel
date palm	die Dattelpalme
palm tree	die Palme
pomegranate	der Granatapfel
pomegranate tree	der Granatapfelbaum
banana tree	die Bananenstaude
pineapple	die Ananas

143

coconut	die Kokosnuß
coconut tree	die Kokospalme
sugar cane	das Zuckerrohr
yam	die Yamwurzel
lychee	die Litschi
kiwi	die Kiwi
ripe	reif
to ripen	reifen
juicy	saftig
strawberry	die Erdbeere

144

strawberry plant	die Erdbeerpflanze

medlar	die Mispel
medlar tree	der Mispelbaum
raspberry	die Himbeere
raspberry bush	der Himbeerbusch
blackcurrant	die schwarze Johannisbeere
currant bush	der Johannisbeerbusch
gooseberry	die Stachelbeere
grape	die Traube
raisin	die Rosine

145

vine	der Weinstock
vineyard	der Weingarten
vintner	der Winzer
grape harvest	die Traubenernte
to gather grapes	Trauben ernten
press	die Presse
to press	pressen
forest trees	die Waldbäume
wood	der Wald
jungle	der Dschungel

146

woody	waldig
wild, uncultivated	wild
ivy	der Efeu
to climb	klettern
creeping	kletternd, Klettter-
wisteria	die Glyzine
mistletoe	die Mistel
rosewood	das Rosenholz
juniper	der Wacholder
fern	der Farn

147

tree	der Baum
bark	die Rinde
branch	der Ast
twig	der Zweig
knot	der Knoten
tree ring	der Jahresring
trunk	der Stamm
oak	die Eiche
acorn	der Ahorn
holm oak	die Steineiche

148

beech	die Buche
ash	die Esche
elm	die Ulme
poplar	die Pappel
aspen	die Espe
lime	die Linde
birch	die Birke
fir	die Tanne
conifer	der Nadelbaum
coniferous	zapfentragend

The Environment

149

cone	der Zapfen
pine	die Kiefer
hop	der Hopfen
monkey puzzle	die Schuppentanne
sycamore	der Bergahorn
maple	der Ahorn
holly	die Stechpalme
alder	die Erle
bamboo	der Bambus
eucalyptus	der Eukalyptus

150

acacia	die Akazie
rubber tree	der Gummibaum
mahogany	das Mahagoni
ebony	das Ebenholz
cedar	die Zeder
cactus	der Kaktus
cacao tree	der Kakaobaum
giant sequoia	der Mammutbaum
bonsai	der Bonsai
yew	die Eibe

151

weeping willow	die Trauerweide
azalea	die Azalee
catkin	das (Weiden-)Kätzchen
spore	die Spore
pollination	die Bestäubung
to pollinate	bestäuben
pollen	der Blütenstaub
to fertilise	befruchten
stock (species)	der Bestand
hybrid	die Hybride

The Environment   Die Umwelt

152

environmental	ökologisch
environmentalist	Ökologe
environmentalism	Ökologie
pollution	die Umweltverschmutzung
conserve	schützen
conservation	der Umweltschutz
waste	die Verschwendung
to waste	verschwenden
rubbish	Abfall
rubbish tip	der Müllhaufen

153

sewage	das Abwasser
spill	das Überlaufen
poisonous	giftig
to poison	vergiften
industrial waste	der Industriemüll

toxic	toxisch
pollutant	das Umweltgift
to pollute	(die Umwelt) belasten
consumerism	die Konsumgesellschaft
consumerist	das Mitglied der Konsumgesellschaft

154

to consume	verbrauchen
solar panel	Solarpanel
windmill	die Windmühle
wind energy	die Windenergie
wave energy	die Wellenenergie
wildlife	das Tierreich
harmful	schädlich
atmosphere	die Atmosphäre
smog	der Smog
unleaded petrol	das bleifreie Benzin

155

ecosystem	das Ökosystem
ecology	die Ökologie
ecologist	der Ökokloge
acid rain	der saure Regen
deforestation	die Entwaldung
to deforest	entwalden
rainforest	der Regenwald
underdeveloped	unterentwickelt
industrialised	industrialisiert
ozone layer	die Ozonschicht

156

oil slick	der Ölteppich
oil spill	die Öllache
greenhouse effect	der Treibhauseffekt
to recycle	recyceln
recycling	das Recycling
renewable	erneuerbar
fossil fuels	die fossilen Brennstoffe *pl*
resource	die Quelle, Ressource
landfill	die Deponie
to waste	verschwenden

157

decibel	das Dezibel
to soundproof	lärmdicht machen
radiation	die Strahlung
radioactive	radioaktiv
nuclear energy	die Kernenergie
fallout	der Fallout
reactor	der Reaktor
fission	die Spaltung
fusion	die Fusion
leak	das Leck

The Home   Das Zuhause

158

house	das Haus
apartment block	der Wohnblock
to let	vermieten
tenant	der Mieter
housing	der Wohnraum
to change	ändern
to move house	umziehen
landlord, owner	der Vermieter,
	der Eigentümer
own	eigen
ownership	das Eigentum

159

country house	das Landhaus
farmhouse	das Bauernhaus
villa	das Chalet
cottage	das Häuschen
chalet	das Chalet
terraced house	das Reihenhaus
semi-detached	
house	die Doppelhaushälfte
country house	das Landhaus
mansion	die Villa
palace	der Palast

160

castle	die Burg
igloo	der Iglu
teepee	das Tipi
log cabin	das Blockhaus
houseboat	das Hausboot
hut	die Hütte
house trailer	der Wohnwagen
penthouse	das Penthaus
lighthouse	der Leuchtturm
shack	der Verschlag

161

building	das Gebäude
to build	bauen
building site	das Baugelände
building contractor	der Bauunternehmer
repair	reparieren
solid	solide
to destroy	zerstören
to demolish	abreißen
garage	die Garage
shed	das Gartenhaus

162

door	die Tür
doorknocker	der Türdrücker
to knock at	
the door	an die Tür klopfen

doormat	der Fußabstreifer
doorbell	die Türklingel
threshold	die Schwelle
bolt	der Riegel
plan	der Plan
foundations	das Fundament
to found	gründen

163

cement	der Zement
concrete	der Beton
stone	der Stein
cornerstone	der Eckstein
angular	eckig
antiquated	veraltet
modern	modern
luxurious	luxuriös
roomy	geräumig
whitewashed	gekalkt
neglected	vernachlässigt

164

worm-eaten	vom Holzwurm befallen
moth-eaten	mottenzerfressen
shanty	der Schuppen
shantytown	die Wellblechhüttensiedlung
brick	der Backstein
sand	der Sand
slate	die Schindel
gutter	die Dachrinne
drainpipe	das Abflußrohr
step	die Stufe

165

plaster	der Verputz
skirting	die Fußleiste
floor	der Boden
wall	die Wand
partition wall	die Trennwand
wood	das Holz
board	das Brett
beam	der Balken
to sustain	stützen
to contain, hold	enthalten

166

facade	die Fassade
outside	die Außenseite
inside	die Innenseite
window	das Fenster
windowsill	das Fensterbrett
venetian blind	die Jalousie
shutter	der Fensterladen
balcony	der Balkon
windowpane	die Fensterscheibe
glass ·	das Glas

The Home

167

porch	der Eingang
door	die Tür
hinge	die Angel
front door	die Eingangstür
doorkeeper	der Pförtner
to open	öffnen
opening	die Öffnung
entrance	der Eingang
to enter	eintreten
to go out	ausgehen

168

way out	der Ausgang
lock	das Schloß
to shut, close	schließen
to lock up	zuschließen, verschließen
key	der Schlüssel
to lock	abschließen
staircase	das Treppenhaus
upstairs	oben
downstairs	unten
landing	die Diele

169

ladder	die Leiter
banisters	das Treppengeländer
lift	der Aufzug
to go up	nach oben gehen
to ascend	nach oben gehen
ascent	der Aufstieg
to go down	nach unten gehen
descent	der Abstieg
low	niedrig
storeys	die Stockwerke

170

ground floor	das Erdgeschoß
first floor	der erste Stock
cellar	der Keller
tile	die Kachel
roof	das Dach
ceiling	die Decke
floor	der Boden
to turn	(sich) drehen
to return	zurückkehren
return	die Rückkehr

171

to give back	zurückgeben
chimney	der Kamin
hearth	die Feuerstelle
fire	das Feuer
spark	der Funke
to sparkle	glitzern
flame	die Flamme
ashes	die Asche *sing*

The Home

stove	der Herd
smoke	der Rauch

172

to smoke (of fire)	rauchen
to burn	brennen
to blaze	lodern
ardent	lodernd
coal	die Kohle
charcoal	die Holzkohle
embers	die Glut
to scorch	versengen
to glow	glühen
firewood	das Feuerholz

173

woodcutter	der Holzhacker
shovel	die Schaufel
poker	dser Feuerhaken
to poke	stochern
matches	die Streichhölzer
wax	das Wachs
to light	anzünden
box	die Schachtel
drawer	die Schublade
chest of drawers	die Kommode

174

comfortable	bequem
uncomfortable	unbequem
lighting	die Beleuchtung
dazzle, splendour	das gleißende Licht
to light up	erleuchten
to put out,	
extinguish	löschen
light	das Licht
lamp	die Lampe
lampshade	der Lampenschirm
wick	der Docht

175

candle	die Kerze
candlestick	der Kerzenhalter
room	das Zimmer
to inhabit	bewohnen
inhabitant	der Bewohner
to reside	wohnen
residence	die Wohnung
hall (large room)	der Saal
furniture	die Möbel
a piece of furniture	ein Möbelstück

176

furnished	möbliert
corridor	der Flur
hall, lobby	die Eingangshalle
hall stand	der Garderobenständer

The Home

sitting room	das Wohnzimmer	photograph	die Fotografie
lounge (of hotel)	das Foyer	photograph album	das Fotoalbum
to serve	einen Gast bedienen	dining room	das Eßzimmer
guest	der Gast	to eat, dine	essen
to invite	einladen	meals	die Mahlzeiten
table	der Tisch	breakfast	das Frühstück
		to breakfast	frühstücken
177		lunch	das Mittagessen
seat	der Platz		
to sit down	sich hinsetzen	**182**	
to be sitting	sitzen	dinner	das Abendessen
cushion	das Kissen	to lunch	zu Mittag essen
stool	der Hocker	supper	das Abendessen
chair	der Stuhl	to have supper	zu Abend essen
armchair	der Sessel	sideboard	das Sideboard
rocking chair	der Schaukelstuhl	larder	der Speiseschrank
sofa	das Sofa	pantry	die Speisekammer
couch	die Couch	shelf	das Regal
bench	die Bank	cup	die Tasse
		draining board	das Abtropfbrett
178			
bookcase	der Bücherschrank	**183**	
bookshelf	das Bücherregal	sugarbowl	die Zuckerdose
bookrest	die Buchstütze	coffeepot	die Kaffeekanne
library	die Bücherei	teapot	die Teekanne
office, study	das Büro	tray	das Tablett
writing desk	der Schreibtisch	table service	das Service
to write	schreiben	tablecloth	das Tischtuch
handwriting	die Handschrift	napkin	die Serviette
paper	das Papier	plate	der Teller
		saucer	die Untertasse
179		serving dish	der Vorlegeteller
record-player	der Plattenspieler		
hi-fi	Hi-Fi	**184**	
television	das Fernsehen	microwave	die Mikrowelle
video recorder	der Videorekorder	to microwave	in der Mikrowelle kochen
radiator	der Heizkörper	food mixer	der Mixer
radio	das Radio	refrigerator	der Kühlschrank
ornament	das Ornament	grater	die Reibe
clock	die Uhr	flowerpot	der Blumentopf
grandfather clock	die Standuhr	(drinking) glass	das Glas
		glassware	das Glas
180		to cook	kochen
tapestry	die Gobelinstickerei	to boil	kochen
a tapestry	ein Wandbehand		
to hang	aufhängen	**185**	
to take down	abnehmen	gas cooker	der Gasherd
wallpaper	die Tapete	electric cooker	der Elektroherd
to wallpaper	tapezieren	grill	der Grill
tile (decorative)	die (Zier-)Kachel	barbecue grill	der Holkohlengrill
floor tile	die Bodenfließe	saucepan	die Kasserole
tiling	das Fließen	refuse, rubbish	der Abfall
picture	das Bild	washing machine	die Waschmaschine
		sewing machine	die Nähmaschine
181		washing powder	das Waschpulver
frame	der Rahmen	vacuum cleaner	der Staubsauger
portrait	das Porträt		

186	
electricity	die Elektrizität
fusebox	der Sicherungskasten
central heating	die Zentralheizung
light bulb	die Glübirne
switch	der Schalter
to switch on	anschalten
to switch off	ausschalten
plug	der Stecker
socket	die Steckdose
air conditioning	die Klimaanlage

187	
lid, cover	der Deckel
to cover	zudecken
to uncover	öffnen
to uncork	entkorken
crockery	das Geschirr
to cover	abdecken
discover	entdecken
spoon	der Löffel
teaspoon	der Teelöffel
spoonful	einen Löffel voll

188	
fork	die Gabel
cutlery	das Besteck
set of cutlery	das Gedeck
knife	das Messer
to carve (meat)	tranchieren
to cut	schneiden
sharp	scharf
bottle	die Flasche
cork	der Korken
corkscrew	der Korkenzieher

189	
to pull out	herausziehen
to drink	trinken
beverage, drink	das Getränk
to toast (health)	zuprosten
oven	die Röhre
(kitchen) utensils	die Küchengeräte *pl*
saucepan	die Kasserolle
frying pan	die Pfanne
pot	der Topf
pitcher	der Krug

190	
bucket	der Eimer
to pour out	ausgießen
basket	der Korb
to fill	füllen
full	voll
empty	leer
to empty	leeren
broom	der Besen

to sweep	kehren
to rub	reiben
to scrub	schrubben

191	
to wash (dishes)	abwaschen
bedroom	
(master bedroom)	das Schlafzimmer
(other) bedroom	das Zimmer
to go to bed	zu Bett gehen
bed	das Bett
bedspread	die Tagesdecke
bunk bed	das Stockbett
cot	das Kinderbett
mattress	die Matratze
sheets	die Bettücher *pl*
electric blanket	die elektrische Wärmdecke

192	
bolster	die Schlummerrolle
pillow	das Kissen
carpet	der Teppich
rug, mat	der Vorleger
to wake	wecken
to awake	aufwachen
to get up early	früh aufstehen
the early hours	die Nacht, nach Mitternacht
curtain	der Vorhang
attic	die Mansarde

193	
alarm clock	der Wecker
hot-water bottle	die Wärmflasche
nightcap	der Bettrunk
to sleepwalk	schlafwandeln
sleepwalker	der Schlafwandler, die Schlafwandlerin
sleepwalking	das Schlafwandeln
wardrobe	der Kleiderschrank
to keep, preserve	behalten
dressing table	der Schminktisch
screen	der Paravent

194	
bathroom	das Badezimmer
bath	das Bad
bathtub	die Badewanne
to bathe	baden
to wash	waschen
to wash oneself	sich waschen
towel	das Handtuch
washbasin	das Waschbecken
shower	die Dusche
to take a shower	sich duschen

The Home

195	
tap	der Wasserhahn
to turn on (tap)	(den Hahn) aufdrehen
to turn off (tap)	(den Hahn) abdrehen
sponge	der Schwamm
facecloth	der Waschlappen
toothbrush	die Zahnbürste
toothpaste	die Zahnpasta
toothpick	der Zahnstocher
toilet paper	das Eau de Toilette
toilet bowl	die Waschschüssel

196	
soap	die Seife
shampoo	das Schampu
makeup	das Makeup
face cream	die Gesichtscreme
face pack	die Gesichtsmaske
compact	der Kompaktpulver
lipstick	der Lippenstift
nail file	die Nagelfeile
nail clippers	die Nagelschere
nail varnish	der Nagellack

197	
hairpin	die Haarnadel
hairdryer	der Föhn
hairspray	das Haarspray
hairslide	die Haarklammer
hairpiece	das Haarteil
hairnet	das Haarnetz
to wipe	wischen
to clean	reinigen
clean	sauber
dirty	schmutzig

198	
mirror	der Spiegel
basin	das Becken, die Schüssel
jug	der Krug
razor (cutthroat)	das Rasiermesser
smoke detector	der Feuermelder
razorblade	die Rasierklinge
electric razor	der Rasierapparat
shaving foam	der Rasierschaum
comb	der Kamm
to comb (oneself)	(sich) kämmen

199	
tools	das Werkzeug
saw	die Säge
to saw	sägen
drill	die Bohrmaschine
drill bit	der Bohrer
sawdust	das Sägemehl
hammer	der Hammer
nail	der Nagel

to nail	nageln
spade	die Schaufel
pickaxe	die Spitzhacke

200	
screw	die Schraube
screwdriver	der Schraubenzieher
axe	die Axt
paint	die Farbe
paintbrush	der Pinsel
to paint	malen, streichen
glue	der Leim
to glue, stick	leimen, kleben
sander	die Schleifmaschine
sandpaper	das Schleifpapier

Society — Die Gesellschaft

201	
street	die Straße
walk, promenade	der Spaziergang
to go for a walk	spazierengehen
passer-by	der Passant, die Passantin
avenue	die Allee
kiosk	der Kiosk
native of	der Einwohner aus, die Einwohnerin aus
compatriot	der Landsmann, die Landsmännin
pavement	der Bürgersteig
gutter	die Gosse

202	
road	die Straße
high road	die Hauptstraße
street lamp	die Straßenlampe
traffic	der Verkehr
frequented	besucht
to frequent	besuchen
pedestrian	der Fußgänger
pedestrian area	die Fußgängerzone
square	der Platz
park	der Park

203	
crossroads	die Kreuzung
corner	die Ecke
alley	der Fußweg
quarter (of town)	das Viertel
slum	der Slum
outskirts	die Außenbezirke
around	um… herum
dormitory town	die Schlafstadt
premises	das Gelände
warehouse	das Lagerhaus

Society   **Society**

204

cul-de-sac	die Sackgasse
one-way	die Einbahnstraße
traffic jam	der Verkehrsstau
rush hour	die Stoßzeit
zebra crossing	der Zebrastreifen
shop window	das Schaufenster
poster	das Plakat
bus stop	die Bushaltestelle
to queue	sich anstellen
routine	die Routine

205

shop	der Laden
shopkeeper	der Ladenführer, die Ladenführerin
counter	die Theke
to show	zeigen
inn	die Gaststätte
innkeeper	der Gaststätteninhaber, die Gaststätteninhaberin
to stay	bleiben, wohnen
lodging house	die Pension
guest	der Gast
board and lodgings	Unterkunft und Verpflegung

206

profession	der Beruf
trade	das Gewerbe
mechanic	der Mechaniker, die Mechanikerin
engineer	der Techniker, die Technikerin
spinner	der Spinner, die Spinnerin
workman	der Arbeiter, die Arbeiterin
operative	der Bediener, die Bedienerin
apprentice	der Lehrling
apprenticeship	die Ausbildung, die Lehre
day labourer	der Tagelöhner

207

fireman	der Feuerwehrmann
fire station	die Feuerwehrstation
fire hydrant	der Hydrant
shop assistant	der Verkäufer, die Verkäuferin
fishmonger	der Fischverkäufer, die Fischverkäuferin
fishmonger's	der Fischladen
street sweeper	der Straßenkehrer, die Straßenkehrerin
library	die Bibliothek
librarian	der Bibliothekar, die Bibliothekarin
notary	der Notar, die Notarin

208

policeman	der Polizist, die Polizistin
police (force)	die Polizei
police station	die Polizeistation
secretary	der Sekretär, die Sekretärin
plumber	der Klempner, die Klempnerin
jeweller	der Juwelier, die Juwelierin
stonecutter	der Steinmetz, die Steinmetzin
hatter	der Hutmacher, die Hutmacherin
hat shop	der Hutladen

209

carpenter	der Zimmermann
ironmonger	der Eisenwarenhändler, die Eisenwarenhändlerin
miller	der Müller, die Müllerin
mill	die Mühle
to grind	mahlen
baker	der Bäcker, die Bäckerin
to knead	kneten
bakery	die Bäckerei
barber	der Friseur, die Friseurin
barbershop	der Frisiersalon

210

tobacconist	der Tabakwarenhändler, die Tabakwarenhändlerin
tobacconist's	das Tabakwarengeschäft, die Traffik (*Austria*)
rag-and-bone-man	der Lumpenhändler, die Lumpenhändlerin
tailor	der Schneider, die Schneiderin
tailor's	die Schneiderei
butcher	der Metzger, der Fleischer
butcher's	die Metzgerei, die Fleischerei
milkman	der Milchmann
dairy	die Molkerei
glazier	der Glasierer, die Glasiererin

211

bricklayer	der Maurer
stationer	der Papierwarenhändler, die Papierwarenhändlerin
stationer's	die Papierwarenhandlung
upholsterer	der Dekorateur
photographer	der Fotograf, die Fotografin
blacksmith	der Schmied
horseshoe	das Hufeisen
to shoe (horses)	behufen
shepherd	der Schafhirte, die Schafhirtin
cowboy	der Kuhhirte, die Kuhhirtin

Society   Society

212	
farm	der Bauernhof
to lease	verpachten
country estate	das Landgut
courtyard	der Hof
well	der Brunnen
stable	der Stall
hayfork	die Heugabel
straw	das Stroh
hay	das Heu
haystack	der Heuhaufen
grain	das Korn

213	
agriculture	die Landwirtschaft
agricultural	landwirtschaftlich
rustic	ländlich
countryside	die Landschaft, das Land
peasant	der Bauer, die Bäuerin
farmer	der Landwirt, die Landwirtin
to cultivate	anbauen
cultivation	der Anbau
tillage	das Pflügen
to plough	pflügen

214	
plough	der Pflug
furrow	die Furche
fertiliser	der Dünger
to fertilise (crop)	düngen
fertile	fruchtbar
barren	unfruchtbar
dry	trocken
to sow	sähen
seed	der Samen
sowing	die Saat

215	
to scatter	verstreuen
to germinate	keimen
to mow	mähen
reaper	der Erntearbeiter
reaping machine	die Erntemaschine
combine harvester	der Mähdrescher
sickle	die Sichel
scythe	die Sense
to harvest	ernten
harvest	die Ernte

216	
rake	der Rechen
to rake	rechen
spade	die Schaufel
to dig	graben
hoe	die Hacke
meadow	die Wiese
silage	das Silofutter

wheat	der Weizen
oats	der Hafer
barley	die Gerste
ear (of wheat)	die (Weizen-)Ähre

217	
maize	der Mais
rice	der Reis
alfalfa	das Alfalfa
pile	der Haufen
to pile up	aufhäufen
tractor	der Traktor
harrow	die Egge
baler	der Stabilistor
rotovator	der Pflug mit
	rotierenden Klingen
milking machine	die Melkmaschine

218	
to milk	melken
stockbreeder	der Viehzüchter,
	die Viehzüchterin
stockbreeding	die Viehzucht
fodder, feed	das Futter
to irrigate	bewässern
greenhouse	das Treibhaus
subsidy	die Unterstützung
grape harvest	die Weinernte
grape picker	der Traubenpflücker

219	
commerce	der Handel
firm	die Firma
branch	die Filiale
export	die Ausfuhr
import	die Einfuhr
company	die Gesellschaft
partner	der Partner
to associate	in Partnerschaft gehen
businessman	der Geschäftsmann
business	das Geschäft

220	
subject	das Thema
to offer	bieten
offer	das Gebot
demand	die Forderung
account	das Konto
current account	das Girokonto
to settle	begleichen
order	der Auftrag
to cancel	annullieren
on credit	auf Kredit

221	
by instalments	auf Raten
for cash	gegen Bargeld

338

Society   **Society**

market	der Markt
deposit	die Kaution
goods	die Waren
bargain	das Sonderangebot
second-hand	aus zweiter Hand
cheap	billig
expensive	teuer
to bargain, haggle	handeln

222

packaging	die Verpackung
to pack up	einpacken
to unpack	auspacken
to wrap	einwickeln
to unwrap	auswickeln
transport	der Transport
to transport	transportieren
carriage	der Wagen
portable	tragbar
delivery	die Lieferung

223

to deliver	liefern
to dispatch	absenden
office	das Büro
manager	der Manager, die Managerin
accountant	der Buchhalter, die Buchhalterin
clerk	der Angestellte, die Angestellte
to depend on	abhängig sein von
to employ	einstellen
employee	der Arbeitnehmer, die Arbeitnehmerin
employment	die Anstellung

224

employer	der Arbeitgeber, die Arbeitgeberin
unemployment	die Arbeitslosigkeit
unemployed	arbeitslos
chief	der Chef, die Chefin
typewriter	die Schreibmaschine
typist	die Schreibkraft
typing	das Maschinenschreiben
shorthand	die Stenographie
shorthand typist	der Stenotypist, die Stenotypistin
audiotypist	der Audiotypist, die Audiotypistin

225

director	das Vorstandsmitglied
managing director	der geschäftsführende Direktor, die geschäftsführende Direktorin

board of directors	der Vorstand
shareholder	der Aktionär, die Aktionärin
dividend	die Dividende
takeover	die Übernahme
to list (shares)	Aktien notieren lassen
asset	das Vermögen
liability	die Verbindlichkeiten *pl*
contract	der Vertrag

226

purchase	der Kauf
to buy	kaufen
sell	verkaufen
sale	der Verkauf
buyer	der Käufer, die Käuferin
seller	der Verkäufer, die Verkäuferin
wholesale	(der Verkauf) en gros
to bid	bieten
bidder	der Steigerer

227

to auction	versteigern
client	der Kunde, die Kundin
clientele	die Kundschaft
catalogue	der Katalog
price	der Preis
quantity	die Menge
gross	bruto
net	netto
to cost	kosten
cost	die Kosten *pl*

228

free of charge	kostenlos
pay	zahlen
wages	der Lohn
salary	das Gehalt
payment	die Bezahlung
in advance	im voraus
invoice	die Rechnung
checkout	die Kasse
cashier	der Kassierer, die Kassiererin
accounts	die Konten

229

balance sheet	die Bilanz
general income	die Einnahmen
expenditure	die Ausgaben
to spend	ausgeben
to acknowledge	
receipt	quittieren
to receive	erhalten
reception	der Empfang

Society

profit	der Gewinn		to inform	unterrichten
loss	der Verlust		warning	die Warnung
loan	das Darlehn		coin	die Münze
			money	das Geld
230			mint	die Münzstätte
to borrow	borgen			
to lend	leihen		**235**	
to prepare	vorbereiten		post office	das Postamt
to obtain	erhalten		mail	die Post
creditor	der Gläubiger		by return of post	postwendend
debt	die Schuld		postcard	die Postkarte
debtor	der Schuldner		letter	der Brief
to get into debt	Schulden machen		postman	der Briefträger
to be in debt	verschuldet sein		letterbox	der Briefkasten
bankruptcy	der Konkurs		collection	die Abholung
			to collect	abholen
231			delivery	die Lieferung
to go bankrupt	in Konkurs gehen			
banking	das Bankwesen		**236**	
bank	die Bank		to distribute	verteilen
banknote	der Geldschein		distributor	der Verteiler
banker	der Bankier		envelope	der Umschlag
bankbook	das Bankbuch		postage	das Beförderungsentgelt
bankcard	die Kreditkarte		to frank	frankieren
bank account	das Bankkonto		to seal	versiegeln
savings bank	die Sparkasse		stamp	der Stempel
			postmark	der Poststempel
232			to stamp	mit Briefmarken versehen
to save (money)	sparen		to pack	verpacken
capital	das Kapital		to unpack	auspacken
interest	das Vermögen			
income	das Einkommen		**237**	
stock exchange	die Börse		to register	einschreiben
share	die Aktie		to forward	zustellen
shareholder	der Aktionär		sender	der Sender
exchange	der Kurs		addressee	der Adressat
rate	der Satz		unknown	unbekannt
to exchange	wechseln		to send	senden
exchange rate	der Wechselkurs		price list	der Tarif
			courier	der Bote
233			air mail	die Luftpost
to be worth	wert sein		by airmail	per Luftpost
value	der Wert			
to value	bewerten		**238**	
discount	der Rabatt		pound sterling	Pfund Sterling
to deduct	abziehen		franc	der Franc (*France*),
to cash a cheque	einen Scheck einlösen			der Franken (*Switzerland*)
payable on sight	auf Sicht zahlbar		mark	die Mark
signature	die Unterschrift		dollar	der Dollar
to sign	unterschreiben		penny	der Penny
draft	der Wechsel		shilling	der Schilling
			ingot	der (Gold-)Barren
234			foreign currencies	die Fremdwährung
postal order	die Postanweisung		speculation	die Spekulation
to fall due	fällig werden		speculator	der Spekulant
date	das Datum			
to date	datieren			

Society

239

wealthy	wohlhabend
wealth	der Reichtum
rich	reich
to get rich	reich werden
to acquire	erwerben
to possess	besitzen
fortune	das Vermögen
to be fortunate	Glück haben
poverty	die Armut
poor	arm
necessity	die Notwendigkeit

240

to need	brauchen
misery	das Elend
miserable	elend
beggar	der Bettler, die Bettlerin
to beg	betteln
homeless	obdachlos
squatter	der Hausbesetzer, die Hausbesetzerin
eviction	die Räumung
malnourished	unterernährt
disadvantaged	unterprivilegiert

241

industry	die Industrie, die Branche
industrialist	der Industrielle
manufacture	die Produktion
to manufacture	produzieren, herstellen
factory	die Fabrik
manufacturer	der Produzent
trademark	das Warenzeichen
machine	die Maschine
machinery	die Maschinerie
to undertake	unternehmen

242

enterprise	das Unternehmen
expert	der Experte
skill	die Fertigkeit
skilful	fähig
ability	die Fähigkeit
clumsy	ungeschickt
to keep busy	sich beschäftigen
busy	beschäftigt
lazy	faul
strike	der Streik

243

striker	der Streikteilnehmer, die Streikteilnehmerin
lock-out	die Aussperrung
blackleg	der Streikbrecher, die Streikbrecherin
picket	der Streikposten

to go on strike	in Streik gehen
trade union	die Gewerkschaft
trade unionist	der Gewerkschaftler, die Gewerkschaftlerin
trade unionism	die Gewerkschaftsbewegung
minimum wage	der Mindestlohn
market economy	die Marktwirtschaft

244

government	die Regierung
to govern	regieren
politics	die Politik
political	politisch
politician	der Politiker, die Politikerin
socialist	sozialistisch
conservative	konservativ
liberal	liberal
fascist	faschistisch
communist	kommunistisch

245

monarchy	die Monarchie
monarch	der Monarch
king	der König
queen	die Königin
viceroy	der Vizekönig
to reign	regieren
royal	königlich
crown	die Krone
to crown	krönen
throne	der Thron

246

court	der Hof
courtier	der Höfling
chancellor	der Kanzler
rank	der Rang
prince	der Prinz
princess	die Prinzessin
title	der Titel
subject	der Untertan, die Untertanin
emperor	der Kaiser
empress	die Kaiserin

247

revolution	die Revolution
guillotine	die Guillotine
to guillotine	guillotinieren
counterrevolution	die Konterrevolution
aristocracy	die Aristokratie
aristocrat	der Aristokrat
confiscate	konfiszieren
confiscation	die Konfiszierung
secular	weltlich
secularisation	die Verweltlichung

Society

248
republic	die Republik
republican	republikanisch
president	der Präsident
embassy	die Botschaft
ambassador	der Botschafter, die Botschafterin
consul	der Konsul, die Konsulin
consulate	das Konsulat
state	der Staat
city state	der Stadtstaat
councillor	das Ratsmitglied

249
council	der Rat
to advise	beraten
to administer	verwalten
minister	der Minister, die Ministerin
ministry	das Ministerium
cabinet	das Kabinett
deputy	der Gesandte, die Gesandte
parliament	das Parlament
senate	der Senat
senator	der Senator, die Senatorin

250
session	die Sitzung
to deliberate	sich beraten
dialogue	der Dialog
discuss	diskutieren
adopt	adoptieren
decree	der Beschluß
to decree	beschließen
to proclaim	ausrufen
election	die Wahl
referendum	die Volksabstimmung

251
to elect	wählen
vote	wählen
vote	die Stimme
town council	der Gemeinderat
mayor	der Bürgermeister
bailiff	der Gerichtsvollzieher, die Gerichtsvollzieherin
justice	die Gerechtigkeit
just	gerecht
unjust	ungerecht
judge	der Richter, die Richterin

252
to judge	richten
court	das Gericht
judgment	das Urteil
injury	die Verletzung
to protect	schützen
law	das Gesetz

legal	legal
illegal	illegal
to bequeath	vererben
beneficiary	der Begünstigte, die Begünstigte

253
to make a will	sein Testament machen
will	das Testament
heir	der Erbe
heiress	die Erbin
to inherit	erben
inheritance	die Erbschaft
tribunal	die Gerichtsverhandlung
to summons	vorladen
summons	die Vorladung
appointment	die Bestellung

254
trial	der Prozeß
lawsuit	das Gerichtsverfahren
lawyer	der Rechtsanwalt
to advocate	verteidigen
to swear	schwören
oath	der Eid
witness	der Zeuge, die Zeugin
to bear witness	bezeugen
testimony	das Zeugnis
evidence	der Beweis

255
to infringe	übertreten
indictment	die Anklage
to plead	plädieren
to accuse	anklagen
accused	der Beklagte, die Beklagte
plaintiff	der Kläger, die Klägerin
defendant	der Angeklagte, die Angeklagte
to sue	verklagen
fault	die Schuld
jury	die Geschworenen *pl*

256
crime	das Verbrechen
murderer	der Mörder, die Mörderin
to murder	ermorden
murder	der Mord
to kill	töten
suicide	der Selbstmord
to commit	begehen
offence	eine Straftat
thief	der Dieb, die Diebin
bandit	der Bandit, die Banditin

Society   **Society**

257

theft	der Diebstahl
to steal	stehlen
traitor	der Verräter, die Verräterin
treason	der Verrat
fraud	der Betrug
bigamy	die Bigamie
bigamist	der Bigamist,
	die Bigamistin
assault	die Körperverletzung
blackmail	die Erpressung
to blackmail	erpressen

258

rape	die Vergewaltigung
rapist	der Vergewaltiger
guilty	schuldig
innocent	unschuldig
defence	die Verteidigung
to defend	verteidigen
to prohibit	verbieten
acquittal	der Freispruch
to acquit	freisprechen

259

sentence	das Urteil
to sentence	verurteilen
verdict	der Urteilsspruch
fine	die Geldbuße
conviction	die Schuldigsprechung
to condemn	schuldig sprechen
prison	das Gefängnis,
	die Justizvollzugsanstalt
to imprison	einsperren
prisoner	der Gefangene,
	die Gefangene
to arrest	verhaften

260

capital punishment	die Todesstrafe
executioner	der Henker, die Henkerin
gallows	der Galgen
firing squad	das Schießkommando
electric chair	der elektrische Stuhl
pardon	die Begnadigung
remission	der Erlaß
parole	die bedingte Strafaussetzung
false imprisonment	die Freiheitsberaubung
self-defence	die Selbstverteidigung

261

army	die Armee
to drill	exerzieren
military	militärisch
soldier	der Soldat, die Soldatin
conscription	die Einberufung
conscript	der Wehrdienstpflichtige

conscientious	
objector	der Wehrdienstverweigerer
recruit	der Rekrut, die Rekrutin
flag	die Fahne
troops	die Truppe

262

officer	der Offizier, die Offizierin
sergeant	der Feldwebel
corporal	der Korporal
rank	der Rang
general	der General
colonel	der Oberst
captain	der Kapitän
lieutenant	der Leutnant
discipline	die Disziplin
order	die Ordnung

263

disorder	die Unordnung
infantry	die Infantrie
cavalry	die Kavallerie
artillery	die Artillerie
cannon	die Kanone
grenade	die Granate
to explode	explodieren
gunpowder	das Schwarzpulver
ammunition	die Munition
bomb	die Bombe

264

to shell	bombardieren
bombardment	die Bombardierung
guard, watch	die Wache
sentry	der Wachposten
garrison	die Garnison
barracks	die Kaserne *sing*
regiment	das Regiment
detachment	die Abkommandierung
reinforcement	die Verstärkung
battalion	das Battallion

265

to equip	ausrüsten
equipment	die Ausrüstung
uniform	die Uniform
flak jacket	die schußsichere Weste
firearm	die Schußwaffe
to arm	bewaffnen
to disarm	entwaffnen
to load	beladen
to unload	entladen
to shoot	schießen

266

| shot | der Schuß |
| bullet | die Kugel |

Society

bulletproof	kugelsicher	**271**	
cartridge	die Kartusche	to pursue	verfolgen
revolver	der Revolver	pursuit	die Verfolgung
bayonet	das Bayonet	to conquer	erobern
dagger	der Dolch	victor	der Sieger, die Siegerin
tank	der Panzer	vanquished	der Unterlegene
armoured car	der Panzerwagen	armistice	der Waffenstillstand
barbed wire	der Stacheldraht	treaty	das Abkommen
		peace	der Frieden
267		captivity	die Gefangenschaft
cold war	der kalte Krieg	to escape	entkommen
superpower	die Supermacht		
rocket	die Rakete	**272**	
nuclear warhead	der Atomsprengkopf	to encamp	lagern
blockade	die Blockade	encampment	das Lager
holocaust	der Holocaust	to manoeuvre	manövrieren
friendly fire	das Freundesfeuer	manoeuvre	das Manöver
ceasefire	der Waffenstillstand	wounded	verwundet
disarmament	die Abrüstung	hero	der Held
pacifism	der Pazifismus	heroine	die Heldin
		medal	die Medaille
268		pension	die Rente
war	der Krieg	war memorial	das Kriegerdenkmal
warlike	kriegerisch		
warrior	der Krieger	**273**	
guerrilla	die Guerilla,	navy	die Marine
	der Guerillero	sailor	der Matrose
guerrilla campaign	der Guerillakampf	admiral	der Admiral
siege	die Belagerung	squadron	das Schwadron
to besiege	belagern	fleet	die Flotte
fort	das Fort	to float	treiben
spy	der Spion, die Spionin	to sail	segeln
		navigator	der Steuermann
269		warship	das Kriegsschiff
attack	der Angriff	battleship	das Kampfschiff
to attack	angreifen		
assault	der Überfall	**274**	
ambush	der Ambusch	aircraft carrier	der Flugzeugträger
to surrender	sich ergeben	fighter plane	das Kampfflugzeug
surrender	die Ergebung	destroyer	der Zerstörer
encounter	das Treffen	minesweeper	das Minenräumboot
to meet	treffen	submarine	das U-Boot
fight	der Kampf	aerodrome	der Flughafen
to fight	kämpfen	spotter plane	das Aufklärungsflugzeug
		air raid	der Luftangriff
270		to bomb	bombardieren
combatant	der Kämpfer	parachute	der Fallschirm
exploit	das Ergebnis		
battlefield	das Schlachtfeld	**275**	
trench	der Graben	parachutist	der Fallschirmspringer,
to repel	abschrecken		die Fallschirmspringerin
retreat	sich zurückziehen	surface to	
flight	die Flucht	air missile	das Land-Luft-Geschoß
to flee	fliehen	helicopter	der Helikopter
defeat	die Niederlage	to bring down	abschießen
to defeat	besiegen	anti-aircraft gun	das Flugabwehrgeschütz
		shelter	der Bunker

Society

bomb disposal	die Entschärfung von Bomben
bomber (plane)	der Bomber
to explode	explodieren
explosion	die Explosion

276

religion	die Religion
religious	religiös
God	Gott
god	der Gott
goddess	die Göttin
monk	der Mönch
nun	die Nonne
divine	göttlich
omnipotent	allmächtig
saviour	der Erlöser

277

safe	sicher
pagan	heidnisch
Christianity	das Christentum
Christian	der Christ, die Christin
Catholic	katholisch
Catholicism	der Katholizismus
Protestantism	der Protestantismus
Protestant	protestantisch
Calvinism	der Calvinismus
Calvinist	calvinistisch

278

Presbyterian	presbiterianisch
Mormonism	das Mormonentum
Mormon	der Mormone, die Mormonin
Bible	die Bibel
Koran	der Koren
Islam	der Islam
Muslim	mohamedanisch
Hindu	hinduistisch
Hinduism	der Hinduismus
Buddhist	buddhistisch

279

Buddhism	der Buddhismus
Jewish	jüdisch
Judaism	das Judentum
Rastafarian	rastafarian
scientology	(die) Scientology
to convert	konvertieren
sect	die Sekte
animism	der Animismus
voodoo	(das) Voodoo

280

shaman	der Schamane
atheist	der Atheist, die Atheistin

atheism	der Atheismus
agnostic	der Agnostiker
agnosticism	das Agnostikertum
heretic	der Ketzer, die Ketzerin
heresy	die Ketzerei
fundamentalist	der Fundamentalist, die Fundamentalistin
fundamentalism	der Fundamentalismus
to believe	glauben

281

believer	der/die Gläubige
belief	der Glaube
faith	der Glaube
church	die Kirche
chapel	die Kapelle
chalice	der Kelch
altar	der Altar
mass	die Messe
blessing	der Segen
to bless	segnen

282

to curse	verfluchen
clergy	der Klerus
clergyman	der Kleriker
to preach	predigen
preacher	der Prediger
sermon	die Predigt
apostle	der Apostel
angel	der Engel
holy	heilig
saint	der Heilige, die Heilige

283

blessed	selig
sacred	heilig
devil	der Teufel
devilish	teuflisch
cult	der Kult
solemn	feierlich
prayer	das Gebet
to pray	beten
devout	fromm
fervent	hingebungsvoll

284

sin	die Sünde
to sin	sündigen
sinner	der Sündiger, die Sündigerin
repentant	reumütig
to baptise	taufen
pope	der Papst
cardinal	der Kardinal
bishop	der Bischof
archbishop	der Erzbischof
priest	der Priester, die Priesterin

285

parish	die Gemeinde
abbot	der Abt
abbess	die Äbtissin
abbey	die Abtei
convent	das Kloster
monastery	das Kloster
minister	der Pfarrer, die Pfarrerin
pilgrim	der Pilgerer, die Pilgerin
pilgrimage	die Pilgerschaft
to celebrate	feiern

The Intellect and Emotions
Der Intellekt und die Emotionen

286

mind	der Geist
thought	der Gedanke
to think of	denken an
to meditate	meditieren
to remember	sich erinnern an
to agree with	übereinstimmen mit
agreement	die Übereinstimmung
soul	die Seele
to occur,	
come to mind	einfallen
recollection	die Erinnerung

287

renown	berühmt
to perceive	wahrnehmen
to understand	verstehen
understanding	das Verständnis
intelligence	die Intelligenz
intelligent	intelligent
clever	klug
stupid	dumm
stupidity	die Dummheit
worthy	würdig

288

unworthy	unwürdig
reason	die Vernunft
reasonable	vernünftig
unreasonable	unvernünftig
to reason	erwägen
to discuss	diskutieren
to convince	überzeugen
opinion	die Meinung
to affirm	bejahen
to deny	verneinen

289

certainty	die Gewißheit
certain	gewiß

uncertain	ungewiß
sure	sicher
unsure	unsicher
security	die Sicherheit
to risk	riskieren
doubt	der Zweifel
doubtful	zweifelhaft
mistake	der Fehler

290

to make a mistake	einen Fehler machen
suspicion	der Verdacht
to suspect	verdächtigen
suspicious	verdächtig
desire	die Sehnsucht
to desire	ersehnen
to grant	gewähren
will	der Wille
to decide	entscheiden
undecided	unentschlossen

291

to hesitate	zögern
capable	fähig
incapable	unfähig
capability	die Fähigkeit
talent	das Talent
disposition, temper	die Veranlagung, das Temperament
character	der Charakter
to rejoice	sich freuen
cheerfulness	die Fröhlichkeit
happiness	das Glück

292

cheerful	fröhlich
sad	traurig
sadness	die Traurigkeit
to grieve	trauern
enjoyment	der Genuß
happy	glücklich
unhappy	unglücklich
unfortunate	unglücklich
contented	zufrieden
discontented	unzufrieden

293

discontent	die Unzufriedenheit
displeased	unerfreut
pleasure	das Vergnügen
to please	gefallen
to displease	mißfallen
pain	der Schmerz
painful	schmerzhaft
sigh	der Seufzer
to sigh	seufzen
to complain	sich beschweren

The Intellect and Emotions

294

complaint	die Beschwerde
to protest	protestieren
depressed	deprimiert
to despair	verzweifeln
despair	die Verzweiflung
hope	die Hoffnung
to hope	hoffen
expectation	die Erwartung
consolation	der Trost
to comfort	trösten

295

consoling	tröstlich
calm	die Ruhe
calm	ruhig
restless	rastlos
anxiety	die Angst, die Unruhe
fear	die Angst, die Furcht
to fear	fürchten
to be afraid	Angst haben
to frighten	erschrecken
to be frightened	Angst haben

296

terror	der Schrecken, der Terror
to terrify	erschrecken
frightful	ängstlich
to astonish	erstaunen
astonishment	das Erstaunen
to encourage	ermuntern
to discourage	abraten
conscience	das Gewissen
scruple	der Skrupel
remorse	die Reue

297

repentance	die Buße
to repent	büßen
to regret	bedauern
sentiment	das Gefühl
consent	die Zustimmung
to consent	zustimmen
mercy	die Gnade
charitable	nächstenliebend
pity	das Mitleid
piety	die Frömmigkeit

298

impiety	die Gottlosigkeit
friendly	freundlich
unfriendly	unfreundlich
favour	der Gefallen
to favour	begünstigen
favourable	günstig
unfavourable	ungünstig
confidence	das Vertrauen

trustful	vertrauensvoll
mistrustful	mißtrauisch

299

to trust	vertrauen
friendship	die Freundschaft
friendly	freundlich
kind	nett
friend	der Freund
enemy	der Feind
hatred	der Haß
to hate	hassen
hateful	verhaßt
contempt	die Verachtung

300

to despise	verachten
to get angry	ärgerlich werden
quarrel	der Streit
to quarrel	streiten
to reconcile	sich versöhnen
quality	die Qualität, die Eigenschaft
virtue	die Tugend
virtuous	tugendhaft
vice	das Laster
vicious	bösartig

301

addicted	abhängig
defect	der Mangel
fault	der Fehler
I lack, fail	mir fehlt
custom	die Sitte
to be necessary	nötig sein
to become accustomed	sich daran gewöhnen
habit	die Gewohnheit
to boast (about something)	sich (einer Sache) rühmen
moderate	gemäßigt

302

goodness	die Güte
good	gut
wickedness	die Schlechtigkeit
gratitude	die Dankbarkeit
ingratitude	die Undankbarkeit
grateful	dankbar
ungrateful	undankbar
to thank	danken
thanks, thank you	danke

303

honesty	die Ehrlichkeit
honourable	ehrbar
to honour	ehren
to dishonour	beleidigen

honour	die Ehre
dishonour	die Ehrlosigkeit
honest	ehrlich
dishonest	unehrlich

304

modesty	die Bescheidenheit
shame	die Scham
shameful	schamhaft
to be ashamed	sich schämen
audacity	die Kühnheit
audacious	kühn
daring	waghalsig
boldness	Wagemut
fearless	furchtlos
to dare	wagen

305

reckless	achtlos
timid	ängstlich
timidity	die Ängstlichkeit
rude	unverschämt
rudeness	die Unverschämtheit
courtesy	die Höflichkeit
polite	höflich
impolite	unhöflich
villain	der Bösewicht
envy	der Neid

306

loyal	loyal
disloyal	unloyal
generous	großzügig
generosity	die Großzügigkeit
selfishness	der Egoismus
selfish	egoistisch
egoist	der Egoist
greed	die Habsucht
stingy	geizig
miser	der Geizhals

307

truth	die Wahrheit
true	wahr
to lie	lügen
liar	der Lügner
lie	die Lüge
hypocritical	scheinheilig
hypocrite	der Scheinheilige
frank	offen
frankness	die Offenheit
accuracy	die Genauigkeit

308

inaccuracy	die Ungenauigkeit
punctuality	die Pünktlichkeit
faithfulness	die Treue

unfaithfulness	die Untreue
faithful	treu
unfaithful	untreu
coward	der Feigling
cowardice	die Feigheit
anger	der Ärger
offence	die Kränkung

309

to offend	kränken
to insult	beleidigen
excuse	die Entschuldigung
to excuse	entschuldigen
humble	demütig
humility	die Demut
pride	der Stolz
proud	stolz
vain	eingebildet
obstinate	starrköpfig

310

obstinacy	die Starrköpfigkeit
whim	die Laune
sober	nüchtern
sobriety	die Nüchternheit
sensual	sinnlich
sensuality	die Sinnlichkeit
hedonistic	hedonistisch
lust	die Lust
revenge	die Rache
to revenge	rächen

311

vindictive	rachsüchtig
jealous	eifersüchtig
temperamental	eigenwillig
affectionate	liebevoll
imaginative	phantasievoll
extrovert	extrovertiert
introvert	introvertiert
demanding	anspruchsvoll
sincere	ehrlich
sincerity	die Ehrlichkeit

312

optimistic	optimistisch
optimist	der Optimist
pessimistic	pessimistisch
pessimist	der Pessimist
perceptive	einfühlsam
cautious	wachsam
sensitive	sensibel
sensitivity	die Sensibilität
sensible	vernünftig
common sense	der gesunde Menschenverstand

Education and Learning
Die Erziehung und das Lernen

313

to educate	erziehen, bilden
educational	erzieherisch
educationalist	der Pädagoge, die Pädagogin
adult education	die Erwachsenenbildung
mixed education	die gemischte Erziehung
primary school	die Grundschule
to teach	lehren, unterrichten
teacher	der Lehrer, die Lehrerin
tutor	der Tutor, die Tutorin
college	das Kolleg

314

university	die Universität
class	die Klasse
pupil	der Schüler
boarder	der Internatsschüler
day pupil	der Tagesschüler
to study	studieren
student	der Student, die Studentin
grant	das Stipendium
scholarship holder	der Stipendiat
desk	der Schreibtisch

315

blackboard	die Tafel
chalk	die Kreide
pencil	der Bleistift
ink	die Tinte
pen	der Federhalter
ruler	das Lineal
line	die Zeile
exercise book	das Schreibheft
to bind (books)	(Bücher) einbinden
page	die Seite

316

to fold	falten
sheet of paper	das Blatt Papier
cover (book)	der Umschlag
work	die Arbeit
to work	arbeiten
hard-working	arbeitsam
studious	lernbegierig
lesson	die Lektion
to learn	lernen
to forget	vergessen

317

forgetful	vergeßlich
forgetfulness	die Vergeßlichkeit
absentminded	abwesend
course	der Kurs

attention	die Aufmerksamkeit
to be attentive	aufpassen
attentive	aufmerksam
inattentive	unaufmerksam
to explain	erklären
explanation	die Erklärung

318

task	die Aufgabe
theme	das Thema
thematic	thematisch
exercise	die Übung
to exercise	üben
practice	die Übung
to practise	üben
easy	leicht
easiness	die Leichtigkeit
difficult	schwierig

319

difficulty	die Schwierigkeit
progress	der Fortschritt
homework	die Hausaufgabe
must	müssen
to owe	schulden
examination	die Prüfung
to sit an examination	eine Prüfung machen
to pass an examination	eine Prüfung bestehen
to copy	kopieren
to swot	abschreiben

320

to examine	prüfen
examiner	der Prüfer
proof	der Beweis
to try	versuchen
to blame	beschuldigen
blame	die Beschuldigung
approve	billigen
disapprove	mißbilligen
mark	die Note
to note	anmerken

321

annotation	die Anmerkung
remarkable	bemerkenswert
prize	der Preis
to reward	belohnen
to praise	loben
praise	das Lob
holidays	die Ferien
vacancy	die freie Stelle
conduct	das Verhalten
to behave	sich verhalten

Education and Learning

Education and Learning

322

effort	die Bemühung
to endeavour	sich anstrengen
to try	versuchen
obedience	die Folgsamkeit
disobedience	die Unfolgsamkeit
obedient	folgsam
disobedient	unfolgsam
to obey	gehorchen
to disobey	nicht gehorchen
laziness	die Faulheit

323

strict	streng
severity	die Strenge
threat	die Drohung
to threaten	drohen
punishment	die Strafe
to punish	bestrafen
to deserve	verdienen
grammar	die Grammatik
to indicate	anzeigen
indication	der Hinweis

324

to point out something	auf etwas hinweisen
spelling	die Rechtschreibung
to spell	schreiben
full stop	der Punkt
colon	der Doppelpunkt
semicolon	der Strichpunkt
comma	das Komma
question mark	das Fragezeichen
exclamation mark	das Ausrufezeichen
to note down	notieren

325

to ask (question)	fragen
to ask for	bitten um
to answer	antworten
answer	die Antwort
to admire	bewundern
admiration	die Bewunderung
to exclaim	ausrufen
article	der Artikel
noun	das Hauptwort, das Substantiv
to name	nennen

326

appointment	die Verabredung
to call	rufen
to be called	heißen
reference	Hinweis
to relate to	sich beziehen auf
fixed	fest

to fix	festlegen
to join	sich zusammentun
together	gemeinsam
join	die Verbindung

327

to correspond	korrespondieren
correspondence	der Briefwechsel, die Korrespondenz
sentence	der Satz
language	die Sprache
idiomatic	idiomatisch
idiom	die Wendung
speech	die Sprache
talkative	gesprächig
voice	die Stimme
word	das Wort

328

to express	ausdrücken
expressive	ausdrucksvoll
vocabulary	das Vokabular
dictionary	das Wörterbuch
letter	der Brief
speech	die Rede
lecture	die Vorlesung
lecturer	der Lektor
orator	der Redner
eloquence	die Beredsamkeit

329

eloquent	beredsam
elocution	die Vortragskunst
to converse	sich unterhalten
conversation	die Unterhaltung
to understand	verstehen
to pronounce	aussprechen
to correct	korrigieren, verbessern
example	das Beispiel
meaning	die Bedeutung
to mean	bedeuten

330

translation	die Übersetzung
to translate	übersetzen
translator	der Übersetzer
interpreter	der Dolmetscher
to interpret	dolmetschen
interpretative	interpretierend
interpretation	die Interpretation
to imagine	sich vorstellen
imagination	die Vorstellungskraft

331

idea	die Idee
essay	der Aufsatz, der Essai
essayist	der Essayist

Education and Learning

thesis	die These
doctorate	die Promovierung
to develop	entwickeln
to roll up	aufrollen
roll	die Rolle
object	der Gegenstand, das Objekt
subject	das Subjekt
describe	beschreiben

332

description	die Beschreibung
fable	die Fabel
drama	das Drama
comedy	die Komödie
comical	komisch
chapter	das Kapitel
to interest	interessieren
interesting	interessant
attractive	attraktiv
to attract	anziehen

333

to publish	veröffentlichen
to print	drucken
printer	der Drucker
printing	der Druck
newspaper	die Zeitung
journalist	der Journalist, die Journalistin
magazine	das Magazin
news	die Nachrichten
to announce	ankündigen
advertisement	die Werbung

334

history	die Geschichte
historian	der Historiker
the Stone Age	die Steinzeit
the Bronze Age	die Bronzezeit
the Iron Age	die Eisenzeit
the Dark Ages	das dunkle Mittelalter
the Middle Ages	das Mittelalter
archaeology	die Archäologie
archaeologist	der Archäologe
to excavate	ausgraben

335

carbon dating	die Radiokohlenstoffdatierung
event	das Ereignis
to happen	sich ereignen
to civilise	zivilisieren
civilisation	die Zivilisation
knight	der Ritter
chivalry	die Ritterlichkeit
explorer	der Entdecker

Education and Learning

to explore	erforschen
discovery	die Entdeckung

336

to discover	entdecken
pirate	der Pirat
piracy	die Piraterie
treasure	der Schatz
conquest	die Eroberung
conqueror	der Eroberer
to conquer	erobern
empire	das Reich
imperial	kaiserlich, souverän
slave	der Sklave

337

emancipation	die Emanzipation
to emancipate	emanzipieren
destiny	das Schicksal
to destine	bestimmen
power	die Macht
powerful	mächtig
to be able, can	können, vermögen
slavery	die Sklaverei
to free	befreien
reformation	die Reformation

338

liberator	der Befreier
nationalism	der Nationalismus
nationalist	der Nationalist
alliance	die Allianz
to ally	sich allieren
ally	der Alliierte
to enlarge	vergrößern
increase	die Zunahme
to increase	zunehmen
to diminish	abnehmen

339

decline	der Untergang
to decay	verfallen
to decline	untergehen
to disturb	stören
to emigrate	auswandern
emigrant	der Auswanderer
rebel	der Rebell
rebellion	die Rebellion
rising	der Aufstand
independence	die Unabhängigkeit

340

geography	die Geographie
map	die Karte
North Pole	der Nordpol
South Pole	der Südpol
north	der Norden

south	der Süden
east	der Osten
west	der Westen
compass	der Kompaß
magnetic north	der magnetische Norden

341

distant	entfernt
distance	die Entfernung
near	nahe
to approach	sich nähern
neighbour	der Nachbar
to determine	bestimmen
limit	die Grenze
region	die Region, die Gegend
country	das Land
compatriot	der Landsmann

342

citizen	der Bürger
city	die Stadt
population	die Bevölkerung
to people	bevölkern
populous	volkreich
village	das Dorf
people	die Leute
province	die Provinz
provincial	provinziell
place	der Ort

Places   Die Orte

343

Africa	Afrika
African	afrikanisch
North America	Nordamerika
North American	nordamerikanisch
South America	Südamerika
South American	südamerikanisch
Central America	Mittelamerika
Central American	mittelamerikanisch
Australia	Australien
Australian	australisch

344

Europe	Europa
European	europäisch
Arctic	die Arktik
Antarctica	die Antarktik
Oceania	Ozeanien
Oceanian	ozeanisch
Asia	Asien
Asian	asiatisch
New Zealand	Neuseeland
New Zealander	der Neuseeländer, die Neuseeländerin

345

Spain	Spanien
Spanish	spanisch
Germany	Deutschland
German	deutsch
Italy	Italien
Italian	italienisch
Greece	Griechenland
Greek	griechisch
Russia	Rußland
Russian	russisch

346

Switzerland	die Schweiz
Swiss	schweizerisch
Holland	Holland
Dutch	holländisch
Portugal	Portugal
Portuguese	portugiesisch
Belgium	Belgien
Belgian	belgisch
Great Britain	Großbritannien
British Isles	die britischen Inseln

347

United Kingdom	das Vereinigte Königreich
British	britisch
England	England
English	englisch
Scotland	Schotland
Scottish	schottisch
Wales	Wales
Welsh	walisisch
Northern Ireland	Nordirland
Northern Irish	nordirisch

348

Ireland	Irland
Irish	irisch
France	Frankreich
French	französisch
Austria	Österreich
Austrian	österreichisch
Scandinavia	Skandinavien
Scandinavian	skandinavisch
Iceland	Island
Icelandic	isländisch

349

Greenland	Grönland
Greenlander	grönländisch
Sweden	Schweden
Swedish	schwedisch
Norway	Norwegen
Norwegian	norwegisch
Finland	Finland
Finnish	finnisch

Places   **Places**

| Denmark | Dänemark |
| Danish | dänisch |

350

Bavaria	Bayern
Bavarian	bayerisch
Saxony	Sachsen
Saxon	sächsisch
Alsace	das Elsaß
Alsatian	elsässisch
Lorraine	Lothringen

351

London	London
London adj	Londoner
Paris	Paris
Parisian	Pariser
Madrid	Madrid
Madrid adj	Madrider
Munich	München
Brunswick	Braunschweig
Cologne	Köln

352

Toulouse	Toulouse
Milan	Mailand
Lisbon	Lissabon
Bordeaux	Bordeaux
Lyons	Lyon
Bratislava	Preßburg
The Hague	den Haag (also der Haag)

353

Rome	Rom
Roman	römisch
Venice	Venedig
Venetian	venezianisch,
	der Venezianer
Naples	Neapel
Neapolitan	neapolitanisch,
	der Neapolitaner
Florence	Florenz
Florentine	florentinisch,
	der Florentiner
Turin	Turin

354

Hamburg	Hamburg
Hanover	Hannover
Basle	Basel
Vienna	Wien
Viennese	Wiener
Antwerp	Antwerpen
Berlin	Berlin
Berlin adj	Berliner
Geneva	Genf
Geneva adj	Genfer

355

Athens	Athen
Brussels	Brüssel
Strasbourg	Straßburg
Bruges	Brügge
Moscow	Moskau
Muscovite	Moskowiter
Warsaw	Warschau
Prague	Prag
Budapest	Budapest

356

Copenhagen	Kopenhagen
New York	New York
New York adj	New Yorker
Cairo	Kairo
Capetown	Kapstadt
Beijing	Peking

357

Poland	Polen
Polish	polnisch
Czech Republic	die Tschechische Republik
Czech	tschechisch
Slovakia	die Slowakei
Slovak	slowakisch
Slovenia	Slowenien
Slovene	slowenisch
Croatia	Kroatien
Croatian	kroatisch

358

Hungary	Ungarn
Hungarian	ungarisch
Bosnia	Bosnien
Bosnian	bosnisch
Serbia	Serbien
Serbian	serbisch
Albania	Albanien
Albanian	albanisch
Romania	Rumänien
Romanian	rumänisch

359

Bulgaria	Bulgarien
Bulgarian	bulgarisch
Macedonia	Mazedonien
Macedonian	mazedonisch
Moldova	Moldawien
Moldovan	moldauisch
Belarus	Weißrußland
Belorussian	weißrussisch
Ukraine	die Ukraine
Ukrainian	ukrainisch

360

| Estonia | Estland |

Places   **Places**

Estonian	estländisch		**365**	
Latvia	Lettland		United States	die Vereinigten Staaten
Latvian	lettisch		North American	nordamerikanisch
Lithuania	Lithauen		Canada	Kanada
Lithuanian	lithauisch		Canadian	kanadisch
Armenia	Armenien		Mexico	Mexico
Armenian	armenisch		Mexican	mexikanisch
Azerbaijan	Aserbaidschan		Colombia	Kolumbien
Azerbaijani	aserbaidschanisch		Colombian	kolumbianisch
			Peru	Peru
361			Peruvian	peruanisch
Georgia	Georgien			
Georgian	georgisch		**366**	
Siberia	Sibirien		Brazil	Brasilien
Siberian	sibirisch		Brazilian	brasilianisch
Turkey	die Türkei		Chile	Chile
Turkish	türkisch		Chilean	chilenisch
Arabia	Arabien		Argentina	Argentinien
Arab	arabisch		Argentinian	argentinisch
Morocco	Marokko		Uruguay	Uruguay
Moroccan	marokanisch		Uruguayan	uruguayisch
			Bolivia	Bolivien
362			Bolivian	bolivianisch
Egypt	Ägypten			
Egyptian	ägyptisch		**367**	
China	China		Pyrenees	die Pyreneen
Chinese	chinesisch		Alps	die Alpen
India	Indien		Atlas Mountains	das Atlasgebirge
Indian	indisch		Dolomites	die Dolomiten
Japan	Japan		Carpathians	die Karpaten
Japanese	japanisch		Andes	die Anden
Ghana	Ghana		Himalayas	der Himalaya
Ghanaian	ghanaisch		Mont Blanc	der Mont Blanc
			Table Mountain	das Tafelgebirge
363			Everest	Mount Everest
Algeria	Algerien			
Algerian	algerisch		**368**	
Tunisia	Tunesien		Amazon	der Amazonas
Tunisian	tunesisch		Nile	der Nil
South Africa	Südafrika		Rhine	der Rhein
South African	südafrikanisch		Rhône	die Rhone
Israel	Israel		Tagus	der Tajo
Israeli	israelisch		Danube	die Donau
Palestine	Palästina		Thames	die Themse
Palestinian	palästinensisch		Seine	die Seine
			Loire	die Loire
364			Ebro	der Ebro
Castile	Kastilien			
Castilian	kastilianisch		**369**	
Andalusia	Andalusien		Atlantic	der Atlantik
Andalusian	andalusisch		Pacific	der Pazifik
Catalonia	Katalonien		Arctic	die Arktik
Catalan	katalonisch		Indian	der Indische Ozean
Galicia	Galizien		Antarctic	die Antarktik
Galician	galizisch		Mediterranean	das Mittelmeer
Basque Country	das Baskenland		North Sea	die Nordsee
Basque	baskisch		Black Sea	das Schwarze Meer

| Red Sea | das Rote Meer |
| Caribbean | die Karibik |

370

Baltic Sea	die Ostsee
English Channel	der Ärmelkanal
Bay of Biscay	die Biskaya
West Indies	die Westindischen Inseln
Canaries	die Kanarischen Inseln
The Philippines	die Philippinen
Balearic Islands	die Balearischen Inseln
Sicily	Sizilien
Sardinia	Sardinien
Corsica	Korsika

371

Corsican	korsisch
Rhodes	Rhodos
Crete	Kreta
Cretan	kretisch
Cyprus	Zypern
Cypriot	zypriotisch
Dardanelles	die Dardanellen
Bosphorus	der Bosporus
Scilly Isles	die Scillyinseln
Falkland Islands	die Falklandinseln

Science Die Wissenschaft

372

weights	die Gewichtsmaße *pl*
weight	das Gewicht
to weigh	wiegen
heavy	schwer
light	leicht
scales	die Wage *sing*
to measure	messen
measure	das Maß
to compare	vergleichen
comparison	der Vergleich

373

to contain	enthalten
contents	der Inhalt
metric system	das metrische System
metre	der Meter
centimetre	der Zentimeter
millimetre	der Millimeter
gram	das Gramm
kilogram	das Kilogramm
litre	der Liter
hectare	der Hektar

374

| kilometre | der Kilometer |
| ton | die Tonne |

inch	der Zoll
foot	der Fuß
mile	die Meile
arithmetic	das Rechnen
mathematics	die Mathematik
to calculate	berechnen
to count	zählen
number	die Zahl

375

figure	die Ziffer
zero	die Null
addition	die Addition
to add	addieren
subtraction	die Subtraktion
remainder	der Rest
equal	gleich
equality	die Gleichheit
to multiply	multiplizieren
product	das Produkt

376

to produce	produzieren
producer	der Produzent
to divide	dividieren, teilen
part	der Teil
fraction	der Bruch
half	die Hälfte
third	das Drittel
quarter	das Viertel
dozen	das Dutzend
double	doppelt

377

triple	dreifach
geometry	die Geometrie
algebra	die Algebra
space	der Raum
spacious	geräumig
parallel	parallel
perpendicular	vertikal
horizontal	horizontal
horizon	der Horizont
right angle	der rechte Winkel

378

triangle	das Dreieck
square	das Quadrat
curved	gebogen
straight	gerade
circumference	der Umfang
circle	der Kreis
centre	das Zentrum
diameter	der Durchmesser
problem	die Aufgabe
correct	richtig

Science   **Communications**

379		science	die Wissenschaft
incorrect	falsch	scientific	wissenschaftlich
wrong	falsch		
simple	einfach	384	
to complicate	komplizieren	scientist	der Wissenschaftler
to demonstrate	demonstrieren	knowledge	das Wissen
to solve	lösen	to know	
result	das Ergebnis	(something)	wissen
to result	ergeben	to know (person)	kennen
physics	die Physik	wisdom	die Weisheit
physical	physikalisch	wise	weise
		sage	der Weise
380		to be ignorant of	nichts wissen von
matter	die Materie	experience	die Erfahrung
pressure	der Druck	inexperience	der Erfahrungsmangel
phenomenon	das Phänomen		
strange	merkwürdig		
movement	die Bewegung		
to move	(sich) bewegen		
mobile	beweglich		
immobile	unbeweglich		
electric	elektrisch		
electricity	die Elektrizität		

Communications
die Kommunikation

381		385	
mechanics	die Mechanik	telegraph	der Telegraph
invent	erfinden	telegram	das Telegramm
optics	die Optik	to telegraph	telegrapghieren
optical	optisch	telex	das Telex
microscope	das Mikroskop	telephone	das Telefon
lens	die Linse	to telephone	telefonieren, anrufen
to reflect	spiegeln	telephonist	der Telefonist,
reflection	die Reflektion		die Telefonistin
chemistry	die Chemie	call	der Anruf
chemical	chemisch	receiver	der Hörer
		mouthpiece	die Sprechmuschel
382			
biology	die Biologie	386	
biological	biologisch	telephone booth	die Telefonzelle
biologist	der Biologe	telephone exchange	die Telefonzentrale
to research	untersuchen	telephone	
researcher	der Forscher	directory	das Telefonbuch
element	das Element	telephone	
oxygen	der Sauerstoff	subscriber	der Telefonbesitzer
hydrogen	der Wasserstoff	answerphone	der Anrufbeantworter
atom	das Atom	to hang up	aufhängen
nucleus	der Kern	engaged	besetzt
		to dial	wählen
383		radiotelephone	das Funktelefon
laboratory	das Labor	videophone	das Bildtelefon
experiment	der Versuch, das Experiment		
mixture	die Mischung	387	
mixed	gemischt	fax	das Fax
to decompose	(sich) zersetzen	to fax	faxen
to compose	zusammensetzen	modem	das Modem
compound	die Verbindung	electronic mail	die elektronische Post
rare	selten	information	
		technology	die Informationstechnologie
		microelectronics	die Mikroelektronik
		screen	der Bildschirm

Communications

keyboard	die Tastatur
key	die Taste
mouse	die Maus

388

computer	der Computer
computer language	die Computersprache
computer literate	computerkundig
computer scientist	der Informatiker, die Informatikerin
computer game	das Computerspiel
computer animation	die Computeranimation
computer aided design	die rechnergestützte Konstruktion
computerese	das Computerchinesisch
to computerise	auf Computer umstellen
computerisation	die Umstellung auf Computer

389

to program	programmieren
programmer	der Programmierer
systems analyst	der Systemanalytiker
wordprocessor	das Textverarbeitungsgerät
memory	der Speicher
disk drive	das Diskettenlaufwerk, das Plattenlaufwerk
software	die Software
hardware	die Hardware
shareware	die Shareware
cursor	der Cursor

390

menu	das Menü
to store	speichern
file	die Datei
to file	ablegen
data	die Daten
database	die Datenbank
desktop publishing	das Desktop Publishing
to lay out	layouten
silicon	das Silikon
silicon chip	der Silikonchip

391

user-friendly	anwenderfreundlich
laser printer	der Laserdrucker
bubble jet printer	der Bubble-Jet-Drucker
scanner	der Scanner
circuit	der Kreislauf
fibreoptics	die Faseroptik
machine translation	die Maschinenübersetzung
network	das Netz

networking	die Vernetzung
information superhighway	der Informations-Superhighway

The Arts and Entertainment
Die schönen Künste und die Unterhaltung

392

painting	die Malerei
painter	der Maler, die Malerin
to paint	malen
picturesque	malerisch
artist	der Künstler, die Künstlerin
museum	das Museum
engraving	die Radierung
to engrave	radieren
print	der Druck
background	der Hintergrund

393

foreground	der Vordergrund
still life	das Stilleben
drawing	die Zeichnung
to draw	zeichnen
draughtsman	der Zeichner
outline	der Umriß
to imitate	imitieren
imitation	die Imitation
abstract	abstrakt
innovative	innovativ

394

to innovate	innovieren
resemblance	die Ähnlichkeit
similar	ähnlich
forgery	die Fälschung
forger	der Fälscher, die Fälscherin
auction	die Versteigerung, die Auktion
to bid	bieten
lot	die Partie
reserve price	der Mindestpreis
exhibition	die Ausstellung

395

antique	die Antiquität
antique dealer	der Antiquitätenhändler
art dealer	der Kunsthändler
palette	die Palette
brush	der Pinsel
easel	die Staffelei

The Arts and Entertainment

colour	die Farbe
to colour	färben
coloured	gefärbt
dull	trüb

396

multicoloured	vielfarbig
contrast	der Gegensatz
to contrast	kontrastieren
white	weiß
black	schwarz
light blue	hellblau
dark green	dunkelgrün
yellow	gelb
brown	braun
chestnut	kastanienbraun

397

pink	rosa
red	rot
violet	violett
mauve	lila
purple	purpurfarben
gilt	vergoldet
to gild	vergolden
grey	grau
patron	der Mäzen
patronage	die Förderung

398

patronise	fördern
oils	das Ölbild
watercolour	das Aquarell
fresco	das Fresko
triptych	das Triptychon
cartoon	der Comic
the Renaissance	die Renaissance
Renaissance art	die Renaissancekunst
crayon	der Wachsmalkreide, die Ölkreide
canvas	die Leinwand

399

gallery	die Gallerie
tone	der Ton
landscape	die Landschaft
portrait	das Porträt
portraitist	der Porträtmaler, die Porträtmalerin
miniature	die Miniatur
miniaturist	der Miniaturenmaler, die Miniaturenmalerin
landscape painter	der Landschaftsmaler, die Landschaftsmalerin
impressionism	der Impressionismus
impressionist	impressionistisch

The Arts and Entertainment

400

surrealism	der Surrealismus
surrealist	surreaslistisch
cubism	der Kubismus
cubist	kubistisch
symbol	das Symbol
to symbolise	symbolisieren
symbolic	symbolisch
sculpture	die Plastik
sculptor	der Bildhauer, die Bildhauerin
workshop	das Atelier

401

to carve	schnitzen
model	das Modell
statue	die Statue
bust	die Büste
group	die Gruppe
chisel	der Meißel
cast	der Guß
shape	die Form
to shape	formen
architecture	die Architektur

402

architect	der Architekt
vault	das Gewölbe
dome	die Kuppel
pillar	die Säule
arch	der Bogen
tower	der Turm
scaffolding	das Gerüst
arch	der Bogen
column	die Säule
plinth	die Fußleiste

403

nave	das Schiff
cathedral	der Dom
cathedral city	die Domstadt
apse	die Apsis
stained glass	das Kirchenfensterglas
transept	das Querschiff
flying buttress	das Strebewerk
font	das Taufbecken
crypt	die Krypta
basilica	die Basilika

404

Gothic	gothisch
Romanesque	romanisch
Baroque	barock
mosque	die Moschee
minaret	das Minarett
synagogue	die Synagoge
pagoda	die Pagode

The Arts and Entertainment

mausoleum	das Mausoleum
pyramid	die Pyramide
Sphinx	die Sphynx

405

temple	der Tempel
Corinthian	korynthisch
Ionian	ionisch
Doric	dorisch
forum	das Forum
amphitheatre	das Amphitheater
aqueduct	das Aquädukt
dolmen	der Dolmen
menhir	der Menhir
cave painting	die Höhlenmalerei

406

illiterate (person)	der Analphabet
literate	lesekundig
oral tradition	die mündliche Tradition
ballad	die Ballade
saga	die Saga
tradition	die Tradition
story	die Geschichte
storyteller	der Geschichtenerzähler
narrative	die Erzählung
to learn by heart	auswendig lernen

407

literature	die Literatur
papyrus	der Papyrus
parchment	das Pergament
alphabet	das Alpbabet
character	die Person
author	der Autor
writer	der Schriftsteller
editor	der Herausgeber
edition	die Ausgabe
copyright	das Urheberrecht

408

style	der Stil
reader	der Leser, die Leserin
biography	die Biographie
biographer	der Biographieautor, die Biographieautorin
biographical	biographisch
autobiography	die Autobiographie
autobiographical	autobiographisch
fiction	die Belletristik
fictional	fiktiv
science fiction	die Science Fictions

409

novel	der Roman
novelist	der Romanautor, die Romanautorin

The Arts and Entertainment

publisher	der Verleger, die Verlegerin
royalties	die Tandiemen
bookshop	die Buchhandlung
bookseller	der Buchhändler, die Buchhändlerin
encyclopaedia	die Enzyklopädie
encyclopaedic	enzyklopädisch
paperback	das Taschenbuch
poetry	die Poesie

410

poet	der Dichter, die Dichterin
poetic	poetisch
rhyme	der Reim
to rhyme	sich reimen
metre	das Metrum
stanza	der Vers
sonnet	das Sonett
assonance	die Assonanz
syllable	die Silbe
nursery rhyme	der Kinderreim

411

fairy tale	das Märchen
Cinderella	Aschenputtel
Red Riding Hood	Rotkäppchen
Snow White	Schneewittchen
dwarf	der Zwerg
goblin	der Kobold
gnome	der Gnom
elf	die Elfe
Sleeping Beauty	Dornröschen
Snow Queen	die Schneekönigin

412

Puss in Boots	der Gestiefelte Kater
Bluebeard	Blaubart
witch	die Hexe
wizard	der Hexer
spell	der Zauberspruch
to cast a spell	verwünschen
magician	der Zauberer
magic	die Zauberei
magical	magisch
mermaid	die Meerjungfrau

413

mythology	die Mythologie
Homer	Homer
Homeric	homerisch
Iliad	die Ilias
Odyssey	die Odyssee
Odysseus	Odysseus
Trojan	trojanisch
Trojan horse	das trojanische Pferd
Achilles	Achilles
Achilles heel	die Achillesferse

The Arts and Entertainment

414

Cyclops	der Zyklop
Atlantis	Atlantis
Romulus	Romulus
Hercules	Herkules
Herculean	herkulisch
The Arabian Nights	Tausendundeine Nacht
Armageddon	der Armageddon
Valhalla	die Walhalla
Thor	Thor
rune	die Rune

415

masterpiece	das Meisterwerk
music	die Musik
musician	der Musiker, die Musikerin
to play	
(an instrument)	spielen
composer	der Komponist, die Komponistin
orchestra	das Orchester
symphony	die Symphonie
aria	die Arie
overture	die Ouvertüre
march	der Marsch

416

soft	sanft
stringed	
instrument	das Seiteninstrument
wind instrument	das Blasinstrument
brass instrument	das Blechblasinstrument
piano	das Piano, das Klavier
pianist	der Pianist
organ	die Orgel
organist	der Organist
harmony	die Harmonie
flute	die Querflöte

417

to blow	blasen
bagpipes	der Dudelsack
cornet	das Horn
violin	die Violine
auditorium	die Zuhörer *pl*
score	die Partitur
opera	die Oper
tenor	der Tenor
soprano	der Sopran
baritone	der Bariton

418

bass	der Baß
conductor	der Dirigent, die Dirigentin
instrumentalist	der Instrumentalist, die Instrumentalistin

rehearsal	die Probe
violin	die Violine, die Geige
viola	die Bratsche
violinist	der Violinist, die Violinistin
cello	das Cello
bow	der Bogen
guitar	die Gitarre

419

to strum	herumklimpern
harp	die Harpe
flute	die Querflöte
oboe	die Oboe
clarinet	die Klarinette
bassoon	das Fagott
trumpet	die Trompete
trombone	die Posaune
French horn	das Waldhorn
tuba	die Tuba

420

songbook	das Liederbuch
singing	der Gesang
to sing	singen
to enchant	bezaubern
enchanting,	
delightful	bezaubernd
spell, charm	der Zauber
singer	der Sänger, die Sängerin
choir	der Chor
to accompany	begleiten
accompaniment	die Begleitung

421

song	das Lied
refrain	der Refrain
concert	das Konzert
to syncopate	synkopieren
jazz	der Jazz
beat	der Beat
saxophone	das Saxophon
rock music	die Rockmusik
rock star	der Rockstar
drums	das Schlagzeug

422

synthesiser	der Synthesizer
folk music	die Volksmusik
mandolin	die Mandoline
ocarina	die Okarina
drum	die Trommel
accordion	das Akordeon
xylophone	das Xylophon
zither	die Zither
concertina	die Concertina

The Arts and Entertainment

423

dance, dancing	der Tanz
to dance	tanzen
ball, dance	der Ball
dancer	der Tänzer, die Tänzerin
theatre	das Theater
theatrical	theatralisch
mask	die Maske
box office	die Kasse
seat, place	der Platz
stalls	der Sperrsitz
box (theatre)	die Loge

424

pit	das Parkett
stage	die Bühne
scene	die Szene
act	der Akt
interval	die Pause
scenery	das Bühnenbild
curtain	der Vorhang
play	das Theaterstück
playwright	der Theaterautor
character	die Person

425

tragedy	die Tragödie
comedy	die Komödie
actor	der Schauspieler
actress	die Schauspielerin
to play a role	eine Rolle spielen
to be word-perfect	seine Rolle genau kennen
costume	das Kostüm
lighting	die Belleuchtung
dénouement	die Auflösung
to stage, represent	auf die Bühne bringen, darstellen

426

performance	die Vorführung
flop	der Flop
to flop	durchfallen
debut, first performance	die Premiere
trapdoor	die Versenkung
to be a success	ein Erfolg sein
audience	das Publikum
spectator	der Zuschauer
applause	der Aplaus
whistling, hissing	die Pfiffe *pl*, die Buhrufe *pl*

427

cinema	das Kino
screen	die Leinwand
to dub	synchronisieren
to subtitle	mit Untertiteln versehen
subtitle	der Untertitel

sequel	die Folge
director	der Regisseur
producer	der Produzent
to censor	zensieren
censorship	die Zensur

428

to whistle, hiss	pfeifen, ausbuhen
amusements	die Unterhaltung
playground	der Spielplatz
to enjoy oneself	sich unterhalten
entertaining	unterhaltsam
amusing	vergnüglich
pastime	der Zeitvertreib
rest	die Ruhe
to rest	ruhen
weariness	die Müdigkeit

429

to get tired	ermüden
tired	müde
to be bored	sich langweilen
boring	langweilig
fair	das Straßenfest, die Kirchweih
festival	das Fest
crowd	die Menge
to assemble	zusammensetzen
circus	der Zirkus
trapeze	das Trapez

430

trapeze artist	der Trapezkünstler, die Trapezkünstlerin
tightrope	das Seil
tightrope walker	der Seiltänzer, die Seiltänzerin
acrobat	der Akrobat, die Akrobatin
acrobatic	akrobatisch
acrobatics	die Akrobatik
clown	der Clown
joke	der Witz
lottery	die Lotterie
to be lucky	Glück haben

431

luck	das Glück
swing	die Schaukel
to swing (oneself)	schaukeln
seesaw	die Wippe
roundabout	das Karusell
game	das Spiel
to play	spielen
player	der Spieler
toy	das Spielzeug
match	das Match

Sport

432

to win	gewinnen
to lose	verlieren
to draw	zeichnen
to cheat	mogeln
deceit	die Täuschung
meeting	das Treffen
to meet	sich treffen
to join	sich zusammenschließen
party	die Gruppe

433

to visit	besuchen
visit	der Besuch
playing cards	die Spielkarten
to deal	handeln
to shuffle	mischen
suit	der Satz
billiards	Billard
cue	das Queue
cannon	die Karambolage
spin	der Effekt

434

chess	das Schach
piece	die Figur
pawn	der Bauer
rook	der Turm
bishop	der Läufer
knight	der Springer
chessboard	das Schachbrett
draughts	das Damespiel
dice	die Würfel *pl*
jigsaw	das Puzzle

Sport — Der Sport

435

swimming	das Schwimmen
to swim	schwimmen
swimmer	der Schwimmer, die Schwimmerin
breaststroke	das Brustschwimmen
crawl	das Kraulen
backstroke	das Rückenschwimmen
butterfly	der Delphinstil
lifeguard	der Bademeister
to dive	tauchen

436

high diving	das Turmspringen
to row	rudern
rower	der Ruderer
oar	das Ruder
canoe	das Kanu
canoeing	das Kanufahren

canoeist	der Kanufahrer
paddle	das Paddel
skate	der Schlittschuh
to skate	Schlittschuh fahren

437

figure skating	der Eistanz
rollerskates	die Rollschuhe
skateboard	das Skateboard
amateur	der Amateur
bet	die Wette
to bet	wetten
odds	die Chancen
ball	der Ball
football (sport)	der Fußball

438

football	der Fußball
footballer	der Fußballer
football pools	die Fußballwetten, das Fußballtoto
referee	der Schiedsrichter
penalty	die Strafe
corner	die Ecke
offside	das Abseits
forward	der Stürmer
defender	der Verteidiger
midfielder	der Mittelstürmer

439

winger	der (Links/Rechts-)Außen
to score	ein Tor schießen
to shoot	schießen
to dribble	dribbeln
goal	das Tor
goalpost	der Torpfosten
goalkeeper	der Torhüter
goalscorer	der Torschütze
goal-kick	der Torschuß
team	die Mannschaft

440

league	die Liga
trophy	die Trophäe
knockout	der Ausschußwettbewerb
rugby	das Rugby
to tackle	angreifen
scrum	das Gedränge
scrum-half	der Gedrängehalbspieler
fly-half	der Öffnungshalbspieler
prop	der Pfosten
fullback	der Verteidiger

441

tennis	das Tennis
lawn tennis	das Rasentennisspiel

Sport

tennis player	der Tennisspieler,
	die Tennisspielerin
set	der Satz
volley	der Flugball
to serve	anschlagen
table tennis	das Tischtennis
racket	der Schläger
boxing	das Boxen

442

boxer	der Boxer
wrestling	das Ringen
champion	der Champion
fencing	das Fechten
fencer	der Fechter, die Fechterin
foil	Florettfechten
gymnast	der Turner, die Turnerin
gymnastics	das Turnen
somersault	die Rolle
cycling	das Radfahren

443

cyclist	der Radfahrer,
	die Radfahrerin
mountain bicycle	das Mountainbike
time trial	der Zeitkampf
stage	das Stadium
yellow jersey	das gelbe Trikot
horseriding	das Reiten
showjumping	das Kunstspringen
dressage	die Dressur
polo	das Polo
horseman	der Reiter, die Reiterin

444

grandstand	die Tribüne
racecourse	die Rennbahn
race	das Rennen
to run	rennen
bullfight	der Stierkampf
bull fighter	der Torero
motor racing	das Motorrennen
scrambling	das Motocross
hockey	das Hockey
bowls	das Kegeln

445

stadium	das Stadium
high jump	der Hochsprung
record	der Rekord
long jump	der Weitsprung
triple jump	der Dreisprung
pole vault	der Stabhochsprung
long-distance	
runner	der Langstreckenläufer,
	die Langstreckenläuferin
lap	der Sprung

Sport

marathon	der Marathon
training	das Training

446

athletics	die Leichtathletik
athlete	der Leichtathlet,
	die Leichtathletin
sprinter	der Sprinter, die Sprinterin
sprint	der Sprint
to sprint	sprinten
shotput	das Kugelstoßen

447

discus	der Diskuswurf
hammer	das Hammerwerfen
relay race	der Staffellauf
baton	der Tambourstock
Olympics	die Olympiade *sing*
triathlon	der Triathlon
triathlete	der Triathlet, die Triathletin
decathlon	der Dekathlon
decathlete	der Deklathlete,
	die Deklathletin
pentathlon	der Pentathlon

448

pentathlete	der Pentathlet,
	die Pentathletin
mountaineering	das Bergsteigen
mountaineer	der Bergsteiger,
	die Bergsteigerin
rock climbing	das Felsklettern
rock climber	der Felskletterer,
	die Felsklettererin
ice-axe	der Eispickel
skiing	das Skifahren
to ski	Ski fahren
ski	der Ski
cross-country skiing	der Langlauf

449

ski-lift	der Skilift
skier	der Skifahrer,
	die Skifahrerin
ski-stick	der Skistock
ski-jump	das Skispringen
snowshoes	Schneeschuhe
ice hockey	das Eishockey
puck	der Puck
water skiing	der Wasserski
outboard motor	der Außenmotor

450

slalom	der Slalom
to abseil	sich abseilen
fish	der Fisch
angling	das Angeln

fishing rod	die Angelrute
reel	die Leine
bait	der Köder
to bait	ködern
hook	der Haken
fly fishing	das Fliegenfischen

Food and Drink
Essen und Trinken

451

food	das Essen
provisions	die Lebensmittel
to nourish	ernähren
appetite	der Appetit
snack	der Imbiß
to have a snack	einen Imbiß einnehmen
hunger	der Hunger
hungry	hungrig
thirst	der Durst
thirsty	durstig

452

to be hungry	Hunger haben
to be thirsty	Durst haben
sweet	süß
to have a	
sweet tooth	eine Schwäche für Süßes haben
sugar	der Zucker
sugary	zuckrig
tasteless	geschmacklos
bitter	bitter
milk	die Milch
to pasteurise	pasteurisieren

453

skimmed milk	die entrahmte Milch
whole milk	die Vollmilch
cream	die Sahne
butter	die Butter
buttermilk	die Buttermilch
cheese	der Käse
egg	das Ei
yolk	das Eigelb
egg white	das Eiweiß
shell	die Schale

454

soft boiled egg	das weichgekochte Ei
scrambled eggs	die Rühreier
omelette	das Omelette
bread	das Brot
brown bread	das Graubrot. das Schwarzbrot

sliced bread	das in Scheiben geschnittene Brot
loaf	der Leib
roll	das Brötchen
crumb	der Krümel, die Krume
crust	die Kruste

455

health foods	die Reformkost
organically grown	aus organischem Anbau
vegetarian	der Vegetarier, die Vegetarierin
fibre	der Ballaststoff
wholemeal bread	das Vollkornbrot
rye bread	das Roggenbrot
to slim	abnehmen
lentil	die Linse
margarine	die Margarine
polyunsaturated	mehrfach ungesättigt

456

fast food	das Fast Food
hamburger	der Hamburger
hot dog	das Hot Dog
pizza	die Pizza
fat	das Fett
fatty food	das fettreiche Essen
frozen food	die Tiefkühlnahrung
french fries	die Pommes frites *pl*
crisps	die Chips
confectionery	die Süßwaren *pl*

457

vegetable	das Gemüse
carrot	die Karottte
broccoli	der Broccoli
onion	die Zwiebel
celery	der Sellerie
radish	das Radieschen
spinach	der Spinat
asparagus	der Spargel
cucumber	die Gurke
gherkin	das Cornichon

458

lettuce	der Salat
tomato	die Tomate
pea	die Erbse
chickpea	die Kichererbse
bean	die Bohne
French bean	die grüne Bohne
haricot bean	die weiße Bohne
cauliflower	der Blumenkohl
Brussels sprout	der Rosenkohl
aubergine	die Aubergine

Food and Drink

Food and Drink

459

salad	der Salat
mixed salad	der gemischte Salat
corn	der Mais
beetroot	die rote Beete
green pepper	der grüne Paprika
mashed potato	das Kartoffelpüree
garlic	der Knoblauch
squash	der Squash
courgette	die Zucchini
marrow	der Markkürbis

460

tomato	die Tomate
mushroom	der Champignon
condiment	das Würzmittel
spice	das Gewürz
coriander	der Koriander
mustard	der Senf
nutmeg	Muskatnuß
cinnamon	der Zimt
turmeric	der Kurkuma
saffron	der Safran

461

soup	die Suppe
soup tureen	die Suppenterrine
broth	die Brühe
beef	das Rindfleisch
veal	das Kalbfleisch
steak	das Steak
rare	blutig
well done	durch
sauce	die Soße
gravy	die Bratensoße

462

cutlet	das Kotelett
ham	der Schinken
bacon	der Speck
sausage	die Wurst
pepperoni	die Pepperoni
blood sausage	die Blutwurst
raw	roh
soft	weich
hard	hart
stew	der Eintopf

463

tripe	die Kutteln *pl*
cooking	das Kochen
cook	der Koch, die Köchin
to cook	kochen
to roast	rösten
roast	der Braten
to stew	schmoren
to slice	in Scheiben schneiden

slice	die Scheibe
to fry	braten

464

fried	gebraten
chicken	das Hähnchen
breast	die Brust
leg	der Schlegel
ham	der Schinken
to cure	pökeln
to smoke (food)	räuchern
lamb	das Lammfleisch
pork	das Schweinefleisch
veal	das Kalbfleisch

465

to grill	grillen
to barbecue	grillen
barbecue	der Holzkohlengrill
to bake	backen
breaded	paniert
scampi	die Scampi *pl*
to stuff	füllen
spit	der Spieß
suckling pig	das Ferkel
shank (lamb)	die (Lamms-)Haxe

466

fish	der Fisch
haddock	der Schellfisch
mussel	die Mießmuschel
mullet	die Meerbarbe
mackerel	die Makrele
clam	die Muschel
sole	die Seezunge
tuna	der Thunfisch
salad	der Salat
oil	das Öl

467

vinegar	der Essig
sour	sauer
cruet	Essig und Öl
salt	das Salz
saltcellar	der Salzstreuer
to salt	salzen
pepper	der Pfeffer
pepperpot	der Pfefferstreuer
mustard	der Senf
mayonnaise	die Mayonnaise

468

jam	die Konfitüre
marmalade	die Marmelade
cake	der Kuchen
pastry-cook	der Konditor
dough	der Teig

Food and Drink

dessert	der Nachtisch
pancake	der Pfannkuchen
rice pudding	der Reispudding
custard	die Eierkrem
roast apple	der Bratapfel

469

caramel cream	die Creme Caramel
ice cream	das Speiseeis
chocolate	die Schokolade
chocolate mousse	die Mousse au Chocolat
fritters	die Beignets
sponge cake	der Biskuitkuchen
fruit salad	der Obstsalat
whipped cream	die Schlagsahne
cheese cake	der Käsekuchen
lemon meringue	die Zitronenbaiserkuchen

470

pudding	die Süßspeise
biscuit	das Plätzchen
baby food	die Babynahrung
flour	das Mehl
self-raising flour	das Mehl mit Backpulver
yeast	die Hefe
baking soda	Natron
lard	das Schmalz
oil	das Öl
sunflower oil	das Sonnenblumenöl

471

olive oil	das Olivenöl
rice	der Reis
yoghurt	der Joghurt
doughnut	der Krapfen, der Berliner
apple compote	das Apfelmuß
sandwich	das Sandwich, das belegte Brot
spaghetti	die Spaghetti
cake	der Kuchen
noodle	die Nudel
frog legs	die Froschschenkel

472

restaurant	das Restaurant
menu	die Speisekarte
starter	die Vorspeise
first course	der erste Gang
waitress	die Bedienung
waiter	der Kellner, der Ober
drink	das Getränk
to drink	trinken
to sip	nippen
to gulp	in großen Zügen trinken

473

to empty	leeren
empty	leer
nonalcoholic drink	das alkoholfreie Getränk
wine	der Wein
red wine	der Rotwein
rosé wine	der Roséwein
vintage	der Jahrgang
beer	das Bier
water	das Wasser
drinking water	das Trinkwasser

474

milkshake	der Milkshake
tonic	das Stärkungsmittel
juice	der Saft
soft drink	das Erfrischungsgetränk
sherry	der Sherry
dry	trocken
sherbet	das Sorbet
lemonade	die Limonade
fizzy	kohlensäurehaltig
to uncork	entkorken

475

corkscrew	der Korkenzieher
liqueur	der Likör
spirits	die alkoholischen Getränke
cognac	der Cognac
tonic water	das Tonicwasser
orange drink	das Orangengetränk
mineral water	das Mineralwasser
cappuccino	der Cappucino
tea	der Tee
camomile tea	der Kamillentee

476

lemon tea	der Zitronentee
coffee	der Kaffee
coffee with milk	der Kaffee mit Milch
decaffeinated coffee	der entkoffeinierte Kaffee
iced coffee	der Eiskaffee
instant coffee	der Instantkaffee
soda	das Sodawasser
whisky	der Whisky
canned beer	das Dosenbier
bottled beer	das Flaschenbier

477

cider	der Cidre, der Apfelwein
champagne	der Champagner, der Sekt
vermouth	der Wermut
vodka	der Wodka
rum	der Rum
Irish coffee	der Irish Coffee
anise	der Anis

brandy	der Weinbrand
cherry brandy	der Kirschlikör
applejack	der Apfelbranntwein

Travel and Tourism
Reise und Tourismus

478

to travel	reisen
traveller	der Reisende
travel agency	das Reisebüro
travel agent	der Reisekaufmann
package holiday	der Pauschalurlaub
tourist	der Tourist, die Touristin
tourist season	die Fremdenverkehrssaison
hotel	das Hotel
hotelier	der Hotelier
reception	die Rezeption

479

information desk	der Informationsschalter
lobby	das Foyer
service	der Service
to book in advance	im voraus buchen
vacant	frei
bill	die Rechnung
tip	das Trinkgeld
hostel	die Herberge
youth hostel	die Jugendherberge
boarding house	die Pension

480

camping	das Zelten, das Camping
campsite	der Zeltplatz
to go camping	zelten gehen
camp-chair	der Klappstuhl
camping-van	der Campingbus
air mattress	die Luftmatratze
bottle-opener	der Flaschenöffner
camp bed	das Klappbett
tin-opener	der Dosenöffner

481

campfire	das Lagerfeuer
flashlight	die Taschenlampe
fly sheet	das Flugblatt
impermeable	
ground	wasserdichter Boden
ground sheet	die Bodenabdeckung
guy line	die Zeltleine
mallet	der Holzhammer
shelter	der Unterschlupf
to take shelter	Unterschlupf suchen
to get wet	naß werden

482

sleeping bag	der Schlafsack
to sleep out	im Freien schlafen
tent	das Zelt
tent peg	der Hering
tent pole	die Zeltstange
thermos flask	die Thermosflasche
caravan	der Caravan
to go caravaning	im Caravan reisen
to live rough	auf der Straße leben
tramp	der Landstreicher, der Stadtstreicher

483

self-catering	
apartment	die Ferienwohnung
day-tripper	der Tagesausflügler
trip	der Ausflug
railway	die Eisenbahn
platform	der Bahnsteig
to derail	entgleisen
derailment	die Entgleisung
to collide	zusammenstoßen
collision	die Kollision, der Zusammenstoß
accident	der Unfall

484

timetable	der Fahrplan
guidebook	der Führer
train	der Zug
express train	der Expreß
through train	der Direktzug
to arrive	ankommen
arrival	die Ankunft
to leave	abfahren
departure	die Abfahrt
departure board	der Abfahrtsfahrplan

485

underground (rail)	die U-Bahn
diesel	der Diesel
steam	der Dampf
corridor	der Korridor
to alight	aussteigen
halt	der Stopp
compartment	das Abteil
tunnel	das Tunnel
viaduct	das Viadukt
cutting	der Durchstich

486

railway network	der Bahnnetz
railhead	der Kopfbahnhof
railtrack	das Bahngleis
railworker	der Bahnarbeiter
stationmaster	der Stationsvorsteher

waiting room	der Wartesaal
single ticket	die Einzelkarte
return ticket	die Rückkarte
to examine	prüfen
ticket inspector	der Fahrkartenkontrolleur

487
guard	die Wache
engine driver	der Zugführer
signalman	der Bahnwärter
locomotive	die Lokomotive
carriage	der Wagen
sleeping car	der Schlafwagen
dining car	der Speisewagen
luggage	das Gepäck
to check in	anmelden
left luggage	die Gepäckaufbewahrung

488
trunk	die Truhe
case	der Koffer
rucksack	der Rucksack
stop	das Stoppsignal
to stop	anhalten
stay	der Aufenthalt
customs	der Zoll
customs officer	der Zollbeamte
examination	die Prüfung
to examine	prüfen

489
duty	der Zoll
tax	die Steuer
to tax	besteuern
declare	anmelden
duty-free	zollfrei
passport	der Paß
identity card	der Personalausweis
bus	der Bus
taxi	das Taxi
taxi driver	der Taxifahrer, die Taxifahrerin

490
driving licence	der Führerschein
to drive	fahren
motor car	das Auto
motoring	der Automobilismus
motorist	der Fahrer
to hire	mieten
trailer	der Anhänger
to give someone a lift	jemanden mitnehmen
hitchhiker	der Anhalter
to hitchhike	per Anhalter fahren

491
hitchhiking	das Fahren per Anhalter
sharp bend	die scharfe Kurve
to skid	schleudern
door (vehicle)	die Tür
window (vehicle)	das Fenster
to park	parken
to slow down	langsamer werden
to accelerate	beschleunigen
to start up	starten
to overtake	überholen

492
aerial	die Antenne
air filter	der Luftfilter
alternator	der Drehstromgenerator
antifreeze	das Frostschutzmittel
gearbox	die Gangschaltung
axle	die Achse
battery	die Batterie
flat	leer
bonnet	die Kühlerhaube
boot	der Kofferraum

493
brake fluid	die Bremsflüssigkeit
brake	die Bremse
to brake	bremsen
bumper	die Stoßstange
carburettor	der Vergaser
child seat	der Kindersitz
choke	der Choke
clutch	die Kupplung
cylinder	der Zylinder
horsepower	die Pferdestärke

494
disc brake	die Scheibenbremse
distributor	der Verteiler
dynamo	die Lichtmaschine
dynamic	dynamisch
engine	der Motor
exhaust	der Auspuff
fan belt	der Keilriemen
fuel gauge	die Benzinanzeige
fuel pump	die Benzinpumpe
fuse	die Sicherung

495
gear lever	der Ganghebel
generator	der Generator
to generate	generieren
alternating current	Wechselstrom
hand brake	die Handbremse
hazard lights	die Warnblinkanlage
horn	die Hupe
ignition	die Zündung

Travel and Tourism

ignition key	der Zündschlüssel
indicator	der Blinker

496

jack	der Wagenheber
silencer	der Schalldämpfer
number plate	das Nummernschild
oil filter	der Ölfilter
points	die Anschlüsse
rear view mirror	das Rückfenster
reflector	das Katzenauge
reverse light	das Rücklicht
roof-rack	der Dachgepäckträger
seat	der Platz

497

seat-belt	der Sicherheitsgurt
shock absorber	der Stoßdämpfer
socket set	das Steckschlüsselset
spanner	der Schraubenschlüssel
spare part	das Ersatzteil
spark plug	die Zündkerze
speedometer	die Geschwindigkeitsanzeige
starter motor	der Anlasser
steering wheel	das Lenkrad
sun roof	das Schiebedach

498

suspension	die Federung
towbar	die Abschleppstange
transmission	die Übersetzung
tyre	der Reifen
wheel	das Rad
windscreen	die Windschutzscheibe
wipers	die Scheibenwischer
wrench	der Schraubenschlüssel
air bag	der Airbag
four-wheel drive	der Vierradantrieb

499

motorbike	das Motorrad
helmet	der Helm
bicycle	das Fahrrad
racing cycle	das Rennrad
pedal	das Pedal
to pedal	die Pedale treten
tube	der Schlauch
to puncture	beschädigt werden
chain	die Kette
pannier bag	die Radtasche

500

ship	das Schiff
boat	das Boot, das Schiff
sail	das Segel
to embark	an Bord gehen
to disembark	von Bord gehen

on board	an Bord
disembarkment	die Ausschiffung
to tow	tauen
tug	der Schlepper
crossing	die Überquerung

501

to cross	überqueren
passage	die Überfahrt
passenger	der Passagier
cabin	die Kabine
deck	das Deck
mast	der Mast
pilot	der Pilot
rudder	das Steuer
crew	die Mannschaft
anchor	der Anker

502

to cast anchor	Anker werfen
anchorage	die Verankerung
cargo	die Ladung
to sink	sinken
sinking	das Sinken
shipwreck	das Schiffswrack
signal	das Signal
to signal	Signal geben
lighthouse	der Leuchtturm
port	der Hafen

503

quay	der Kai
oil tanker	der Öltanker
to launch	vom Stapel lassen
salvage	die Bergung
to salvage	bergen
free on board	frei Bord
waybill	der Frachtbrief
hovercraft	das Hovercraft
hoverport	der Hovercraft-Hafen

504

stern	das Heck
bows	die Knoten
prow	der Bug
starboard	das Steuerbord
port	der Hafen
keel	der Kiel
figurehead	die Bugfigur
funnel	der Schornstein
rigging	die Takelage
sail	das Segel

505

raft	das Floß
galley	die Galeere
clipper	der Schnellsegler

Travel and Tourism

schooner	der Schoner
whaler	der Walfänger
trawler	der Trawler
to trawl	mit Schleppnetz fischen
factory ship	das Fabrikschiff

506

hydrofoil	das Luftkissenboot
powerboat	das schnelle Motorboot
dinghy	das Beiboot
pontoon	der Ponton
liferaft	das Rettungsboot
aqualung	die Taucherlunge
diver	der Taucher, die Taucherin
navigation	die Steuerung
to navigate	steuern
to weigh anchor	die Anker lichten

507

balloon	der Ballon
airship	der Zeppelin
aviation	die Luftfahrt
airplane	das Flugzeug
flying boat	das Flugboot
airport	der Flughafen
air terminal	das Flughafenabfertigungsgebäude
passenger	der Passagier
business class	die Business Class
tourist class	die Tourist Class

508

farewell	die Verabschidung
air hostess	die Stewardess
to land	landen
forced landing	die Notlandung
to take off	abheben
takeoff	der Start
seatbelt	der Sicherheitsgurt
to fly	fliegen
propeller	der Propeller
pilot	der Pilot

509

autopilot	der Autopilot
black box	die Black Box
runway	die Startbahn, die Landebahn
undercarriage	das Fahrwerk
sound barrier	die Schallgrenze
to crash	abstürzen
glider	das Segelflugzeug
to glide	gleiten
hang-glider	der Drachensegler
autogyro	das Drehflügelflugzeug

Days of the week — Die Tage der Woche

Monday	Montag
Tuesday	Dienstag
Wednesday	Mittwoch
Thursday	Donnerstag
Friday	Freitag
Saturday	Samstag, Sonnabend
Sunday	Sonntag

Months — Die Monate

January	Januar
February	Februar
March	März
April	April
May	Mai
June	Juni
July	Juli
August	August
September	September
October	Oktober
November	November
December	Dezember

Seasons — Die Jahreszeiten

spring	der Frühling, das Frühjahr
summer	der Sommer
autumn	der Herbst
winter	der Winter

Numbers — Die Zahlen

1	eins
2	zwei
3	drei
4	vier
5	fünf
6	sechs
7	sieben
8	acht
9	neun
10	zehn
11	elf
12	zwölf
13	dreizehn
14	vierzehn
15	fünfzehn
16	sechzehn
17	siebzehn
18	achtzehn
19	neunzehn

20	zwanzig
21	einundzwanzig
22	zweiundzwanzig
23	dreiundzwanzig
24	vierundzwanzig
25	fünfundzwanzig
26	sechsundzwanzig
27	siebenundzwanzig
28	achtundzwanzig
29	neunundzwanzig
30	dreißig
40	vierzig
50	fünfzig
60	sechzig
70	siebzig
80	achtzig
90	neunzig
100	hundert
200	zweihundert
300	dreihundert
400	vierhundert
500	fünfhundert
600	sechshundert
700	siebenhundert
800	achthundert
900	neunhundert
1000	tausend
2000	zweitausend
1000000	eine Million
1st	erste(r, s)
2nd	zweite(r, s)
3rd	dritte(r, s)
4th	vierte(r, s)
5th	fünfte(r, s)
6th	sechste(r, s)
7th	siebte(r, s)
8th	achte(r, s)
9th	neunte(r, s)
10th	zehnte(r, s)
11th	elfte(r, s)
12th	zwölfte(r, s)
13th	dreizehnte(r, s)
14th	vierzehnte(r, s)
15th	fünfzehnte(r, s)
16th	sechzehnte(r, s)
17th	siebzehnte(r, s)
18th	achtzehnte(r, s)
19th	neunzehnte(r, s)
20th	zwanzigste(r, s)
21st	einundzwanzigste(r, s)
30th	dreißigste(r, s)
31st	einunddreißigste(r, s)
40th	vierzigste(r, s)
50th	fünfzigste(r, s)
60th	sechzigste(r, s)
70th	siebzigste(r, s)
80th	achtzigste(r, s)

90th	neunzigste(r, s)
100th	hundertste(r, s)
200th	zweihundertste(r, s)
300th	dreihundertste(r, s)
400th	vierhundertste(r, s)
500th	fünfhundertste(r, s)
600th	sechshundertste(r, s)
700th	siebenhundertste(r, s)
800th	achthundertste(r, s)
900th	neunhundertste(r, s)
1000th	tausendste(r, s)
2000th	zweitausendste(r, s)
millionth	millionste(r, s)
two millionth	zweimillionste(r, s)

Proverbs and Idioms
Sprichwörter und Idiome

to be homesick — Heimweh haben

I have pins and needles in my foot — mir ist der Fuß eingeschlafen

it's none of your business — es geht dich (Sie) nichts an

it's all the same to me — das ist mir egal

as deaf as a post — völlig taub

to sleep like a log — schlafen wie ein Murmeltier

as drunk as a lord — stockbesoffen

a bird in the hand is worth two in the bush — lieber der Spatz in der Hand als die Taube auf dem Dach

to kill two birds with one stone — zwei Fliegen mit einer Klappe schlagen

at full speed — mit voller Geschwindigkeit

no sooner said than done — gesagt, getan

birds of a feather flock together — gleich und gleich gesellt sich gern

every cloud has a silver lining — es gibt immer einen Morgen

a chip off the old block — der Apfel fällt nicht weit vom Stamm

out of sight, out of mind — aus dem Auge, aus dem Sinn

practice makes perfect — Übung macht den Meister

many hands make light work — viele Hände machen kurze Müh

First Names

better late than never — besser spät als nie

at first sight — auf den ersten Blick

in the short term — kurzfristig

in the long run — langfristig

on the other hand — andererseits

in my opinion — meiner Meinung

in fact — in der Tat

in other words — mit anderen Worten

First Names — Vornamen

Alexander	Alexander
Andrew	Andreas
Anthony	Anton
Bernard	Bernhard
Charles	Karl
Christopher	Christoph
Edward	Eduard
Francis	Franz
George	Georg
Henry	Heinrich
James	Jakob
John	Johann, Hans
Joseph	Joseph
Lawrence	Laurenz
Louis	Ludwig
Martin	Martin
Michael	Michael
Nicholas	Niklas
Paul	Paul
Peter	Peter
Philip	Philip
Raymond	Raimund
Thomas	Thomas
Vincent	Vinzenz
Alice	Alice
Anne	Anna
Catherine	Katharina
Charlotte	Charlotte
Deborah	Deborah
Eleanor	Leonore
Elizabeth	Elisabeth
Ellen	Ellen
Emily	Emilie
Esther	Esther
Frances	Franzisca
Josephine	Josefine
Louise	Luise
Margaret	Margarete
Mary	Maria
Matilda	Mathilde
Ophelia	Ophelia

Patricia	Patricia
Pauline	Paula
Rachel	Rachel
Rose	Rosa
Susan	Susanne
Sylvia	Sylvia
Veronica	Veronika

Signs of the Zodiac — Die Tierkreiszeichen

Aquarius	der Wassermann
Pisces	die Fische
Aries	der Widder
Taurus	der Stier
Gemini	die Zwillinge
Cancer	der Krebs
Leo	der Löwe
Virgo	die Jungfrau
Libra	die Wage
Scorpio	der Scorpion
Sagittarius	der Schütze
Capricorn	der Steinbock

Prepositions, adverbs and conjunctions — Präpositionen, Adverben und Konjunktionen

against	gegen
at	bei
between	zwischen
for	für
from	von
in	in
of	von
on	auf
to	zu
with	mit
without	ohne
above	oben
down	unten
under	unter
in front of	vor
opposite	gegenüber
forward	vorwärts
behind	dahinter
backwards	rückwärts
close to	nahe bei
near	nahe
far from	weit von
before	vor
after	nach

Prepositions, Adverbs and Conjunctions

here	hier
there	da, dort
inside	innen
within	darin
outside	außen
where	wo (place).
	wohin (direction)
during	während
except	außer
towards	auf... zu
until	bis
according to	gemäß
now	nun, jetzt
often	oft
then	dann
never	nie
always	immer
at once	sofort
soon	bald
still	noch
already	schon
like	wie
how	wie

Prepositions, Adverbs and Conjunctions

neither... nor	weder... noch
why	warum
because	weil
yes	ja
no	nein
well	gut
badly	schlecht
quickly	schnell
slowly	langsam
enough	genug
when	wann
too	auch
more	mehr
less	weniger
much	mehr
nothing	nichts
nobody	niemand
never	nie
perhaps	vielleicht
once	einmal
instead of	anstatt
often	oft
at times	manchmal

German Phrases

Key to Pronunciation

Guide to German Pronunciation Scheme

Vowels

a	as in b<u>a</u>d, f<u>a</u>ther
e	as in b<u>e</u>d, fath<u>e</u>r
ee	as in s<u>ee</u>
i	as in b<u>i</u>t
y	as in b<u>i</u>te
o	as in h<u>o</u>t
oa	as in b<u>oa</u>t
w	as in f<u>ow</u>l
oo	as in p<u>oo</u>l
û	as in French t<u>u</u>

Consonants have approximately the same sounds as in English, but note the following:

g	as in g<u>e</u>t
kh	as in the German name Ba<u>ch</u>, Scottish lo<u>ch</u>
zh	as in mea<u>s</u>ure

Getting Started
Everyday words and phrases

Yes
Ja
ya

Yes, please
Ja bitte
ya bit-e

No
Nein
nyn

No, thank you
Nein danke
nyn dank-e

OK
In Ordnung
in ord-noong

Please
Bitte
bit-e

Thank you
Danke
dank-e

Excuse me
Entschuldigung
ent-shoold-ee-goong

Good
Gut
goot

I am very sorry
Es tut mir sehr leid
es toot meer zayr lyt

Being understood

I do not speak German
Ich spreche kein Deutsch
eekh shprekh-e kyn doytsh

I do not understand
Ich verstehe nicht
eekh fer-shtay-e neekht

**Can you find someone who
speaks English?**
Könnten Sie jemanden finden, der
Englisch spricht?
*koent-en zee yay-mand-en find-en der
eng-leesh shprikht*

Can you help me, please?
Können Sie mir bitte helfen?
koen-en zee meer bit-e helf-en

It does not matter
Keine Ursache
kyn-e oor-zakh-e

I do not mind
Macht nichts
makht neekhts

Please repeat that slowly
Bitte wiederholen Sie das langsam
bit-e veed-er-hoal-en zee das lang-zam

Greetings and exchanges

Hello
Hallo
ha-loa

Hi
Hallo
ha-loa

Good evening
Guten Abend
goot-en a-bent

Good morning
Guten Morgen
goot-en mor-gen

Good night
Gute Nacht
goot-e nakht

Goodbye
Auf Wiedersehen
owf veed-er-zay-en

How are you?
Wie geht es Ihnen?
vee gayt es een-en

I am very well, thank you
Danke, es geht mir sehr gut
dank-e es gayt meer zayr goot

It is good to see you
Schön, Sie zu sehen
shoen zee tsoo zay-en

It is nice to meet you
Angenehm, Ihre Bekanntschaft zu machen
an-ge-naym eer-e be-kannt-shaft tsoo makh-en

There are five of us
Wir sind zu fünft
veer zint tsoo fûnft

Here is my son
Hier ist mein Sohn
heer ist myn zoan

This is— my daughter
Das ist   — meine Tochter
das ist   — myn-e tokht-er

— my husband
— mein Mann
— myn man

— my wife
— meine Frau
— myn-e frow

My name is . . .
Mein Name ist . . .
myn nam-e ist . . .

What is your name?
Was ist Ihr Name?
vas ist eer nam-e

You are very kind
Sehr nett von Ihnen
zayr net fon een-en

You are very welcome!

Bitte sehr
bit-e zayr

See you soon
Bis bald
bis balt

I am on holiday
Ich bin auf Urlaub
eekh bin owf oor-lowp

I live in London
Ich wohne in London
eekh voan-e in lon-don

I am a student
Ich bin Student
eekh bin shtoo-dent

I am from America
Ich komme aus Amerika
eekh kom-e ows a-may-ree-ka

I am from — Australia
Ich komme aus   — Australien
eekh kom-e ows — ow-stra-lee-en

— Britain
— Großbritannien
— groas-bri-ta-nee-en

— Canada
— Kanada
— ka-na-da

— England
— England
— eng-lant

— Ireland
— Irland
— eer-lant

— New Zealand
— Neuseeland
— noy-zay-lant

— Scotland
— Schottland
— shot-lant

— South Africa
— Südafrika
— zûd-af-ree-ka

Common questions

Where?
Wo?
voa

Where is...?
Wo ist...?
voa ist

Where are...?
Wo sind...?
voa zint

When?
Wann?
van

What?
Was?
vas

How?
Wie?
vee

How much?
Wieviel
vee-feel

Who?
Wer?
vayr

Why?
Warum?
va-room

Which?
Welcher / Welche / Welches
velkh-er / velkh-e / velkh-es

Do you know a good restaurant?
Kennen Sie ein gutes Restaurant?
ken-en zee yn goot-es rest-oa-rong

How can I contact American Express / Diners Club?
Wie kann ich mich mit American Express / dem Diners Club in Verbindung setzen?
vee kan eekh meekh mit A-mer-ican Express / dem Dyn-ers Club in fer-bind-oong zets-en

Do you mind if I . . .
Stört es Sie, wenn ich . . .
stoert es zee ven eekh . . .

Have you got any change?
Können Sie wechseln?
koen-en zee veks-eln

How long will it take?
Wie lange dauert das?
vee lang-e dow-ert das

May I borrow your map?
Darf ich Ihre Karte borgen?
darf eekh eer-e kart-e borg-en

What is the problem?
Was ist das Problem
vas ist das prob-laym

What is this?
Was ist das?
vas ist das

What is wrong?
Was ist nicht in Ordnung? / Was ist los?
vas ist neekht in ord-noong / vas ist loas

What time do you close?
Wann schließen Sie?
van shlees-en zee

Where can I buy a postcard?
Wo kann ich eine Postkarte kaufen?
voa kan eekh yn-e post-kart-e kowf-en

Where can I change my clothes?
Wo kann ich mich umziehen?
voa kan eekh meekh oom-tsee-en

Where can we sit down?
Wo können wir uns hinsetzen?
voa koen-en veer oons hin-zets-en

Who did this?
Wer hat das getan?
vayr hat das ge-tan

Who should I see about this?
Mit wem müßte ich darüber sprechen?
mit vaym müst-e eekh da-rûb-er shprekh-en

Will you come?
Kommen Sie?
kom-en zee

Asking the time

What time is it?
Wieviel Uhr ist es?
*vee-feel **oor** ist es*

It is —
Es ist —
*es **ist** —*

> **— a quarter past te*n***
> — viertel elf / viertel nach zehn
> *— **feer**-tel **elf** / **feer**-tel nakh **tsayn***

> **— a quarter to eleven**
> — viertel vor elf / dreiviertel elf
> *— **feer**-tel foar **elf** / **dry**-veer-tel **elf***

> **— after three o'clock**
> — nach drei Uhr
> *— nakh **dry** oor*

> **— early**
> — früh
> *— frû*

> **— eleven o'clock**
> — elf Uhr
> *— **elf** oor*

> **— five past ten**
> — fünf nach zehn
> *— **fûnf** nakh **tsayn***

> **— five to eleven**
> — fünf vor elf
> *— **fûnf** foar **elf***

> **— half past eight exactly**
> — genau halb neun
> *— ge-**now** halp **noyn***

> **— half past ten**
> — halb elf
> *— halp **elf***

> **— late**
> — spät
> *— spet*

> **— midnig*h*t**
> — Mitternacht
> *— **mit**-er-nakht*

> **— nearly five o'clock**
> — fast fünf Uhr
> *— fast **fûnf** oor*

> **— ten o' clock**
> — zehn Uhr
> *— **tsayn** oor*

> **— ten past ten**
> — zehn nach zehn
> *— tsayn nakh **tsayn***

> **— ten to eleven**
> — zehn vor elf
> *— tsayn foar **elf***

> **— twelve o'clock (midday)**
> — zwölf Uhr (Mittag)
> *— **tsvoelf** oor (**mi**-tag)*

> **— twenty-five past ten**
> — fünfundzwanzig Minuten
> nach zehn
> *— fûnf-oont-**tsvan**-tseekh mee-**noo**-
> ten nakh **tsayn***

> **— twenty-five to eleven**
> — fünfundzwanzig Minuten vor elf
> *— fûnf-oont-**tsvan**-tseekh mee-**noo**-
> ten voar **elf***

> **— twenty past ten**
> — zwanzig Minuten nach zehn
> *— **tsvan**-tseekh mee-**noo**-ten nakh
> **tsayn***

> **— twenty to eleven**
> — zwanzig Minuten vor elf
> *— **tsvan**-tseekh mee-**noo**-ten
> foar **elf***

at about one o'clock
etwa um ein Uhr
*et-va oom **yn** oor*

at half past six
um halb sieben
*oom halp **zeeb**-en*

at night
nach*t*s
nakhts

before midnight
vor Mitternacht
*foar **mit**-er-nakht*

Getting Started

in an hour's time
in einer Stunde
*in yn-er **shtoond**-e*

in half an hour
in einer halben Stunde
*in yn-er halb-en **shtoond**-e*

soo*n*
bald
balt

this afternoon
heute Nachmittag
*hoyt-e **nakh-mi**-tag*

this evening
heute Abend
*hoyt-e **a**-bent*

this morning
heute morgen
*hoyt-e **mor**-gen*

tonight
heute nacht
*hoyt-e **nakht***

two hours ago
vor zwei Stunden
*foar tsvy **shtoond**-en*

Common problems

I am late
Ich bin schon zu spät
*eekh bin **shoan** tsoo **shpet***

I have dropped a contact lens
Mir ist eine Kontaktlinse heruntergefallen
*meer ist yn-e kon-**takt**-linz-e hayr-**oont**-er-ge-fal-en*

I have no currency
Ich habe nicht die richt*ige Währung*
*eekh **hab**-e neekht dee **reekht**-eeg-e **ver**-oong*

I haven't enough money
Ich habe nicht genug Geld
*eekh **hab**-e neekht ge-**noog** gelt*

I have lost my — **credit cards**
Ich habe meine — Kreditkarten verloren
*eekh **hab**-e myn-e — kray-**deet**-kart-en
fer-**loar**-en*

— **key**
— Schlüssel verloren
*— shlûs-el fer-**loar**-en*

— **ticket**
— Karte verloren
*— kart-e fer-**loar**-en*

— **traveller's cheques**
— Reiseschecks verloren
*— ryz-e-sheks fer-**loar**-en*

My car has been stolen
Mein Wagen wurde gestohlen
*myn **vag**-en voord-e ge-**shtoal**-en*

My handbag has been stolen
Meine Handtasche wurde gestohlen
*myn-e **hant**-tash-e voord-e ge-**shtoal**-en*

My wallet has been stolen
Mein Geldbeutel wurde gestohlen
*myn **gelt**-boyt-el voord-e ge-**shtoal**-en*

My son is lost
Ich habe meinen Sohn verloren
*eekh **hab**-e myn-en **zoan** fer-**loar**-en*

Arriving in Germany

By air

The major airlines operating from the UK to Germany are British Airways, Lufthansa and Air UK, which offer regular daily departures. There are also low cost alternatives with a limited number of flights.

International airports are situated at Berlin, Bremen, Dusseldorf, Dresden, Frankfurt on Main, Hamburg, Hannover, Cologne/Bonn, Leipzig, Munich, Münster/Osnabrück, Nuremberg, Stuttgart and Saarbrücken. All airports have quick and easy links to the road network of a given city and Lufthansa offers a train service for air ticket holders between Cologne and Frankfurt. Frankfurt has the biggest airport in Europe, which is linked to the InterCity rail network by a station under the terminal.

For cheap flights on major airlines look into APEX or Super-APEX ticket options, which should be booked in advance and have certain restrictions.

Germany's internal air network is excellent, and it is possible to travel from north to south or from east to west in little over an hour. Services are operated by Deutsche BA, Lufthansa and LTU. In addition, smaller airlines offer a limited service to the North Frisian Islands.

By ferry

The following companies operate car ferries from the UK: Sealink, Eurolink Ferries, P&O European Ferries, North Sea Ferries, and Motorail. The only direct ferry link from the UK to Germany goes to Hamburg. Other popular connections are from Dover, Ramsgate, Harwich, Hull and Newcastle to Calais, Ostende, Rotterdam, Zeebrugge or Esbjerg.

By train

There are several ways to reach Germany from London by rail. Travellers may take the Channel Tunnel to save time, leaving London on the Eurostar hourly from Waterloo. To proceed to Germany they would have to change trains in Brussels. Much cheaper and slower are the regular departures from Victoria using the Ramsgate-Ostend ferry, Jetfoil or SeaCat service.

By coach

There are three departures a day from London's Victoria Coach Station. The buses cross the channel on Sealink's Dover-Zeebrugge ferry service and then drive via the Netherlands and Belgium to Cologne, Frankfurt, Mannheim, Stuttgart/Nurnberg, and Munich. Hoverspeed runs buses from Victoria Station to Berlin.

Arrival

Here is my passport
Da ist mein Paß
da ist myn pas

I am attending a convention
Ich wohne einer Versammlung bei
eekh voan-e yn-er fer-zam-loong by

I am here on business
Ich bin geschäftlich hier
eekh bin ge-sheft-leekh heer

I will be staying here for eight weeks
Ich bleibe acht Wochen lang hier
eekh blyb-e akht vokh-en lang heer

We are visiting friends
Wir besuchen Freunde
veer be-zookh-en froynd-e

We have a joint passport
Wir haben einen Sammelpaß
veer hab-en yn-en zam-el-pas

I have nothing to declare
Ich habe nichts anzumelden
eekh hab-e neekhts an-tsoo-meld-en

I have the usual allowances
Ich habe die üblichen zollfrei erlaubten
Mengen
eekh hab-e dee ûb-leekh-en tsol-fry er-lowp-ten meng-en

How long will this take?
Wie lange dauert das?
vee lang-e dow-ert das

How much do I have to pay?
Was habe ich zu zahlen?
vas hab-e eekh tsoo tsal-en

This is for my own use
Das ist für meinen eigenen Gebrauch
das ist fûr myn-en yg-en-en ge-browkh

Common problems and requests

Can I upgrade to first class?
Kann ich ein Upgrade zur ersten
Klasse haben?
kan eekh yn up-grayd tsoor erst-en klas-e hab-en

How long will the delay be?
Wie groß ist die Verspätung?
vee groas ist dee fer-spet-oong

I am in a hurry
Ich bin in Eile
eekh bin in yl-e

I have lost my ticket
Ich habe mein Ticket verloren
eekh hab-e myn tik-et fer-loar-en

I have missed my connection
Ich habe meinen Anschluß verpaßt
eekh hab-e myn-en an-shloos fer-past

Where is the toilet?
Wo finde ich eine Toilette?
voa find-e eekh eyn-e toy-let-e

Where is   — the bar?
  Wo ist   — die Bar?
  voa ist   — dee bar

        — the information desk?
        — der Informationsschalter?
        — der in-for-ma-tsee-oans-shalt-er

        — the departure lounge?
        — der Wartesaal?
        — voa ist der vart-e-zal

        — the transfer desk?
        — der Transfer-Schalter
        — der trans-fer-shalt-er

Where can I buy currency?
Wo kann ich Landeswährung kaufen?
voa kan eekh land-ez-ver-oong kowf-en

Where can I change traveller's cheques?
Wo kann ich meine Reiseschecks
umwechseln?
voa kan eekh myn-e ryz-e-sheks oom-veks-eln

Where can I get a taxi?
Wo kann ich ein Taxi nehmen?
voa kan eekh yn tax-ee naym-en

Where do I get the connection flight to Cologne?
Wo finde ich einen Anschlußflug nach
Köln?
voa find-e eekh yn-en an-shloos-floog nakh koeln

Where will I find the airline representative?
Wo finde ich einen Vertreter der
Fluggesellschaft?
voa find-e eekh yn-en fer-trayt-er der floog-ge-zel-shaft

My flight was late
Mein Flug hat sich verspätet
myn floog hat zeekh fer-shpet-et

I was delayed at the airport
Ich wurde am Flughafen aufgehalten
eekh woord-e am floog-haf-en owf-ge-halt-en

I was held up at immigration
Ich wurde bei den
Einwanderungsbehörden aufgehalten
eekh woord-e by den yn-vand-er-oongs-be-hoerd-en owf-gehalt-en

The people who were to meet me have not arrived
Die Leute, die mich abholen sollten, sind
nicht angekommen
dee loyt-e dee meekh ap-hoal-en zolt-en zint neekht an-ge-kom-en

Luggage

Where is the baggage from flight number...?
Wo ist das Gepäck von Flug Nummer...?
voa ist das ge-pek fon floog noom-er...

Are there any baggage trolleys?
Gibt es hier Gepäckwagen?
gipt es heer ge-pek-vag-en

Can I have help with my bag?
Könnte mir jemand mit meiner Tasche
helfen?
koent-e meer yay-mant mit myn-er tash-e help-en

Careful, the handle is broken
Achtung, der Griff ist kaputt
akh-toong der grif ist ka-poot

I will carry that myself
Das trage ich selbst
das trag-e eekh zelpst

Is there a left-luggage office?
Gibt es hier eine Gepäckverwarung?
gipt es heer yn-e ge-pek-fer-var-oong

Is there any charge?
Kostet das etwas?
kost-et das et-vas

Where is my bag?
Wo ist meine Tasche?
voa ist myn-e tash-e

I have lost my bag
Ich habe meine Tasche verloren
eekh hab-e myn-e tash-e fer-loar-en

It is	— a large suitcase
Es ist	— ein großer Koffer
es ist	— *yn gros-er kof-er*
	— a rucksack
	— ein Rucksack
	— *yn rook-zak*
	— a small bag
	— eine kleine Tasche
	— *yn-e klyn-e tash-e*

My baggage has not arrived
Mein Gepäck ist nicht angekommen
myn ge-pek ist neekht an-ge-kom-en

Please take these bags to a taxi
Bitte bringen Sie diese Taschen in ein Taxi
bit-e bring-en zee deez-e tash-en in yn tax-ee

These bags are not mine
Das ist nicht mein Gepäck
das ist neekht myn ge-pek

This package is fragile
Dieses Paket ist zerbrechlich
deez-es pa-kayt ist tser-brekh-leekh

No, do not put that on top
Nein, stellen Sie das bitte nicht darauf
nyn shtel-en zee das bit-e neekht da-rowf

At the Hotel

Types of Hotel

The standard of German hotels is very high. There are great variations in prices, and although there is no official grading system for German hotels, you are usually welcomed politely and courteously and polite service. Rooms are clean and comfortable and breakfast is usually included. It is worth asking for non-smoking rooms in larger hotels.

If you are looking for a guest house or B & B, there are many *Gasthöfe* or *Gasthäuser*, country inns offering food and rooms, *Fremdenheime* or *Pensionen* (guest houses), with *Fremdenzimmer*, which are rooms in private houses, at the lowest end of the scale. The words *Zimmer frei* or *zu vermieten* on a green background means there are vacancies while *besetzt*, on a red background, means no vacancies.

Most hotels have restaurants but those listed as *Garni* provide breakfast only. Lists of German hotels are available from the German National Tourist Office, 65 Curzon Street, London W1Y 8NE.

Castle Hotels

Germany's castle, or *Schloss*, hotels are of considerable interest. They are privately owned and run, and the majority offer four star luxury combined with the atmosphere of antique furnishings and stone passageways. For a brochure listing these hotels, write to Gast im Schloss e.V., D-34388 Trendelburg.

Romantik Hotels

These are of similar interest to castle hotels, being privately run in historic buildings with an emphasis on excellent food.

Spas

Taking the waters in Germany has been popular since Roman times. There are over 300 health resorts and mineral springs in the country. The word 'Bad' at the beginning of a place name usually indicates a spa, offering treatment at fairly high prices. Although there are spas in eastern Germany, most are in need of renovation. For information, write to Deutscher Bäderverband e.V., Schumannstr. 111, D-53113 Bonn.

Farm holidays

More and more holiday makers are opting for a holiday on a farm (*Urlaub auf dem Bauernhof*). Brochure listings are available from local tourist offices or from DLG Verlags GmbH, Eschenheimer Landstrasse 122, D-60489 Frankfurt am Main.

Reservations and enquiries

I am sorry I am late
Bitte entschuldigen Sie die Verspätung
bit-e ent-shoold-eeg-en zee dee fer-shpet-oong

I have a reservation
Ich habe gebucht
eekh hab-e ge-bookht

I shall be staying until July 4th
Ich werde bis vierten Juli bleiben
eekh vayrd-e bis feer-ten yool-ee blyb-en

I want to stay for 5 nights
Ich möchte fünfmal übernachten
eekh moekht-e fûnf-mal û-ber-nakht-en

Do you have a double room with a bath?
Haben Sie ein Doppelzimmer mit Bad?
hab-en zee yn dop-el-tsim-er mit bat

Do you have a room with twin beds and a shower?
Haben Sie ein Zweibettzimmer mit Dusche?
hab-en zee yn svy-bet-tsim-er mit doosh-e

Do you have a single room?
Haben Sie ein Einzelzimmer?
hab-en zee yn yn-tsel-tsim-er

I need a double room with a bed for a child
Ich brauche ein Doppelzimmer mit Kinderbett
eekh browkh-e yn dop-el-tsim-er mit kind-er-bet

I need — a single room with a shower or bath
Ich brauche — ein Einzelzimmer mit Dusche oder Bad
eekh browkh-e —yn yn-tsel-tsim-er mit doosh-e oad-er bat

— a room with a double bed
— ein Doppelzimmer
— yn dop-el-tsim-er

— a room with twin beds and bath
— ein Zweibettzimmer mit Bad
— yn tsvy-bet-tsim-er mit bat

— a single room
— ein Einzelzimmer
— yn yn-tsel-stim-er

How much is — full board?
Wieviel kostet — Vollpension?
vee-feel kost-et — fol-pen-see-oan

— half-board?
— Halbpension?
— halp-pen-see-oan

— it per night?
— es pro Nacht?
— es pro nakht

— the room per night?
— das Zimmer pro Nacht?
— das tsim-er pro nakht

Do you take traveller's cheques?
Nehmen Sie Reiseschecks?
naym-en zee ryz-e-sheks

Does the price include — room and breakfast?
Beinhaltet der Preis — Übernachtung und Frühstück
be-in-halt-et der prys — ûb-er-nakht-oong oont frûshtook

— room and all meals?
— Übernachtung und alle Mahlzeiten
— ûb-er-nakht-oong oont al-e mal-tsyt-en

— room and dinner?
— Übernachtung und Abendessen
— ûb-ernakht-oong ont ab-ent-es-en

At the Hotel

Can we have adjoining rooms?
Könnten wir Zimmer nebeneinander haben?
*koent-en veer **tsim**-er nay-ben-yn-**and**-er **hab**-en*

Do you have a car park?
Haben Sie einen Gästeparkplatz?
***hab**-en zee yn-en **gest**-e-park-plats*

Do you have a cot for my baby?
Haben Sie ein Kinderbett für mein Baby?
***hab**-en zee yn **kind**-er-bet für myn **bayb**-ee*

Are there supervised activities for the children?
Gibt es beaufsichtigte Aktivitäten für Kinder?
***gipt** es be-**owf**-zeekht-eegt-e ak-teev-ee-**tet**-en für **kind**-er*

Can my son sleep in our room?
Kann mein Sohn in unserem Zimmer schlafen?
*kan myn **zoan** in oonz-er-em **tsim**-er shlaf-en*

Are there other children staying at the hotel?
Wohnen noch andere Kinder in diesem Hotel?
voan**-en nokh **and**-er-e **kind**-er in **deez**-em hoa-**tel

Do you have a fax machine?
Haben Sie ein Faxgerät?
***hab**-en zee yn **fax**-ge-ret*

Do you have a laundry service?
Haben Sie einen Waschdienst?
***hab**-en zee yn-en **vash**-deenst*

Do you have a safe for valuables?
Haben Sie einen Safe für Wertsachen?
***hab**-en zee yn-en **sayf** für **vert**-zakh-en*

Do you have any English newspapers?
Haben Sie englische Zeitungen?
***hab**-en zee **eng**-leesh-e **tsyt**-oong-en*

Do you have satellite TV?
Haben Sie Satellitenfernsehen?
***hab**-en zee za-te-**leet**-en-**fern**-zay-en*

Which floor is my room on?
Auf welchem Stock ist mein Zimmer?
*owf **velkh**-em shtok ist myn **tsim**-er*

Is there a casino?
Gibt es hier ein Kasino?
***gipt** es **heer** yn ka-**see**-noa*

Is there a hairdryer?
Gibt es einen Föhn?
gipt** es yn-en **foen

Is there a lift?
Haben Sie einen Aufzug?
***hab**-en zee yn-en **owf**-tsoog*

Is there a minibar?
Gibt es eine Minibar?
***gipt** es yn-e **meen**-ee-bar*

Is there a sauna?
Haben Sie eine Sauna?
***hab**-en zee yn-e **zown**-a*

Is there a swimming pool?
Haben Sie ein Schwimmbecken?
***hab**-en zee yn **shvim**-bek-en*

Is there a telephone?
Gibt es ein Telefon?
gipt** es yn tay-lay-**foan

Is there a television?
Gibt es ein Fernsehgerät?
***gipt** es yn **fern**-zay-ge-ret*

Is there a trouser press?
Gibt es eine Hosenpresse?
***gipt** es yn-e **hoaz**-en-pres-e*

What is the voltage here?
Wie hoch ist die Spannung hier?
*vee **hoakh** ist dee **shpan**-oong heer*

Is the voltage 220 or 110?
Beträgt die Spannung 220 oder 110 Volt?
*be-**tregt** dee **shpan**-oong tsvy-hoond-ert tsvan-tseekh oad-er hoond-ert-**tsayn** volt*

Is this a safe area?
Ist das eine sichere Gegend?
*ist das yn-e **zeekh**-er-e gay-**gent***

Is there a market in the town?
Gibt es in dieser Stadt einen Markt?
gipt** es in deez-er **shtat** yn-en **markt

At the Hotel Service

Can you recommend a good local restaurant?
Können Sie ein gutes Restaurant in der Nähe empfehlen?
koen-en zee yn goot-es rest-oa-rong in der ne-e emp-fayl-en

Is there a Chinese restaurant?
Gibt es hier ein chinesisches Lokal?
gipt es heer yn khee-nayz-eesh-es loa-kal

Is there an Indian restaurant?
Gibt es hier ein indisches Lokal?
gipt es heer yn in-deesh-es loa-kal

Can I use traveller's cheques?
Kann ich mit Reiseschecks zahlen?
kan eekh mit ryz-e-sheks tsal-en

Has my colleague arrived yet?
Ist mein Kollege schon angekommen?
ist myn ko-layg-e shoan an-ge-kom-en

What time does the restaurant close?
Wann schließt das Restaurant?
van shleest das rest-oa-rong

When does the bar open?
Wann öffnet die Bar?
van oef-net dee bar

What time does the hotel close?
Wann schließt das Hotel?
van shleest das hoa-tel

What time is — breakfast?
Wann wird das — Frühstück — serviert?
van virt das — frû-shtûk — zer-veert

— dinner?
— das Abendessen?
— das a-bent-es-en

— lunch?
— das Mittagessen?
— das mi-tag-es-en

Service

Can I make a telephone call from here?
Kann ich von hier aus telefonieren?
kan eekh fon heer ows tay-lay-fo-neer-en

Can I dial direct from my room?
Kann ich von meinem Zimmer aus direkt wählen?
kan eekh fon myn-em tsim-er ows dee-rekt vel-en

Can I have an outside line?
Könnte ich eine Verbindung nach draußen haben?
koent-e eekh yn-e fer-bind-oong nakh drows-en hab-en

Can I charge this to my room?
Kann ich das auf meine Rechnung setzen lassen?
kan eekh das owf myn-e rekh-noong zets-en las-en

Can I have my key, please?
Kann ich bitte meinen Schlüssel haben?
kan eekh bit-e myn-en shlûs-el hab-en

Can I have — a newspaper?
Kann ich — eine Zeitung haben?
kan eekh — yn-e tsyt-oong hab-en

— an ashtray?
— einen Aschenbecher?
— yn-en ash-en-bekh-er

— another blanket?
— noch eine Decke?
— nokh yn-e dek-e

— another pillow?
— noch ein Kissen?
— nokh yn kis-en

Can I have my wallet from the safe?
Könnten Sie mir bitte meine Brieftasche aus dem Safe geben?
koent-en zee meer bit-e myn-e breef-tash-e ows dem sayf gayb-en

Can I hire a portable telephone?
Kann ich ein tragbares Telefon mieten?
kan eekh yn trag-bar-es tay-lay-foan meet-en

At the Hotel

Can I send this by courier?
Kann ich das per Kurier schicken?
*kan eekh das per koo-**reer** shik-en*

Can I use my charge card?
Kann ich meine Kundenkreditkarte
verwenden?
*kan eekh myn-e **koond**-en kray-**deet**-kart-
e fer-**vend**-en*

Can I use my personal computer here?
Kann ich meinen Computer hier
verwenden?
*kan eekh myn-en com-**pyoot**-er heer
fer-**vend**-en*

**Can we have breakfast in our room,
please?**
Können wir bitte in unserem Zimmer
frühstücken?
*koen-en veer **bit**-e in oons-er-em **tsim**-er
frû-**shtûk**-en*

Is there a room service menu?
Gibt es eine Karte für den Zimmerservice?
*gipt es yn-e **kart**-e fûr den **tsim**-er-zer-**vees***

I need an early morning call
Ich möchte morgen früh geweckt werden
*eekh **moekht**-e **mor**-gen frû ge-**vekt** vayrd-en*

Is there a trouser press I can use?
Gibt es eine Hosenpresse, die ich
verwenden kann?
*gipt es yn-e **hoaz**-en-pres-e dee eekh fer-
vend-en kan*

I am expecting a fax
Ich erwarte ein Fax
*eekh er-**vart**-e yn **fax***

Where can I send a fax?
Wo kann ich ein Fax senden?
*voa kan eekh yn **fax** send-en*

I need to charge these batteries
Ich muß diese Batterien aufladen
*eekh **moos** deez-e bat-er-ee-en **owf**-lad-en*

Please can I leave a message?
Kann ich bitte eine Nachricht
hinterlassen?
*kan eekh **bit**-e yn-e **nakh**-reekht **hint**-er-
las-en*

My room number is 22
Meine Zimmernummer ist 22
*myn-e **tsim**-er-noom-er ist tsvy-oont-
tsvan-tseekh*

Please fill the minibar
Würden Sie bitte die Minibar wieder
auffüllen?
*vûrd-en zee **bit**-e dee **meen**-ee-bar veed-er
owf-**fûl**-en*

I need — **a razor**
Ich brauche — einen Rasierapparat
*eekh **browkh**-e — yn-en ra-**zeer**-a-pa-rat*

— **some soap**
— Seife
— *zyf-e*

— **some toilet paper**
— Toilettenpapier
— *toy-**let**-en-pa-**peer***

— **some towels**
— Handtücher
— *hant-**tûkh**-er*

— **some coat hangers**
— ein paar Bügel
— *yn par **bûg**-el*

Please turn the heating off
Würden Sie bitte die Heizung abschalten?
*vûrd-en zee **bit**-e dee **hyts**-oong **ap**-shalt-en*

**Please, wake me at 7 o'clock in the
morning**
Wecken Sie mich bitte um 7 Uhr.
*vek-en zee meekh **bit**-e oom **zeeb**-en oor*

Please send this fax for me
Bitte senden Sie dieses Fax für mich
*bit-e **zend**-en zee deez-es **fax** fûr **meekh***

Where is the manager?
Wo ist der Manager?
*voa ist der **man**-a-ger*

Can I speak to the manager?
Kann ich mit dem Manager sprechen?
*kan eekh mit dem **man**-a-ger **shprekh**-en*

Hello, this is the manager
Guten Tag, hier spricht der Direktor
*goot-en **tag** heer sprikht der di-**rek**-tor*

Problems

I cannot close the window
Ich kann das Fenster nicht schließen
*eekh kan das **fenst**-er neekht **shlees**-en*

I cannot open the window
Ich kann das Fenster nicht öffnen
*eekh kan das **fenst**-er neekht **oef**-nen*

The air conditioning is not working
Die Klimaanlage funktioniert nicht
*dee **kleem**-a-an-lag-e foonk-tsee-o-**neert** neekht*

The bathroom is dirty
Das Badezimmer ist schmutzig
*das **bad**-e-tsim-er ist **shmootz**-eekh*

The heating is not working
Die Heizung funktioniert nicht
*dee **hyts**-oong foonk-tsee-o-**neert** neekht*

The light is not working
Das Licht funktioniert nicht
*das **leekht** foonk-tsee-o-**neert** neekht*

The room is not serviced
Für dieses Zimmer besteht kein
Zimmerservice
*fûr dees-es **tsim**-er be-shtayt kyn **tsim**-er-ser-vees*

The room is too noisy
Das Zimmer ist zu laut
*das **tsim**-er ist tsoo **lowt***

The room key does not work
Der Zimmerschlüssel funktioniert nicht
*der **tsim**-er-shlûs-el foonk-tsee-o-**neert** neekht*

There are no towels in the room
In dem Zimmer sind keine Handtücher
*in dem **tsim**-er zint kyn-e **hant**-tûkh-er*

There is no hot water
Wir haben kein heißes Wasser
*veer **hab**-en kyn **hys**-es **vas**-er*

There is no plug for the washbasin
Im Waschbecken ist kein Stöpsel
*im **vash**-bek-en ist kyn **shtoep**-sel*

Checking out

We will be leaving early tomorrow
Wir werden morgen früh abfahren
*veer vayrd-en **morg**-en frû **ap**-far-en*

I have to leave tomorrow
Ich muß morgen wegfahren
*eekh **moos** morg-en **vayg**-far-en*

I want to stay an extra night
Ich möchte eine Nacht länger bleiben
*eekh **moekht**-e yn-e **nakht** leng-er **blyb**-en*

Do I have to change rooms?
Muß ich in ein anderes Zimmer ziehen?
*moos eekh in yn **and**-er-es **tsim**-er **tsee**-en*

Could you have my bags brought down?
Könnten Sie mein Gepäck bitte herunter-
bringen lassen?
*koent-en zee myn ge-**pek** bit-e hayr-**oont**-er-**bring**-en **las**-en*

Can I have the bill please?
Kann ich bitte die Rechnung haben?
*kan eekh bit-e dee **rekh**-noong hab-en*

Please leave the bags in the lobby
Lassen Sie das Gepäck bitte in der
Eingangshalle stehen
*las-en zee das ge-**pek** bit-e in der **yn**-gangs-hal-e **shtay**-en*

Could you order me a taxi?
Könnten Sie bitte ein Taxi rufen?
*koent-en zee bit-e yn **tax**-ee **roof**-en*

Thank you, we enjoyed our stay
Vielen Dank, wir hatten einen sehr
angenehmen Aufenthalt
*feel-en **dank** veer hat-en yn-en **zayk** an-gen-naym-en **owf**-ent-halt*

Other Accommodation

Apartment and villa rental

A furnished rental with cooking facilities can save money, but they are often luxury properties, economical only if your party is large. The German Automobile Association issues listings of family holiday apartments or contact local tourist offices.

Renting a house

We have rented this villa
Wir haben dieses Ferienhaus gemietet
veer hab-en deez-es fayr-i-en-hows ge-meet-et

Here is our booking form
Hier ist unser Buchungsformular
heer ist unz-er bookh-oongs-form-oo-lar

We need two sets of keys
Wir brauchen die Schlüssel in zweifacher Ausführung
veer browkh-en dee shlûs-el in tsvy-fakh-er ows-fûr-oong

When does the cleaner come?
Wann kommt die Putzfrau?
van komt dee poots-frow

Where is the bathroom?
Wo ist das Badezimmer?
voa ist das bad-e-tsim-er

Can I contact you on this number?
Kann ich Sie unter dieser Nummer erreichen?
kan eekh zee oont-er deez-er noom-er er-rykh-en

Can you send a repairman?
Können Sie jemanden zum Reparieren schicken?
koen-en zee jaym-an-den tsoom re-pa-reer-en shik-en

How does this work?
Wie funktioniert das?
vee foonk-tsee-o-neert das

I cannot open the shutters
Ich kann die Fensterläden nicht öffnen
eekh kan dee fenst-er-led-en neekht oef-nen

Is the water heater working?
Funktioniert der Warmwasserbereiter
foonk-tsee-o-neert der varm-vas-er-be-ry-ter

Is the water safe to drink?
Kann man das Wasser unbedenklich trinken?
kan man das vas-er oon-be-denk-leekh trink-en

Is there any spare bedding?
Gibt es zusätzliches Bettzeug?
gipt es tsoo-zets-leekh-es bet-tsoyg

The cooker does not work
Der Herd funktioniert nicht
der hert foonk-tsee-o-neert neekht

The refrigerator does not work
Der Kühlschrank funktioniert nicht
der kûl-shrank foonk-tsee-o-neert neekht

The toilet is blocked
Die Toilette ist verstopft
dee toy-let-e ist fer-shtopft

There is a leak
Da ist eine undichte Stelle
da ist yn-e oon-deekht-e shtel-e

We do not have any water
Wir haben kein Wasser
veer hab-en kyn vas-er

Where is the fuse box?
Wo ist der Sicherungskasten?
voa ist der zeekh-er-oongs-kast-en

Where is the key for this door?
Wo ist der Schlüssel für diese Tür?
voa ist der shlûs-el fûr deez-e tur

Where is the socket for my razor?
Wo ist die Steckdose für meinen Rasierapparat?
voa ist dee shtek-doz-e fûr myn-en ra-zeer-ap-a-rat

Around the house

bath
Bad
bat

bathroom
Badezimmer
bad-e-tsim-er

bed
Bett
bet

brush
Bürste
bûrst-e

can opener
Dosenöffner
doaz-en-oef-ner

chair
Stuhl
shtool

cooker
Herd
hert

corkscrew
Korkenzieher
kork-en-tsee-er

cup
Tasse
tas-e

fork
Gabel
gab-el

glass
Glas
glas

kitchen
Küche
kûkh-e

knife
Messer
mes-er

mirror
Spiegel
shpeeg-el

pan
Pfanne
pfan-e

plate
Teller
tel-er

refrigerator
Kühlschrank
kûl-shrank

sheet
Bettuch
bet-tookh

sink
Spüle
shpû-le

spoon
Löffel
loef-el

stove
Ofen
oa-fen

table
Tisch
tish

tap
Wasserhahn
was-er-han

vacuum cleaner
Staubsauger
shtowp-zowg-er

toilet
Toilette
toy-let-e

washbasin
Waschbecken
vash-bek-en

Camping

There are some 2000 camp sites scattered all over Germany, 400 of which are open in the winter. If you enjoy a down-to-earth holiday, this is for you. Some sites will lend you a tent for a small fee. Blue signs with a black tent on a white background indicate official sites. The German Camping Club (DCC, Mandlstrasse 28, D-80802 Munich) publishes a list of sites, including details about trailer and caravan facilities.

If you want to camp rough, you need the permission of the landowner. The police will help you to contact him or her.

Caravans may be parked by the roadside for one night only but you may not set up equipment there.

Camping questions

Can we camp in your field?
Können wir auf Ihrem Feld zelten?
koen-en veer owf eer-em felt tselt-en

Can we camp near here?
Können wir hier in der Nähe zelten?
koen-en veer heer in der ne-e tselt-en

Can we park our caravan here?
Können wir unseren Caravan hier parken?
koen-en veer oons-er-en ka-ra-van heer park-en

Do I pay in advance?
Zahle ich im voraus?
tsal-e eekh im foar-ows

Do I pay when I leave?
Zahle ich bei der Abreise?
tsal-e eekh by der ap-ryz-e

Is there a more sheltered site?
Gibt es einen geschützteren Platz?
gipt es yn-en ge-shûts-ter-en plats

Is there a restaurant or a shop on the site?
Gibt es auf dem Platz ein Restaurant oder einen Laden?
gipt es owf dem plats yn rest-o-rong od-er yn-en lad-en

Is there another camp site near there?
Gibt es einen anderen Campingplatz in der Nähe?
gipt es yn-en and-er-en kamp-ing-plats in der ne-e

Is this the drinking water?
Ist das Trinkwasser?
ist das trink-vas-er

Please can we pitch our tent here?
Können wir bitte unser Zelt hier aufstellen?
koen-en veer bit-e oons-er tselt heer owf-shtel-en

The site is very wet and muddy
Das Gelände ist sehr naß und schlammig
das ge-lend-e ist zayr nas oont shlam-eekh

Other Accomodation   Around the camp site

Where are the toilets?
Wo sind die Toiletten?
voa zint dee toy-*let*-en

Where can we wash our dishes?
Wo kann ich unser Geschirr abspülen?
voa kan eekh oons-er ge-*shir* ap-shpûl-en

Where can I have a shower?
Wo kann ich mich duschen?
voa kan eekh meekh *doosh*-en

Around the camp site

air mattress
Luftmatratze
looft-ma-trats-e

frying pan
Bratpfanne
brat-pfan-e

bottle-opener
Flaschenöffner
flash-en-oef-ner

ground sheet
Bodenabdeckung
boad-en-ap-dek-oong

bucket
Eimer
ym-er

guy line
Zeltleine
tselt-lyn-e

camp bed
Feldbett
felt-bet

knife
Messer
mes-er

camp chair
Klappstuhl
klap-shtool

mallet
Holzhammer
holts-ham-er

can-opener
Dosenöffner
doz-en-oef-ner

matches
Streichhölzer
shtrykh-hoelts-er

candle
Kerze
kerts-e

penknife
Taschenmesser
tash-en-mes-er

cup
Tasse
tas-e

plate
Teller
tel-er

fire
Feuer
foy-er

rucksack
Rucksack
rook-zak

fly sheet
Fliegennetz
fleeg-en-nets

sleeping bag
Schlafsack
shlaf-zak

fork
Gabel
gab-el

spoon
Löffel
loef-el

stove
Ofen
oaf-en

tent peg
Hering
hayr-ing

tent pole
Zeltstange
tselt-shtang-e

tent
Zelt
tselt

thermos flask
Thermosflasche
ter-moas-flash-e

torch
Taschenlampe
tash-en-lamp-e

Hostelling

German youth hostels (*Jugendherberge*) have long lost their army camp atmosphere and are probably the most efficient and up-to-date in the world. There are more than 600, and many of the originally low budget dormitories have been turned into new leisure centres, which also offer courses. A new development is that of offering insights into ecological issues with excursions and open-air studies.

Many eastern youth hostels had to close down following reunification, but efforts are currently being made to bring them up to western standards. Apart from Bavaria, where there is an age limit of 27, there are no restrictions of age, although those under 20 get preference. For information, write to Deutsches Jugendherbergswerk, Bismarckstrasse 8, Postfach 1455, 32756 Detmold.

Are you open during the day?
Sind Sie tagsüber geöffnet?
*zint zee **tags**-ûb-er ge-**oef**-net*

Can I join here?
Können wir hier Mitglied werden?
***koen**-en veer heer **mit**-gleet vayrd-en*

Can I use the kitchen?
Kann ich die Küche benutzen?
*kan eekh dee **kûkh**-e be-**noots**-en*

Can we stay five nights here?
Können wir fünf Nächte hier bleiben?
***koen**-en veer fûnf **nekht**-e heer blyb-en*

Can we stay until Sunday?
Können wir bis Sonntag bleiben?
***koen**-en veer bis **zon**-tag blyb-en*

Is there a youth hostel near here?
Gibt es eine Jugendherberge in der Nähe?
***gipt** es yn-e **yoog**-ent-hayr-berg-e in der **ne**-e*

Do you serve meals?
Servieren Sie auch Mahlzeiten?
*ser-**veer**-en zee owkh **mal**-tsyt-en*

— to take away?
— zum Mitnehmen?
*— tsoom **mit**-naym-en*

Here is my membership card
Hier ist meine Mitgliedschaftskarte
***heer** ist myn-e **mit**-gleet-shafts-**kart**-e*

I do not have my card
Ich habe meine Karte nicht
*eekh **hab**-e myn-e **kart**-e neekht*

What time do you close?
Wann schließen Sie?
*van **shlees**-en zee*

Childcare

There is plenty of entertainment available for young travellers. Most cities have children's theatres, numerous playgrounds, theme parks, children's movies at the cinemas during the daytime, and the country's puppet theatres rank among the best in the world. If you are renting a car, be sure to arrange for a child seat. For recommended baby sitters check with your hotel desk. Updated lists are also available from the local tourist office.

Can you warm this milk for me?
Können Sie mir diese Milch aufwärmen?
*koen-en zee meer deez-e **milkh** owf-verm-en*

Do you have a high chair?
Haben Sie einen Hochstuhl?
*hab-en zee yn-en **hoakh**-shtool*

How old is your daughter?
Wie alt ist Ihre Tochter?
*vee **alt** ist eer-e **tokht**-er*

I am very sorry. That was very naughty of him
Tut mir sehr leid. Das war sehr böse von ihm.
***toot** meer zayr **lyt** das var zayr **boez**-e fon eem*

Is there a baby-sitter?
Haben Sie einen Babysitter?
*hab-en zee yn-en **bayb**-ee-sit-er*

Is there a cot for our baby?
Haben Sie ein Kinderbett für unser Baby?
*hab-en zee yn **kind**-er-bet für oons-er **bayb**-ee*

Is there a paddling pool?
Haben Sie ein Planschbecken?
*hab-en zee yn **plansh**-bek-en*

Is there a swimming pool?
Haben Sie ein Schwimmbecken?
*hab-en zee yn **shvim**-bek-en*

Is there a swing park?
Haben Sie Schaukeln?
*hab-en zee **showk**-eln*

It will not happen again
Es wird nicht wieder vorkommen
*es virt **neekht** veed-er **foar**-kom-en*

My daughter is 7 years old
Meine Tochter ist sieben Jahre alt
*myn-e **tokht**-er ist zeeb-en **yar**-e alt*

My son is 10 years old
Mein Sohn ist zehn Jahre alt
*myn **zoan** ist tsayn **yar**-e alt*

She goes to bed at nine o'clock
Sie geht um neun Uhr ins Bett
*zee gayt oom **noyn** oor ins **bet***

We will be back in two hours
Wir sind in zwei Stunden zurück
*veer zind in **tsvy shtoond**-en tsoo-**rük***

Where can I buy some disposable nappies?
Wo kann ich Wegwerfwindeln kaufen?
*voa kan eekh **veg**-verf-vin-deln **kowf**-en*

Where can I change the baby?
Wo kann ich das Baby wickeln?
*voa kan eekh das **bayb**-ee **vik**-eln*

Where can I feed/breastfeed my baby?
Wo kann ich mein Baby füttern/stillen?
*voa kan eekh myn **bayb**-ee **füt**-ern/**shtil**-en*

Getting Around

Tourist offices

Most German towns are served by a local tourist office, which is usually located in the town square or the main train station. These offices can have a variety of bewildering names – *Verkehrsamt, Fremdenverkehrsbüro, Fremdenverkehrsverein, Tourist-Information, Gemeindeamt,* and in spa-towns *Kurverwaltung* or *Kurverein.*

Business hours

Bank opening times vary from state to state, but they are generally open on weekdays from 8.30am or 9am to 2pm or 3pm (5pm or 6pm on Thursday) with a lunchbreak of about an hour. Most museums are open from Tuesday to Sunday 9am–6pm, many stay open late on Wednesday and Thursday. Post offices in larger cities are usually open from 8am to 6pm Monday to Friday and on Saturday until noon. Department stores are generally open from 9am or 9.15am to 8pm on weekdays and until 2pm on Saturdays. Many shops, however, still stick to the business hours in operation before liberalisation in 1996 and close at 6pm or 6.30pm. In 1997 some department stores were thinking of following suit.

Asking for directions

Where is — **the art gallery?**
Wo ist — die Kunstgalerie?
voa ist — *dee **koonst**-gal-er-ee*

— **the post office?**
— das Postamt?
— *das **post**-amt*

— **the Tourist Information Service?**
— die Tourist Information?
— *dee too-**reest** in-form-a-tsee-**oan***

Can you show me on the map?
Können Sie mir das auf der Karte zeigen?
*koen-en zee meer **das** owf der **kart**-e t syg-en*

Can you tell me the way to the station?
Können Sie mir den Weg zum Bahnhof sagen?
*koen-en zee meer den **vayg** tsoom **ban**-hoaf zag-en*

Can you walk there?
Kann man dorthin zu Fuß gehen?
*kan man **dort**-hin tsoo **foos** gay-en*

I am looking for the Tourist Information Office
Ich suche die Tourist Information
*eekh **zookh**-e dee too-**reest** in-form-a-tsee-**oan***

Where are the toilets?
Wo sind die Toiletten?
*voa zint dee toy-**let**-en*

Getting Around

I am lost
Ich habe mich verlaufen
*eekh **hab**-e meekh fer-**lowf**-en*

I am lost. How do I get to the Krone Hotel?
Ich habe mich verlaufen. Wie finde ich das Hotel Krone?
*eekh **hab**-e meekh fer-**lowf**-en vee find-e eekh das hoa-**tel kroan**-e*

I am trying to get to the market
Ich versuche, zum Markt zu gehen
*eekh fer-**zookh**-e tsoom **markt** tsoo **gay**-en*

I want to go to the theatre
Ich möchte ins Theater gehen
*eekh **moekht**-e ins tay-a-ter **gay**-en*

Is it far?
Ist es weit?
*ist es **vyt***

Is there a bus that goes there?
Gibt es einen Bus, der dorthin fährt?
***gipt** es yn-en **boos** der **dort**-hin fert*

Is there a train that goes there?
Gibt es einen Zug, der dorthin fährt?
***gipt** es yn-en **tsoog** der **dort**-hin fert*

Is this the right way to the supermarket?
Ist das der richtige Weg zum Supermarkt?
*ist **das** der **reekht**-ig-e **vayg** tsoom **soop**-er-markt*

We are looking for a restaurant
Wir suchen ein Restaurant
*veer **zookh**-en yn rest-oa-**rong***

Where do I get a bus for the city centre?
Wo finde ich einen Bus zur Innenstadt?
***voa** find-e eekh yn-en **boos** tsoor **in**-en-shtat*

Directions — by road

Do I turn here for Bad Windsheim?
Muß ich nach Bad Windsheim hier abbiegen?
*moos eekh nakh bat **vints**-hym heer **ap**-beeg-en*

How far is it to Dresden?
Wie weit ist es nach Dresden?
*vee **vyt** ist es nakh **drays**-den*

How long will it take to get there?
Wie lange dauert es, bis man dorthin kommt?
*vee **lang**-e dow-ert es bis man **dort**-hin komt*

Is there a filling station near here?
Gibt es hier in der Nähe eine Tankstelle?
***gipt** es heer in der **ne**-e yn-e **tank**-shtel-e*

I am looking for the next exit
Ich suche die nächste Ausfahrt
*eekh **zookh**-e dee nekst-e **ows**-fart*

Where does this road go to?
Wohin führt diese Straße?
***voa**-heen **fürt** deez-e **shtras**-e*

How do I get onto the motorway?
Wie komme ich auf die Autobahn?
*vee **kom**-e eekh owf dee **owt**-o-ban*

Which is the best route to Frankfurt?
Wie komme ich am besten nach Frankfurt?
*vee **kom**-e eekh am **best**-en nakh **frank**-foort*

Which road do I take to Aachen?
Welche Straße muß ich nach Aachen nehmen?
*velkh-e **shtras**-e moos eekh nakh **akh**-en **naym**-en*

Which is the fastest route?
Was ist die schnellste Route?
***vas** ist dee **shnelst**-e **root**-e*

Will we arrive in time for dinner?
Werden wir rechtzeitig zum Abendessen ankommen?
***vayrd**-en veer **rekht**-tsyt-eekh tsoom **ab**-end-es-en **an**-kom-en*

Directions — what you may hear

Sie fahren
zee far-en
You go

— **bis...**
— *bis...*
— as far as...

— **nach links**
— *nakh links*
— left

— **nach rechts**
— *nakh rekhts*
— right

— **auf ... zu**
— *owf ... tsoo*
— towards ...

Es ist
es ist
It is

— **an der Kreuzung**
— *an der kroyts-oong*
— at the crossroads

— **unter der Brücke**
— *oont-er der brûk-e*
— under the bridge

— **nach der Ampel**
— *nakh der amp-el*
— after the traffic lights

— **um die Ecke**
— *oom dee ek-e*
— around the corner

— **neben dem Kino**
— *nayb-en dem keen-o*
— next to the cinema

— **auf dem nächsten Stockwerk**
— *owf dem nekst-en shtok-verk*
— on the next floor

— **gegenüber dem Bahnhof**
— *gayg-en-ûb-er dem ban-hoaf*
— opposite the railway station

— **da drüben**
— *da drûb-en*
— over there

Überqueren Sie die Straße
ûb-er-kvayr-en zee dee shtras-e
Cross the street

Biegen Sie links ab
beeg-en zee links ap
Turn left

Biegen Sie rechts ab
beeg-en zee rekhts ap
Turn right

Folgen Sie den Zeichen nach . . .
folg-en zee den tsykh-en nakh . . .
Follow the signs for . . .

— **die Autobahn**
— *dee owt-o-ban*
— the motorway

— **die nächste Abzweigung**
— *dee nekst-e ap-tsvyg-oong*
— the next junction

— **der Platz**
— *der plats*
— the square

Fahren Sie gerade aus
far-en zee ge-rad-e ows
Keep going straight ahead

Biegen Sie bei der nächsten Straße rechts ab
beeg-en zee by der nekst-en shtras-e rekhts ap
Take the first road on the right

Sie müssen zurückfahren
zee mûs-en tsoo-rûk-far-en
You have to go back

Nehmen Sie die Straße nach Bamberg
naym-en zee dee stras-e nakh bam-berg
Take the road for Bamberg

Biegen Sie bei der zweiten Straße links ab
beeg-en zee by der tsvyt-en stras-e links ap
Take the second road on the left

Sie müssen eine Gebühr zahlen
zee mûs-en yn-e ge-bûr tsal-en
You have to pay the toll

Hiring a car

Major car hire agencies are: Budget, Eurodollar, Hertz and Europcar Inter-Rent. To get the best deal, book through a travel agent who is prepared to shop around and look into wholesalers (Auto Europe, Europe by Car, DER Tours, the Kemwel Group).

You are generally responsible for any damage or loss of the vehicle. It is best to check what coverage you have under your own personal insurance as well as credit card insurance. Stolen vehicles are often not covered by insurance sold by car-rental companies. Ask about drop-off charges, if you plan to pick up your car in one city and leave it in another.

You will not need your driving licence translated if you are from Andorra, Belgium, Cyprus, Denmark, Finland, France, Great Britain, Greece, Hong Kong, Hungary, Ireland, Italy, Luxembourg, Monaco, the Netherlands, New Zealand, Norway, Portugal, San Marino, Sweden, Switzerland, Senegal or Spain.

Can I hire a car?
Kann ich einen Wagen mieten?
*kan eekh yn-en **vag**-en **meet**-en*

Can I hire a car with an automatic gearbox?
Kann ich einen Wagen mit Automatikschaltung mieten?
*kan eekh yn-en **vag**-en mit owt-o-**mat**-eek-**shalt**-oong **meet**-en*

I want to hire a car
Ich möchte einen Wagen mieten
*eekh **moekht**-e yn-en **vag**-en **meet**-en*

I need it for 2 weeks
Ich brauche ihn für zwei Wochen
*eekh **browkh**-e een für **tsvy vokh**-en*

We will both be driving
Wir werden beide fahren
*veer **vayrd**-en **byd**-e far-en*

Do you have	— a large car?
Haben Sie	— einen großen Wagen?
hab-en zee	— *yn-en **gros**-en **vag**-en*
	— a smaller car?
	— einen kleineren Wagen?
	— *eyn-en **klyn**-er-en **vag**-en*
	— an automatic?
	— einen Wagen mit Automatikschaltung?
	— *yn-en **vag**-en mit owt-oa-**mat**-ik-**shalt**-oong*
	— an estate car?
	— einen Kombiwagen?
	— *yn-en **kom**-bee-**vag**-en*

I would like to leave the car at the airport
Ich möchte den Wagen am Flughafen stehen lassen
*eekh **moekht**-e den **vag**-en am **floog**-haf-en **shtay**-en las-en*

I want to leave the car at the airport
Ich möchte den Wagen am Flughafen lassen
*eekh **moekht**-e den **vag**-en am **floog**-haf-en las-en*

Is there a charge per kilometre?
Gibt es eine Gebühr pro Kilometer?
*gipt es yn-e ge-**bûr** pro keel-o-**mayt**-er*

Must I return the car here?
Muß ich den Wagen hierher zurückbringen?
*moos eekh den **vag**-en **heer**-hayr tsu-**rûk**-bring-en*

Please explain the documents
Bitte erklären Sie mir die Unterlagen
*bit-e er-**kler**-en zee meer dee **oont**-er-lag-en*

How much is it per kilometre?
Wieviel kostet es pro Kilometer?
*vee-feel **kost**-et es pro keel-o-**mayt**-er*

Can I pay for insurance?
Kann ich gegen Gebühr eine Versicherung abschließen?
*kan eekh **gayg**-en ge-**bûr** yn-e fer-**zeekh**-er-oong **ap**-shlees-en*

Getting Around   **By taxi**

Do I have to pay a deposit?
Muß ich etwas anzahlen?
*moos eekh et-vas **an**-tsal-en*

I would like a spare set of keys
Ich hätte gerne Extraschlüssel
*eekh **het**-e gern-e **ex**-tra-shlûs-el*

How does the steering lock work?
Wie funktioniert das Lenkradschloß?
*vee foonk-tsee-o-**neert** das **lenk**-rat-shlos*

Where is reverse gear?
Wo ist der Rückwärtsgang?
*voa ist der **rûk**-verts-gang*

Where is the tool kit?
Wo ist das Werkzeug?
*voa ist das **verk**-tsoyg*

Please show me how
— **to operate the lights**
Zeigen Sie mir bitte, wie
— die Scheinwerfer bedient werden
*tsyg-en zee meer **bit**-e vee*
— *dee **shyn**-verf-er be-**deent** vayrd-en*

— **to operate the windscreen wipers**
— die Scheibenwischer betätigt
werden
— *dee **shyb**-en-vish-er be-**tet**-eegt vayrd-en*

By taxi

German taxis are easily distinguished by the 'taxi' sign on the top. They are usually cream coloured, comfortable saloon cars, which can be hailed at stations, taxi ranks or in the street, and rates are metered.

There are also some private hire firms with cars displaying phone numbers. In general try to use the efficient public transport services available in the cities in preference to taxis, which are very expensive.

Please show us around the town
Zeigen Sie uns bitte die Stadt
*tsyg-en zee oons **bit**-e dee **shtat***

Please take me to this address
Bringen Sie mich bitte zu dieser Adresse
*bring-en zee meekh **bit**-e tsoo **deez**-er a-**dress**-e*

Take me to the airport, please
Bringen Sie mich bitte zum Flughafen
*bring-en zee meekh **bit**-e tsoom **floog**-haf-en*

The bus station, please
Die Bushaltestelle, bitte
*dee **boos**-halt-e-shtel-e **bit**-e*

Turn left, please
Nach links, bitte
*nakh **links** bit-e*

Turn right, please
Nach rechts, bitte
*nakh **rekhts** bit-e*

Can you come back in one hour?
Können Sie in einer Stunde
zurückkommen?
*koen-en zee in **yn**-er **shtoond**-e tsoo-**rûk**-kom-en*

Will you put the bags in the boot?
Könnten Sie das Gepäck bitte in den
Kofferraum legen?
*koent-en zee das ge-**pek** bit-e in den **kof**-er-rowm **layg**-en*

I am in a hurry
Ich bin in Eile
*eekh bin in **yl**-e*

Please hurry, I am late
Bitte beeilen Sie sich, ich habe bereits
Verspätung
*bit-e be-**yl**-en zee zeekh eekh **hab**-e be-**ryts** fer-**shpet**-oong*

Please wait here for a few minutes
Bitte warten Sie hier ein paar Minuten
*bit-e **vart**-en zee **heer** yn par mee-**noot**-en*

Wait for me please
Bitte warten Sie auf mich
*bit-e **vart**-en zee owf **meekh***

Please, stop at the corner
An der Ecke bitte halten
*an der **ek**-e bit-e **halt**-en*

How much is that, please?
Was macht das, bitte?
*vas **makht** das **bit**-e*

Please, wait here
Bitte warten Sie hier
*bit-e **vart**-en zee **heer***

Keep the change
Der Rest ist für Sie
*der **rest** ist **für** zee*

By bus

Germany's urban bus services are very efficient, but there is no nationwide network. The railways operate some services (*Bahnbus*), which link with the rail network. For special touring programmes along fascinating tourist routes, write to Deutsche Touring, Am Römerhof 17, D–60426 Frankfurt am Main, or local tourist offices.

All towns operate their own local buses, which often link up with local trams, S-Bahn (local rail links) and U-Bahn (underground). Tickets usually allow you to transfer freely between the various forms of transport. Public transport in cities is invariably fast, clean and efficient.

Does this bus go to the castle?
Fährt dieser Bus zur Burg?
*fert deez-er **boos** tsoor **boorg***

How frequent is the service?
In welchen Abständen fährt der Bus?
*in velkh-em **ap**-stend-en **fert** der **boos***

How long does it take to get to the park?
Wie lange dauert es bis zum Park?
*vee **lang**-e **dow**-ert es bis tsoom **park***

Is there a bus into town?
Gibt es einen Bus in die Stadt?
*gipt es yn-en **boos** in dee **shtat***

What is the fare to the city centre?
Was kostet die Fahrt in die Innenstadt?
*vas **kost**-et dee **fart** in dee **in**-en-shtat*

When is the last bus?
Wann geht der letzte Bus?
*van **gayt** der **letst**-e **boos***

Where do I get the bus for the airport?
Wo kann ich den Bus zum Flughafen nehmen?
*voa kan eekh den **boos** tsoom **floog**-haf-en **naym**-en*

Where should I change?
Wo muß ich umsteigen?
*voa moos eekh **oom**-shtyg-en*

Which bus do I take for the football stadium?
Welcher Bus fährt zum Fußballstadium?
*velkh-er **boos** fert tsoom **foos**-bal-stad-ee-oom*

Will you tell me when to get off the bus?
Könnten Sie mir sagen, wann ich aussteigen muß?
*koent-en zee meer **zag**-en van eekh **ows**-shtyg-en **moos***

By train

In 1994 the rail networks of the former East and West Germany were merged under the name of Deutsche Bahn (DB), which is currently being privatised. The renovation of the ancient tracks of the old German Democratic Republic is progressing fast, allowing the extension into there of the high-speed InterCity Express (ICE). InterCity, EuroCity and InterRegio services have also been improved and expanded.

Depending on classification of service, there are varying surcharges on ticket prices, with InterCity Express fares being about 20 per cent more expensive than normal ones. The cheapest and slowest option are the D-class trains.

All overnight InterCity and D-class services have sleepers with a first class service including breakfast. InterCity and InterCity Express trains have restaurant cars or trolley service, while the InterRegio trains have bistro cars.

Major route connections and their timetables are well coordinated and changing trains is easy as usually you need only cross the platform.

You are strongly advised to book your ticket and seat reservation in advance.

There are various rail passes available offering attractive discounts on rail travel. The German Rail Pass allows unlimited travel over a certain period of time and can also be used on KR River Steamers. The EurailPass provides unlimited first-class travel in participating countries as long as the pass is valid, and there is the cheaper and more limited Europass. In addition there are special passes for young people, senior citizens, groups or those combining rail and car travel. Whichever you are considering, you must purchase your pass before arrival, and none of the passes includes seat reservation.

A return (ticket) to Hamburg, please
Eine Rückfahrkarte nach Hamburg, bitte
*yn-e **rûk**-far-kart-e nakh **ham**-boorg **bit**-e*

A return to Paris, first-class
Eine Rückfahrkarte erster Klasse nach Paris, bitte
*yn-e **rûk**-far-kart-e erst-er **klas**-e nakh pa-rees **bit**-e*

A single (one-way ticket) to Hanover, please
Eine Einzelfahrkarte (Rückfahrkarte) nach Hannover, bitte
*yn-e **yn**-tsel-far-kart-e (**rûk**-far-kart-e) nakh han-oaf-er **bit**-e*

Can I buy a return ticket?
Kann ich eine Rückfahrkarte kaufen?
***kan** eekh yn-e **rûk**-far-kart-e **kowf**-en*

I want to book a seat on the sleeper to Paris
Ich möchte einen Platz im Schlafwagen nach Paris buchen
*eekh **moekht**-e yn-en **plats** im **shlaf**-vag-en nakh pa-**rees bookh**-en*

Second class. A window seat, please
Zweiter Klasse. Einen Fensterplatz, bitte
***tsvyt**-er **klas**-e yn-en **fenst**-er-plats **bit**-e*

What are the times of the trains to Paris?
Was sind die Zeiten für die Züge nach Paris?
vas** zint dee **tsyt**-en fûr dee **tsûg**-e nakh pa-**rees

Where can I buy a ticket?
Wo kann ich eine Fahrkarte kaufen?
***voa** kan eekh yn-e **far**-kart-e **kowf**-en*

A smoking compartment, first-class
Ein Raucherabteil erster Klasse
yn rowkh-er-ap-tyl erst-er klas-e

A non-smoking compartment, please
Ein Nichtraucherabteil bitte
yn neekht-rowkh-er-ap-tyl bit-e

When is the next train to Munich?
Wann geht der nächste Zug nach
München?
van gayt der nekst-e tsoog nakh mûn-khen

When is the next train to Stuttgart?
Wann geht der nächste Zug nach
Stuttgart?
van gayt der nekst-e tsoog nakh shtoot-gart

**How long do I have before my next train
leaves?**
Wieviel Zeit habe ich bis zur Abfahrt
meines nächsten Zuges?
*vee-feel tsyt hab-e eekh bis tsoor ap-fart
myn-es nekst-en tsoog-es*

Do I have time to go shopping?
Habe ich noch Zeit zum Einkaufen?
hab-e eekh nokh tsyt tsoom yn-kowf-en

Can I take my bicycle?
Kann ich mein Rad mitnehmen?
kan eekh myn rat mit-naym-en

What time does the train leave?
Wann fährt der Zug ab?
van fert der tsoog ap

What time is the last train?
Wann geht der letzte Zug?
van gayt der letst-e tsoog

Where do I have to change?
Wo muß ich umsteigen?
voa moos eekh oom-shtyg-en

**I want to leave these bags in the
left-luggage**
Ich möchte diese Taschen bei der
Gepäckverwahrung lassen
*eekh moekht-e deez-e tash-en by der ge-pek-fer-
var-oong las-en*

Can I check in my bags?
Kann ich mein Gepäck aufgeben?
kan eekh myn ge-pek owf-geb-en

How much is it per bag?
Wieviel kostet es pro Gepäckstück?
vee-feel kost-et es pro ge-pek-shtûk

I shall pick them up this evening
Kann ich sie heute Abend abholen?
kan eekh zee hoyt-e ab-ent ap-hoal-en

Where do I pick up my bags?
Wo kann ich mein Gepäck abholen?
voa kan eekh myn ge-pek ap-hoal-en

Is there	**— a buffet car/club car?**
Gibt es	— eine Snackbar / einen
	Salonwagen?
gipt es	— *yn-e snak-bar / yn-en za-*
	loang-vag-en

	— a dining car?
	— einen Speisewagen?
	— *yn-en shpyz-e-vag-en*

Is there a restaurant on the train?
Hat der Zug einen Speisewagen?
hat der tsoog yn-en shpyz-e-vag-en

Where is the departure board (listing)?
Wo ist der Abfahrtsplan?
voa ist der ap-farts-plan

Which platform do I go to?
Zu welchem Bahnsteig muß ich gehen?
tsoo velkh-em ban-shtyg moos eekh gay-en

Is this the platform for Mannheim?
Ist das der richtige Bahnsteig für den Zug
nach Mannheim?
*ist das der reekht-ig-e ban-shtyg fûr den tsoog
nakh man-hym*

Is this a through train?
Ist das ein Direktzug?
ist das yn dee-rekt-tsoog

Is this the Bonn train?
Ist das der Zug nach Bonn?
ist das der tsoog nakh bon

Do we stop at Schwabach?
Halten wir in Schwabach?
halt-en veer in shvab-akh

What time do we get to Hildesheim?
Wann kommen wir in Hildesheim an?
*van kom-en veer in **hild**-es-hym an*

Are we at Hof yet?
Sind wir schon in Hof?
*zint veer shoan in **hoaf***

Are we on time?
Haben wir Verspätung?
*ha-ben veer fer-**shpe**-toong*

Can you help me with my bags?
Könnten Sie mir bitte mit meinem
Gepäck helfen?
*koent-en zee meer **bit**-e mit myn-em **ge-pek**
helf-en*

I have lost my ticket
Ich habe meine Fahrkarte verloren
*eekh **hab**-e myn-e **far**-kart-e fer-**loar**-en*

My wife has my ticket
Meine Frau hat meine Fahrkarte
*myn-e **frow** hat myn-e **far**-kart-e*

Is this seat taken?
Ist dieser Platz besetzt?
*ist **deez**-er **plats** be-**zetst***

May I open the window?
Darf ich das Fenster öffnen?
*darf eekh das **fenst**-er **oef**-nen*

This is a non-smoking compartment
Das ist ein Nichtraucherabteil
*das ist yn **neekht**-rowkh-er-ap-**tyl***

This is my seat
Das ist mein Platz
*das ist myn **plats***

Where is the toilet?
Wo sind die Toiletten?
*voa zint dee toy-**let**-en*

Why have we stopped?
Warum haben wir angehalten?
*va-**room** hab-en veer **an**-ge-halt-en*

Driving

What you need

Entry formalities are few: you need your domestic licence (*see* Hiring a Car, page 75) and proof of insurance. It is recommended that drivers get a green card from their insurance company, which extends insurance coverage to driving in continental Europe. Extra breakdown insurance and vehicle and personal security coverage are advisable. All foreign cars need a country sticker, and right-hand-drive vehicles should have their headlights adjusted.

Roads

There are many specially designated tourist roads, covering areas of specific scenic or historic interest. The longest one is the *Deutsche Ferienstrasse*, the German Holiday Road, which runs from the Baltic to the Alps, a distance of around 1,720 kilometres (1,070 miles). The most famous, however, is the *Romantische Strasse*, the Romantic Road, which runs from Würzburg in Franconia to Fussen in the Alps, spanning 355 kilometres (220 miles) and passing through some of the most historic cities in Germany.

Roads in the western part of Germany are excellent, with 10,500 kilometres (6,500 miles) of toll-free motorways (*Autobahnen*) in ultramodern condition. There is no speed limit on motorways except the recommended one of 130 kilometres per hour (62 miles per hour). Germans drive fast, and it is advisable to be very familiar with rules and signs before venturing onto the roads. There are 169 motorway service stations and 268 petrol and diesel stations offering a round-the-clock service. In the east, many road surfaces are still in urgent need of repair and generally the road system is not yet as well developed, especially the main links across the former border, which are insufficient for the increased volume of traffic.

Rules

Driving on the right – it is illegal to pass on the right side of the road, even on motorways. Travellers used to driving on the left should take care on quiet roads, and when taking a left-hand turn should not revert to the left side of the road.

Traffic signs – traffic signs in Germany are international.

Priority to the right – at intersections priority is usually indicated by signs, even when there are traffic lights.

Speed limits – built up areas: 50 kilometres per hour (31 miles per hour); outside built-up areas: 100 kilometres per hour (62 miles per hour). Place-name signs mark the boundaries of built-up areas. The recommended speed limit on motorways: 130 kilometres per hour (62 miles per hour). It is not advisable to drive slowly in the left-hand (fast) lane, as you will soon see cars looming in your rear mirror with headlights flashing. This lane is for overtaking. Cars pulling trailers are limited to 80 kilometres per hour (50 miles per hour).

Seatbelts – seatbelts are required by law, front and back. *Children* – children under 12 may not sit in the front seat unless a special seat has been installed; children up to four need a special child seat.

Motorcyles – motorcyclists require helmets.

Snow tyres – studded snow tyres are not allowed.

Alcohol limit – the alcohol limit on drivers is 0.8 per cent, equivalent to two small beers or a quarter of a litre of wine.

Traffic and weather conditions

Are there any hold-ups?
Gibt es Verkehrsstörungen?
gipt es fer-kayrs-stoer-oong-en

Is there a different way to the stadium?
Gibt es eine andere Route zum Stadium?
gipt es yn-e and-er-e root-e tsoom shtad-ee-oom

Is there a toll on this motorway?
Ist diese Autobahn gebührenpflichtig?
ist deez-e owt-o-ban ge-bûr-en-pfleekht-eekh

What is causing this traffic jam?
Wodurch wird dieser Stau verursacht?
voa-doorkh virt deez-er shtow fer-oor-zakht

What is the speed limit?
Was ist die Höchstgeschwindigkeit?
vas ist dee hoekst-ge-shvind-eekh-kyt

When is the rush hour?
Wann sind die Stoßzeiten?
van zint dee shtoas-tsyt-en

Is the traffic heavy?
Gibt es viel Verkehr
gipt es feel fer-kayr

Is the traffic one-way?
Ist das eine Einbahnstraße?
ist das yn-e yn-ban-shtras-e

When will the road be clear?
Wann ist die Straße wieder frei?
van ist dee stras-e veed-er fry

Do I need snow chains?
Brauche ich Schneeketten?
browkh-e eekh shnay-ket-en

Is the pass open?
Ist der Paß geöffnet?
ist der pas ge-oef-net

Is the road to Saarbrücken snowed up?
Ist die Strecke nach Saarbrücken verschneit?
ist dee shtrek-e nakh zar-brûk-en fer-shnyt

Parking

There are no yellow lines along the kerbs in Germany. Parking regulations are indicated on road signs.

Where is there a car park?
Wo gibt es hier einen Parkplatz?
voa gipt es heer yn-en park-plats

Can I park here?
Kann ich hier parken?
kan eekh heer park-en

Do I need a parking disc?
Brauche ich hier eine Parkscheibe?
browkh-e eekh heer yn-e park-shyb-e

Where can I get a parking disc?
Wo kann ich eine Parkscheibe bekommen?
voa kan eekh yn-e park-shyb-e be-kom-en

How long can I stay here?
Wie lange kann ich hier bleiben?
vee lang-e kan eekh heer blyb-en

Is it safe to park here?
Kann man hier unbesorgt parken?
kan man heer oon-be-zorgt park-en

What time does the car park / multi-storey car park close?
Wann schließt der Parkplatz / Parkhaus?
van shleest der park-plats / das park-hows

Where do I pay?
Wo kann ich zahlen?
voa kan eekh tsal-en

Do I need coins for the meter?
Brauche ich Münzen für die Parkuhr?
browkh-e eekh mûnts-en fûr dee park-oor

Do I need parking lights?
Brauche ich eine Parkleuchte?
browkh-e eekh yn-e park-loykht-e

At the service station

As part of the anti-pollution effort, most German cars now run on lead-free fuel and leaded petrol is becoming increasingly difficult to find. Super leaded may be phased out by 1998. If you are renting a car, find out which fuel it requires as some cars take diesel. German filling stations are highly competitive and it is worth shopping around for bargains, but not on the *Autobahn*. Self-service (*SB Tanken*) is cheapest. Pumps marked *bleifrei* contain unleaded fuel.

Do you take credit cards?
Kann ich mit Kreditkarte zahlen?
kan eekh mit kray-deet-kart-e tsal-en

Fill the tank please
Voll bitte
fol bit-e

25 litres of
                    — unleaded petrol
fünf und zwanzig Liter
                    — bleifreies Benzin
fûnf-oont-tsvant-seekh lee-ter
                    — *bly-fry-es ben-tseen*

                    — 3 star
                    — Normalbenzin
                    — *nor-mal-ben-tseen*

                    — 4 star
                    — Super
                    — *soop-er*

                    — diesel
                    — Diesel
                    — *deez-el*

Can you clean the windscreen?
Können Sie die Windschutzscheibe putzen?
koen-en zee dee vint-shoots-shyb-e poots-en

Check   — the oil
Prüfen Sie bitte — den Ölstand
prûf-en zee bit-e — den oel-shtant

                    — the water
                    — das Wasser
                    — *das vas-er*

Check the tyre pressure please
Bitte prüfen Sie den Reifendruck
bit-e prûf-en zee den ryf-en-drook

The pressure should be 2.3 at the front and 2.5 at the rear
Der Druck sollte vorne zwei Komma drei und hinten zwei Komma fünf sein
der drook solt-e forn-e tsvy comma dry oont hint-en tsvy comma fûnf zyn

I need some distilled water
Ich brauche destilliertes Wasser
eekh browkh-e de-steel-eert-es vas-er

Breakdowns and repairs

There are three automobile clubs in Germany: ADAC (*Allgemeiner Deutscher Automobil Club*), Am Westpark 8, D-81373 Munich; AvD (*Automobilclub von Deutschland*), Lyonerstrasse 16, D-60528 Frankfurt; DTC (*Deutscher Touring-Automobil Club*), Amalienburgstrasse 23, D-81247 Munich. ADAC or AvD operate tow trucks on all motorways, and ADAC maintains the *Strassenwachthilfe*, which patrols roads to assist disabled vehicles.

There are orange emergency roadside telephones every 3 kilometres (1.8 miles), which are announced by blue *Notruf* (emergency) signs. ADAC will provide road assistance free of charge if the damage can be repaired within half an hour. If not, you will pay repair and towing fees. On minor roads find the nearest phone box, dial 19211 and ask, in English, for road service.

Driving

Is there a telephone nearby?
Gibt es hier in der Nähe ein Telefon?
*gipt es heer in der **ne**-e yn **tay**-lay-foan*

Can you send a recovery truck?
Können Sie einen Abschleppdienst
senden?
*koen-en zee yn-en **ap**-shlep-deenst **zen**-den*

Can you take me to the nearest garage?
Können Sie mich zur nächstenWerkstatt
bringen?
*koen-en zee meekh tsoor **nekst**-en **verk**-shtat
bring-en*

I have run out of petrol
Ich habe kein Benzin mehr
*eekh **hab**-e kyn ben-**tseen** mayr*

Can you give me a can of petrol, please?
Könnten Sie mir bitte einen Kanister
Benzin geben?
*koent-en zee meer **bit**-e yn-en kan-**eest**-er ben-
tseen gayb-en*

Can you give me — a push?
Könnten Sie mich bitte — anschieben?
*koent-en zee meekh **bit**-e* — **an**-sheeb-en

— a tow?
— abschleppen?
— **ap**-shlep-en

Is there a mechanic here?
Ist ein Mechaniker da?
*ist yn me-**khan**-ee-ker da*

Do you have an emergency fan belt?
Haben Sie einen Reservekeilriemen?
*hab-en zee yn-en re-**zerv**-e-kyl-reem-en*

Do you have jump leads?
Haben Sie ein Starthilfekabel?
*hab-en zee yn **shtart**-hilf-e-kab-el*

Can you find out what the trouble is?
Können Sie feststellen, was das
Problem ist?
*koen-en zee **fest**-shtel-en vas das
prob-laym ist*

There is something wrong
Etwas funktioniert nicht
*et-vas **foonk**-tsee-oa-**neert** neekht*

There is something wrong with the car
Mit dem Auto stimmt etwas nicht
*mit dem **owt**-oa **shtimt** et-vas **neekht***

Will it take long to repair it?
Würde eine Reparatur lang dauern?
*vûrd-e yn-e re-pa-ra-**toor** lang **dow**-ern*

Is it serious?
Ist es etwas Größeres / Ernsthaftes?
*ist es et-vas **groes**-er-es / **ernst**-haf-tes*

Can you repair it for the time being?
Können Sie es übergangsweise
reparieren?
*koen-en zee es **ûb**-er-gangz-vyz-e re-pa-**reer**-en*

**Can you replace the windscreen wiper
blades?**
Können Sie die Scheibenwischergummis
ersetzen?
*koen-en zee dee **shyb**-en-vish-er-goom-eez
er-**zets**-en*

Can you repair a flat tyre?
Können Sie einen platten Reifen reparieren?
*koen-en zee yn-en **plat**-en **ryf**-en re-pa-**reer**-en*

Do you have the spare parts?
Haben Sie Ersatzteile?
*hab-en zee er-**zats**-tyl-e*

I have a flat tyre
Ich habe einen platten Reifen
*eekh **hab**-e yn-en **plat**-en **ryf**-en*

I have locked myself out of the car
Ich habe mich aus dem Wagen
ausgesperrt
*eekh **hab**-e meekh ows dem **vag**-en
ows-ge-spert*

**I have locked the ignition key inside
the car**
Ich habe den Zündschlüssel im Auto
eingeschlossen
*eekh **hab**-e den **tsûnt**-shlûs-el im **owt**-oa
yn-ge-shlos-en*

I need a new fan belt
Ich brauche einen neuen Keilriemen
*eekh **browkh**-e yn-en **noy**-en **kyl**-reem-en*

I think there is a bad connection
Ich glaube, da ist ein Wackelkontakt
*eekh **glowb**-e da ist yn **vak**-el-kon-takt*

Driving

My car has been towed away
Mein Wagen wurde abgeschleppt
*myn **vag**-en voord-e **ap**-ge-shlept*

My car has broken down
Mein Auto hatte eine Panne
*myn **owt**-o hat-e yn-e **pan**-e*

My car will not start
Mein Wagen springt nicht an
*myn **vag**-en **shpringt neekht** an*

My windscreen has cracked
Meine Windschutzscheibe ist gesprungen
*myn-e **vint**-shuts-shyb-e ist ge-**shproong**-en*

The air-conditioning does not work
Die Klimaanlage funktioniert nicht
*dee **klee**-ma-an-lag-e **foonk**-tsee-oa-neert neekht*

The battery is flat
Die Batterie ist leer
*de bat-e-**ree** ist **layr***

The engine — **has broken down**
Der Motor — ist kaputt
*der **moa**-toar — ist ka-**poot***

— **is overheating**
— ist überhitzt
*— ist ûb-er-**hitst***

The exhaust pipe has fallen off
Der Auspuff ist abgefallen
*der **ows**-poof ist **ap**-ge-fal-en*

There is a leak in the radiator
Die Kühlung ist undicht
*dee **kûl**-oong ist **oon**-deekht*

Accidents and the police

Although German police officers are polite and businesslike, they are not to be messed with. If you fail to treat an officer with the proper respect, you may receive an on-the-spot fine. Not many of them speak more than a bit of English. Germans are very law-abiding, so beware of petty offences, which are subject to

fines and will mark you out as a foreigner (for instance, littering or ignoring the red light at a pedestrian crossing, even if there are no people in sight). There are two emergency numbers that are common to all areas: 110 for accidents and police, 112 for fire services.

There has been an accident
Ein Unfall ist passiert
*yn **oon**-fal ist pa-**seert***

We must call — **an ambulance**
Wir müssen — den Notarzt rufen
*veer **mûs**-en — den **noat**-artst **roof**-en*

— **the police**
— die Polizei rufen
*— dee pol-ee-**tsy roof**-en*

What is your name and address?
Was sind Ihr Name und Ihre Adresse?
*vas zint eer **nam**-e oont eer-e a-**dress**-e*

You must not move
Sie dürfen sich nicht bewegen
*zee **dûrf**-en zeekh neekht be-**vayg**-en*

I did not see the bicycle
Ich habe das Fahrrad nicht gesehen
*eekh **hab**-e das **far**-rat neekht ge-**zay**-en*

I could not stop in time
Ich konnte nicht rechtzeitig zum Stehen kommen
*eekh **kont**-e neekht **rekht**-tsyt-eekh tsoom **shtay**-en kom-en*

I did not know about the speed limit
Ich wußte nichts von der Geschwindigkeitsbegrenzung
*eekh **voost**-e neekhts fon der ge-**shvind**-eekh-kyts-be-grents-oong*

He did not stop
Er hat nicht angehalten
*er hat neekht **an**-ge-halt-en*

He is a witness
Er ist Zeuge
*er ist **tsoyg**-e*

He overtook on a bend
Er überholte in einer Kurve
*er ûb-er-**holt**-e in yn-er **koorv**-e*

Driving

He ran into the back of my car
Er fuhr auf meinen Wagen auf
er foor owf myn-en vag-en owf

He stopped suddenly
Er bremste plötzlich
er bremst-e ploets-leekh

He was moving too fast
Er ist zu schnell gefahren
er ist tsoo shnel ge-far-en

I did not see the sign
Ich habe das Zeichen nicht gesehen
eekh hab-e das tsykh-en neekht ge-zay-en

Here are my insurance documents
Hier sind meine Versicherungs unterlagen
heer zint myn-e fer-seekh-er-oongs-oont-er-lag-en

Here is my driving licence
Da ist mein Führerschein
da ist myn fûr-er-shyn

I cannot find my driving licence
Ich kann meinen Führerschein nicht finden
eekh kan myn-en fûr-er-shyn neekht find-en

Do you want my credit card?
Brauchen Sie meine Kreditkarte?
browkh-en zee myn-e kray-deet-kart-e

Do you want my passport?
Brauchen Sie meinen Paß?
browkh-en zee myn-en pas

I am very sorry. I am a visitor
Es tut mir sehr leid. Ich bin nur zu Besuch hier
es toot meer zayr lyt eekh bin noor tsoo be-zookh heer

I did not understand the sign
Ich habe das Zeichen nicht verstanden
eekh hab-e das tsykh-en neekht fer-shtand-en

How much is the fine?
Wie hoch ist die Geldbuße?
vee hoakh ist dee gelt-boos-e

I have not had anything to drink
Ich habe nichts getrunken
eekh hab-e neekhts ge-troonk-en

I have not got enough money. Can I pay at the police station?
Ich habe nicht genug Geld. Kann ich bei der Polizeiwache zahlen?
eekh hab-e neekht ge-noog gelt. kan eekh by der pol-ee-tsy-vakh-e tsal-en

I was only driving at 50 kilometres an hour
Ich bin nur fünfzig Kilometer pro Stunde gefahren
eekh bin noor fûnf-tseekh kee-loa-mayt-er pro shtoond-e ge-far-en

I was overtaking
Ich habe überholt
eekh hab-e ûb-er-hoalt

I was parking
Ich habe geparkt
eekh hab-e ge-parkt

That car was too close
Dieser Wagen hielt nicht genügend Abstand
deez-er vag-en heelt neekht ge-nûg-end ap-stand

The brakes failed
Die Bremsen versagten
dee bremz-en fer-zagt-en

The car number was...
Das Nummernschild war...
das noom-ern-shilt var...

The car skidded
Der Wagen schleuderte
der vag-en shloyd-ert-e

The car swerved
Der Wagen scherte aus
der vag-en shayrt-e ows

The car turned right without signalling
Der Wagen bog rechts ab, ohne zu blinken.
der vag-en boag rekhts ap oan-e tsoo blink-en

The road was icy
Die Straße war vereist
dee stras-e var fer-yst

The tyre burst
Der Reifen platzte
der ryf-en platst-e

413

Car parts

accelerator
Gaspedal
gas-pay-dal

aerial
Antenne
an-ten-e

air filter
Luftfilter
looft-filt-er

alternator
Drehstromgenerator
dray-stroam-gay-nay-ra-tor

antifreeze
Frostschutzmittel
frost-shoots-mit-el

automatic gearbox
Automatikschaltung
owt-oa-ma-teek-shalt-oong

axle
Achse
aks-e

battery
Batterie
bat-e-ree

bonnet
Kühlerhaube
kûl-er-howb-e

boot
Kofferraum
kof-er-rowm

brake fluid
Bremsenflüssigkeit
bremz-en-flûs-eekh-kyt

brake light
Bremsleuchte
bremz-loykht-e

brakes
Bremsen
bremz-en

bulb
Glühbirne
glû-birn-e

bumper
Stoßstange
shtoas-shtang-e

car-phone
Autotelefon
owt-oa-tay-lay-foan

carburettor
Vergaser
fer-gas-er

child seat
Kindersitz
kind-er-zits

choke
Choke
tshoak

clutch
Kupplung
koop-loong

cooling system
Kühlung
kûl-oong

cylinder
Zylinder
tsû-lind-er

disc brake
Scheibenbremse
shyb-en-bremz-e

distributor
Verteiler
fer-tyl-er

door
Tür
tûr

dynamo
Lichtmaschine
leekht-ma-sheen-e

electrical system
Stromanlage
shtroam-an-lag-e

engine
Motor
moa-toar

Driving

exhaust system
Auspuffanlage
ows-poof-an-lag-e

fan belt
Keilriemen
kyl-reem-en

foot pump
Fußpumpe
foos-poomp-e

fuel gauge
Benzinanzeige
ben-tseen-an-tsyg-e

fuel pump
Benzinpumpe
ben-tseen-poomp-e

fuse
Sicherung
zeekh-er-oong

gear box
Gangschaltung
gang-shalt-oong

gear lever
Ganghebel
gang-hayb-el

generator
Generator
gay-nay-ra-tor

hammer
Hammer
ham-er

hand brake
Handbremse
hant-bremz-e

hazard lights
Warnblinkanlage
varn-blink-an-lag-e

headlights
Scheinwerfer
shyn-verf-er

heating system
Heizung
hyts-oong

hood
Haube
howb-e

horn
Hupe
hoop-e

hose
Schlauch
shlowkh

ignition key
Zündungsschlüssel
tsûnd-oongs-shlûs-el

ignition
Zündung
tsûnd-oong

indicator
Blinker
blink-er

jack
Wagenheber
vag-en-hayb-er

lights
Leuchten
loykht-en

lock
Schloß
shlos

oil filter
Ölfilter
oel-filt-er

oil
Öl
oel

oil pressure
Ölstand
oel-shtant

petrol
Benzin
ben-tseen

points
Anschlüsse
an-shlûs-e

Driving   Car parts

pump
Pumpe
poomp-e

radiator
Kühlung
kûl-oong

rear-view mirror
Rückscheibe
rûk-shyb-e

reflectors
Reflektoren
reflek-toar-en

reversing light
Rückfahrscheinwerfer
rûk-far-shyn-verf-er

roof-rack
Dachgepäckträger
dakh-ge-pek-treg-er

screwdriver
Schraubenzieher
shrowb-en-tsee-er

seat belt
Sicherheitsgurt
zeekh-er-hyts-goort

seat
Platz
plats

shock absorber
Stoßdämpfer
shtoas-dempf-er

silencer
Schalldämpfer
shal-dempf-er

socket set
Steckschlüsselset
shtek-shlûs-el-set

spanner
Schraubenschlüssel
shrowb-en-shlûs-el

spare part
Ersatzteil
er-zats-tyl

spark plug
Zündkerze
tsûnd-kerts-e

speedometer
Geschwindigkeitsmesser
ge-shvind-eekh-kyts-mes-er

starter motor
Anlasser
an-las-er

steering
Lenkung
lenk-oong

steering wheel
Lenkrad
lenk-rat

sun roof
Schiebedach
sheeb-e-dakh

suspension
Federung
fay-der-oong

tools
Werkzeug
verk-tsoyg

towbar
Abschleppstange
ap-shlep-shtang-e

transmission
Getriebe
ge-treeb-e

tyre pressure
Reifendruck
ryf-en-drook

tyre
Reifen
ryf-en

warning light
Warnleuchte
varn-loykht-e

water
Wasser
vas-er

Driving

wheel
Rad
rat

windshield
Frontscheibe
front-shyb-e

windscreen
Windschutzscheibe
vint-shoots shyb-e

wipers
Scheibenwischer
shyb-en-vish-er

Road signs

bitte rechts fahren
bit-e rekhts far-en
keep to the right

private Zufahrt
pree-vat-e tsoo-fart
private road

Durchfahrt verboten
doorkh-fart fer-boat-en
no thoroughfare

Parken nur für Anwohner
park-en noor für an-voan-er
parking for residents only

kein Eingang
kyn-yn-gang
no entry

Umleitung
oom-lyt-oong
diversion

Eating Out

Where to eat

There is a great variety in restaurants and eating places, with the most sophisticated and expensive ones usually in the cities. For the most authentic and down-to-earth options, there is a *Gaststätte* in almost every street, and every village has its *Gasthof*, and such establishments are almost as easy to find in the east.

The emphasis in the Gasthof or Gaststätte is on good home cooking – simple food, wholesome rather than refined, at reasonable prices. These are also places where people will meet in the evening for a chat, a beer and a game of cards. They normally serve hot meals from 11.30am to 9 or 10pm, but many places stop serving between 2 and 6pm except for cold snacks.

Lunch rather than dinner is the main meal of the day in Germany, followed by *Abendbrot* or *Abendessen* (supper) in the evening. Coffee and cake are still often enjoyed in the afternoon, and some bakeries (*Konditorei*) double as cafés for this purpose. It is also perfectly acceptable to visit a Gaststätte or Gasthof for just a pot of coffee outside the busy lunch hour.

To save money in the cities, consider dining in restaurants serving foreign cuisine. Germany has a vast number of moderately priced Turkish, Italian, Greek, Chinese and Balkan restaurants.

Unpretentious restaurants expect you to seat yourself. In traditional restaurants the waiter is addressed as 'Herr Ober', waitresses as 'Fräulein' ('Miss' – the address of Fräulein is no longer acceptable in other situations, since there is now no distinction made between married and single women).

A number of fast food chains exist all over Germany, including McDonald's, Pizza Hut, Burger King, Wienerwald (chicken) and Nordsee fish bars. However, the small take-away kiosks or snack bars (*Imbiss*) selling *Bratwurst* (fried or grilled sausage), *Bockwurst* (frankfurter) and *Pommes frites* (chips) are still popular. Sometimes you find butcher shops (*Metzgerei*) serving warm snacks on their premises.

Reservations

Should we reserve a table?
Sollten wir einen Tisch bestellen?
sollt-en veer yn-en tish be-shtel-en

Can I book a table for four at 8 o'clock?
Kann ich für acht Uhr einen Tisch für vier Personen buchen?
kan eekh für akht oor yn-en tish für feer per-zoan-en bookh-en

Can we have a table for four?
Könnten wir bitte einen Tisch für vier Personen haben?
koent-en veer bit-e yn-en tish für feer per-zoan-en hab-en

I am a vegetarian
Ich bin Vegetarier
eekh bin veg-e-ta-reer-er

We would like a table
      — by the window
Wir hätten gerne einen Tisch
      — am Fenster
verr het-en gern-e yn-en tish
      — am fenst-er

      — on the terrace
      — auf der Terrasse
      — owf der te-ras-e

Useful questions

Do you have a local speciality?
Haben Sie eine Spezialität des Ortes?
hab-en zee yn-e shpe-tsee-a-lee-tet des ort-es

Do you have a set menu?
Haben Sie ein Menü
hab-en zee yn me-nû

Do you have yoghurt?
Haben sie Joghurt?
hab-en zee yoa-goort

What do you recommend?
Was können Sie empfehlen?
vas koen-en zee emp-fayl-en

What is the dish of the day?
Was ist das Gericht des Tages?
vas ist das ge-reekht des tag-es

What is the soup of the day?
Was ist die Tagessuppe?
vas ist dee tag-es-zoop-e

What is this called?
Wie heißt das?
vee hyst das

What is this dish like?
Wie schmeckt dieses Gericht?
vee shmekt deez-es ge-reekht

Which local wine do you recommend?
Welchen hiesigen Wein empfehlen Sie?
velkh-en heez-ig-en vyn emp-fayl-en zee

How do I eat this?
Wie esse ich das?
vee es-e eekh das

Are vegetables included?
Ist das Gemüse inbegriffen?
ist das ge-mûz-e in-be-grif-en

Is the local wine good?
Ist der hiesige Wein gut?
ist der heez-ig-e vyn goot

Is this cheese very strong?
Ist das ein sehr kräftiger Käse?
ist das yn zayr kreft-eg-er kez-e

Is this good?
Ist das gut?
ist das goot

Ordering your meal

I will take the set menu
Ich nehme das Menü
eekh naym-e das me-nû

The menu, please
Die Karte, bitte
dee kart-e bit-e

I will take that
Ich nehme das
eekh naym-e das

That is for me
Das ist für mich
das ist fûr meekh

Can we start with soup?
Können wir mit einer Suppe anfangen?
koen-en veer mit yn-er zoop-e an-fang-en

I like my steak
   — very rare
Ich bevorzuge mein Steak
      — sehr wenig durchgebraten
eekh be-foar-tsoog-e myn stayk
      — zayr vayn-eekh doorkh-
        ge-brat-en

   — medium rare
   — mittel
   — *mit-el*

   — rare
   — nicht sehr stark durchgebraten
   — *neekht zayr shtark
     doorkh-ge-brat-en*

   — well done
   — durchgebraten
   — *doorkh-ge-brat-en*

Eating Out

I will have salad
Ich hätte gerne einen Salat
*eekh **het**-e **gern**-e yn-en za-**lat***

Could we have some butter?
Könnten wir etwas Butter haben?
*koent-en veer et-vas **boot**-er **hab**-en*

Can we have some bread?
Können wir Brot haben?
*koen-en veer **broat** hab-en*

Could we have some more bread, please?
Könnten wir bitte noch etwas Brot haben?
*koent-en veer **bit**-e nokh et-was **broat** hab-en*

Can I see the menu again, please?
Kann ich bitte die Karte noch einmal
sehen?
*kan eekh **bit**-e dee **kart**-e nokh yn-mal **zay**-en*

Ordering drinks

The wine list, please
Die Weinkarte bitte
*dee **vyn**-kart-e **bit**-e*

We will take the Riesling
Wir nehmen den Riesling
*veer **naym**-en den **reez**-ling*

A bottle of house red wine, please
Eine Flasche roten Hauswein, bitte
*yn-e **flash**-e roat-en **hows**-vyn **bit**-e*

A glass of dry white wine, please
Ein Glas trockenen Weißwein, bitte
*yn **glas** trok-en-en **vys**-vyn **bit**-e*

Another bottle of red wine, please
Noch eine Flasche Rotwein, bitte
*nokh yn-e **flash**-e **roat**-vyn **bit**-e*

Another glass, please
Noch ein Glas, bitte
*nokh yn **glas** bit-e*

Black coffee, please
Schwarzen Kaffee, bitte
***shvarts**-en **ka**-fay bit-e*

Coffee with milk, please
Kaffee mit Milch, bitte
***ka**-fay mit **milkh** bit-e*

Some plain water, please
Könnten wir bitte etwas Leitungswasser
haben?
*koent-en veer **bit**-e et-was **lyt**-oongs-vas-er
hab-en*

Can we have some mineral water?
Können wir Mineralwasser haben?
*koen-en veer min-er-**al**-vas-er **hab**-en*

Two beers, please
Zwei Bier, bitte
*tsvy **beer** bit-e*

Paying the bill

German restaurateurs are very accommo-
dating when it comes to splitting the bill
and paying separately, and waitresses in
small establishments often add up individual bills at the table. Tipping in Germany

is purely voluntary (up to 10 per cent of
the total bill) and indicates your particular
satisfaction with the service you have
received.

Can we have the bill, please?
Könnten wir bitte die Rechnung haben?
*koent-en veer **bit**-e dee **rekh**-noong hab-en*

Can I have an itemized bill?
Könnte ich bitte eine spezifizierte
Rechnung haben?
***koent**-e eekh **bit**-e yn-e **shpets**-æ-fee-**tseert**-e **rekh**-noong
hab-en*

Eating Out

Do you accept traveller's cheques?
Nehmen Sie Reiseschecks?
naym-en zee ryz-e-sheks

Is service included?
Ist die Bedienung im Preis inbegriffen?
ist dee be-deen-oong im prys in-be-grif-en

Is tax included?
Ist die Steuer mitinbegriffen?
ist dee shtoy-er mit-in-be-grif-en

Is there any extra charge?
Gibt es zusätzliche Gebühren?
gipt es tsoo-zets-leekh-e ge-bûr-en

Can I have a receipt?
Könnte ich bitte eine Quittung haben?
koent-e eekh bit-e yn-e kvit-oong hab-en

I would like to pay with my credit card
Ich möchte mit meiner Kreditkarte zahlen
eekh moekht-e mit myn-er kray-deet-kart-e tsal-en

I do not have enough currency
Ich habe nicht genug Landeswährung
eekh hab-e neekht ge-noog land-es-ver-oong

This is not correct
Das stimmt nicht
das shtimt neekht

This is not my bill
Das ist nicht meine Rechnung
das ist neekht myn-e rekh-noong

You have given me the wrong change
Sie haben mir falsch herausgegeben
zee hab-en meer falsh hayr-ows-ge-gayb-en

Complaints and compliments

This is cold
Das ist kalt
das ist kalt

This is not what I ordered
Das ist nicht, was ich bestellt habe
das ist neekht vas eekh be-shtellt hab-e

Waiter! We have been waiting for a long time
Herr Ober! Wir warten jetzt schon sehr lange
her oab-er veer vart-en yetst shoan zayr lang-e

The meal was excellent
Das Essen war ausgezeichnet
das es-en var ows-ge-tsykh-net

This is excellent
Das ist ausgezeichnet
das ist ows-ge-tsykh-net

Can I have the recipe?
Könnte ich bitte das Rezept haben?
koent-e eekh bit-e das re-tsept hab-en

Food

Nowadays Germany has a large number of good ethnic restaurants in larger towns and cities, but if your taste runs more towards meat and potatoes rather than tofu and yoghurt, you will find the food in Germany hearty and satisfying. Be careful when you order from a German menu if you don't speak the language, because ingredients like eel, blood sausage and brains are not uncommon. But don't let this deter you from taking risks – they are often tastier than you think.

The typical German breakfast (*Frühstück*) consists of coffee or tea with rolls or bread, jam, cold meat and cheese, sometimes boiled eggs. Lunch (*Mittagessen*) as the main meal of the day can consist of a variety of hot meals, usually with meat, potatoes and vegetables or salad. *Eintopf* can be found on menus of traditional restaurants. It is a hearty stew cooked in one pot, as the name indicates, often containing meat, vegetables, potatoes and beans. Supper (*Abendbrot* or *Abendessen*) is a re-enactment of breakfast with a wider choice of meat and cheese and often accompanied by beer.

German bread (*Brot*) is of astounding quality and variety. *Vollkornbrot* is whole-wheat, which has a different meaning in Germany. *Schwarzbrot* (black bread) is dense, dark and slightly acidic and *Roggenbrot* is rye bread. *Brötchen* are rolls, which also come in different shapes and styles. Many Germans indulge in the ritual of *Kaffee und Kuchen* (*see* page 115), which is a fourth meal taken in the afternoon.

In addition to bread, the staples of the German diet are *Wurst* (sausage in various shapes and sizes), *Schweinefleisch* (pork), *Rindfleisch* (beef), *Kalbfleisch* (veal), *Kartoffeln* (potatoes) and *Eier* (eggs). Dairy products include cheese and butter and especially *Schlagsahne* (whipped cream).

To sample local specialities as you travel around Germany is to appreciate the diversity of its food. Everyone has heard of *Sauerkraut* (pickled cabbage) or *Sauerbraten* (pickled beef), but there is much more to German cuisine. In Bavaria there are various kinds of *Knödel* (potato dumplings with fillings) and *Weisswurst*, which is a sausage made with milk. In Swabia and Baden there are *Spätzle* (noodles) and *Maultaschen* ('pasta pockets'). *Pfannekuchen* (pancakes) are universal, while *Kaiserschmarren*, a southern version, are pancakes chopped up and served with powdered sugar, raisins and sometimes boiled fruit. Hessians do amazing things with potatoes, and in the northern regions you can enjoy the tradition of a *Kohl und Pinkelfahrt*. This usually involves a long walk on a bitterly cold day, accompanied by some warming *Schnaps* and culminating at a rural inn, where a large meal of *Kohl* (kale), *Kasseler* (smoked pork) and *Pinkel* (sausage containing offal and cereal) is consumed, with more *Schnaps*. Because of the fishing industry, fish specialities are popular in the north. Herring used to be cheap and is still used in a variety of ways, either fried (*Brathering*), pickled in different ways (*Matjeshering*, *Bismarckhering*), rolled and pickled (rollmops), in salads (*Heringsalat*) and in many other ways.

Menu reader

Ananas
an-an-as
pineapple

Äpfel
ep-fel
apples

Apfelkompott
ap-fel-kom-pot
apple compote

Apfelkuchen
ap-fel-kookh-en
apple cake

Apfelpüree/Apfelmus
ap-fel-pû-re / ap-fel-moos
apple sauce

Aprikosen
ap-ree-koaz-en
apricots

Artischocken
ar-tee-shoak-en
artichoke

Aubergine
oa-ber-zheen-e
aubergine

Austern
owst-ern
oysters

Avocado
a-voa-ka-doa
avocado

Backhuhn/Brathuhn
bak-hoon / brat-hoon
baked / roasted chicken

Bananen
ba-na-nen
bananas

Barbe
barb-e
mullet

Basilikum
ba-zee-lee-koom
basil

Beefsteak
beef-stayk
beefsteak

belegtes Brot
be-laygt-es broat
cold sandwich

Birne
birn-e
pear

Biskuitkuchen
bees-kveet-kookh-en
sponge cake

Blaue Zipfel
blow-e tsip-fel
sausages cooked with vinegar and onions
(Franconia)

Blumenkohl
bloom-en-koal
cauliflower

Blut- und Leberwurst
bloot oont layb-er-woorst
black pudding and liver sausage
(Franconia)

Bohneneintopf
boan-en-yn-topf
bean stew

Bratapfel
brat-ap-fel
baked apple

Brathuhn/Backhuhn
brat-hoon / bak-hoon
fried / breaded chicken

Bratkartoffeln
brat-kar-tof-eln
roast potatoes

Brötchen
broet-khen
bread rolls

Brunnenkresse
broon-en-kres-e
watercress

Butter
boot-er
butter

Champignoncremesuppe
*sham-peen-yoang-**kraym**-zoop-e*
cream of mushroom soup

Champignons mit Knoblauch
*sham-peen-yoans mit **knoab**-lowkh*
mushrooms with garlic

Champignons mit Soße
*sham-peen-yoans mit **zoas**-e*
mushrooms in sauce

Chicorée
shee-koa-ray
chicory

Cornichon
kor-nee-shoang
gherkin

Creme Caramel
*kraym ka-ra-**mel***
crème caramel

Datteln
dat-eln
dates

Dessert
*de-**sert***
pudding

dünne Pfannkuchen/Crêpes
*dûn-e **pfan**-kookh-en / krep*
thin pancakes

　　　　　　— mit Marmelade
　　　　　　*— mit mar-me-**lad**-e*
　　　　　　— with jam
　　　　　　— mit Schokolade
　　　　　　*— mit shok-oa-**lad**-e*
　　　　　　— with chocolate

Eier mit Schinken
*y-er mit **shink**-en*
eggs with ham

Eier mit Speck
*y-er mit **shpek***
eggs with bacon

Eiernudeln
y-er-nood-eln
egg noodles

einfaches Kotelett
*yn-fakh-es ko-te-**let***
plain cutlet

eingelegte Makrele
*yn-ge-laygt-e mak-**rayl**-e*
marinated mackerel

Eiskrem
ys-kraym
ice cream

Ente
ent-e
duck

Erbsen
erp-sen
peas

Erbsensuppe
erp-sen-soop-e
pea soup

Erdbeeren
ert-bayr-en
strawberries

Erdbeeren mit Sahne
*ert-bayr-en mit **zan**-e*
strawberries with cream

Essig
es-eekh
vinegar

Estragon
es-tra-gon
tarragon

Fasan
*fa-**zan***
pheasant

Filet
*fee-**lay***
steak fillet

Fisch
fish
fish

Fleisch
flysh
meat

Fleisch vom Grill
flysh fom gril
grilled meats

Flußkrebs
floos-krayps
crayfish

Forelle
fo-rel-e
trout

Forelle blau
fo-rel-e blow
boiled trout

Forelle gebraten
fo-rel-e ge-brat-en
fried trout

französische Bohnen
fran-tsoe-zeesh-e boan-en
French beans

Gaisburger Marsch
gys-boorg-er marsh
stew with pasta and potatoes

Gans
gans
goose

gebratene Froschschenkel
ge-brat-en-e frosh-shenk-el
fried frog legs

gefüllter Hase
ge-fûl-ter haz-e
stuffed rabbit

gemischter Salat
ge-misht-er za-lat
mixed salad

Gemüse
ge-mûz-e
vegetables

Gemüsecremesuppe
ge-mûz-e-kraym-zoop-e
cream of vegetable soup

Granatäpfel
gra-nat-ep-fel
pomegranates

Grapefruit / Pampelmuse
grayp-froot / pam-pel-mus-e
grapefruit

grüne Paprika
grûn-e pap-ree-ka
green pepper (vegetable)

grüner Pfeffer
grûn-er pfef-er
green pepper (spice)

Gurke
goork-e
cucumber

Gurkensalat
goork-en-za-lat
cucumber salad

Halve Hahn
halv-e han
cheese roll (Cologne)

Haxe (Lammshaxe)
haks-e (lams-hax-e)
leg (of lamb, etc)

Hechtfilet
hekht-fee-lay
hake fillet

Himbeeren
him-bayr-en
raspberries

Hühnerbrühe
hûn-er-brû-e
chicken broth

Hühnereintopf
hûn-er-yn-topf
chicken stew

Hühnersuppe
hûn-er-zoop-e
chicken soup

Hummer
hoom-er
lobster

Joghurt
yoa-goort
yoghurt

Kalbskotelett
kalps-ko-te-let
veal cutlet

Karotten
ka-rot-en
carrots

Kartoffelpüree
kar-tof-el-pû-ray
mashed potatoes

Kartoffelsalat
kar-to-fel-za-lat
potato salad

Käsekuchen
kez-e-kookh-en
cheese cake

Kerbel
ker-bel
chervil

Kirschen
kirsh-en
cherries

Knoblauch
knoab-lowkh
garlic

Knödel/Klöße
knoed-el / kloes-e
dumplings

Kohl/Weißkohl
koal / vys-koal
cabbage

Kopfsalat
kopf-za-lat
lettuce

Krapfen
krapf-en
doughnuts

Kuchen
kookh-en
cake

Pastete
pas-tay-tuh
pie

Kürbis
kûr-bees
squash

Kutteln
koot-eln
tripe

Lamm am Spieß
lam am shpees
lamb on the spit

Lammkotelett
lam-kot-e-let
lamb cutlet

Lammshaxe
lams-hax-e
leg of lamb

Lauch
lowkh
leeks

Lauchsuppe
lowkh-zoope
leek soup

Leberkäse
layb-er-kez-e
processed meat (Bavaria)

Lorbeerblätter
loar-bayr-blet-er
bayleaf

Mais
ma-ees
sweet corn

Maissalat
ma-ees-za-lat
corn salad

Makrele
mak-rayl-e
mackerel

Mandelkuchen
mand-el-kookh-en
almond cake

marinierter Fisch
ma-ree-neert-er fish
marinated fish

Markkürbis
mark-kûr-bis
marrow

Marmelade
mar-me-lad-e
jam

Maultaschen
mowl-tash-en
pasta filled with spinach and chopped meat

Melone
me-loan-e
melon

Miesmuscheln
meez-moosh-eln
mussels

Milchreis
milkh-rys
rice pudding

Minze
mints-e
mint

Mousse au Chocolat
moos oa sho-koa-la
chocolate mousse

Muscheln
moosh-eln
clams

Niereneintopf
neer-en-yn-topf
stewed kidney

Nudeln
nood-eln
pasta

Obst mit Schlagsahne
obst mit shlag-zan-e
fruit with whipped cream

Obstsalat
obst-za-lat
fruit salad

Ochse am Spieß
oks-e am shpees
ox on the spit

Öl
oel
oil

Oliven
o-leev-en
olives

Orangen/Apfelsinen
o-ranzh-en / ap-fel-zeen-en
oranges

Palatschinken
pa-lat-shink-en
Austrian pancakes

Pasternake
past-er-nak-e
parsnip

Petersilie
payt-er-zeel-ee-e
parsley

Pfirsich
pfir-zeekh
peach

Pflaumen
pflowm-en
plums

Pilze/Champignons
pilts-e / sham-peen-yoans
mushrooms

Pommes frites
pom freet
French fries

Pumpernickel
poomp-er-nik-el
wholemeal bread

Radieschen
ra-dees-khen
radishes

Eating Out

Räucherschinken
roykh-er-shink-en
cured ham

Reineclauden
ryn-e-kload
greengages

Rindereintopf
rind-er-yn-topf
beef stew

Rindsbrühe
rints-brû-e
beef broth

Rosenkohl
roaz-en-koal
Brussels sprouts

Rosmarin
roaz-mar-reen
rosemary

Rote Bete
roat-e bayt-e
beetroot

rote Paprika
roat-e pap-ree-ka
red pepper

Rote-Bohnen-Suppe
rot-e-boan-en-zoop-e
kidney-bean soup

Rühreier
rûr-y-er
scrambled eggs

russischer Salat
roos-eesh-er za-lat
Russian salad

Salat
za-lat
lettuce

Salbei
zal-by
sage

Sardinen
zar-deen-en
sardines

Sauerkraut
zow-er-krowt
pickled white cabbage

Saumagen
zow-mag-en
pork and processed meat

Scampi
skamp-ee
scampi

Schalotten
sha-lot-en
shallots

Schinkenbrot
shink-en-broat
ham sandwich

Schmorbraten
shmoar-brat-en
braised beef

Schnittbohnen
shnit-boan-en
broad beans

Schnittlauch
shnit-lowkh
chives

schwarze Johannisbeeren
shvarts-e joa-han-is-bayr-en
blackcurrants

Schweinebraten
shvyn-e-brat-en
pork roast

Schweinskotelett
shvyns-ko-te-let
pork cutlet

Soße mit grünem Pfeffer
zoas-e mit grûn-em pfef-er
green pepper sauce

Spaghetti
shpa-get-ee
spaghetti

Spanferkel
shpan-ferk-el
suckling pig on the spit

Spargel
shparg-el
asparagus

Spiegeleier
shpeeg-el-y-er
eggs sunny side up

Spinat
spi-nat
spinach

Squash
skwosh
squash

Staudensellerie
shtowd-en-zel-er-ee
celery

Tafelspitz mit Kren
*taf-el-spits mit **krayn***
beef and horseradish

Thunfisch
toon-fish
tuna

Tintenfisch
tint-en-fish
cuttlefish

Tintenfisch
tint-en-fish
squid

Tomaten
*toa-**mat**-en*
tomatoes

Tomatensalat
*toa-**mat**-en-za-la*t
tomato salad

Tomatensoße
*toa-**mat**-en-zoas-e*
tomato sauce

Tomatensuppe
*toa-**mat**-en-**zoop**-e*
tomato soup

Trauben
trowb-en
grapes

Truthahn
troot-han
turkey

Vanillesauce
*va-**neel**-e-zoas-e*
custard

vom Grill
*fom **gril***
grilled/barbecued

Wassermelone
vas-er-me-loan-e
watermelon

weichgekochtes Ei
*vykh-ge-kokht-es **y***
soft boiled egg

Weinsoße
vyn-zoas-e
wine sauce

weiße Rüben
*vys-e **rûb**-en*
turnip

Würstchen
vûrst-khen
sausage

Zitrone
*tsee-**troan**-e*
lemon

Zitronenbaiserkuchen
*tsee-**troan**-en-be-**zay**-kookh-en*
lemon meringue

Zucchini
*tsoo-**kee**-nee*
courgettes

Zuckererbsen
tsook-er-erps-en
sweet peas

Zwiebel
tsveeb-el
onion

Zwiebelsoße
tsveeb-el-zoas-e
onion sauce

Drinks

Beer

Germans have been brewing beer since the eighth century, but in the Middle Ages the lucrative trade of the monastic orders was taken over by the lords of the land.

The variety of German beers is astonishing. *Vollbier* contains 4 per cent alcohol, *Export* 5 per cent, *Bockbier* 6.25 per cent and *Doppelbock* should be reserved for special occasions. There are also different colours, *ein Helles* being of a standard light colour, while *ein Dunkles* could be as dark as Coca-Cola. *Pils* is popular in the north, *Weissbier* in the south, *Kölsch* in Cologne and *Altbier* in Dusseldorf. *Fassbier* is a draught straight from the barrel.

Venues for drinking beer vary. There are *Biergärten* (beer garden) and *Bierkeller* (the indoor version meaning beer cellar). Many *Gaststätten* have a *Stammtisch* (locals' table) for their regular visitors, who sit around this table playing cards while drinking.

Wines and spirits

Although Germans are known to consume vast quantities of beer, they also produce some excellent wines in various famous wine growing areas. The main concentrations of viniculture lie around the Rhine and Mosel valleys, the Main River, Franconia and Baden-Baden. Rhine wine bottles are brown, all others are green, and the Franconian wines may be bottled in the characteristically shaped *Boxbeutel*.

Most German wines are white, but they vary a lot in sweetness and alcohol content. The cheapest are called *Tafelwein* (table wine), while *Qualitätswein* (quality wine) is better and *Qualitätswein mit Prädikat* (quality wine with distinction) is even superior. *Prädikat* wines are further subdivided according to the ripeness of grapes at harvest time: *Kabinett, Spätlese, Auslese, Beerenauslese* or *Trockenbeerenauslese.*

The most famous grapes grown in Germany are *Riesling, Muller-Thurgau* and *Traminer,* which produces the *Gewürztraminer.* In wine-growing areas, the thirsty traveller can stop at a *Weinstube* to sample the local produce. Many places celebrate annual wine festivals.

After a meal, many Germans aid their digestion by throwing back a *Schnaps* distilled from barley (*Korn*) or various fruit-like cherries (*Kirschwasser*), plums (*Zwetschgenwasser* or *Sliwowitz*), raspberries (*Himbeergeist*) and apricots (*Aprikosenlikör*). A popular strong-tasting herb liqueur is called *Jagermeister.*

If you order water (*Wasser*) in a restaurant you will be given mineral water. Tap water is called *Leitungswasser,* which Germans would find odd to drink with a meal.

Drinks reader

Apfelsaft
ap-fel-zaft
apple juice

Aprikosensaft
ap-ree-koz-en-zaft
apricot juice

Bananenmilch
ba-na-nen-milkh
banana milkshake

Bier
beer
beer

Bierflasche/Flaschenbier
beer-flash-e / flash-en-beer
bottled beer

Bowle
bow-le
punch

Calvados
kal-va-dos
apple brandy

Cappuccino
ka-poo-tshee-no
cappuccino

Champagner/Sekt
sham-pan-yer / zekt
champagne

Cidre/Apfelwein
seedr / ap-fel-vyn
cider

Cola
koal-a
coke

Dosenbier
doaz-en-beer
canned beer

ein Glas Rotwein
yn glas roat-vyn
a glass of red wine

ein Glas Weißwein
yn glas vys-vyn
a glass of white wine

ein großes Bier
yn gros-es beer
a large beer

ein Kännchen Kaffee
yn ken-khen ka-fay
small pot of coffee

ein Weinbrand
yn vyn-brant
a brandy

eine Tasse Kaffee
yn-e tas-e ka-fay
a cup of coffee

Eiskaffee
ys-ka-fay
iced coffee

entkoffeinierter Kaffee
ent-ko-fee-neert-er ka-fay
decaffeinated coffee

Grog
grog
tea with rum

Kaffee
ka-fay
coffee

Kaffee mit Milch
ka-fay mit milkh
coffee with milk

Kaffee mit Milch
ka-fay mit milkh
white coffee

Kamillentee
ka-meel-en-tay
camomile tea

Likör
lee-koer
liqueur

Eating Out

Limonade
*lee-mo-**nad**-e*
lemonade

löslicher Kaffee
***loes**-leekh-er **ka**-fay*
instant coffee

Mineralwasser
*mee-ner-**al**-vas-er*
mineral water

Orangengetränk
o-**ranzh**-en-ge-**trenk**
orange drink

Orangensaft
*o-**ranzh**-en-zaft*
orange juice

Pfirsichsaft
***pfir**-zeekh-zaft*
peach juice

Pharisäer
fa-reez-e-er
coffee with rum and cream

Roséwein
*roa-**zay**-vyn*
rosé wine

Rum
room
rum

Schnaps
shnaps
liquor

Sodawasser
***zoad**-a-vas-er*
soda

Starkbier
***shtark**-beer*
stout

Tee mit Milch
tay** mit **milkh
tea with milk

Tee mit Zitrone
***tay** mit tsee-**troan**-e*
lemon tea

Tonic Wasser
***ton**-ik vas-er*
tonic water

Traubensaft
***trowb**-en-zaft*
grape juice

Wermut
***vayr**-moot*
vermouth

Whisky
whisk-ee
whisky

Out and About

The weather

Germany's climate is predominantly mild and temperate, but there are regional variations. Cold snaps can plunge the temperatures well below freezing, particularly in the Alps, which makes winter sports possible from December to March. Regular snow and frost is also common in inland regions and the hills of the Harz, the Black Forest, Lower Saxony and Franconia. Summers are usually sunny and warm, although you should be prepared for some cloudy and wet days. Seasonal temperature differences are more pronounced in southern regions, while the north is kept temperate by the vicinity of the North Sea. Near the Alps, particularly in higher regions, the summer often starts late. Autumn can be warm and soothing. A peculiar weather condition called *Föhn* can be experienced in southern parts. This is a warm Alpine wind, often associated with atmospheric pressure changes, which may cause headaches for some people. Average summer temperatures range from 20°C to 30°C. The average winter temperature is 0°C.

Is it going to get any warmer?
Wird es wärmer werden?
*virt es **verm**-er vayrd-en*

Is it going to stay like this?
Wird es so bleiben?
*virt es zo **blyb**-en*

Is there going to be a thunderstorm?
Wird es ein Gewitter geben?
*wirt es yn ge-**vit**-er gayb-en*

Isn't it a lovely day?
Ist es nicht ein wunderschöner Tag?
*ist es neekht yn **voond**-er-shoen-er **tag***

It has stopped snowing
Es hat aufgehört zu schneien
*es hat **owf**-ge-hoert tsoo **shny**-en*

It is a very clear night
Es ist eine sehr klare Nacht
*es ist yn-e **zayr** klar-e **nakht***

It is far too hot
Es ist viel zu heiß
*es ist **veel** tsoo **hys***

It is foggy
Es ist neblig
*es ist **nay**-bel-eekh*

It is raining again
Es regnet wieder
*es **rayg**-net veed-er*

It is very cold
Es ist sehr kalt
*es ist zayr **kalt***

It is very windy
Es ist sehr windig
*es ist zayr **vind**-eekh*

It is going   — to be fine
Es wird   — schön
*es virt   — **shoen***

           — to be windy
           — windig
           *— **vind**-eekh*

           — to rain
           — regnen
           *— **rayg**-nen*

           — to snow
           — schneien
           *— **shny**-en*

There is a cool breeze
Es geht ein kühler Wind
*es gayt yn kûl-er **vint***

What is the temperature?
Welche Temperatur haben wir?
*velkh-e tem-per-a-**toor** hab-en veer*

Will it be cold tonight?
Wird es heute nacht kalt werden?
*virt es **hoyt**-e **nakht** kalt vayr-den*

Will the weather improve?
Wird das Wetter besser werden?
*virt das **vet**-er bes-er **vayrd**-en*

Will the wind die down?
Wird sich der Wind legen?
*virt zeekh der **vint** layg-en*

On the beach

Western mainland beaches often consist of grass bordering onto mudflats, but there are beautiful sandy beaches on the East and North Frisian Islands, which are easily accessible by regular ferry services. Local authorities often charge a fee for the use of beaches, and on the islands you can hire a *Strandkorb* (wicker beach seat). Because currents around the islands can be treacherous, bathers should stick to the areas designated for swimming. Taking a walk on exposed mudflats can be quite spectacular and is supposed to be healthy, but beware of getting trapped on banks by the incoming tide. In the east there are spectacular chalk cliffs on the coast at the island of Rügen and there are many sandy beaches on the Baltic coast and islands.

Can you recommend a quiet beach?
Können Sie einen ruhigen Strand empfehlen?
*koen-en zee yn-en **roo**-eeg-en **shtrant** emp-fayl-en*

Is it safe to swim here?
Kann man hier unbesorgt schwimmen?
*kan man heer **oon**-be-zorgt **shvim**-en*

Is the current strong?
Ist die Strömung stark?
*ist dee **stroem**-oong **shtark***

Is the sea calm?
Ist das Meer ruhig?
*ist das **mayr roo**-eekh*

Is the water warm?
Ist das Wasser warm?
*ist das **vas**-er **varm***

Is there a lifeguard here?
Gibt es hier einen Bademeister?
*gipt es heer yn-en **bad**-e-myst-er*

Can we change here?
Können wir uns hier umziehen?
*koen-en veer oons heer **oom**-tsee-en*

Is this beach private?
Ist das ein Privatstrand?
*ist das yn pree-**vat**-shtrant*

Is it possible to go	**— sailing?**
Kann man hier	— segeln — gehen?
kan man heer	— **sayg**-eln gay-en
	— surfing?
	— Wellenreiten?
	— **vel**-en-ryt-en
	— water skiing?
	— Wasserski fahren?
	— **vas**-er-shee-far-en
	— wind surfing?
	— Windsurfen
	— **vint**-surf-en

When is high tide?
Wann ist Flut?
*van ist **floot***

When is low tide?
Wann ist Ebbe?
*van ist **eb**-e*

Sport and recreation

Among the popular sports in Germany are fishing, tennis, swimming, water sports, hiking and rock climbing, winter sports and cycling. Germany's lakes and rivers have a variety of fish including carp, pike, eel, bream, zander and trout, but you need a licence and a local permit to fish in the open season. Tennis courts can be found in virtually all major tourist spots, where you can usually hire rackets. There are plenty of heated outdoor and indoor swimming pools in the country in addition to swimming beaches on lakes and seaside resorts, where water sports facilities can also be found. Germany has 180 yachting schools along the coast and on major inland lakes. There is a network of hiking routes in the lowlands and highlands for rambling and rock-climbing enthusiasts, and the Alpine region offers plenty of opportunity for winter sports. Many resorts offer bicycles for hire and so do the railways. In urban areas the bike can be one of the most efficient ways of getting around. Because it is regarded as a form of transport rather than of recreation, towns and cities are well equipped with designated cycle lanes, sometimes in the street, sometimes on the pavement. For touring purposes, good maps and routes are available from ADFC-Bundesverband, Postfach 10 77 47, D-28077 Bremen.

Is there a heated swimming pool?
Haben Sie ein beheiztes Schwimmbecken?
hab-en zee yn be-hytst-es shvim-bek-en

Can I rent the equipment?
Kann ich die Ausrüstung mieten?
kan eekh dee ows-rûst-oong meet-en

Can we go riding?
Können wir Reiten gehen?
koen-en veer ryt-en gay-en

Where can we fish?
Wo können wir fischen?
voa koen-en veer fish-en

Do we need a permit?
Brauchen wir eine Lizenz?
browkh-en veer yn-e lee-tsents

Can I rent
Kann ich
kan eekh

— **a sailing boat?**
— ein Segelboot — mieten?
— *yn zayg-el-boat meet-en*

— **a rowing boat?**
— ein Ruderboot?
— *yn rood-er-boat*

Can we
Können wir
koen-en veer

— **play tennis?**
— Tennis spielen?
— *te-nees shpeel-en*

— **play golf?**
— Golf spielen?
— *golf shpeel-en*

— **play volleyball?**
— Volleyball spielen?
— *vo-lay-bal shpeel-en*

Entertainment

Germans call their country the land of *Dichter und Denker* (poets and philosophers), and indeed Germany's cultural legacy is rich, richer almost than that of any other nation in Europe. This international inheritance extends to the visual arts, music, architecture, literature and film. Opportunities for an evening's entertainment are virtually limitless. Whether it is a pub, cinema, theatre, concert, disco or something entirely different, most cities have a lot to offer.

Is there	**— a disco?**
Gibt es hier	— eine Disco?
gipt es heer	— *yn-e disk-oa*

— **a casino?**
— ein Kasino?
— yn ka-**see**-noa

— **a theatre?**
— ein Theater?
— *yn tay-a-ter*

— **a good nightclub?**
— einen guten
   Nachtclub?
— *yn-en goot-en nakht-kloob*

Are there any films in English?
Werden hier auch englische Filme gezeigt?
vayrd-en heer owkh eng-leesh-e film-e ge-tsygt

How much is it per person?
Wieviel kostet es pro Person?
vee-feel kost-et es pro per-zoan

How much is it to get in?
Wieviel kostet es hineinzugehen?
vee-feel kost-et es heen-yn-tsoo -gay-en

Is there a reduction for children?
Gibt es eine Ermäßigung für Kinder?
gipt es yn-e er-mes-eeg-oong für kind-er

Two stall tickets, please
Zwei Karten für Sperrsitze, bitte / Zwei Karten im Parkett, bitte
tsvy kart-en für shper-sits-e bit-e / tsvy kart-en im par-ket bit-e

Two tickets, please
Zwei Karten, bitte
tsvy kart-en bit-e

Sightseeing

On many inland waters in Germany there are river-boat and motorboat services available, and very often rail passes are valid for boat trips too. In addition to connecting towns within Germany, there are passenger and car ferries operating to offshore islands in the North and Baltic Sea. KD Rhine Line offers a programme of luxury cruises along the Rhine, Main, Mosel, Neckar, Saar, Elbe and Danube rivers. During the summer there are good services between Bonn and Koblenz as well as Koblenz and Bingen. Other cruises are offered on the Oder, Saale and Weser. Boat trips are very popular and advance booking is advisable.

Are there any boat trips on the river?
Gibt es Bootsfahrten auf dem Fluß?
gipt es boats-fart-en owf dem floos

Are there any guided tours of the castle?
Gibt es Führungen durch die Burg?
gipt es für-oong-en doorkh dee boorg

Are there any guided tours?
Gibt es Führungen?
gipt es für-oong-en

Is there a tour of the cathedral?
Gibt es eine Führung durch den Dom?
gipt es yn-e für-oong doorkh den doam

Is there an English-speaking guide?
Haben Sie einen Englisch sprechenden
Führer?
*hab-en zee yn-en **eng**-leesh shprekh-end-en*
***fûr**-er*

How long does the tour take?
Wie lange dauert die Rundfahrt?
*vee lang-e **dow**-ert dee **roont**-fart*

When is the bus tour?
Wann findet die Busrundfahrt statt?
*van **find**-et dee **boos**-roont-fart **shtat***

What is there to see here?
Was gibt es hier zu sehen?
*vas gipt es heer tsoo **zay**-en*

What is this building?
Was für ein Gebäude ist das?
*vas fûr yn ge-**boyd**-e ist das*

When was it built?
Wann wurde es gebaut?
*van voord-e es ge-**bowt***

Can we go in?
Können wir hineingehen?
***koen**-en veer heen-**yn**-gay-en*

Is it open to the public?
Ist es für die Öffentlichkeit zu betreten?
*ist es fûr dee **oef**-ent-leekh-kyt tsoo be-*
***trayt**-en*

Is there a guidebook?
Haben Sie einen Ortsführer?
*hab-en zee yn-en **orts**-fûr-er*

What is the admission charge?
Was kostet der Eintritt?
*vas **kost**-et der **yn**-tritt*

How much is it for a child?
Wieviel kostet es für ein Kind?
*vee-feel **kost**-et es fûr yn **kint***

When is the bus tour?
Wann findet die Busrundfahrt statt?
*van **find**-et dee **boos**-roont-fart **shtat***

Can we go up to the top?
Können wir nach oben gehen?
***koen**-en veer nakh **oab**-en gay-en*

Is this the best view?
Ist das die beste Aussicht?
*ist das dee **best**-e **ows**-zeekht*

What time does the gallery open?
Wann öffnet die Galerie?
*van **oef**-net dee gal-e-**ree***

Can I take photos?
Können wir Fotos machen?
***koen**-en veer **foa**-toas **makh**-en*

Can I use flash?
Kann ich mein Blitzlicht verwenden?
*kan eekh myn **blits**-leekht fer-**vend**-en*

Souvenirs

Where can I buy postcards?
Wo kann ich Postkarten kaufen?
*voa kan eekh **post**-kart-en **kowf**-en*

Where can we buy souvenirs?
Wo kann ich Andenken kaufen?
*voa kan eekh **an**-denk-en **kowf**-en*

Have you got an English guidebook?
Haben Sie einen Führer in englischer
Sprache?
*hab-en zee yn-en **fûr**-er in **eng**-leesh-er*
shprakh-e

Have you got any colour slides?
Haben Sie Farbdias?
*hab-en zee **farb**-dee-as*

Going to church

In Germany, the church and the state are separate and there is complete religious freedom. Three-quarters of all Germans claim a Christian faith, half belonging to the Roman Catholic Church and half to the Protestant branch of the church (*Evangelische Kirche*) that was based on the teachings of Martin Luther. Other Christian denominations are also active, including predominantly the Evangelical Free Church, Baptists, Old Catholics and Quakers. There are distinct Catholic and Protestant areas in Germany, the north being predominantly Protestant, while southern areas and the Rhineland tend to be Catholic. With the arrival of ethnic minorities, Islamic and Orthodox cultures are growing, and there are also some Jewish communities.

Where is the
Wo ist die
voa ist dee

— **Catholic church?**
— katholische Kirche?
— *ka-toal-eesh-e kirkh-e*

— **Baptist church?**
— Baptistenkirche?
— *bap-teest-en-kirkh-e*

— **mosque?**
— Moschee?
— *mo-shay*

— **Protestant church?**
— evangelische Kirche?
— *ay-fan-gay-lish-e kirkh-e*

— **synagogue?**
— Synagoge?
— *zû-na-goag-e*

I would like to see
Ich möchte

eekh moekht-e

— **a priest**
— einen Priester — sehen,
— *yn-en preest-er zay-en*

— **a minister**
— einen Pfarrer
— *yn-en pfar-er*

— **a rabbi**
— einen Rabbiner
— *yn-en ra-been-er*

What time is the service?
Wann findet der Gottesdienst statt?
van find-et der got-es-deenst shtat

Shopping

General information

Business hours vary and are detailed under Getting Around (*see* page 67). On Sunday most shops are closed, apart from bakeries (for fresh bread and cake), florists (if invited to a private house, fresh flowers are a traditional present for your host) and newsagents. Shops also close on public holidays (*see* page 227). Most towns and city centres have their pedestrian shopping precincts with department stores, boutiques, hairdressers', pharmacies, butchers, bakers, cafés and specialist shops. Some old towns still have their weekly markets.

Outside the centres there are supermarkets, DIY stores, car showrooms, carpet warehouses and petrol stations. World-famous shopping centres are the Kurfürstendamm in Berlin, the Königsallee in Düsseldorf, the Hansequarter in Hamburg and the Zeil in Frankfurt / Main. Watch out for the 'Tax-free' sign, where you will receive a tax-free cheque with your purchase. This will need a stamp at the check-in at the start of your homeward journey.

When buying souvenirs or gifts, most shops will offer to gift-wrap your purchase.

General phrases and requests

How much is this?
Was macht das?
*vas **makht** das*

How much does that cost?
Was kostet das?
*vas **kost**-et das*

How much is it — **per kilo?**
Wieviel kostet es — pro Kilo?
*vee-feel **kost**-et es* — *pro **keel**-oa*

— **per metre?**
— pro Meter?
— *pro **mayt**-er*

I like this one
Das gefällt mir
*das ge-**felt** meer*

I do not like it
Das gefällt mir nicht
*das ge-**felt** meer **neekht***

I will take that one
Ich nehmen das
*eekh **naym**-e das*

I will take the other one
Ich nehmen das andere
*eekh **naym**-e das and-er-e*

I will take this one
Ich nehmen dieses
*eekh **naym**-e deez-es*

No, the other one
Nein, das andere
*nyn das **and**-er-e*

Have you got anything cheaper?
Haben Sie etwas Billigeres?
***hab**-en zee et-vas **bil**-ig-er-es*

Can I have a carrier bag?
Könnte ich eine Tragetasche haben?
***koent**-e eekh yn-e **trag**-e-tash-e hab-en*

Can I pay for air insurance?
Kann ich gegen Gebühr eine Luftfrachtversicherung abschließen?
***kan** eekh gayg-en ge-**bûr** yn-e **looft**-frakht-fer-zeekh-er-oong **ap**-shlees-en*

Shopping

Can I see that one over there?
Könnte ich mir das da drüben ansehen?
koent-e eekh meer das da -drûb-en an-zay-en

Can I see that umbrella?
Könnte ich mir diesen Schirm anschauen?
koent-e eekh meer deez-en shirm an-show-en

Can you deliver to my hotel?
Können Sie es mir in meinem Hotel
liefern?
*koen-en zee es meer in myn-em hoa-tel
leef-ern*

Do you sell sunglasses?
Verkaufen Sie Sonnenbrillen?
fer-kowf-en zee zon-en-bril-en

I am looking for a souvenir
Ich suche ein Andenken
eekh zookh-e yn an-denk-en

I do not have enough money
Ich habe nicht genug Geld
eekh hab-e neekht ge-noog- gelt

Please forward a receipt to this address
Bitte schicken Sie eine Rechnung an diese
Adresse
*bit-e shik-en zee yn-e rekh-noong an deez-e
a-dres-e*

Will you send it by air freight?
Schicken Sie es per Luftfracht?
shike-en zee es per looft-frakht

Please pack it for shipment
Bitte packen Sie das für den Transport ein
bit-e pak-en zee das fûr den trans-port yn

Please wrap it up for me
Bitte packen Sie es mir ein
bit-e pak-en zee es meer yn

There is no need to wrap it
Einzupacken ist nicht nötig
yn-tsoo-pak-en ist neekht noet-eekh

We need to buy some food
Wir müssen etwas zu essen kaufen
veer mûs-en et-vas tsoo es-en kowf-en

What is the total?
Was macht das zusammen?
vas makht das tsoo-zam-en

Where can I buy some clothes?
Wo kann ich Kleidung kaufen?
voa kan eekh kly-doong kowf-en

**Where can I buy cassette tapes and
compact discs?**
Wo kann ich Tonbandkassetten und
Compact Disks kaufen?
*voa kan eekh toan-bant-ka-set-en oont
kom-pakt disks kowf-en*

**Where can I buy tapes for my
camcorder?**
Wo kann ich Kassetten für meinen
Camcorder kaufen?
*voa kan eekh ka-set-en fûr myn-en
kam-kord-er kowf-en*

Where can I get my camcorder repaired?
Wo kann ich meinen Camcorder
reparieren lassen?
*voa kan eekh myn-en kam-kord-er
re-pa-reer-en las-en*

Where is the children's department?
Wo ist die Kinderabteilung?
voa ist dee kind-er-ap-tyl-oong

Where is the the food department?
Wo ist die Lebensmittelabteilung?
voa ist dee layb-ens-mit-el-ab-tyl-oong

Buying groceries

You can buy all your groceries under one roof at a supermarket, but you might prefer small shops with a wider choice. The displays in bakeries (*Bäckerei* for bread, *Konditorei* more for pastry and cakes) are astounding and mouth-watering. The butcher's is called *Metzgerei* or *Schlachterei*, where you will find a large variety of fresh and cooked meats and sausages. The greengrocer's is *Obst- und Gemüsehandlung*, where produce is usually very fresh and plentiful. *Lebensmittel* are general groceries.

Can I please have — some sugar?
Kann ich bitte — etwas Zucker — haben?

kan eekh bit-e — et-vas tsook-er — hab-en

— **a bottle of wine?**
— eine Flasche Wein?
— *yn-e flash-e vyn*

— **a kilo of sausages?**
— ein Kilo Würste?
— *yn keel-oa vûrst-e*

— **a leg of lamb?**
— eine Lammshaxe?
— *yn-e lams-haks-e*

— **a litre of milk?**
— einen Liter Milch?
— *yn-en leet-er milkh*

— **two steaks?**
— zwei Steaks?
— *tsvy stayks*

— **a kilo of potatoes?**
— ein Kilo Kartoffeln?
— *yn keel-oa kar-tof-eln*

— **a bar of chocolate?**
— eine Tafel Schokolade?
— *yn-e taf-el shok-oa-lad-e*

Can I please have — 5 slices of ham?
Kann ich bitte — fünf Scheiben Schinken haben?

kan eekh bit-e — fûnf shyb-en shink-en— hab-en

— **100 grams of ground coffee?**
— hundert Gramm gemahlenen Kaffee?
— *hoond-ert gram ge-mal-en-en ka-fay?*

— **half a dozen eggs?**
— ein halbes Dutzend Eier?
— *yn halb-es doots-ent y-er?*

— **half a kilo of butter?**
— ein halbes Kilo Butter?
— *yn halb-es keel-oa boot-er?*

Groceries

baby food
Babynahrung
bayb-ee-nar-oong

biscuits
Kekse
kayk-se

bread
Brot
broat

butter
Butter
boot-er

cheese
Käse
kez-e

coffee
Kaffee
ka-fay

cream
Sahne
zan-e

eggs
Eier
y-er

flour
Mehl
mayl

groceries
Lebensmittel
layb-enz-mit-el

jam
Marmelade
mar-me-lad-e

margarine
Margarine
mar-ga-reen-e

milk
Milch
milkh

mustard
Senf
zenf

oil
Öl
oel

pasta
Nudeln
nood-eln

pepper
Pfeffer
pfef-er

rice
Reis
rys

salt
Salz
zalts

soup
Suppe
zoop-e

sugar
Zucker
tsook-er

tea
Tee
tay

vinegar
Essig
es-eekh

yoghurt
Joghurt
yoa-goort

Meat and fish

beef
Rindfleisch
rint-flysh

chicken
Huhn
hoon

cod
Kabeljau
kab-el-yow

fish
Fisch
fish

hake
Hecht
hekht

ham
Schinken
shink-en

herring
Hering
hayr-ing

kidneys
Nieren
neer-en

lamb
Lamm
lam

liver
Leber
layb-er

meat
Fleisch
flysh

mussels
Muscheln
moosh-eln

pork
Schweinefleisch
shvyn-e-flysh

sole
Seezunge
zay-tsoong-e

tuna
Thunfisch
toon-fish

veal
Kalbsfleisch
kalps-flysh

At the newsagent's

These usually sell tobacco, too, and are often situated in tiny premises or kiosks. Germans are avid newspaper readers and virtually every city has its own daily newspaper. These are supplemented by a number of major national papers and a wide selection of magazines.

In the major cities you can buy all the important international newspapers and periodicals.

Do you have
Haben Sie
hab-en zee

— English newspapers?
— englische Zeitungen?
— eng-leesh-e tsyt-oong-en

— English books?
— englische Bücher?
— eng-leesh-e bûkh-er

— postcards?
— Postkarten?
— post-kart-en

Shopping

Do you sell — **English paperbacks?**
Verkaufen Sie — englische
Taschenbücher?
fer-kowf-en zee — *eng-leesh-e tash-
en-bûkh-er*

— **coloured pencils?**
— Farbstifte?
— *farb-shtift-e*

— **drawing paper?**
— Zeichenpapier?
— *tsykh-en-pa-peer*

— **felt pens?**
— Filzschreiber?
— *filts-shryb-er*

— **street maps?**
— Stadtpläne?
— *shttat-plen-e*

I need — **some writing paper**
Ich brauche — Schreibpapier
eekh browkh-e — *shryb-pa-peer*

— **a local map**
— einen Stadtplan
— *yn-en shtat-plan*

— **a road map**
— eine Straßenkarte
— *yn-e shtras-en-kart-e*

I would like — **some postage stamps**
Ich hätte gerne — ein paar Briefmarken
eekh het-e gern-e — *yn par breef-mark-en*

— **a bottle of ink**
— einen Behälter mit Tinte
— *yn-en be-helt-er mit tint-e*

— **a pen**
— einen Federhalter
— *yn-en fayd-er-halt-er*

— **a pencil**
— einen Bleistift
— *yn-en bly-shtift*

— **some adhesive tape**
— etwas Klebstreifen
— *etvas klayb-shtryf-en*

— **some envelopes**
— Umschläge
— *oom-shleg-e*

At the tobacconist's

I would like — **a box of matches**
Ich hätte gerne — eine Packung
Streichhölzer
eekh het-e gern-e — *yn-e pak-oong
shtrykh-hoelts-er*

— **a cigar**
— eine Zigarre
— *yn-e tsee-gar-e*

— **a cigarette lighter**
— ein Feuerzeug
— *yn foy-er-tsoyg*

— **a gas (butane) refill**
— eine Nachfüllpackung
Butangas
— *yn-e nakh-fûl-pak-oong
boo-tan-gas*

— **a pipe**
— eine Pfeife
— *yn-e pfyf-e*

— **a pouch of pipe tobacco**
— ein Päckchen
Pfeifentabak
— *yn pek-khen
pfyf-en-ta-bak*

— **some pipe cleaners**
— ein paar Pfeifenreiniger
— *yn par pfyf-en-ryn-eeg-er*

Do you have cigarette papers?
Haben Sie Zigarettenpapier?
hab-en zee tsee-ga-ret-en-pa-peer

Do you have rolling tobacco?
Haben Sie Tabak zum Selberdrehen?
hab-en zee ta-bak tsoom zelb-er-dray-en

Have you got any American brands?
Führen Sie amerikanische Marken?
fûr-en zee a-may-ree-ka   n-eesh-e mark-en

Have you got any English brands?
Führen Sie englische Marken?
fûr-en zee eng-leesh-e mark-en

A packet of ... please
Bitte eine Packung ...
bit-e yn-e pak-oong...

— with filter tips
— mit Filter
— mit filt-er

— without filters
— ohne Filter
— oan-e filt-er

At the chemist's

Dispensing chemists are called *Apotheke*, where you can buy medicines and take your doctor's prescription. A *Drogerie* is a drugstore, which sells cosmetics, soap, toothpaste and the like as well as over-the-counter remedies. Both are open during normal business hours. There are notices with information about night-time and Sunday services.

I need some high-protection suntan cream
Ich brauche Sonnencreme mit hohem Schutzfaktor
eekh browkh-e zon-en-kraym-e mit hoa-em shoots-fak-tor

Can you give me something for a headache?
Können Sie mir etwas gegen Kopfschmerzen geben?
koen-en zee meer et-vas gayg-en kopf-shmerts-en gayb-en

Can you give me something for a cold?
Können Sie mir etwas gegen eine Erkältung geben?
koen-en zee meer et-vas gayg-en yn-e er-kelt-oong gayb-en

Can you give me something for a cough?
Können Sie mir etwas gegen Husten geben?
koen-en zee meer et-vas gayg-en hoost-en gayb-en

Can you give me something for a sore throat?
Können Sie mir etwas gegen Halsentzündung geben?
koen-en zee meer et-vas gayg-en hals-ent-tsûnd-oong gayb-en

Can you give me something for an upset stomach?
Können Sie mir etwas gegen eine Magenverstimmung geben?
koen-en zee meer et-vas gayg-en yn-e mag-en-fer-shtim-oong gayb-en

Can you give me something for sunburn?
Können Sie mir etwas gegen Sonnenbrand geben?
koen-en zee meer et-vas gayg-en zon-en-brant gayb-en

Can you give me something for chapped lips?
Können Sie mir etwas gegen aufgesprungene Lippen geben?
koen-en zee meer et-vas gayg-en owf-ge-shproong-en-e lip-en gayb-en

Can you give me something for swollen feet?
Können Sie mir etwas gegen geschwollene Füße geben?
koen-en zee meer et-vas gayg-en ge-shvol-en-e fûs-e gayb-en

Can you give me something for toothache?
Können Sie mir etwas gegen Zahnschmerzen geben?
koen-en zee meer et-vas gayg-en tsan-shmerts-en gayb-en

Can you give me something for insect bites?
Können Sie mir etwas gegen Insektenstiche geben?
koen-en zee meer et-vas gayg-en in-zekt-en-shtikh-e gayb-en

I need some antibiotics
Ich brauche Antibiotika
eekh browkh-e an-tee-bee-o-tee-ka

Do I need a prescription?
Brauche ich dafür ein Rezept?
browkh-e eekh da-fûr yn re-tsept

How many do I take?
Wieviel nehme ich davon?
vee-feel naym-e eekh da-fon

How often do I take them?
Wie oft nehme ich sie?
vee oft naym-e eekh zee

Are they safe for children to take?
Können sie auch bedenkenlos Kindern gegeben werden?
koen-en zee owkh be-denk-en-loas kind-ern ge-gayb-en vayrd-en

Do you have toothpaste?
Haben Sie Zahnpasta?
hab-en zee tsan-past-a

Medicines and toiletries

aftershave
Rasierwasser
ra-zeer-vas-er

antihistamine
Antihistamin
ant-ee-his-ta-meen

antiseptic
Antiseptikum
ant-ee-zep-tee-koom

aspirin
Aspirin
as-pee-reen

Band-aid
Pflaster
pflast-er

bandage
Verband
fer-bant

bubble bath
Schaumbad
showm-bat

cleansing milk
Reinigungsmilch
ryn-ee-goongs-milkh

contraceptive
Empfängnisverhütungsmittel
emp-feng-nis-fer-hût-oongs-mit-el

cotton wool
Watte
vat-e

deodorant
Deodorant
day-oad-oa-rant

disinfectant
Desinfektionsmittel
dayz-in-fek-tsee-oans-mit-el

eau de Cologne
Eau de Cologne
oa de ko-lon-ye

eye shadow
Lidschatten
leed-shat-en

Shopping

Medicines and toiletries

hair spray
Haarspray
har-shpray

hand cream
Handcreme
hant-kraym

hay fever
Heuschnupfen
hoy-shnup-fen

insect repellent
Insektenspray
in-zekt-en-shpray

Kleenex
Tempo
temp-oa

laxative
Abführmittel
ap-fûr-mit-el

lipstick
Lippenstift
lip-en-shtift

mascara
Wimperntusche
vim-pern-toosh-e

mouthwash
Mundspülung
moont-shpûl-oong

nail file
Nagelfeile
nag-el-fyl-e

nail varnish
Nagellack
nag-el-lak

nail varnish remover
Nagellackentferner
nag-el-lak-ent-fern-er

perfume
Parfüm
par-fûm

powder
Puder
pood-er

razor blades
Rasierklingen
ra-zeer-kling-en

sanitary towels
(Hygiene)binden
(hûg-ee-ayn-e) bind-en

shampoo
Haarshampoo
haar-sham-poo

shaving cream
Rasiercreme
ra-zeer-kraym

skin moisturiser
Feuchtigkeitscreme
foykht-eekh-kyts-kraym

soap
Seife
zyf-e

suntan oil
Sonnenöl
zon-en-oel

talc
Puder
pood-er

toilet water
Eau de Toilette
oa de twa-let

toothpaste
Zahnpasta
tsan-past-a

447

Shopping for clothes

Generally, Germans dress informally, especially in the summer. Even visits to the theatre do not require special dress. The spirit of the age tends towards a con-servative elegance with plenty of scope for individual taste and style. Only in casinos are jacket and tie mandatory while in many discos jeans and trainers are taboo.

I am just looking, thank you
Danke, ich schaue mich nur um
dank-e eekh show-e meekh noor oom

I like it
Es gefällt mir
es ge-felt meer

I do not like it
Es gefällt mir nicht
es ge-felt meer neekht

I would like	**— this hat**
Ich hätte gerne	— diesen Hut
eekh het-e gern-e	*— deez-en hoot*
	— this suit
	— diesen Anzug
	— deez-en an-tsoog

I like	**— this one**
Mir gefällt	— dieses
meer ge-felt	*— deez-es*
	— that one there
	— das da
	— das da
	— the one in the window
	— das im Fenster
	— das im fenst-er

I will take it
Ich nehme es
eekh naym-e es

Can I change it if it does not fit?
Kann ich es umtauschen, falls es nicht paßt?
kan eekh es oom-towsh-en fals es neekht past

Can you please measure me?
Können Sie mich bitte messen?
koen-en zee meekh bit-e mes-en

I take continental size 40
In Europa brauche ich Größe 40
in oy-roa-pa browkh-e eekh groes-e feer-tseekh

Have you got	**— a large size?**
Haben Sie eine	— größere Größe
hab-en zee yn-e	*— groes-er-e groes-e*
	— a smaller size?
	— kleinere Größe
	— klyn-er-e groes-e

Have you got this in other colours?
Haben Sie das auch in anderen Farben?
hab-en zee das owkh in and-er-en farb-en

Where are the changing (dressing) rooms?
Wo sind die Umkleidekabinen?
voa zind dee oom-klyd-e-ka-been-en

Where can I try it on?
Wo kann ich es anprobieren?
voa kan eekh es an-pro-beer-en

Is there a full-length mirror?
Gibt es hier einen großen Spiegel?
gipt es heer yn-en groas-en shpeeg-el

May I see it in daylight?
Kann ich das im Tageslicht anschauen?
kan eekh das im tag-es-likht an-show-en

It does not fit
Es paßt nicht
es past neekht

Is it too long?
Ist es zu lang?
ist es tsoo lang

Is it too short?
Ist es zu kurz?
ist es tsoo koorts

Is this all you have?
Ist das alles, was Sie haben?
ist das al-es vas zee hab-en

It does not suit me
Es steht mir nicht
es shtayt meer neekht

Shopping

I would like one
Ich hätte gerne eines

*eekh **het**-e gern-e yn-es*

— with a zip
— mit
    Reißverschluß
— mit
    rys-fer-shloos

— without a belt
— ohne Gürtel
— oan-e **gûrt**-e

Is it guaranteed?
Gibt es dafür eine Garantie?
*gipt es da-fûr yn-e ga-ran-**tee***

What is it made of?
Woraus besteht das?
***voa**-rows be-**shtayt** das*

Is it drip-dry?
Muss man es schleudern?
*moos man es **shloyd**-ern*

Is it dry-clean only?
Muß man es chemisch reinigen?
*moos man es **khaym**-eesh **ryn**-ee-gen*

Is it machine-washable?
Kann ich es in der Maschine waschen?
*kan eekh es in der mas-**sheen**-e vash-en*

Will it shrink?
Läuft es ein?
*loyft es **yn***

Clothes and accessories

acrylic
Acryl
*a-**krûl***

belt
Gürtel
***gûrt**-el*

blouse
Bluse
***blooz**-e*

bra
BH
*bay-**ha***

bracelet
Armband
***arm**-bant*

brooch
Brosche
***broash**-e*

button
Knopf
knopf

cardigan
Strickjacke
***shtrik**-yak-e*

coat
Mantel
***mant**-el*

corduroy
Cord
kord

denim
Jeansstoff
***jeens**-shtof*

dress
Kleid
klyt

dungarees
Latzhose
***lats**-hoaz-e*

earrings
Ohrringe
***oar**-ring-e*

fur
Pelz
pelts

gloves
Handschuhe
***hant**-shoo-e*

handbag
Handtasche
***hant**-tash-e*

handkerchief
Taschentuch
-en-tookh

Shopping

hat
Hut
hoot

jacket
Jacke
yak-e

jeans
Jeans
jeenz

jersey
Pulli/Pullover
pool-ee/pool-oav-er

lace
Spitze
shpits-e

leather
Leder
layd-er

linen
Leinen
lyn-en

necklace
Halskette
hals-ket-e

night-dress
Nachthemd
nakht-hemt

nylon
Nylon
ny-lon

panties
Unterhosen
oont-er-hoaz-en

pendant
Anhänger
an-heng-er

petticoat
Unterrock
oont-er-rok

polyester
Polyester
pol-ee-est-er

poplin
Popeline
pop-e-leen-e

pullover
Pullover
pool-oav-er

purse
Geldbeutel
gelt-boyt-el

pyjamas
Schlafanzug
shlaf-an-tsoog

raincoat
Regenmantel
rayg-en-mant-el

rayon
Kunstseide/Rayon
koonst-zyd-e/ray-on

ring
Ring
ring

sandals
Sandalen
zan-dal-en

scarf
Schal
shal

shirt
Hemd
hemt

shorts
kurze Hosen / Shorts
koorts-e hoaz-en

silk
Seide
zyd-e

skirt
Rock
rok

slip
Unterrock
oont-er-rok

Shopping

socks
Socken
zok-en

tights
Strumpfhose
shtroompf-hoaz-e

stockings
lange Strümpfe
lang-e shtrûmpf-e

towel
Handtuch
hant-tookh

suede
Wildleder
vilt-layd-er

trousers
Hose
hoaz-e

suit (men's)
Anzug
an-tsoog

umbrella
Schirm
shirm

suit (women's)
Kostüm
kos-tûm

underpants
Unterhose
unt-er-hoaz-e

sweater
Pullover
pool-oaf-er

velvet
Samt
zamt

swimming trunks
Badehose
bad-e-hoaz-e

vest
Unterhemd
oont-er-hemt

swimsuit
Badeanzug
bad-e-an-tsoog

wallet
Brieftasche
breef-tash-e

T-shirt
T-shirt
tee-shirt

watch
Armbanduhr
arm-bant-oor

terylene
Terylen
ter-ee-layn

wool
Wolle
vol-e

tie
Krawatte/Schlips
kra-vat-e/shlips

zip
Reißverschluß
rys-fer-shloos

Photography

I need a film — for this camera
Ich brauche
einen Film — für diese Kamera
*eekh **browkh-e***
*yn-en **film*** — *fûr deez-e **ka-me-ra***

— for this camcorder
— für diesen Camcorder
— *fûr deez-en **kam**-kord-er*

— for this cine camera
— für diese Filmkamera
— *fûr deez-e **film**-ka-me-ra*

— for this video camera
— für diese Videokamera
— *fûr deez-e **vid**-e-oa-ka-me-ra*

Can you develop this film, please?
Könnten Sie bitte diesen Film entwickeln?
*koent-en zee bit-e deez-en **film** ent-**vik**-eln*

I would like this photo enlarged
Ich hätte dieses Foto gerne vergrößert
*eekh **het**-e deez-es **foa**-toa gern-e fer-**groes**-ert*

I would like two prints of this one
Ich hätte gerne zwei Abzüge davon
*eekh **het**-e gern-e tsvy **ap**-tsûg-e da-fon*

When will the photos be ready?
Wann werden die Bilder fertig sein?
*van vayrd-en dee **bild**-er **fert**-eekh zyn*

I want — a black and white film
Ich möchte — einen Schwarzweißfilm
*eekh moekht-e — yn-en shvarts-**vys**-film*

— a colour print film
— einen Farbbildfilm
— *yn-en **farb**-bilt-film*

— a colour slide film
— einen Farbdiafilm
— *yn-en **farb**-dee-a-film*

— batteries for the flash
— Batterien für den Blitz
— *bat-e-**ree**-en fûr den **blits***

Camera repairs

I am having trouble with my camera
Ich habe Probleme mit meiner Kamera
*eekh hab-e prob-**laym**-e mit myn-er **ka**-mer-ra*

The film is jammed
Der Film klemmt
*der **film** klemt*

There is something wrong with my camera
Mit meiner Kamera stimmt etwas nicht
*mit myn-er **ka**-me-ra **shtimt** et-vas **neekht***

Can you repair it?
Können Sie es reparieren?
*koen-en zee es re-pa-**reer**-en*

Where can I get my camera repaired?
Wo kann ich meine Kamera reparieren
lassen?
*voa kan eekh myn-e **ka**-me-ra re-pa-**reer**-en
las-en*

Camera parts

accessory
Zusatzteil
***tsoo**-zats-tyl*

blue filter
Blaufilter
***blow**-filt-er*

camcorder
Camcorder
***kam**-kord-er*

cartridge
Patrone
*pa-**troan**-e*

Shopping

cassette
Kassette
ka-set-e

cine camera
Filmkamera
film-ka-me-ra

distance
Entfernung
ent-fern-oong

enlargement
Vergrößerung
fer-groes-er-oong

exposure
Belichtung
be-leekht-oong

exposure meter
Belichtungsmesser
be-leekht-oongs-mes-er

flash
Blitz
blits

flash bulb
Blitzlichtbirne
blits-leekht-birn-e

flash cube
Blitzlichtwürfel
blits-leekht-vûrf-el

focal distance
Entfernung
ent-fern-oong

focus
Brennpunkt
bren-poonkt

image
Abbildung
ap-bild-oong

in focus
scharf eingestellt
sharf yn-ge-shtelt

lens cover
Linsendeckel
linz-en-dek-el

Camera parts

lens
Linse
linz-e

negative
Negativ
nay-ga-teef

out of focus
nicht scharf eingestellt
neekht sharf yn-ge-stelt

over-exposed
zu stark belichtet
tsoo shtark be-leekht-et

picture
Bild
bilt

print
Papierbild
pa-peer-bilt

projector
Projektor
proa-yek-tor

red filter
Rotfilter
roat-filt-er

reel
Spule
shpool-e

rewind mechanism
Rückspulmechanismus
rûk-shpool-may-kha-neez-moos

shade
Schatten
shat-en

shutter
Blende
blend-e

shutter speed
Belichtungszeit
be-leekht-oongs-tsyt

slide
Dia
dee-a

transparency
Transparenz
*trans-pa-**rents***

viewfinder
Sucher
***zookh**-er*

tripod
Stativ
*shta-**teef***

wide-angle lens
Weitwinkelobjektiv
vyt**-vink-el-ob-yek-**teef

under-exposed
zu wenig belichtet
*tsoo **vayn**-eekh be-**leekht**-et*

yellow filter
Gelbfilter
***gelp**-filt-er*

At the hairdresser's

I would like to make an appointment
Ich möchte mich anmelden
*eekh **moekht**-e meekh **an**-meld-en*

I would like — a perm
Ich hätte gerne — eine Dauerwelle
*eekh **het**-e gern-e — yn-e **dow**-er-vel-e*

— **a blow-dry**
— Föhnen
— *foen-en*

— **my hair dyed**
— Haare Färben
— *har-e ferb-en*

— **my hair streaked**
— Strähnchen
— *stren-khen*

— **shampoo and cut**
— Waschen und
    Schneiden
— *vash-en oont shnyd-en*

— **shampoo and set**
— Waschen und Legen
— *vash-en oont layg-en*

I want a haircut
Ich möchte meine Haare schneiden lassen
*eekh **moekht**-e myn-e har-e shnyd-en **las**-en*

I want a trim
Ich möchte meine Haare nachschneiden lassen
*eekh **moekht**-e myn-e har-e **nakh**-shnyd-en **las**-en*

Please cut my hair — short
Schneiden Sie meine
Haare bitte — kurz
shnyd-en zee myn-e
har-e bit-e — koorts

— **fairly short**
— ziemlich kurz
— *tseem-leekh*
   koorts

— **in a fringe**
— zu einem Pony
— *tsoo yn-em poan-ee*

— **not too short**
— nicht allzu kurz
— *neekht al-tsoo*
   koorts

Take a little more off the back
Schneiden Sie hinten bitte noch etwas weg
*shnyd-en zee **hint**-en bit-e nokh et-vas **vek***

Not too much off
Nicht zu viel weg
*neekht tsoo **feel** vek*

I would like — a conditioner
Ich hätte gerne — Conditioner
*eekh **het**-e gern-e — kon-**dish**-en-er*

— **hair spray**
— Haarspray
— *har-shpray*

That is fine, thank you
Das ist gut so, danke
*das ist **goot** zoa **dank**-e*

The dryer is too hot
Die Trockenhaube ist zu heiß
*dee **trok**-en-howb-e ist tsoo **hys***

The water is too hot
Das Wasser ist zu heiß
*das **vas**-er ist tsoo **hys***

Laundry

Is there a launderette nearby?
Gibt es in der Nähe einen Waschsalon?
*gipt es in der **ne**-e yn-en **vash**-za-loan*

How does the machine work?
Wie funktioniert dieses Gerät?
*vee foonk-tsee-o-**neert** deez-es ge-**ret***

How long will it take?
Wie lange dauert das?
*vee lang-e **dow**-ert das*

I will come back in an hour
Ich komme in einer Stunde
*eekh **kom**-e in yn-er **shtoond**-e*

What time do you close?
Wann schließen Sie?
*van **shlees**-en zee*

Can you	**— clean this skirt?**
Können Sie	— diesen Rock reinigen?
***koen**-en zee*	*— deez-en **rok ryn**-ee-gen*

— clean and press these shirts?
— diese Hemden reinigen und bügeln?
*— deez-e **hemd**-en **ryn**-ee-gen oont **bûg**-eln*

— wash these clothes?
— diese Kleider waschen?
*— deez-e **klyd**-er **vash**-en*

This stain is	**— oil**
Das ist ein	— Ölfleck
das ist yn	*— **oel**-flek*

— blood
— Blutfleck
*— **bloot**-flek*

— coffee
— Kaffeefleck
*— **ka**-fay-flek*

— ink
— Tintenfleck
*— **tint**-en-flek*

I will come back later
Ich komme später zurück
*eekh kom-e **shpet**-er tsoo-**rûk***

When will I come back?
Wann soll ich zurückkommen?
*van zol eekh tsoo-**rûk**-kom-en*

When will my things be ready?
Wann sind meine Sachen fertig?
*van zint myn-e zakh-en **fert**-eekh*

Can you do it quickly?
Können Sie es schnell machen?
*koen-en zee es **shnel** makh-en*

Please send it to this address
Bitte schicken Sie es an diese Adresse
*bit-e **shik**-en zee es an deez-e a-**dres**-e*

General repairs

This is	— broken
Das ist	— kaputt
das ist	— *ka-poot*

	— damaged
	— beschädigt
	— *be-shed-eekht*

	— torn
	— zerrissen
	— *tser-ris-en*

Can you repair it?
Können Sie es reparieren?
koen-en zee es re-pa-reer-en

Have you got a spare part for this?
Haben Sie ein Ersatzteil dafür?
hab-en zee yn er-zats-tyl da-für

Would you have a look at this please?
Könnten Sie sich das bitte einmal
anschauen?
*koent-en zee zeekh das bit-e yn-mal
an-show-en*

Here is the guarantee
Hier ist die Garantie
heer ist dee ga-ran-tee

I need new heels on these shoes
Ich brauche an diesen Schuhen neue
Absätze
*eekh browkh-e an deez-en shoo-en noy-e
ap-zets-e*

At the post office

The post office symbol is a black post-horn on a yellow background. and mailboxes and post vans are all yellow. Opening times for post offices are as under Getting Around (*see* page 67). In small villages the post office may be run from a home and opening times may vary. At stations and airports post offices often stay open longer than normal and may even be open on Sundays. Foreign money orders are paid out in German Marks.

12 stamps please
zwölf Briefmarken bitte
tsvoelf breef-mark-en bit-e

Can I have a telegram form, please?
Könnte ich bitte einen
Telegrammvordruck haben?
*koent-e eekh bit-e yn-en tay-lay-gram-foar-
drook hab-en*

I need to send this by courier
Ich muß das per Kurier schicken
eekh moos das per koo-reer shik-en

I want to send a telegram
Ich möchte ein Telegramm schicken
eekh moekht-e yn tay-lay-gram shik-en

I want to send this by registered mail
Ich möchte das per Einschreiben schicken
eekh moekht-e das per yn-shryb-en shik-en

I want to send this parcel
Ich möchte dieses Paket abschicken
eekh moekht-e deez-es pa-kayt ap-shik-en

When will it arrive?
Wann wird es ankommen?
van virt es an-kom-en

How much is	
a letter	— **to Britain?**
Wieviel kostet	
ein Brief	— nach Großbritannien?
vee-feel kost-et	
yn breef	— *nakh groas-bri-tan-ee-en*

	— **to the United States?**
	— in die Vereinigten Staaten
	— *in dee fer-yn-eeg-ten shtat-en*

Using the telephone

After reunification, telephone links between east and west had to be established, upgraded and new area codes introduced or changed. This complex process is now complete. You can make local and long-distance calls from all post offices and public call boxes. Most kiosks accept phone cards, which are available at any post office. Phone boxes usually have instructions in English and German and can be operated with coins or cards, although the card phones are rapidly taking over. The ringing tone in Germany is a slowly repeating tone rather than a double ring, while the engaged sound consists of quickly repeating tones.

Germany's country code is 49, so from Britain you dial 0049, then leave the initial 0 of the area code, dialling straight through. To phone Britain from Germany dial 0044, and similarly skip the 0 of the area code, dialling straight through.

Can I use the telephone, please?
Kann ich bitte das Telefon benutzen?
kan eekh bit-e das tay-lay-foan be-noots-en

Can you connect me with the international operator?
Könnten Sie mich bitte mit der internationalen Telefonvermittlung verbinden?
koent-en zee meekh bit-e mit der in-ter-na-tsee-oa-nal-en tay-lay-foan-fer-mit-loong fer-bind-en

Can I dial direct?
Kann ich direkt wählen?
kan eekh dee-rekt vel-en

How do I use the telephone?
Wie verwendet man dieses Telefon?
vee fer-vend-et man deez-es tay-lay-foan

I must make a phone call to Britain
Ich muß mit Großbritannien telefonieren
eekh moos mit groas-bri-tan-ee-en tay-lay-fo-neer-en

I need to make a phone call
Ich muß telefonieren
eekh moos tay-lay-fo-neer-en

The number I need is...
Die Nummer, die ich brauche, lautet...
dee noom-er dee eekh browkh-e lowt-et...

How much is it to phone to London?
Wieviel kostet es nach London anzurufen?
vee-feel kost-et es nakh lon-don an-tsoo-roof-en

What is the charge?
Was kostet das?
vas kost-et das

Please, call me back
Bitte rufen Sie mich zurück
bit-e roof-en zee meekh tsoo-rûk

I am sorry. We were cut off
Es tut mir leid. Die Leitung wurde unterbrochen
es toot meer lyt dee lyt-oong voord-e oont-er-brokh-en

I would like to make a reversed charge call
Ich möchte gerne einen vom Empfänger bezahlten Anruf machen
eekh moekht-e gern-e yn-en fom emp-feng-er be-tsalt-en an-roof makh-en

What is the code for the UK?
Was ist die Vorwahl für Großbritannien?
vas ist dee foar-val fûr gros-bri-tan-ee-en

What you may hear

Bitte, tun Sie das
Please go ahead
*bit-e **toon** zee das*

Die Leitung ist belegt
The line is engaged
*dee **lyt**-oong ist be-**laygt***

Ich komme bei dieser Nummer nicht durch
I cannot obtain this number
*eekh **kom**-e by deez-er **noom**-eer neekht doorkh*

Die Nummer funktioniert nicht
The number is out of order
*dee **noom**-er foonk-tsee-o-**neert** neekht*

Ich stelle Sie an Herrn Smith durch
I am putting you through to Mr Smith
*eekh **stel**-e zee an hern **smith** doorkh*

Ich versuche, Sie zu verbinden
I am trying to connect you
*eekh fer-**zookh**-e zee tsoo fer-**bind**-en*

Changing money

Bank opening times are given under in Getting Around (*see* page 67). Bureaux de Change at airports and border crossings are usually open from 6am to 10pm. At border stations they open for all international trains.

Germany offers fewer opportunities to use credit cards than most other western countries, as the Germans still prefer to use cash. It is a good idea to carry traveller's cheques in case your credit cards are not accepted.

Can I contact my bank to arrange for a transfer?
Kann ich mich mit meiner Bank über die Regelung einer Überweisung in Verbindung setzen?
*kan eekh meekh mit myn-er **bank** ûb-er dee **rayg**-el-oong yn-er ûb-er-**vyz**-oong in fer-**bind**-oong **zets**-en*

I would like to obtain a cash advance with my credit card
Ich hätte gerne eine Bargeldauszahlung auf meine Kreditkarte
*eekh **het**-e gern-e yn-e **bar**-gelt-ows-tsal-oong owf myn-e kray-**deet**-kart-e*

I would like to cash a cheque with my Eurocheque card
Ich möchte gerne mit meiner Eurocheque-Karte einen Scheck einlösen
*eekh **moekht**-e gern-e mit myn-er **oy**-roa-shek-kart-e yn-en **shek yn**-loez-en*

Has my cash arrived?
Ist mein Geld angekommen?
*ist myn **gelt** an-ge-kom-en*

Here is my passport
Hier ist mein Paß
heer** ist myn **pas

This is the name and address of my bank
Das sind Name und Adresse meiner Bank
*das zint **nam**-e oont a-**dres**-e myn-er **bank***

What is the rate of exchange?
Was ist der Wechselkurs?
***vas** ist der **veks**-el-koors*

Shopping Changing money

What is your commission?
Wie hoch ist Ihre Kommission?
*vee **hoakh** ist eer-e ko-mee-see-**oan***

Can I change Kann ich ***kan** eekh*	**— these traveller's cheques?** — diese Reiseschecks — hier umtauschen? *— deez-e **ryz**-e-sheks — heer **oom**-towsh-en*
	— these notes? — diese Banknoten? *— deez-e **bank**-noat-en*
What is the rate for Was ist der gängige Kurs für *vas ist der **geng**-eeg-e- **koors** für*	**— sterling?** — britische Pfund? *— **brit**-eesh-e **pfoont***
	— dollars? — Dollars? *— **dol**-ars*

Health

Before you go

Nobody plans to fall sick while on holiday, but it can happen. If you are British, you should obtain an E111 form from a post office, which entitles you to medical treatment in other European Union countries.

In addition to this, it is advisable to take out travel insurance. If you are not from an EU country, you should consider signing up with a medical-assistance company.

Hours and numbers

Surgery hours are generally from 10am to 12 noon and 4pm to 6pm, except for Wednesdays and the weekend.

In an emergency, call 110 for accidents and emergencies or 112 for fire services.

At the moment you are not required to be immunised before making your trip.

What's wrong?

I need a doctor
Ich brauche einen Arzt
*eekh **browkh**-e yn-en **artst***

Can I see a doctor?
Kann ich einen Arzt sehen?
*kan eekh yn-en **artst** zay-en*

He has been badly injured
Er wurde schwer verletzt
*er voord-e **shvayr** fer-**letst***

He is unconscious
Er ist bewußtlos
*er ist be-**voost**-loas*

He has burnt himself
Er hat sich verbrannt
*er hat zeekh fer-**brant***

He has dislocated his shoulder
Er hat sich die Schulter verrenkt
*er hat zeekh dee **shoolt**-er fer-**renkt***

He is hurt
Er ist verletzt
*er ist fer-**letst***

My son is ill
Mein Sohn ist krank
*myn **zoan** ist **krank***

I am a diabetic
Ich bin Diabetiker
*eekh bin dee-a-**bay**-teek-er*

I am allergic to penicillin
Ich bin gegen Penizillin allergisch
*eekh bin gayg-en pe-nee-tsee-**leen** a-**lerg**-eesh*

I am badly sunburnt
Ich habe einen starken Sonnenbrand
*eekh hab-e yn-en **shtark**-en **zon**-en-brant*

I am constipated
Ich habe Verstopfung
*eekh hab-e fer-**shtopf**-oong*

I cannot sleep
Ich kann nicht schlafen
*eekh kan neekht **shlaf**-en*

I feel dizzy
Ich fühle mich schwindelich
*eekh fûl-e meekh **shvinde**-leekh*

I feel faint
Ich fühle mich sehr schwach
*eekh fûl-e meekh zayr **shvakh***

I feel nauseous
Mir ist übel
*meer ist **ûb**-el*

Health

I fell
Ich bin gefallen
*eekh bin ge-**fal**-en*

I have a pain here
Ich habe hier Schmerzen
*eekh hab-e heer **shmerts**-en*

I have a rash here
Ich habe hier einen Ausschlag
*eekh hab-e heer yn-en **ows**-shlag*

I have been sick
Ich habe mich übergeben
*eekh hab-e meekh ûb-er-**gayb**-en*

I have been stung
Ich wurde gestochen
*eekh voord-e ge-**shtokh**-en*

I have cut myself
Ich habe mich geschnitten
*eekh hab-e meekh ge-**shnit**-en*

I have diarrhoea
Ich habe Durchfall
*eekh hab-e **doorkh**-fal*

I have pulled a muscle
Ich habe einen Muskel gezerrt
*eekh hab-e yn-en **moosk**-el ge-tsert*

I have sunstroke
Ich habe einen Sonnenstich
*eekh hab-e yn-en **zon**-en-shtikh*

I suffer from high blood pressure
Ich leide an hohem Blutdruck
*eekh **lyd**-e an **hoa**-em **bloot**-drook*

I think I have food poisoning
Ich glaube ich habe eine
Lebensmittelvergiftung
*eekh **glowb**-e eekh hab-e yn-e*
***layb**-enz-mit-el-fer-**gift**-oong*

It is inflamed here
Es ist hier entzündet
*es ist **heer** ent-**tsûnd**-et*

My arm is broken
Mein Arm ist gebrochen
*myn **arm** ist ge-**brokh**-en*

My stomach is upset
Ich habe einen verdorbenen Magen
*eekh hab-e yn-en fer-**dorb**-en-en **mag**-en*

What's wrong?

My tongue is coated
Meine Zunge ist belegt
*myn-e **tsoong**-e ist be-**laygt***

She has a temperature
Sie hat erhöhte Temperatur
*zee hat er-**hoe**-te tem-pe-ra-**toor***

She has been bitten
Sie wurde gebissen
*zee voord-e ge-**bis**-en*

She has sprained her ankle
Sie hat sich den Knöchel verstaucht
*zee hat zeekh den **knoekh**-el fer-**shtowkht***

There is a swelling here
Da ist es geschwollen
*da ist es ge-**shvol**-en*

I have hurt	**— my arm**
Ich habe	— meinen Arm verletzt
eekh hab-e	*— myn-en **arm** fer-**letst***
	— my leg
	— mein Bein verletzt
	*— myn **byn** fer-**letst***

It is painful	**— to walk**
Ich habe Schmerzen	
beim	— Gehen
*eekh hab-e **shmerts**-en*	
bym	*— **gay**-en*
	— to breathe
	— Atmen
	*— **at**-men*
	— to swallow
	— Schlucken
	*— **shlook**-en*

I have	**— a headache**
Ich habe	— Kopfschmerzen
eekh hab-e	*— **kopf**-shmerts-en*
	— a sore throat
	— Halsschmerzen
	*— **hals**-shmerts-en*
	— earache
	— Ohrenschmerzen
	*— **oar**-en-shmerts-en*
	— cramp
	— einen Krampf
	*— yn-en **krampf***

I am taking these drugs
Ich nehme diese Medikamente
*eekh **naym**-e deez-e may-dee-ka-**ment**-e*

Can you give me a prescription for them?
Können Sie mir ein Rezept dafür geben?
*koen-en zee meer yn re-**tsept** da-für **gayb**-en*

Do I have to go into hospital?
Muß ich ins Krankenhaus gehen?
*moos eekh ins **krank**-en-hows **gay**-en*

Do I need an operation?
Brauche ich eine Operation?
browkh**-e eekh yn-e o-pe-ra-tsee-**oan

I am ill
Ich bin krank
*eekh bin **krank***

I am on the pill
Ich nehme die Pille
*eekh naym-e dee **pil**-e*

I am pregnant
Ich bin schwanger
*eekh bin **shvang**-er*

My blood group is . . .
Meine Blutgruppe ist . . .
*myn-e **bloot**-groop-e ist . . .*

I do not know my blood group
Ich kenne meine Blutgruppe nicht
*eekh **ken**-e myn-e **bloot**-groop-e **neekht***

At the hospital

Here is my E111 form
Hier ist mein E111
*heer ist myn **ay**-hoond-ert-**elf***

How do I get reimbursed?
Wie bekomme ich die Kosten
zurückerstattet?
*vee be-kom-e eekh dee **kost**-en
tsoo-**rûk**-er-shtat-et*

Must I stay in bed?
Muß ich im Bett bleiben?
*moos eekh im **bet** blyb-en*

When will I be able to travel?
Wann werde ich in der Lage sein,
zu reisen?
***van** vayrd-e eekh in der **lag**-e zyn tsoo
ryz-en*

Will I be able to go out tomorrow?
Werde ich morgen das Haus verlassen
können?
*vayrd-e eekh **morg**-en das **hows** ver-**lass**-en
koen-en*

Parts of the body

ankle
Fußgelenk
***foos**-ge-lenk*

arm
Arm
arm

back
Rücken
***rûk**-en*

bone
Knochen
***knokh**-en*

breast
Brust
broost

cheek
Wange
***vang**-e*

chest
Brust
broost

ear
Ohr
oar

Health

elbow
Ellbogen
el-boag-en

liver
Leber
layb-er

eye
Auge
owg-e

lungs
Lunge
loong-e

face
Gesicht
ge-zeekht

mouth
Mund
moont

finger
Finger
fing-er

muscle
Muskel
moosk-el

foot
Fuß
foos

neck
Hals
hals

hand
Hand
hant

nose
Nase
naz-e

heart
Herz
herts

skin
Haut
howt

kidney
Niere
neer-e

stomach
Magen
mag-en

knee
Knie
knee

throat
Hals
hals

leg
Bein
byn

wrist
Handgelenk
hant-ge-lenk

At the dentist's

I have toothache
Ich habe Zahnschmerzen
eekh hab-e tsan-shmerts-en

Can you repair them?
Können Sie sie reparieren?
koen-en zee zee re-ar-reer-en

I have broken a tooth
Ich habe einen zerbrochenen Zahn
eekh hab-e yn-en tser-brokh-en-en tsan

My gums are sore
Mein Zahnfleisch ist entzündet
myn tsan-flysh ist ent-tsûnd-et

I have to see the dentist
Ich muß zum Zahnarzt gehen
eekh moos tsoom tsan-artst gay-en

Please give me an injection
Geben Sie mir bitte eine Spritze
gayb-en zee meer bit-e yn-e shprits-e

My false teeth are broken
Meine dritten Zähne sind kaputt
myn-e drit-en tsen-e zint ka-poot

That hurts
Das tut weh
das toot vay

Health

The filling has come out
Die Plombe ist herausgefallen
*dee **blomb**-e ist hayr-**ows**-ge-fal-en*

This one hurts
Der tut weh
*dayr toot **vay***

Are you going to fill it?
Werden Sie ihn füllen?
*vayrd-en zee een **fûl**-en*

Will you have to take it out?
Müssen Sie ihn ziehen?
*mûs-en zee een **tsee**-en*

For Your Information

Numbers, etc

Cardinal numbers

0	null *nool*	26	sechsundzwanzig *zeks-oont-tsvan-tseekh*
1	eins *yns*	27	siebenundzwanzig *zeeb-en-oont-tsvan-steekh*
2	zwei *tsvy*	28	achtundzwanzig *akht-oont-tsvan-tseekh*
3	drei *dry*	29	neunundzwanzig *noyn-oont-tsvan-tseekh*
4	vier *feer*	30	dreißig *dry-seekh*
5	fünf *fûnf*	40	vierzig *feer-tseekh*
6	sechs *zeks*	50	fünfzig *fûnf-tseekh*
7	sieben *zeeb-en*	60	sechzig *zekh-tseekh*
8	acht *akht*	70	siebzig *zeeb-tseekh*
9	neun *noyn*	80	achtzig *akh-tseekh*
10	zehn *tsayn*	90	neunzig *noyn-tseekh*
11	elf *elf*	100	hundert *hoond-ert*
12	zwölf *tsvoelf*	200	zweihundert *tsvy-hoond-ert*
13	dreizehn *dry-tsayn*	300	dreihundert *dry-hoond-ert*
14	vierzehn *feer-tsayn*	400	vierhundert *feer-hoond-ert*
15	fünfzehn *fûnf-tsayn*	500	fünfhundert *fûnf-hoond-ert*
16	sechzehn *zekhs-tsayn*	600	sechshundert *zeks-hoond-ert*
17	siebzehn *zeeb-tsayn*	700	siebenhundert *zeeb-en-hoond-ert*
18	achtzehn *akht-tsayn*	800	achthundert *akht-hoond-ert*
19	neunzehn *noyn-stayn*	900	neunhundert *noyn-hoond-ert*
20	zwanzig *tsvan-tseekh*	1000	tausend *towz-ent*
21	einundzwanzig *yn-oont-tsvan-tseekh*	2000	zweitausend *tsvy-towz-ent*
22	zweiundzwanzig *tsvy-oont-tsvan-tseekh*	3000	dreitausen *dry-towz-ent*
23	dreiundzwanzig *dry-oont-tsvan-tseekh*	4000	viertausend *feer-towz-ent*
24	vierundzwanzig *feer-oont-tsvan-steekh*	1000000	eine Million *yn-e mee-lee-oan*
25	fünfundzwanzig *fûnf-oont-tsvan-tseekh*		

Ordinal numbers

1st erster *erst-er*
2nd zweiter *tsvyt-er*
3rd dritter *drit-er*

4th vierter *feert-er*
5th fünfter *fûnft-er*
xth xter *xt-er*

Fractions and percentages

a half ein halb *yn halp*
a quarter ein Viertel *yn feert-el*
a third ein Drittel *yn drit-el*

two thirds zwei Drittel *tsvy drit-el*
10 per cent zehn Prozent *tsayn pro-tsent*

Time

Days

Sunday Sonntag *zon-tag*
Monday Montag *moan-tag*
Tuesday Dienstag *deens-tag*
Wednesday Mittwoch *mit-vokh*

Thursday Donnerstag *don-ers-tag*
Friday Freitag *fry-tag*
Saturday Samstag *zams-tag*

Dates

on Friday am Freitag *am fry-tag*
next Tuesday nächsten Dienstag
nekst-en deens-tag
last Tuesday letzten Dienstag
letst-en deens-tag
yesterday gestern *gest-ern*
today heute *hoyt-e*

tomorrow morgen *morg-en*
in June im Juni *im yoon-ee*
7th July siebter Juli *zeept-er yool-ee*
next week nächste Woche
nekst-e vokh-e
last month letzten Monat
letst-en moa-nat

The seasons

spring Frühjahr *frû-yar*
summer Sommer *zom-er*

autumn Herbst *herpst*
winter Winter *vint-er*

Times of the year

in spring im Frühjahr *im frû-yar*
in summer im Sommer *im zom-er*

in autumn im Herbst *im herpst*
in winter im Winter *im vint-er*

466

Months

January	Januar *ya-noo-ar*		**July**	Juli *yool-ee*
February	Februar *fayb-roo-ar*		**August**	August *ow-goost*
March	März *merts*		**September**	September *zep-temb-er*
April	April *a-preel*		**October**	Oktober *ok-toab-er*
May	Mai *my*		**November**	November *noa-vemb-er*
June	Juni *yoon-ee*		**December**	Dezember *day-tsemb-er*

Public holidays

The following holidays are observed in Germany:

1 January, New Year's Day
Neujahr
noy-yar

6 January, Twelfth Night
(Bavaria and Baden Württemberg only)
Heilige Dreikönige / Epiphania
hyl-eege dry-koen-eege

Good Friday
Karfreitag
kar-fry-tag

Easter Sunday
Ostersonntag
oast-er-zon-tag

Easter Monday
Ostermontag
oast-er-moan-tag

1 May, May Day
Maifeiertag / Tag der Arbeit
my-fy-er-tag

Ascension
(Christi) Himmelfahrt
krist-ee him-el-fart

Whit Sunday
Pfingstsonntag
pfingst-zon-tag

Whit Monday / Pentecost
Pfingstmontag
pfingst-moan-tag

Corpus Christi
(southern Germany only)
Fronleichnam
fron-lykh-nam

Feast of the Assumption
Mariä Himmelfahrt
(Bavaria and Saarland only)
ma-ree-e him-el-fart

3 October, German unification
Tag der Einheit
tag der yn-hyt

1 November, All Saints' Day
Allerheiligen
al-er-hyl-eeg-en

24 December, Christmas Eve
Heilig Abend
(shops closed in afternoon)
hyl-eekh a-bent

25 December, Christmas Day
erster Weihnachtsfeiertag
erst-er vy-nakhts-fy-er-tag

26 December, Boxing Day
zweiter Weihnachtsfeiertag
tsvyt-er vy-nakhts-fy-er-tag

31 December, New Year's Eve
Sylvester
zil-vest-er

Colours

beige	**mauve**
beige	violett
bayzh	*vee-oa-**let***
black	**orange**
schwarz	orange
shvarts	*o-**ranzh**-e*
blue	**pink**
blau	rosa
blow	***roaz**-a*
brown	**purple**
braun	lila
brown	***lee**-la*
cream	**red**
cremefarben	rot
***kraym**-farb-en*	*roat*
fawn	**silver**
khaki	silbern
***ka**-kee*	***zilb**-ern*
gold	**tan**
golden	gelbbraun
***gold**-en*	*gelp-brown*
green	**white**
grün	weiß
grûn	*vys*
grey	**yellow**
grau	gelb
grow	*gelp*

Common adjectives

bad	**cheap**
schlecht	billig
shlekht	***beel**-eekh*
beautiful	**cold**
schön	kalt
shoen	*kalt*
big	**expensive**
groß	teuer
groas	***toy**-er*

difficult
schwierig
shveer-eekh

easy
leicht
lykht

fast
schnell
shnel

good
gut
goot

high
hoch
hoakh

hot
heiß
hys

little
wenig
vayn-eekh

long
lang
lang

new
neu
noy

old
alt
alt

short
kurz
koorts

slow
langsam
lang-zam

small
klein
klyn

ugly
häßlich
hes-leekh

Signs and notices

These are some of the signs and notices you may see in Germany.
See also Road signs, page 114.

Achtung
akh-toong
caution

Aufzug
owf-tsoog
lift / elevator

Ausgang
ows-gang
exit

Information
in-for-ma-tsee-oan
information

Ausverkauf
ows-fer-kowf
sale

Verkauft
fer-kowft
sold out

besetzt
be-zetst
occupied

nicht auf das Gras gehen
neekht owf das gras gay-en
keep off the grass

bitte klingeln
bit-e kling-eln
please ring

drücken
drûk-en
push

For Your Information

Eingang
yn-gang
entrance

Eintritt frei
yn-trit fry
no admission charge

Telefon
tay-lay-foan
telephone

Feuerwehr
foy-er-vayr
fire brigade

frei
fry
vacant

Fundamt
foont-amt
Lost Property Office

Betreten verboten
*be-**trayt**-en fer-**boat**-en*
No trespassing

Gefahr
*ge-**far***
danger

geschlossen
*ge-**shlos**-en*
closed

Gift
gift
poison

heiß
hys
hot

kalt
kalt
cold

Kasse
kas-e
cashier

Durchfahrt verboten
*doorkh-fart fer-**boat**-en*
no thoroughfare

kein Eingang
*kyn **yn**-gang*
no entry

Krankenhaus
***krank**-en-hows*
hospital

Sanitäter
*zan-ee-**tet**-er*
ambulance

Lebensgefahr
***layb**-ens-ge-far*
danger of death

Nachmittags geschlossen
***nakh**-mit-ags-ge-shlos-en*
closed in the afternoon

nicht berühren
*neekht be-**rûr**-en*
do not touch

nicht nach außen lehnen
neekht nakh ows-en layn-en
do not lean out

Rauchen verboten
rowkh-en fer-boat-en
no smoking

Notausgang
noat-ows-gang
emergency exit

private Zufahrt
pree-vat-e tsoo-fart
private road

Radweg
rat-vayg
cycle path

Raucherabteil
rowkh-er-ap-tyl
smoking compartment

Geschäftsauflösung
ge-shefts-owf-loez-oong
closing down sale

bitte rechts fahren
bit-e rekhts far-en
keep to the right

Andenken
an-denk-en
souvenirs

Reiseagentur
ryz-e-a-gen-toor
travel agency

Sonderangebot
zond-er-an-ge-boat
special offer

Trinkwasser
trink-vas-er
drinking water

Umleitung
oom-lyt-oong
diversion

ziehen
tsee-en
pull

zu verkaufen
tsoo-fer-kowf-en
for sale

zu mieten
tsoo meet-en
to let / for hire

Preisliste
prys-list-e
price list

willkommen
vil-kom-en
welcome

Gepäck
ge-pek
baggage

Bank
bank
bank

Zoll
tsol
Customs

Notfall
noat-fal
Emergency

Feuermelder
foy-er-meld-er
fire alarm

reserviert
re-zer-veert
reserved

Raucherbereich
rowkh-er-be-rykh
smoking area

nur für ... erlaubt
noor für ... er-lowpt
allowed only for ...

Achtung vor dem Hund
akh-toong foar dem hoont
beware of the dog

Polizei
po-lee-tsy
police

Feuergefahr
foy-er-ge-far
danger of fire

Nur für Mitarbeiter
noor für mit-ar-byt-er
employees only

Abfahrt / Abflüge
ap-fart / ap-flug-e
departures

Abfall
ap-fal
litter

offen
of-en
open

klingeln
kling-eln
ring

Ankunft
an-koonft
arrivals

Schule
shool-e
school

For Your Information

Eingang
yn-gang
entrance

Zeitplan
tstyt-plan
timetable

Herren
her-en
gentlemen

Damen
dam-en
ladies

Fotografieren verboten
foa-toa-gra-feer-en fer-boat-en
no picture taking

Notbremse
noat-bremz-e
communication cord (rail)

nur zur äußerlichen Anwendung
noor tsoor oys-er-leekh-en an-vend-oong
for external use only

eintreten, ohne zu klopfen
yn-trayt-en oan-e tsoo klopf-en
enter without knocking

Parken nur für Anwohner
park-en noor fûr an-voan-er
parking for residents only

Es ist verboten, während der Fahrt mit dem Fahrer zu sprechen
es ist fer-boat-en ver-ent der fart mit dem far-er tsoo shprekh-en
It is forbidden to speak to the driver while the bus is moving

In an Emergency

What to do

The German police force is called Polizei and officers are dressed in green uniforms with white caps, while their patrol cars are also green and white. Police officers should be approached with due respect and most of them do not speak more than basic English.

If you witness an accident or criminal activity, you should phone the emergency services on 110. The call is free from anywhere, including public phone boxes. You will also find clearly marked emergency phones (*Notruf*) in railway stations and on main roads and motorways.

In the case of fire, the fire-fighting services can be reached by dialling 112 free of charge.

Each town and city has its own medical emergency service organised to offer assistance night and day. You will find the phone number in the local telephone directory. Chemist shops also have a night and Sunday service, and in each chemist shop you will find the address of the nearest duty chemist.

Embassies will provide lists of doctors or pertinent legal advice, and can also contact your relatives in an emergency. Consulates can be found in major cities.

Call — **the fire brigade**
Rufen — Sie die Feuerwehr
roof-en — *zee dee **foy**-er-vayr*

— **the police**
— Sie die Polizei
— *zee dee po-lee-**tsy***

— **an ambulance**
— Sie die Sanitäter
— *zee dee zan-ee-**tet**-er*

Get a doctor
Holen Sie einen Arzt
hoal-en zee yn-en **artst**

There is a fire
Es brennt
*es **brent***

Where is — **the police station?**
Wo ist — die Polizeiwache?
voa ist — *dee po-lee-**tsy**-vakh-e*

— **the British consulate?**
— das britische Konsulat?
— *das bri-**tish**-e **koan-soo**-lat*

473

Appendix:
English Irregular Verbs

Present tense	Past tense	Past participle	Present tense	Past tense	Past participle
arise	arose	arisen	come	came	come
awake	awoke	awaked, awoke	cost	cost	cost
			creep	crept	crept
be [I am, you/ we/they are, he/she/it is, g≥rondif being]	was, were	been	cut	cut	cut
			deal	dealt	dealt
			dig	dug	dug
			do [he/she /it does]	did	done
bear	bore	borne	draw	drew	drawn
beat	beat	beaten	dream	dreamed, dreamt	dreamed, dreamt
become	became	become			
begin	began	begun	drink	drank	drunk
behold	beheld	beheld	drive	drove	driven
bend	bent	bent	dwell	dwelt, dwelled	dwelt, dwelled
beseech	besought , beseeched	besought, beseeched			
			eat	ate	eaten
beset	beset	beset	fall	fell	fallen
bet	bet, betted	bet, betted	feed	fed	fed
bid	bade, bid	bid, bidden	feel	felt	felt
bite	bit	bitten	fight	fought	fought
bleed	bled	bled	find	found	found
bless	blessed, blest	blessed, blest	flee	fled	fled
			fling	flung	flung
blow	blew	blown	fly [he/she/ it flies]	flew	flown
break	broke	broken			
breed	bred	bred	forbid	forbade	forbidden
bring	brought	brought	forecast	forecast	forecast
build	built	built	forget	forgot	forgotten
burn	burnt, burned	burnt, burned	forgive	forgave	forgiven
			forsake	forsook	forsaken
burst	burst	burst	forsee	foresaw	foreseen
buy	bought	bought	freeze	froze	frozen
can	could	(been able)	get	got	got, (US) gotten
cast	cast	cast			
catch	caught	caught	give	gave	given
choose	chose	chosen	go [he/she/ it goes]	went	gone
cling	clung	clung			

475

Present tense	Past tense	Past participle	Present tense	Past tense	Past participle
grind	ground	ground	ride	rode	ridden
grow	grew	grown	ring	rang	rung
hang	hung, hanged	hung, hanged	rise	rose	risen
			run	ran	run
have [I/you/ we/they have, he/she/it has, g≥rondif having]	had	had	saw	sawed	sawn, sawed
			say	said	said
			see	saw	seen
hear	heard	heard	seek	sought	sought
hide	hid	hidden	sell	sold	sold
hit	hit	hit	send	sent	sent
hold	held	held	set	set	set
hurt	hurt	hurt	sew	sewed	sewn, sewed
keep	kept	kept	shake	shook	shaken
kneel	knelt	knelt	shall	should	-
know	knew	known	shear	sheared	sheared, shorn
lay	laid	laid			
lead	led	led	shed	shed	shed
lean	leant, leaned	leant, leaned	shine	shone	shone
leap	leapt, leaped	leapt, leaped	shoot	shot	shot
			show	showed	shown, showed
learn	learnt, learned	learnt, learned	shrink	shrank	shrunk
leave	left	left	shut	shut	shut
lend	lent	lent	sing	sang	sung
let	let	let	sink	sank	sunk
lie [g≥rondif lying]	lay	lain	sit	sat	sat
			slay	slew	slain
light	lighted, lit	lighted, lit	sleep	slept	slept
lose	lost	lost	slide	slid	slid
make	made	made	sling	slung	slung
may	might	-	smell	smelt, smelled	smelt, smelled
mean	meant	meant			
meet	met	met	sow	sowed	sown, sowed
mistake	mistook	mistaken			
mow	mowed	mowed, mown	speak	spoke	spoken
			speed	sped, speeded	sped, speeded
must	(had to)	(had to)			
overcome	overcame	overcome	spell	spelt, spelled	spelt, spelled
pay	paid	paid			
put	put	put	spend	spent	spent
quit	quit, quitted	quit, quitted	spill	spilt, spilled	spilt, spilled
read	read	read	spin	spun	spun
rid	rid	rid	spit	spat	spat

Present tense	Past tense	Past participle	Present tense	Past tense	Past participle
split	split	split	think	thought	thought
spoil	spoilt	spoilt	throw	threw	thrown
spread	spread	spread	thrust	thrust	thrust
spring	sprang	sprung	tread	trod	trodden, trod
stand	stood	stood			
steal	stole	stolen	understand	understood	understood
stick	stuck	stuck	upset	upset	upset
sting	stung	stung	wake	woke	woken
stink	stank	stunk	wear	wore	worn
stride	strode	stridden	weave	wove,	wove, woven
strike	struck	struck			
strive	strove	striven	wed	wedded	wed, wedded
swear	swore	sworn			
sweep	swept	swept	weep	wept	wept
swell	swelled	swelled, swollen	win	won	won
			wind	wound	wound
swim	swam	swum	withdraw	withdrew	withdrawn
swing	swung	swung	withhold	withheld	withheld
take	took	taken	withstand	withstood	withstood
teach	taught	taught	wring	wrung	wrung
tear	tore	torn	write	wrote	written
tell	told	told			